Encyclopedia of
CAPITALISM

Volume I
A–G

SYED B. HUSSAIN, Ph.D.

GENERAL EDITOR

Facts On File, Inc.

9486162

Encyclopedia of Capitalism

Facts On File, Inc.
132 West 31st Street
New York NY 1001

Library of Congress Cataloging-in-Publication Data

Encyclopedia of capitalism / Syed B. Hussain, general editor
 p. cm.
  Includes bibliographical references and index.
  ISBN 0-8160-5224-7 (alk paper)
   1. Capitalism—Encyclopedias.   I. Hussain, Syed B.

   HB501.E558 2004
   330'.03—dc22   2003064170

Facts On File books are available at special discounts when purchased in bulk quantities for businesses, associations, institutions, or sales promotions. Please call our Special Sales Department in New York at (212) 967-8800 or (800) 322-8755.

You can find Facts On File on the World Wide Web at http://www.factsonfile.com

GOLSON BOOKS, LTD.

Geoff Golson, President and Editor

Syed B. Hussain, Ph.D., General Editor, Encyclopedia of Capitalism

Kevin Hanek, Design Director

Brian Snapp, Copyeditor

Gail Liss, Indexer

PHOTO CREDITS
Bank of Sweden Prizes in Memory of Alfred Nobel: Pages 20, 193, 281, 320, 380, 488, 553, 614, 735, 780. Kenneth Gabrielsen Photography: Pages 11, 14, 27, 52, 60, 72, 75, 137, 139, 150, 152, 160, 188, 189, 212, 217, 238, 243, 248, 249, 275, 278, 281, 329, 372, 391, 413, 422, 495, 527, 556, 596, 617, 656, 659, 669, 674, 696, 708, 709, 758, 765, 768, 784, 801, 818, 831, 841, 872, 883, 889. PhotoDisc, Inc.: Pages 55, 133, 214, 269, 310, 355, 408, 433, 469, 516, 546, 675, 870, 934. U.S. Senate: 442.

Printed in the United States of America

VB PKG 10 9 8 7 6 5 4 3 2 1

This book is printed on acid-free paper.

Contents

Foreword

The Rebirth of Capitalism

Robert J. Samuelson

ONE OF THE REMARKABLE STORIES of our time is the fall and rise of capitalism. If you go back 30 or 40 years, hardly anyone talked about "capitalism." The word existed in dictionaries and history books, but it had virtually disappeared from everyday conversation and political debate. It connoted a bygone era (it was thought) of cruel and crude business titans who abused their workers and presided over an inherently unstable economic system. It was bad news.

We had moved on. People thought the economic system had fundamentally changed. Government supervised markets; modern managers, not the old moguls, were more sensitive to workers and communities. They had more "social responsibility." A new vocabulary was needed to signify the progress. People talked of a "mixed economy" of shared power between government and business. Sometimes there was mention of "free enterprise" and "private enterprise." Hardly anyone advocated unadulterated "capitalism."

There were a few conspicuous exceptions. In 1962, a little-known economist named Milton Friedman published a book titled *Capitalism and Freedom*. The title was catchy precisely because it praised a system that was so unfashionable that it was hardly mentionable.

Four decades later, we have come a long way. Friedman became famous and won a Nobel Prize. His title no longer seems controversial, and the relationship it suggests—that capitalism promotes political freedom—is widely, if not universally, accepted. (Freidman cited many connections. By allowing consumers more choices, capitalism nurtures a taste for choice in many areas, including politics. Capitalism dilutes political power with

"widely dispersed" economic power. And it enables people to criticize government because most workers do not depend on government for a job.)

What explains the reversal? Well, the answer isn't shrinking government. When Friedman wrote his book, government did less than it does now. It spent less as a percentage of national income (gross domestic product—GDP) and taxed less. It had fewer regulations. In 1965, Congress created Medicare and Medicaid, federal health-insurance programs for the elderly and poor. Programs to provide college aid, food assistance, and housing expanded. In 1960, governments at all levels—federal, state and local—spent 26 percent of GDP. In 2002, they spent 32 percent of a much larger GDP. Government regulation of the environment, workplace safety, and consumer products had increased dramatically.

Generally speaking, the story is similar in Europe. In the 1980s and 1990s, some nationalized industries (airlines, telecommunications, steel) were converted to private companies. But government spending has progressively grown, as has regulation. From 1960–2002, government spending rose from 30–45 percent of GDP in Germany, from 28–46 percent of GDP in Italy, and from 37–49 percent of GDP in France (1963–2002). Almost everywhere the "welfare state" has grown.

Still, capitalism has regained respectability for two reasons: fading memories and the end of the Cold War.

Nothing discredited capitalism more than the Great Depression, which seemed to be a climactic crisis. In the 1930s, the unemployment rate in the United States averaged 18 percent. High joblessness in Europe helped cause World War II by bringing Hitler to power. Raw capitalism, in the popular view, could no longer be trusted. At a minimum, it needed to be reformed and regulated. Other critics thought it should be abolished. Among some intellectuals, communism was fashionable.

So much suffering and political instability made capitalism a scourge. But as the Depression-era generation has died, so have the personal memories of the decade's horrors. The anti-capitalist stigma has faded.

Simultaneously, the collapse of communism in the 1980s and the early 1990s seemed to confirm capitalism's superiority as a wealth-generating machine, a system that could raise mass living standards. Governments everywhere were obsessed with improving the well-being of their citizens. For roughly four decades, communism (and its many variants) vied with "free enterprise" to see which could do better.

Under communism, government ruled the economy. There was collective ownership of industry and agriculture in communist states; in socialist countries, the government controlled critical industries (power, communications, railroads, airlines, oil). Central planners coordinated production, made investment decisions, and decided which industries would expand. On the other side was free enterprise. Private companies competed for customers and profits. Private "markets"—responding to consumers' preferences and corporate profitability—made the basic decisions of what would be produced, what prices would be charged, and what sectors would flourish or falter.

By the early 1980s, even before communism's political collapse, the economic competition was essentially over. People could see that the communist world (the old Soviet Union, most of Eastern Europe, China, and Cuba) was vastly poorer than Western Europe, the United States, and Japan. They could see that it wasn't just elites who benefited; average families enjoyed riches that, 50 years earlier, had been virtually unimaginable. The contrast was so obvious that even some communist states began abandoning the orthodoxy. In the late 1970s, China started to introduce personal ownership and private markets into its farming system. Once the Soviet Union and Eastern Europe discarded communism, it became commonplace to dramatize the outcome: "Capitalism" and "freedom" had conquered "communism" and "tyranny."

But if "capitalism" was no longer a dirty word, its triumph was also misleading. Lost in all the celebration and rhetoric was a simple reality: Capitalism itself is a vague concept. Its meaning is unclear. Capitalism requires more than the legality of private property or the ability to accumulate profits—wealth. After all, even feudal societies had private property and permitted some members (monarchs, lords, barons) to become rich. But feudal societies restricted property ownership and, through law and custom, decided what people could do. Serfs were tied to lords, who promised them protection. In turn, the serfs had to farm their lords' lands.

Capitalism is larger than property and profits. It's an economic system that depends on some common social and political arrangements that guide the behavior of people and enterprises. A capitalist society has at least three defining characteristics.

First, it settles most economic questions through decentralized markets and free prices. If people want more widgets, then widget prices rise and production increases. If there are too many widgets, prices will drop, profits will fall and, ultimately, production will decline. Decisions about which industries will grow (or shrink) and what occupations will increase (or decline) are mostly resolved by markets.

Second, it creates a motivational system because it allows people and companies to keep much of the reward from their own work. Capitalism presumes that people want to better themselves. The theory is that they will work harder, invest more, and take more risks if they benefit from their own ambition, inventiveness, or imagination. Incomes are generally not determined by law, custom, or politically set "needs."

Finally, capitalism establishes a permanent system of "trial and error." Without centralized control of what's produced—and because people and firms can profit from satisfying "the market"—everyone is free to experiment. The experimentation is a basic source of higher living standards, because it leads to new technologies, products, and services or better ways (including cheaper ways) of making and selling existing products and services.

What this means is that, as a social system, capitalism inevitably involves inequality. Some win more than others. The whole theory is that the possibility of exceptional reward inspires people to make exceptional effort. Similarly, capitalism virtually ensures constant change. The "market" is not wedded to the present. Its demands and desires can shift. The economist Joseph Schumpeter (1883–1950) called this process "creative destruction." At its best, it improves people's well-being. But sometimes the constant change leads to economic and social instability—financial panics, depressions, and industrial and agricultural displacement. Economic stability requires that supply and demand roughly match; that workers who want jobs can find them; that what's produced will be consumed; that what's saved will be invested. Though "the market" does well at making these matches, it doesn't succeed at all times and in all places.

Because all societies cope with these twin problems—inequality and instability—there is no ideal form of capitalism. Every country, including the United States, modifies capitalism's dictates to satisfy its own political preferences and cultural tastes. Few markets are totally free. Most involve some government regulation. Labor markets in the United States have, among other things, a minimum wage, limits on working hours, and rules for pensions. Some prices are regulated or controlled; in many countries, governments set power, water, and phone rates. People and companies typically can't keep everything they earn; there are taxes. Government regulation and social custom limit "trial and error." In Japan, government regulations protected small family-owned stores against larger chains. Almost all societies regulate scientific experimentation.

Capitalism is thus a term of art. All advanced economies remain "mixed economies" with power shared between private markets and government. It is a matter of degree. Similarly, capitalism is conditioned by culture. It is not the same in the United States as in, say, Japan, Brazil, Germany, or South Korea. If government suppresses the power of markets too much—through taxes, restrictions, regulations, subsidies, and politically inspired privileges—then capitalism is a misnomer. It is a label without meaning. Similarly, if culture checks markets too much—by, for example, awarding wealth and status on the basis of birth, custom, political connections, or corruption—then capitalism is also a misnomer.

Capitalism is always a work in progress, and at the dawn of the 21st century, this is especially true. In the past half century, it has grown more global in two senses.

First, more and more countries are trying the capitalist "model"—China, India, and Russia being the largest of recent converts—and hoping to fit it to their own values and social systems. Because Friedman was at least partially correct, this involves social and political transformations as well as economic change. Relying more on "markets" means giving people more freedom and allowing status and income to be settled more by economic competition rather than by birth, ethnic background, or political standing. Conflicts between the past and present are not only possible; they are inevitable.

Capitalism has also grown more "global" in a second sense: Reduced barriers to international trade and investment have resulted in more of both. Countries that decide to try capitalism need not decide simultaneously to join the world economy; they could keep their capitalism at home and restrict dealings with the outside world. But in practice, countries are doing both. Almost all countries have become more dependent on worldwide flows of trade and investment funds for their own prosperity. This creates new opportunities for gains—cross-border flows of products, technologies, and management techniques. Countries can specialize in what they do best; investors can seek out the highest returns. But the same interdependence also creates new opportunities for instability if there's a breakdown in global trade or investment flows.

There has been a rebirth of capitalism, but it is not the capitalism of 30, 50, or 100 years ago. It is a new version—or rather many new versions—of an old idea. How it evolves and fares is a fascinating story that is fateful for us all.

ROBERT J. SAMUELSON writes a column for *Newsweek* and the *Washington Post*. He is author of *The Good Life and Its Discontents: the American Dream in the Age of Entitlement* (1995) and *Untruth: Why the Conventional Wisdom is (Almost Always) Wrong* (2001).

Introduction

THE FACT THAT WE live in an era of capitalism is universally acknowledged by both the laity and the priesthood of social sciences. The dynamism in the production of wealth and the social progress associated with the historical development of capitalism are also generally conceded. However, passionately controversial debates ensue as soon as an effort is made to specify the defining elements—the essence—of the social system called capitalism.

What is capitalism? A dictionary definition, for example, is generally stated as an economic system characterized by freedom of the market, along with private ownership of the means of production and distribution. Simple enough at the outset. But, if one looks at the institution of markets, one finds them in primitive, slave, feudal, and even socialist societies. Perhaps, one could assign a teleological design to an ever-expanding market as an indicator of choice and freedom achieving its zenith in the full flowering of capitalism. The fully fledged actualization of a market system in this view, in a way, is a herald of the end of history: Capitalism *must* reign forever since it is coeval with human freedom.

Another view explains the pervasive and guiding role of markets under capitalism—the invisible hand metaphor of Adam Smith. While individual human beings pursue their own selfish interests, the market forces bring about not only a technical equalization of things bought and sold (i.e., produced and consumed) but also, as if behind the backs of the unsuspecting operators, a socially beneficent outcome is generated—an optimum optimorum—the best of all possible worlds. The implied belief system is to yield to the deity of the inherently virtuous invisible hand.

Yet another strand of thinking questions the wisdom of reposing such sovereignty in the market forces—expressing our productive potential as producing commodities for the market, satisfying our human needs through buying from the market—as it bypasses direct human interaction, thus leading to alienation from other human beings, and creating a profound malaise of the modern capitalist era. Does the freedom of the market take precedence over the freedom of human beings? The question remains.

A second defining element of capitalism has to do with the private ownership of the means of production, presumably to effect efficient utilization as well as efficacious stewardship of resources. Those who produce the smartest get to receive the most returns. And the expectation of future returns assures a rational interest in the proper maintenance of productive resources—the cliché of "nobody ever washes a rented car" is invoked to reinforce private ownership. True enough.

However, if one examines the actual state of the relationship between private (individual, corporate) and collective (government) ownership in the advanced capitalist economies, it becomes obvious that the collective control of national income (the gross national product) varies from a third in North America to about a half in Western Europe. This, of course, does not take account of the collective ownership of stocks and bonds through pension funds, etc. Also, despite repeated and frequent spates of privatizations, the average weight of collective ownership has been on the rise. This can be explained by examining the role of the state in a private market economy. A market economy is premised on the notion of private property, which in its essence requires the exclusion of potential claimants. The enforcement of this exclusion requires a potential, sometimes actual, use of coercive power. Individually centered protection of private property can be awfully expensive, hence irrational. Therefore, we have the historically concomitant rise of state power along with the development of capitalism, as well as its public acceptance even when grudging, as in the "necessary evil" conceptualization of government.

This formulation of the collective in service of, and subservient to, the private ownership concept tends to leave out a prior theoretical issue. How does private ownership of the means of production come about in the first place? The textbook economic literature essentially assumes the problem away. The problematic is defined to focus on efficient allocation of resources in the market setting where the economic agents appear with varying initial endowments. This truly is rephrasing the myth of the proverbial stork randomly granting the baby in the pouch with certain gifts—initial endowment. A more sophisticated explanation would rest on the obvious laws of inheritance, talent, industriousness, and a random factor of luck—not an entirely robust explanatory formulation, much less a morally defensible one.

The skeptic must look for a sharper angle to discover the deeper meaning of this emphasis on the private ownership (by some) of the means of production. By the same token, it implies that there are others (indeed many, the majority) who are deprived of their own independent means of survival under capitalism. This introduces the notion of social classes in the system—those who own the means of production (the capitalists) and those who do not (the workers) and must access them via the courtesy of the former—a relationship of dependence, inequality, and possibly exploitation.

The real significance of private property in the means of production is that a worker can be excluded from the use of tools necessary for productive activity unless the worker agrees to share the produce of labor with those who own capital, the tools of production. An obvious corollary of this is that as in feudalism, where the serf did the producing and the lord got most of the share of total product, under capitalism the actual production is undertaken by the workers, and the capitalist is assured of a lion's share of the produce. Not only that. The market mechanism, through competition, allows only a socially determined subsistence to the worker whereas the capitalists get the residual—the social surplus—as their reward. Thus, capitalists have a basis for enhancing their property of the means of production, and maintaining and consolidating their class privilege.

The creation of wealth. A stellar characteristic of capitalism is its fantastic capacity to produce goods and services: wealth. Much as it is celebrated, it is also mostly justifiable. By any measure, if one were to stack the millennia of production of all previous social formations—primitive, slave, feudal—it would pale into insignificance when compared to the production of this relatively young, in a historical sense, social system that, according to varying accounts, established itself during the so-called long century, 1350–1550. The transformation of feudalism into capitalism, initially in western Europe, is accompanied with an era of enlightenment, scientific discovery, industrialization of production, expanding trade, and dissolution of many social barriers. The transformation involves not just the application of scientific technique to production, but also the necessity of continuous innovation that is required by the inexorable forces of market competition.

It is in this context that one can appreciate the unique category of capital as being similar to wealth in the sense of accumulation of social objects of use, but also quintessentially distinct in the sense of its drive to dissolve into money capital, to buy physical commodities to produce more commodities that in turn had to be sold for more money for their realization as capital, and so on as a continuous circuit of production and circulation. This ceaseless and insatiable quality of investing for production and reinvesting for more production in the face of competition from market adversaries lends capitalism a special penchant for excellence in production. Mercifully, all schools of thought are in happy unison in praise of this aspect. But there is more.

Whereas the earlier social formations concentrated the wealth objects in the exclusive possession of the ruling classes, the dialectic of capitalist production requires that, as part of the efficiency of production, the commodities produced should be cheapened enough for the working classes to partake of this abundance, and experience a relatively higher standard of living. Money, the common denominator of all valuations in the system, requires that produced commodities be sold in the market to realize their money value. That is the secret of appropriating social surplus: the making of profits in the system.

Thus, the expanded production leads to a commensurately expanded market. For all of the products to be sold, the efficiency in production shows up as cheaper products, which in turn enables the working classes to participate in the market to raise their standard of living. The historically unprecedented high standards of living of advanced countries are a testimony to this dynamic. The partisan champions of the system emphasize this empirical reality as proof-positive that capitalism equals prosperity.

In this view, capitalism's frontiers are described by the geographical areas of Western Europe, North America, and Japan. But capitalism, from its very inception, is a global system—the long-distance trading, ocean-faring adventures, colonial capture of far-flung areas for resources and markets are essential features of its development. The social systems of Honduras, Guatemala, Bangladesh, Botswana (and most of the so-called Third World countries) are shaped by and in the image of western capitalism. A cursory look at these societies negates the equation of capitalism equaling prosperity. One way to look at the system is to suggest a differential system of distribution within countries (favoring the governing classes), and between countries (favoring the core countries). This hierarchy of privilege can explain, to some degree, the existence of scarcity and deprivation in some social classes and some geographical areas under the sway of capitalism. While capitalism helps dissolve and destroy the hierarchy of pre-capitalist eras, it establishes a new hierarchy of its own with consequent deleterious effects.

The politics of capitalism. Another major claim often asserted vociferously is that capitalism equals freedom and democracy. Again, the empirical evidence of advanced capitalist countries is cited to stunning effect. The logic of market is truly democratic: one dollar one vote, more dollars more votes. Indeed, the market recognition of any human need is in proportion to the money endowment one commands. This leads to the hierarchy of the elite. However, there is another side to it. If you have money, you can overcome the barriers of caste, creed, race, and social status—an amazingly leveling phenomenon. In addition, anyone can strive to earn, to accumulate money (at least in theory), thus overcoming shortcomings of birthrights, conferred honors, etc. Since the universe of capital runs on the measuring rod of money, anybody with money can express freedom commensurate with that valuable commodity.

As for democracy, the record is at best mixed. We need only cite the varyingly undemocratic governments of today's Third World countries, but can also look to the easy historical co-existence of capitalism with fascism, militarism, and allied totalitarianisms. It is for this reason that critics of capitalism can, with some effect, decry the extant modes of democracy as, in reality, dictatorships of the bourgeoisie. We have some ways to go to achieve true democracy in the field of the economy as we have done in the sphere of the polity: one person, one vote!

The mainstream expositions assiduously avoid the issue of fairness or equitability (perhaps exploitation) in the market setting as a value judgment beyond the domain of scientific analysis. Is market price of labor (wages) a fair compensation for work in some sense? The question is obviated if we accept a market determination of personal or social values as not only inevitable, but inherently desirable. This view is buttressed by the notion of the social contract between capital and labor. Since, in this view, workers voluntarily agree to a specific wage (presumably market determined, directly or indirectly), there is no sense of unfairness or exploitation in this relationship. Perhaps. But what, as some have pointed out, if the workers have no choice but to enter into an agreement with capital, since they do not have their own independent means of production or survival? Could this, then, be a contract between un-equals subject to nullification?

Generally, it is claimed that capitalists sacrifice through saving (not consuming) and workers do not, hence the extra share for the capitalists is justified. But, if one examines this closely—just as a thought experiment—one may arrive at a divergent conclusion. When investment goods (machines) production increases to expand investment, the consumption goods (bread) production declines, thus leading to relatively higher prices for consumption goods—the marketplace expression of belt-tightening. But who ends up consuming less bread as a result? The workers or capitalists? And when investment does expand the overall production, who controls the additional benefits of production? Workers or capitalists? The best we can say is that, through a trickle down, workers also gain at the end. They do, but in relation to each one's sacrifice? A corollary of this thought experiment is that the slave and the serf could clearly see the obvious exploitation by the overlord as expropriation of the produced value. The expropriation of surplus under capitalism is veiled through the mechanism of the market that, like many things in the system, renders it invisible.

A more formal presentation equates land, labor, and capital as factors of production—each factor in turn receiving its due desserts—the so-called theory of marginal productivity. Since all produce is exhausted as a result of compensating the three contributing factors, there remains no social surplus to fuss over, and hence no possibility of exploitation. The fact that it is the landlords and capitalists, not the inanimate objects—land and capital—who are receiving the share of the produce, without contributing their labor directly to the process, remains elusive. Here, there is no friction, conflict, or contradiction of subordination. Therefore, there is no reason for resistance to the system or appeal for reform.

Capitalism and human beings. Lastly, how is the logic of capitalism related, if at all, to the nature of social construction and the essence of human beings? Here, the mainstream view is crystal clear. Human beings are, and have always been, essentially homo-economicus—i.e., they are by nature self-interested (selfish?), individualistic (self-centered?), acquisitive (greedy?), and rational (calculating?). And if you do not agree, observe them in a market setting, we are told. Sure enough. How would anybody, with some modicum of common sense, react to the exacting conditions of survival in a market setting? Besides, the notion of labor as a commodity, something produced for and purchased from the market, is repeated incessantly in the same breath with land and capital. Labor is co-equal with land and capital, to be bought and sold and pressed into service for production at the beck and call of capitalism.

This, in a way, is an example of dehumanization *par excellence*. There are no human beings in this model, just commodities—commodities that acquire the social attributes of interacting with each other in exchange through the market. That the commodities for sale represent purposeful labor of a human being is lost in the shuffle. People do not interact with, or depend on, or express their sociality with other people—all this is mediated in the market through commodities' purchase and sale. There is no temporal transcendence, no reform, no resistance—the peaceful reproduction of the capitalist system continues. Of course, one still has to confront the daily world of capitalism full of roiling resentments, wars of conflicting interests, and general chaos of humanity under duress. But, still capitalism continues on.

No introduction can be concluded without some future prognosis of the system. This is the trickiest area in social sciences, hence left untouched for better or worse. However mystical this terrain, one can take a bit of a risky peek. The economic side of the system is prone to recurring ebbs and flows—expansion, contraction, recession, depression, and stagnation and resurgence yet again. Many theorists have suggested tentative remedies of reform and control of the system. Some have argued for a structural rearrangement. Others have argued for a romantic return to the earlier (more pristine) formulations. One thing is clear. Through the zigs and zags, trial and error were built into the ever-changing nature of the system, and an abiding drive of humanity has been to raise its level of humane consciousness. The system of capitalism, by the end of the 21st century, is likely to be a lot more democratic, with freer access to its productions, less rapacious of environment, and more receptive to the better instincts of human beings.

The Encyclopedia of Capitalism. Any work with pretensions of being encyclopedic is a daunting enterprise. To carry out this project on the topic of capitalism—itself a tricky subject—is doubly intimidating. Even so, the organizing principle of the work is to present topics and articles that describe the historical evolution of capitalism as a system of social relations in production and distribution. This evolution essentially relates to a transformation from feudalism into the meteoric rise of industrialism. At the same time, a system of ideas came into social acceptance after vigorous debate. We present this strand of ideas as a history of economic thought—a new lexicon, a different perspective, the capitalist paradigm. We also present the advance of capitalism through wars, colonization, and imperialism to the modern day: the ultimate triumph of unchallenged domination. This encyclopedia covers

not only the spread of the system itself but its myriad benefits to humanity that make it so universally appealing: the "Why?" of capitalism, if you will.

Here, along with commentaries, debates, and points-of-view, we strive for objectivity and balanced perspective. Yet, we emphasize the nature of the system's vigor that compels and nourishes innovation of technique as well as organization—the real secret of capitalistic success. Lastly, we include reference to capitalism's effect on the overall condition of humanity both in the United States and internationally. To accomplish this task, more than 700 articles were prepared with the following features in mind:

- Descriptions of major world countries and their economic histories as they relate to capitalism.

- Biographies of winners of the Nobel Prize in Economics and how their theories and discoveries affected capitalism.

- Profiles of the top global companies and explanations of how each employed the tenets of capitalism in achieving their global status.

- Descriptions of all U.S. presidential administrations with a focus on how their policies affected the development of American capitalism.

- Historical biographies of American and international capitalistic entrepreneurs and how their ideas, inventions, or discoveries led to the creation of enterprise.

- More than 100 article entries on major historical events, social movements, technological advances, and personalities that affected the development of capitalism.

- Definitions of economic business terms and theories relating to capitalism.

More than 100 authors, affiliated with universities, research organizations, and business activities around the world were invited to write on the topic of their specialization. We hope the Encyclopedia will serve as a useful and outstanding reference work, as well as a resource for teaching courses in economics, political science, history, international relations, sociology and other related fields.

SYED B. HUSSAIN, PH.D.
GENERAL EDITOR OF THE *ENCYCLOPEDIA OF CAPITALISM*
UNIVERSITY OF WISCONSIN, OSHKOSH
MAY 1, 2003

List of Contributors

Abugri, Benjamin
Department of Economics and Finance
Southern Connecticut University

Aka, Arsène
The Catholic University of America

Azari-Rad, H.
Department of Economics
State University of New York, New Paltz

Balak, Benjamin
Department of Economics
Rollins College

Barnhill, John
Independent Scholar

Batchelor, Bob
Independent Scholar

Becker, Klaus
Texas Tech University

Berkley, Holly
Department of History
Hardin-Simmons University

Bhattacharya, Tithi
Department of History
Purdue University

Bishop, Elizabeth
Institute for Gender and Women's Studies
American University in Cairo, Egypt

Blankenship, Cary
Department of History, Geography, Political Science
Tennessee State University

Block, Walter
Loyola University, New Orleans

Boettcher, Susan R.
Department of History
University of Texas

Borden, Timothy G.
Independent Scholar

Bradley, Robert L., Jr.
Institute for Energy Research

Braguinsky, Serguey
Department of Economics
State University of New York, Buffalo

Caplan, Bryan
Department of Economics
George Mason University

Carton, Joel
Department of Economics
Texas Tech University

Cawley, John H.
Department of Economics
Cornell University

Chen, Shehong
University of Massachusetts, Lowell

Chung, Wai-keung
Department of Sociology
University of Washington

Coelho, Alfredo
University of Montpellier, France

Cruz, Laura
Department of History
Western Carolina University

Cundiff, Kirby R.
Hillsdale College

Dadres, Susan
Department of Economics
Southern Methodist University

DeCoster, Karen
Walsh College

Dolenc, Patrick
Department of Economics
Keene State College

Dompere, Kofi Kissi
Department of Economics
Howard University

Douglas, R.M.
Department of History
Colgate University

DuBose, Mike
American Culture Studies
Bowling Green State University

Dynan, Linda
Independent Scholar

Elvins, Sarah
Department of History
University of Notre Dame

Erickson, Christian
Roosevelt University

Evrensel, Ayşe Y.
Department of Economics
Portland State University

Ewing, Bradley T.
Department of Economics
Texas Tech University

Ferguson, William
Institute for Experiential Living
Grinnell College

Foster, Kevin R.
City College of New York

Fowler, Russell
University of Tennessee, Chattanooga

Fuming, Jiang
Charles Sturt University, Australia

Gabriel, Satya J.
Department of Economics
Mount Holyoke College

Gallois, William
American University of Sharjah
United Arab Emirates

Geringer, Joseph
Essays On History

Gerlach, Jeffrey
Department of Economics
College of William & Mary

Grassl, Wolfgang
Department of Economics
Hillsdale College

Haworth, Barry
University of Louisville

Hill, Kirstin
Merrill Lynch & Company
London, England

Holst, Arthur
Widener University

Howell, Chris
Red Rocks College

Hussain, Akmal
Institute of Development Economics
Pakistan

Hussain, Syed B.,
General Editor of the Encyclopedia

Işcan, Talan
Department of Economics
Dalhousie University, Canada

Jacobson, Katherine
Department of History
Metropolitan State University

Jeitschko, Thomas D.
Department of Economics
Michigan State University

Kinni, Theodore
Independent Scholar

Kline, Audrey D.
University of Louisville

Klumpp, Tilman
Economics Department
Indiana University

Kosar, George
Brandeis University

Kozlov, Nicholas N.
Economics Department
Hofstra University

Kucsma, Kristin
Economics Department
Seton Hall University

Kypraios, Harry
Rollins College

Laberge, Yves
Institut Québécois des
Hautes Études Internationales, Canada

Larudee, Mehrene
Department of Economics
University of Kansas

Lawrence, Taresa
Howard University

Lawson, Russell M.
Independent Scholar

Lewis, David
Citrus College

Luque, Emilio
UNED University, Madrid, Spain

MacKenzie, D.W.
George Mason University

Mahmud, Tayyab
Ohio State University

Malik, Farooq
Pennsylvania State University, Berks

Matheson, Victor
Department of Economics
Williams College

Matraves, Catherine
Department of Economics and Management
Albion College

Mattson, Kevin
Department of History
Ohio University

Mazzoleni, Roberto
Department of Economics and Geography
Hofstra University

McGee, Kevin
University of Wisconsin

McGregor, Michael
Fannie Mae

Mitchell, David
George Mason University

Mocnik, Josip
Bowling Green State University

Moiz, Syed
Marian College

Moore, Karl
McGill University, Canada

Motluck, Mark E.
Anderson University

Mozayeni, Simin
State University of New York, New Paltz

Nesslein, Thomas
Urban and Regional Studies
University of Wisconsin, Green Bay

Neumann, Caryn
Department of History
Ohio State University

Odekon, Mehmet
Skidmore College

Ornelas, Emmanuel
University of Georgia

Paas, David
Hillsdale College

Palmer, Scott
RGMS Economics

Papageorgiou, Chris
Department of Economics
Louisiana State University

Petrou, Linda L.
Department of History
and Political Science
High Point University

Phelps, Chris
Ohio State University

Prieger, James E.
Department of Economics
University of California, Davis

Prono, Luca
University of Nottingham, England

Pullin, Eric
College of Business
Cardinal Stritch University

Purdy, Elizabeth
Independent Scholar

Rabbani, Mahbub
Temple University

Raman, Jaishankar
Department of Economics
Valparaiso University

Reagle, Derrick
Department of Economics
Fordham University

Robinson, Charles
Brandeis University

Rodríguez-Boetsch, Leopoldo
Portland State University

Rubel, Shawn
Independent Scholar

Saeed, Agha
University of California, Berkeley

Sagers, John
Department of History
Linfield College

Schrag, Jonathan
Harvard University

Schuster, Zeljan
School of Business
University of New Haven

Silver, Lindsay
Brandeis University

Sorrentino, John A.
Department of Economics
Temple University

Subramanian, Narayanan
Brandeis University

Sullivan, Timothy E.
Department of Economics
Towson University

Swanson, Paul
Department of Economics
and Finance
William Patterson University

Syed, Aura
Department of Political Science
Northern Michigan University

Thompson, Mark A.
Sephen F. Austin State University

Traflet, Janice
Columbia University

Troy, Michael J.
Michigan State University

Turdaliev, Nurlan
Department of Economics
McGill University

Vavrik, Ursula
Vienna University of Economics, Austria

von Ende, Terry
Texas Tech University

Walsh, John
Shinawatra University, Thailand

Weed, Charles
Department of Social Science
Keene State College

Weston, Samuel
Economics Department
University of Dallas

Whaples, Robert
Department of Economics
Wake Forest University

Wu, Xiadong
University of North Carolina, Chapel Hill

Young, Derek Rutherford
Department of History
University of Dundee, Scotland

Young, Ronald
Georgia Southern University

Zaccarini, Cristina
Adelphi University

List of Articles

Timeline of Capitalism

1964	Civil Rights movement gains momentum in United States	2/446
	Robert W. Fogel publishes *Railroads and American Economic Growth*	1/303
	Gary Becker publishes *Human Capital*	1/85
	Lyndon Johnson begins War on Poverty	2/446
1968	Protests spread against U.S. Vietnam War policy	3/902
1971	Richard Nixon abandons gold standard, Bretton Woods	2/602
1973	OPEC begins oil embargo against western nations	2/621
1979	Margaret Thatcher pushes privatization in UK	3/835
1981	France experiments with nationalization	1/309
	Ronald Reagan engages supply-side economics	2/702
1987	U.S. stock market crash causes deep recession	2/704
	Single Market Act approved in Europe, EU groundwork	1/271
1988	Japanese economic confidence peaks	2/438
1991	First introduction of the World Wide Web	3/829
	Soviet Union breaks into separate states	3/864
1992	Russia launches privatization program	2/729
1993	U.S. Congress passes NAFTA	2/581
1994	United States enters economic expansion	3/874
	Apartheid falls in South Africa, opens economy	3/777
1998	Asian financial crisis spreads fear of contagion	1/49
1999	Seattle WTO meeting draws strong protest	3/922
2001	Terrorist attacks in United States as nation enters recession	3/874
2002	Euro replaces currencies of 12 European nations	1/268

SOURCES. "Commanding Heights: Timemap" www.pbs.org; "Top 100 Business Events" www.thestreet.com; Harry Landreth and David Colander, *History of Economic Thought* (Houghton Mifflin, 1993).

Encyclopedia of
CAPITALISM

VOLUME I

accounting

IDENTIFYING, MEASURING, and communicating economic information is the process of accounting that permits informed judgments and decisions by the users of the information. Accordingly, accounting is not an end in itself but an information system that measures, processes, and communicates financial information about an identifiable economic entity. An economic entity is a unit that exists independently and includes both for-profit and not-for-profit organizations. Examples include a business, a hospital, a governmental body, a church, or a professional football team.

Accounting should not be confused with bookkeeping. Bookkeeping is the process of recording financial transactions and maintaining financial records. Accounting, on the other hand, includes the bookkeeping function, but goes well beyond that. While bookkeeping is an important part of accounting and is mechanical as well as often repetitive in nature, accounting includes design of accounting systems, interpretation and analysis of data, and communicating this information to its intended users.

Who benefits from accounting? As the definition of accounting indicated, after identifying the economic events having financial consequences, the accountant measures, records, and communicates this information. The accounting information may be communicated to two main groups: Insiders (people belonging to the organization) and outsiders, to help them make sound business decisions.

Inside users include: Management, which has the responsibility for operating a business and for meeting its profitability, liquidity, and investment goals; and other non-management employees who may need the information to help negotiate contracts with management, salary increases, and other benefits.

Outside users include: Existing and prospective owners (investors) who have the highest stake in the company. They would like to know if they are making enough money on their investment. If they donated money to a charitable organization, their interest would be to ensure the money was spent on the purpose it was meant for. Potential investors judge the prospects for a profitable investment using the information provided by the accountants in the financial statements.

Accounting information provides detailed pertinent data that help creditors assess the profitability of the debtor and hence the chances of the return of their capital together with the interest. Potential creditors are interested in making the assessment of whether the company will be able to pay back its debts when they become due. Creditors would also be interested in assessing the prospects of the continuity and the existence of the company in future. Accounting information provided in the financial statements, when used with other criteria, may be a very useful tool in making such determinations.

Accounting information also helps customers and clients get the answers to their concerns that may include questions such as: Will the company survive long enough to honor its product warranties or provide after-sales service provided in the sales agreement? Accountants have developed analytical procedures that provide answers to such concerns.

Government, at all levels, depends on the TAX revenues to finance its operations and business. Companies and individuals pay many types of taxes. These taxes are based on net sales (excise and sales tax), net income (income tax), or on some other basis. Whatever tax amount is computed, it is the accounting information that is used as the basis to compute the taxes.

Types of accounting. There are mainly two types of accounting: Managerial accounting that is geared to the needs of the internal users in the company and financial accounting, which is basically meant for the external users.

Managerial accounting provides internal decision makers working for the company at various levels information that is needed for making sound business decisions, relating to profitability and liquidity of the company. The reports produced by the management accountants are called management reports. The range of these reports may include production department cost reports, product cost reports, direct labor cost reports, sales force traveling expenses in a particular area, expense reports of various departments, budgets, variance analysis, and projections. These reports help management identify areas of relative strengths and weaknesses and focus on increasing the efficiency at various levels and measure the effectiveness of the past decisions. In essence, these reports relate more to the day-to-day operations of the business and do not follow the accounting principles known as GENERALLY ACCEPTED ACCOUNTING PRINCIPLES (GAAP).

Financial accounting, on the other hand is primarily focused on the information needs of the outside users, including creditors, investors (owners), prospective investors, governmental and regulatory agencies, and the public in general. Accounting information is provided to the external users through reports called FINANCIAL STATEMENTS. These outside users make decisions pertaining to the company, such as whether to extend credit to a company or to invest in a company. Consequently, financial accounting information relates to the company as a whole, while managerial accounting focuses on a part or a segment of a company. It follows, therefore, that financial accounting is "macro" whereas managerial accounting is "micro" in nature.

Because of the diverse type of businesses companies may engage in, it is imperative to use uniform standards to record, process, accumulate and communicate the accounting information to outsiders. In the absence of such reporting standards or principles, accountants of a company or different companies may report their financial statements differently from year to year based on their personal goals or preferences. This would make the comparisons of financial statements very difficult from year to year and, at times, would be misguiding.

At the very early stage of its development, the accounting profession recognized the need to address this issue of adopting uniform standards for the preparation and reporting of financial statements. These standards or guidelines developed over a period of time, collectively, are called GAAP. All the external financial reports should be prepared in accordance with the GAAP. GAAP also requires providing adequate disclosures in the notes to the financial statements. By doing so, chances are that different readers or users of the financial statements will interpret the data in the same way and the leeway for subjectivity is minimized. The five organizations most influential in the establishment of GAAP for business and non-business organizations are the American Institute of Certified Public Accountants (AICPA), the Financial Accounting Standard Board (FASB), the Governmental Accounting Standard Board (GASB), the SECURITIES AND EXCHANGE COMMISSION (SEC), and the American Accounting Association.

With the increase in cross-border financial activities, there has been an increased focus on international accounting diversity. The International Federation of Accountants (IFAC) established the International Accounting Standards Committee (ISAC) in 1973 (now replaced by International Accounting Standards Board) in order to address this emerging issue. The ISAC has 142 accounting organizations from 103 countries as its members. More and more countries are recognizing International Accounting Standards (IAS) as acceptable standards for reporting their financial statements.

As a further measure to protect the interests of the financial statement users, SEC requires all the public companies whose stocks are listed on stock exchange to include "audited" financial statements in their annual reports. An audited financial statement means that a Certified Public Accountant (CPA) has to examine the financial statements of the company to give the reader an assurance that GAAP was followed in recording and processing the financial transactions as well as reporting standards required by GAAP have consistently been followed by the company. CPAs conduct their audits in accordance with Generally Accepted Auditing Standards (GAAS). The essential role of CPAs is to provide attestation and assurance services.

Basic financial statements. GAAP requires businesses to prepare and include four types of financial reports and include them in the annual report of the business. These reports, when used collectively, provide external users enough information about the financial position of a company and the results of its operations.

A balance sheet, also called the statement of financial position, shows the total economic resources at the disposal of a company on the date of the report and the sources of those resources. These economic resources, used to generate revenues for the company, are also called assets. By definition, assets are the economic resources owned by a business that are expected to benefit future operations. Examples are cash, amounts receivable from customers, inventory to be sold in the future, machinery and equipment used in production, furniture used in the office, land and building, etc. Assets can also be intangible (non-physical) such as patents, trademark, goodwill, software, etc. Assets have value to the company because it uses them to run its business.

The accounting system is based on a double entry system. Thus, for every resource, there has to be a source. The sources of these resources (assets) or claims on the resources are called equities. These sources can be either from the owners (owners' equity) or from the creditors (creditors' equity) or from both the sources. The relationship between the two may be expressed in any of the following ways:

Resources = Sources
Assets = Equities
Assets = Creditors' Equity + Owners' Equity
Assets = Liabilities + Owners' Equity

The last equation above is called the accounting equation and a balance sheet merely further provides details of the two sides of this equation.

Liabilities are present obligations of a business to pay cash, transfer assets or provide services to other entities in the future. Among these obligations are the debts of the business, amounts owed to suppliers for goods or services bought on credit (called accounts payable), borrowed money (for example money on loans payable to banks), taxes owed to the government, and services to be performed.

The equity of owners, shareholders, or stockholders represents the amount invested by the investors as CAPITAL. It is the claim of the owners to the assets of the business.

A company's assets are financed either by creditors, investors (owners or shareholders), or by both. Stockholders' equity, thus, is the portion of the assets financed by (owned by) the investors. Owners' equity is therefore also called the residual interest or the residual equity in the assets of the company. Owners' equity comes from two sources: a) contributed capital, which is the cash or other investments in the business by the owners; and b) earned capital, which is the earnings of the business kept in the business. It follows that owners' equity is increased by capital contributions and earnings of the business and decreased by the dividends paid out to shareholders and losses incurred by the business. Earned capital is also called retained earnings. Since the amount of the assets of a business changes continuously as a result of its operations, the balance sheet is ever-changing and therefore, at a point in time the financial position of a business will be different from other points in time.

In summary, by looking at the balance sheet of an entity, and comparing it with the balance sheet of the previous period, its user can ascertain what economic resources are at the disposal of the company, how they are financed, and what changes took place over a period of time.

The income statement, also called the statement of income, statement of earnings, or statement of operations, reports the revenues and expenses for a period. The excess of revenues over expenses is called net income. An accounting principle, called the matching concept, is applied in recognizing the revenues and expenses for the period. The term, PROFIT, is also widely used for this measure of performance but accountants prefer to use the technical terms net income or net earnings. If the expenses used in generating the revenue exceed the revenue, the excess is the net loss for the period.

GAAP requires that financial statements should be prepared in accordance with the accrual basis accounting principles. The matching concept is the essence of accrual basis accounting. Therefore, an understanding of the matching concept is important to grasp the concept of the accrual basis accounting. In its simplest form, the matching concept requires that all the expenses incurred to generate a period's revenue should be recorded (matched) in the same period regardless of when paid. Conversely, if the expenses of the next accounting period are paid in the current period, they cannot be deducted in the current year; they need to be deducted (matched) with the revenues of the next year.

Accrual basis accounting also requires that revenues should be recorded when earned, regardless of the timing of the cash receipts. There is another form of accounting, called cash basis accounting, which is usually used by very small businesses. It is based on the actual cash receipt and payment system. Therefore, under this system, revenue would not be recognized (included) in the income statement until actually collected. Similarly, only those expenses which have actually been paid, are recorded as expenses. Because, by choosing the timing of the payment of expenses or collection of revenues, income of the business can be manipulated, GAAP does not recognize the cash method of accounting as an acceptable method of reporting income.

The statement of retained earnings is also sometimes called the statement of owners' equity. This statement explains the changes in retained earnings during the accounting period. Such changes are usually due to the net income of the business, which increases the retained earnings, and dividend payments to shareholders which decreases the retained earnings.

While the income statement focuses on a company's profitability goal, the statement of cash flows is directed toward a company's liquidity goals. CASH FLOWS are the inflows of cash in the business (from customers, loans from banks and individuals, sale of assets, capital contributions, and investment income, etc.) as well as outflows from the business (payments to suppliers, employees, purchase of new equipment, etc.). The statement of cash flows summarizes the net cash flow in each of the three types of activities: Operating activities of business, investing activities, and financing activities. A user of this financial report, after carefully reading this statement can see how much cash from different sources was collected, and how much and in which areas it was spent.

GAAP and organizations influencing GAAP. It is important for the user of a financial statement to understand the measurement rules that were used in developing the information provided in the financial statements. These GAAP rules recognize the importance of adopting uniform rules for treating financial transactions and issues and presenting them in the financial statements. In the absence of these rules, the management of a company could record and report financial transactions as it sees fit and comparisons among companies would be difficult. GAAP takes away this liberty from the individual entities to use their own methods of reporting the financial information and brings uniformity in the accounting practices of different companies.

Historically, it was the SEC that took the initiative to work out detailed rules relating the recognition and measurement of accounting transactions and reporting them in the financial statements. However, the SEC very soon recognized that the development of accounting standards should be in the hands of the professional accountants. Since the late 1930s, the American Institute of Certified Public Accountants (AICPA) gradually took over the major work of standard development through its sub-organizations. From 1939 through 1959, the AICPA Committee on Accounting Procedures issued 51 Accounting Research Bulletins relating to various accounting issues. In 1959, AICPA created the Accounting Principles Board (APB), which was charged with the responsibility of guiding on matters of accounting principles. From 1959 until 1973 when it was replaced by another body of AICPA, Financial Accounting Standards Board (FASB), APB issued 31 "opinions" that accountants are required to follow while preparing the financial statements.

APB was replaced in 1973 by an independent, full-time, seven-member Financial Accounting Standard Board (FASB). The FASB issues Statements of Financial Accounting Standards and there are currently 148 such statements. A few more statements on some new emerging issues were in the development stage at the time of the writing of this article in 2003.

Governmental Accounting Standard Board (GASB) established in 1984 is responsible for issuing accounting and financial accounting standards in the government area.

The SEC, created under the Securities and Exchange Act of 1934, works very closely with the accounting profession to influence its work. The SEC indicates to the FASB the accounting topics it believes should be addressed. The American Accounting Association, consisting largely of accounting educators, influences GAAP by conducting research and studies.

Certified Public Accountants. Financial reports should be prepared in accordance with GAAP. But what is the assurance that GAAP has been followed consistently and if a departure from GAAP was necessitated, what was the support or justification for such a departure? Certified Public Accountants (CPAs) are charged to answer this question by providing assurance and attestation services. In their role as the auditor, CPAs are independent of the company's management. An audit is an examination of the company's financial statements as well as an evaluation of the accounting system, accounting controls used by the company, and records maintained by the company. CPAs state their opinion of the fairness of the financial statements and evidence gathered to support them in the Independent Auditor's Report, which is included in the annual report of a public company. The CPA, in this role as an auditor, conducts the audit of the financial statements in accordance with Generally Accepted Auditing Standards (GAAS).

The SEC requires that all the public companies should include their audited financial statements in their annual reports. The accountants' report does not preclude minor or unintentional errors and omissions in the financial statements. However, it does provide an assurance to the users of the financial statements that, on the whole, the financial statements are reliable.

BIBLIOGRAPHY. American Accounting Association, "A Statement of Basic Accounting Theory," (1966); Financial Accounting Standard Board, Statement of Financial Accounting Concept No. 1, "Objectives of Financial Reporting by Business Enterprises," (1979); Debra Jeter and Paul Chaney, *Advanced Accounting* (John Wiley & Sons, 2001); International Accounting Standard Board, www.isab.org.uk; Needles, Powers, Mills, and Anderson, *Principles of Accounting* (Houghton Mifflin, 1999); Financial Accounting Standard Board, www.fasb.org.

SYED MOIZ, PH.D.
MARIAN COLLEGE

Adams, John (1735–1826)

AMERICA'S FIRST vice president and second president seemed a bundle of contradictions. He was a leading advocate for American independence who admired British institutions; a fiery radical who became a pillar of order and conservatism; a revolutionary who defended British soldiers in court; an accomplished diplomat who was all but impossible to deal with; a champion of the rights of man who squelched freedom of speech; an architect of democracy who distrusted the people; and a politician who hated politics. Yet with all the contradictions of his long life and complex personality, John Adams was one of his nation's greatest statesmen.

Born on a small farm in Braintree (now Quincy), Massachusetts, outside Boston, Adams proved to be a voracious reader and an outstanding scholar. At the age of 16 he entered Harvard University and graduated in 1755. His parents hoped he would enter the ministry but he studied law in the evenings while teaching school in Worcester, Massachusetts in the day. After admission to the bar, he started a law practice in Braintree. In 1764, he married Abigail Smith, together sharing a love of books. They would eventually have five children. Although Adams would be known for his honesty, courage, and patriotism, and recognized as a legal and political thinker, he would also be known for his stubbornness, irritability, egotism, and suspicion of others.

The events leading to the AMERICAN REVOLUTION gave Adam's life new purpose and showcased his abilities as a lawyer, politician, and revolutionary. Displaying courage, in 1770, he successfully represented a British officer and six soldiers accused of murder during the Boston Massacre, but rejoiced when tea was dumped in Boston Harbor during the Boston Tea Party, and wrote masterful attacks on British tax policies in the Boston *Gazette.*

After election to the First Continental Congress, which convened in 1774, and the Second Continental Congress, which first met in 1775, he became an early and ardent advocate for American independence and proposed the appointment of George WASHINGTON as commander of the American Army assembled outside Boston. Even though written by Thomas JEFFERSON, Adams served on the committee assigned the task of drafting the Declaration of Independence and led the effort on the floor of Congress to secure its adoption in July, 1776. As Chairman of the Continental Board of War and Ordinance, he was in effect a single-man department of war. In 1779, he served as the chief drafter of the Massachusetts Constitution.

Adams believed that all men were created equal, but in a limited way. He argued that men are born equal in certain natural rights and desires, but unequal in characteristics like talent, wisdom, and temperament. This inequality of ability results in inequality of property and thus inequality of social status. He thought those favored by nature form an aristocracy of merit, an elite destined to rule for the good of society. These rulers are best able to fulfill the chief function of government: control man's passions. Adams also believed man had an inclination toward forming governments and without a ruling aristocracy of the "wise and good," anarchy results.

Therefore, Adams opposed the concept of democracy granting political equality to all. He believed in a republican government of aristocratic representatives. Because his ideal aristocracy was based on merit, he disfavored the hereditary aristocracy prevalent in Europe. His views also led him to support independence, for although he admired British institutions of governance in the abstract, including parliament and constitutional monarchy, he saw Britain as having slipped into corruption and ruled by a degenerate, unmeritorious aristocracy. He also believed in the protections of separation of powers within government to prevent concentration of power, even in the hands of aristocracy, but because of continual fear of mob rule, he found the American Constitution too liberal because of the popular elections it sanctioned.

Adams was sent to France to assist with the negotiation of a treaty of alliance. By 1780, he was back in Europe on a mission to obtain trade agreements and loans with the Netherlands and France, and, along with Benjamin Franklin and John Jay, negotiated a peace treaty known as "The Treaty of Paris," which was signed on September 3, 1783, formally ending the war. He was named the United States' first ambassador to Great Britain in 1785.

In 1789 and 1792, Adams was elected vice president serving under Washington, but found his eight years in the largely ceremonial position frustrating. When opposing political factions began to form around Secretary of the Treasury Alexander HAMILTON and Secretary of State Thomas Jefferson, Adams became a principal leader of the Hamiltonian forces that coalesced into the Federalist Party. As the Federalist nominee for president in 1796, Adams defeated Jefferson, and, under the terms of the Constitution at the time, Jefferson became vice president. Despite the victory, Adams' presidency soon became one of turmoil and disappointment.

When in 1797 American diplomats were asked to pay a bribe to three French agents (referred to by Adams as X, Y, and Z) to obtain a treaty with France, Americans were enraged and an undeclared war developed between the United States and France. Despite demands that a formal declaration of war be adopted, Adams bravely resisted the pressure feeling that the country was unprepared for such an engagement, and he eventually reached an understanding with France in 1800. Although a full-scale war was prevented, Adam's popularity was damaged and the Federalists were split.

Believing that foreign agents and spies were fomenting trouble, the Federalist Congress passed, and Adams signed, the Alien and Sedition Act in 1798. This measure made it harder to become a citizen and empowered the president to deport aliens deemed troublemakers. More importantly, it sought to silence domestic opposition by permitting the criminal prosecution of those falsely or maliciously criticizing the Congress or the president. The law was then used against Jeffersonian Republican newspapermen. Due to these unpopular policies, Jefferson defeated Adams in the bitter election of 1800.

After leaving the White House, Adams returned to Braintree and his books, and he and Jefferson rekindled their friendship in a remarkable series of letters. Both died on the same day, July 4, 1826, the 50th anniversary of the Declaration of Independence.

BIBLIOGRAPHY. L. H. Butterfield, ed., *Diary and Autobiography of John Adams* (Holiday House, 1962); Joseph Ellis, *Passionate Sage: The Character and Legacy of John Adams* (W.W. Norton, 1993); David McCullough, *John Adams* (Simon & Schuster, 2001); Peter Shaw, *The Character of John Adams* (1976); Jack Shephard, *The Adams Chronicles: Four Generations of Greatness* (1975).

RUSSELL FOWLER, J.D.
UNIVERSITY OF TENNESSEE, CHATTANOOGA

Adams, John Quincy (1767–1848)

THE SIXTH PRESIDENT of the UNITED STATES, John Quincy Adams was born in Braintree, Massachusetts, the oldest son of John ADAMS. At age 10, during the AMERICAN REVOLUTION, he began to accompany his father on diplomatic trips to Europe and attended schools in Paris, FRANCE, and Leiden, the NETHERLANDS. Adams returned to attend Harvard University and, after graduating in 1787, he studied law and began a legal practice in 1790.

Adams' public support for President WASHINGTON's neutrality policy won him an appointment as minister to the Netherlands in 1794. After three years he was appointed minister to Berlin. In 1801, his father, President John Adams, recalled him immediately following the election of Thomas JEFFERSON.

After several years in private practice, Adams was elected to the U.S. Senate. His support for President Jefferson's embargo, however, enraged his Massachusetts constituents who forced him to resign his seat.

In 1809, Adams once again left private practice and a professorship at Harvard to become President James MADISON's minister to Russia. In 1814, he served as chief negotiator to end the WAR OF 1812, and became minister to Great Britain the following year.

President James MONROE recalled Adams in 1817 to appoint him secretary of state. Adams had developed many relationships in Europe and remained on good terms with the heads of state and the diplomatic corps. However, he continued to believe in the U.S. policy of neutrality towards European affairs. He also negotiated

several agreements, including getting SPAIN to give up its claims on Florida, and with Britain over the boundaries of the Oregon Territory and for trade with the British West Indies. Yet his most significant contribution to foreign policy was drafting the Monroe Doctrine, which proclaimed that the United States would oppose any European intervention in the Americas.

Adams was one of four candidates running to succeed President Monroe in 1824. Andrew JACKSON received the most popular and electoral votes, but failed to carry a majority. That threw the election to the House of Representatives for the first time in U.S. history.

Henry Clay had great influence in the House, but had finished fourth. Only the top three candidates could be considered. Both Adams and Clay believed that Jackson would be a dangerous president. After meeting with Adams, Clay had his supporters vote for Adams, allowing Adams to win the presidency. Shortly thereafter, Adams announced that Clay would be his secretary of state, causing Jackson supporters to declare a "corrupt bargain" had been struck.

As president, Adams supported the Bank of the United States, a national tariff to protect domestic industries, greater infrastructure improvements such as canals and railroads, and government involvement in education and the sciences. A hostile Congress, however, kept him from enacting most of his proposals.

Congress did send him a Tariff Act in 1828 that raised tariffs on many manufactured goods to 50 percent of their value. The Act protected domestic industries in New England and the western states, but harmed southerners who bought most of their goods abroad. It also reduced British demand for southern cotton. Some Jackson supporters who normally opposed such tariffs supported the increases, with the hope such outrageous increases would either kill the bill altogether, or would kill Adams' chances of re-election if passed. Adams signed the bill, termed the "Tariff of Abominations," into law, virtually ending his chances for re-election.

Strong southern opposition to the bill led to a new movement for nullification, similar to the Virginia and Kentucky Resolutions of 1798. Southern leaders such as Vice President John Calhoun took the view that the states could nullify actions of the federal government. They also began to discuss more seriously the right of states to secede from the Union.

At the end of four years, Jackson swept Adams from power in 1828, and Adams returned to Massachusetts, content to finish his life in private practice.

Despite the fact that Adams did not seek office nor campaign for it, his friends and neighbors elected him to the House of Representatives in 1830. Adams found himself returning to Washington.

Congressman Adams remained prominent as an antislavery advocate. He spent more then a decade fighting to end the gag rule that prevented Congressional debate over the slavery issue. He repeatedly submitted petitions calling for the end of SLAVERY, in violation of House rules. Eventually the House voted to overturn the gag rule. Less successful was his attempt to amend the Constitution in 1839 to declare that no one born after 1845 could be kept in slavery.

Adams also donated his legal services to a group of Africans who had mutinied on the slave ship *Amistad.* Adams argued that these men who had been bound for slavery were free men, kidnapped from Africa, and should be allowed to return. The U.S. Supreme Court agreed and allowed the men to return to Africa.

Adams continued to be a vocal advocate for internal improvements as well as investment in scientific research. His work focused on founding the Smithsonian Institute and a failed attempt to establish a federal astronomical observatory.

Adams was also a vocal opponent of the MEXICAN-AMERICAN WAR. For 10 years, he had thwarted attempts to annex Texas before the annexation passed in 1845. In 1848, as he was standing on the floor of the House, protesting a Congressional grant of honorary swords to the men who won the war, he suffered a cerebral stroke and collapsed. He died two days later.

BIBLIOGRAPHY. Charles Francis Adams, *Memoirs of John Quincy Adams* (1874-77, Best Books, 1974); Mary W.M. Hargreaves, *The Presidency of John Quincy Adams* (University Press of Kansas, 1985); Paul C. Nagel, *John Quincy Adams: A Public Life, A Private Life* (Harvard University Press, 1997); Robert Remini, "Martin Van Buren and the Tariff of Abominations," *American Historical Review* (v.63/4, 1958); Robert Remini, *John Quincy Adams* (Times Books, 2002).

THOMAS D. JEITSCHKO, PH.D.
MICHIGAN STATE UNIVERSITY
MICHAEL J. TROY, J.D.

Afghanistan

A LAND-LOCKED COUNTRY bordered by IRAN, Turkmenistan, Uzbekistan, Tajikistan, CHINA, and PAKISTAN, Afghanistan has an area of 251,739 square miles (a bit larger than France), and has a population of 27 million people. Four ethnic groups inhabit the majority of Afghanistan, making up 88 percent of the population. The Pashtun people comprise 38 percent, the Tajiks 25 percent, the Hazara 19 percent, the Uzbeks 6 percent, and the remaining 12 percent are categorized as "other."

Afghanistan has never experienced an industrial revolution, mostly due to the near constant state of war in the country and partly because of the extremely rugged terrain. Without an industrial revolution, the major industries in Afghanistan have remained nearly unchanged in the past 200 years since its lawful foundation in 1774. The major industries are textiles and rugs, fruits and nuts, wool, cotton, fertilizer, soap, fossil fuels and gemstones. Afghanistan's GROSS DOMESTIC PRODUCT (GDP) in 2000 was $21 billion and the exchange rate of an Afghanis to a U.S. dollar in January, 2000, was 4,700:1.

Export commodities include opium, fruits and nuts, hand-woven carpets, wool, cotton, hides and pelts and precious and semi-precious gems. In 2001, exported commodities totaled $1.2 billion. Major import commodities include capital goods, food and petroleum products and most consumer goods. The import commodities totaled $1.3 billion in 2001. It is no surprise then, that in 1996 Afghanistan claimed $5.5 billion in external debt.

In January, 2002, $4.5 billion was collected at the Tokyo Donors Conference for Afghan Reconstruction following the United States–led removal of the Taliban regime. The money will be distributed by the World Bank to the Afghan Interim Authority, headed by Chairman Hamid Karzai, and is slated for rebuilding the country's infrastructure.

BIBLIOGRAPHY. *The CIA World Factbook 2002*; Sayed Qasim Reshtya, *The Price of Liberty: The Tragedy of Afghanistan* (Bardi Editore, 1984).

ARTHUR HOLST, PH.D.
WIDENER UNIVERSITY

Afrocentrism

AT THE SURFACE LEVEL, Afrocentrism is a variation on ethnocentrism in general and Eurocentrism in particular, designed to circumvent the inherent flaws of both, and yet to disclose and assert the self-reflective African consciousness. Based on a worldview that is derived from an ideologically constructed African perspective based on African ideals such as balance and harmony, Afrocentrism calls for "literally, placing African ideals at the center of any analysis that involves African culture and behavior." Though, simply put, it means looking at world with African eyes whose gaze is inspired by African experiences, its exponents are careful to qualify that "To be an African is not necessarily to be Afrocentric."

Its constitutive elements include, but are not limited to, Egyptcentrism, Negritude, Black Nationalism, and Pan-Africanism. Articulated by a number of competing schools of thought, the Afrocentric project alternately seeks: authenticity; recognition for its uniqueness; parity with every culture including European; and centrality as torch bearers of the first human civilization, as well as the progenitors of uniquely American music and other cultural forms. Moreover, it is defined by its zeal to contribute to the world civilization from a non-European visionary perspective. To that end, broadly speaking, it seeks influence in five main areas: 1) axiology, 2) education, 3) culture, 4) literature, and 5) politics.

The pursuit of authenticity is executed in two realms: Afrocentricity, that is, acquisition of agency and action and Africanity, or means to broadcast identity and being. In those realms, Afrocentric assertions can be summarized in terms of Edward Said's contrapuntal method, Malcolm X's retrieval method, and Frantz Fanon's critical self-evaluation method. The contrapuntal method is supposed to provide missing links in the collective memory and insert a multi-perspective corrective connection into historical narratives; the retrieval method is designed to recover forcefully alienated aspects of the self, (name, language, culture, art, religion, dress, cuisine, ritual, etc.) and restore them to their existential significance; and, finally, the critical method grew out of the need to for internal reform and improvement. Afrology, yet another related construct, denotes a particular method of knowledge production that is characterized by "the Afrocentric study of African concepts, issues and behavior."

Rooted in the politics of recognition, Afrocentrism seeks to rectify problems of both non-recognition and mis-recognition of the African identity. Typified by Ralph Ellison's novel, *Invisible Man*, it is based on the underlying conception that, to a large extent, our identity is shaped by recognition or mis-recognition of others, and to use Taylor's words, "a person or group of people can suffer real damage, real distortion, if the people or society around them mirror back to them a confining or demeaning or contemptible picture of themselves." The exponents of Afrocentrism seek recognition on their own terms by way of substantive affirmation of African ideals, values, symbols, heroes, and visions.

Its visionary goals, and here one could refer to Frantz Fanon for a clear example, are to not to create a third Europe but to "try to create the whole man, whom Europe has been incapable of bringing to triumphant birth."

Concerning axiology, or conceptualization of values, Afrocentrism at its philosophical center involves a revaluation of values in matters pertaining to morality, the arts, science, religion, economics, politics, laws, and customs, etc., and it seeks to disentangle them from hegemonic and self-perpetuating cultural claims of the West. Its approach to education involves a critique of

Eurocentric claims of universalism and permanence. It is in the writing and teaching of history, and history of civilizations above all, that (the non-essentialist and non-Manichean) Afrocentrism calls for a multicultural and multi-perspective approach.

If art "expresses the transformation of the spirit in the pursuit of value," and if culture can be seen, as Mathew Arnold has put it, as the pursuit of perfection, then Afrocentrism offers a definition of perfection significantly different than that of the West. But invested in the concrete historical context of the UNITED STATES, this definition gains added significance as a liberation aesthetic: "It has long been a commonplace that the achievements of the black music have far outstripped those of black literature," observes Henry Louis Gates, Jr., and, therefore, black intellectuals such as Albert Murray have "sought to process the blues into a self-conscious aesthetic, to translate the deep structure of the black vernacular into prose." This literature is to be a "statement about perseverance and about resilience and thus also about the maintenance of equilibrium despite precarious circumstances and about achieving elegance in the very process of coping with the rudiments of subsistence."

Derived from its institutional memory of slavery and colonialism, its politics is crystallized through various readings of the civil rights and human rights movements and, centrally focused on human liberation.

What underlies all five areas—at least from the perspective of non-Manichean and non-universalist Afrocentrism—is a conception of history, culture, and society that is open to and characterized by numerous perspectives, voices, and methodologies. It seeks, to use Mikhail Baktin's terms, a public space capable of inspiring and accommodating polyphony—an orchestra-like social interaction with each voice having its place and significance—and heteroglossia, that is to say, a wide variety of speaking consciousnesses, each with its own agency and autonomy.

Like many other ideological formulations, Afrocentrism, too, has its moderate and radical as well as essentialist and non-essentialist versions. The non-essentialist formulation invokes a common historico-cultural experience of subjugation, and bases itself, to use Aimé Césaire's words, not on "a cephalic index, or a plasma, or a soma, but . . . the compass of suffering." This school limits the claims of its applicability only to Africans or even more narrowly, as W.E.B. Du Bois postulates it, to soul-searching and self-reconciliation by African-Americans.

The non-essentialists exhort that Afrocentricity is not ethnocentric in two senses: "It does not valorize the African view while downgrading others," and, "It is a systematic approach to presenting the African as a subject rather than object."

The essentialist school, however, sees much broader application based on the achievements and contributions of the Egyptian civilization, on the one hand, and by the universal significance of black music, art and politics—civil rights movement, in particular—on the other. The essentialist and non-essentialist schools also, roughly, overlap with Manichean, a point of view that divides the world into two morally irreconcilable opposites, and non-Manichean tendencies within the Afrocentric project.

Third, apparently antithetical, school symbolized by Albert Murrary and seen as integrationist is also, paradoxically, Afrocentric at its core: "In its bluntest form, their assertion was that the truest Americans were the black Americans." . . . [In their] discourse, American, roughly speaking, means black." This school, however, does not anchor its claims in African culture and history but in the black experience in the United States.

The Afrocentrism debate. The idea and theory of Afrocentrism has had its share of criticism and controversy. Some critics have accused Afrocentrists of promoting "bad" history in order to invent a glorious past and to "provide themselves with an ancient history with links to that of the high civilization of ancient Egypt." This, the critics claim, is a "myth based on the flimsiest kind of evidence. The Egyptians were a mixed people, as all Mediterranean people are mixed." The charges leveled against Afrocentrists include: poor scholarship, reverse racism, sectarianism, and pursuit of therapeutic education which amounts to projecting ideological self-glorification into the academy, through the trap door of agitation and militancy.

Critics of Afrocentrism raise many of the same objections that others have raised against Eurocentrism. The debate, both sides agree is, in part, a debate about the future of the United States and how this future will be impacted by the emergent forms, types and hierarchies of knowledge.

Most of the critics, writing from a mainstream U.S. perspective, allege that Afrocentrism will lead to multicentrism that will weaken the United States by promoting "fragmentation and ethnocentrism," in effect resulting in rejection of multiculturalism. The critics fear the Afrocentric project is propelling the United States towards *E Pluribus Pluribus* instead of *E Pluribus Unum.* It is also perceived as implicitly anti-capitalistic as it seeks to overthrow Eurocentrism, capitalism's overarching and unifying ideology.

A sublime Afrocentric response in the American context, however, was given by Du Bois, even before the current debate had formally started: "The history of the American Negro is the history of this strife, this longing to attain self-conscious manhood, to merge his double self into a better and truer self. In this merging he wished neither of the older selves to be lost. He would not Africanize America, for America has too much to teach the world and Africa. He would not bleach his Negro soul in a flood of white Americanism, for he knows that the Negro blood has a message for the world."

Afrocentrism as a method of critiquing Eurocentrism. The exponents of Afrocentrism argue that a colonizing system is premised on the demand that the history of a state should also become the history of its varied peoples. One task of Afrocentrism, they contend, is to furnish a diversity-enhancing critique of all-homogenizing Eurocentrism that aims at inculcating the same values and aspirations in all peoples. Unless they are subjected to severe criticism, the preponderant Eurocentric myth of universalism, objectivity, and classical traditions retain a provincial European cast. And therefore Afrocentrism challenges European hegemony in the realms of:

1. production and dissemination of information

2. naming of things

3. propagation of concepts

4. dissemination of interpretations.

The final aim is abolishing the dominance and hegemony of the Eurocentric view of reality on a multicultural society.

The future significance of Afrocentrism can be contemplated in the dual cultural context characterized by Americanization of globalization and ethno-diversification of America. African-American intelligentsia has played a pivotal role in the cultural life of the United States with the aim of diversifying it from within. Afrocentrism can, among other things, serve as a convenient short hand for comprehending and discussing the role of black intellectuals and artists in the ethno-diversification of the globalization process.

BIBLIOGRAPHY. Molefi Kete Asante, *The Afrocentric Idea* (Temple University Press, 1997); Elijah Muhammad, *Message to the Black Man in the United States* (M.E.M.P.S, 1997); W.E.B. Dubois, *The Negro* (Oxford University Press, 1990); Frantz Fanon, *The Wretched of the Earth* (Grove/Atlantic, Inc., 1976); Cornel West, *Race Matters* (Random House, 1994); Martin Barnal, *Black Athena: The Afroasiatic Roots of Classical Civilization* (Rutgers University Press,1989-1990); Mary R. Lefkowitz and Guy Rogers, eds., *Black Athena Revisited* (University of North Carolina Press, 1996); Arthur M. Schlesinger Jr., *The Disuniting of America: Reflections on a Multicultural Society* (Norton, 1998); Wilson J Moses, *Afrotopia: The Roots of African American Popular History* (Cambridge University Press, 1998); Martin Bernal, David Chioni

Moore, eds., *Black Athena Writes Back: Martin Bernal Responds to His Critics* (Duke University Press, 2001).

AGHA SAEED, PH.D.
UNIVERSITY OF CALIFORNIA, BERKELEY

agriculture

SIMPLY DEFINED, agriculture is the production of crops, but there is nothing simple about the importance of agriculture to human evolution. Agriculture has been and continues to be the foundation of the economies of many societies. Agriculture is not an unchanging system of production, but has been in a continual state of transformation throughout human history, interacting with and often acting as the catalyst for changing technological, social, and environmental conditions.

Early agriculture. Agriculture first developed within settled human communities in Africa. Specifically, there is the region of the Sahara that, at one time, was wetter than it is now. Little is known about the early farming communities of the Sahara, except that they did not rely on farming alone, but engaged in fishing and hunting and gathering activities as well. These communities seem to have cultivated grain crops. Due to environmental and climatic change they were pushed out of the steadily growing arid desert region of the Sahara to the Nile Valley and surrounding areas.

The Nile River Valley experienced seasonal flooding that produced rich silt deposits of minerals and highly fertile soil. The early settlers to this region lived communally in small kinship units. Inhabitants engaged in the cultivation and harvest of a wide range of seeds, fruits, tubers, and the wild nut-grass that is still grown today. In the beginning, subsistence farming was practiced, but as cultivation practices improved with invention and innovation of new farming practices and materials, including pottery, storage facilities, grindstones, sickles, wheels, ploughs, hoes, mattocks, ox-driven water-wheels, and cantilevered water-buckets to irrigate fields, SURPLUS production became possible and with it trade between kinship groups and eventually between communities throughout the region. The extension of land under cultivation and the increasing surplus made it possible for greater specialization in labor. Artisans, merchants, and administrators became possible occupations with the advance of surplus production within agriculture.

Surplus production in agriculture also made it possible and necessary to have more advanced means for organizing production. A system of crop management was developed. In addition, a system for meeting spiritual needs was also developed. Over time, the changes in agricultural techniques helped to create the basis for a highly centralized, theocratic society in the Nile River Valley that would eventually evolve into a monarchical society grounded in feudal, rather than communal, labor.

Another side effect of the successes in expanding agricultural output and generating a surplus was that it made possible what Thorstein VEBLEN called "conspicuous consumption" of the ruling elite. Farmers not only had to give up their surplus in kind to the elite but were also forced to perform surplus labor on public works projects. These projects were sometimes beneficial to the larger public, such as the production of irrigation networks. However, this surplus labor was often expended in the creation of monuments to the ruling elite, including the construction of the Pyramids, tombs to house the mummified corpses and some of the precious possessions of the elite (conspicuous consumption in death).

On the east coast of Africa, in what is now called Ethiopia, the Aksum Kingdom rose to prominence based on its agricultural prowess. Aksum was situated in the highlands that receive an ample amount of rainfall and has a relatively temperate climate. These conditions made it possible for the Aksum farmers to produce and harvest a diversity of plant life. A number of the world's major food crops originated from this one area in Africa, including coffee. This area was so rich in genetic plant material that, in the 1920s, Russian plant geneticist Nikolai Vavilov claimed that Ethiopia was one of just eight centers in which the entire world's stock of cultivated plants originated. Although this claim was later refuted, Ethiopia is, nevertheless, the origin of a number of species of wheat, barley, sorghum, millet, lentils, legumes, and other staple crops. The ancient kingdom of Aksum took advantage of its geographical and climatic advantages and a flourishing agricultural society was established. Being on the coast also gave it trading advantages. Trade with Mesopotamia and the Mediterranean states introduced terracing in the area, helping to increase land cultivation.

About the time of Christ, climatic change increased rainfall in Aksum so that crops could be increased to two harvests a year, even on poor soil. This allowed for the production of an agricultural surplus and led to specialization in trades, the rise of merchants, and the gradual formation of a ruling elite of Aksum kings. Aksum was so prosperous that it became a metropolis with satellite urban centers sprawling across the northern plateau of Ethiopia. Aksum became a trading center, controlling most of the trade on the east coast of Africa and the hinterland. It established long-distance trading relationships with INDIA, CHINA, the Black Sea area, and SPAIN.

The widening market for Aksum's agricultural goods resulted in continued expansion in production and more intensive use of existing farm areas. The result was environmental degradation. The rapid growth of Aksum generated not only an increased need for agricultural lands but also increased demand for fuels and construction materials. These factors combined to result in deforestation, as trees were felled to supply fuel, used in metallurgy, and for construction. Overuse of the soil and deforestation led to soil erosion. Aksum suffered a sharp drop in agricultural output that triggered a commercial and political crisis. These problems were exacerbated by another change in climate. This time average rainfall went down just as dramatically as it had earlier risen. The crisis in Aksum led to the collapse in the centralized power of the monarchy. Around 800 C.E. what was left of the royal elite moved, along with their retainers, to settle in current-day central Ethiopia.

But while Africa may represent the earliest agricultural communities, it had no monopoly on this development. Other agricultural communities formed independently in other parts of the world, mostly notably in CHINA in the Hwang Ho Valley, in Mesopotamia or the Fertile Crescent, the Indus River Valley in present-day Pakistan, and in MEXICO in Central America.

Colonialism and the beginning of an international food system.

Settlements in western Europe are relatively recent, particularly in comparison to Africa, Asia, and Mesoamerica. From 500 to 1150 C.E., agriculture was largely based on a feudal system for organizing the production and distribution of agricultural goods. During this period there was a rise in a merchant class that traded agricultural goods produced on the feudal manors to the growing towns, which were dominated by self-employed artisans. The lords found that they could gain significant additional wealth by selling agricultural goods to these merchants. From 1200 to 1400 there were numerous revolts of the feudal direct-producers (peasants) in response to increased demands from lay and ecclesiastical feudal lords. However, most feudal direct-producers could not increase production sufficiently to meet these new demands on their output, forcing them to give up part of their family's subsistence, causing an increase in malnutrition and, in extreme cases, famines. The weakened state of the peasantry contributed to an increase in disease, including epidemics. The ensuing wars of resistance, famines, and epidemics led to many feudal serfs running away from the areas where the lords had authority, even if this meant abandoning relatively fertile for less fertile soil. Whole villages disappeared. The lords responded, eventually, by reducing their demands on the peasantry. In many cases, the crisis led to a complete abandonment of feudal relations in agriculture as lords sold or rented the land to farmers, who became self-employed like the artisans in the relatively prosperous towns.

In the 14th and 15th centuries western Europeans colonized Mediterranean and Atlantic islands, then north and west Africa and the Americas. Trade relations were expanded with eastern Europe, the Russian Steppes, and eventually central Asia in the search for food and fuel. Wheat was a central focus of new production and commerce. Exploration, colonization, and trade not only provided new sources of existing foods, but also introduced new foodstuffs into the European diet. Sugar cane, introduced from Asia, became one of the most important additions to the European diet, a major impetus for island expansion and colonization. The introduction of slave labor to sugar cultivation began in the eastern Mediterranean in the 12th century and then moved westward. Sugar was lucrative and demanding. Its production surpassed that of wheat. However, sugar production exhausted the soil requiring ever new lands and people to harvest it. Other crops that were, like sugar, not indigenous to Europe rose to prominence during this period, such as bananas, tea, coffee, and indigo. This was a period of sustained and widespread diffusion of plant genetic material around the world.

European agriculture benefited considerably from the transfer of such plant genetic material from the so-called New World. Two crops from the New World that became a staple for factory workers during the industrialization of Europe were corn and potatoes. These two crops offered lots of calories and made it possible to cheaply feed the worker population of Europe. European countries organized botanic gardens in the 10th century to collect plant specimens from around the world. Botanists would sometimes illegally remove plants from other countries in order to secure specimens for their research. Intellectual property rights were largely nonexistent, particularly in an international context, and the source countries would sometimes suffer serious economic harm as a result of

The spread of once-indigenous plants fueled the growth of population and trade in the 14th and 15th centuries.

losing control of plants that were the basis of lucrative foreign trade. Many of these plants would eventually become important commercial crops in the colonies and hybrids developed from such plants would improve yields on the slave plantations of the New World. Fortunes were made on these plants for British, mainland European and American companies. By the late 1800s, British and mainland European food supplies were coming from all over the world. The food and other agricultural resources flooding in from colonial possessions helped to fuel, sustain, and expand the European INDUSTRIAL REVOLUTIONS.

The agricultural basis of American hegemony. Originally, the European settlers to the American colonies brought European seed crops to establish a subsistence food supply. Many of these crops were unsuited to the environmental conditions in the Americas, and the settlers were forced to rely on indigenous crops, such as maize, squash, and beans. Many expeditions to America carried seeds to the new settlers for experimentation, and eventually many new plant species were added to the food supply and to plant species used for non-food purposes. Following the tradition of the botanical gardens of Europe, elites in the colonies had experimental stations built that would focus on the growing of cash crops in the New World. After American independence, this practice continued and plant experimentation took place on many plantations, including those of George WASHINGTON and Thomas JEFFERSON. Imported crop varieties would provide the basis for new hybrids, some of which proved useful, and the variety of subsistence and cash crops continued to grow.

The U.S. government played an important role in increasing American seed and plant diversity. The U.S. Naval fleets and U.S. embassies would often collect plant material from around the world and ship it back to the United States. But this approach was disorganized and in 1862 the United States Department of Agriculture (USDA) was formed and given powers to oversee plant collection and selective breeding. The USDA was able to speed up the development of new crop species by using extension agents and government-funded research sites for agricultural experimentation. The primary objective of the USDA was to significantly increase crop yields and, by any estimate, this new government institution was a success.

In 1926, Henry A. Wallace, who would later become first secretary of agriculture and then vice president of the United States, founded the first company devoted specifically to the commercialization of hybrid corn. This initiated patents for plant seed varieties. Before this innovation, seed was open-pollinated and farmers were able to reproduce seed needed for next year's crop. Under the new system of patented seed, farmers were forced to buy seed from capitalist firms specializing in the production of patented hybrid seeds before they could plant the next year's crop. This spurred private investment in plant research. Because hybrid corn increased yields and lowered the cost to farmers, it was widely adopted and by 1965 over 95 percent of U.S. corn acreage was planted with this variety. Because hybrid corn yields were so much greater than the original yields, the use of mechanization and hired labor increased.

At the end of WORLD WAR II, the military had accumulated a large store of nitrogen. The USDA, working with the military, created a special program to sell, at very low prices, this nitrogen to farmers as a substitute for organic fertilizers. Unfortunately, the highly concentrated form of nitrogen sold by the USDA damaged some plants. So, in the 1950s and 1960s breeders came out with new plant varieties that were bred to grow in nitrogen-rich soil. The richer soil made it possible to grow more plants in the same space, but the richer soil also allowed for the proliferation of weeds. The concentration of plants, and monoculture, also attracted more insects and plant disease. USDA provided a solution to the problem it had, in fact, helped to create by encouraging farmers to use insecticides, fungicides, and herbicides. This led to the growth of the agrichemical industry in the United States.

Green revolution. American hybrid corn breeding programs extended to the rest of the world through governmental and nongovernmental organizations. Primarily, this began in Mexico and extended out to other Latin American countries. It was the design of the U.S. government to create stronger economic ties between U.S. agribusiness firms and growers in these other nations. U.S. agrichemical companies, seed companies, and other agribusinesses set up divisions in Latin America for the sale of seeds, fertilizers, and other inputs to the Latin American market. As hybrid seeds were adopted, agriculture in Mexico and many other Latin American countries shifted from smaller scale farms to large mechanized farms using imported equipment, seeds, fertilizers, and other inputs. Since these inputs had to be paid for in U.S. dollars, the most successful farmers were those who could generate U.S. dollars to pay for these inputs. In other words, agriculture became more export-oriented (to the United States) than before the green revolution. Self-employed farmers were replaced by capitalist farms employing wage laborers. The total number of people who could make a living from agriculture declined, forcing many who had been farmers to migrate to the cities seeking wage employment. On the other hand, U.S. companies gained a lucrative new market for their goods and services.

Since the 1960s, there has been a growing recognition of the loss of plant species because of the smaller number of open-pollinated varieties in cultivation, and the patenting of some of these varieties so that it is illegal to grow them without permission from and royalties paid to the patent-holding corporations. The growth in capitalist agriculture, displacing self-employment in many places, has raised awareness of unfair labor practices in agriculture and the unsafe working conditions that many farm workers endure.

And, finally, there has been greater concern for the impact of agriculture on the environment. In particular, concern has been expressed about the poisons contained in herbicides and pesticides used in crop production. And there is a strong movement in opposition to genetically modified crops. One result of these concerns has been an increase in sales of organically grown foods and many states have passed organic-food laws that regulate the organic food industry.

BIBLIOGRAPHY. Albert Hourani, *A History of the Arab Peoples* (Belknap Press, 1991); Jack Ralph Kloppenburg, Jr., *First the Seed* (Cambridge University Press, 1988); John Reader, *Africa: A Biography of the Continent* (Vintage Books, 1998); Kevin Shillington, *History of Africa* (Palgrave Macmillan, 1989); Immanuel Wallerstein, *The Modern World-System: Capitalist Agriculture and the Origins of the European World-Economy in the Sixteenth Century* (Academic Press, 1974).

SATYA J. GABRIEL
MOUNT HOLYOKE COLLEGE

airlines

WHEN THOMAS BENOIST introduced air service between Tampa and St. Petersburg, Florida, on January 1, 1914, his airline lasted through the tourist season but shut down in the spring. For several years thereafter, there was no American passenger service. The UNITED STATES had a quarter of a million miles of railroad track and railroad service from convenient downtown locations. Airplanes could not compete. Woodrow WILSON's government allowed airline pioneers to carry the U.S. mail for a living.

Between WORLD WAR I and WORLD WAR II, transportation technology improved markedly, not just in aircraft but also in trains, ships, and automobiles. Still, flying was dangerous, uncomfortable, and potentially fatal in the primitive aircraft of the early postwar years. Noise, vibration, cold at higher altitudes, airsickness, claustrophobia—air travel was definitely uncomfortable. With government assistance, commercial aviation began in the 1920s and slowly blossomed in the 1930s once the competition from airships ended with the *Hindenburg* disaster of 1937. The flying boats peaked in the late 1930s, fading when runway technology evolved from grass or dirt to paved and grooved surfaces. Modern airports such as in New York City and Los Angeles, initially close to water for the convenience of flying boats, adapted to faster and larger commercial land planes, including jets. Airlines and airports alike developed aircraft service capabilities and passenger amenities. But late in the 20th century, airlines, especially American carriers, struggled to survive.

Early technology. With the onset of World War I, in 1915 the United States instituted the National Advisory Committee for Aircraft (NACA), that established a research facility at Langley Field, Virginia, to compete with the English Royal Aircraft Factory, Farnborough. By the 1930s Langley was home to the largest aircraft research facility in the world. Scientists used wind tunnels and advanced photography to study potential problems of high performance aircraft, commonly years before the manufacturers had the capability to apply the research.

Langley research explored airflows and allowed rapid development of aircraft with such innovations as wing flaps and slats, cowling that streamlined the area around the engine, and engines incorporated into the wing structure. These innovations reduced drag, allowed for better control on landing and takeoff. The Lockheed Vega was first to use the cowl. Engines on the wings were standard on the Douglas DC-3 and Boeing 247 and eventually all commercial aircraft. Between 1917 and its conversion to NASA in 1958, NACA made American aircraft science the leader in the world. By 1935, the United States had technology that far surpassed the Europeans who had started earlier.

The first modern commercial airplane was the Boeing 247-B, introduced in 1933 as an all-metal, low wing, twin-engine aircraft with retractable landing gear. With autopilot, de-icing equipment, and cabin air conditioning, it served as the standard configuration as well as the standard for crew and service for two decades. It was larger than earlier commercial aircraft. The 247 required 20 hours for the trip between New York to Los Angeles, with seven refueling stops and an air speed of 189 miles per hour. Carriers that used it included Boeing Air Transport, United Aircraft Corporation (United Airlines), Deutsche Lufthansa and a private owner in China. After World War II, some 247s were converted to C-73 transports and trainers, with some still flying into the late 1960s.

But air travel was still not the norm. Although world passenger miles nearly reached 1.9 billion in 1934, a marked increase over the 66 million passenger miles of 1929, this was less than 2 percent of all intercity travel. In 1934, the novelty was gone; those who would willingly fly had already done so, and the rest of

From humble beginnings in the early 20th century, airlines carried millions of passengers by 2000.

the traveling public required enticement. The industry recognized the need for a safer and more comfortable airplane that could fly above turbulence, that had a sealed and air-conditioned passenger compartment that could take off and land safely. They needed government assistance.

Government aid. The barnstormers of the postwar era went the way of the innovative risk-takers of the prewar era. The age of commercial aviation would be a time for cautious capitalists and sympathetic governments. Legislation, which had favored the RAILROADS in the 19th century, and the AUTOMOBILE industry early in the century, shifted to airlines in the 1930s. Clearly it would take time for the airlines to become profitable, so governments began providing contracts for army transport or mail delivery. Outright purchase of aircraft was another form of subsidy to the industry. Government research at the NACA or the Institute Aerotechnique, justified for military or pure scientific reasons, moved quickly to Lockheed or Breguet as governments thought open publication would deter military competition.

Interwar Germany, denied secret research of its own, quickly managed to develop civilian aircraft convertible to military use. And Japan also used NACA and other government research information to develop its military aircraft.

Initially, the mail service contracts were limited. Trains competed for local routes, so the airlines bid for transcontinental routes in 1921, routes finally marked with beacon lights in 1924. Scheduled service began in 1924, leading the railroads to protest. Congress cooperated by passing the Kelly Act of 1925, privatizing the airlines. The government became responsible for aircraft safety in 1926. When it was all done, the United States had commercial air transport regulated and subsidized

by the government. When Charles Lindbergh flew nonstop from New York to Paris in 1927, interest in aviation soared. Passengers for all of 1926 totaled only 5,800; four years later the total was 417,000.

The Postmaster General of the United States provided a final ingredient. Walter Folger Brown, in the Herbert HOOVER administration, pressed Congress to enact the McNary Waters Act of 1930, which gave Brown almost total control of awarding postal contracts. By paying for carrying capacity instead of volume of mail, Brown encouraged the use of larger aircraft. This harmed the small companies with small aircraft, forcing them to merge with the larger companies that had the mail routes. By the time Brown was through, 24 of the 27 contracts belonged to four carriers. The Big Four were United, American Airways, Transcontinental and Western air, and Eastern Air Transport. Gone into the merger were Boeing Air Transport, Varney, National, Stout, Pacific, Robertson, Embry-Riddle, Colonial, Thompson, Texas Air, Western air Express, and others.

When the Democrats came to power in 1933, they investigated Brown's dealings with the airlines. After a Congressional investigation, in 1934 the Big Four lost their mail contracts. The army would carry the mail. It was a disaster. The army was unprepared. In six months, 11 people died in 16 crashes. Nearly half of the 26 mail routes, 12, were not flown regularly.

Postmaster General James Farley returned the contracts to the commercial lines at much reduced rates. To avoid Farley's prohibition of awards to the Big Four because of their participation in Brown's division of the routes, three of the airlines altered their names. Transcontinental and Western air became Trans-World Airlines (TWA), and American Airways became American Airlines. United Airlines retained its name. Bill Boeing of United had other problems.

Boeing had developed a vertically integrated corporation. His company built the engines, built the planes that used the engines, built the airline that used the planes that used the engines. New Deal ANTITRUST legislation outlawed this configuration, and Boeing had to split his manufacturing companies from his airline. Boeing retired as his company dissolved.

European governments also involved themselves with private operators. France split Aeropostale from a manufacturing company in 1927, forced its sale to another owner, who managed to run a deficit for four years before the airline dissolved in1931. France nationalized Aeropostale and four smaller airlines in 1933, naming the new carrier Air France.

Germany established a state airline in 1926, Deutsche LuftHansa, renamed Lufthansa in 1934. LuftHansa flew Junkers aircraft and took passenger service seriously, so it competed strongly throughout Europe. Its South American subsidiary, VARIG, replaced Aeropostale as the major provider between Europe and South America. By encouraging local management, contrasted to Aeropostale's central control, LuftHansa gave Germany a diplomatic edge in South America.

Commerce and diplomacy: Pan Am. Competing with the Germans in South America was Juan Trippe. Using Charles Lindbergh as technical advisor and his connections to the Washington, D.C., elites, Trippe made his airline, Pan Am, into the largest and best run long-distance airline in the world. He lasted four decades, too. Trippe began with a small line that used navy war surplus planes to ferry passengers from Long Island, New York, to resorts. In 1922, his Colonial Air Transport won the mail contract for the New York-Boston route. In 1927, he won the contract for a route from Florida to Havana, Cuba. Competing with the likes of Henry "Hap" Arnold and Eddie Rickenbacker, Trippe convinced the Cuban dictator, Garado Machad, to give his airline monopoly landing rights in Havana. He forced Arnold's company out of business, adding insult to injury by taking over the name Pan American. In 1930, Pan Am had 20,308 miles of airway in 20 Latin American countries. Through the 1930s, Pan Am expanded into the Pacific and more deeply into Latin America. Trippe was a large purchaser of aircraft, and he favored no manufacturer, keeping all suppliers competitive. He also used Pan Am as a surrogate of the U.S. State Department against LuftHansa and Germany in Latin America. Trippe's Pan Am also had the advantage that its chief pilot, Eddie Musick, built the best training, weather-forecasting, and communications systems in the industry, holding the edge for decades.

Trippe also worked with others to create the S-40 "Clipper" flying boat, first introduced to service in 1931. Slow and luxurious, as was the S-42 of 1934, the Clippers were also safe. Trippe and W.R. Grace Company joined to form Panagra, the subsidiary that serviced the west coasts of North and South America. In 1935, Pan Am entered the Pacific as Trippe worried about Japanese expansion. His new Clipper for this route was built by Glenn Martin, and had a range of 3,000 miles. The ultimate Clipper, 1939's Boeing B-3 14, had room for 70 passengers, a crew of 16, sleeping quarters, dining rooms, bars, and powder rooms and deluxe suites.

Europe could not compete with the Clippers. The Short Company of England built the Empire flying boat to carry mail and passengers across the Atlantic. When Pan Am decided to compete in Europe and the Atlantic in the late 1930s, the Empire was no match for the Clipper.

The German flying boat effort culminated in the Dornier Do X, a plane with twelve engines and capacity for 169 passengers. Its maiden voyage in 1931 was un-

successful, and the plane became a museum piece. The Russians built the largest plane of the era, the Maxim Gorky with eight engines and a 210-foot wingspan, which crashed in 1935, killing all forty aboard and raising the question of the value of such large aircraft.

In the late 1930s Donald Douglas' DC-3 was the dominant aircraft. But the airlines on the eve of the war wanted larger planes that could carry more passengers faster and over longer distances. Douglas and Howard Hughes competed to build the new plane. Hughes controlled TWA, and he worked with Lockheed to create the Constellation, with range to fly across the United States nonstop. Douglas responded with the DC-6 and DC-7. This technology served until the jet age.

War and its legacies. While Douglas and Hughes competed, the world went to war. WORLD WAR II was pivotal for the development of aviation because it compressed decades of technological improvement into a matter of years. When it was done, the flying boat was obsolete, even though the British built the Saunders-Roe "Saro" Princess as late as 1952. And cities began recognizing the status and economic benefits of attractive and convenient international airports.

After the war, many airlines used converted warplanes such as the Douglas DC-3 and DC-4 or the Lockheed Constellation. And with the rise of the military-industrial complex during the Cold War, military technology translated to commercial planes. When Boeing built the Stratocruiser from its B-29, Lockheed upgraded to a Super Constellation in 1950. Douglas, Lockheed, and Boeing made the United States the predominant builder of civilian aircraft. With three large and comfortable passenger aircraft, the United States was ready to dominate the market for long-distance travel.

The British wartime Brabazon Committee planned the postwar future, determining that jet power was the future of commercial aviation. First into the fray was the Vickers Viscount, a turboprop good for short distance flights. The Saro Princess was also a product of this plan, as was the oversized Bristol Brabazon turbojet that died after eight empty years of development.

The British were planners, trying to anticipate the market of a decade out. The Americans responded more quickly to the market. While the Americans were flourishing, filling seats, the British were building planes they couldn't sell. But the British did create the de Havilland Comet, a four-engine jet that went through four models from 1949. When two planes crashed in 1954, even though the cause was quickly identified and corrected, confidence in the plane was destroyed. Eighty percent of the commercial market belonged to the Americans, with Douglas holding more than half. But while Douglas waited to read the fallout of the Comet disaster, in

1954 Boeing introduced the 707, based on the B-52. Pan Am bought large numbers of 707s, giving Boeing market dominance even though Douglas and Convair offered jets as well. Boeing also had more willingness than the others to customize its planes to the customer's taste.

Jet age. The war generated jet engines. Boeing led the way with the B-47 and B-52, fuel guzzlers unacceptable to airline executives who did not want to lose money just for greater speed. Juan Trippe disagreed as usual. Pan Am's lead forced the other lines to order jets to remain competitive. But 1950s jets were too fast, as proved by the 1956 collision over the Grand Canyon that killed 128 people. The government stepped in, funding radar and navigational aids that made air travel much safer, even at jet speed.

During the 1960s, jets, fast and comfortable, began to dominate the market. Passenger miles soared. Between 1960 and 1970 passengers increased from 62 million to 169 million. The soaring demand encouraged Trippe and Boeing's William Allen to commit to building the 747. Boeing took on massive debt. Then delivery was delayed because the engines were not ready. Then a recession hit and orders dried up. Boeing avoided bankruptcy by offering still more variations of the 707. Pan Am struggled too, having taken on high-interest debt to buy the 747s. It struggled through the 1970s thanks mostly to the International Air Transport Association, the cartel that held worldwide fares high.

The Europeans didn't quit, joining forces in 1962 to develop a supersonic transport, the Concorde. The Americans assumed this would be another Brabazon fiasco, a plane built even though the market would not support it. Government support was not enough to counter lack of market support and the likely environmentalist protest over air and noise pollution. Nevertheless, the Concorde came into being and never made a profit. For the British and French governments, prestige was at stake. In the late 1970s, the Russians built the Tupolev Tu-144, the "Concordski" for service between Moscow and Vladivostok. After a crash at the 1973 Paris Air Show, this plane too was mothballed.

The Europeans did have more success when they formed Airbus, whose wide-body A340 was competitive with Boeing's finest, forcing Boeing to develop the 777, luxurious but as with all contemporary liners, but a pale shadow of the luxury planes of the 1930s.

Deregulation and dire straits. By century's end the airlines were struggling with labor problems, mismanagement, congested airports, and rising costs of fuel. Government intrusion and questions of safety after various aircraft losses were also of concern. And there were alarms over air pollution and possible health hazards within the aircraft. Terrorism was a problem from the 1970s on as well.

For half a century the American airline industry was highly regulated. The airline deregulation act of 1978 lowered fares overall while maintaining service to larger cities, and initially it brought increased competition by start-ups. But travelers found their choices limited as smaller cities lost service. The major airlines quickly developed hub cities, restricted competition by dividing the territory, and froze out the smaller lines as well as decreased service to the smaller airports. Many of the smaller lines went bankrupt in the face of inability to get slots at hub airports, and the major airlines, with cut-rate prices squeezing their profits as they squeezed the competition, experienced difficulty in surviving without major government assistance.

In 25 years after deregulation, 11 American airlines went bankrupt. Old carriers such as Pan Am and TWA and Braniff were no more.

American and United were among those that found even more difficulty after the trauma of hijacked planes in 2001, that produced airport delays for security and shrinking numbers of passengers. Airlines, at least in America, had not recovered previous levels of passenger miles by early 2003. Costs continued to rise as virtually every American line operated at a deficit. The survival of the industry involved massive layoffs, bankruptcy restructurings, and additional fees for what before had been amenities.

BIBLIOGRAPHY. T.A. Heppenheimer, *Turbulent Skies: The History of Commercial Aviation* (John Wiley & Sons, October 1995); Wernher Krutein, Photovault Museum, www.photovault.com; National Advisory Committee for Aircraft, *NACA Technical Reports*, www.naca.larc.nasa.gov; Geza Szurovy and Martin Berinstein, *Classic American Airlines* Osceola (Motorbooks International, 2000); U.S. General Accounting Office, *Report to Congressional Requestors: Airline Deregulation; Change in Airfares, Service Quality, and Barriers to Entry*, www.swaaae.org, (March, 1999) Sarah Ward, *The Airline History*, www.airlines.freeuk.com.

JOHN H. BARNHILL, PH.D.
YUKON, OKLAHOMA

Akerlof, George A. (1940–)

GEORGE AKERLOF HAS BUILT a career on his quirky, unconventional insights: his papers are titled with redolent words such as "Lemons," "The Rat Race," "Gift Exchanges," "Fair Wage," "Gang Behavior," and "Looting." Underneath the casualness has been a serious research program: to provide underlying behavioral models to Keynesian theory, importing knowledge from other social sciences. He was awarded the 2001 Nobel Prize with A. Michael SPENCE and Joseph E. STIGLITZ for work that the three men did (separately) on markets with asymmetric information, in Akerlof's case, on "lemon" markets. Other papers on the importance of fairness and other sociological norms have been incorporated into efficiency wage theories in labor economics. Akerlof's works form a comprehensive "behavioral" paradigm, which he explicitly contrasts with the Neo-classical explanations.

It is worth carefully examining the "lemons" model. Akerlof analyzed a market where a certain fraction of the goods sold were "lemons"—poor quality items that were indistinguishable from the higher-quality ones. Suppose these are used cars, where some cars are of high quality and some of low. Buyers are willing to pay up to $8000 for a high-quality car but only up to $2000 for a low-quality car. Sellers are willing to sell their high-quality cars if they can get at least $6000, but will sell low-quality cars (lemons) for as little as $1000. Clearly, then, if buyers can differentiate between high and low quality cars, there will be two separate markets. But what happens if buyers can't tell high-quality from low-quality cars? Then their willingness to pay will be based on the probability that they will get a high or low quality car.

Suppose that buyers initially believe that half the cars are high quality and half are bad. In this case, they would be willing to pay (50 percent)(8000) + (50 percent)(2000) = $5000, if they believe that the outcome is purely random. But there's the problem: no seller is willing to supply a high-quality car at a price of just $5000! So fewer than 50 percent of the cars will be high quality, so consumers will be willing to pay even less, and so on in a downward spiral. All of the high-quality cars will be driven out of the market by the lemons.

If there is a continuum of grades of quality, the market may not even exist. This market is characterized by asymmetric information: buyers can't tell if they're getting a high or low quality car, but sellers know. So the market must be somehow fixed, by government action or by the traders themselves, to get sellers to reveal their knowledge. A seller might offer a warranty, offering to fix any problems that are revealed. Or certain sellers might gain a reputation for selling high-quality products, a brand name. The good traded need not be cars, it could be insurance, or products in developing countries, or new hires, or myriad other goods, which Akerlof only began to explore.

For macroeconomics the most important market is the LABOR market, and here Akerlof has devoted much of his theoretical and empirical work. Classical economic theory wonders why wages don't fall enough in recessions to eliminate unemployment. In various papers Akerlof (with others, notably Janet Yellen) has imported from other social sciences reasons why firms might choose to pay higher wages: from psychology, equity theory highlights considerations of fairness; from anthropology, gift exchange notes the importance of reciprocity; and from sociology come notions of the importance of group norms. Additionally, in work with Dickens and Perry, he has shown that near-rational decision rules may explain the "money illusion" of wage setting.

These are just a few of the many ways in which Akerlof has posited that people's behaviors differ from that of the standard rational actor model. A richer understanding of human behavior, grounded in experimental evidence rather than faith in rationality, can solve many of the puzzles of economics.

BIBLIOGRAPHY. George Akerlof, "The Market for 'Lemons:' Quality Uncertainty and the Market Mechanism," *Quarterly Journal of Economics* (August, 1970); George Akerlof, William T. Dickens and George L. Perry, "The Macroeconomics of Low Inflation," *Brookings Papers on Economic Activity* (1996); George Akerlof and Janet Yellen, "The Fair Wage-Effort Hypothesis and Unemployment," *Quarterly Journal of Economics* (May, 1990); George Akerlof, "Behavioral Macroeconomics and Macroeconomic Behavior," Nobel Prize Lecture, www.nobel.se.

KEVIN R FOSTER, PH.D.
CITY COLLEGE OF NEW YORK

Alger, Horatio Jr. (1832–99)

HORATIO ALGER GAINED FAME as a writer of children's fiction during the late 19th century. His "rags-to-riches" tales of young orphans and scrappy street kids who managed to triumph over their humble beginnings struck a chord with generations of young Americans. A highly prolific author, he produced well over one hundred novels and numerous short stories, that remained in print well into the 20th century.

Alger was born in Massachusetts. His father was a Unitarian minister who was paid a meager salary, and the family lived in relative poverty. Alger entered the freshman class of Harvard College at the age of 16 and graduated in 1852. He experimented with work as a freelance writer before entering Harvard Divinity School, eventually taking a position in a parish in Brewster, Massachusetts. His career in the church was cut short when parishioners accused him of engaging in improper behavior with young boys in his charge. To avoid scandal, Alger agreed to resign from the ministry and left Brewster, eventually settling in New York City, where he began to work full time as a writer.

His first literary attempts were not notable, but when Alger sent a series of stories entitled, "Ragged Dick, or, The Streets of New York," to a magazine aimed at young people, he found his calling. He was hired as a regular contributor, and the stories were eventually collected and published in book form. This work contained many elements that would recur in later Alger novels. The protagonist was a poor boy who lived on the streets of New York, polishing boots. The novel recounts many of Ragged Dick's adventures in the city, including incidents where he saves a child from drowning and catches a thief. The boy's honesty and strength of character impress a wealthy man, who takes Dick into his charge. By the end of the story, the hero has acquired an education and is starting a new job as a clerk, destined for great things.

Although Alger's critics charged that his stories were highly formulaic, young readers did not tire of reading about the rise of poor boys to success, the kind of success envisioned by eager young capitalists. Novels with titles like *Strive and Succeed* (1872), *Risen from the Ranks* (1874), and *Julius, the Street Boy* (1874) were snapped up by the public. It is estimated that over 250 million copies of his works have been sold around the world. In addition to his fiction, he wrote biographies of important historical figures who could also serve as inspiration for young boys. In Alger's hands, the life of President James GARFIELD became *From Canal Boy to President* (1881).

Alger's work is often cited as a celebration of the possibilities of capitalism. He chose the modern city as the setting for his tales, and followed young newsboys and peddlers as they rose to achieve the "American Dream." It is worth noting, however, that Alger's heroes succeed not only due to their own perseverance but also because of the kindness of a wealthy benefactor. Many of the novels feature chance meetings that change the lives of the characters forever. Nevertheless, Alger's name has entered the popular lexicon as typifying the values of individualism and self-reliance. More than a century after his death, Alger is still cited as an influence and is honored by the Horatio Alger Association, a scholarship program.

BIBLIOGRAPHY. Glenn Handler, "Pandering in the Public Sphere: Masculinity and the Market in Horatio Alger," *American Quarterly* (v.48/3, 1996); Edwin P. Hoyt, *Horatio's Boys: The Life and Works of Horatio Alger, Jr.* (Chilton Book Co., 1974); Carol Nackenoff, *The Fictional Republic: Horatio Alger and American Political Discourse* (Oxford University Press, 1994); Gary Scharnhorst with Jack Bales, *The Lost Life of Horatio Alger, Jr.* (Indiana University Press, 1985).

SARAH ELVINS
UNIVERSITY OF NOTRE DAME

Algeria

THE MODERN ALGERIAN STATE came into being in 1962, but this is not to say that Algeria did not have a significant economic history before that date. In the period between the 8th and the 19th centuries, Algeria had been a part of different Islamic states and empires, some of which (such as the Almoravid and Almohad empires) had been centered on the Maghreb.

Considerable trade existed across the Mediterranean and Islamic worlds at this time, while high levels of education, literacy and scientific development were actively promoted by the state. Between 1830 and 1962 Algeria was a French colony, incorporated into metropolitan FRANCE in a manner unique in the French Empire. The legacy of French imperialism, especially in the political and economic spheres, is still evident today. In the post-independence period the leading resistor of the French, the FLN (Front de Libération Nationale), instituted a one-party state with the task of restructuring an economy that had been designed for the benefit of the colonial power, rather than the Algerian people.

The FLN's program of bureaucratic state capitalism and technocratic modernization was strongly influenced by French models (although its political ideology, which combined Marxism with nationalism and Islamism, was distinctly Algerian). Early leaders such as Ben Bella, Boumedienne and Chadli achieved some economic growth, but economic development was almost secondary to the tasks of nation-building and forging a viable political consensus. From the late 1970s there was a concurrent growth in political pluralism and the private economic sector, under the auspices of the one-party state.

Economic liberalization has been arguably more successful than its political counterpart (which suffered greatly during the Algerian civil war of 1992–98), though an increasing acceptance of neo-liberal economic principles and an integration into world markets have done little to conceal the structural flaws of the Algerian economy. These include massive unemployment (and concomitant social unrest), an over-reliance on oil (which made up 96 percent of exports in 2000) and the limited profits Algerians themselves make from oil production which is part-contracted to foreign corporations, the vulnerability of the economy to exogenous shocks (such as the 1986 oil price collapse), low levels of competition and diversification, large debts owed to western banks, and the stifling effects of the one-party state and its military backers.

It remains unclear whether Algeria's recent integration into international networks such as the INTERNATIONAL MONETARY FUND (IMF) and the EUROPEAN UNION (EU) will have long-term gains for an economy that has not fully realized an independent identity since the French withdrawal.

BIBLIOGRAPHY. Kay Adamson, *Algeria: A Study in Competing Ideologies* (Continuum, 1998); Phillip Chiviges Naylor and Alf Andrew Heggoy, *Historical Dictionary of Algeria* (Scarecrow Press, 1994); Michael Kettle, *De Gaulle and Algeria 1940–1960* (Quartet Books, 1990); Ricardo René Laremont, *Islam and the Politics of Resistance in Algeria* (Africa World Press, 1999); Benjamin Stora, *Algeria 1830–2000* (Cornell University Press, 2001).

WILLIAM GALLOIS, PH.D.
AMERICAN UNIVERSITY OF SHARJAH

alienation

THE CONCEPT OF ALIENATION is generally employed to describe feelings of isolation and powerlessness, and is common to many teleological theories of societies, rooted as it is in the idea that in the past people lived in harmony, which was then broken causing people to feel like foreigners in the world. In the future, according to the theories, this alienation would be overcome and humanity would again live in harmony.

The most famous theorist of alienation related to capitalism was Karl MARX, who developed the concept particularly in his early writings. Marx specifically focused on the experience of alienation in modern bourgeois society and he developed his understanding of the process through his critique of Georg W.F. HEGEL. According to Hegel, people create a culture by means of their actions, which were the expression of the Spirit. Such culture eventually becomes an entity alien from the people who produce it. Giving a materialist base to Hegel's mystical conception, Marx insists that it is human labor which creates culture and history: "Precisely because Hegel starts from the predicates of universal determination instead of from the real subject, and because there must be a bearer of this determination, the mystical idea becomes this bearer." What Hegel calls the Spirit is, according to Marx, a human product. Thus, the history of mankind is marked by a paradox: man increasingly controls nature yet he becomes alienated from and dominated by forces of his own creation.

According to Marx, the labor process is an objectification of human powers. Yet workers are unable to relate to their product as an expression of their own essence and thus fail to recognize themselves in their product. This lack of recognition is the basis for alienation. The specific form of LABOR characteristic of bourgeois society, wage labor, corresponds to the most profound form of alienation. Since wage workers sell their labor power to earn a living, and the capitalist *owns* the labor process, the product of the workers' labor is in a very real sense *alien* to the worker as it becomes property of the capitalist and not of its maker. The workers' alienation worsens during the regime of industrial capitalism where workers are attached to a machine and are themselves a mere unit along an assembly line, performing a meaningless task which is only part of a larger process.

Marx describes the concept of alienation as fourfold: workers are alienated from work, from the objects they make, from their fellow workers, and from their potential for creative production. This is because labor is a commodity that can be bought and sold under capitalist economic relations. Employers also control the means of production and the cooperation between workers is destroyed as is their creativity in the name of a higher and more effective production.

In Marx's later writings, the concept of alienation is subsumed under the idea of "fetishism of commodities." In *Capital*, Marx argues that social relations between human beings becomes relations between things:

> In order, therefore, to find an analogy, we must have recourse to the mist-enveloped regions of the religious world. In that world the productions of the human brain appear as independent beings endowed with life, and entering into relation both with one another and the human race. So it is in the world of commodities with the products of men's hands. This I call the fetishism which attaches itself to the products of labor, so soon as they are produced as commodities, and which is therefore inseparable from the production of commodities. This fetishism of commodities has its origin, as the foregoing analysis has already shown, in the peculiar social character of the labor that produces them.

Marx's prescription to overcome alienation is of course the transformation of the economic system from capitalist to socialist. In socialist economies, work and products are no longer commodities and the rigid distinction between mental and physical work breaks down thus allowing the full development of every worker's potential.

BIBLIOGRAPHY. Istvan Meszaros, *Marx's Theory of Alienation* (Prometheus Books, 1986); Bertell Ollman, *Alienation: Marx's Conception of Man in Capitalist Society* (Cambridge University Press, 1973); Wolfgang Schirmacher, ed., *German Socialist Philosophy* (Continuum Publishing Company, 1997); Simon H. Simon, ed., *Karl Marx: Selected Writings* (Hackett Publishing Company, 1994).

LUCA PRONO, PH.D.
UNIVERSITY OF NOTTINGHAM, ENGLAND

Allais, Maurice (1911–)

WINNER OF THE 1988 Nobel Prize in Economics, Maurice Allais is perhaps best known for the Allais Paradox and his important contributions in the fields of economics and physics. Born in Paris, FRANCE, to a working class family, Allais intended to study history, but at the insistence of a mathematics teacher, entered a special mathematics class to prepare for the Ecole Polytéchnique. Allais himself reports that he was "generally first in my year in almost all subjects," and in 1933, he graduated first in his class.

After a year of military service and two years at the Ecole Nationale Supérieure des Mines in Paris, Allais became the head of the Nantes Mines and Quarries Service. With the outbreak of WORLD WAR II in 1939, Allais was sent to the Italian front and given command of a heavy artillery battery near Briancon. Following the French surrender on June 25, 1940, Allais returned to his position in Nantes, which was then in the German occupation zone, and remained there until he became director of the Bureau of Mines Documentation and Statistics in Paris in 1943.

During this tumultuous period, Allais wrote the first of his major works, *In Quest of an Economic Discipline, Part I, Pure Economics*, published in 1943. He

Maurice Allais, best-known for the Allais Paradox, has emerged as a sharp critic of globalization.

turned to economics as a means to prepare for the aftermath of the war with the intent of solving what he regarded as the fundamental problem of any economy: "How to promote the greatest feasible economic efficiency while ensuring a distribution of income that would be generally acceptable." The book focused on the proofs of two fundamental propositions regarding efficiency. First, any state of EQUILIBRIUM of a market economy is efficient in the sense that no one can become better off without someone else becoming worse off. Second, any state of maximum efficiency can be achieved through the redistribution of initial resources and a system of equilibrium prices.

In 1947, Allais published *Economy and Interest*, which focused on efficiency in an intertemporal setting. He found that accounting for future generations altered his analysis considerably, and concluded that a policy of compulsory saving for old age is perfectly compatible with economic efficiency. In two papers published in 1954 and 1955, Allais developed the foundations of his general theory of monetary dynamics. He tested the model with empirical data and concluded that the "observed reality is represented in an almost perfect manner" by his theory. He called the empirical verifications of his work on monetary policy "the most extraordinary ones that have ever been found in the Social Sciences."

Today, Allais is best known for the Allais Paradox, which demonstrated that standard expected utility theory does not apply to many empirically realistic decisions under risk and uncertainty. Given the paradox, some economists have concluded that individuals are irrational in that they are unable to calculate the probabilities necessary to conform to expected utility theory. Allais himself, however, believed that this result was a paradox in appearance only and represented instead "the preference for security in the neighborhood of certainty."

Throughout his life, Allais was concerned with political and economic policies. He believed that "a man of science cannot fail to take an interest in the fundamental problems of his time." In the 1950s and 1960s, he participated in many of the international conferences aimed at establishing the EUROPEAN UNION (EU). In recent years, Allais has continued his interest in public policy, emerging as a sharp critic of globalization. The publisher of his 1999 book, *Globalization: The Destruction of Growth and Employment*, described the work as "the passionate battle of a man of science against globalization." In the book, Allais argues for free trade within the European Community, but a system of quotas designed to ensure that an average of about 80 percent of the goods consumed within Europe Community are produced by member countries.

BIBLIOGRAPHY. Maurice Allais, *In Quest of an Economic Discipline, Part One, Pure Economics* (Kluwer Academic, 1943); Maurice Allais, *Economy and Interest* (Kluwer Academic, 1947); Maurice Allais, "An Outline of My Main Contributions to Economic Science," Nobel Lecture (1988); www.allais.maurice.free.fr.

JEFFREY R. GERLACH
COLLEGE OF WILLIAM & MARY

Allianz

ALLIANZ VERSICHERUNGS was founded in Berlin, GERMANY, in 1890. Now headquartered in Munich, it is one of the leading global service providers in insurance, banking, and asset management. Allianz has approximately 182,000 employees worldwide, and customers in more than 70 countries, significantly expanding its international market presence in the 1990s and early 21st century. Examples of key international acquisitions include Cornhill Insurance (UK) in 1986; the Fireman's Fund Insurance Company (U.S.) in 1991; the ELVIA Group (Switzerland) in 1995; Assurances Générales de France in 1997; and Pimco (U.S.) in 2000. Allianz first moved into the banking industry with the acquisition of Dresdner Bank (Germany) in 2001.

In 2002, premiums in property and casualty insurance amounted to €43.3 billion (9.8 billion from Germany), with a claims ratio of 78.2 percent. Total revenue in life and health insurance amounted to €40.1 billion (12.6 billion from Germany). In both insurance markets, Allianz is the market leader in Germany, and is one of the strongest firms in Europe.

In banking and asset management, Allianz faced a difficult year in 2002. The banking sector (essentially Dresdner Bank) had a loss of €1.4 billion, and Turnaround 2003 was launched (a program aimed at restructuring the banking sector to cut costs and improve efficiency, as well as minimizing the impact of "impaired loans"). In asset management, given falling stock prices and the depreciation of the dollar, Allianz made an (expected) loss of €405 million, but currently manages approximately €1 billion, and is one of the five leading asset managers in the world.

Given its decentralized organization and strong local presence, Allianz believes it is well placed to meet the needs of regional and national markets. Ranked as the 18th largest company in the world in 2002, Allianz's strategic objective is to further strengthen its global positions in INSURANCE and asset management, as the world recovers from loss of investor confidence in the early 21st century.

BIBLIOGRAPHY. "Allianz Investor Relations," www.allianz.com; "Global 500: World's Largest Companies," *Fortune* (July, 2002).

CATHERINE MATRAVES
ALBION COLLEGE

Altria (Philip Morris)

PHILIP MORRIS COMPANIES, INC., or Altria, is a multinational corporation, producing and distributing consumer products worldwide. It divides its products and services into four categories: tobacco, food, beer, and financial. With over 200 manufacturing facilities in 50 countries, Philip Morris ranks as the largest producer and marketer of consumer packaged goods in the world. The Philip Morris "family" consists of PM USA, Philip Morris International Inc., and the Philip Morris Capital Corporation. As of April 25, 2002, shareholders approved a name change of the parent corporation to Altria Group, Inc.

Philip Morris was founded by Philip Morris, Esquire, in London during the mid-19th century. What began as a self-proprietorship in London became a leviathan of an organization. In 2001, the company reported approximately $80 billion in underlying net revenues. Altria owns 83.9 percent of the outstanding shares of Kraft Foods Inc. and holds 36 percent of the economic interest in the newly created SABMiller, the result of a 2002 merger between Miller Brewing Company and South African Breweries.

Tobacco is the company's primary revenue maker; the cigarette division controls 51 percent of the U.S. market and ranks as the largest tobacco company in the country. The company produces the best-selling brand Marlboro. Four out of every 10 cigarettes sold is a Marlboro, granting the company more market share than the next seven largest brands combined. Likewise, in the international cigarette market, Marlboro is the top-selling brand and has been since 1972.

In 1988, Philip Morris acquired Kraft at a price of $12.9 billion—the largest non-oil acquisition in the history of the United States. The largest branded food company in North America, Kraft brands include: Kool-Aid, Maxwell House, Cool Whip, Jell-O, 20 or so brands of cereal, Oreo, Ritz, Chips Ahoy, Planters, Grey Poupon, Miracle Whip, DiGiorno, and many more.

As shown by the company's vast holdings throughout the world, Philip Morris or Altria is one of the world's largest and most powerful corporations. Through billion-dollar acquisitions and continual restructuring, it has remained the dominant player in the market and outlasted many of its competitors.

BIBLIOGRAPHY. Altria, www.philipmorris.com; Active Media Guide Company Snapshot, www.activemedia-guide.com; "Global 500: World's Largest Companies," *Fortune* (July, 2002).

ARTHUR HOLST, PH.D.
WIDENER UNIVERSITY

American Civil War

EVEN BEFORE THE United States came into being, the economic interests, and hence to some degree the political interests, of the northern and the southern states had begun to diverge. The South developed on the basis of large plantations run by a few families; the North tended to have smaller farms and began to focus more on manufacturing, fishing, and foreign trade. Although all colonies permitted SLAVERY at one time or another, the system was much more critical to the maintenance of the South's large plantation system.

After the AMERICAN REVOLUTION, slavery had been largely banned in the North, which became more focused on trade and industry. The South continued to concentrate on agriculture. After the introduction of the cotton gin by Eli WHITNEY, the South turned primarily to a single crop, cotton.

Thus, at the eve of the Civil War (1861–65), in the 1850s, the degree of the urbanization and the level of the industrial labor force in the South was less than half of that of the North, and even the more industrial southern states were producing at less than half the per-capita rates of northern states.

As a consequence of these differences there were frequent political clashes between North and South centered on economic policy. Thus, a perennial source of conflict was federal tariff policy. The northern states regularly pushed for high tariffs on manufactured products in order to protect their industries from foreign competition. While this was perceived to be beneficial to the economic interests of the North, it raised the prices of many goods that the South consumed, and was thus in direct opposition to the interests of the South.

Events leading up to the war. Although the sectional differences between the North and South pre-date the Revolution, the debate leading to the Civil War was framed in 1820 with the admission of Missouri to the union. By 1820, there were 11 free and 11 slave states. Northerners, concerned over the expansion of slavery northward, sought to admit Missouri only if it outlawed slavery. Southerners opposed a precedent that allowed the federal government to dictate to states whether or not they could have slaves. If slavery could not expand, it would eventually become a minority interest that could be ended by the majority. The Missouri Compromise permitted Missouri to enter as a slave state while Maine was admitted as a free state, thus keeping the balance. It also forbade slavery in any other state that was formed on the northern portions of the Louisiana Purchase.

The Compromise held for the next 30 years. However, following the MEXICAN-AMERICAN WAR, ceded lands sought entry as free states with no slave state to counterbalance it. The Compromise of 1850, among other things, permitted California to be admitted as a free state, but gave Southerners more powerful fugitive slave laws to capture runaway slaves. It also introduced the idea of "popular sovereignty," which permitted the residents of each territory to decide for themselves whether to be admitted as slave or free.

While the purpose of the Compromise was to quiet the debate, it swelled the abolitionist movement in the North. No longer did Northerners merely have to tolerate slavery; now they were forced to assist in arresting their runaway slave neighbors and returning them to slavery.

In 1854, the Kansas-Nebraska Act permitted those territories to decide for themselves whether to be admitted as slave or free. The "debate" soon turned into a bloody war as abolitionists and slaveholders, primarily from Missouri, used violence, intimidation, and murder to take control of the territory.

Southerners, who were already on the defensive now that they were outnumbered in Congress, relied on the Supreme Court to assert their demands for expanding slavery. In 1857, the U.S. Supreme Court further inflamed the sectional dispute by issuing its opinion in *Dred Scott v. Sanford*. It held in part that the Missouri Compromise was unconstitutional and that slave owners could take their slaves wherever they liked.

In 1859, John Brown attacked the federal arsenal at Harper's Ferry, Virginia. His hope was to foment a slave rebellion that would spread throughout the South. He captured the arsenal but failed to spark the uprising he had hoped for. He was quickly captured and hanged, but the Southern fear of slave revolt had been resurrected and Southerners now saw Northern abolitionists as a potential cause of such an insurrection.

With the election of the Republican Abraham LINCOLN in 1860, Southerners decided the federal government had become too hostile to their interests. After the election, but before Lincoln's inauguration, 11 southern states seceded from the Union and formed the Confederate States of America.

Economic significance of slavery. The institution of slavery was an outgrowth of economic and socio-cultural differences, with an obvious moral dimension to it as well. It had been argued that slavery was doomed as a form of economic organization; had compromise between the northern and the southern states succeeded a bit longer, then slavery would have naturally perished.

Recent research indicates that the rate of return on investing in slaves in the ante-bellum South was close to 10 percent—well above the return that was available to southern planters in other ventures, such as railroads. And indeed, a higher return than most textile mills were able to achieve in New England in the 1840s and 1850s. Further, indications are that slavery was becoming even more profitable leading up to the Civil War. In an amoral, objective view, if one uses market prices for slaves as a proxy for what returns were expected to be obtainable from exploiting slave labor, then there is a clear upward trend in the profitability of slavery, subsequent to the widespread introduction of the cotton gin around the turn of the century.

Charting the course of slavery absent the Civil War is clearly speculative. The answer, perhaps, follows upon one primary supposition: Would slavery have been permitted to expand beyond the South, in particular might it have expanded to the west and northwest? Given that the North seemed to be gaining more political power and that most unsettled western lands were not useful for cotton farming, it seems unlikely. Further, the fact that Britain, the main market for southern cotton, was developing a strong anti-slavery movement and was finding alternatives to cotton for its clothing industry; means that Britain likely would have begun to exert economic pressure to end slavery.

Brief summary of the war. The war began when South Carolina troops fired on federal troops who refused to surrender Fort Sumter in Charleston Harbor. Northerners were outraged by this act and rallied around the war cause. Both sides thought the war would be over in a matter of weeks or months. Volunteers signed up for 90-day enlistments.

Northerners emphasized that they had a larger population and industrial base, and hence, more arms and the capacity to manufacture arms. Southerners had a superior officer corps and potential allies in Europe.

Federal troops marched from Washington, D.C., into Virginia where they engaged the Confederates in the Battle of Bull Run/Manassas. Confederate troops routed the Union soldiers who fled back to Washington. For the next three years, a series of Union generals would attempt to invade Virginia with the hope of capturing the Confederate capital of Richmond. Each time, they would be outmaneuvered, out-generaled, and ultimately defeated by the Army of Northern Virginia, commanded by General Robert E. Lee.

The Southerners attempted twice to take the war to the North. The first attempt was an invasion of Maryland in the fall of 1862. On September 17th, the armies met at the battle of Antietam/Sharpsburg. After a day of bloody fighting, the Confederates withdrew to Virginia. Lincoln seized on the Confederate's withdrawal as the opportunity to announce the Emancipation Proclamation, which declared all slaves in rebel territory to be free.

The following year, the Confederates made another attempt to move northward as they entered Pennsylvania. The two armies clashed for three days in July, in and around the town of Gettysburg. In a final charge on July 3rd, the Confederate Army was decimated in what became known as Pickett's Charge (General George Pickett led the charge). Despite the loss, Lee successfully retreated back to Virginia and retained his forces. The stalemate in the eastern theater continued.

The only real Union progress came in the west. Generals Ulysses GRANT and William Tecumseh Sherman captured Tennessee and had begun moving down the Mississippi River. On July 4, 1863, Union troops broke the siege of Vicksburg, giving them full control of the river. These western generals defied military convention by ignoring their own supply lines. Their armies moved hard and fast, capturing whatever food and supplies they needed from the enemy.

In March 1864, Lincoln put Grant in charge of all Union armies. As with all the other generals who tried to march on Richmond, Grant was outmaneuvered and suffered heavy losses. However, unlike previous generals who retreated after a loss, Grant continued to send in more reinforcements, relying on the fact that the North had far greater reserves than the South and could afford to sustain much heavier losses.

At the same time, Grant had Sherman push in from the west, eventually capturing and burning Atlanta and beginning his well-known march to the sea. The purpose of this move was not only to demoralize the South, but also to cut the Confederacy in half, which it did. Sherman also wanted to ensure that the war experience would be so horrible that the South would never rise in arms again. Consequently, Sherman destroyed almost anything that could be of value to the Confederacy. The Confederate Army, and Southern people generally, were cut off from all food and supplies.

Despite massive casualties, Grant's relentless assault resulted in the capture of Richmond within a year. Within days, Lee surrendered his army, effectively ending the war on April 9, 1865.

Economic and war policies in the North. The Union recognized its clear naval advantage over the Confederacy, as well as the South's complete dependence on foreign trade for most of its necessities. Consequently, it employed a naval blockade on all trade to or from the Confederacy. At first, the blockade was unable to prevent the bulk of merchant vessels, known as blockade runners, from engaging in trade. Over the course of the war, however, the blockade became more effective in starving the South of weapons, ammunition, food, and other necessities.

In the final years of the war, the Union embarked on a scorched-earth policy further designed to break the Confederate economy. Northern armies confiscated or destroyed farm animals, crops, and anything else of value to the South.

The Union also introduced a military draft for the first time. Prior to this, the federal government had always depended on volunteers. But as a protracted war became evident, the government could not keep up enlistments, even with generous bounties. In order to help raise needed funds, draftees were permitted to hire a replacement or pay the government $300—causing considerable resentment among those who could not buy their way out.

With tariff revenues down because the war prevented much trade, the government also instituted a tax on incomes as a temporary war measure.

Finally, the emancipation of slaves had strategic significance as well. When Lincoln declared the slaves free in 1863, it made the war about more than saving the Union. While this provoked mixed feelings among Northerners, it convinced the British, many of whom had strong anti-slavery sentiments, to forgo allying themselves with the Confederacy.

Economic and war policies in the South. The South had a more difficult strategy. Because of its lack of a manufacturing base, it relied on Europe. The Confederacy hoped that it could draw Britain into the conflict as an ally. Britain was heavily dependant on the South's cotton, and could have viewed the war as an opportunity to regain influence in America. However, once the Union successfully made slavery the main issue of the War, Britain decided to stay out of it.

Later, the Confederacy hoped to drag out the war, making it costly enough on the North that a friendlier president would be elected who would grant them peaceful separation. However, a string of Union victories helped Lincoln's re-election in 1864 and the Confederacy surrendered a few months later.

The cost of the Civil War. The total costs of the Civil War to the U.S. economy are immeasurable. Even a rough estimate would require that one determine how the economy might have developed without the enormous amount of destruction, in terms of both physical capital as well as human lives. There were well over 1 million military casualties, including over a half-million lost lives. Given a total population of a little over 31 million according to the 1860 census, war casualties amounted to over 3.5 percent of the entire population. If one attempts to estimate the lost lifetime earnings of these casualties, and adds to them the military expenditures, and the value of the property destroyed in the course of the conflict, one estimate of the total direct costs of the war is $3.4 billion for the North and $3.3 billion for the South—together more than the total annual production of the U.S. economy preceding the war. In fact, a much higher figure than what it would have cost to purchase all slaves into freedom at the prevailing prices just before the War.

Of course, these are only monetary losses to the economy, and these figures cannot capture the total costs to American society, which would have to include costs in terms of the immense suffering. By the same token, however, it is not possible to measure accurately what American society has gained through the liberation of the nearly four million slaves. Not only is their mere freedom invaluable, but one also cannot even begin to estimate the contributions to American society and the American economy made by African-Americans, despite organized and inadvertent setbacks that reverberate to this day.

BIBLIOGRAPHY. W. Elliot Brownlee, *Dynamics of Ascent: A History of the American Economy* (Random House, 1978); Henry Steele Commanger, *The Blue and the Gray* (Fairfax, 1950); Susan B. Dixon, *History of the Missouri Compromise and Slavery in American Politics* (Johnson Reprint, 2003); Don E. Feherenbacher, *The Sectional Crisis and Southern Constitutionalism* (Louisiana State University Press, 1995); Shelby Foote, *The Civil War* (Vintage Books, 1974); Jonathan Hughes and Louis P. Cain, *American Economic History* (Addison-Wesley, 1998).

THOMAS D. JEITSCHKO, PH.D.
MICHIGAN STATE UNIVERSITY
MICHAEL J. TROY, J.D.

American Electric Power

RANKED AS THE 36TH LARGEST company in the world by *Fortune* magazine in 2002, American Electric Power (AEP) is the largest electricity generator in the UNITED STATES.

The company is marked indelibly by its geographic location, which provides both its most important strength and deepest future worry: It is in the middle of the Ohio coal-mining region, which provides cheap but high-sulphur, high-ash coal. At the beginning of the 1990s, as deregulation began, approximately 90 percent of its power was generated in coal-fired plants; by the end of the decade coal still made up a three-quarter share.

The specter of environmental regulation hangs darkly. When the Clean Air Act introduced sulphur-dioxide tradable permits in 1995, the utility was allocated sufficient allowances to burn coal of up to approximately 2 percent to 2.5 percent sulphur. Any amount of sulphur in the coal over that level means that AEP must either increase its cleanup efforts or buy permits. Although some of its subsidiaries get low-sulphur western coal, its Columbus Southern and Ohio Power operations use eastern coal that averages 3 percent.

Changing to low-sulphur coal is complicated by local political pressure to continue mining employment in Midwest fields. New efforts to curtail emission of nitrogen-oxide, regulate haze, or even tax carbon output will continue to obscure the company's financial future.

As the company expands to overseas markets, its exposure to foreign regulation also grows. From this multinational standpoint, AEP admitted that government regulations on greenhouse gases were inevitable. However, AEP has some confidence in its ability to dance with regulators, since it was one of the few U.S. utilities to survive NEW DEAL regulations (the Public Utility Holding Company Act, PUHCA, in 1935) virtually unscathed.

BIBLIOGRAPHY. AEP 10-K Report (1992); www.aep.com; "Global 500: World's Largest Companies," *Fortune* (July 2002).

KEVIN R FOSTER, PH.D.
CITY COLLEGE OF NEW YORK

American International Group

AN INSURANCE COMPANY that began in Shanghai, CHINA—American International Group (AIG)—was founded by Cornelius Vander Starr in 1919 as American Asiatic Underwriters, which later became affiliated with American International Underwriters (AIU). Starr later expanded his business with the founding of the Asia Life Insurance Company. He moved forward with this enterprise despite the fact that there were no available statistics on Chinese life expectancy.

In 1931, Starr formed the International Assurance Company as a partnership with British and Chinese investors. In 1932, American International Underwriters expanded into Central America. By the end of the 1930s, impending war forced Starr to close his Shanghai office and move his headquarters to New York City. Though WORLD WAR II interfered with AIU's European and Asian interests, the company continued to rapidly expand into Central America during the early 1940s.

After the war, the Shanghai office reopened, but communist domination of mainland China shut down the Shanghai office once again, in 1950. AIU's post-war entry into West GERMANY and JAPAN proved more lasting, with U.S. occupation troops serving as primary customers. In 1948, Starr reorganized the International Assurance Company as the American International Assurance Company, and became involved in MALAYSIA, THAILAND, and SINGAPORE. He then formed the American International Reinsurance (AIRCO) and American International Underwriters Overseas Companies, and the American International Underwriters Association.

In 1952, AIRCO acquired Globe and Rutgers Insurance, along with American Home Assurance. American International interests continued to grow during the 1950s and 1960s, with expansion into the Caribbean, the Middle East, and some African nations. The communist takeover in CUBA represented a serious loss, as private enterprise in the small country was nationalized. However, the New Hampshire Insurance Company, Commerce and Industry Insurance Company, and the National Union Fire Insurance Company of Pittsburgh were added during this period to American International's portfolio.

During the 1970s, the American International Credit Corporation and North American Managers Inc. were formed as new divisions. NAM sold insurance to foreign companies operating in the United States. AIG Oil Rig Inc. was also formed at this time to sell insurance to offshore drilling operations. AIG profits grew rapidly during the 1970s, and by the end of the decade, AIG had entered Eastern Europe, re-entered mainland China, and increased its size tenfold.

During the 1980s, AIG expanded further into health-care services and real estate. Profits declined in 1984, but improved in 1985. 1988 was also a difficult year, because AIG lost an arbitration case that cost the company more than $100 million. In the late 1980s, AIG consolidated many of its operations, but continued to expand in other areas, including divisions that lease commercial jet airliners, and that provide financial services.

In 1999, AIG merged with Sun America and acquired licenses to operate in Azerbaijan, Bulgaria, and Sri Lanka. In 2003, AIG operated in more than 130 countries, with more than 80,000 employees, and reported $67.5 billion in sales, making it the 25th largest company in the world. With hundreds of billions of dollars in assets, AIG is as massive as it is innovative and complex; it is one of the most remarkable business enterprises of modern times.

BIBLIOGRAPHY. "American International Group History," www.aig.com; "American International Group," *Hoover's Handbook of American Business 2003* (Hoover's Business

Press, 2002); Roger W. Rouland, "American International Group," *The International Directory of Companies* (St. James Press, 1991).

D.W. MacKenzie
George Mason University

American Revolution

THROUGHOUT MUCH of the 17th and 18th centuries, the UNITED KINGDOM and FRANCE struggled for domination of North America. Britain took control of most of the east coast, while France controlled CANADA and the Mississippi Valley. By the mid-18th century British colonists moving westward began encroaching on territories claimed by France. Both powers tried to strengthen their positions and harass the other. Eventually this touched off what became known in America as the French and Indian War, otherwise also known as the Seven Years' War, 1756–63. When the war ended, Britain retained undisputed control as far west as the Mississippi river. France gave up all claims on the continent.

Until that time, Britain had strongly encouraged colonization by allowing the colonists certain liberties (particularly religious freedom) not available in Britain. Britain also left the colonists virtually untaxed, and failed to enforce effectively many of the tariffs in place. Prior to 1767 it cost Britain £9,000 annually in order to collect £2,000 in customs duties from the colonies. The mass colonization of British subjects who took advantage of these incentives helped Britain to take control of the continent. With control over the continent secured, however, Britain hoped to recoup the costs of the war and make the colonies profitable. A series of laws from Parliament created a rift between Britain and its colonies.

The growing rift. Thus, the Proclamation of 1763 banned further expansion westward. The Crown hoped to reserve that land for Native Americans and to make them loyal subjects of the empire. Colonists, however, viewed this ban as a dangerous limitation on the expansion of their growth.

The Currency Act of 1764 limited the issuance of paper money through colonial governments. This limited colonial power to shape fiscal policy. It also made trade more difficult given a shortage of specie (gold and silver) in the colonies.

The Sugar Act of 1764 imposed taxes on sugar and molasses not imported from the West Indies, raising prices and limiting supplies of sugar in the colonies.

This was supported by increased enforcement against smuggling.

In 1765, the Stamp Act introduced taxes on legal documents, newspapers, and virtually all other printed materials. This was the first direct tax levied by Britain on the colonists. Since these duties were to be collected by the local colonial governments and then transferred to England, the effect was to pit colonial governments against their own citizens who resented this form of "taxation without representation." Britain further inflamed the issue by passing the Quartering Act, requiring the colonies to house and feed British soldiers, sent to enforce the laws.

While there had been displeasure over the earlier taxes, the Stamp Act caused the first true resistance. The Sons of Liberty organized in Boston to fight the tax and collectors were threatened or beaten to prevent collection. Colonial leaders throughout the continent urged resistance. Parliament quickly repealed the Stamp Act (having been largely ineffectual for not having been enforced), but reasserted its prerogative by passing the Declaratory Act, establishing the right of the Crown to impose direct taxes on the colonists without their consent.

In 1767, Parliament passed the Townsend Acts, which introduced customs duties on tea, glass, and paper. Though they were not direct taxes, the colonists responded with boycotts on imports and violence against tax collectors. Britain repealed these duties, leaving only a small tax on tea in order to assert the principle of its right to impose such taxes. It also sent British troops to Boston to stop the acts of violence and resistance to British laws.

Opposition to British occupation led to frequent riots, and eventually the Boston Massacre, in which British troops shot at an unarmed albeit threatening mob, shooting six colonists in 1770. In 1773 the Sons of Liberty boarded a ship that had been waiting to unload its fares and dumped British tea into Boston Harbor. In response to the "Boston Tea Party," Britain closed the port of Boston until the colonists paid for the destroyed property.

In the wake of this rupture, the First Continental Congress met in Philadelphia in 1774, passing resolutions that, in effect, demanded nullification of all British policies taken toward the colonies since the end of the French and Indian War. Britain refused to recognize the Congress and even disbanded a number of Colonial Legislatures that had been hostile to British policies.

The American sentiment. Many have asked, on the eve of the Revolution, why a relatively prosperous and free people would risk armed conflict with the world's undisputed superpower over a few taxes. Indeed, American colonists of the 1770s may very well have enjoyed the highest per capita income levels of anyone in the world at the time, and were surely among the least taxed people in Europe and America.

In fact, most people did not oppose the Crown. On the eve of independence, one of its most powerful advocates, John ADAMS, estimated that only one-third of the country supported the patriot cause, with another third supporting the Crown, and the rest remaining neutral, hoping only to avoid harm.

The great concern among those supporting the patriot cause was precedent. Colonists had seen how Britain had treated other colonies, culling their wealth for the benefit of the mother country, and drafting their men for fighting in seemingly continuous wars with the other European powers. By accepting the principle of direct taxation without representation, the American colonies would begin down this road. They would become subservient to Britain, never full partners.

Brief chronology of the Revolution. Most historians consider the real beginning of the war to be the battles of Lexington and Concord. Boston patriots had stored a large stash of arms and ammunition in Concord, and in April 1775, the military governor directed 700 British troops to destroy the cache. Patriots were tipped off and assembled to block the British. At Lexington, the troops met about 70 armed Patriots and demanded they disperse. No one is sure who fired first, but the British shot 18 militiamen. The remainder scattered. The British continued on to Concord where they met further resistance. By this time, local farmers had turned out and began shooting at the British, who then retreated back to Boston. By the time they had returned, 250 British had been killed or wounded.

The Second Continental Congress convened a month later and declared war. George WASHINGTON was appointed commander of the Continental Army. Although Congress attempted to resolve the matter diplomatically, Britain refused to negotiate while violence continued. A year later, in July 1776, Congress declared the colonies to be "free and independent states."

At the time Washington took command, the British troops were concentrated in Boston, with American troops in the surrounding hills. The British had captured the nearby hills at great cost in the Battle of Bunker Hill. The two sides had reached a standoff. Washington needed artillery to take on the British effectively.

Fortunately for Washington, a small contingent of patriots under Ethan Allen and Benedict Arnold had captured Fort Ticonderoga in northern New York. Even more impressively, these men dragged one hundred cannons through the wilderness to Boston. When the Americans put the cannon in place, the British retreated to Canada without a shot fired.

The British next decided to take New York as a base of operations. Washington's Army took up the defenses

Modern day re-enactments celebrate the Revolution and its unleashing of American economic ascent.

of New York, but his militia were quickly scattered by the professional soldiers employed by the British. It was a humiliating defeat from which Washington was lucky to retreat with his army mostly intact. By the winter of 1776, the Continental Army had retreated through New Jersey to Philadelphia. Continental soldiers were demoralized and planned to leave when their enlistments ended at the end of the year. A desperate Washington planned a surprise Christmas Day attack on the British and their Hessian mercenary soldiers in Trenton and Princeton, New Jersey. The resulting victory increased morale and saved the Army from disbanding.

The British, however, pressed on, capturing Philadelphia. Nevertheless, a subsequent American victory at Saratoga impressed the French sufficiently so that they began to provide support to the American cause. The French were still smarting from their losses to the British a decade earlier, and saw an opportunity to regain influence over the continent by providing covert aid. By 1778, France made its support public and went to war against Britain.

That same year, Washington's victory at Monmouth, New Jersey forced the British to retreat to New York City. The British sent peace commissioners, promising to end all taxation, but the Americans refused to end hostilities unless the British were to recognize their independence.

In 1780, the British attempted to reclaim control of the southern colonies by capturing Charleston. They met with initial success, capturing thousands of American troops. However, American counter-attacks pushed the British northward into Virginia. Finally, in 1781, the British forces became trapped at Yorktown, Virginia, surrounded by French and American troops and cut off from the sea by the French Navy. General Cornwallis surrendered his army, effectively ending hostilities. The following year, peace negotiations began in Paris, which lead to agreements that were ratified in 1783.

The financing of the Revolution. With the battle cry "no taxation without representation" and the colonies being a disparate lot, levying taxes in order to finance the war effort was neither technically nor politically possible. Instead, the American government used four methods to finance the war: printing money, borrowing money, promising lands, and confiscating property, including reneging (at least temporarily) on some obligations.

The Continental Congress issued approximately $226 million in paper money, with the states issuing roughly another $200 million. When, in 1780, Congress devalued its currency at the rate of $40 of paper money to $1 of specie, it still continued to print more virtually worthless Continental dollars, giving rise to the expression "not worth a Continental." Price limits set by Congress caused people to refuse to sell or produce goods, leading to even greater shortages.

To support its worthless paper money and to continue the cause, Congress sought loans from abroad. France provided several loans and grants. Merchants in the NETHERLANDS also provided loans. John ADAMS and Benjamin FRANKLIN spent most of their time in Europe either seeking loans or trying to defer repayment of past loans. Such loans were very risky since the lender would incur the wrath of Britain, the loans would not be repaid if the Americans lost, and might not be repaid for some time even if the Americans won. In the end, foreign loans paid for only about eight percent of the war's expenses.

Without anything of value to pay its troops, Congress kept an army in the field with a series of promises. Many soldiers enlisted with promises of hundreds of acres of western land after the war. Toward the end of the war, officers and men were promised generous pensions for those who stayed with the army until the end.

Finally, Congress confiscated lands and other property from Tories (British loyalists) who had fled the country. All debts to British merchants prior to the war were not paid, as well as debts incurred with others during the war were deferred. Although private debts and confiscated property was to be repaid as part of the peace treaty, much of it was never recovered.

Despite all these measures, the Americans were regularly at the point of desperation. Just before the Battle of Trenton, Washington had to promise a $10 bounty, paid in sterling, to keep many men from leaving when their enlistments ended. This money came from the personal fortune of Robert Morris, a Philadelphia merchant and financier, who became the head of the Continental Congress' finance committee. Morris used his personal credit on numerous occasions to help bail out the cause. His contacts and good reputation in the Netherlands were also critical to receiving loans from neutral merchants.

The Continental Army almost never had sufficient food or clothing, let alone arms and ammunition. On several occasions, Washington had to put down mutinies of soldiers who had faced too many deprivations.

Economic consequences of the Revolution. The colonies had been net benefactors of the Crown, even just prior to the Revolution. Consequently, early U.S. governments had to impose much higher taxes and became much more restrictive than the Crown had ever been. Indeed, the monetary situation had become precarious. Financing the war by printing money had lead to a severe depreciation of the Continental dollar, ultimately to below one percent of its face value. Moreover, outflows of specie (gold) to finance the war had lead to a strong deflation (decrease in prices) that increased the burden on all who owed money.

New England farmers, being heavily indebted, revolted in Shay's rebellion. The rebellion gave added impetus to create a stronger national government, which ultimately led to the drafting of a new Constitution of the United States. The new Constitution, which allowed for direct taxation of imports, finally gave Congress the ability to begin regular and reliable repayment on its debts.

American trade remained limited in part because continuing wars between Britain and France prevented unimpaired trade, even of neutral merchant vessels. Despite obstacles, however, over the next few decades, U.S. merchant vessels expanded trade all over the world, taking a major role in world business.

With the stability created by the new Constitution and westward expansion possible, these trade patterns laid the foundation of significant economic growth and, ultimately, the economic ascent of the United States.

BIBLIOGRAPHY. Bernard Bailyn, *Ideological Origins of the American Revolution* (Belknap Press, 1992); W. Elliot Brownlee, *Dynamics of Ascent: A History of the American Economy* (Random House, 1978); Jonathan Hughes and Louis P. Cain, *American Economic History* (Addison-Wesley, 1998); Pauline Maier, *From Resistance to Revolution* (W.W. Norton, 1992); Robert Middlekauff, *The Glorious Cause: The American Revolution, 1763–1789* (Oxford University Press, 1982).

THOMAS D. JEITSCHKO, PH.D.
MICHIGAN STATE UNIVERSITY
MICHAEL J. TROY, J.D.

American Stock Exchange

THE AMERICAN STOCK EXCHANGE (Amex) is the second largest stock exchange in the UNITED STATES, the first being the NEW YORK STOCK EXCHANGE (NYSE). The

Amex is often defined in terms of its relationship with, and distinction from, the NYSE.

The Amex was originally called the New York Curb Market (or simply, the Curb). The term originated from the fact that the brokers once conducted their auctions in the open air. Yet, in fact, the NYSE (then called the New York Stock and Exchange Board) also originated as an outdoor marketplace. However, the NYSE quickly moved inside in 1792 after formalizing their organization with the Buttonwood Agreement. The Amex traces its roots to the curbstone brokers who did not sign that agreement and who chose to remain outside to trade, among themselves, stocks that were not traded on the formal exchange. The practice of convening outside the New York Stock Exchange to trade securities alongside the curbs of Wall Street remained intact for more than a century. Commenting on this long tradition of a lack of a central marketplace, Wall Street historian Charles Geisst credits the New York Curb Market as being the forerunner of not just the Amex, but also the over-the-counter market.

At first, the Curb and the NYSE competed for business. Gradually, however, the two exchanges reached an informal arrangement whereby the Curb established a niche that did not directly encroach the NYSE's territory. The Curb traded in securities that tended to be smaller and less established than those traded on the NYSE. The listing requirements for Curb stocks were less stringent as well.

Besides dealing with a different type of clientele, the curbstone brokers historically had a less aristocratic culture than that which prevailed at the private club-like atmosphere pervading the NYSE. Fewer members hailed from prestigious families; in fact, many were immigrants or children of immigrants who had come to the United States with little money. In addition to this socioeconomic difference, the curbstone broker group was more religiously diverse than the mostly Protestant NYSE. The Curb attracted a significant number of Jews and Catholics, some of whom were able to rise to leadership positions there.

Due to the above reasons, a certain bias existed that the Curb was second in status to the NYSE. In the 1920s, Curb president Edward R. McCormick was determined to elevate the reputation of the institution. In 1921, upon his urging, the Curb finally moved indoors (more than a century after the NYSE). The move from the street curbs to formal offices was a symbol of the Curb's newfound respectability.

At the same time, the Board members of the Curb, inspired by McCormick's leadership, tightened standards for member firm conduct. They also enforced stricter listing standards. While these reforms were successful in building the Curb's image, the exchange remained predominantly a place where smaller stocks could be traded until they gained sufficient stature to advance to the more illustrious NYSE. As financial journalist Martin Mayer described it, the Curb functioned as a "seasoning exchange," which "took the stock of corporations not large enough or national enough to qualify for listing on the New York Stock Exchange."

This pattern of firms listed on the Curb eventually migrating to the NYSE diminished in the 1950s. This time period, at least in the early years of the decade, may be perceived as a Golden Age for the Curb.

Confident in President Dwight EISENHOWER's administration, American investors displayed heightened interest in new industries, seeking unusual growth opportunities. This was a boom for the Curb due to its specialization in trading securities of mid-size companies. Many of its listed firms now excited investor attention because they seemed to be on the verge of major success, propelled by technological advancements in such fields as computers and television. During this time, the Curb changed its name to the American Stock Exchange, another effort to give the institution a more solid and more national image. The newly amended constitution of the American Stock Exchange, in 1953, declared that "the purposes of this Association shall be to provide a securities marketplace where high standards of honor and integrity shall prevail to promote and maintain just and equitable principles of trade and business."

While the 1950s began as a time of hope and expansion for the Amex, the decade ended in crisis, as the SECURITIES AND EXCHANGE COMMISSION (SEC) exposed the illegal dealings of brokers Jerry Re and James Patrick Gilligan. Bringing more disgrace to the Amex, Edward T. McCormick, its president, was implicated in this scandal and was forced to resign in 1961.

In the wake of the scandal, the Amex underwent a series of reforms, led by Ralph Saul, Edwin Posher, David Jacobs, among others. The exchange also underwent modernization, as the Amex adapted new technological innovations to its trading procedures. This paralleled a similar movement at the NYSE, which was forced to prioritize computerization after the famous "back office crisis" of the late 1960s, when the NYSE became mired in paperwork resulting from increased trading volume.

In the late 1960s and 1970s, Amex and NYSE officials often discussed the possibility of merging the two exchanges. A merger, however, never took place because it was clear to Amex officials that it would not be a merger of equals, but rather, would be the submerging of the junior Amex into the more senior NYSE.

In 1998, a combination did occur, but it was not between Amex and the NYSE. Rather, the parent company of the NASDAQ purchased Amex and combined their markets. Amex, though, continues to operate separately.

BIBLIOGRAPHY. Stuart Bruchey, *The Modernization of the American Stock Exchange* (Garland, 1991); Constitution of the American Stock Exchange (1953); Walter Geisst, *Wall Street: A History* (Oxford University Press, 1997); Martin Mayer, *Wall Street: Men and Money* (Harper and Row, 1959): Robert Sobel, *Amex: a History of the American Stock Exchange, 1921–1971* (Weybright & Talley. 1972); Robert Sobel, *Inside Wall Street: Continuity and Change in the Financial District* (W.W. Norton, 1977); Robert Sobel, *The Curbstone Brokers: The Origins of the American Stock Exchange* (Macmillan, 1970).

JANICE TRAFLET
COLUMBIA UNIVERSITY

Andorra

A TINY COUNTRY LOCATED in the Pyrenées mountains between FRANCE and SPAIN, Andorra was originally created by Charlemagne in the 8th century to serve as a buffer between Christian Europe and Muslim Spain.

The traditional economy was based on subsistence agriculture, especially sheep-raising. In the 20th century, many Andorran farmers switched to growing tobacco which proved to be more profitable. In the 1990s, the economy of Andorra greatly benefited from a customs-union agreement with the EUROPEAN UNION (EU) that permitted it to sell duty-free items that it combined with minimal sales taxes. Because of the appeal of shopping (prices are as much as 40 percent lower than in neighboring countries) and natural scenery, the primary basis of Andorra's economy is tourism, accounting for 80 percent of employment and GROSS DOMESTIC PRODUCT (GDP). Andorra also has had a strong banking sector. Investors have been attracted by its strict privacy laws, but these practices have come under criticism from foreign agencies seeking to crack down on under-regulated tax havens.

The country is so small (468 square miles) that economist Simon KUZNETS once held it up as an example of why scholars should not use nation states as the primary units of economic research.

BIBLIOGRAPHY. U.S. Department of Commerce, "Andorra," (U.S. Government Printing Office, 2001); Derwent Whittlesey, "Andorra's Autonomy," *Journal of Modern History* (v.9, 1934); Elena Sanchez, "Finding Andorra's Place in the World: A Micro-state Adjusts to Europe's Wider Perspective," *The Washington Times* (1999).

LAURA CRUZ
WESTERN CAROLINA UNIVERSITY

Angell, Sir Norman (1872–1967)

RALPH NORMAN ANGELL LANE, journalist and pacifist, used the pen-name Norman Angell. Author of the most widely read anti-war manifesto of the early 20th century, Angell became the leading spokesman of the "New Pacifist" movement and was awarded the Nobel Peace Prize in 1933.

Born in Holbeach in northeastern England to a prosperous commercial family and educated in FRANCE and SWITZERLAND as well as his native country, Angell spent nine years working in a variety of menial occupations in the UNITED STATES before drifting into journalism. Returning to Europe in 1898, he settled in Paris and rose to become editor of the continental edition of the *London Daily Mail*. From this vantage point he observed the dramatic escalation of international tensions between GERMANY and its neighbors and the growth of a seemingly uncontrollable arms race.

In 1909, Angell published an analysis of these developments, *Europe's Optical Illusion*, that after revision was reissued the following year under the title, *The Great Illusion*.

The central argument of *The Great Illusion* was an inversion of the Marxist proposition that the root causes of war lay in competition between rival capitalist groups seeking to enrich themselves by monopolizing foreign markets and natural resources. Angell sought to show that, to the contrary, modern warfare had become so expensive and economically disruptive that, even if successful, the costs of a war of conquest would vastly exceed the expected benefits. In a rapidly integrating and interdependent world economy, territorial expansion could offer no tangible or lasting commercial advantage to the victors.

War was therefore futile and obsolete, as was the possession of colonies and the creation of exclusive trading blocs. Upon the broadest possible recognition of these truths depended the only possibility of averting a conflict that threatened to wreck the continent of Europe. Angell's ideas were far from original, having been anticipated in substance by the French essayist Jacques Novikow and the Polish industrialist Ivan S. Bloch, among others. Nonetheless, *The Great Illusion* enjoyed an immense success, selling two million copies in 25 languages in the years before the WORLD WAR I. An extensive network of clubs and societies dedicated to the spread of its doctrines sprang up throughout Europe and North America, and Angell himself, abandoning journalism, embarked upon a new career as a peace activist.

The rise of "New Pacifism" or "Norman Angellism" met with mixed reactions from established pacifist organizations. Some decried his appeal to material self-interest rather than morality as the principal reason for opposing war, condemning in particular his acceptance of the legitimacy of military establishments as a safeguard against aggression. Many others interpreted his work to mean that armed conflict, being unprofitable, had become economically impossible as opposed to self-defeating, a misapprehension which Angell would spend much of his life attempting to dispel.

A more serious criticism leveled against his work, however, was that *The Great Illusion* spoke only to those liberal Western elites who shared Angell's assumptions about the desirability of preserving modern industrial society in its existing form, and ignored the very different priorities of extremists on both the Left and Right who posed the chief threat to peace.

After the Great War (that Angell regarded as a vindication of his warnings), he joined the British Labor Party, serving as Member of Parliament for North Bradford in the short-lived MacDonald administration of 1929-31. Although he quickly became disillusioned both with politics and with the Labor party, a knighthood in 1931 maintained him in the public eye, as did the award of the Nobel Prize two years later. During the 1930s, Angell campaigned energetically in support of the League of Nations, advocating the creation of a more effective system of collective security to check fascist expansionism. This stance further alienated him from traditional pacifists, while the outbreak of the WORLD WAR II seemed to contradict his faith in the ability of rational self-interest to counteract the forces militating in favor of armed conflict. Nevertheless, Angell remained active in publication and pacifist activism almost to the end of his long life, by which time he had produced no fewer than 42 books and an immense volume of lesser writings on various aspects of international affairs.

BIBLIOGRAPHY. N. Angell, *The Great Illusion: A Study of the Relation of Military Power in Nations to Their Social and Economic Advantage* (Heinemann, 1910). *After All: The Autobiography of Norman Angell* (Hamish Hamilton, 1951). A. Marrin, *Sir Norman Angell* (Twayne, 1979). J.D.B. Miller, *Norman Angell and the Futility of War: Peace and the Public Mind* (Macmillan, 1986).

R.M. DOUGLAS, PH.D.
COLGATE UNIVERSITY

annual report

ALL PUBLICLY TRADED COMPANIES, holdings, mutual funds, public services, agencies, ministries, and many private and public institutions have to publish every year an annual report. In most cases, the annual report is an institutional portrait, a means of communication, a synthesis of activities during the past 12 months, explaining in words, numbers and figures the reasons behind the successes and failures of an organization or a company.

In order to be listed on a stock exchange, publicly traded companies have to include in their annual reports some specific elements: statistics and detailed financial results according to specific rules edited by the government, national trade commission, or commerce department. This data includes sales, revenues, profits (or losses in parentheses), earnings per share, cash flow, capital spending, and balance sheet with assets. The company has to explain where their stores (branches or laboratories) are located, if new acquisitions were made (or branches sold). The annual report has to state as well the company's dividend policy. There also has to be the report of an independent auditor that confirms the company's financial statements are accurate.

For a stock shareholder, an annual report will explain why the company he or she owns has grown or not, succeeded or failed. It is therefore a way to check if the company is well managed or not. For example, if members of the BOARD OF DIRECTORS get bonuses even during bad years, it will be indicated in the annual report and a shareholder could possibly react or even complain about that situation at the annual meeting, that is usually held a few weeks after the annual report's release.

The message from the president, chair or CHIEF EXECUTIVE OFFICER (CEO) is a key element, almost a telltale story, in every annual report. In fact, these opening lines are sometimes written by communication consultants or marketing specialists, because they have to reassure and even improve confidence for the stockholders (and the public in general). This is the place where vague terms such as "challenging year," and "difficult environment" are used in place of "bad results and problems" to describe the less-favorable economic context. Other, frequent excuses for bad performance include unfavorable currency conversion, weak demand, and an unstable economic context. Optimism and confidence in the future are unavoidable mottoes in the conclusion. This means: "Please, stay with us!"

An annual report is an important part of a company's image. It has to be well-written, elegant, appealing, impressing; it must inspire confidence, honesty, wealth, prosperity. Employees and shareholders, as well as members of the Board, have to look proud of their institution. The annual report not only includes information about the company's aims, balance sheet, financial data; it features graphs, sometimes color photographs of products, employees, members of the board of directors and executive officers.

In the first pages of pharmaceutical manufacturer MERCK's annual report, we can see clear, regular graphs of the continuously rising sales, earnings, and dividend payments over 10 years. Coca-Cola Enterprises' annual reports have become collectibles through the years because they feature classic photographs of Coke logos, marketing products, and publicity. Berkshire Hathaway's annual report always includes a sage sermon from the famous billionaire Warren Buffet. Luxurious annual reports are not always done by the biggest or most flamboyant companies. AOL's annual reports (prior to its merger with Time Warner) in 2000 and 2001 were plain documents on thin paper, without any photographs or embellishments.

As an annual report must explain what the company does, their brands, projects, goals, and guidance, this information is especially useful when the company does business dealing with scientific research, or any uncommon field difficult to explain to the general public.

If the company is traded on a stock market, its annual report has to indicate many specific elements such as where it is traded (name of the stock exchanges and respective stock symbols), the number of shares outstanding, and what were the highest and lowest levels of the shares for each quarter in the last two years. It also has to state the age and compensation for every member of the board of directors, including their amount of stock options earned for the company's shares during the year.

For many stockholders, the annual report is the source to check if the company is profitable, if its value improves, if its shares deliver a higher dividend compared to recent years. Then, according to these results, the shareholder will or will not reconsider holding the stock and might abandon it, either to cash out the capital gains that were made or to reinvest the remaining invested amount in another stock.

Usually, an annual report can be obtained for free from most companies; it is more and more possible to find them on the internet and on the company's own web site. In order to receive a copy of a company's annual report, one has just to own one share; therefore, the shareholder is considered as a co-owner of the company and is thus entitled to get legitimate information about his or her company's directors. An annual report that is delayed, postponed, or re-stated automatically raises suspicion among shareholders, the media, and the public.

BIBLIOGRAPHY. AOL *Annual Report* (2001); Berkshire Hathaway *Annual Report* (2001); Coca-Cola Enterprises *Annual Report* (2001); France Telecom *Annual Report* (2001); Merck *Annual Report* (2001); Nortel Networks *Annual Report* (2001); Global Reports Library, www.global-reports.com.

Yves Laberge, Ph.D.
Institut québécois des
hautes études internationales

anti-globalization

ANTI-GLOBALIZATION IS A TERM that refers to a grassroots movement in opposition to the concentration of economic and political power in transnational corporations and supranational institutions, such as the WORLD TRADE ORGANIZATION (WTO) and the INTERNATIONAL MONETARY FUND (IMF). These institutions are seen as usurping some of the democratic decision-making powers of ordinary citizens in more developed nations, and taking actions that lower the quality of life in all parts of the world, but particularly in the less developed nations. It would be simplistic to argue that the anti-globalization movement is against the idea of a global economy. Many of those involved in the movement promote closer economic, political, and cultural ties between self-employed artisans, collectives, and non-governmental organizations across the globe. Some have worked for the development of global grassroots markets for crafts, open pollination seeds, and other goods. Thus, rather than broadly opposing global economic relationships, the movement is against what its participants and supporters perceive as a drift away from a more democratic economy.

The anti-globalization movement is comprised of a diverse collection of organizations and individuals. The movement is not guided by a coherent theoretical framework or paradigm, nor is there general agreement on strategies for either democratizing the globalization process or reversing the trend toward the concentration of political and economic power in transnational corporations and multilateral organizations. It is, instead, a populist movement united as much by what it opposes as by what it hopes to build. This is the reason it is possible for anarchists, environmentalists, socialists, and a wide range of other marginalized political groups to cooperate, despite significant differences in their underlying philosophies.

In some very fundamental sense, the anti-globalization movement is anti-capitalist. WTO, the IMF, and transnational corporations are, in many ways, complementary institutions. The transnational corporations are mostly industrial capitalist firms, dependent on wage laborers, or non-industrial firms with close relationships to such industrial capitalist firms. It is the drive by such firms to lower costs and to find new markets that drives the globalization process that the anti-globalization movement opposes. And WTO and the IMF help to break down institutional barriers to such growth.

Transnational expansion. Capitalist firms expand geographically for a wide range of reasons. For example, such firms may build facilities in a foreign country in order to tap into low-cost inputs. The exploitation of labor in poor countries has been of particular concern to anti-globalization activists because it is understood that these firms may use existing authoritarian political arrangements as a tool for guaranteeing cheap and compliant labor. In many countries workers are not allowed to organize into independent labor unions. Further, they risk physical harm for speaking out against unfair labor practices, and may be forced to work under feudal bondage conditions. Thus, what may be in the labor-cost-minimizing interests of the transnational firm may not be consistent with widely supported ideals of human rights and equity. Labor unions based in the UNITED STATES, and other more industrialized nations, have complained about these problems, in part, because firms often shift existing production and wage-labor jobs out of higher-cost areas to lower-cost areas. This trend is not simply a transnational issue. In the United Sates, thousands of jobs were shifted from the higher-cost northern states to lower-cost southern states. Now the southern states are losing jobs to the so-called Third World countries.

In addition to reducing labor costs, other reasons for the transnational firms to expand overseas operations include:

1. accessing subsidies or other special benefits provided by a foreign government

2. improving access to the market in a specific foreign country or related trading bloc partner countries

3. reducing foreign exchange rate risks

4. reducing total tax costs

5. reducing risk of disruption to operations due to country specific political risks, including labor disputes.

The globalization of the production process (creating a "factory" that is geographically de-centered) weakens the power of labor to organize itself, and the power of sovereign states to police production practices, including those relating to the health and safety of the workers, strengthening transnational management's control over the globalized production processes.

Transnational corporations have, to some extent, tried to shield themselves from criticism by investing indirectly in foreign companies. These firms generally have the option of either building their own facilities, that are operated as integral parts of the parent company, or entering into joint ventures or subcontracts with external firms, although often these subcontractors are nothing more than loosely affiliated subsidiaries of the parent company. Joint-venture agreements with external firms can include developing relationships with state-owned enterprises, as is often the case with foreign direct investment in China. Using subcontractors often shields the parent company from accusations of abuse of workers or other offenses related to the behavior of the subcontractor.

However, it is becoming increasingly difficult for transnationals to shield themselves in this way. The anti-globalization movement has targeted certain transnational firms, such as Nike, by exposing the links between parent transnationals and subcontractors who engage in unfair labor practices and pay wages that are considered to be barely above subsistence. The negative publicity can be harmful to the targeted company. This has pushed many firms to alter their business practices.

Cultural imperialism. The anti-globalization movement also includes critics of cultural imperialism, which follows globalization. By cultural imperialism they mean that the United States, in particular, but also other Western nations are imposing their cultural icons, language, and way of life upon other peoples, leading to erosion in the cultural diversity on the planet. These critics tend to look at the cultural impact of globalization in only one direction: the way the transnational corporation brings "Western" culture into the environment where its foreign facilities are located.

However, when transnational firms expand to new environments, the choice of location influences the future culture of the transnational. Ex-pat, or foreign-based managers will be changed by their experiences in the country where facilities are located. The culture of the company will be influenced by the interaction of management with officials and others in the countries where such facilities are located. Foreign managers and workers will bring their own ideas into the corporation. Indeed, this is a powerful intangible benefit to transnational corporations (and potentially to their home countries). These effects are likely to be all the stronger if the transnational acquires an existing firm in another country. Cross-border mergers and acquisitions are becoming more frequent. This is another outcome of the speed-up of globalization: creating more cultural diversity expands the range of ideas possible within the firm, making it more likely the firm can compete effectively in a global market. Research by the American Management Association found a strong correlation between diversity (different demographic characteristics) of top management at corporations and corporate performance (as measured by profitability, productivity, and shareholder value creation). The study of 1,000 firms provides support for the concept that cultural diversity among top management can improve corporate results and give genuinely multinational firms an edge in competition with more culturally homogeneous firms. If this is, indeed, the case then the anti-globalization view of the transnational corporation as a carrier of Western hegemonic culture may cease to be relevant.

Some of the other arguments against globalization have included arguments that transnationals:

1. typically wield greater political power than the governments of the countries where they locate facilities, reducing the degree to which such governments can act independently of the wishes of the transnational

2. use their extraordinary economic and political power to super-exploit local environmental resources and the labor of local people, resulting in environmental destruction and a decline in the quality of life for the local population

3. come to dominate the local economies where they locate facilities, resulting in greater vulnerability of the local economy to shifts in transnational investment strategies.

The ability of transnationals to pull out their investment (or, alternatively, to expand such investments) can have a decisive impact on policy decisions by foreign political leaders. It is clearly in the interest of transnationals to wield as much influence as possible on the policies of governments in nations and localities where they build facilities or carry out operations. Such influence satisfies both the desire to maximize the net present value of corporate investments and the desire of corporate managers to wield greater social and political power for status acquisition or other personal gain.

The hegemony of transnationals over many national governments is facilitated, and perhaps dramatically expanded, by international trade agreements, such as WTO, which severely constrain national sovereignty and guarantee a more favorable environment for trade and foreign direct investment. It is, in fact, the rapid expansion of the scope and reach of these international agreements that has sparked both an explosion in international trade and economic relationships, as well as in the anti-globalization movement. This is the reason the anti-globalization coalition has organized demonstrations targeted at cities where the WTO negotiations or meetings were held in an effort to slow down, if not stop, the process of extending these agreements into new areas of local and national sovereignty.

The grassroots opposition to globalization is a David against Goliath battle and the anti-globalization activists are forced to rely primarily upon street demonstrations and rhetoric. They argue that globalization is having severe negative consequences in both the more industrialized and less industrialized world, from damage to the environment to lost jobs in the northern hemisphere, and substandard wages and working conditions in the southern hemisphere.

The globalization debate. However, supporters of globalization counter with the argument that the increased integration of national economies through investment activities of transnational corporations and the increased

flow of global portfolio investments to domestic firms is a key catalyst for more rapid economic growth in the less industrialized world, as well as in the more developed economies. Indeed, it is argued that globalization improves global equity because, in an open economic environment, more investment will flow to the less industrialized economies (due to diminishing returns to investment) sparking rapid rates of economic growth. And the accelerated growth in less industrialized economies creates expanded markets for the output of the more industrialized nations. Everyone is better off, the argument goes, if global trading, manufacturing, and financial relationships expand.

The problem with the above argument is that the evidence does not support it. Growth in the less-industrialized world has been rather spotty and largely concentrated in a few countries. The supposed wonderful opportunities for high rates of return in the poorest countries are either nonexistent or largely unexploited, despite increasingly favorable rules for foreign direct investment in many of these countries. Some of the supporters of globalization have given up and thrown in the towel on the idea that open economies are sufficient to generate the necessary growth in less developed nations. They have come to recognize that more developed nations may, indeed, have advantages that are reproduced over time.

Richer countries have better infrastructure (roads, airports, seaports, telecommunications, etc.), more educated and healthy citizens, and a generally more favorable living environment than the poorer countries, attracting the lion's share of foreign direct investment, particularly the most sophisticated forms of such investment (and the talents of many of the best educated citizens born in the less industrialized world—the brain drain). Is Intel likely to build its new manufacturing plant in Mali or in Malaysia? Perhaps labor would be cheaper in Mali, but Malaysia already has the necessary infrastructure to support Intel's plant. On the other hand, it would be incorrect to assume that more advanced existing infrastructure is *the* determinant of location choices for new investments. These decisions, even when predominantly based on a net present value decision, are functions of a wide range of economic, political, cultural, and environmental factors.

Other supporters of globalization (including Jeffrey Sachs, arguably the leading intellectual voice in favor of globalization) have argued that the evidence in favor of more rapid growth rates in the poorer countries ("convergence") is much stronger than has been recognized. They argue that the less industrialized economies with poor growth records are those with the greatest impediments to open trade. In other words, globalization works when it is allowed to work.

The anti-globalization movement is critical, both implicitly and explicitly, of the tendency of social analysts, whether neoliberals, Marxian theorists, or institutionalists, to focus so much attention on government as the sole subject of the economic growth story. Nevertheless, the anti-globalization movement is particularly hostile to the neoliberal/neoclassical point of view that capitalist firms are, in the best of all possible worlds, benign forces for economic growth and development. The anti-globalization leaders argue that transnational firms, financial and industrial, grow in political, economic, and cultural influence and power every day. And they also argue that supranational (multilateral) institutions, like the IMF and WTO, play an increasing role in directing public policy, both through direct interventions and through "jaw boning" at the expense of democracy. The ability of local governments to act independently is seriously constrained within this environment. Thus, many participants in the anti-globalization movement believe that their struggle is ultimately a pro-democracy movement.

BIBLIOGRAPHY. Jeremy Brecher and Tim Costello, *Global Village or Global Pillage* (South End Press, 1998); Louis Ferleger and Jay R. Mandle, eds., *Dimensions of Globalization* (University of Minnesota Press, 2000); John Gray, *False Dawn: The Delusions of Global Capitalism* (New Press, 1998); Noreena Hertz, *The Silent Takeover: Global Capitalism and the Death of Democracy* (Free Press, 2001); Richard H. Robbins, *Global Problems and the Culture of Capitalism* (Allyn and Bacon, 1999); Dan Schiller, *Digital Capitalism* (MIT Press, 1999); Joseph E. Stiglitz, *Globalization and Its Discontents* (W.W. Norton, 2002).

SATYA J. GABRIEL
MOUNT HOLYOKE COLLEGE

antitrust

COMBATING BUSINESS MONOPOLIES and unfair commercial practices, antitrust laws are designed to restrict business activities that constitute a threat to free-market competition. Antitrust laws prohibit price fixing, outlaw mergers that will interfere with competition, and prohibit companies from using their economic power to create or maintain a monopoly. While the UNITED STATES was the first country to pioneer such laws, many countries have followed suit in adopting similar laws.

The years after the AMERICAN CIVIL WAR saw a dramatic increase in competition among businesses due in large part to geographic expansion of business markets and to technological innovations that boosted productivity. In order to successfully compete, American business leaders, such as John D. ROCKEFELLER, began to create larger firms by combining smaller firms. At first, these larger businesses were in the form of CARTELs, but

as the years went on the businesses became more fully integrated, and by the 1880s were taking the forms of trusts, holding companies, and outright mergers. The effect of these trusts was to increase prices and limit production. By the late 1880s, public outcry against the abuses by these trusts led to the passage of the Sherman Antitrust Act in 1890.

Sherman Antitrust Act. Named for Senator John Sherman, an expert on the regulation of commerce, the Sherman Antitrust Act has two sections. Section 1 states: "Every contract, combination in the form of trust or otherwise, or conspiracy, in restraint of trade or commerce among the several States, or with foreign nations, is hereby declared to be illegal." Section 2 states: "Every person who shall monopolize, or attempt to monopolize . . . any part of the trade or commerce among the several States, or with foreign nations, shall be deemed guilty of a misdemeanor." The act is enforced by the Department of Justice through litigation in federal court. Companies found in violation of the act can be enjoined from continuing illegal practices. And if the court determines that violations warrant it, the courts can even dissolve the company. Violations are punishable by fines and imprisonment. The act also provides for private parties injured by violations to seek civil remedies, which can be upwards of triple the amount of damages done to them.

The first case in which the U.S. Supreme Court interpreted the Sherman Antitrust Act was *United States v. E.C. Knight Co.* (1895). This case stemmed from the E.C. Knight Company gaining control of the American Sugar Refining Company and thus enjoying a virtual monopoly of sugar refining in America. In its decision, the Court ruled against the government, finding that manufacturing was a local activity not subject to regulation of interstate commerce. Given the Court's restrictive reading of antitrust law, there was very little enforcement of the Sherman Antitrust Act in the decade or so after its passage.

As the turn of the century approached, the Supreme Court began to apply the act in a variety of contexts—first with regard to railroad cartels and then to a rash of new mergers. This increase in application culminated with the 1911 Supreme Court's decisions in *Standard Oil Co. v. United States* and *United States v. American Tobacco Co.* In both these decisions, the Court found that the Sherman Antitrust Act was violated and ordered the dissolution of the companies. However, these decisions did not establish the proper general standard to be applied. Rather, the court was divided over applying Justice Rufus W. Peckham's versus Justice Edward D. White's reasoning. Justice Peckham's reasoning, which rejected any defense of "reasonableness," condemned "per se" any agreement that directly and immediately restricted competition and therefore trade in interstate or foreign commerce. While Justice White's reasoning, which was the standard applied in the *Standard Oil* and *American Tobacco* opinions, called for applying a "rule of reason." Under the "rule of reason" analysis only unreasonable restraint of trade is a violation of the Sherman Act.

The application of the "rule of reason" approach to the Sherman Act allowed companies far more latitude in their behavior and revitalized political debate over antitrust law. During the 1912 presidential race between Theodore ROOSEVELT, William Howard TAFT, and Woodrow WILSON the "rule of reason" approach was a major issue. After Wilson's election, efforts were made to strengthen the Sherman Act, which in 1914 resulted in the passage of the Clayton Antitrust Act and the Federal Trade Commission Act.

Clayton Antitrust Act. Named after its sponsor, Alabama congressman Henry De Lamar Clayton, the Clayton Antitrust Act was specifically designed to address the competitive dangers arising from price discrimination, tying and exclusive-dealing contracts, mergers, and interlocking boards of directors, where the effect may be to substantially lessen competition or tend to create a MONOPOLY in any line of commerce. The act also forbade intercorporate stock holdings allowing one company to gain control over another and affirmed the right of unions to boycott, picket, and strike.

The provisions of the act specifically dealing with labor issues limited the use of federal injunctions in labor disputes and excluded unions from the restrictions of antitrust regulations. The act permitted individual suits for damages from discrimination or exclusive selling or leasing; and made corporation directors or officers responsible for infractions of antitrust laws. In 1936, the Robinson-Pateman Act strengthened Section 2 of the Clayton Antitrust Act. Both the Department of Justice and the Federal Trade Commission enforce the Clayton Act.

Federal Trade Commission Act. The Federal Trade Commission Act of 1914 created the Federal Trade Commission (FTC), whose basic objective is to promote free and fair trade competition in the American economy. The FEDERAL TRADE COMMISSION was given power to investigate suspected violations of law, hear evidence, and issue cease-and-desist orders when illegal activities have been proven. Under the Clayton Antitrust Act the FTC also hears appeals. Section 5 of the Federal Trade Commission Act declares that "unfair methods of competition in commerce are hereby declared unlawful." A 1938 amendment extended the prohibition to include "unfair or deceptive acts or practices in commerce," whether or not in competition. Only the FTC can enforce Section 5 of the Act.

The FTC also provides guidance to business and industry on what is allowable under the law; and gathers and makes available to Congress, the president, and the public information on economic and business conditions. The FTC consists of five commissioners, one of whom serves as Chair, appointed for seven-year terms by the president, with the advice and consent of the U.S. Senate. No more than three commissioners may be members of the same political party.

As America's economy prospered in the years after the passage of the Clayton Antitrust and the Federal Trade Commission Acts, and through the 1920s, Americans were less concerned with anti-competitive behavior, and, in fact, had begun to accept the Progressive Era's increased level of economic concentration. With the stock market crash of 1929, though, American confidence in business and in the health of the American markets collapsed. Initially, the government's reaction was to expand business cooperative efforts under the National Industrial Recovery Act, however the Supreme Court in *Schechter Poultry Corporation v. United States* (1935) ruled this act to be unconstitutional.

Due in part to an economic downturn in 1937 and concerns regarding the growth of European cartels, as well as to recent economic scholarship arguing that concentrated markets were a contributing factor in troubling economic performance, the late 1930s began to see a significant increase in federal antitrust activity. These increased efforts did not reduce the levels of economic concentration that occurred in the early 20th century, but they did establish a bipartisan commitment to a greater level of antitrust activity than had been seen in the years before the NEW DEAL.

Rule of reason reversal. In 1945, the Supreme Court in *United States v. Aluminum Company of America* reversed its stance regarding the "rule of reason" analysis and found that the size and structure of a corporation were sufficient grounds for antitrust action. In his landmark opinion, Justice Billings Learned Hand found that evidence of greed or lust for power was inessential; monopolies were unlawful, even if they resulted from otherwise unobjectionable business practices.

As Hand wrote, "Congress did not condone 'good trusts' and condemn 'bad ones;' it forbade all." While the ruling established that both dominant market power, and its acquisition or maintenance through wrongful conduct, were distinguishable from competition on the merits, both were needed to establish a monopoly under the Sherman Antitrust Act, the decision limited the range of conduct deemed to be mere skill, foresight, and industry. Through this decision, the Court established a two-element test that would be followed for years to come, but otherwise left the concept of monopolization open to question.

After its decision in *United States v. Aluminum Company of America*, the Supreme Court greatly increased its application of per se rules to condemn certain collective agreements, such as price-fixing and output limitation, as well as to condemn vertical restrictions, such as resale price maintenance restrictions and manufacturer imposed restrictions on dealers' geographic territories and customers. The Court also established a "partial" per se test that condemned most tying arrangements that conditioned the purchase of a desired good on the simultaneous purchase of a second, different good. Though sympathetic toward dealing agreements that required a purchaser to deal exclusively in a particular manufacturer's brand, the Court declared that such agreements were illegal whenever they threatened to "foreclose" a substantial share of market sales.

Partly because the Clayton Antitrust Act's anticompetitive merger clause only applied to stock and not market acquisitions, as well as only to horizontal mergers and not vertical or conglomerate mergers, the Supreme Court's merger decisions in the years after the New Deal were in favor of large acquisitions. This, along with concerns regarding renewed economic concentration, led to the Celler-Kefauver Act of 1950.

This act strengthened the Clayton Antitrust Act, specifically Section 7, by prohibiting one company from securing either stocks or physical assets of another firm when the acquisition would reduce competition. The Act also extended coverage of antitrust laws to all forms of mergers whenever the effect would substantially lessen competition and tend to create a monopoly. By the 1960s, the Supreme Court had reversed its approach to mergers and was even ruling against mergers that might lead to cost savings and lower consumer prices.

In the mid 1970s, due to, among other things, a decline in support for government regulation, new economic analysis that argued for the efficiency-enhancing potential of horizontal and vertical agreements, and increased foreign imports that were heightening the competitiveness of American markets, the Supreme Court's approach to antitrust enforcement began to evolve. In *Continental T.V., Inc. v. GTE Sylvania, Inc.* (1977), the Supreme Court overturned its per se condemnation of nonprice vertical restrictions on dealers and found that such restraints often generated greater increases and benefits than competition among brands. The Court also began to reapply the "rule of reason" approach to the evaluation of horizontal agreements and to look to whether gains in efficiency offset the specific anti-competitive behavior in question.

Less restriction. The Supreme Court's approach to mergers also began to become less restrictive. In *United States v. General Dynamics Corp.* (1974), the Supreme Court determined that a deeper economic assessment of the likely competitive impact of an acquisition was needed before a merger could be declared illegal. In the years since, the Justice Department has revised its merger guidelines to emphasize the possible economic benefits a merger might have and has established much higher thresholds for antitrust challenges to mergers than were previously required. One example of the changing approach to mergers is the telecommunications industry.

In 1984 the government determined that the American Telephone & Telegraph Company (AT&T) was in violation of the Sherman Antitrust Act and broke the company up into several smaller, regional telecommunication companies ("baby bells"). In the years since many of these "baby bells" have merged back together with the government's approval.

The approach to monopolization issues has continued to remain unsettled. In *Aspen Skiing Co. v. Aspen Highlands Skiing Corp.* (1985) the Supreme Court held that in the absence of any plausible efficiency justification a dominant firm could not severely hamper a smaller competitor by discontinuing a long-established cooperative marketing arrangement. With the government's 1982 dismissal of its longstanding suit against the International Business Machines (IBM) and the 1984 divestiture of AT&T, the federal government did not initiate any major monopolization cases for many years. This changed in 1998 when the Justice Department, along with 20 state attorney generals, filed an antitrust suit against the MICROSOFT Corporation.

The Microsoft suit. The Microsoft suit alleged that Microsoft had used monopoly power to restrict competition and maintain its strong market position. Microsoft countered by insisting that its policies had benefited consumers. Initially focused on the contention that Microsoft had improperly attempted to gain control of the internet browser market to the disadvantage of Netscape, the case grew to include broader allegations of anti-competitive behavior on the part of Microsoft. In 2000, United States District Court Judge Thomas P. Jackson determined that Microsoft "enjoys monopoly power" and that "some innovations that would truly benefit consumers never occur for the sole reason that they do not coincide with Microsoft's self-interest." In his final ruling Judge Jackson decreed that Microsoft should be split into two companies. Microsoft appealed the decision, and in 2001 a federal appeals court overturned the breakup order but agreed that Microsoft had abused its monopoly power.

Several full or partial exemptions are permitted under the provisions of antitrust law, including agriculture marketing cooperatives, export associations, labor unions, and major league baseball. In 1970, Curt Flood with the backing of the Major League Players Association sued Major League Baseball, challenging the reserve clause, which gave the St. Louis Cardinals the right to trade him without his permission. Flood lost his case, but his suit paved the way for the abolishment of the reserve clause and the institution of free agency. Other than baseball, no professional sports league is exempt from antitrust law. In the early 1980s, Al Davis owner of the Oakland Raiders wanted to move the football team to Los Angeles, but was blocked from doing so by league owners. Davis sued the National Football League on antitrust grounds and won, thus paving the way for numerous moves of sports teams from city to city.

International antitrust laws. Internationally, it was not until after WORLD WAR II that other countries began to embrace antitrust regulation. In 1948, Britain created a Monopolies and Restrictive Practices Commission and in 1956 it passed a Restrictive Trade Practices Act. Other countries to pass antitrust regulations since 1945 include AUSTRIA, DENMARK, FRANCE, GERMANY, IRELAND, and SWEDEN. After the collapse of communism, both POLAND and RUSSIA passed similar regulations. However, for much of the second half of the century JAPAN did not have any antitrust regulations. Only after the mid-1990s financial crisis in Asia did Japan adopt some antitrust reforms.

With the spread of globalization there has been a significant lowering of international trade barriers and with it an increase in corporate mergers. Debate continues over the level of need and effectiveness of antitrust protection, with some arguing that businesses can best respond to their customer's needs if left alone and others arguing that vigilant application of antitrust law is essential to protect competition. In the years to come, antitrust law and theory will continue to evolve and adapt to the changing economic and global trends of the 21st century.

BIBLIOGRAPHY. Robert H. Bork, *The Antitrust Paradox: A Policy at War with Itself* (The Free Press, 1993); Herbert Hovenkamp, *Federal Antitrust Policy: The Law of Competition and Its Practice* (West Wadsworth, 1994); Ernest Gellhorn and William E. Kovacic, *Antitrust Law and Economics in a Nutshell* (West Wadsworth, 1994); Dominick T. Armentano, *Antitrust: The Case for Repeal* (Mises Institute, 1999); Lawrence Anthony Sullivan and Warren S. Grimes, *The Law of Antitrust: An Integrated Handbook* (West Wadsworth, 2000); Richard A. Posner, *Antitrust Law* (University of Chicago Press, 2001); Richard B. McKenzie, *Trust on Trial* (Perseus Publishing, 2001); David B. Kopel, *Antitrust after Microsoft: The Obsolescence of Antitrust in the Digital Era* (Heartland Institute, 2001).

S.J. RUBEL, J.D.
NEW YORK CITY

AOL Time Warner

RANKED NUMBER 37 in 2002 on the *Fortune* magazine Global 500 list of the largest companies in the world, AOL Time Warner is the leading entertainment company in the world. The company is the result of several layers of mergers, and its holdings extend throughout the entertainment industry.

The earliest components of AOL Time Warner, Warner Bros. (a motion picture company founded 1918), and Time Inc. (publisher of *Time* magazine, incorporated in 1923), stuck to their respective fields through the 1980s: Time Inc. diversifying only into print holdings, while Warner Bros. expanded mainly into film companies. The two companies merged and became Warner Communications in 1986, the same year that America Online, an internet service provider began operations. Warner Communications merged in 1996 with Turner Broadcasting System, a company of cable television networks (such as CNN and TBS) owned by Ted Turner. America Online, meanwhile, became the dominant internet provider and continued to acquire internet companies, most notably the web browser company Netscape in 1999. In 2001, America Online (which had grown to 27 million customers) merged with Warner Communications, and the new company was titled AOL Time Warner.

AOL Time Warner's operations extend across the entertainment industry. All told, AOL Time Warner holdings include (in addition to those listed above) book publishing companies (most notably Little, Brown and Company and Warner Books), over 35 magazines (including *Sports Illustrated* and *Entertainment Weekly*), several film studios (New Line Cinema among them), over a dozen cable television networks (including HBO, BET, and the myriad of Turner networks), several music labels (including Atlantic and Electra), DC Comics, and several sports teams. The conglomerate also owns a number of television network affiliates, a large cable television company, and its own television network.

One impetus for the merger from AOL's point of view was to provide potential programming for its internet service; of particular interest was AOL's ability to stream Time Warner properties over its high-speed (broadband) internet service in the future. As is, the vast holdings of AOL Time Warner allow for marketing to apply synergy (a product being marketed simultaneously on several media) on a vast scale. For instance, any future movie in the Batman franchise could be cross promoted with a corresponding DC comic, a show on the Cartoon Network, a book adaptation published by Little, Brown & Company, a soundtrack released on Atlantic Records, and a film rebroadcast on HBO, promoted in Time Warner Cable advertisements. All products in such a scheme would be produced by AOL Time Warner–owned companies.

AOL Time Warner has not, however, performed according to financial expectations, and the company posted a $5 billion deficit for 2002. AOL Time Warner stocks have similarly dropped by a significant amount. Industry analysts argue that AOL's stock prior to the merger was severely overvalued, and indeed AOL has been accused of artificially inflating its value as early as 1996 by spreading out member acquisition costs over several years rather than when the expenses actually occurred. As of 2003, AOL's accounting practices are under investigation by the SECURITIES & EXCHANGE COMMISSION (SEC). These financial uncertainties led to AOL Time Warner chairman Steve Case (who was AOL chairman before the merger) to resign in 2002.

AOL Time Warner's economic strategy as of 2003 is based around increased cross-promotion on their internet service. *Time* magazine is advertising on AOL, as are Warner movies and the pay cable HBO service; this cross-selling is expected to benefit from AOL's dominance of the internet market. However, the original grand synergistic plans envisioned by the merger of AOL and Time Warner still elude the company, and some observers wonder whether convergence is ever possible. Indeed, the company ended up in 2003 dropping the AOL part of its name, thus reverting to one of its original names, Time Warner.

BIBLIOGRAPHY. United State Senate, *The AOL Time Warner Merger: Competition and Consumer Choice in Broadband Internet Services and Technologies* (U.S. Government Printing Office, 2001); Marc Gunther, "Understanding AOL's Grand Unified Theory of the Media" *Fortune* (January 8, 2001); Kara Swisher, *AOL.com: How Steve Case Beat Bill Gates, Nailed the Netheads, and Made Millions in the War for the Web* (Random House, 1998); Marc Gunther and Stephanie N. Mehta, "Can Steve Case Make Sense of this Beast?" *Fortune* (April 28, 2002).

MIKE S. DUBOSE
BOWLING GREEN STATE UNIVERSITY

Aquila

HEADQUARTERED IN Kansas City, Missouri, Aquila, Inc., owns electricity and natural gas distribution systems in the UNITED STATES, CANADA, UNITED KINGDOM, and AUSTRALIA. Aquila also owns and operates power plants in the United States.

The company began in 1917 as Green Light and Power Company. For the next half century, the renamed Missouri Public Service (MPS) operated as a state-regulated public utility distributing gas and power in the state.

In 1985, Aquila (then UtiliCorp United) purchased Peoples Natural Gas, a gas distribution company with operations in five states. PSI, a small wholesale natural gas marketing company within Peoples, was renamed Aquila Energy. Aquila's profitable gas trading in the short-term "spot" market led to the creation of risk-management products to serve the long-term market. Aquila was following the lead of ENRON and other companies anxious to diversify away from regulated rates of return, and into lucrative new areas.

Aquila added electricity to its portfolio in the mid-1990s, making a market between regulated utilities and volatile energy markets. Aquila soon became, in industry parlance, a "total gas and power risk merchant and energy solution provider." UtiliCorp changed its name to the better known Aquila in 2002.

In the late 1990s Aquila began building power plants in response to rising electricity prices. Aquila's leveraged "merchant" plants were not backed by long-term purchase contracts but short-term power prices.

When power prices began to fall in mid-2001, Aquila was hurt in three ways. First, trading margins were squeezed by reduced volatility. Second, the cash flow and capital value of merchant power plants plummeted. Third, the company's credit worthiness fell below the grade needed to support its trading books.

Bad investments were also part of the overall problem. Aquila, like other high-flying energy marketers, structured deals that accelerated revenue that was then invested as VENTURE CAPITAL. As Aquila's telecommunications investments soured, the company was left with its energy contract obligations but less cash flow to cover them.

Aquila embarked on asset sales and closed its U.S. and European trading operations in 2002. The market value of Aquila, which peaked at $4.3 billion in May 2001, had fallen 95 percent to under $300 million as of first quarter 2003. With much learned, Aquila has returned to its roots as a gas and electric utility.

BIBLIOGRAPHY. Missouri Public Service, *Power: The Story of Missouri Public Service* (The Lowell Press, 1992). *Annual Reports,* www.aquila.com.

ROBERT L. BRADLEY, JR.
INSTITUTE FOR ENERGY RESEARCH

Arab nationalism

A SOCIO-HISTORIC FRAMEWORK to define a collective identity, Arab nationalism enunciates a shared ethos and imagines a pan-ethnic moral, intellectual, cultural and political unity among the 22 Arab countries. Gamal Abdel Nasser, one of its principal exponents saw it as a "dawn after a terribly long night," a "genuine spiritual unity," and "a solidarity emanating from the heart." It was designed to repulse imperialist aggression but also to "shun extremism" from the political or religious left and the right.

Scholars differentiate between four overlapping labels: Arabism, Arab nationalism, Arab unity, and Arab world. The first refers to a unique cultural personality born of Arab language, memory, and imagination and privileged by Islamic and pre-Islamic Arab values, symbols, and ideals; the second refers to a group solidarity, national solidarity, and regional solidarity; the third refers to a timeless affinity expressed through corporate forms and concrete manifestations of solidarity aimed at region-wide interest aggregation and interest maximization "within," to use Ahmed Ben Bella's words, "a unified framework of unified tendencies;" and the fourth refers to a self-contained universe of discourse and action complete with its own cosmology, ontology, and epistemology, on the one hand, and its own architecture, language, literature, myth, poetry, food, dress, music, and more, on the other.

All four concepts are underpinned by a common belief that as a culturally homogeneous people, Arabs could realize their potential only by turning themselves into a single political entity. And such a transformation could be achieved through self-conscious adoption of Arab-Islamic values, symbols, heroes, texts, and norms which furnish a framework to conceptualize both Arab unity and Arab nationalism, and by making Arabs aware of their own creative capacities and the spiritual and intellectual essence of their own existence.

Social, political, and intellectual antecedents. In a large measure, Arab nationalism was a product of the age of COLONIALISM. However, the rise of Arab nationalism was not just a label for struggles against Ottomans, Europeans, or the Zionists; it resulted from the convergence of many socio-historic factors and efforts of numerous institutions, movements, and intellectuals working for cultural, social, political, and ideological revival of the "Arab soul."

It was actually a unique blend of nationalism, anti-imperialism, SOCIALISM, modernism, and internationalism. Rooted in multifarious responses to colonization and foreign domination, social backwardness, and economic stagnation; and further motivated by need for modernization, internal reform, strategic depth and international esteem, Arab nationalism was accentuated by convergence of religious and cultural revivalists, on the one hand, and by Israeli occupation of Arab lands, on the other. It arose and was widely accepted as an ideology of self-empowerment with the promise of rejuve-

nating the Arab mind, heart, and soul. In sum, it resulted from the convergence of efforts aimed at overthrowing colonialism, resisting imperialism, and seeking religious reform, modernization, self-empowerment, intellectual renaissance, and material development.

In the final analysis, it was an ideology of a region and not of a single nation-state. The history of Arab nationalism is a history of building regional unity and then seeking inter-regional cooperation; the non-aligned movement being a monumental example of that spirit of reaching out to other groups and peoples. Ali Mazrui has perceptively pointed out: "European Nationalism generally has had a pervasive influence on much of the Third World, including the Arab world. . . . It was not the Arabs, however, but the Jews who rejected the idea of Arabs and Jews living together in a united Palestine."

Arab wa Ajam. On one of its many contours, Arab nationalism seeks to recover and restore the original "purity" of Arab identity, culture, and religion along with the authenticity of its freedom and independence. To that end, the concept of *Arab wa Ajam*, Arab and non-Arab, is applied to sift and separate un-Islamic ideas, beliefs, values and practices from the genuinely Islamic ideas, beliefs, values, and practices. The historical fact that Prophet Muhammad was an Arab, that Islam was revealed first to Arabs, and that the Qu'ran was revealed in the Arabic language, created a high degree of co-extensiveness, indistinguishability and inseparability, between Islam and Arabism. And thus recovery of pristine and unadulterated Islam became synonymous with shedding of all *Ajami*, non-Arab, ideas and influences. Thus the religious purists became inadvertent allies of Arabism.

While religious theorists were seeking to separate Arab thought and belief from non-Arab thought and belief, the political thinkers and theorists were seeking to unify, first, Muslim and Christian Arabs, and, then, through the non-aligned movement, Arabs with other newly independent nations. As, inspired by Elijah Muhammad, many African-Americans saw Islam as one more, albeit historic, dimension of black nationalism, Arab nationalists saw it as a key dimension of Arab nationalism, identity and ideology. It is in this context, that a number of Christian Arabs, ranging from Michel Aflak to Edward Said to Clovis Muksoud, have talked of being "Muslim by culture."

Understandably, Arab unity was the main theme around which the Arab nationalist narrative was organized. But, for sure, that was not the only theme. Other themes included de-colonization, liberation, independence, freedom, equality, and individual and collective dignity. In sum, this ideological edifice was built on the five pillars of unity, democracy, socialism, industrialization, and progress.

Each of these public values and goals, it was argued, necessitates specific groundwork. Unity presupposes mutual understanding, respect and trust, as democracy presupposes elimination of FEUDALISM and sectarianism. It was obvious to the exponents that democracy will not succeed, as long as voters are controlled by landlords or are themselves motivated by tribal, religious, or regional considerations. The task of Arab nationalism was to help the Arab nation overcome these impediments.

Since the material conditions in the Middle East were significantly different than Europe, the task of building a real and consequential socialist movement also had to be different. Here, the term "socialism" was used to invoke socially sanctioned conceptions and norms of social justice in the Arab-Islamic context. However, it required transforming ideological affinities from tribes and communities to classes and institutions and movements. This had the inherent difficulty of calling for an overall Arab unity and then asking the Arab masses to struggle against some of those with whom they had just been asked to form a fraternal bond.

Progress was perceived in both material and intellectual terms. Promoted as a positive and a forward-looking approach to life, this public value was to inculcate a spirit of self-reliance based on a rational outlook on life and a scientific approach to socio-economic problems. Industrialization was to be the engine of this progress but not at the cost of Arab identity, so one had to strive for industrialization without westernization.

Nasserism. The more prominent among those who had articulated and popularized the cause of Arab nationalism included Sharif Husayn (1859–1931), Zaki al-Arsuzi (1899–1968), Abd al-Rahman Shahbandar (1879–1940), Michel Aflak (1910–89), Salah al-Din al-Baytar (1912–80), and Gamal Abdel Nasser (1918–70).

For many, Nasserism, named after Nasser, one of the foremost theoreticians and practitioners of Arab nationalism, was simply another name for Arab nationalism. Nasser, described by one biographer as "a man of ice and fire," believed that EGYPT's historical destiny was defined by three concentric circles: Arab, African, and Islamic. "There is no doubt," Nasser had emphasized, "that the Arab circle is the most important and the most closely connected with us." The fourth circle of NON-ALIGNMENT and THIRD WORLD INTERNATIONALISM was to emerge in Nasser's thought and Egypt's foreign policy at a later date.

In his speech on "Rise of Arab Nationalism" in the Indian Parliament on August 14, 1958, Jawaharlal Nehru, the prime minister of INDIA, and one of the most astute participant-observers of 20th-century national liberation movements, expressed his support for Arab nationalism by arguing that it represents "the urge of the people" who are "trying to push out this foreign domination." Complimenting Nasser for his able leadership and for having become "the most prominent symbol of Arab nationalism," Nehru observed that Arab nationalism had become a "dominant force" in the region and must be treated with respect and dignity by Europeans.

Though Nasser had paid lofty tributes to Shukry Al-Kuwatly and called him "the first protagonist and herald of Arab nationalism after the Great Egyptian Revolution," it is he, Nasser, who became the most widely known leader, symbol, and spokesperson of this cause. In reflecting on the meaning and significance of Arab unity, Nasser told the Egyptian National Assembly on February 5, 1958: "The Arab unity goes back to time immemorial. For this unity existed from the very beginning of the Arab nation's existence, grew on the same soil, lived through the same events, and moved toward the achievement of the same aims, so when our nation was able to lay down the base of its existence in the area, and to affirm them, it was certain that unity was rapidly approaching."

It was only though Nasser and his colleagues among the Free Officers (an organization formed to defeat neo-colonialism, end feudalism, liquidate monopolies, institute strong defense, establish social justice, and introduce democracy) that the various streams of Arabism became the mighty river of Arab nationalism.

Nasser argued that this unity was built upon many layers of history: first it was achieved through the "force of arms at the time when arms were the means by which humanity in its infancy made itself understood," then it was confirmed by holy prophecies; third, it was reinforced by the "power of faith" under the banner of Islam, and fourth, it was further cemented by "the interaction of various elements in a singly Arab nation."

For Nasser the true nature of Arab nationalism was clearly demonstrated "when the Christianity of the Arab Orient joined the ranks of Islam to battle the Crusaders until victory." While Arab nationalism became the dominant ideology of the region, Nasserism became its dominant form during the second half of the 20th century. For Nasser the primary unit of thought was region and not an individual country. He saw Middle Eastern countries as so many ingredients for the unified Arab nation and his goals were internal unity, reform, revival, empowerment, and prosperity.

Arab nationalism and Islam. Arab nationalism had a complex, intricate, mutually enhancing, and mutually delimiting relationship with Islam. Interestingly, Christian Arabs played a prominent role in articulating Islam as the defining essence of the high Arab culture and a factor common to all Arabs. Michel Aflak, a Christian Arab, believed that once the Arab Christians "were awakened to their true identity, Islam would become for them 'a national culture' and an expression of their living heritage."

Though at one level, Arab nationalism was an attempt to link Islamic culture with pre-Islamic Arab heritage, ranging from Mesopotamia to Babylon and Nineveh, and from legal codes of Hammurabi to the poetic vision of the Saba Mualaqat (the seven great poets), and though many scholars have discussed the dialectical link between Islamic reform—a cultural revolution of sorts to rid Islam of various distortions and contaminations—and Arab nationalism, yet the movement for pan-Arabism was not a movement for pan-Islamism. Actually, the two became rival movements in the Middle East. In the 1960s, Egypt and SAUDI ARABIA were competing for the leadership of the Arab world, first through the civil war in Yemen, and later through the rival ideologies of pan-Arabism and pan-Islamism.

In fact, the popularity of pan-Islamism in the Muslim world during the 1980s and 1990s, accelerated by the Islamic revolution in IRAN and the war against Soviet invasion and occupation of AFGHANISTAN, had coincided with the decline if not demise of Arab nationalism in the Middle East. Arab nationalists see Islam as a culture, more than as a religion, and thus feel intellectually and morally consistent in asserting their profound admiration and even celebration of Islam while professing a secular creed.

One task for Arab nationalist was to renegotiate political geography by shifting centers of hope and inspiration from foreign lands to the heart of Arabia. Al-Husri has suggested that in being a project of unifying all—Muslim and Christian—Arabs, the exponents of Arab nationalism, had to steer Muslims away from the Ottomans and Christians and their European power.

Arab nationalism and capitalism. Despite the generalized focus of many Arab states on economic development through heavy investment in the public sector and despite the avowed sympathy of Arab nationalists for different varieties of non-Marxian socialism (including Michel Aflak's Arab socialism, and Habib Bourghiba's constitutional socialism) and non-capitalist paths to development, Arab states always remained open to capitalism, and followed capitalist principles in banking, TRADE, investment, MARKETING, and management. An important consequence, flowing from both Arab nationalism and non-alignment, was the public attitude toward foreign aid. Though it is impossible to generalize the economic and fiscal policies of 22 Arab countries, which exhibited significant differences among themselves, the public attitude toward foreign aid, particularly from previous colonizers, such as the UNITED KINGDOM and FRANCE, as well as other capitalist countries such as the UNITED STATES, was one of caution and careful negotiation. Other significant policy implications

included land reforms, (subsequent enfranchisement of peasants), preferential trade relations with Arab and African countries, and knowledge and technology transfer from the socialist bloc.

Critical evaluation. Arab nationalism has been criticized from three perspectives: Western, Religious, and Nationalist.

Some Western powers saw it as an attempt to replace the Ottoman Empire with a nascent Arab empire. Responding to the western critics of Arab nationalism, Nehru said: "It was said that some kind of an Arab empire was being built up, which was dangerous. I do not know about the future, but I see no empire, much less an Arab empire."

While Muslim religious leaders equated it with secularization of the Islamic creed, critical secular thinkers saw it saddled with the under-development and incompetence of Arab ruling elites, a nascent bourgeoisie, and a sprawling petty-bourgeoisie. In addition, it was seen as handicapped by both internal and external factors including tribalism, despotism, illiteracy, single-commodity economies, emergence of rentier states, and crafty manipulations of western oil companies and multinational corporations.

Future prospects: Neo-Arabism. At the dawn of the 21st century, PALESTINE has become the central focus of Arab nationalism and has brought a sense of urgency and global visibility to its cause, yet the future of Arab nationalism remains uncertain. It remains uncertain in terms of its direction, goals and strategies, and moral-philosophical orientations. Those matters, it may be safe to say, will be decided in part by the ability of the Arab nations to respond to the long-standing challenges of modernity and post-modernity, particularly challenges in the areas of social reform, democracy, gender equality, rule of law, human rights, and social justice. It will also depend on increased rates of literacy, knowledge acquisition, technology transfer, infrastructural development, conflict management and conflict resolution.

BIBLIOGRAPHY. Gamal Abdel Nasser, *The Philosophy of the Revolution* (Economica Books, 1959); Gamal Abdel Nasser, Speeches and Press Interviews (Information Department, Government of Egypt, 1962); Jawaharlal Nehru, Speeches 1957-1963 (Publications Division, Government of India, 1983); Youssef Choueiri, *Arab Nationalism: A History* (Blackwell, 2000); Gauri Viswanathan, ed., *Power, Politics and Culture: Interviews with Edward Said* (Vintage, 2001); Edward Said, *Culture and Imperialism* (Random House, 1994); Zeine N. Zeine, *Arab-Turkish Relations and the Emergence of Arab Nationalism* (Greenwood Publishing, 1981); Hilal Khashan, *Arabs at the Crossroads: Political Identity and Nationalism* (University Press of Florida, 2000); James Jankowsi, *Rethinking Nationalism in the Arab Middle East* (Columbia University

Press, 1997); James Jankowsi, *Nasser's Egypt, Arab Nationalism and the United Arab Republic* (Lynne Rienner, 2001); Rashid Khalid, et. al., eds., *The Origins of Arab Nationalism* (Diane Publishing, 1998); Samir Amin, *Arab Nation: Nationalism and Class Struggle* (St. Martin's Press, 1976).

AGHA SAEED, PH.D.
UNIVERSITY OF CALIFORNIA, BERKELEY

arbitrage

THE PURCHASE AND immediate sale of an asset or a commodity to reap a guaranteed instant profit from the difference in their respective prices is known as arbitrage. People who engage in arbitrage are called arbitrageurs. The concept of arbitrage is very closely related to the law of one price, which states that in competitive markets identical assets or commodities should have the same price. If prices are different, then there is an opportunity for arbitrage and arbitrageurs will trade, equalizing the prices.

Consider the following example. Let us look at the price of gold, usually measured as the price of a standard quality of one ounce of gold. Assume that the price of gold in New York is $250 per ounce and the price of the same quality of gold in Los Angeles is $300 per ounce. This implies that there exists a price differential and someone can potentially gain profit by buying gold in New York and selling it in Los Angeles. If the transportation cost is $3 per ounce, each time you buy gold in New York and sell in Los Angeles, you make a profit of $47 per ounce. In this example there is no risk associated with this trade as long as the prices do not change while you are transporting gold. However, in some cases you can even avoid this risk by signing a contract with someone in Los Angeles that you will sell gold in the future at a specific price which is agreed upon today. Additionally if you can delay payment when you buy gold from New York, you will gain a guaranteed profit without taking any risk at all. This is called pure risk-less arbitrage.

As more traders buy gold from New York, the increased demand for gold will drive up gold prices in New York. Similarly, an increase in supply will put a downward pressure on gold prices in Los Angeles. Prices in both markets will continue to move as long as the price in New York is lower than the price in Los Angeles by more than $3. The process will stop when the price differential is only $3, as there is no opportunity for arbitrage and thus no pressure on prices to move. Note that in the real world opportunities like these do not exist for long as arbitrageurs are constantly on the lookout for them. In the above example, if you further assume that there is no cost of undertaking this trade, and

there are no other trade barriers, then you should expect the same price to prevail in both markets. This is the law of one price: prices move in markets based on supply and demand conditions until there is no opportunity for arbitrage and one price prevails.

The law of one price and the concept of arbitrage carry over to financial markets as well. If you look at price of a share of stock of GENERAL MOTORS on the NEW YORK STOCK EXCHANGE and London Stock Exchange, you will see almost the same price in both markets because the share of stock is identical, and trading costs are very low in financial markets. Because a substantial price differential would result in arbitrage, so it will result in price equality. The law of one price and arbitrage are very important in valuation of assets in finance.

However, in the real world, financial-asset prices sometimes differ by more than the trading costs. Does that mean that law of one price sometimes does not apply to real life? Actually, it simply means that the underlying assets could be different or the markets are not competitive. In competitive markets, arriving information is processed very quickly, and if markets are not competitive, price differentials will prevail as traders will not know about these differentials and, thus, will not engage in arbitrage.

Interest rates on financial assets are also related to arbitrage and the law of one price. For example consider the bond market, where BONDS are debt securities issued by a government or a corporation to finance borrowing needs. When you buy a bond you are essentially lending your money to the bond issuer, and you get compensation through earned interest. If two bonds in the economy are very similar in their characteristics, such as risk, then you should expect almost the same interest rate on both of them. The reason is that no company will pay a higher interest rate since it does not want to increase its borrowing cost; likewise, it will not pay a lower interest rate because the public will then buy bonds from another company. If interest rate differentials exist, then an entity can possibly borrow where interest rates are low and lend where interest rates are high. This is the concept of interest-rate arbitrage. Corporations use the concept of interest-rate arbitrage to calculate how much interest they should pay on bonds when they need to borrow money. They just look at what the market is paying on a similar bond to the one they plan to issue.

There are numerous applications of arbitrage in the foreign-exchange market. Perhaps the most important one is in determining currency exchange rates. An EXCHANGE RATE is the rate at which one country's currency can be traded for another country's currency. Exchange rates are very important since they directly impact the exports and imports of a country and thus affect its economy.

Various theories have emerged in the literature for exchange-rate determination in the foreign-exchange market. However, the Purchasing Power Parity (PPP) theory is used extensively to explain the determination of exchange rate between two currencies. The absolute version of the theory states that the exchange rate between two currencies is equal to the ratio of their respective price levels. For example, if the price of one bushel of wheat is $2 in the UNITED STATES and £1 in the UNITED KINGDOM, then the exchange rate should be $2 for £1. In other words, according to law of one price, a given commodity should have the same price across countries so purchasing power is at parity. If that is not the case, then traders can buy a commodity from a country where it is cheap and sell in a country where it is expensive and gain an instant profit. This commodity arbitrage will result in equal commodity prices across countries so purchasing power parity is established.

Of course this theory assumes no trade barriers, no transportation cost, and only looks at commodities and ignores capital flows. In real life, the relative version of PPP is followed which states that changes in exchange rates are proportional to relative changes in price levels in two nations. In the real world, PPP is only valid over long periods of time and is more relevant for individual traded goods, and does not work well for non-traded goods.

Due to arbitrage you will not find differences in exchange rates across countries. Also arbitrageurs ensure that if you know the exchange rate between two currencies you can calculate the third one. For example, let us say that the Japanese YEN price of a U.S. DOLLAR is ¥100 and the yen price of the UK pound is ¥200. It follows from the law of one price that the cross rate, which is the dollar price of one pound, is $2. This is due to triangular arbitrage, the concept of arbitrage extended to three commodities or assets. In today's world of computers and high speed of information flow, arbitrage opportunities exist only for very brief time periods.

Modern FINANCE theory has spent a considerable amount of time studying the relationship between interest rates and returns on stocks. The Nobel Prize in Economics for 1991 was awarded to Harry MARKOWITZ, Merton MILLER and William SHARPE for development of a theory that relates interest rates to stock returns. They developed the Capital Asset Pricing Model (CAPM), which is still widely used by academia and practitioners on Wall Street. CAPM, like most other modern finance theories, relies on the concept of arbitrage. CAPM assumes absence of arbitrage profits to arrive at the formulae for predicting stock prices.

Sometimes, without even knowing it, people use the law of one price in their daily lives. Suppose you want to know, what is the value of your house? An easy way is to find out what a similar house on your street was sold for recently. You are basically using law of one price here. Arbitrage is a very simple process but its applications in real life are endless.

BIBLIOGRAPHY. Zvi Bodie and Robert C. Merton, *Finance* (Prentice Hall, 2000); Dominick Salvatore, *International Economics* (John Wiley & Sons, 2001); Burton G. Malkiel, *A Random Walk Down Wall Street* (Norton & Company, 1999); Bruce Tuckman, *Fixed Income Securities* (John Wiley & Sons, 2002); Robert E. Hall and John B. Taylor, *Macroeconomics* (W.W. Norton, 1997); Stephen A. Ross, Randolph W. Westerfield, and Bradford D. Jordan, *Essentials of Corporate Finance* (McGraw Hill, 2004).

FAROOQ MALIK, PH.D.
PENN STATE UNIVERSITY, BERKS

Argentina

COMPRISING MORE THAN a million square miles in South America, Argentina is a vast country with a relatively small population of 37 million, a third of which concentrates in the Buenos Aires metropolitan area. Argentina's territory provides great geographic diversity including high peaks in the Andes along the western border with CHILE, flat expanses of fertile soil in the central Pampas, high arid plateaus bordering Bolivia to the northwest, marshlands and tropical forests in the northeastern border with Paraguay and BRAZIL, and the remote and scarcely populated regions of Patagonia to the south. The rich agricultural lands of the central plains, source of vast amounts of grains and cattle, have been determinant in shaping of the nation's economic and political institutions since the early Spanish settlement.

Under Spanish colonial rule, the territory that currently includes Argentina was a neglected province, part of the *Virreinato del Peru* and administered from Lima. The territory did not have precious metals, and generally lacked concentrations of indigenous people readily available as labor. Northwestern regions adjacent to Potosi enjoyed some prosperity as suppliers of beasts of burden for the silver mines, food for the miners, and a few manufactures. The port of Buenos Aires began to acquire salience with the establishment of the *Virreinato del Rio de la Plata* in 1776. It acted primarily as a center for the smuggling of manufactures from PORTUGAL and Britain, and the export of hides and dried meat to slave plantations in the West Indies and the southern UNITED STATES.

In 1806, and again in 1807, British troops attempted to take Buenos Aires from the Spanish, but were defeated by local militias with little support from Spain. Napoleon's occupation of Spain (1808–13) provided the local elites an opportunity to declare autonomy from the Spanish government in 1810, leading to full independence on July 9, 1816. The territory split into rival factions with diverse visions of nationhood, but a liberal constitution was finally adopted in 1853, which, having undergone significant amendments through the years, is still in force today.

On a course of economic LIBERALISM, Argentina experienced rapid export expansion during the second half of the 1800s. Technological innovations significantly cut the costs of transportation of grains and meat to European markets. The economic boom was primarily financed by British investment in railways connecting Buenos Aires with the Pampas, and the labor provided by massive immigration from Europe, primarily Spaniards and Italians, but also Welsh, Germans, Eastern European Jews, and Syrian-Lebanese.

By the early 1900s, the export bonanza had placed Argentina among the richest nations in GROSS DOMESTIC PRODUCT (GDP) per capita. However, this wealth had weak foundations as it was highly dependent on agricultural exports to Britain and supported by large income inequalities among the population and between regions. Immigrants were accused of bringing with them socialist and anarchist ideologies, contrary to the interests of the ruling oligarchy. The demands of syndicalist labor unions placed strains on the established order, and were generally met with repression, persecution, and deportation of its leaders. The middle class, represented by the *Unión Cívica Radical* (UCR), also pressed for reforms. A new electoral law in 1912 guaranteed universal male suffrage and the secret ballot, resulting in the 1916 election of the UCR leader, Hipólito Yrigoyen, to the presidency.

The disruption of world trade caused by World War I opened opportunities for the manufacture of import substitutes. The vulnerability of the country to events beyond its borders also awoke nationalist sentiments and a desire for greater self-reliance. The inter-war years did not bring the expected return to normalcy. Britain never fully recovered its dominant position in world affairs and the UCR dominated domestic politics to the dismay of conservative opposition parties. The onset of the Great DEPRESSION provided an opportunity for the old oligarchy to return to power through a coup d'etat in 1930. The Depression had catastrophic effects on the Argentine economy, but it served to reinforce fledgling industrial development and strengthen nationalist resolve and political ambitions in the military.

The country lacked political stability until the election to the presidency of Colonel Juan D. Perón in 1946. His pro-labor stance during a brief tenure at the Ministry of Labor a few years earlier had won him the support of labor unions. Armed with a significant reserve of foreign exchange accumulated through World War II, and enjoying high commodity prices in the post-war years, Perón set out to implement a state-centered policy of import substitution, industrialization, and nationalization of key sectors of the economy such as the railways and oil production. He also enacted legislation favorable to labor unions and industrialist development, often at the expense of landed elites and the agricultural sector.

A military coup in 1955 sent Perón into exile in Spain, and the military establishment banned him from politics for nearly two decades. Civilian governments were replaced by military administrations at a dizzying rate until Perón was allowed to return to politics, winning elections in 1973. Perón's untimely death in 1974 led to the escalation of political violence between leftist urban guerrillas and paramilitary forces, resulting in a military coup in 1976.

The military junta that followed (1976–83) engaged in the brutal repression of leftist groups resulting in the disappearance of 9,000 to 30,000 people. Countless others were tortured or fled into exile. The military also implemented economic liberalization policies with disastrous consequences including the ballooning of the foreign debt from $8 billion to $50 billion in the seven years they were in power. By 1982, the junta faced economic collapse and was devoid of political support. Seeking instant popularity through a burst of nationalism it embarked on a military adventure in the *Islas Malvinas* (Falkland Islands), trying to enact their claim of the British-ruled islands in the south Atlantic. After a quick conflict, the Argentine junta's incompetence was confirmed on the battlefield, and the military had no choice but to return the nation to democratic rule.

In 1983, Raúl Alfonsín, candidate of the UCR, became president. His administration struggled with the enormous burden of the foreign debt during what has come to be known as the "lost decade" in Latin America. In 1989, toward the end of his administration, renewed bouts of hyperinflation forced an early transfer of power to president-elect Carlos S. Menem of Perón's *Partido Justicialista*.

Menem implemented a staunchly neo-liberal program of economic reforms that included rapid trade and capital account liberalization, and the widespread privatization of state enterprises. Menem's success in eliminating inflation and accelerated rates of growth caused his popularity to soar, resulting in his re-election in 1995. Privatization and the curtailment of the role of the state in the economy resulted in the rapid concentration of wealth, the erosion of the middle class and the weakening of labor unions. Another important accomplishment of his administration was the creation of Mercosur, a regional customs union, by Argentina, Brazil, Uruguay and Paraguay.

The cornerstone of the economic model was the Convertibility Plan; essentially monetary policy based on a fixed exchange rate of the Argentine peso to the

U.S. dollar. Its viability relied on heavy inflows of foreign capital, but the Mexican peso crisis of 1995 and the ASIAN FINANCIAL CRISIS of 1997 caused international capital flows to emerging markets to dry up. The peso also became severely overvalued with respect to the currency of Argentina's top trade partners, particularly after the devaluation of the Brazilian real in 1999 and the decline in value of the euro in 2000. The possibility of a balance of payments crisis emerged and the INTERNATIONAL MONETARY FUND demanded the implementation of austerity measures. In 1998, the economy entered a recession that would last until 2002. Menem's second term, started in euphoria, closed in disappointment as the unemployment rate reached 15 percent in 2000, up from 7 percent in 1989.

Fernando de la Rúa, Menem's successor, was unable to re-establish growth. In December 2001, food riots turned into massive protests demanding his resignation. After de la Rúa's resignation and a political compromise in Congress, Eduardo Duhalde emerged as president in January, 2002. He immediately declared an end to the fixed exchange rate and the largest default of sovereign debt in history. By late 2002, more than a decade of reforms to the Argentine economy had resulted in unemployment at 19 percent, population below the poverty line at 54 percent, a decline in GDP of 12 percent, and a public foreign debt of $160 billion. It should come as no surprise that Argentines have lost faith both in statist and neoliberal models. In the midst of social, political, and economic crisis, civil society has been strengthened in neighborhood assemblies, workers' takeover of shut-down factories, and organizations of the unemployed.

BIBLIOGRAPHY. James Scobie, *Argentina: A City and a Nation* (Oxford University Press, 1964); David Rock, *Argentina, 1516-1987: From Spanish Colonization to the Falklands War and Alfonsín* (University of California Press, 1987); Guido di Tella and Rudiger Dornsbusch, eds., *The Political Economy of Argentina, 1976-1983* (University of Pittsburgh Press, 1989); E. Epstein, ed., *The New Argentine Democracy: The Search for a Successful Formula* (Praeger, 1992); Michael Mussa, *Argentina and the Fund: From Triumph to Tragedy* (Institute for International Economics, 2002).

LEOPOLDO RODRÍGUEZ-BOETSCH, PH.D.
PORTLAND STATE UNIVERSITY

Armenia

THE SECOND MOST densely populated of the former Soviet Republics, Armenia is landlocked between the Black and Caspian Seas, with the capital at Yerevan.

The first Armenian state was founded in 190 B.C.E., and for a time, Armenia was the strongest state in the Roman East. In 301 C.E., it became the first nation to adopt Christianity. It was incorporated into RUSSIA in 1828, and the SOVIET UNION in 1920.

Armenian citizens voted overwhelmingly for independence in 1991, at the dissolution of the Soviet Union, and held their first presidential election that year. Armenia has had periods of political instability since then, struggling with the transformation from a communist country to a stable, Western-style parliamentary democracy. Armenia has registered steady economic growth since 1995.

As a member of the UNITED NATIONS, INTERNATIONAL MONETARY FUND, WORLD BANK, and other international institutions, Armenia had a population of 3.3 million people in 2001 and a GROSS DOMESTIC PRODUCT (GDP) of $11.2 billion.

BIBLIOGRAPHY. The Department of State Background Note, www.state.gov; *CIA World Factbook* (2002); Armenia, A Country Study, The Library of Congress, lcweb2.loc.gov.

LINDA L. PETROU, PH.D.
HIGH POINT UNIVERSITY

Arrow, Kenneth J. (1921–)

AWARDED THE 1972 Nobel Prize in Economics (with John R. HICKS), Kenneth Arrow was cited by the Nobel Committee for "pioneering contributions to general economic equilibrium theory and welfare theory."

Arrow made significant contributions to the development of more refined analytical techniques in economics, and helped introduce the economics of uncertainty and monetary economics. He also made a major contribution in the field of public choice, proposing the concept of the social welfare function.

Born and raised a true New Yorker, Arrow obtained his B.S. in social science from the City College of New York, and his M.A. in mathematics and Ph.D. in economics from Columbia University.

Arrow's graduate study was interrupted by WORLD WAR II, when he served as a weather officer in the U.S. Army Air Corps, rising to the rank of captain. Returning to Columbia after the war, Arrow also conducted research at the Cowles Commission for Research in Economics at the University of Chicago. The years at Cowles (1946–49) were important for the young economist. Arrow writes in his Nobel autobiography: "The brilliant intellectual atmosphere of the Cowles Commission, with eager young econometricians and mathematically inclined economists under the guidance of Tjalling KOOPMANS and Jacob Marschak, was a basic formative influence for me, as was also the summers of 1948 and subsequent years at the RAND Corporation in the heady days of emerging game theory and mathematical programming. My work on social choice and on Pareto efficiency dated from this period."

Arrow is probably best known for his book *Social Choice and Individual Values* (1951), based on his Ph.D. dissertation, in which he proved his famous "Impossibility Theorem." As described by author David R. Henderson, Arrow showed that under certain assumptions about peoples' preferences between options, it is impossible to find a voting rule under which one person emerges as the most preferred. Arrow went on to show that a competitive economy in equilibrium is efficient and that any efficient allocation could be reached by having the government use lump-sum taxes to redistribute, and then letting the markets work.

Arrow's research led to the economic proposition that the government should not control prices to redistribute income, but rather if it must redistribute at all, do so directly.

Another example of Arrow's contribution includes being one of the first economists to deal with the existence of a learning curve in production. In simple terms, Arrow showed that as producers increase output of a product, they gain experience and become more efficient. "The role of experience in increasing productivity has not gone unobserved, though the relation has yet to be absorbed into the main corpus of economic theory," Arrow wrote in a 1962 article. Some economists argue that even today, Arrow's insight into the learning curve has not been fully integrated into mainstream economic analysis.

Arrow has taught at several universities in the United States and Europe and in early 2003, he was Joan Kenney Professor of Economics and Operations at Stanford University. His professional affiliations include the U.S. National Academy of Sciences, the American Academy of Arts and Sciences, the American Philosophical Society, the British Academy, and the Finnish Academy of Sciences. Arrow has received 16 honorary degrees from American and European universities, and has served as president of Econometric Society, the American and the International Economic Associations, and the Western Economic Association.

In addition to *Social Choice and Individual Values*, Arrows other important works include *General Competitive Analysis* (with F. Han, 1971) and the *Collected Papers of Kenneth J. Arrow* (1984).

BIBLIOGRAPHY. Kenneth J. Arrow Autobiography, www.nobel.se; David R. Henderson, "Kenneth Arrow," *The Concise Encyclopedia of Economics* (Liberty Fund, 2002); Kenneth Arrow, "The Economic Implications of Learning by Doing," *Review of Economic Studies* (v.29, 1962); Kenneth Arrow, *Social Choice and Individual Values* (Yale University Press, 1970).

SYED B. HUSSAIN, PH.D.
UNIVERSITY OF WISCONSIN, OSHKOSH

Arthur, Chester A. (1829–86)

THE 21ST PRESIDENT of the UNITED STATES, Chester Alan Arthur was born in Fairfield, Vermont. When he was five, his family moved to upstate New York. Arthur graduated from Union College in 1848, then studied law and joined a New York City law firm.

Arthur's strongly held anti-slavery views motivated him to join the new Republican Party. In 1857, he became a judge advocate in the state militia and was called to active duty during the AMERICAN CIVIL WAR. After leaving the Army in 1863, Arthur resumed his legal practice as well as his involvement in local politics.

In 1871, President Ulysses GRANT appointed Arthur collector of customs for the Port of New York. This was considered a plum position because of the many patronage jobs it controlled, and Arthur satisfied the patronage demands of the city's political machine, hiring many more people than were needed for the work. In response to demands by reformers, President Rutherford HAYES removed Arthur in 1878.

In 1880, the Republican Convention deadlocked in a fight between reformer and machine politicians, known as Stalwarts. Eventually, they settled on moderate reformer James GARFIELD for president and nominated Arthur as vice president to satisfy the Stalwarts. Although Arthur's political boss ordered him to reject the nomination, Arthur accepted.

Given Garfield's youth and vigor, reformers saw the vice presidency as a relatively harmless place for a machine politician like Arthur. They were horrified the following summer when Garfield was assassinated.

Despite his background, President Arthur became a powerful advocate of political reform. Garfield's death resulted in a public outcry for civil service reform, and in 1883, Arthur signed the Pendleton Act into law, banning political kickbacks from public employees. The Act also began to protect many government jobs from political litmus tests and established a bipartisan Civil Service Commission to administer it.

Arthur championed attempts to reduce the amount of federal funds wasted on patronage and pork-barrel (special-interest) spending. He attempted to reduce tariffs to prevent large surpluses of money that the government wasted, though this met with limited success. He was more successful in moving surplus away from patronage and toward paying off debt. He reduced the national debt from $2.1 billion in 1881 to just over $1.8 billion when he left office in 1885.

Many applauded Arthur's reforms, but it also made him many enemies in the political establishment. In 1884, he lost his party's nomination, and also failed in an attempt to be nominated for a New York senate seat. He died two years later.

BIBLIOGRAPHY. Justus Doenecke, *The Presidencies of James A. Garfield and Chester A. Arthur* (University Press of Kansas, 1981); George Howe, *Chester A. Arthur: A Quarter Century of Machine Politics* (Reprint Services, 1935); Thomas Reeves, *Gentleman Boss* (American Political Biography, 1975).

THOMAS D. JEITSCHKO, PH.D.
MICHIGAN STATE UNIVERSITY
MICHAEL J. TROY, J.D.

Asian developmental state

ASIAN DEVELOPMENTAL STATES emerged during the Cold War in JAPAN, SOUTH KOREA, TAIWAN, and SINGAPORE as a controversial hybrid of Soviet Union-style central planning and American free market capitalism. Governments promoted industries judged to be "strategic" in enhancing overall economic growth, while nonstrategic sectors were left to market forces.

The industries chosen for promotion reflected the developmental states' nationalist orientation to economic activity. In contrast to neo-classical economists' internationalist ideas of comparative advantage and mutual gains from trade across national boundaries, developmental states viewed trade as a national struggle with clear winners and losers. Producers of technologically sophisticated products became rich while countries that concentrated on light manufactures and commodities remained poor. Developmental states, therefore, raised their country's standard of living by promoting industries with high paying jobs such as automobiles, computers, shipbuilding, and petrochemicals.

Government pilot institutions emerged to plan and coordinate the systematic development of these industries. The Japanese Ministry of International Trade and Industry (MITI), for example, drafted the Petrochemical Nurturing Plan in 1955 and provided initial capital investment through the government's Japan Development Bank. MITI also assisted the industry with technology import licenses, tax exemptions, and facilities constructed at government expense. Once the industry was underway, MITI organized the petrochemical companies into an "administrative guidance cartel" to facilitate government coordination. During Japan's rapid economic growth in the 1950s and 1960s, MITI also played a pivotal role in the growth of the automobile, computer, and steel industries.

Close business-government relations clearly favored large business conglomerates over smaller firms. Japanese *keiretsu* and Korean *chaebol*, for example, were large corporate groups uniting manufacturers, suppliers, and distributors. These groups developed a symbiotic relationship with their governments. Governments needed trustworthy companies to carry out development plans and the firms were happy to receive government subsidies and windfall profits from these new businesses.

The Korean government's cooperation with the gigantic Hyundai Group to promote shipbuilding in the 1970s and 1980s is a good example. The government subsidized Hyundai with lucrative contracts for ships, infrastructure at Hyundai facilities, and financial guarantees to foreign investors and Hyundai's first customers. With this support from the government, Hyundai grew into one of the world's largest shipbuilders by the late 1980s.

Government subsidy of new industries required a redistribution of resources within society. Big companies and their urban employees generally prospered. Farmers, small businesses, and laborers were less fortunate. To maintain political stability, Asian developmental states developed authoritarian political systems dominated by a single party like the Liberal Democratic Party in Japan, the Kuomintang in Taiwan, and the People's Action Party in Singapore. These regimes suppressed independent labor unions to keep wages low for the sake of international competitiveness. Governments often tempered this repression with paternalistic policies assisting workers with housing, healthcare, and recreational facilities.

With their systematic intervention in markets, close relations with big business, and authoritarian politics, developmental states have drawn substantial criticism. Some economists believe that developmental states' importance in promoting economic development has been exaggerated. Growth rates, they argue, might have been even higher if entrepreneurs had devoted all of their resources to innovation rather than soliciting political favors. The SONY Corporation spent months in the 1950s lobbying government officials for a permit to license American semiconductor technology. In the early 1960s, motorcycle manufacturer Honda Soichiro had to overcome stiff government resistance to his company's diversification into passenger automobiles.

International trading partners have criticized the developmental states' predatory "neo-mercantilist" promotion of exports and "crony capitalist" exclusion of outsiders from their domestic markets. These accusations peaked in the late 1980s and early 1990s as Japanese automobiles, semiconductors, and consumer electronics became popular in American markets. American firms complained that the Japanese developmental state's policies gave Japanese companies an unfair competitive advantage. After protracted negotiations and threats of U.S. government retaliation, the Japanese deregulated several of their industries.

Finally, critics suggest that Asian developmental states owe much of their success to favorable Cold War international conditions. The United States gave its Cold War allies unusually open access to American military assistance, capital, technology, and markets. After the Cold War ended in 1989, Americans demanded reciprocal access to Asian markets. Developmental states also faced growing pressure for political reform as international opinion sided with local democratic movements seeking an end to authoritarian repression. Nevertheless, governments in Thailand, VIETNAM, CHINA and elsewhere continue to follow the developmental state model to promote economic growth.

The developmental states in Japan, Korea, Taiwan, and Singapore took advantage of Cold War opportunities and pursued policies contributing to rapid economic development. This development came at the price of political repression at home and strained relations abroad. Although controversial, the Asian developmental state remains an important form of capitalism.

BIBLIOGRAPHY. Alice Amsden, *Asia's Next Giant* (Oxford University Press,1989), Marie Anchordoguy, *Computers Inc.* (Harvard University Press, 1989), Frederic C. Deyo, *Political Economy of the New Asian Industrialism* (Cornell University Press, 1987), Stephan Haggard, *Pathways from the Periphery* (Cornell University Press, 1990), Chalmers Johnson, *MITI and the Japanese Miracle* (Stanford University Press, 1982), Meredith Woo-Cumings, *The Developmental State* (Cornell University Press, 1999).

JOHN SAGERS, PH.D.
LINFIELD COLLEGE

Asian Financial Crisis

FINANCIAL CRISES REFER TO currency crises (also called balance of payments crises) during which a country's CENTRAL BANK loses international reserves and is eventually forced to allow the depreciation of the domestic currency. Countries with pegged (managed) EXCHANGE RATE regimes are particularly prone to currency crises. While first-generation (canonical) currency crises models support the view that deteriorating country fundamentals are at the core of such crises, second-generation

(self-fulfilling) currency crises models suggest that currency crises may occur despite strong fundamentals. Self-fulfilling currency crises may take place because of the possibility of multiple equilibria, which means that, despite strong fundamentals, currency crisis may be one of the possible outcomes.

Since THAILAND, INDONESIA, and South KOREA experienced currency crises in August, October, and November, 1997, respectively, researchers have been discussing the causes of the Asian Financial Crisis. Although there is disagreement as to the causes of this crisis, some characteristics of capital inflows into Asian countries have remained undisputed. Following the fall in world interest rates in 1989, Asian countries attracted large capital inflows because of their high and solid GROSS DOMESTIC PRODUCT (GDP) growth rate. By the mid-1990s, the capital inflows as a percentage of the GDP were almost in the mid-teens in some Asian countries, whereas the same ratio was less than 1 percent in G8 countries. As capital flows increased through the mid-1990s, countries such as Thailand and South Korea had total external debt/GDP ratios of almost 200 percent.

As to the reason for the Asian currency crisis, the basic first-generation currency crisis model explains the cause of currency crises based on the coexistence of a pegged exchange rate regime and expansionary fiscal and monetary policies. However, before the financial crisis struck, Asian countries successfully stabilized inflation by maintaining fiscal and monetary discipline under pegged exchange rate regimes. Therefore, researchers working with first-generation currency crisis models have used a different set of fundamentals to discuss the cause of the Asian Financial Crisis. Increasing foreign liabilities of the commercial banking system, maturity mismatches, and asset price bubbles are assumed to have made the financial systems in some Asian countries vulnerable to capital inflows of substantial magnitudes.

Some economists argue that financial liberalization precedes banking and currency crises. As financial liberalization allows a country to enjoy the inflow of foreign investors, the outflow may be substantial and speedy, which leads to a boom-bust cycle. This particular point has been made with respect to the Asian crisis. Financial liberalization may have led to the maturity mismatch between assets and liabilities of the banking system because of over-lending and excessive risk, especially in short-term external debt. International investors may have become wary and expected financial problems in the future. Therefore, based on the first-generation currency crisis model, systemic banking problems lay at the roots of the substantial devaluation of the Thai baht, Korean won, and Indonesian rupiah in 1997.

Researchers who focus on the self-fulfilling nature of the Asian Financial Crisis argue that markets' reaction to news demonstrates the possibility of currency crisis despite strong fundamentals. Some argue that the largest daily swings in financial markets in Asia during the crisis period cannot be explained by any apparently relevant economic or political news. Empirical studies indicate that news releases that contribute to significant movements in financial markets are releases that are about agreements with the international community, and about announcements by credit-rating agencies. Some also suggest that news releases about monetary and fiscal policies do not affect financial markets in a predictable fashion.

In some instances, tight policies may contribute to financial market rallies or lead to a slowdown in financial markets. There is also evidence that investors react more strongly to bad news than to good news. Generally speaking, investors' reactions to information have been used to argue that bad news in crisis episodes may increase uncertainty, which may lead to herding behavior.

In addition to first- and second-generation currency crisis models, some researchers suggest the possibility that a country may experience a currency crisis, even though the crisis cannot be explained based on either currency crisis model. There is empirical evidence that CONTAGION, regional spread of currency crises, may occur through trade linkage among countries.

BIBLIOGRAPHY. R. Chang and A. Velasco, "The Asian Financial Crisis in Perspective," *Private Capital Flows in the Age of Globalization: The aftermath of the Asian Crisis* (International Bank for Reconstruction and Development, 2000); G. Kaminsky and C. Reinhart, "The Twin Crises: The Causes of Banking and Balance-of-Payments Problems," *American Economic Review* (v.89/3, 1999); G. Kaminsky and S.L. Schmukler, "What Triggers Market Jitters? A Chronicle of the Asian Crisis," *Journal of International Money and Finance* (v.18, 1999); P. Krugman, "A Model of Balance-of-Payments Crisis," *Journal of Money, Credit, and Banking* (v.11, 1979); M. Obstfeld, "Models of Currency Crises with Self-Fulfilling Features," *European Economic Review* (v.40, 1996); W.T. Woo, J.D. Sachs, and K. Schwab, eds., *The Asian Financial Crisis: Lessons for a Resilient Asia* (MIT Press, 2000).

AYŞE Y. EVRENSEL
PORTLAND STATE UNIVERSITY

Assicurazioni Generali

THE LARGEST ITALIAN INSURER was established at the beginning of the 19th century in the city of Trieste, which was then a natural outlet to the sea for the inter-national commerce of the Austro-Hungarian Empire. Because of its unique position, the city enjoyed a remarkable economic growth. Several local businessmen felt the need for the creation of an insurance company and on December 26th, 1831, they established Assicurazioni Generali.

The company's initial capital was quite a large sum for the period (2 million florins), revealing the company's ambitious programs. A few months after its foundation, Generali began to spread within the Hapsburg Empire and branches were established in Vienna, Budapest, and Prague. In July, 1832, the important Venetian branch was founded by Samuele della Vida to develop the insurance sector in the many states of the fragmented Italian peninsula. The Venetian office has played a particularly important part in the development of the insurance company and, tellingly, its symbol is also the symbol of the city of Venice: a winged lion protecting a copy of the Gospel. Generali soon expanded in other European countries such as FRANCE, GERMANY and SWITZERLAND. It then stretched into the Balkans and Eastern Europe and reached separate continents such as Africa and Latin America.

The end of WORLD WAR I and the new political scene created several problems for the group. The Hapsburg Empire dissolved and Trieste was absorbed into the Italian Kingdom, thus losing its privileged position. Yet Generali confronted this difficult period with a program of structural reforms designed to consolidate and expand its organization in ITALY. New companies were set up, and the group acquired significant stakes in existing insurance companies. In the 1920s and 1930s, the Generali Group played a crucial role in the development of the Italian economy through investments in the industrial and agricultural sectors.

The Generali Group was faced with another crisis at the end of the WORLD WAR II and the outbreak of the Cold War. The establishment of the Iron Curtain meant the loss of 14 insurance companies operating in eastern European countries. However, the Generali did not relinquish its worldwide presence and successfully focused on the development of important markets in the following decades outside Europe in Latin America, Asia, and Africa. In 2002, Generali ranked as the 50th largest company in the world with sales of more than $52 billion.

BIBLIOGRAPHY. Francesco Balletta, *Mercato Finanziario e Assicurazioni Generali: 1920–1961* (Edizioni Scientifiche Italiane, 1995); "The Years of the Lion," www.generali.com; "Global 500: World's Largest Companies," *Fortune* (July, 2002).

LUCA PRONO, PH.D.
UNIVERSITY OF NOTTINGHAM, ENGLAND

Astor, John Jacob (1763–1848)

BORN IN WALDORF, GERMANY, a butcher's son, John Jacob Astor arrived in Baltimore by way of London at the end of the AMERICAN REVOLUTION. Nearly penniless, his assets included $50, seven flutes from his brother's musical instrument shop, experience in trade, and determination.

By 1786, he was able to open his own fur shop in New York City. In 1790, he married Sarah Todd, gaining entrée into New York's old line Dutch society. His wife was highly knowledgeable about furs too, and the marriage was either a successful partnership in all respects or a stormy affair, depending on the source. Astor wasted no time, developing a fleet of clipper ships to capitalize on the demand for China tea. Soon he was a leader in the China trade, shipping furs out, bringing tea in. But tea, while lucrative, was not his path to fame. His fortune came from the fur trade.

After the Lewis and Clark expedition revealed the potential of newly acquired territory, he sent out expeditions of his own to explore the fur country. In 1808, he capitalized the American Fur Company at $500,000, a very sizeable amount in that time. He planned to compete with the British Hudson's Bay Company in the American northwest. He later established the Pacific Fur Companies and the Southwest Fur Company, establishing trading posts everywhere the trappers might congregate. One major failure was Astoria, Oregon, that Astor established in 1811 with the aim of penetrating the Far East market. The WAR OF 1812 intervened, and the naval blockade was a factor in Astor's decision to sell the post to the British.

For Astor, the fur trade was worldwide. It was a business that brought beaver, otter, muskrat, and mink furs from the native or company trapper to the trader to the exporter to the maker of hats for fashion conscious women and men—and, in return, it gave the natives and other trappers muskets, blankets, tools, and utensils. The trade had a long history, from the early French couriers *du bois* and their colonial British rivals. In the early years of the UNITED STATES government-supported factories carried on the trade. From the presidency of George WASHINGTON, the trade had received federal subsidies because it was thought to be in the national interest to compete with the British companies in CANADA. Astor challenged the government system by establishing a new style of fur company.

Astor's fur companies were modern with a division of labor, specialists, and vertical integration. Astor ran the business from his headquarters in New York City, but the actual trading took place on Mackinac Island, out where the business was, in present-day Michigan. There, Astor's men bought furs, packed boats, and sent them to the East Coast for further distribution to the world markets. Astor also sent his employees throughout the trapping regions, going where the business was. From log cabins, they supplied the fur traders with the goods they needed. Credit was available as well.

Astor sent his men out to where the trappers were, traded fairly and in quality goods of the sort the Native Americans wanted, with low prices. He gave them the muskets and kettles they wanted, not the plows and other sometimes inferior and overpriced goods the government tried to trade. Astor also traded in liquor, albeit reluctantly. He understood that drunken trappers were worthless to his business, but he recognized that the British were dealing in liquor and he had to match the competition. Astor also established a merit system and paid his managers good salaries and shares of the profits. And he took his trade worldwide, refusing to sell when and where the price didn't suit him. The government factories had fixed-salary employees and no market control, selling at auction each year regardless of price.

By 1808, Astor was the leading exporter in the United States, and his edge grew after the War of 1812. By the 1820s he had 750 men in his employ, and connections to untold numbers of fur sources. Annual harvests reached $500,000. Government efforts to ban private companies complicated his life, but eventually his ability to profit while the government was losing money consistently killed that effort.

But the trade began to wane in the 1820s and 1830s as fashion changed, pelts became scarce, and silk and cheap cloth took market share. Astor held a monopoly on the fur trade until he retired in 1834, turning his attention to New York real estate and making himself the first millionaire in the United States.

By 1810, Astor had a fortune of at least $2 million. Shrewdly, he bought lots in desolate north Manhattan, calculating that the city would eventually grow and make his investments valuable. He also did his part to fund the War of 1812; typically, when he bought $2 million worth of government bonds; he paid 88 cents on the dollar. Other than the Manhattan properties, he also invested in the Park Theater, the Mohawk and Hudson Railroad, and the Astor House Hotel.

Astor became America's first world-class entrepreneur and, at his death, its richest man. He could be ruthless, he could be tight with a dollar, but he understood how to organize a business, how to deal with his employees and his customers. His empire was worldwide due to his skills and, to an extent to his knack for getting out of a venture at the top, as when he sold his fleet of China clipper ships just before Chinese tea faded in the face of competition from India and Japan. He also anticipated the end of the fur trade, selling his interests before the fur business fell to increased scarcity, fashion shifts, and the boom in ready-made, cheap clothing.

At his death Astor left a fortune variously estimated at $10–20 million. Astor did leave $400,000 in his will for the establishment of a library in New York City. The Astor Library opened in 1849.

A measurement of the magnitude of Astor's wealth is that $20 million from the 1840s equates to late-20th century fortunes in the billions. One estimate is that his modern day net worth would be $78 billion, ranking him behind only John D. ROCKEFELLER, Andrew CARNEGIE, and Cornelius VANDERBILT. Bill GATES of Microsoft ranked just behind Astor in 1999.

Rising from the penniless immigrant to by far the richest man of his time, John Jacob Astor epitomized rags-to-riches American dream, and he was one of the prototypes for the rise of big business in America.

BIBLIOGRAPHY. Burton W. Folsom, Jr., "John Jacob Astor and the Fur Trade: Testing the Role of Government" *The Freeman* (v.47/6, 1997); www.libertyhaven.com; John Denis Haeger, *John Jacob Astor: Business and Finance in the Early Republic* (Wayne State University Press, 1991); Axel Madsen, *John Jacob Astor: America's First Multimillionaire* (John Wiley & Sons, 2002).

JOHN H. BARNHILL, PH.D.
INDEPENDENT SCHOLAR

AT&T

ALEXANDER GRAHAM BELL, Gardiner Hubbard, and Thomas Sanders founded the Bell Telephone Company, later known as the American Telephone and Telegraph Corporation, in 1877. Bell was the telephone inventor, Hubbard and Sanders were the men who financed his work. The first telephone exchange was opened in New Haven, Connecticut, in 1878; within

In more than 100 years of business AT&T has gone through multiple competitive phases, from monopoly to breakup.

three years, telephone exchanges existed in most major cities in the UNITED STATES.

The American Telephone and Telegraph Company was created with the charter to provide long-distance telephone service. The first lines were built between New York and Chicago and were completed in 1892. AT&T's long distance telephone system was extended from coast to coast when San Francisco was added in 1915. In 1927, AT&T inaugurated commercial transatlantic telephone service to London using two-way radio. Radiotelephone service to Hawaii began in 1931 and to Tokyo in 1934. In 1956, service to Europe moved to the first transatlantic submarine telephone cable. Transpacific cable service began in 1964. AT&T opened its first microwave relay system between the cities of New York and Boston in 1948. In 1962, AT&T placed the first commercial communications satellite in orbit, offering an additional alternative especially suited to international communications.

During its life, AT&T Bell Laboratories has been the home of more than 22,000 patents and seven Nobel-Prize winners. Its most significant, single invention is probably the transistor, which replaced large, less efficient vacuum tubes. Other inventions include gas and semiconductor lasers, the UNIX operating system, the C computer programming language, the touch-tone telephone, the first artificial larynx, and the first fax machine. Bell scientists A.A. Penzias and R.W. Wilson discovered the universe's "background radiation" posited by cosmologists who favored the Big Bang theory of creation and were awarded a Nobel Prize in Physics in 1978 for their discovery.

During its life, AT&T has gone through multiple MONOPOLY and competitive phases. Before 1894, Bell Telephone's patents protected it from competition. After Bell's patents expired in 1894 many telephone companies began to provide telephone service particularly in the rural areas and Bell's profits dropped drastically. The number of telephones exploded from approximately 266,000 in 1893 to 6.1 million in 1907, and about half of all new telephone installations were controlled by Bell's competitors.

In 1907, AT&T's president wrote in the annual report that the telephone, by the nature of its technology, would operate most efficiently as a monopoly. While independent companies provided the first service available to many customers, the multiple telephone systems were not interconnected until after the 1913 Kingsbury Commitment. As a result of the agreement, the government of each local community would allow only one telephone company to operate and this local company would be connected to the Bell long-distance system. Since Bell was the largest single company, it was in the best position to lobby the state utility commissions and was generally chosen over its competitors to provide local phone service. Bell soon became a monopoly again.

The U.S. government, in 1974 filed the antitrust suit that finally led to a competitive market in long distance. In 1982, AT&T agreed to sell those parts (the local exchanges) where the natural monopoly argument was still considered valid from those parts (long distance, manufacturing, research and development), where competition was thought appropriate. Divestiture took place in 1984. Many new long distance companies soon entered the market and long distance rates dropped 30 percent over the next five years. Local phone service, still a monopoly, went up 50 percent in price during the same period.

Since its breakup, AT&T has been restructured numerous times. On September 20, 1995, AT&T announced that it would split into three separate publicly traded companies: a systems and equipment company (Lucent Technologies,) a computer company (NCR) and a communications services company (AT&T). It was the largest voluntary break-up in the history of American business. In October, 2000, AT&T announced another restructuring. AT&T would be split into three companies: AT&T Wireless, AT&T Broadband, and AT&T. On December 9, 2001, AT&T and the cable-operator Comcast reached agreement to combine AT&T Broadband with Comcast in a new company to be known as AT&T Comcast.

Fortune magazine ranked AT&T as the world's 40th largest company in 2002 with revenues of $59 billion.

BIBLIOGRAPHY. Sheldon Hochheiser, "AT&T: A Brief History," www.att.com; Mary J. Ruwart, *Healing Our World* (Sunstar Press, 1993); Peter Samuel, *Telecommunications: After the Bell Break-Up* (1985); Peter Temin, *The Fall of the Bell System* (Cambridge University Press, 1987).

KIRBY R. CUNDIFF, PH.D.
HILLSDALE COLLEGE

audit

A SYSTEMATIC PROCESS, an audit involves the examination of accounting information by a third party other than the preparer or user, and the verification of data to determine the reliability and accuracy of accounting statements and reports. Audits are used to evaluate all kinds of information and data, and can be divided into three main categories.

An audit can be a compliance audit, which is performed to determine whether certain activities of an entity conform to specified rules, conditions, or regulations.

An audit can also be an operational audit, wherein the efficiency and effectiveness of specified operating objectives can be assessed. For instance, the functionality and reliability of information systems are often audited, as are elections and various lottery functions. Additionally, the annual Academy Award voting process is audited by a top accounting firm.

Nonetheless, the financial statement audit is by far the most common and valued form of audit. This audit procedure involves obtaining and evaluating evidence about an entity's financial statements, which are based on assertions made by the entity's management. The overall goal of the auditor in a financial statement audit is to increase the usefulness of the compiled accounting information to interested users such as creditors, investors, labor unions, investment bankers, and government.

The final product of an audit is the auditor's report. The audit report consists of an entity's financial statements and any applicable disclosures. It is a means of communicating the overall conclusions about the audited financial statements in a way that users can understand.

The audit opinion, which is included in the auditor's report, is the backbone of the report because it tells the user of an entity's financial statements whether or not they were presented fairly according to GENERALLY ACCEPTED ACCOUNTING PRINCIPLES (GAAP). When the financial statements are judged to be in conformity with GAAP, the auditor issues an unqualified opinion. Other opinions may be issued by the auditor if the financial statements contain a material departure from GAAP, or if the auditor is unable to obtain sufficient evidence regarding one or more management assertions, and therefore cannot reasonably issue an unqualified opinion. Bear in mind that an audit opinion applies to the financial statements as a whole. The other opinions that can be issued are:

1. *Qualified opinion.* The auditor expresses certain reservations concerning the scope of the audit or the financial statements. Since the departure is not extremely material or significant, the auditor states that except for effects of the matter to which the qualification relates, the financial statements are in conformity with GAAP.

2. *Adverse opinion.* The auditor states that the financial statements are not presented fairly due to a material or significant departure from GAAP.

3. *Disclaimer of opinion.* Auditor does not give an opinion on the presentation of the financial statements.

The quality of performance and general objectives to be achieved in a financial-statement audit are identified by a set of Generally Accepted Auditing Standards (GAAS), the most recognized set of auditing standards in the industry. In essence, GAAS is comprised of 10 standards divided into three distinct categories that prescribe certain considerations for accepting and assigning an audit, performing the actual fieldwork, and issuing the audit report. Though GAAS are not statutory laws, they were originally put in place by the American Institute for Certified Public Accountants (AICPA) as valid standards of the profession, and thus they are used by government agencies, industry peers, and courts of law in evaluating the performance of financial statement audits.

The execution of an audit is a complicated and varied process. First, the auditor goes into an audit with a preliminary audit strategy that involves assessing materiality and risk, two important factors in the audit planning process. Materiality is the magnitude of an omission or misstatement of accounting information that makes it likely that the judgment of a person relying on the information would have been different or otherwise drastically influenced by the omission or misstatement. The auditor may encounter various omissions or misstatements that may or may not be material, depending upon the overall audit objective and strategy. Also, the auditor looks at audit risk, which relates to the risk that the auditor may unknowingly fail to properly modify an audit opinion in regard to financial statements that are in fact materially misstated. Understanding the nature of both of these components assists the auditor in deciding upon the scope of the audit and the testing approach to be used.

Essentially, the overall methodology of an audit involves identifying that which needs to be evidenced, for example, the existence or occurrence of an assertion or an account balance. The auditor collects relevant evidence for that which he needs to express his judgment on, and assesses the fairness of the data through the use of various testing procedures. In applying a range of tests, the auditor deals in probabilities through statistical sampling. Small sample units that represent larger populations are observed in order to evaluate relevant characteristics that the auditor needs to identify.

Auditing also involves less systematic means of evidence collection such as inquiring, observing, and the application of analytical procedures. The auditor may observe and inquire about procedures for recording transactions, or apply analytical procedures to compare current year assertions to the prior year, often helping him to pinpoint items that may need to be further investigated.

It is important to remember that the auditing of financial statements is an attest function, meaning that after conducting an audit of the accounting system of a business, the independent auditor issues an opinion on the fairness of the presentation of the financial state-

ments and their conformity to GAAP. Essentially, an attestation is an evaluation of the quality of the information presented under GAAP rules. An attest function differs from the definitive substantiation of facts or truths because "attest" merely means to "bear witness" or, more specifically, to attest to the reliability of an entity's financial statements. The financial statement assertions of a company are the responsibility of its management. The auditor is merely expressing judgment—in a separate report—on the basis of being a trained observer performing a critical review of the data.

Auditing, in general, is about maintaining a healthy skepticism. In spite of the excellent credentials of most auditors, accounting scandals have put the audit profession in the limelight, and not in the laudable sense. Since the mid-1990s, there has been a parade of corporate wrongdoings wherein questionable accounting approaches are said to have led to bankruptcies and/or numerous financial statement restatements, in order to accurately quantify previous earnings reports.

The accounting industry, as a whole, faces vast restructuring. However, the new wave of regulatory oversight may be unwelcome if the governance of the audit sector shifts from the private realm to the bureaucratic government sector.

BIBLIOGRAPHY. R.K. Mautz and Hussein A. Sharaf, *The Philosophy of Auditing* (American Accounting Association, 1961); David Kent, Michael Sherer, and Stuart Terley, *Current Issues in Accounting* (Harper & Row, 1985); W. Thomas Porter, Jr. and John C. Burton, *Auditing: A Conceptual Approach* (Wadsworth, 1971); William C. Boynton and Walter G. Kell, *Modern Auditing* (John Wiley & Sons, 1996); Walter B. Meigs, E. John Larsen, and Robert F. Meigs, *Principles of Auditing* (Irwin, 1973); R.K. Mautz, *Fundamentals of Auditing* (John Wiley & Sons, 1967).

KAREN DE COSTER
WALSH COLLEGE

Australia

LYING BETWEEN THE Pacific and Indian Oceans in the southern hemisphere, the continent of Australia is one of the world's largest and most isolated countries. A member of the British Commonwealth of Nations, Australia is a political federation with a central government and six member states that enjoy limited sovereignty, as well as two territories. Canberra is the capital.

The population of Australia is approximately 19.5 million, with approximately 90 percent white, seven percent Asian, and the balance Aborigines and Torres Strait Islanders. Approximately 85 percent of the population lives in urban areas. English is the official language, though Aboriginal and other native languages are also spoken. The coastal plains near the mainland capitals in the east, southeast, and southwest are Australia's fastest growing areas—about four-fifths of Australians live in these areas, which make up only about three percent of the total land area.

The Aborigines were the first to live in Australia and are believed to have migrated there about 40,000 years ago. Until the 17th century the continent was relatively unknown. In 1788, the first European settlement by British convicts was established at Botany Bay. During the 19th century, British colonies continued to be established, and in 1901, the colonies united to form an independent nation, and Australia became a member of a commonwealth of the British Empire.

Taking advantage of its natural resources, Australia quickly developed its agricultural and manufacturing industries, and was able to make a significant contribution to Britain's efforts in both WORLD WAR I and WORLD WAR II. After World War II, Australia entered a long period of political stability and built further upon the development foundations established during the war. In the early 1970s, the government attempted to institute plans for increased social services, but these came into conflict with Australia's declining economic prosperity and state rights. In the mid-1970s the government reinstated domestic and foreign policies previously followed and laid a foundation for land claims by Aboriginals. In the 1980s, the government attempted to promote labor-management cooperation and had a foreign policy that was emphatically pro-American. Mired in a recession, the government, in the early 1990s, began the process of changing Australia's status from a commonwealth headed by the British monarchy to a republic. Acknowledging the proximity of huge potential markets in Asia, the government continued its re-orientation toward Asia. But in 1999, a referendum to change Australia's status to a republic was defeated.

MINING has long been a major factor in Australia's economic growth, and in certain instances is among the world's leading producers. Minerals mined include gold, iron ore, diamonds, uranium, coal, titanium, nickel, and aluminum. Wheat is the main crop, but other crops include oats, fruit, and sugarcane. Australia is also a leading producer of wine and the leading producer and exporter of wool. Australia raises both beef and dairy cattle.

Due to Australia's large size and relatively small population, transportation has historically been expensive and has utilized a high proportion of the work force. The road network radiates from the ports and state capitals, and continues to be in need of upgrade. There are both private rail systems and a government owned system, however rail transport has declined due to competition with road and air services. Australians

Australia's Sydney Opera House has become an icon of the country's strong growth in tourism.

have become especially accustomed to flying, and an inclusive network of air service links the major cities as well as remote areas.

Industry accounts for about one-quarter of Australia's GROSS DOMESTIC PRODUCT (GDP), services about 72 percent, and agriculture the rest. Central components of the industrial sector are the manufacture of metals, food, transportation equipment, textiles, and printed materials. Australia's tourism industry has experienced strong growth, and has enabled each state to capitalize on its own attractions.

Australia's currency is the Australian dollar (AUD) and it is freely traded on global currency markets. The reserve bank of Australia manages the central banking system, including the issuance of notes. Australia's stock exchange is well connected to the global network. Local, state, and federal governments impose taxes.

Australia's exports are valued at approximately $68.8 billion annually and its imports at $70.2 billion; partners include the UNITED STATES, JAPAN, SOUTH KOREA, SINGAPORE, NEW ZEALAND, GERMANY, and the UNITED KINGDOM. Under Australian tariff policy, Australian industries are protected and imports from certain Commonwealth countries are given preference.

Soon after the year 2000, Australia's per capita GDP was level with the major West European economies, and a strong domestic economy enabled Australia to be resilient in dealing with an international economic downturn.

BIBLIOGRAPHY. Rodney Maddock and Ian W. McLean, eds., *The Australian Economy in the Long Run* (Cambridge University Press, 1987); Kevin O'Connor, Maurice T. Daly, Maurie Daly, and Robert J. Stimson, *Australia's Changing Economic Geography: A Society Dividing* (Oxford University

Press, 2002); R.C. Mascarenhas, *Government and the Economy in Australia and New Zealand: The Politics of Economic Policy Making* (Austin & Winfield, 2002); *CIA World Factbook* (2002).

S.J. Rubel, J.D.
Independent Scholar

Austria

THE REPUBLIC OF AUSTRIA borders Switzerland and Liechtenstein to the west, Germany to the northwest, the Czech Republic to the north, Slovakia to the northeast, Hungary to the east, Italy to the southwest, and Slovenia to the south. Vienna is the capital.

Austria's population in 2002 was approximately 8.1 million, with the majority being Austrian, though increasingly immigrants, especially Croats, Hungarians, and Turks are contributing to the ethnic mix. About 60 percent of the population lives in urban areas, with 20 percent living in the Vienna capital area. A high life expectancy offsets a declining birth rate in the German-speaking nation.

At one time the center of power for the Austro-Hungarian Empire, Austria was downsized into a small republic after its defeat in World War I. Subsequently, Austria experienced more than 25 years of economic and social upheaval, annexation by Nazi Germany, and subsequent occupation by the Allies. In 1955, the State Treaty ended Austria's occupation, recognized its independence, and prohibited unification with Germany. As a condition for the withdrawal of the Soviet Union, a constitutional law declared Austria's "perpetual neutrality."

Since 1955, Austria has developed into a stable nation characterized by a vibrant cultural life and a spirit of cooperation between its social and economic institutions. In the 1990s, Austria began to struggle with growing resentment towards ethnic minorities and the growing strength of the right-wing Freedom Party. Germany's unification and the subsequent takeover of major industries and newspapers by German companies have led to a questioning of Austria's role in the united Europe. In 1990, the government revoked several provisions of the 1955 State Treaty regarding neutrality. In 1995, Austria joined the European Union (EU), and in 1999 it entered the European Monetary Union, adopting the Euro currency.

Austria is an essential link between central, northern, and western Europe, as well as Italy, Eastern Europe, and the Balkans. It has an intricate road system, which it continues to develop. Being a mountainous and landlocked country, Austria depends on rail passage for a large share of its foreign trade. The rail network is managed by the state owned OBB, or Austrian Federal Railways, which operates as an independent commercial enterprise.

Industry accounts for about 30 percent of Austria's Gross Domestic Product (GDP), services comprise almost 70 percent, and agriculture plays a minor role in the country's economy. Components of the industrial sector include machinery, metals, food products, and wood and paper products. Austria's manufacture industry is composed of a few large enterprises and many small- and medium-sized production facilities. Many of these smaller enterprises make traditional Austrian products including wood, glass, and ceramic handicrafts.

With its beautiful landscape, historic villages and cities, and highly developed hospitality industry, Austria is a major tourism destination. More than half of Austria's annual tourists come from Germany, with the remainder primarily from the Netherlands, Italy, United Kingdom, Switzerland, France, and the United States.

The Ministry of Finance and the Austrian National Bank determine Austrian monetary policy in conjunction with EU policy.

Austria's exports in 2002 were approximately $70 billion annually and its imports $73 billion. Exports included motor vehicles and parts, metal goods, textiles, chemicals, and iron and steel. Imports included oil and oil products, foodstuffs, and machinery and equipment. In the early 2000s, Austria's membership in the EU attracted foreign investors. However, slowing growth in Germany, and globally, also affected Austria's growth. In order to compete with both the EU and central Europe, economists suggest Austria needs to emphasize its knowledge-based sectors of the economy, while continuing to deregulate the service sector and lower tax burdens.

BIBLIOGRAPHY. Elizabeth Barker, *Austria: 1918–1972* (University Press of Texas, 1973); Kurt Steiner, ed., *Modern Austria* (Sposs, 1981); Richard Rickett, *A Brief Survey of Austrian History* (I.B.D. Ltd., 1985); *CIA World Factbook* (2002); Barbara Jelavich, *Modern Austria: Empire and Republic, 1815–1986* (Cambridge University Press, 2003).

S.J. Rubel, J.D.
Independent Scholar

Austrian School

THE AUSTRIAN SCHOOL, also called the Vienna School or Austrian School of Marginal Utility, describes a school of economic thought whose main contribution relies on the development of the theory of marginal UTIL-ITY, and the related price and distribution theory. In comparison to classical (objective) ECONOMIC THEORY, the theory of marginal utility defends a subjectively based price, wage, and interest theory. Marginal utility is defined as the last disposable unit of a good that fulfils the least urgent need. Through several generations of economists, the Austrian School produced additional pioneer theories, which became, to a large extent, part of mainstream economics.

In the beginning the term "Austrian School" was derisively used by German economists, following a historic approach, to distinguish different schools of thought; later on the Austrian School became the prevailing economic school until WORLD WAR II. At the same time, Vienna was considered a center of theoretical economics in Europe. In the early 2000s, the Austrian School experienced a revival after having fallen into oblivion in the aftermath of World War II.

With the publication of *Principles of Economics* in 1871, by Carl MENGER (1840–1921) came the foundation of the Austrian School. Together with Leon WALRAS and William Stanley JEVONS, Menger "spelled out the subjective basis of economic value, and fully explained, for the first time, the theory of marginal utility (the greater the number of units of a good that an individual possesses, the less he will value any given unit). In addition, Menger showed how money originates in a free market when the most marketable commodity is desired, not for consumption, but for use in trading with other goods," explains the Mises Institute.

Menger, a professor of economics at the University of Innsbruck, Austria, was considered a classical liberal and methodological individualist. Contrary to the German Historical School understanding of economics as the accumulation of data in service of the state, Menger described economics as the science of individual choice and human action based on deductive logic. He thus prepared the ground for later writings against socialist thought.

Menger's students, Friedrich von Wieser (1851–1926) and Eugen von BÖHM-BAWERK (1851–1914) are the two main representatives of the First Generation of the Austrian School. Von Wieser formulated the most comprehensive economic theory based on the principle of marginal utility and influenced the older Swedish School, namely K. Wicksell and E. Lindhal. He further contributed with the landmark *Social Economics* (1914) and a revolutionary interpretation of cost showing that "the value of production factors does not only lie in the money spent, but on the opportunities missed by not spending that money on something else." This concept was later referred to as opportunity COST. Böhm-Bawerk applied the marginal utility principle to value, price, capital and interest theories. In his *History and Critique of Interest Theories*, Böhm-Bawerk

showed that "the interest rate is not an artificial construct but an inherent part of the market" reflecting the universal fact of time preference (people tend to satisfy preferences sooner rather than later).

In *Positive Theory of Capital*, Böhm-Bawerk demonstrated that "the normal rate of business profit is the interest rate. Capitalists save money, pay laborers, and wait until the final product is sold to receive profit." He further wrote against the socialist doctrine of capital and wages and interventionism. During the period when Böhm-Bawerk served as finance minister (three times) for the Habsburg monarchy, he fought for "balanced budgets, sound money and the gold standard, free trade, and the repeal of export subsidies and other monopoly privileges."

The Second Generation of the Austrian School includes, in particular, Ludwig von MISES (1881–1973) and Joseph SCHUMPETER (1883–1950). Von Mises developed the theory of marginal utility further, applying it to money (*The Theory of Money and Credit*, 1912). In *Socialism* (1921) he predicted the end of SOCIALISM. While the debate between the Austrian School and the socialists continued, and many academics thought the debate resolved in favor of socialism, world socialism collapsed in 1989.

In the 1920s and 1930s, von Mises wrote a series of essays on the deductive method in economics, later called the logic of action. It should be noted that in 1934, the Austrian philosopher Sir Karl Popper published the first edition of his epochal book *The Logic of Scientific Discovery*, which includes a pleading for deductive methodology to be applied in science, and relates scientific progress to trial and error processes. Von Mises further worked, with his student Friedrich von HAYEK, on the Austrian theory of the BUSINESS CYCLE, at the same time warning of the danger of credit expansion and predicting the coming currency crises. Mises founded the Austrian Institute of Business Cycle Research and put Hayek in charge of it. In 1974, Hayek was awarded the Nobel Prize in Economics for this work. Since life for economists was difficult in Austria due to the economic crises and the Nazi regime, von Mises came to the UNITED STATES where his book, *Human Action*, appeared in 1949 and remains the economic treatise that defines the school.

Schumpeter's notoriety relates to his sensational book, *Theory of Economic Development*, representing the first analysis of capitalism's inherent dynamism: The ENTREPRENEUR becomes the crucial part of the economic system, his or her innovations constantly revive the capitalist market system, naturally never in equilibrium. Schumpeter is considered the economist of the 1990s, since his theories contributed to a smoother transition from socialism to capitalism in post-communist economies. A Schumpeterian process does not start on its own. Framework conditions are necessary, including a functioning financial sector, a certain level of education and motivation of the population, as well as a certain pro-capitalist value system.

With von Mises, many other Austrian economists of the so-called Third Generation including von Hayek (1889–1992), Oskar Morgenstern (1902–76), Gottfried von Haberler (1900–) and Fritz Machlup (1902–83) went to the United States and taught at universities such as Princeton, Harvard, or Columbia. Von Hayek can be considered as the central leader of conservative economists, and later became a prime opponent of Keynesian economics, publishing books on exchange rates, capital theory, and monetary reform. His popular book, *Road to Serfdom*, helped revive the classical liberal movement in America after the NEW DEAL and World War II. In his writings, von Hayek particularly attacked mixed economies, "the muddle of the middle," defending at the same time a spontaneous order, the rule of law, the necessary cultural preconditions for a market economy, and social minimum standards.

In 1982, Machlup summarized six main tenets of the Austrian School encompassing methodological individualism; methodological subjectivism; marginalism; tastes and preferences; opportunity costs; and time structure of consumption and production that entered mainstream economics.

Israel M. Kirchner (1930–) together with Murray N. ROTHBARD (1926–) and James M. BUCHANAN (1919–) belong to the Fourth (American) Generation of the Austrian School. They define two tenets, namely markets as process and radical uncertainty that distinguish the Austrian School from mainstream thought. For this latter generation, as well as the Fifth and Sixth Generations of Austrian economists (including Rizzo, Lavoie, Garrison, White, Block and Salerno as well as Selgin, Boettke, Horwitz and Prychitko) the ideas spelled out particularly by Von Mises and Hayek became the framework for an alternative paradigm in economic science and have thus reborn the Austrian School as a distinct school of economic thought, further developing capital-based macroeconomics and trade cycle theory.

BIBLIOGRAPHY. Ludwig Von Mises, *Human Action: A Treatise on Economics* (Mises Institute, 1998); Joseph Alois Schumpeter, *Theory of Economic Development: An Inquiry into Profits, Capital, Credit, Interest and the Business Cycle* (Transaction Publishing, 1983); Carl Menger, *Principles of Economics* (Libertarian Press, 1994); Peter Boettke and Peter Leeson, "Austrian School of Economics: 1950–2000," www.gmu.edu; Ludwig von Mises, "Address at New York University Faculty Club," May 1962, www.mises.org.

URSULA A. VAVRIK, PH.D.
UNIVERSITY OF ECONOMICS, VIENNA, AUSTRIA

autarky

A SITUATION WHERE A country does not TRADE with other nations is referred to as an autarky. The immediate implication is that an autarkic country can consume only what it produces.

Theoretically, exceptionally high transportation and communication costs could make a country autarkic. In practice, however, in at least the last few centuries these costs have not been high enough to fully prevent a country from trading. Therefore, in practice a country can become autarkic only as a result of extremely restrictive trade policies.

A government may, for instance, simply enforce direct restrictions to block trade. Alternatively, it may impose trade barriers high enough to fully discourage trade with outsiders. A country may become autarkic involuntarily as well, in the event all other countries, perhaps motivated by political and diplomatic strains, decide to stop trading with it.

Throughout history, and especially in recent years, the concept of autarky has become mainly theoretical. The last country that could have been characterized as an approximate autarky was Albania, which adopted an increasingly strict policy of self-reliance from 1945 until 1991, when it rejected its isolationist socialist regime. Albania's economic inward orientation reflected, essentially, its government's political orientation at that time.

Despite its practical irrelevance, the concept of autarky is analytically very helpful. It is by comparing autarky relative prices—that is, the relative prices countries would face in the absence of trade—that one can theoretically determine countries' comparative advantages (a key concept in international trade), and the resulting pattern of trade among them. The concept of autarky is useful as well to highlight the gains from its antipode, free trade. In fact, most international trade textbooks rely heavily on the contrast between autarky and free trade to draw attention to the effects of the latter. It can be used as a benchmark in sophisticated analyses as well. A recent example is Philip Levy (1997), who analyzes the impact of free trade areas on the political support for liberalization at the multilateral level.

BIBLIOGRAPHY. Max Kreinin, *International Economics: A Policy Approach* (South-Western, 2003); Paul R. Krugman and Maurice Obstfeld, *International Economics: Theory and Policy* (Addison Wesley, 2003); Philip Levy, "A Political Economic Analysis of Free Trade Agreements," *American Economic Review* (v.87/4, 1997).

EMANUEL ORNELAS, PH.D.
UNIVERSITY OF GEORGIA

automobiles

THE KEY MANUFACTURING SECTOR for many nations in the 20th century, the automobile has transformed everyday life in most regions of the world, from transportation and travel to social customs and domestic life, even affecting national economic planning. Nowhere have the automobile's effects been more apparent than in North America, where car ownership consistently ranked as the highest in the world after 1900. Despite its mass popularity with consumers, however, the automobile has been blamed for some of the scourges of the 20th century: suburban sprawl, air pollution, and declining social cohesion.

From craft production to mass production. The modern automobile—typically a four-wheeled vehicle powered by a gasoline- or diesel-fueled, internal combustion engine—dates to the last decades of the 19th century. Germans Gottlieb Daimler and Karl Benz were two of the first European inventors to conduct successful trial runs of automobiles in 1885 and 1886. Within five years, Benz earned the distinction of becoming the first automobile manufacturer in the world. In 1893, Charles and Frank Duryea staged a pioneering automobile run in the UNITED STATES in Springfield, Massachusetts. Two years later, the first auto race in the Americas took place to great public acclaim. The interest translated into strong consumer demand for the new "horseless carriages," and the Duryeas became the first American automobile manufacturers in 1897.

By the turn of the century more than 30 other companies joined them in selling over 2,500 cars annually. In 1900, about 8,000 automobiles were registered in the United States. Like their European counterparts, American models were expensive—essentially luxurious, motorized carriages—and considered a plaything of the rich.

In 1901, Ransom E. Olds produced the first cars aimed at the lower-priced market, the Oldsmobile, which retailed for about $650. Olds was joined in the mid-priced market by Henry FORD, who founded the FORD MOTOR COMPANY in 1903. The success of Ford's Model N, which sold for $700 in 1907, proved that automakers could succeed by selling to a broader range of consumers. Ford sold over 8,000 Model Ns in 1907-8 and amassed a million-dollar profit. By WORLD WAR I, the Ford Motor Company was the world's largest automobile maker due to the success of the Model T, which debuted in 1908–09. More than any other car of its era, the Model T revolutionized the automobile industry and transformed American society.

Ford's first plant, on Mack Avenue in Detroit, Michigan, was essentially an assembly site for components produced elsewhere. Ford's car bodies, for example, were built by the Dodge Brothers before being sent to the Mack Avenue assembly line. Ford streamlined many of the operations on the assembly line and began to produce many of the automobile components himself in order to guarantee their delivery and keep production flowing. It was not until Ford built his Highland Park, Michigan, plant in 1909 that mass production of automobiles began in earnest. Under the system that came to be known as "Fordism," each task on the assembly line was simplified and routinized, de-skilling each step and lessening Ford's dependence on more expensive, skilled labor. Wherever machines could be used in place of human labor, Ford made the technological investment. His managers also experimented endlessly with the pace of the production line, seeking the highest possible rate of production without jeopardizing the quality of the final product.

To contemporary observers, Ford's Highland Park plant seemed a technological and managerial marvel. To those who worked there, though, the place was dehumanizing, the work monotonous, and the pace brutalizing. By 1913, the daily absentee rate at Highland Park stood at 10 percent and the annual turnover rate reached 380 percent. Searching for solutions, Ford hit upon the idea of a major wage increase, that he publicized as an unprecedented "Five-Dollar Day" for Ford workers. Although the widely praised Five-Dollar Day was actually comprised of the same $2.34 base wage that had previously been in place, it contained a profit-sharing provision that indeed brought some workers' wages to the five-dollar-a-day level. Other automobile manufacturers were soon forced to match Ford's wages, but Ford reaped most of the publicity; his act seemed almost philanthropic and he was even accused of "spoiling" his workers. The high wages of the American automobile industry, however, which remained its hallmark for generations, came at the price for workers of ceding control of their labor on the assembly line. The issue was revisited after World War II, when Walter Reuther of the United Automobile Workers (UAW) union attempted to gain a voice for labor in production and management decisions, but latter-day Fordism prevailed.

Although Ford was no philanthropist in raising his workers' wages, his announcement of the Five-Dollar Day in January, 1914, brought thousands of workers and their families into the consumer class for mass-production items such as automobiles. In the 1920s, about 47 percent of Ford workers were car owners, a figure that dwarfed the rate of car ownership for other unskilled, working-class groups in the United States and seemed impossible to imagine in any other country.

Competition and the rise of General Motors. Between 1900 and 1910 the number of automobile registrations jumped from about 8,000 to 469,000 in the United

States. Despite the rapid and continuous growth in sales, the industry itself was characterized by volatility and uncertainty. At least three hundred of the five hundred automobile companies that set up shop between 1900 and 1908 in North America went out of business. The typical fledgling automaker during this period was undercapitalized and under constant—and unreasonable—demands for quick returns by its investors, most of who saw the new industry as a speculative venture. After Olds and Ford started drastically increasing production on their assembly lines, most other auto makers were unable to keep up the pace necessary to compete in the industry. With capital requirements for larger factories, more tools and machines, and—eventually—higher wages even for unskilled workers, the barriers to entering the auto market became prohibitive for all but the most determined—and well-funded—prospective manufacturer.

A cartel of 32 manufacturers further attempted to limit new entrants into the industry by enforcing the Selden Patent, which appeared to retain the rights to all gasoline-engine-powered automobiles, in the first decade of the 20th century. By the time the Selden Patent was voided by a court in 1911, largely on the efforts of Henry Ford, the Association of Licensed Automobile Manufacturers (ALAM) had driven or bought out several smaller auto companies. The lead advocate of the ALAM, William C. Durant, soon emerged as Ford's chief competitor in the industry as the founder of GENERAL MOTORS (GM), organized in 1908 after merging several automobile lines.

Although GM shared the basics of Fordism in its manufacturing, the company took a different approach to marketing. In contrast to Ford, who relied on lowering the price of the Model T in the 1920s to gain market share, GM presented an entire line of automobiles across the consumer market. The luxurious Cadillac, aimed at the high-end market, was followed by the Buick and Oldsmobile, also marketed to the established professional class, the Pontiac, for the upwardly mobile middle-class, and the Chevrolet, an economy car that competed most directly for Ford buyers. Annual style updates, usually mere cosmetic changes, also generated consumer interest in GM's new models each year. The biggest contrast between Ford and GM, however, was the installment-buying that GM offered through its General Motors Acceptance Corporation, which it established as its consumer-credit arm in 1919. By 1921, about half of American cars were purchased on installment and GM succeeded Ford as the country's largest auto maker in 1930; Ford later battled with the Chrysler Corporation for second place among American automobile manufacturers.

Along with Chrysler, Ford and GM comprised the "Big Three" American automakers. A few smaller, "independent" automakers continued to struggle along in North America, but the Big Three's market share was not seriously challenged from the 1930s through the 1970s. GM had 43 percent of the American auto market in 1936, with Chrysler holding 25 percent and Ford holding 22 percent. The remaining 10 percent of the market was held by a few independent companies—Hudson, Packard, Studebaker, and Willys among them—that would merge or disappear altogether by the 1960s.

Unionization in the American auto industry. Through installment-buying and a generally prosperous economy, most American automobile manufacturers enjoyed steady sales and profits through the 1920s. In contrast, the decade of the Great DEPRESSION brought an abrupt downturn to the industry. GM stock went from a high of $91 a share in 1929 to $13 per share in 1933. The industry was also rocked by the demands for union representation in its plants, which gathered in force after President Franklin D. ROOSEVELT's administration implemented such NEW DEAL measures as the National Recovery Act of June 1933 and the Wagner Labor Relations Act of 1935.

Seeking job security, higher wages, and improved working conditions, many auto workers attempted to

By the late 1990s, the automobile added $100 billion annually in gross domestic product to the American economy.

form independent labor unions to engage in collective bargaining with the auto makers. Workers were met with a brutal, and sometimes patently illegal, response by almost every automaker. After trying to allay the unionization impulse by forming company-controlled employee relations programs (ERPs), the Big Three resorted to intimidation—sometimes including physical violence—legal maneuvering, and public-relations campaigns throughout the 1930s. A strike wave that began in 1934 culminated in a series of sit-down strikes in GM plants throughout the Midwest in the winter of 1936–37, in which workers occupied GM property and refused to move until their union gained recognition by management.

Although the sit-down strikes were illegal, federal and state governments refused to remove the strikers and GM capitulated, becoming the first of the Big Three to recognize the United Auto Workers (UAW) union as the collective bargaining agent of its work force. With the collective bargaining agreement between the Ford Motor Company and the UAW of June, 1941, the unionization of the Big Three was essentially complete.

In exchange for agreeing to a no-strike pledge during WORLD WAR II, the UAW completed the unionization of the entire auto industry by the end of the war. The postwar era in the auto industry focused, then, not on the issues of the right to collective bargaining, but rather on how far the process would go in terms of wages, benefits, and working conditions. The UAW attempted to modify the Ford arrangement of higher wages in exchange for ceding managerial control of the shop floor, which they had established even before the union came into existence. Although the union introduced the topic of managerial decision-making into collective bargaining throughout the 1940s, it failed to make headway on the issue. The legal climate, which had been more favorable to labor's agenda in the 1930s and during World War II, had again turned against labor again with the passage of the Taft-Hartley Act of 1947, which limited labor's ability to engage in general strikes and other collective actions.

It was the 1950 agreement between General Motors and the UAW, publicized as the "Treaty of Detroit," that formed the outlines of collective bargaining for the next generation in the American automobile industry. In exchange for improved wages and benefits—including cost-of-living adjustments, pensions, and health care provisions—automakers retained all managerial prerogatives, including production and investment decisions. The framework of the Treaty of Detroit allowed automakers to enjoy a measure of stability in their work force and autoworkers to expand their wage and benefits packages in succeeding years. Supplemental unemployment benefits were added to collective bargaining agreements between the UAW and the Big Three in 1955 and early retirement provisions came into effect in 1964.

The golden age of the automobile. The 1950s and 1960s were the golden age of the American automobile industry as it shared in the nearly continuous economic prosperity in North America. Foreign automakers, recovering from the devastation of World War II, had not yet geared up major exporting efforts, and instead concentrated on rebuilding their domestic markets. Although sales of the German Volkswagen Beetle were on the rise, there was little foreign competition in North America, particularly among the ranks of the most profitable, full-sized luxury cars that dominated the marketplace. Despite the publicity over consumer advocate Ralph Nader's *Unsafe at Any Speed* in 1965, automakers concentrated more on annual style updates on the larger, more profitable models, instead of technological and safety innovations or the introduction of smaller, more efficient cars in the 1960s.

Not that most North American consumers *wanted* smaller cars. One of the last of the independent automakers, Studebaker, tried to capture the small-car market with its Lark in the early 1960s and was out of business by 1965. Another independent, Nash Motors, had somewhat better success with its Rambler line; it managed to stave off bankruptcy by merging with some of the other independents to form the American Motors Corporation in 1959. The Big Three occasionally made forays into the small-car market, but its most notable effort, the Chevrolet Corvair, ended in an unqualified disaster.

After Nader exposed crucial design flaws in the car—with its rear-wheel drive and concentration of weight in the rear part of the vehicle, the Corvair had an increased chance of rolling over if a driver lost control while turning—General Motors eased the car out of production, even though it had corrected the problem in its later-model Corvairs. GM's heavy-handed tactics against Nader, including the use of private detectives to dig up dirt on the irrepressible crusader, backfired when the company was forced to pay a settlement to its adversary for its questionable actions.

Although some consumers turned away from the Big Three's products, foreign automakers held just 5 percent of the American market in 1963. By 1971, however, their share had increased to 16 percent, an ominous trend once gasoline prices skyrocketed after the ORGANIZATION OF PETROLEUM EXPORTING COUNTRIES (OPEC) oil embargoes of the early 1970s. Although many of the imported autos were luxury makes such as the Mercedes-Benz or sports cars from Fiat or MG, increasingly they were fuel-efficient Japanese models from Honda and Toyota.

Consumerism and criticism. Critics of the automobile also accused the industry of fostering detrimental long-range social trends, including urban sprawl. The 1970 U.S. Census revealed that for the first time in American history, more people lived in suburban areas than in cities or on farms. It was a trend that began with the post-World War II building boom, when returning veterans and their growing families took advantage of high wages, low interest rates, and a booming economy to buy their piece of the American Dream: a new home. The federal government encouraged Americans to buy their own homes with low-interest loans through the Veterans Administration, and by investing billions of dollars in a new interstate highway system. As a result, 83 percent of America's population growth took place in the suburbs between 1950–70. Almost all of the new suburbanites required an automobile to take them from their homes to shopping centers, schools, and places of work.

Critics of suburbanization duly noted that the new developments took up huge amounts of land, much of it in prime agricultural areas, and made automobile ownership a necessity, as most cities did not expand their mass transit operations into suburban areas. As social critics castigated the typical suburbanite as an apolitical conformist, obsessed with status symbols and fitting in, the American luxury cruiser came to symbolize the materialism and superficiality of American life.

The energy crisis. On October 6, 1973, EGYPT and SYRIA launched a military offensive against ISRAEL in a conflict that came to be known as the Yom Kippur War, after the Jewish holy day that marked the conflict's first day. After the United States came to Israel's aid, the seven Arab nations in OPEC announced an oil embargo against Israel's supporters, including the United States, JAPAN, and most western European countries. The embargo, lasting from October 1973 to March 1974, created fundamental changes in the global economy and had an immediate impact on American society as well. In 1967, 2.2 million barrels of oil were imported each day that represented 19 percent of American oil consumption. On the eve of the energy crisis in late 1973, America imported six million barrels of oil a day—36 percent of its total oil consumption.

The most visible change induced by the oil embargo was the long lines at gas pumps around the country; only during World War II had gasoline been rationed, and gas prices had remained low in the United States by world standards since then. Suddenly, the average American had to contend with a peacetime gasoline shortage; when there was gas, its price had increased by 40 percent in just a few months. The American economy, which had been built in large part upon the availability of cheap oil, experienced a sharp recession.

Along with the INFLATION triggered by higher energy prices, a period of "stagflation"—an economic downturn accompanied by persistent inflation and unemployment—shook the confidence of the American consumer in 1973 and 1974. After another price hike by OPEC near the end of the decade, energy prices rose an additional 60 percent, contributing to a 14 percent U.S. inflation rate in 1979.

It seemed that the American Dream—symbolized by a new home in a far-flung suburb with an ever-larger automobile in the driveway—had reached the end of the road. The energy crisis thus led to a fundamental reevaluation of the typical American's lifestyle. Conservation and fuel efficiency became the bywords of the new era, accompanied by an uncertainty about the country's economic prospects and its ability to influence the foreign policies of OPEC members.

Although domestic automobile manufacturers later blamed unfair trade regulations and a supposedly high wage rate for their slumping competitiveness in the 1970s, their own decisions had laid the groundwork for the decline. In the days of little foreign competition, cheap gasoline, and a ready consumer market, the Big Three had passed numerous opportunities to diversify their product lineup to include additional smaller models. Convinced that the American driver would never purchase an economy car, even the smaller-sized, less expensive domestic makes were sold as aspiring full-sized luxury cars.

Reorganization and internationalization. Scrambling to recapture their market share throughout the 1970s, American automakers responded with a series of cost-cutting measures that undermined their relationship with their work force. In addition to speeding up production lines in older factories, auto makers attempted to replace workers with robotic machines in their newer plants. The Big Three also relocated many of their parts and assembly plants in non-unionized, lower-wage locations outside of the United States. Although GM had operated factories outside the States since the 1920s to serve various domestic markets, it now made autos for the American market in its international plants. By 1980, GM operated 23 plants outside of the United States, a trend followed by the other members of the Big Three. Although some consumers responded with a "Buy American" campaign in the 1980s, the trend toward foreign assembly and components production continued unabated.

In contrast, foreign automakers such as Honda, Mercedes-Benz, Subaru-Isuzu, and Toyota invested billions of dollars to build assembly plants in the United States in the 1980s and 1990s, beginning with Honda's operation of a plant in Marysville, Ohio, in November 1982. Rejecting attempts by the UAW to unionize their work forces, the so-called "transplant" producers instead focused on quality circles and other employee-involvement programs to boost production and morale in their plants. As of 1998, over 990,000 full-time workers were employed in the automobile manufacturing sector; those in the Big Three largely remained unionized, while only those in joint-manufacturing operations among the transplant companies were unionized.

The 1990s were generally favorable to the North American auto industry, which remained a major contributor to the American economy with over $105 billion added to the GROSS DOMESTIC PRODUCT (GDP) in 1998 alone. While Ford and Chrysler seemed to adapt to the demands of lean manufacturing to remain competitive and offered numerous successful smaller models, however, GM was often criticized for organizational disarray and lackluster product development. In 1991 and 1992, the company was estimated to have lost $15 billion in North America alone. Even its attempts to diversify its core businesses by purchasing Hughes Aircraft and Electronic Data Systems kicked off a storm of controversy and criticism. Like their transplant counterparts, however, American automakers (still known as the Big Three, even after Chrysler's purchase by Daimler-Benz in 1997) continued to emphasize the principles of total quality management to achieve impressive results over the past two decades.

Indeed, by the late 1990s the automobile industry added $100 billion in GDP to the American economy. The automobile industry also fostered a rising standard of living for its workers by paying wages that ranked at the top of the industrial sector, a trend that had begun with Henry Ford's announcement of a Five-Dollar Day in 1914. The industry's almost complete unionization by 1941, however, was even more crucial in establishing the autoworker's reputation among the elite of industrial workers. In addition to its economic and technological accomplishments, so too did the industry transform the social and cultural life of the American nation.

With almost 208 million motor vehicles registered in the United States in 1997, the country ranked as the most automobile-dependent nation on earth, with almost 458 cars per 1,000 persons.

BIBLIOGRAPHY. Donald T. Critchlow, *Studebaker: The Life and Death of an American Corporation* (Indiana University Press, 1996); James J. Flink, *The Automobile Age* (MIT Press, 1988); Robert Freeland, *The Struggle for Control of the Modern Corporation: Organizational Change at General Motors, 1924–1970* (Cambridge University Press, 2000); Laurie Graham, *On the Line at Subaru-Isuzu: The Japanese Model and the American Worker* (Cornell University Press, 1995); Ben Hamper, *Rivethead: Tales from the Assembly Line* (1991); Paul Ingrassia and Joseph B. White, *Comeback: The Fall and Rise of the American Automobile Industry* (Warner Books, 1994); Kenneth T. Jackson, *Crabgrass Frontier: The Suburbanization of the United States*, (Oxford University Press, 1985); Maryann Keller, *Rude Awakening: The Rise, Fall, and Struggle for Recovery of General Motors* (William Morrow and Company, 1989).

TIMOTHY G. BORDEN, PH.D.
INDEPENDENT SCHOLAR

Aviva

HEADQUARTERED IN LONDON, ENGLAND, Aviva places seventh in the list of the world's largest insurance groups, one of the top five insurance companies in Europe and the UNITED KINGDOM's top insurer (*Fortune* magazine estimates). While 50 percent of its business lies in the UK, Aviva also has strong markets in AUSTRALIA, CANADA, FRANCE, IRELAND, ITALY, the NETHERLANDS, POLAND and SPAIN. Besides offering general insurance, its two other main activities include the services of long-term savings and fund management. It has worldwide premium income and investment sales of £28 billion from ongoing operations, plus more than £200 billion in assets under management. According to July 2002 figures, it had 25 million customers with 68,000 employees.

Formerly called CGNU Insurance, Aviva created a new name that "represents part of the group's planned journey towards being recognized as a world-class financial services provider." As of July 1, 2002, the Aviva brand brought together 50 different trading units from around the world to generate further opportunities to harness the benefits of size and international advantage.

Envisioned change is significant, allowing Aviva to make more of the corporate brand, benefit its trading businesses, and fine-tune marketing, advertising, and sponsor relationships.

By the close of 2001, Aviva's operating profit (before tax) was up 41 percent and new business increased 10 percent. At mid-year 2002, these figures remained steady, and Aviva reported $52 billion in annual 2001 revenue.

BIBLIOGRAPHY. "Global 500: The World's Largest Companies," *Fortune* (July, 2002); Aviva *Annual Reports*, www.aviva.com.

JOSEPH GERINGER
SYED B. HUSSAIN, PH.D.
UNIVERSITY OF WISCONSIN, OSHKOSH

AXA

WHEN CLAUDE BÉBÉAR TOOK OVER at Anciennes Mutuelles, a regional French insurer, no one would have believed that it would one day be one of the world's major financial companies. Bébéar made a reputation for acquiring distressed companies, making a specialty of turning around businesses that others thought were hopeless.

His first large coup was taking over Drouot, one of FRANCE's largest insurers, in 1982 even as the newly elected government mulled nationalizing the industry. In 1985, he renamed the company, foreseeing a world financial role: AXA is not an abbreviation but a simple name that can be pronounced in many languages.

In 1991 AXA made its first large foray into the United States, securing the Equitable (hit by huge losses in real estate and junk bonds) with its Donaldson, Lufkin & Jenrette trading group. In 1996 AXA took over the larger Union des Assurances de Paris (UAP) in a merger that catapulted AXA into the world's top league of insurers.

Fortune magazine ranked AXA as the 31st largest company in the world in 2003, with revenues exceeding $62 billion.

BIBLIOGRAPHY. AXA *Annual Reports,* www.axa.com; "Global 500: World's Largest Companies," *Fortune* (July, 2002).

KEVIN R FOSTER, PH.D.
CITY COLLEGE OF NEW YORK

B

Bahamas

THE COMMONWEALTH of the Bahamas is located on the northwest edge of the West Indies, and is comprised of approximately 700 islands and cays and more than 2,000 rock formations. The capital is Nassau, located on New Providence Island. Other islands include Grand Bahama, with the cities of Freeport and West End, and Great Inagua Island.

In 2002, the population of the Bahamas was approximately 300,000 and concentrated in the urban centers of Nassau and Freeport. The population is largely of African descent, a result of the Bahamas' early days as a slave-trading center, with a minority descended from English settlers, as well as from Syrians, Greeks, Haitians, and other West Indians. English is the native language and Creole is spoken among Haitians. Due to immigration from the United States and other West Indian islands, the Bahamas' rate of population growth is substantially greater than the Caribbean average.

In 1492, Christopher Columbus landed in the Bahamas. However it was not until the mid-1600s that a permanent European settlement was established by the British. In 1964, the Bahamas was granted internal autonomy and in 1973 it was granted independence.

Until the mid-1900s, farming and fishing were the major economic activities. Since attaining independence, the Bahamas has become a stable, developing nation with an economy heavily dependent on tourism and offshore banking. Due to a wonderful climate and beautiful beaches, the Bahamas is one of the most popular year-round travel destinations in the western hemisphere. Tourism continues to grow and has led to a boom in construction of hotels, resorts, and residences, and to solid economic growth. Tourism accounts for more than 60 percent of the GROSS DOMESTIC PRODUCT (GDP) and directly or indirectly employs approximately half of the country's labor force.

Because of favorable tax laws, the Bahamas has become a growing international financial center, and banking has become its second most important industry. Manufacturing, agriculture, and industry, including the production of petroleum, salt, and rum, contribute about one-tenth of the GDP and show minimal growth. The Bahamas is also a major shipping point for illegal drugs and its territory is used for smuggling illegal immigrants into the UNITED STATES.

In the short run, overall economic growth prospects rest heavily on the tourism industry, which itself depends on growth in the United States, the major source of tourists who visit the Bahamas.

BIBLIOGRAPHY. Paul Albury, *The Story of the Bahamas* (Macmillan, 1975); Michael Craton, *A History of the Bahamas* (Media Enterprises Ltd, 1986); Michael Craton and Gail Saunders, *Islanders in the Stream: A History of the Bahamian People: From the Ending of Slavery to the 21st Century* (University of Georgia Press, 1998); *CIA World Factbook* (2002).

S.J. RUBEL, J.D.
INDEPENDENT SCHOLAR

Bahrain

THE KINGDOM OF BAHRAIN is an archipelago in the Persian Gulf consisting of 33 islands, only six of which are inhabited. Its capital is Manama, and it is a constitutional hereditary monarchy in the form of an emirate with an executive-cabinet form of government and a separate judiciary.

The emir, or head of state, is also supreme commander of the Bahrain Defense Force (BDF). Although the king has substantial executive powers, in practice he has delegated decision-making authority to a cabinet since 1956, when a decree created the Administrative Council, an 11-member body that advised the ruler on policy and supervised the growing bureaucracy.

In 1970, this was transformed into a 12-member Council of Ministers. The president of the Council of Ministers, the prime minister, serves as the head of government. The emir appoints the prime minister, who then forms a government by selecting members of the Council of Ministers, albeit in consultation with the emir. The ministers are directly responsible to the prime minister, who, like the emir, has authority to veto a decision by any member of the council. Bahrain formally gained its independence from the UNITED KINGDOM in 1971.

Unlike other Persian Gulf countries, Bahrain possesses minimal oil reserves, but has become an international banking center and is involved with petroleum processing and refining.

The constitution was suspended in 1975; amended and ratified again in 2001. Bahrain has a high rate of literacy of 88 percent. Both men and women over the age of 18 may vote. Islam is the official religion and its judicial system is based partly on Islamic law and English Common Law. Bahrain has a mixed economy with government control of many basic industries. However, the emir is slowly privatizing all industries and reforming the political system.

With a population of just over 650,000 in 2001, Bahrain had a GROSS DOMESTIC PRODUCT (GDP) of $8.4 billion.

BIBLIOGRAPHY. The Department of State Background Note, www.state.gov; *CIA World Factbook* (2002); "Bahrain, A Country Study," The Library of Congress, lcweb2.loc.gov.

LINDA L. PETROU, PH.D.
HIGH POINT UNIVERSITY

Bank of America

BANK OF AMERICA IS THE THIRD LARGEST bank in the United States with assets of $638 billion (2002). It derives 92 percent of its revenues from domestic operations in 21 states and the District of Columbia making it the nation's largest consumer bank—a fact that would have surely given its founder, A.P. Giannini, a great deal of pleasure.

A.P. (Amadeo Peter) Giannini (1870–1949), known as the father of retail banking and one of the industry's great innovators, led the Bank of America through its first five decades. He was born in San Jose, California, and by age 31, had already made his fortune as a produce wholesaler. While serving as a director for a local bank in San Francisco, Giannini realized that the financial needs of the burgeoning population of Italian immigrants located in city's North Beach neighborhood was being ignored and he urged the bank to extend its services to "the little people." The bank's leaders did not see any profit potential in small customers and refused to implement his ideas. Frustrated, Giannini organized his own bank and on October 15, 1904, Bank of Italy (eventually to become Bank of America) opened for business.

Bank of Italy was the first to cater to an immigrant population previously forced to go to loan sharks and hide their savings in their homes. Many of Bank of Italy's early patrons had never been inside a bank before and did not speak or write English. At a time when bankers toiled behind closed doors and ignored the working class, Giannini placed his desk on the lobby floor and took to the streets to convince the local residents to put their savings in his bank. He advertised his bank's willingness to make loans under $100 and employed Italian-speaking tellers. He also insisted that Bank of Italy's stock be widely distributed among local investors and he limited the bank's directors and executives to 100 shares each of the initial 3,000-share offering.

Bank of Italy's reputation in San Francisco was secured during the Great Earthquake and Fire of 1906, which destroyed the city, including the bank's offices as well as 3,700 of North Beach's 4,000 residences. Seeing opportunity in the disaster, Giannini made a great show of setting up a makeshift counter on the Washington Street wharf and proclaiming the bank open for business. He extended loans to ship captains to bring in loads of lumber and to local residents who were struggling to restore their homes and businesses. As a result, North Beach became the first area of the city to rebuild. Giannini became a local hero and customers flocked to the bank.

Once Giannini proved the efficacy of his business model, he quickly extended it to other underserved ethnic groups. Bank of Italy created departments to cater to Chinese, Greek, Portuguese, Slovenian, Spanish, Latin, and Russian immigrants.

Giannini's greatest ambition, and the challenge that would consume him until his death, was the establishment of branch banking. At that time, the industry was composed of many independent banks and the only branches that existed were local offices in the same city as the parent bank. A wider system of branches was illegal in many states and in others, such as California, was dependent on the permission of state regulators.

Nevertheless, Giannini envisioned Bank of Italy as a statewide system of branches that would serve all of California. He understood that the branch system would create a wide and ever-growing deposit base for Bank of Italy and enable it to offer a higher level of financial services to smaller towns and cities. Thus, in October 1909, Bank of Italy acquired the Commercial and Savings Bank of San Jose and established it as its first branch outside of San Francisco. Giannini had set in motion a strategy of acquisition and expansion that put the Bank of Italy at odds with its industry as well as state and federal governments.

Over the next two decades, Bank of Italy, under Giannini's generalship, used savvy strategies to create new branches. In order to gain branch approvals from state officials, it acquired many ailing independent banks, extending its reach while bolstering the condition of the state banking system. When state officials refused to approve further growth, the bank used legal loopholes to form new companies that were outside the scope of state authority and established the branches under federal authority. When neither state nor federal authorities would approve further growth, the bank took its case to the courts. Bank of Italy's competitors often complained bitterly about its expansion, but the bank's aggressive sales force and exceptional service made it a success with consumers throughout California.

In 1927, with the passage of the McFadden Act, Giannini was able to unite all of the companies he had formed in order to expand as one entity, Bank of Italy National Trust and Savings Association. It was the third largest bank in the United States with 276 branches in 199 communities. In the process, it became a primary lender for California's agriculture and movie industries.

Unsatisfied, Giannini turned his sights toward creating a national branch banking system. In 1929, he created a holding company named Transamerica Corporation and used it to begin buying banks across the country. Planning to retire, he turned over the leadership of Transamerica to two executives recruited from outside the bank, who promised to carry on his program of expansion. During the Great DEPRESSION, however, the new leaders announced plans to sell off many of the company's banks. Giannini returned with a vengeance to defend his vision. He waged a successful proxy battle and regained control of the bank in 1932.

By 1945, the year Giannini retired, his bank was the largest in the United States with just over $5 billion in assets. The bank's asset base and the strong corporate culture that Giannini had fostered put it in an excellent position to profit from the growth of California and emergence of the United States as a global superpower. By 1957, the bank boasted $10 billion in assets. In 1958, it introduced the BankAmericard credit card (now known as Visa). The 1960s and 1970s brought a grow-ing wave of international expansion. In 1968, a new holding company named BankAmerica Corp. was formed and by 1979, it held $108 billion in assets.

BankAmerica remained the nation's largest bank until 1980. By then, international lending had become a minefield as countries, such as BRAZIL and MEXICO, began defaulting on their loans. Many major banks, including BankAmerica, incurred billions of dollars in losses as their loans were restructured. The 1980s also brought the deregulation of the banking industry, which radically altered the competitive environment. The bank's leadership had not foreseen these developments and it staggered through the decade. By 1989, its assets were $98 billion, $20 billion less than a decade before.

By 1990, the bank's downward trend stabilized and it began to grow once again. In 1992, BankAmerica set off a round of industry consolidation when it made the largest banking acquisition to that date, the purchase of California's Security Pacific. In 1993, it acquired Texas-based First Gibraltar. By 1997, its asset base had grown to $260 billion and it was the fourth largest bank in the United States.

In 1998, BankAmerica merged with the nation's third largest bank, Charlotte, North Carolina-based NationsBank. NationsBank dominated the merger. The headquarters of the combined banks was Charlotte and its new leader was NationsBank head Hugh McColl. The new bank was named Bank of America and held assets of $617 billion. A.P. Giannini's vision of a nationwide chain of branch banks operating under a single charter had finally been achieved.

BIBLIOGRAPHY. Marquis James and Bessie R. James, *Biography of a Bank: The Story of Bank of America* (Harper & Brothers, 1954); Felice A. Bonadio, *A.P. Giannini: Banker of America* (University of California Press, 1994); Moira Johnston, *Roller Coaster: the Bank of America and the Future of American Banking* (Ticknor & Fields, 1990); Ross Yockey, *McColl: The Man with America's Money* (Longstreet, 1999); Gary Hector, *Breaking the Bank: The Decline of Bank America* (Little, Brown, 1998); *Bank of America Fact Book* (www.bankofamerica.com).

THEODORE B. KINNI
INDEPENDENT SCHOLAR

Bank of England

THE BANK OF ENGLAND was chartered as a joint-stock company in 1694 to provide financial assistance to the British government for war efforts on the European continent. Over the next three centuries the Bank would shift from a private, profit-making enterprise to a government-owned CENTRAL BANK, and expand its role to become one of the most important financial institutions in the world.

Though not the oldest (that honor belongs to the Sverige Riksbank of Sweden, established in 1668), the Bank of England is internationally recognized as one of the premier central banks. A central bank is a monetary authority that oversees the banking, financial, and monetary affairs of a nation. Central banks (161 existed as of 1990) are very important for contemporary capitalism because they issue currency, oversee banking systems, implement exchange-rate policy, and conduct monetary policy. Although these responsibilities give these institutions tremendous power in manipulating economic performance, such was not always the case. The long history of the Bank of England provides an opportunity for examining the evolving role of central banking over recent centuries.

In the early years of its existence the Bank functioned as a private bank with important obligations to the British government. Indeed, the primary function of the Bank of England throughout the 18th century was financing government debt through the sale of securities. This was an era when modern central banking did not exist and the concepts of monetary policy and "lender of last resort" had yet to be conceived.

During the years when the UNITED KINGDOM followed the GOLD STANDARD (1816–1914 and 1925–31), the Bank of England was expected to convert its bank notes to gold on demand. This restriction limited the Bank's discretionary power to issue CURRENCY, however, it provided a clear rule that fostered confidence in the Bank's autonomy. Nonetheless, monetary crises throughout the first half of the 19th century led to increased regulation of the Bank's actions.

By the middle of the 19th century, the Bank had been granted the exclusive right to issue bank notes. This power helped shift the Bank's responsibility away from commercial operations and in the direction of serving the government and other banks. Financial crises in 1866 and 1890 raised awareness that the Bank of England should serve as "lender of last resort." In this capacity the Bank was expected to provide emergency liquidity to other institutions to address bank runs and panics.

With the demise of the gold standard in the early 20th century, the rationale for the Bank's independence disappeared. This change, coupled with the emergence of Keynesian economics after WORLD WAR II, raised new awareness of monetary policy as a political tool. With a greater interest in government control of the economy, the Bank of England was nationalized in 1946. For the next four decades, the government conducted monetary policy with the Bank's support. Not surprisingly, there was relatively little interest in restoring the autonomy the Bank enjoyed under the gold standard.

Recent studies of central banking practices around the world suggest greater bank autonomy is correlated with greater success against INFLATION. These studies have renewed the question of whether the Bank of England should enjoy greater freedom from the Treasury.

In 1993 and 1994 the British government instituted a series of reforms in this direction including formalizing monthly meetings between the Bank governor and the Chancellor of the Exchequer and giving the bank greater discretion in the timing of interest rate changes.

In 1997, the Bank was given responsibility for setting interest rates. This power, previously held by the Chancellor, was transferred to a newly created Monetary Policy Committee consisting of members of the Bank Governors and Bank Directors. The Monetary Policy Committee meets each month and immediately announces their interest rate decisions. This move is yet another step in the direction of greater Bank autonomy.

In the first decade of its fourth century, the Bank of England has a very different set of responsibilities than it did in 1694. Today's Bank views its first task as fighting inflation through monetary policy. In addition to this responsibility, the Bank implements the British government's exchange-rate policy, maintains foreign-exchange reserves, and is responsible for ensuring a sound and stable financial system including serving as the "lender of last resort" to the British banking system. This last responsibility has been tempered somewhat by the transfer of supervisory and regulatory powers from the Bank to the Financial Services Authority.

The Treaty on Economic and Monetary Unification (also known as the Maastricht Treaty) was negotiated in the early 1990s to establish European Monetary Unification. Monetary unification began January 1, 1999, and included the creation of the EURO currency (first issued in 2002) and the EUROPEAN CENTRAL BANK. As a member of the European Community, the United Kingdom participated in the treaty process. Although Britain endorses the idea of the European Central Bank and has indicated a desire to eventually join the European Monetary Unification, in early 2003 it had not yet done so.

Given the terms of the Maastricht Treaty, such a decision will require granting the Bank of England additional autonomy from the British government. With a history of Bank subordination to the government throughout the 20th century, such a move would be a dramatic change. Nonetheless, recent reforms suggest this direction is possible.

Clearly the future role of the Bank is tied to the evolution of central banking practices around the globe. More importantly, however, the future of the Bank of England seems strongly linked to the continuing issue of Bank autonomy and to the fate of the newly created European Central Bank.

BIBLIOGRAPHY. "The Bank of England Fact Sheet," (The Bank of England, 1988); H.V. Bowen, "The Bank of England During the Long Eighteenth Century, 1694–1820," Roberts, et al., eds., *The Bank of England: Money, Power and Influence, 1694–1994* (Oxford University Press, 1995); John Clapham, *The Bank of England: A History* (Cambridge University Press, 1966); Barry Eichengreen, *Globalizing Capital: A History of the International Monetary System* (Princeton University Press, 1996); John Giuseppi, *The Bank of England: A History from its Foundation in 1694* (Evans Brothers, 1966).

PATRICK DOLENC, PH.D.
KEENE STATE COLLEGE

Bank of France

FOUNDED JANUARY 18, 1800, by the administration of Napoleon Bonaparte, the Bank of France was part of a broader reorganization of the French state by Napoleon (including, for example, the establishment of a national legal code and departmental system), that aimed at creating a post-revolutionary nation state, combating the economic depression of the Revolutionary era, and invigorating the relatively weak French economy.

It had not escaped Napoleon's notice that dynamic European military and economic powers in the 18th century, such as England and the Netherlands, had benefited in many spheres from the creation of central banks. However, the first charter of the Bank of France did not accord it the status of a CENTRAL BANK, nor give it a monopoly on note issue, but instead limited its actions to the provision of credit and the issuing of notes in Paris. This charter established an administrative structure that placed great power in the hands of the two hundred largest shareholders, known as *Les deux cent familles*, who formed the General Assembly of the Bank. This term has since become synonymous in France with the idea that a powerful sociopolitical class controls the strings of the French economy, and this idea was given support by the fact that Napoleon, and many of his political associates, were among the first members of the General Assembly. In 1806–08 the Bank was reorganized, with the Governor and his deputies appointed directly by the Emperor. This move initiated a long-running debate, in common with other central banks, concerning the role of the state in the management of the Bank of France, and the extent to which it should be independent of government.

One might argue that this has been the central question in the history of the Bank of France, for the character of the Bank has certainly often changed according to the prevailing political orthodoxy on central bank independence at different moments in history.

The Bank gradually became a national, central bank in the period after 1848 when it began to expand its operations outside Paris. The Bank started to develop an extensive national branch network at this time, taking the place of many of the small regional banks that had collapsed in 1848. By 1900, the Bank had representation in 411 towns, including 120 full branches, and this regional spread also marked an extension of the bank's issuing powers. Economist Glyn Davies, among others, has suggested that "Owing to its very extensive network of branches and offices, [French] commercial banks have not developed as rigorously as their British or German counterparts." Margaret G. Myers notes that this period saw the origins of the entrenched rivalry between the larger, joint-stock commercial banks in France and the Bank of France, and observes that such competition was enhanced by the fact that larger commercial banks (unlike many private and provincial banks) had little influence on the governance of the Bank of France. Nevertheless, the scope and scale of operations of the Bank were limited compared with other central banks.

Before World War I, the Bank was relatively uninvolved in currency markets or in lending money abroad, and the chief task of the bank was the maintenance of a sense of macroeconomic stability, often through rediscounting for other banks, and through lending money to the French state in return for its issuing privileges. Suggestions have been made that the Bank was responsible for France's consistently low interest rates, though France's traditional position as a net exporter of capital offers another possible cause of those low rates.

The Popular Front government of 1936–38 began a process of democratization of the Bank that culminated in its nationalization in 1945. In 1936, more than 40,000 investors owned shares in the Bank, but this figure concealed the fact that most of its shares were held by a small number of institutions and individuals. The Popular Front government altered the administrative structure of the Bank, by increasing the number of regents appointed directly by government and by including one worker's representative.

In 1945, the Bank of France and the largest deposit banks were nationalized, along with other major economic entities such as Renault car company, the coal industry, and public utilities. Post-war French governments advocated a strong role for technocratic government in the rebuilding of the postwar economy, and in many respects they were successful in this aim, using the Bank of France in furthering such policies. In the postwar period the Bank continued its policy of limiting its role in managing the value of the franc, tracking the dollar for much of the period, before linking the value of the franc to that of the deutschmark. More recently, the franc has been incorporated into the EURO and the Bank of France forms one part of the European System of Central Banks that coordinates the management of monetary policy and common interest rates across the euro-zone. The Bank is also heavily involved in the management of the "zone franc" in 15 African states, and with other international networks such as the INTERNATIONAL MONETARY FUND (IMF) and the WORLD BANK.

The Bank retains its local functions, with an obligation to retain a branch in each French department (region), acting as an agent of the state in the receipt of taxes and the provision of detailed, economic data on the regions to central government. In theory, the Bank has been independent of government since 1993, but given its remit (which also includes the ensuring of price stability and the support of governmental economic policies such as the promotion of economic growth and job creation), it is hardly independent in any meaningful sense. One might, however, say that the Bank of France does have a clear sense of its mission and that it does function as a central bank, which was not true for much of its history.

BIBLIOGRAPHY. Glyn Davies, *A History of Money* (University of Wales Press, 2002); *Banque de France: Deux siècles d'histoire* (Paris); Margaret G. Myers *Paris as a Financial Centre* (Garland, 1936); Marjorie Deane and Robert Pringle, *The Central Banks* (Viking, 1994); Roger Price, *A Concise History of France* (Cambridge University Press, 1993).

WILLIAM GALLOIS, PH.D.
AMERICAN UNIVERSITY OF SHARJAH

Bank of Japan

THE CENTRAL BANK OF JAPAN, entrusted with the task of maintaining the stability of the Japanese currency (the YEN) and the country's financial system, the Bank of Japan (BOJ) was set up in 1882. It is a corporation whose legal status is governed by a special law (the most recent version enacted in 1998), and although the government owns 55 percent of BOJ shareholders' capital, the law makes BOJ independent (in particular, there is no provision in the law for shareholders' meetings). The governing body of BOJ is its Policy Board. The BOJ Governor is appointed by the Cabinet for the term of five years and has to be approved by the Parliament. By law, the Governor cannot be dismissed during the term of tenure except in some well-defined cases.

Japan's economy and its financial sector were devastated after the defeat in WORLD WAR II. Although the 1949 version of the law on the Bank of Japan formally gave it a certain degree of independence from the Ministry of Finance and the government, in practice BOJ acted as part of the broad government. In particular, the main goal of its monetary policy throughout the 1950s and 1960s was not so much price level stability as providing the economy with "money for growth."

With the Japanese economy growing very rapidly, private investment demand was so high, compared to the amount of savings that the economy could generate, that BOJ had to step in aggressively to support the market for corporate loans. The financing of investment by Japanese firms relied heavily on the country's banking system, which, lacking the necessary liquid resources, was itself in the state of "overlending," meaning that reserves were often negative. Under these circumstances, BOJ acted as a lender of last resort to commercial banks, but it also used its position as the banking system's most important creditor to impose certain limits on the credit lines extended by commercial banks (the so-called window guidance). Compared to this administrative guidance, other, more conventional methods of monetary policy, such as open market operations played a much smaller role (in particular, because the bonds market itself was very undeveloped).

Things changed dramatically when the era of high growth came to an end in the 1970s. The real growth rate in the Japanese economy declined sharply and so did private investment demand. Two oil shocks created significant inflationary pressures and also led to big government budget deficits and the issuance of large quantities of government bonds. BOJ was forced to change both the goals and the means of its monetary policy. Since the second half of the 1970s it had decisively shifted its focus to combating inflation. In the wake of reduced corporate investment demand, commercial banks no longer needed access to the BOJ line of credit to secure enough reserves, so that "window guidance" was no longer an option as an instrument of monetary policy either. Instead, BOJ started relying more and more on standard means of monetary policy, such as changing its official DISCOUNT RATE and using open market operations by utilizing the growing market for government bonds.

The new MONETARY POLICY initiated in the late 1970s was initially successful. Inflation was brought under control and economic growth resumed. There were different problems, however, and BOJ was slow in realizing the risks associated with deregulation and globalization of the Japanese capital markets. With real investment demand still much below that which had existed prior to the 1970s, Japanese corporations and wealthy individuals had amassed huge financial assets that sought profitable investment opportunities everywhere, from real estate in Japan to U.S. government bonds and foreign currency assets. Money supply was growing fast but BOJ, seeing no signs of consumer price inflation, failed to implement tighter monetary policy and curb the build-up of a speculative bubble.

On the last day of trading in 1989, the stock price index (NIKKEI 225) at the Tokyo stock exchange reached its all-time peak of 38,916 yen (13 years after that, on the last day of trading in 2002, it was down 78 percent at 8,579 yen). In the next year, the bubble burst, leading to the most protracted depression in the history of the Japanese economy, with the real growth rate averaging 1.4 percent over the period of 1991–2000. In response, BOJ implemented the zero-interest rate policy, supplying the economy with enough liquidity to keep long-term interest rates at virtually zero. This, into early 2003, was not enough to revive the economy, however, and pressure built on BOJ to supply even more liquidity by buying government debt. The new law enacted in 1998 considerably strengthened the political independence of BOJ, however, and it continued to emphasize the stability of the national currency and the prevention of inflation as its primary goal while stressing the government's responsibility to implement structural reform and the reform of the banking sector needed to steer Japan out of its economic conditions.

BIBLIOGRAPHY. *Annual Review* (Bank of Japan, 2002); Thomas M. Cargill, Michael M. Hutchison, and Takatoshi Ito, *Financial Policy and Central Banking in Japan* (MIT Press, 2001).

SERGUEY BRAGUINSKY, PH.D.
STATE UNIVERSITY OF NEW YORK, BUFFALO

banking, commercial

COMMERCIAL BANKS ARE in the business of providing banking services to individuals, small businesses, and government organizations. They act as financial intermediaries by accepting deposited funds in a large variety of forms and lending the money to households, businesses, and government agencies. Examples of major American commercial banks include Citigroup Inc., Bank of America, J.P. Morgan Chase, Bank One Corp., Wells Fargo & Co. Inc, Fleet Financial Group, Sun Trust Banks Inc., and National City Corp.

Bank sources of funds. The major sources of commercial bank funds come in three forms: deposit accounts, borrowed funds, and long term funding. Deposit accounts are composed of transaction deposits, savings deposits, time deposits, and money market funds. Transaction deposits are funds kept in a bank for easy transfer to others and include checking accounts and NOW accounts. NOW accounts, or negotiable order of withdrawal accounts, are checking accounts that pay interest. This was legalized for banks in 1981 as a response to competition

from money market funds offered by non-bank institutions. Traditional savings accounts or passbook accounts pay interest, but do not provide checking services. From the 1930s until 1986, under Regulation Q, the government restricted the interest rates banks and savings and loans could pay on savings accounts, 5.5 percent for savings and loans, and 5.25 percent for banks. The federal government believed that competition could cause bank failures. Regulation Q was repealed when inflation in the UNITED STATES and therefore INTEREST RATES on Treasury Bills and Commercial Paper exceeded 10 percent and people moved their funds from regulated savings accounts to non-regulated money market funds.

Borrowed funds are federal funds purchased, borrowing from the Federal Reserve banks, repurchase agreements, and eurodollar borrowing. The federal funds rate is the lending rate between banks that are members of the FEDERAL RESERVE system. It is the lending rate that the Federal Reserve targets to control the money supply. Federal funds purchased (borrowed) represent a liability to the borrowing bank and an asset to the lending bank. Loans in the federal funds market are typically for one to seven days. Another source of funds for banks is borrowing directly from the Federal Reserve (the United States central bank) at the discount window. Loans from the discount widow are short term, commonly from one day to a few weeks and are designed to resolve a temporary shortage of funds. The discount rate at which these loans takes place is set by the Federal Reserve Board and is generally below the federal funds rate.

Banks are, nonetheless, reluctant to borrow from the discount window since they need direct approval from the Federal Reserve to do so, and borrowing will result in more intense regulatory attention. A repurchase agreement (repo) represents the sale of securities by one party to another with an agreement to repurchase the securities at a specified date and price. The bank sells some of its government securities to another bank or corporation with a temporary excess of funds and agrees to buy them back at some short time in the future. The yield on repo agreements is slightly less than the federal funds rate since the loans are of about the same duration and repo loans are less risky—they are backed by the collateral of government securities.

Banks may also obtain dollar denominated loans, generally in transactions involving $1 million or more, outside the United States in the eurodollar market at the London Interbank Offer Rate (LIBOR). Eurobanks, banks that participate in this currency market, are located not only in Europe but also in the BAHAMAS, CANADA, JAPAN, HONG KONG, and several other countries. Because interest rate ceilings were historically imposed on dollar deposits in U.S. banks, corporations with large dollar balances moved much of their business overseas during the high inflation of the 1970s and 1980s. By the turn of the century, there were more U.S. dollars outside of the United States then in it; thus, the eurodollar market was the largest market for dollars in the world.

The remaining sources of funds for banks are long-term bonds and equity capital. Like other corporations, banks own some fixed assets such as land, buildings, and equipment. These assets are long term in nature, and are therefore funded with long-term sources of money such as equity and long-term debt. This debt is not guaranteed by the Federal Deposit Insurance Corporation (FDIC), and trades on the open market just like the debt issues of other corporations. Bank debt is followed by the rating agencies (S&P and Moody's) and its behavior is a good indication to government regulators of the financial strength of a bank. Equity capital is composed of stock purchased by investors and the retained earnings of the bank. Since capital can absorb bank losses so the FDIC does not have to, bank regulators control the level of capital banks must hold. In 1981 bank regulators imposed a minimum primary

Commercial banks open their vaults for loans—business loans, consumer loans, and real-estate loans.

capital requirement of 5.5 percent of assets. Since 1992, regulators have imposed new risk-based capital requirements, so riskier banks are subject to higher capital requirements.

Bank uses of funds. The common uses of bank funds include cash, bank loans, investment in securities, federal funds sold, repurchase agreements, eurodollar loans, and fixed assets. Banks must hold cash to maintain liquidity and accommodate any withdrawal demands from depositors. The level of cash they maintain is controlled by reserve requirements imposed by the Federal Reserve. Altering the reserve requirement is one of the means the Fed uses to control the money supply.

The main use of bank funds is for loans. These include business loans, consumer loans, and real-estate loans. A common type of business loan is the working capital loan—these loans are short term, but may be renewed by businesses on a frequent basis. They are used to purchase short-term assets such as inventory. Another type of business loan is the term loan, which is primarily used to purchase fixed assets such as machinery. Term loans usually have a fixed interest rate and maturities ranging from 2 to 10 years. Term loans commonly have protective covenants attached to them that restrict what the borrower may do with the funds and are also commonly backed with the collateral of the asset they are used to purchase. A more flexible financing arrangement is the informal line of credit, which allows businesses to borrow up to a specified amount within a specific time period. This is useful for firms that may experience a sudden need for funds but do not know precisely when.

The interest rate charged by banks on loans to their most creditworthy customers is known as the prime rate. The prime rate goes up and down with market conditions and is generally adjusted with the fed funds rate. For large loans several banks generally pool their funds in what is referred to as loan participation. The most common form of loan participation involves a lead bank arranging for the documentation, disbursement, and payment structure of the loan and other banks supplying some of the funds to distribute the risk of the loan.

Commercial banks provide installment loans to individuals to finance the purchase of cars and household items. These loans require the borrowers to make periodic payments over time. Banks also provide credit cards to consumers enabling purchases of various goods without the customer reapplying for credit on each purchase. A maximum limit is assigned to credit-card holders, depending on their income and employment record—this service commonly involves an agreement with either VISA or MasterCard. State regulators may impose usury laws that control the maximum interest rate that banks may charge consumers.

Banks also provide real-estate loans. For residential real-estate loans, the maturity on a mortgage is typically 15 to 30 years, although shorter loans with a large one-time (balloon) payment are also common. Real-estate loans are backed by the residence that the borrower purchases. They are commonly securitized and sold in secondary markets.

History of bank regulation. The regulatory structure of the banking system in the United States is dramatically different from that of other countries. The United States has a dual banking system since either the state or the federal government may regulate banks. A bank that obtains a state charter is referred to as a state bank; a bank that obtains a federal charter is known as a national bank. National banks are regulated by the Comptroller of the Currency, and state banks are regulated by their respective state agencies. Banks that are members of the Federal Reserve system are also regulated by the Fed. Banks that are insured by FDIC are also regulated by the FDIC.

Members of the Monetarist and AUSTRIAN SCHOOL of economics believe that the Great DEPRESSION was largely caused by mismanagement at the Federal Reserve system, and abuses at the banks certainly did occur. The stock market crash of 1929 and the depression that followed inspired significant new banking regulation in the 1930s. Prior to 1933, most commercial banks offered investment-banking services. The Banking Act of 1933 also known as the Glass-Steagall Act required banks belonging to the Federal Reserve system to divorce themselves from their security affiliates. Commercial banks were still allowed to underwrite general obligation bonds of federal, state, and municipal bodies and of government corporations, but were prohibited from underwriting equities and corporate bonds. The act also prohibited partners and officials of security firms from serving as directors or officers of commercial banks that were members of the Federal Reserve system, and created the FDIC. As a result many banks were broken in two. The Morgan Bank, for example, was split into a commercial bank, the Morgan Guaranty Trust Company, known as J.P. MORGAN CHASE and an investment bank, Morgan Stanley, known as Morgan Stanley Dean Witter (2003).

While it took many years to recover from the Great Depression and adjust to all of the new banking regulations, banking was largely successful and stable from World War II until the 1970s. In the 1970s and 1980s excess inflation caused by government overprinting of money to finance the national debt resulted in significant bank losses and Savings and Loan (S&L) failures. The S&Ls ran into trouble when the interest they paid to depositors, which floated with market interest rates, exceeded the income they received from their long-term fixed-rate home mortgages. What followed was a multi-decade wave of regulatory restructuring.

The Deregulation and Monetary Control Act of 1980 (DIDMCA) gradually phased out deposit-rate ceilings (enforced by Regulation Q) between 1980 and 1986 and increased the maximum deposit insurance level from $40,000 to $100,000. It allowed the creation of checkable deposits (NOW accounts) for all depository institutions (previously it was illegal for banks to pay interest on checking accounts), and it allowed S&Ls to offer limited commercial and consumer loans in competition with commercial banks. It also created the explicit pricing of Fed services like check clearing, so the Fed would have to compete with private organizations for this business.

Banks and other depository institutions were further deregulated in 1982 as a result of the Garn-St. Germain Act. The Act allowed the merger of failing financial institutions across state lines; the McFadden Act of 1927 had previously prevented this sort of bank branching. In 1991, Congress passed the Federal Deposit Insurance Corporation Improvement Act (FDICIA), which was intended to penalize banks that engaged in high-risk activities. Its most important provision was to make FDIC insurance more resemble private insurance. Deposit insurance premiums were to be based on the risk of banks, rather than on a traditional fixed rate. Risk-based deposit insurance premiums are now based on a regulatory rating and the financial institution's capital levels.

In 1999, the Financial Services Modernization Act was passed, which allowed commercial banks, securities firms, and insurance companies to merge—essentially repealing the Glass-Steagall Act. The most prominent example of bank expansion into securities services is Citicorp's merger with Traveler's Insurance Company, which resulted in the financial conglomerate named Citigroup. Since Traveler's Insurance Group already owned the investment bank Salomon Smith Barney, the merger was a massive consolidation of banking, securities, and insurance services. This merger occurred in 1998, the year before the passage of the Financial Services Modernization Act. Yet, the Act was still critical, because it allowed Citigroup to retain its banking, securities, and insurance services.

Too big to fail. Some troubled banks have received preferential treatment from bank regulators. The most obvious example is Continental Illinois Bank, which was rescued by the federal government in 1984. Roughly 75 percent of the time-deposits at Continental were in accounts in excess of $100,000. Under FDIC insurance rules, only deposits up to $100,000 were guaranteed against default, nonetheless, the FDIC bailed out all depositors. During this time period, other banks were allowed to fail without any rescue attempt from the federal government. The reason for the Continental rescue plan was, as one of the largest banks in the country,

Continental's failure could have resulted in a loss of public confidence in the U.S. banking system and a subsequent run on other U.S. banks.

While these concerns could be justified, the government rescue also caused a MORAL HAZARD problem. If the federal government rescues a large bank, it sends a message to the banking industry that large banks will not be allowed to fail. Consequently, large banks may take excessive risks without concern about failure. If risky ventures of a large bank (such as loans to very risky borrowers) pay off, then the return will be high, but if they do not pay off, the federal government will bail out a large bank.

BIBLIOGRAPHY. Eugene F. Brigham and Michael C. Ehrhardt, *Financial Management Theory and Practice* (South-Western, 2002); Vincent P. Carosso, *Investment Banking in America* (Harvard University Press, 1970); Richard M. Ebeling, "The Austrian Economists and the Keynesian Revolution: The Great Depression and the Economics of the Short-Run," *Human Action: A 50-Year Tribute* (Hillsdale College Press, 2000); Milton Friedman and Anna Schwartz, *Great Contraction, 1929–1933* (Princeton University Press, 1963); Jeff Madura, *Financial Market and Institutions* (South-Western, 2001); Murray N. Rothbard, *America's Great Depression* (Mises Institute, 1963); Paul B. Trescott, *Financing American Enterprise: The Story of Commercial Banking* (Greenwood Publishing, 1963); Ingo Walter, *Deregulating Wall Street: Commercial Bank Penetration of the Corporate Securities Market* (John Wiley & Sons, 1985).

KIRBY R. CUNDIFF, PH.D.
HILLSDALE COLLEGE

banking, consumer

ALSO KNOWN AS RETAIL BANKING or commercial banking, consumer banks provide checking, savings, credit, and other banking services to individuals and small businesses, typically handling very large numbers of relatively small transactions. They are distinguished from investment banks that raise capital for large businesses and operate in fundamentally different ways from consumer banks.

In the UNITED STATES and UNITED KINGDOM, consumer banking and investment banking are largely separate. In the United States, this separation is legally required by the Glass-Steagall Act of 1933, while in the United Kingdom it is a matter of customary business practice. Other countries allow banks to combine the two types of activity. Banks that offer both consumer and investment banking services are called "universal banks."

Consumer banks are a mainstay of individual and business savings. However, as other savings and invest-

ment vehicles became more widely available and popular, the percentage of household financial assets deposited in consumer banks declined in the United States from 39 percent in 1978 to below 17 percent at the end of the 20th century. This article refers primarily to U.S. consumer banks and the U.S. banking system, but it applies with minor differences to banks in other countries.

Types of consumer banks. In the United States, consumer banking institutions include commercial banks, savings institutions (Savings & Loan associations and mutual savings banks), and credit unions, with each type regulated by a different government agency and organized in a different way. Other countries have similar types of banking institutions, though legal requirements and business customs vary widely from country to country.

Commercial banks, the most common type of depository institution, accept deposits and use them to make loans for a wide range of uses, such as automobile purchases, business equipment, and lines of credit at interest rates that vary just as widely. Though they were once the main providers of both deposit accounts and loans, banks now face competition from other institutions such as money-market funds that allow smaller depositors to invest and write checks against their accounts. Free of some of the legal restrictions placed on banks, such non-bank funds can make more diversified investments and offer higher returns than banks. However, non-bank funds lack deposit protection provided by the U.S. Federal Deposit Insurance Corporation, which insures bank deposits up to $100,000. And banks are still the primary source of loans for individuals and smaller businesses.

Savings institutions include savings and loan associations and mutual savings banks. They started out as "Building & Loan societies" (immortalized in Frank Capra's 1939 film, "It's a Wonderful Life") whose members deposited their money to provide home loans to other members. In the 1930s, the U.S. national government began to subsidize home ownership. In 1934, it extended deposit insurance to savings institutions, putting them on a par with bank deposits.

Until deregulated in the late 1970s, savings institutions invested mainly in home loans. Deregulation allowed them to make riskier loans, but left in place the deposit insurance of $100,000 per depositor by the now-defunct Federal Savings and Loan Insurance Corporation. This led some institutions to offer higher interest rates and make risky loans, confident that government would cover any losses. The combination of deregulation with government protection against risk caused widespread savings institution bankruptcies in the 1980s as risky loans went sour and taxpayers had to foot the bill.

As banks and other financial institutions offer more options to depositors and borrowers, savings institutions seem to be merging into those other institutions and disappearing as a separate type of consumer bank.

Credit unions perform the same functions as banks and savings and loans, but only for members of specific groups, such as employees of the same company, members of the same union, or workers in the same industry who also belong to the credit union. This reduces their risk of making bad loans because borrowers are members and are already known to the credit union.

The two fundamental types of bank deposit are demand deposits and time deposits.

Demand deposits can be withdrawn on demand, as their name implies. Checking accounts and other checkable deposits are the most common type of demand-deposit accounts, and though savings accounts sometimes theoretically require advance notice to withdraw funds, banks usually allow depositors to withdraw their money on demand.

Checkable deposits are accounts against which a depositor can write checks, meaning that money on deposit can be demanded any time a check is presented for payment. Checkable deposits include traditional non-interest checking accounts, negotiable order of withdrawal (NOW) accounts, and super-NOW accounts. Checkable deposits have steadily decreased as a portion of bank funds. In 1960, they accounted for over 60 percent of bank funds, but by the year 2000 had decreased to only 13 percent of bank funds.

Time deposits are left with the bank for an agreed-upon period of time, such as six months, one year, or longer. A depositor who wishes to withdraw the money early must forfeit some of the interest that the money would have earned. Banks offer two main classes of time deposits. Time deposits under $100,000 are considered small-denomination time deposits, while those for $100,000 or more are considered large-denomination time deposits. However, because the Federal Deposit Insurance Corporation only insures deposits up to $100,000, a portion of the money in large-denomination time deposits is uninsured like any other investment.

Time deposits are often made by purchasing certificates of deposit (CDs). Large-denomination time deposits can be bought and sold in bond markets, so depositors can get their money out without penalty if a buyer is willing to pay enough. Large-denomination time deposits are typically made by corporations and financial institutions as one alternative to U.S. Treasury bonds. Such time deposits are an important source of funds for consumer banks.

How consumer banks operate. Consumer banks (including commercial banks, savings institutions, and credit unions) accept deposits from some individuals and busi-

Consumer banking often involves personal consultation to determine the best investment options.

nesses and loan out the money to other individuals and businesses. The difference between the interest they pay to their depositors and the interest they charge to lend out the money is called "the spread," and it is how banks make their money.

A typical passbook savings account, for example, might pay an interest rate of 2 percent. On the other hand, a bank might charge 6 percent for a home loan and 18 to 20 percent for an unsecured credit card loan. This spread is the banking equivalent of "buy low, sell high." Banks "buy" deposits at a relatively low rate of interest and "sell" loans and credit at relatively high rates.

Deposit funds (reserves) that are lent or invested can make a profit for the bank, but funds held by the bank do not. Therefore, consumer banks lend or invest all but a fraction of their deposits, which they keep on hand as vault cash or on deposit at a branch of the U.S. FEDERAL RESERVE, the U.S. central bank. Banks use this held-back fraction of reserves to pay depositors who wish to withdraw funds or who wish to write checks that draw on their accounts. This is called fractional-reserve banking.

The Federal Reserve requires banks to keep a minimum percentage of their demand-deposit funds available to satisfy withdrawals. This minimum is called the reserve requirement. In February, 2002, the reserve requirement was 10 percent of demand deposits. Because time deposits are left with the bank for a specified period, they are less likely to be withdrawn before maturity, so there is no reserve requirement for time deposits.

Fractional-reserve banking has been both a blessing and a curse to Western economies. It gives banks both the ability and incentive to expand a country's money supply, as economist Adam SMITH noted in 1776:

> A particular banker lends among his customers his own promissory notes, to the extent, we shall suppose, of a hundred thousand pounds. As those notes serve all the purposes of money, his debtors pay him the same interest as if he had lent them so much [gold or silver]. This interest is the source of his gain. Though some of the notes are continually coming back upon him for payment, part of them continue to circulate for months and years. Though he has generally in circulation [paper currency of] a hundred thousand pounds, twenty thousand pounds in gold and silver may, frequently, be a sufficient for answering occasional demands. By this operation, therefore, twenty thousand pounds in gold and silver perform all the functions which a hundred thousand could otherwise have performed.

Fractional-reserve banking gives government, through the banking system, the ability to make more money available to stimulate business activity in economic downturns. For example, the Federal Reserve can lower the reserve requirement, enabling banks to loan out a larger portion of funds from their demand deposits.

However, fractional-reserve banks are inherently at risk because they never have enough assets on hand to pay off all their depositors. This has led to numerous problems, including "bank runs" in which too many depositors try to withdraw their money from a shaky bank, thereby causing the bank to fail. Moreover, erratic fluctuations in the money supply are a major cause of the business cycle of boom and bust.

History of consumer banks. Consumer banks as we know them today began to evolve in medieval Europe. In the 12th century, deposit banks opened in Italian trading centers such as Venice and Genoa. These banks were not allowed to earn money by loaning deposits and keeping only fractional reserves, but they did facilitate business transactions by transferring money on order from buyers' to sellers' accounts. They also allowed some depositors to write overdrafts on their accounts, in effect loaning them money. Soon, similar banks operated in major cities such as London, Barcelona, and Geneva.

Banks also facilitated long-range trade by buying and selling bills of exchange. Because shipping gold was time-consuming, expensive, and hazardous, many merchants preferred to use bills of exchange. By this means, merchants could sell goods on credit in a distant market, use one of the market's local banks to invest the proceeds in local goods, and then have the goods shipped back to the home market. Because all the transactions were based on bank credit, no actual gold shipments were required. By the beginning of the INDUSTRIAL REVOLUTION, fractional-reserve banking had become common in Europe and elsewhere around the world, and institutions recognizable as the ancestors of modern consumer banks were in widespread operation.

BIBLIOGRAPHY. R. Glenn Hubbard, *Money, the Financial System, and the Economy* (Addison-Wesley, 2000); Adam Smith, *The Wealth of Nations* (University of Chicago Press, Chicago, 1976); Ludwig von Mises, *Theory of Money and Credit* (Liberty Classics, 1980); Murray N. Rothbard, *America's Great Depression* (Mises Institute Press, 2000); Milton Friedman and Anna Schwartz, *A Monetary History of the United States* (Princeton University Press, 1963); Rondo Cameron, *A Concise Economic History of the World* (Oxford University Press, 2002).

SCOTT PALMER, PH.D.
RGMS ECONOMICS

banking, investment

INVESTMENT BANKS, OR I-BANKS, assist with a large variety of financial transactions generally involving the restructuring of the ownership of firms. These transactions include private placements, initial public offerings, mergers and acquisitions, leverage buyouts, and securitization. The role of an investment bank is generally that of a financial intermediary or advisor rather than a lender or investor so most of its compensation is in the form of fees. The most active investment banking houses in recent years have been: Merrill Lynch, Salomon Smith Barney, Morgan Stanley Dean Witter, CREDIT SUISSE First Boston, J.P. MORGAN CHASE, Goldman Sachs, Deutsche Bank, Lehman Brothers, UBS Warburg, and Banc of America Securities.

Private placements and venture capital funds. Most businesses begin life as proprietorships or partnerships, and then, as the more successful ones grow, at some point they find it desirable to become corporations. Initially, its founders and key employees own most of a firm's corporate stock. Founding firms that are extremely successful tend to grow very quickly and therefore need expansion funds beyond the resources of the initial founders.

The first outside source of funds usually obtained by startup firms come from private placements. Private placements are stock issues that do not have to be registered with the SECURITIES AND EXCHANGE COMMISSION (SEC), and are therefore highly restricted in who may purchase them. In a non-registered private placement, the company may issue securities to an unlimited number of accredited investors, but to only 35 non-accredited investors. Accredited investors include the officers and directors of the company, high wealth individuals, and institutional investors. An additional restriction on private placements is that none of the investors can sell their securities in the secondary market to the general public.

For most startup companies, the first private-equity placements are to a small number of individual investors called angels. The angels tend to be high net-worth people with significant knowledge about the industry they are investing in, and commonly sit on the company's board of directors. As a company's financial needs grow, the next step is commonly to seek support from a venture capital fund. Venture capital funds are private limited partnerships that typically raise $10 million to $100 million from a small group of primarily institutional investors, including pension, funds, college endowments, and corporations. The managers of venture capital funds (venture capitalists) are typically very knowledgeable about a given industry, and limit their investments to only one investment sector.

Initial public offerings (IPOs). Going public means selling some of a company's stock to outside investors and then letting the stock trade in secondary public markets such as the NEW YORK STOCK EXCHANGE. Taking companies public is the primary business of most investment banks. Investment bankers assist firms by helping to determine the stock's initial offering price and selling the stock to its existing clients—generally a mix of institutional investors and high net-worth individuals. After the stock is sold, the I-Bank, through its brokerage house, will have an analyst "cover" the stock to maintain investor interest in it. This analyst will regularly distribute reports to investors describing the stock's future growth prospects.

When taking firms public, the firm and its investment bankers must decide whether the bankers will work on a best-efforts basis or will underwrite the issue. In a best-efforts sale, the banker does not guarantee that the securities will be sold or that the company will get the cash it needs, only that it will put forth its "best efforts" to sell the issue. On an underwritten issue, the company does get a guarantee, because the banker agrees to buy the entire issue and then resell the stock to its customers. Except for extremely small issues, virtually all IPOs are underwritten. Investors are required to pay for securities

within 10 days, and the investment banker must pay the issuing firm within four days of the official commencement of the offering.

Typically, the banker sells the stock within a day or two after the offering begins, but on occasion, the banker miscalculates the offering price and is unable to sell the issue. If this occurs, the investment bank must absorb any losses. Because investment bankers bear significant risk in underwriting sock offerings, large-issues bankers tend to form underwriting syndicates. The banking house that sets up the deal is called the lead, or managing, underwriter and the other banks share in the initial purchase and distribution of the shares.

Since the creation of the SEC in 1933, investment-banking services have been highly regulated. The SEC has jurisdiction over all interstate public offerings in excess of $1.5 million. State agencies also regulate the securities market. Newly issued securities (stocks and bonds) must be registered with the SEC at least 20 days before they are publicly offered. The registration statement, called Form S-1 provides financial, legal, and technical information about the company to the SEC. A prospectus, which is embedded in the S-1, summarizes this information for investors. After the SEC declares the registration to be effective, new securities may be advertised, but a prospectus must accompany all sales. Preliminary, or "red herring," prospectuses may be distributed to potential buyers during the 20-day waiting period after the registration is effective.

After the registration statement has been filed, the senior management team, the investment bankers, and the company's lawyers go on a road show during which the management team will make multiple presentations each day to potential institutional investors—generally existing clients of the underwriters. During the presentations potential investors may ask questions, but the management team may not give out any information that is not already included in the registration due to a SEC mandated quiet period. The quiet period begins when the registration statement is filed and lasts for 25 days after the stock begins trading. After a presentation, the investment bankers will ask the investors for an indication of interest in the new company based on the range of offering prices shown in the registration statement. The investment bankers will record the number of shares that each investor is interested in buying. This process is called book building. If there are more investors interested in purchasing the company than there are shares available, then the offer is oversubscribed and the I-Bankers may increase the offering price, if there is little interest in the new company, then they may lower the offering price or withdraw the IPO.

Mergers and acquisitions. A merger occurs when two or more firms become one firm with approximately equal control of the combined firm going to both management teams. An acquisition occurs when one firm takes control of another, generally smaller firm. From the stockholder's point of view there are good reasons for mergers such as firm synergies, and bad reasons for mergers such as diversification. If two companies merge and the value of the whole is greater than the sum of its parts, then a synergy is said to exist. Synergistic effects can arise from five sources:

1. operating economies, which result from economies of scale in management, marketing, production, or distribution

2. financial economies, including lower transaction costs and better coverage by security analysts

3. tax effects, where the combined enterprise pays less in taxes than the separate firms would pay

4. differential efficiency, which implies that the management of one firm is more efficient and that the weaker firm's assets will be better managed after the merger

5. increased market power due to reduced competition.

Some of these reasons for mergers are good for the economy and consumers since they will receive equal or better goods and services for lower prices, and other reasons, such as decreased competition, may hurt consumers. The ANTITRUST division of the Justice Department regulates mergers and acquisitions.

Managers often cite diversification as a reason for a merger. While this makes sense from the point of view of the manager, it makes little sense from the point of view of the stockholders in the firm. If a manager controls a larger firm involved in multiple different industries, he will collect a larger salary and control more assets than if he only manages a small specialized firm, so diversification helps management. If a stockholder wants to be diversified, he need only buy stock in multiple different firms. Furthermore, since management may only be knowledgeable in one specialized area, mergers based on diversification may actually make the combined firm less valuable than its individual components. As of October 2002, the five largest corporate mergers or acquisitions in the United States were: America Online Inc. acquiring Time Warner; Pfizer Inc. acquiring Warner-Lambert; Exxon Corp. acquiring Mobil Corp; Travelers Group Inc. acquiring Citicorp; and SBC Communications Inc. acquiring Ameritech Corp.

Leveraged buyouts. In a private transaction, the entire equity of a publicly held firm is purchased by a small group of investors that usually includes the firm's current senior management. In some of these transactions, the current management group acquires all of the equity of the company. In others, current management participates in the ownership with a small group of outside investors who typically place directors on the now-private firm's board and arrange for the financing needed to purchase the publicly held stock. Such deals almost always involve substantial borrowing, often up to 90 percent of assets, and thus are known as leverage buyouts (LBOs). The acquirer believes the firm is drastically undervalued in the market or that the firm's value can be increased by changes current management is unwilling to make. Thus, a group of investors might take a firm private, fire the management, and restructure the firm to making a profit. For example when Kohlberg, Kravis, Roberts, & Company (KKR) won the battle for RJR Nabisco, they removed the top management and terminated a money-losing "smokeless" cigarette project. LBOs tend to take place when the stock market is depressed and debt financing is more appealing. Many LBOs were financed with junk bonds issued by Michael Milken and Drexel Burnham Lambert during the early 1980s. Subsequently, Morgan Stanley Dean Witter, Merrill Lynch, Salomon Smith Barney, and other major investment banks have entered the junk bond market.

Securitization. A security refers to a publicly traded financial instrument, as opposed to a privately placed instrument. Thus, securities have greater liquidity than otherwise similar instruments that are not traded in an open market. In recent years, procedures have been developed to securitize various types of debt instruments, thus increasing their liquidity, lowering the cost of capital to borrowers, and generally increasing the efficiency of the financial markets. The oldest type of asset securitization is the mortgage-backed market. Here, individual home mortgages are commonly combined into pools, and then bonds are created that use the pool of mortgages as collateral. The financial institution that originated the mortgage generally continues to act as the servicing agent, but the mortgage itself is sold to other investors. Savings and Loans (S&Ls) are in the business of borrowing money on a short-term basis through passbook accounts and short-term certificates of deposit, and lending money to home purchasers through long-term fixed-rate home mortgages. During the high inflation period of the late1970s and early1980s many S&Ls went bankrupt due to this duration mismatch between their assets and liabilities. When inflation increased, the value of their assets (home mortgages) went down drastically, but the value of their liabilities (passbook accounts) did not change. The securitization of home mortgages is one of the ways developed to help S&Ls and banks limit their exposure to this type of interest-rate risk. Today, many different types of assets are securitized, including auto loans, credit card balances, home loans, and student loans.

History of investment banking. Investment banking services have been available since the early days of the United States. Before the 1850s, when the financial needs of the railroads gave rise to some of the first investment banking houses, the business in securities was conducted by various kinds of unspecialized middlemen. In the United States, as in Europe, investment banking started out as a sideline to some other business. In America this role usually was filled by speculators and merchants, since relatively few other men of large wealth were willing to take the risks entailed in buying securities or had funds other than those invested in land or trade. Early securities trading mainly involved government and railroad bonds.

Of the many incorporated commercial banks performing an investment banking function before 1840, none was more deeply involved in the business than the United States Bank of Pennsylvania, which took over the nongovernmental affairs of the second Bank of the United States, when its charter expired in 1836. Nicholas Biddle, its first president and former head of the Bank of the United States, contracted and negotiated for all kinds of public and private securities, including some of the first railroad issues. Like some large commercial banks doing an investment banking business a half-century later, he tried to attract the deposits of the companies and governmental units whose securities he distributed. His most important innovation, which was partly responsible for the institution's ultimate collapse in 1841, was the practice of lending issuers money on securities he was trying to sell on commission.

By the outbreak of the Civil War, investment banking in the United States had achieved a significant degree of maturity and specialization. During the Civil War, the Union government was having significant difficulty raising funds, so Abraham LINCOLN's first Secretary of the Treasury, Salmon P. Chase called on his brother-in-law, Jay Cooke, who had opened a private banking house in Philadelphia in 1861. Cooke proposed a hard-selling, well-organized, campaign to appeal to the patriotism and self-interest of the small investor. Chase accepted the banker's suggestion since bankers and large investors, the usual purchasers of debt securities, were unwilling to buy the bonds; thus, the first mass marketing of securities was born. Subscriptions ranged from $300,000 to as little as $50. After the war, Cooke attempted the same techniques selling railroad bonds. He was not as successful, and in 1873, Cooke & Co. went out of business due to unpaid debt and unsold bonds of the Northern Pacific Railroad.

After Cooke's failure, a new financial giant—J. Pierpont MORGAN—rose to prominence. His father, Junius Spenser Morgan was born on a Massachusetts farm, but became a powerful international banker as a partner with George Peabody & Co. in London. The younger Morgan, after a brief apprenticeship with Duncan, Sherman, & Co, opened his own banking house in New York, dealing largely in foreign exchange, gold, and securities. In 1871, J.P. Morgan entered into a partnership with Anthony Drexel of Philadelphia. With his advantageous foreign connections, he soon became prominent in underwriting securities issues. In 1879, Morgan took on the important responsibility of helping William H. Vanderbilt sell a large portion of his enormous holdings in the New York Central Railroad. Morgan found English buyers for the stock, and became their representative on Central's board.

From this time period until his death in 1913, Morgan was the dominant figure in American finance. In 1893, the U.S. Treasury suffered from a run on gold reserves motivated by fear that free-silver legislation would end the gold standard causing a depression in the dollar. Morgan organized a marketing syndicate to issue new government bonds and replenish the gold reserve. In 1901, Morgan was one of the key figures in the formation of United States Steel Corporation—at the time the largest business corporation in the world. And in 1907, when Wall Street was swept by a financial panic, Morgan acted as a "one-man Federal Reserve bank" by organizing the heads of New York City's leading banks to put up enough cash to prevent suspension of payment by weaker banks.

Members of the Monetarist and AUSTRIAN SCHOOLS of economics believe that the Great DEPRESSION was largely caused by mismanagement at the FEDERAL RESERVE system, but there were also abuses at the banks. The stock market crash of 1929 and the depression that followed inspired significant new banking regulation. Prior to 1933, most commercial banks offered investment-banking services. The Banking Act of 1933 also known as the Glass-Steagall Act required banks belonging to the Federal Reserve System to divorce themselves from their security affiliates within one year. Commercial banks were still allowed to underwrite general obligation bonds of federal, state, and municipal bodies, and of government corporations, but were prohibited from underwriting equities and corporate bonds. The act also prohibited partners and officials of security firms from serving as directors or officers of commercial banks that were members of the Federal Reserve system, and created the Federal Deposit Insurance Corporation (FDIC). As a result many banks were broken in two. The Morgan Bank, for example, was split into a commercial bank, the Morgan Guaranty Trust Company, now known as J. P. Morgan Chase and an investment bank, Morgan Stanley, now know as Morgan Stanley Dean Witter. Also passed during this time period were the Truth in Securities Act of 1933, and the Securities and Exchange Act of 1934. The provisions of the Truth in Securities Act were discussed in the section on IPOs. The Securities and Exchange Act created the Securities and Exchange Commission, established a minimum margin requirement of 55 percent, and put regulation of broker's loans under the control of the Federal Reserve system.

While it took many years to recover from the Great Depression and adjust to all of the new banking regulations, banking was largely successful and stable from World War II until the 1970s. In the 1970s and 1980s excess inflation caused by government overprinting of money to finance the national debt resulted in significant bank failures. What followed was a multi-decade wave of regulatory restructuring. Most of this deregulating was related to commercial banking. In 1999, the Financial Services Modernization Act was passed, which allowed commercial banks, securities firms, and insurance companies to merge—essentially repealing the Glass-Steagall Act. The most prominent example of bank expansion into securities services is Citicorp's merger with Traveler's Insurance Company, which resulted in the financial conglomerate named Citigroup. Since Traveler's Insurance Group already owned the investment bank Salomon Smith Barney, the merger was a massive consolidation of banking, securities, and insurance services. This merger occurred in 1998, the year before the passage of the Financial Services Modernization Act.

Yet, the act was still critical, because it allowed Citigroup to retain its banking, securities, and insurance services. Since the re-merger of investment and commercial banking there have been accusations of tying (given loans only under the condition of receiving I-Banking business) and of large banks giving questionable loans in exchange for I-Banking business.

BIBLIOGRAPHY. Eugene F. Brigham and Michael C. Ehrhardt, *Financial Management Theory and Practice* (South-Western, 2002); Vincent P. Carosso, *Investment Banking in America* (Harvard University Press, 1970); Richard M. Ebeling, "The Austrian Economists and the Keynesian Revolution: The Great Depression and the Economics of the Short-Run," *Human Action: A 50-Year Tribute* (Hillsdale College Press, 2000); Daniel Fischel, *Payback: The Conspiracy to Destroy Michael Milken and His Financial Revolution* (HarperCollins, 1996); Milton Friedman and Anna Schwartz, *Great Contraction, 1929-1933* (Princeton University Press, 1963); Jeff Madura, *Financial Market and Institutions* (South-Western, 2001); Murray N. Rothbard, *America's Great Depression* (Mises Institute, 1963); Paul B. Trescott, *Financing American Enterprise: The Story of Commercial Banking* (Greenwood Publishing, 1963); Ingo Walter, *Deregulating Wall Street: Commercial Bank Penetration of the Corporate Securities Market* (John Wiley & Sons, 1985).

KIRBY R. CUNDIFF, PH.D.
HILLSDALE COLLEGE

bankruptcy

DATING BACK TO the ancient Romans, bankruptcy has been the course of action for when a business or individual is unable to repay outstanding debts owed to creditors, or avoids repayment. In the last 400 years, governments have put formal laws in place that penalize debtors, while at the same time protecting the rights of creditors.

Bankruptcy, in its early form, was viewed as debtor fraud. Those who were bankrupt were severely punished and laws were created to ensure creditors were repaid.

Bankruptcies mainly took place in the business world and were involuntary, in that a business was charged with bankruptcy when it could not repay creditors. The penalties for merchants and individuals charged with bankruptcy included prison, public flogging, and in some instances, execution.

The meaning of bankruptcy has changed dramatically in today's society. Rather than being charged with bankruptcy, it is now something that businesses and individuals declare, which eliminates virtually all the criminality involved in its original definition. In modern times, bankruptcy has evolved into a practice that centers on eliminating debts, particularly as personal bankruptcy has become a more common practice. In cases of personal bankruptcy, the process of declaring oneself bankrupt—filing for bankruptcy— is viewed as a cleansing act, giving the debtor a fresh start economically and relief from creditors.

Some believe the term bankruptcy was derived from the words *bancus* (tradesman's counter) and *ruptus* (broken), meaning that a person's business was gone. Others see the word coming from the Italian *banca rotta*, or "broken bench," for the practice in medieval times of destroying a businessman's trading bench if he did not repay outstanding debts.

Early bankruptcy. In ancient Rome, under the Caesars, debt collection laws were enacted to make certain that creditors were repaid. A trustee (often referred to as a protector or caretaker) auctioned off the debtor's property to the bidder who agreed to pay the most to the creditors. The trustee was either chosen by the creditors or appointed by a magistrate. In severe cases, a debtor could be sold into slavery.

Historians disagree about the date of the first English bankruptcy law. Some think it was enacted in 1542, while others believe the first law was passed in 1570. The 1542 edict, passed under the rule of Henry VIII, established harsh penalties against the debtor to prevent fraud committed on creditors. Bankrupt individuals appeared before a chancellor, faced examination under oath at the discretion of the creditor, and if the debtor failed to surrender his possessions to repay the debt, the offender was sent to debtors' prison.

The 1570 law passed because the earlier statute put so many people in prison that it became a national epidemic. The penalties, however, were no less severe. All assets were taken, sold, and distributed to creditors. Bankruptcy officials even had the right to break into a person's home to seize property that could be used to repay debts. Unlike today's less hostile version of bankruptcy, there was no discharge of the remaining debt, regardless of the penalty the debtor faced. Debt collection continued until all creditors were satisfied. As the debtors' prisons filled, new forms of punishment took place that did not include jail time. Debtors could be publicly flogged, while others had an ear cut off or had an ear nailed, while still attached, to a pillory in a public forum. The 1705 Statute of Anne law gave prosecutors the right to execute debtors and approximately five people were put to death under this law.

Bankruptcy in America. Given the chaotic state of the economy in early America and large debts the nation owed for financing the AMERICAN REVOLUTION, the founders were not willing to enact punitive bankruptcy laws in the young country. The federal government empowered the individual states to dictate bankruptcy laws. Many of these mimicked the English in harshness, including nailing convicted debtors to the pillory and branding a "T" on the thumb of debtors for "thief."

The first official bankruptcy law in the UNITED STATES was passed in 1800 to regulate land speculation deals. The law was later repealed in 1803. Although modeled after English bankruptcy law, American federal laws were less punitive and allowed the debtor to discharge some debts. The rest of the 19th century saw similar bankruptcy laws enacted in response to specific economic crises. Each of these was followed by repeal, usually after the law proved too cumbersome or people figured out ways to defraud the system using the new law.

The Bankruptcy Act of 1898 began a new era of bankruptcy laws, favoring the debtor over the creditor and giving the bankrupt party legal protection from those who were owed money. The Great DEPRESSION forced more bankruptcy legislation, with new laws being passed in 1933 and 1934. With the Chandler Act of 1938, Congress revamped the laws. Chapter 13 bankruptcy was introduced, which gave debtors the ability to repay over a three- to five-year plan, while retaining their property and residence. The Chandler Act also defined how businesses could reorganize during bankruptcy.

During the long economic boom that took place after World War II, bankruptcy did not change significantly until the 1970s. The Bankruptcy Reform Act of 1978 overhauled bankruptcy practices. Chapter 11 was created to help businesses reorganize, while a new Chapter 13 replaced the old program. Both made it easier for corporations and people to file for bankruptcy and emerge with much less financial damage. Much of the bankruptcy news in the 1980s occurred as the 1978 Act was tweaked and new laws were passed to include groups that were not given special treatment in the earlier laws, such as the Chapter 12 provision created for family farms in 1986.

Boom and bust bankruptcy. The boom and bust economy of the 1980s and 1990s caused record numbers of corporations and individuals to declare bankruptcy. The leniency of modern bankruptcy laws has made it, to some people's viewpoint, an attractive alternative to actually repaying creditors. Many of the world's most well-known companies have filed for bankruptcy, including Continental Airlines, Texaco, and LTV Steel. In 1997, nearly 1.4 million people filed for personal bankruptcy, an average of one for every 76 American households.

Most people filing for bankruptcy now use Chapter 7 liquidation, which discharges all unpaid debts, but does not allow creditors to place a lien on property or garnish wages. In the business world, Chapter 11 reorganizations are the most common form of bankruptcy. Under this program, businesses are allowed to continue operations with their own management teams in place, while assets are protected from creditors. Management has 120 days to propose a plan of reorganization to creditors, but the deadline can be extended for years.

While corporate bankruptcies, such as those by ENRON and WORLDCOM still receive the most media attention, consumer filings dwarf those of business. In 2002, 1.57 million were filed, but only 38,540 were businesses. Yet it is difficult to quantify the true economic effect of the largest bankruptcy filings, such as WorldCom with nearly $104 billion in assets when it filed in 2002, or Enron totaling $63 billion.

BIBLIOGRAPHY. Bruce H. Mann, *Republic of Debtors: Bankruptcy in the Age of American Independence* (Harvard University Press, 2003); Francis R. Noel, *History of the Bankruptcy Law* (C.H. Potter, 1919); Joseph Pomykala, *The Division and Destruction of Value: An Economic Analysis of Bankruptcy Law* (UMI, 1997); Charles Warren, *Bankruptcy in United States History* (Harvard University Press, 1935).

BOB BATCHELOR
INDEPENDENT SCHOLAR

Barclays Bank

BARCLAYS IS A FINANCIAL services group, based in the UNITED KINGDOM, engaged primarily in banking, investment banking, and investment management. It is one of the largest, oldest, and most revered financial services groups in England, Scotland, Wales and Ireland, and a leading provider of coordinated global services to multinational corporations and financial institutions worldwide. As a whole, it is comprised of seven business groupings: Barclays Africa; Barclaycard; Barclays Capital; Barclays Global Investors; Barclays Private Clients; Business Banking; and Personal Financial Services.

In 2003, Barclays had 74,400 employees operating within those groups, spread throughout 60-plus countries. All corners of the world—in Europe, the North America, Latin America, Africa, the Caribbean, Asia, the Middle East and Australia—are represented as Barclays' markets. Barclays has 2,088 branches in the United Kingdom alone, 564 branches overseas, and an online banking service, to which nearly 3.5 million users are registered.

The history of Barclays can be traced back 300 years to when banking partners John Freame and Thomas Gould founded the institution in 1690. The name Barclay came about when a third partner, James Barclay, joined the firm. Since then, it has remained at the physical center of London's financial district, and also the metaphorical center of London's finance business.

By 1896, when a new, realigned bank was formed from mergers, it had 182 branches and deposits of £26 million, a vast sum in Victorian England. After another series of amalgamations, the bank claimed more than a thousand branches in 1926. In 1969, it acquired Martin's Bank, the largest bank outside of London, and in 2000 The Woolwich, a principal lending bank.

According to its 2002 annual report, Barclays aspires to be "recognized as an innovative, customer-focused company that delivers superb products and services, ensures excellent careers and contributes positively to the communities." Striving to uphold a long and honored legacy, it continues to build its business in retail and commercial banking outside the United Kingdom and to nurture global business in the areas of investment banking and credit cards. In 2002, the group achieved a sales of $27.5 billion with profits of $3.7 billion.

BIBLIOGRAPHY. "Global 500: World's Largest Companies," *Fortune* (July, 2002); Barclays PLC, www.personal.barclays. col.uk; Hoover's, "Barclays PLC," www.hoovers.com.

JOSEPH GERINGER
SYED B. HUSSAIN, PH.D.
UNIVERSITY OF WISCONSIN, OSHKOSH

barter

THE EXCHANGE OF ONE COMMODITY for another, barter is used in the absence of any widely accepted type of money, where money is defined as any commodity, coin, or paper currency whose primary value is as a medium of exchange, not as a good or service. Barter evolved early in the history of mankind as individuals recognized the benefits of a fundamental component of capitalism: exchange. Historical evidence suggests barter developed as early as 9000 B.C.E. when human beings exchanged cattle and plant products such as grain.

Before they integrated barter into their daily lives, societies were largely self-sufficient. Individual households provided the necessities of food, clothing, and housing for themselves and consequently had little time to pursue leisure, education, research, or any of the other activities generally associated with economic growth and improved standards of living. The existence of sustained hunter-gatherer and agrarian societies in the early history of man proved that individuals could coexist in communities. The endurance of such living arrangements proved significant for two reasons. First, it exposed individuals to a wide array of different talents and skill sets. Second, community living provided a certain level of trust among its inhabitants.

It was not long before individuals recognized the high costs of remaining self-sufficient. By exchanging with one another, individuals could take advantage of diverse specialization talents and, in so doing, rid themselves of the limitations of remaining self-reliant. Consumption and production were no longer constrained by the type and amount of resources that one possessed. Through specialization and exchange, an individual could produce those items for which his resources and abilities were best suited, trade with someone else to get goods and services he could not otherwise obtain and subsequently free up time and other valuable resources.

Adam SMITH formally recognized the benefits of such specialization when he outlined his "Theory of Absolute Advantage" in his 1776 work, *An Inquiry into the Nature and Causes of the Wealth of Nations*. The rewards of exchange were further endorsed by David RICARDO when he formulated his "Theory of Comparative Advantage." Individuals grew more dependent on one another as barter spread. This, however, did little to negate the tremendous gains from exchange as community living typically fostered a certain degree of trust among individuals.

Specialization and the division of labor have long been acknowledged as driving forces of improvements in productivity and living standards. Not only does a system based on exchange allow individuals access to a greater number of goods and services, it also permits individuals to obtain these commodities more easily and at a lower cost to themselves as well as society. The repetitive nature of specialization leads to improved factor productivity as individuals become better skilled and find more efficient methods of production. Advancements in social and economic welfare accelerate as specialization leads to cultural, technological, and intellectual progress that would be unattainable with self-sufficient systems. Such achievements ultimately promote economic growth and advances in a society's standard of living.

The substantial benefits of specialization could not be realized as long as individuals remained self-sufficient. Hence, barter was a necessary prerequisite for specialization, the division of labor, and the ensuing increase in economic activity. Despite that, few cultures presently exist in which barter continues to be used as a principal method of exchange. In nearly all cultures in the world today, exchange involves the use of some generally accepted form of money.

The Chinese used bronze knives and the Lydians, electrum ingots, to facilitate exchange as early as the 7th century B.C.E. By the 4th century B.C.E., disks of metal that mimicked today's coins were circulating as a medium of exchange throughout the Greek world. Barter systems were replaced quickly by money systems as the high costs of barter became apparent. While the use of barter allowed civilizations to prosper in ways that would have been impossible under self-sufficient regimes, the substantial transactions costs associated with barter placed limits on social and economic advancements.

Barter required what has become known as the double coincidence of wants. A pig farmer who finds himself in need of a sweater would have to find an individual who had sweaters to trade and who also wanted pork (i.e., the desires of the pig farmer and sweater-maker would have to coincide before the two would barter with one another). Assuming the pig farmer could find a sweater-maker in need of pork, the search costs could be prohibitive and hence the pig farmer may choose to retreat to a self-sufficient lifestyle.

Even if the pig farmer were able to overcome the double coincidence of wants, other impediments exist. The durability and portability of the pigs may pose a problem should the farmer live a great distance from the producer of the sweaters. Assessing the true value of the pigs may prove difficult as all pigs are neither uniform in size nor quality. Because one pig is likely to be worth more than one sweater, barter may be further hindered due to the fact that pigs are not divisible. The pig farmer would have to agree to take ownership of a large number of sweaters or find something other than a pig to offer for the sweater. Lastly, a barter system is typically characterized by a large number of exchange rates where the number of exchange rates, E, in a barter economy with n goods will be equal to $1/2n(n-1)$. This further increases the difficulty of quickly assigning a value to a particular commodity and hence discourages exchange.

Barter provided an important impetus for specialization and the division of labor without which social,

cultural, and technological advancements would most likely have been hindered. High transactions costs, however, frequently led to the replacement of barter by money systems. Despite that, barter did not disappear altogether. It continued to crop up throughout modern history particularly during periods of high inflation (e.g., hyperinflations). During the German hyperinflation of 1923, for example, rapid declines in the purchasing power of money caused "lifetime savings to vanish overnight, while economic life was reduced to barter." Similar episodes occurred as recently as the early 1990s at which time hyperinflations in Yugoslavia caused many individuals to return to barter as their primary means of exchange.

BIBLIOGRAPHY. William J. Barber, *A History of Economic Thought* (Viking Press, 1967); Glyn Davies, *A History of Money from Ancient Times to the Present Day* (University of Wales Press, 1996); Timothy Holian, *The German Hyperinflation of 1923: A Seventy-Fifth Anniversary Retrospective* (Peter Lang, 1998); Michael Latzer and Stefan W. Schmitz, eds., *Carl Menger and the Evolution of Payments Systems: From Barter to Electronic Money* (Edward Elgar, 2002).

KRISTIN KUCSMA, PH.D.
SETON HALL UNIVERSITY

Bastiat, Frédéric (1801–50)

ARGUABLY HISTORY'S MOST persuasive and influential popularizer of free-market economics, Bastiat explains, with clarity and humor, the LAISSEZ-FAIRE lessons of economists such as Adam SMITH and Jean-Baptiste Say. For example, in his "Candlemakers' Petition," Bastiat proposes that government end "unfair competition" by blotting out the sun.

The point is to ridicule protectionists who seek to stop the "flood" of "cheap foreign products." Replacing the sun's competition with man-made illumination indeed increases the demand for candles, but consumers lose far more than producers gain. In his other writings, Bastiat spreads his ridicule widely. Protectionism is his favorite target, but he also goes after socialism, redistribution, make-work programs, and debunks critics of thrift, middlemen, and mechanization.

Bastiat is also the author of what some economists consider the finest essay on opportunity cost ever written, "What Is Seen and What Is Not Seen." He begins with a parable: a boy breaks a window. What is the effect on society? The benefits seem to ripple out: the shopkeeper pays the glassmaker to replace the window, the glassmaker in turn buys something else, and so on. But this analysis ignores "the unseen," what the shopkeeper would have bought instead of replacing the window—perhaps a new pair of shoes. As Bastiat puts it:

> There are not only two people, but three, in the little drama that I have presented. The one . . . represents the consumer, reduced by destruction to one enjoyment instead of two. The other, under the figure of the glazier, shows us the producer whose industry the accident encourages. The third is the shoemaker . . . whose industry is correspondingly discouraged by the same cause. It is the third person who is always in the shadow, and who, personifying *what is not seen*, is an essential element of the problem.

One interpretive lesson includes: When government acts, weigh the observed gains against whatever government crowds out. Military spending may employ millions; but imagine what those millions would have accomplished if taxpayers had been allowed to keep their money and spend it as they pleased.

Bastiat was an original theorist as well as an educator. Economists have often wondered why foolish economic policies come into existence and Bastiat has an intriguing answer to this important question. The proximate cause of protectionism may well be industry lobbying, but the root cause is the public's lack of economic understanding: "I am not one of those who say that the advocates of protectionism are motivated by self-interest. Instead, I believe that opposition to free trade rests upon errors, or, if you prefer, upon *half-truths*," Bastiat explains.

According to Bastiat, then, the primary reason for protectionism and other wealth-reducing policies is not the machinations of special interests, but democracy's tendency to heed public opinion—right or wrong. Modern research suggests that this simple explanation has much to recommend it.

BIBLIOGRAPHY. Frédéric Bastiat, *Economic Sophisms* (The Foundation for Economic Education, 1964). Frédéric Bastiat, *Selected Essays on Political Economy* (The Foundation for Economic Education, 1964). Bryan Caplan, "Systematically Biased Beliefs About Economics: Robust Evidence of Judgmental Anomalies from the Survey of Americans and Economists on the Economy," *Economic Journal* (v.112).

BRYAN CAPLAN, PH.D.
GEORGE MASON UNIVERSITY

Beard, Charles Austin (1874–1948)

BORN INTO A PROSPEROUS Indiana mercantile family, Charles Beard was educated in the UNITED STATES and Britain. A scholar who argued forcefully that the function of history was not merely to describe the past but provide guidance for contemporary public policy, Beard was the prototype for the generation of politically engaged "New Left" historians that rose to prominence 20 years after his death.

Of Beard's many works, *An Economic Interpretation of the Constitution* (1913) best displayed both his originality and his talent for generating controversy. In this book, Beard suggested that the founders of the United States had been motivated above all by their own material and political interests, and that the system of government adopted by the infant republic was best understood as a conservative device aimed at protecting the property and status of a planter elite.

Though subsequent research has failed to uphold the more provocative aspects of Beard's thesis, *An Economic Interpretation of the Constitution* nonetheless stands as a landmark in American historical scholarship that opened up to critical debate a topic that had traditionally been treated with considerable deference.

Subsequent works, notably the immensely popular *Rise of American Civilization* (1927), co-written with his wife Mary Ritter Beard, elaborated upon similar themes, depicting material forces, especially the turbulent process of industrialization, as the locomotive driving the historical development of the United States.

Beard's reputation suffered during the last decade of his life, a result of his outspoken opposition to American participation in WORLD WAR II. Persuaded by the work of "revisionist" historians of WORLD WAR I, such as his former student Harry Elmer Barnes, that proposed GERMANY was a country more sinned against than sinning, Beard concluded that Franklin Delano ROOSEVELT's increasingly antagonistic demeanor toward the Nazi regime was motivated above all by a desire to divert public attention from the shortcomings of the NEW DEAL.

In his final years, Beard published several works purporting to prove that Roosevelt had engineered the Japanese attack on Pearl Harbor in an attempt to draw the United States into the war, and spoke in condemnation of the trial of German war criminals at Nuremberg. In the 1960s, however, Beard's attacks on American liberal interventionism enjoyed a partial revival, being echoed by a new generation of historians who, in the light of the VIETNAM WAR, had come to share his critical stance against the United States' record in foreign policy during the 20th century.

BIBLIOGRAPHY. B.C. Borning, *The Political and Social Thought of Charles A. Beard* (University of Washington Press, 1962); R. Hofstadter, *The Progressive Historians: Turner, Beard, Parrington* (Knopf, 1968): T.C. Kennedy, *Charles A. Beard and American Foreign Policy* (University Presses of

Florida, 1975); E. Nore, *Charles A. Beard: An Intellectual Biography* (Southern Illinois University Press, 1983).

R.M. DOUGLAS, PH.D.
COLGATE UNIVERSITY

Becker, Gary (1930–)

AN INNOVATIVE ECONOMIST, Gary Becker has applied the tools of microeconomics to fields of inquiry that were not traditionally recognized as the purview of economics, such as racial discrimination, marriage and divorce, fertility, crime, and addiction. Whereas previously such behaviors were assumed to be determined by habit, culture, or irrationality, Becker's research shows that behavior in such areas is consistent with models of rational choice, in which individuals maximize their utility subject to constraints of time and finances.

Becker also increased the flexibility of the rational choice model. While early models of MICROECONOMICS posited that people were selfish, Becker allows agents in his models to be altruistic or selfish, discriminatory or egalitarian. In recent work, Becker has developed models in which people can choose their preferences.

One of Becker's most significant contributions is *Human Capital*, which studies the relationship between earnings and human capital (i.e., skills and knowledge), and how people choose to invest in their human capital. Becker argues that people will invest in their skills when the net present value of the future benefits of the investment exceeds the net present value of the costs. This work has been the foundation for research in education, on-the-job training, job search, migration, and wage inequality.

Becker was born in Pottsville, Pennsylvania, and grew up in Brooklyn, New York. He received his undergraduate degree from Princeton University and earned a Ph.D. in economics from the University of Chicago; his dissertation addressed the economics of discrimination. He has served on the faculties of the University of Chicago and Columbia University. In 1992 he was awarded the Bank of Sweden Prize in Economic Sciences in Memory of Alfred Nobel "for having extended the domain of microeconomic analysis to a wide range of human behavior and interaction, including non-market behavior."

BIBLIOGRAPHY. Gary S. Becker, "The Economic Way of Looking at Life," Nobel Lecture (1992); Gary S. Becker, *A Treatise on the Family: Enlarged Edition* (Harvard University Press, 1991); Gary S. Becker, *Human Capital: A Theoretical and Empirical Analysis with Special Reference to Education: Third Edition* (University of Chicago Press, 1993); Gary S. Becker, *The Economic Approach to Human Behavior* (University of Chicago Press, 1976); Gary S. Becker, *The Economics of Discrimination: Second Edition* (University of Chicago Press, 1971).

JOHN CAWLEY, PH.D.
CORNELL UNIVERSITY

Belgium

THE MODERN COUNTRY of Belgium did not exist until the 19th century. In the Middle Ages, it formed part of a loose conglomeration of 17 provinces known as the Low Countries. When the seven northern provinces split off to form the NETHERLANDS at the end of the 16th century, the area usually shared the designation of its imperial overseers, either by family name (Habsburg Netherlands) or country of origin (Spanish or Austrian Netherlands). The north and south briefly reunited in 1815 until the southern provinces again broke free and took the name Belgium.

In the Middle Ages, the southern provinces of Flanders and Brabant were among the most dynamic areas in the western world. Towns such as Bruges, Ypres, and Ghent pioneered the techniques of early industry and the area was a major exporter of luxury textiles, practically Europe's only industry. Those seeking work flocked to the towns, and the area was the most heavily urbanized in Europe outside of northern Italy.

The textile industry formed an important trading link to the rest of Europe. In the 12th and 13th centuries, the Flemish established outlets in northern Italy and became important merchants at the great international fairs. Shortly thereafter, many of the Flemish textile towns joined the Hanseatic League. Between 1250 and 1450, this commercial network united northern Europe in a trading nexus that stretched from England to Russia. For a brief period, the Brabant town of Antwerp functioned as the fulcrum of Europe and was a major center for trade, re-exporting and processing, and finance.

The reign of the southern Low Countries would come to an end with the Dutch Revolt from Spain at the end of the 16th century. The Spanish armies occupied the southern provinces for most of the Eighty Years War. Facing stricter Spanish religious policies, tens of thousands of merchants and textile workers fled to the independent provinces in the north, leaving the industry in the south sorely depleted. To add insult to injury, the newly formed United Provinces of the Netherlands placed a full embargo on trade with the south and blockaded the Scheldt river, the major artery for ships to reach Antwerp. With the flourishing of the Dutch republic, the southern Low Countries were relegated to relative economic obsolescence and obscurity.

The situation reversed in the late 18th century when Belgium became the first continental European country to embrace the INDUSTRIAL REVOLUTION. At first, Belgians did so by learning from the masters. In 1799, British industrial expert William Cockerill came to Belgium and developed a factory system that made use of their considerable coal reserves. Cockerill's factory, which produced metals and machinery as well as textiles, was for a time the largest in the world. Belgians also hired George Stephenson, credited with developing the first steam locomotive in England, to help them create an efficient railway system. By the World War I, per capita industrial output in Belgium equaled Great Britain's and Belgians were a leading world producer of steel.

In the 20th century, Belgium has shown remarkable resilience to the ravages of war. Thanks in part to post-WORLD WAR II economic aid such as the MARSHALL PAN, the non-coal producing regions in the north became the home to a variety of light industrial and chemical producing corporations, that helped the country to be one of the first to recover its balance of trade. These boosts worked to offset increasing losses in the aging and increasingly inefficient steel industry. The country remains prosperous and productive, with GROSS DOMESTIC PRODUCT (GDP) levels among the highest in the world, though Belgium also carries large amounts of debt.

The industries of Belgium consume enormous quantities of raw materials and the country's economic growth remains dependent on imports, most of which come from other European countries. Belgium also relies on European countries to purchase over three quarters of its exports. This dependence, along with small territory, has turned the Belgians into major supporters of European integration. They joined Benelux (1921) the European Coal and Steel Commission (1952), the European Monetary Union (1999), and currently the capital city of Brussels serves as the headquarters of the EUROPEAN UNION (EU).

BIBLIOGRAPHY. E.H. Kossman, *The Low Countries 1780–1940* (Oxford University Press,1978); Sidney Pollard, *Peaceful Conquest: The Industrialization of Europe 1760–1970* (Oxford University Press, 1981); Herman van der Wee, *The Low Countries in the Early Modern World* (Variorum, 1994).

LAURA CRUZ
WESTERN CAROLINA UNIVERSITY

Bentham, Jeremy (1748–1832)

THE SON OF A WEALTHY London lawyer, Jeremy Bentham studied law but had little interest in pursuing an active legal practice. He was known to his English contemporaries as a dedicated reformer and as a philosopher of reform rather than as an economist.

The reforms he championed encompassed a wide variety of programs ranging from prison to parliamentary reform, and his influence eventually changed the look of 19th-century England. Yet the philosophical radical movement associated with Bentham also exerted significant influence on post-Smithian (Adam SMITH) economic theory.

This movement attempted to develop principles, analogous to Isaac Newton's in the natural sciences, on which moral and social science could be built. These scientific principles were intended also to serve as the basis for social reform. However, it was not Bentham's technical economics but his utilitarianism mixed with hedonism that affected the future development of economics.

Bentham was influenced by the 18th-century Scottish historian and philosopher David HUME, who taught that human behavior was ultimately the product of sensation rather than reason. Consequently, from this perspective, Bentham developed his social ethics with an association of pleasure with moral goodness and pain with evil. With the underlying doctrine that one's objective should be to seek one's own greatest happiness, Bentham argued that government policies ought to be designed toward promoting the greatest happiness for the greatest number of persons. Such policies should include legal, moral, and social sanctions constraining any individual self-interest that might impede the greater good.

This was clearly a departure from the strict LAISSEZ-FAIRE philosophy of Smith that was based on a natural harmony of self-interests. Moreover, Bentham devised a social arithmetic or felicific calculus to add up pleasures and subtract pains from them, and hence made an early attempt to measure social welfare. According to Bentham, the social welfare was equal to the total welfare of all individuals in the society, an approach that was both democratic and egalitarian. He used money as a measure of pleasure and pain, and formulated the premise behind the principle of the diminishing marginal utility of money: that each extra unit of money provided less additional pleasure than the last.

Bentham's focus on the maxima and minima of pleasures and pains set a precedent for the search for optimum positions that is central to modern microeconomic theory. Bentham was a prolific writer, but the best of his expositions concerning human nature is *An Introduction to the Principles of Morals and Legislation* that remains a classic still today. Though utilitarianism no longer exerts the influence that it had in Bentham's day, the conceptual mechanism that Bentham used addressed many problems, such as the measurability of utility and of social welfare, and is still debated in WELFARE economics today.

BIBLIOGRAPHY. Robert B. Ekelund, Jr. and Robert F. Hebert, *A History of Economic Theory and Method* (McGraw-Hill, 1997); Philip C. Newman, *Development of Economic Thought* (Princeton University Press, 1952); Ingrid H. Rima, *Development of Economic Analysis* (McGraw-Hill, 2001).

ELEANOR T. VON ENDE, PH.D.
TEXAS TECH UNIVERSITY

Berle, Adolf A. (1895–1971)

BEST KNOWN FOR PROMOTING governmental supervision of corporations, Adolf Berle was a member of Franklin D. ROOSEVELT's brain trust, and formed government economic policy in the 1930s. His other significant contributions came in the form of legal scholarship, especially the seminal *The Modern Corporation and Private Property* published in 1932. In this work, Berle argued that the concentration of wealth and power in corporations had robbed stockholders of their ownership, and that the government should intervene to remedy this situation.

After graduating from Harvard Law School in 1916, Berle practiced corporate law while continuing a scholarly career. His legal articles in the 1920s focused on the lack of defined stockholder rights in an unregulated securities market. His first book, *Studies in the Law of Corporation Finance* (1928), favored corporate self-regulation rather than federal oversight to give greater control to stockholders.

In 1932, Berle joined Roosevelt's presidential campaign as an advisor on corporations. Primarily serving as a speechwriter, he developed the theme that speculators had to be curbed to allow the economic management that would create stability and security. With these words, Berle established the planning manifesto of the NEW DEAL. *The Modern Corporation*, an attack on large corporations written in conjunction with Gardiner C. Means, gave further support to the New Deal by arguing that the very size of modern industry meant that those outside of corporate management could only ensure that companies served the community by employing collective action to make small voices heard.

Berle spent the rest of his life serving in various political positions while also teaching and publishing. His legacy lies in his definition of government as the liberator of individuals from the tyrannies of large corporations.

BIBLIOGRAPHY. Beatrice Bishop Berle and Travis Jacobs, *Navigating the Rapids, 1918–1971: From the Papers of Adolf A. Berle* (Harcourt, 1973); Jordan A. Schwarz, *Liberal: Adolf A. Berle and the Vision of an American Era* (Free Press, 1987).

CARYN E. NEUMANN, PH.D.
OHIO STATE UNIVERSITY

Bismarck, Otto von (1815–98)

BORN IN BRANDENBURG, Germany, Otto von Bismarck studied law and agriculture and in 1847 entered the new Prussian Parliament as an ultra-royalist who was totally opposed to democracy. During the 1848 revolutions, he argued against constitutional reform, but as a member of the Federal German Diet at Frankfurt he demanded equal rights for Prussians.

Bismarck served as a foreign ambassador to RUSSIA (1859) and FRANCE (1862). Recalled in 1862, he became the leader of Prussia. At that time the kingdom was universally considered the weakest of the five European powers. Less than nine years later, Prussia had been victorious in three wars, and a unified German Empire had emerged in the heart of Europe, arousing envy and fear among its rivals. All of Bismarck's considerable tactical skills had been successful in creating a powerful German Empire in his first decade in power. For the next two decades these same skills maintained the peace.

In 1878–79, Bismarck initiated a significant change in economic policy, which coincided with his new alliance with the conservative parties at the expense of the liberals. Tariffs were introduced on iron as well as on major grains. The new policy was a result of the DEPRESSION that had swept Europe and the UNITED STATES in the mid-1870s. Bismarck's shift had serious political implications. It signified his opposition to any further evolution in the direction of political democracy. From 1879 onward, the landed elite, major industrialists, the military, and higher civil servants formed an alliance to forestall the rise of social democracy.

Ever since the Commune of Paris of 1871, Bismarck had developed an uncompromising hatred for socialists and anarchists. His attacks on them were egregious. At one point he wrote, "They are this country's rats and should be exterminated." Another time he called them "a host of enemies bent on pillage and murder." He thus introduced a crude and unsavory discourse into everyday German politics that was to be long-lived. Although only two socialists sat in the Reichstag parliament in 1871, their number and support grew with each election, until they had 35 seats in 1890. As early as 1876 Bismarck had sought legislation to outlaw the party but failed to get a majority. After two assassination attempts against

William I, Bismarck ran a campaign in which the socialists (quite unjustly) were blamed for the failed efforts to kill the emperor. The conservative parties triumphed and the Social Democratic Party was banned in 1878. The ban was renewed until 1890.

The second part of Bismarck's strategy to destroy social democracy was the introduction of social legislation to woo the workers away from political radicalism. During the 1880s, accident and old-age insurance as well as a form of socialized medicine were introduced and implemented by the government.

Bismarck was motivated to introduce social insurance in Germany both in order to promote the well-being of workers in order to keep the German economy operating at maximum efficiency, and to stave-off calls for more radical socialist alternatives. However, despite his impeccable right-wing credentials, Bismarck would be called a socialist for introducing these programs, as would U.S. President Franklin ROOSEVELT 70 years later. In his own speech to the Reichstag during the 1881 debates, Bismarck would reply: "Call it socialism or whatever you like. It is the same to me."

The German system provided contributory retirement benefits and disability benefits as well. Participation was mandatory and contributions were taken from the employee, the employer, and the government. Coupled with the workers' compensation program established in 1884 and the "sickness" insurance enacted the year before, this gave the Germans a comprehensive system of income security based on social insurance principles. (They would add unemployment insurance in 1927.)

But Bismarck's two-pronged strategy to win the workers for the conservative regime did not succeed. Support for the Social Democrats increased with each election. The election of 1890 was a disaster for Bismarck. The Centre, the Social Democrats, and the Progressives, the parties that he had termed enemies of the empire, gained more than half of the seats in the new Reichstag. The new young emperor, William II, did not want to begin his reign with a bloodbath or a coup d'état by the state. Seventy-five years old in 1890, Bismarck resigned with a sense of having failed. The antisocialist law was not revived, and the new government set out to win the workers to the regime.

Bismarck retired to his estate an embittered man. That he was now a prince and extremely wealthy did not ease his retirement. For the next eight years he issued sharp critiques of his successors. Elected to the Reichstag, he chose not to take his seat. He wrote his memoirs, which became bestsellers. He died July 30, 1898.

BIBLIOGRAPHY. Alan John Percivale Taylor, *Bismarck: The Man and Satesman* (Random House, 1975); Theodore S. Hamerow, *Otto von Bismarck: A Historical Assessment* (Heath, 1962); Geoff Eley, *Reshaping the German Right* (University of Michigan Press, 1991).

SYED B. HUSSAIN, PH.D.
UNIVERSITY OF WISCONSIN, OSHKOSH

black market

THE BLACK MARKET is the sector of economic activity that involves illegal activities. The term can be used to indicate different phenomena. It can be used to describe the illegal avoidance of TAX payments, the profits of narcotic trafficking, or profits made from theft. Black economy or black market affairs are conducted outside the law, and so are necessarily conducted metaphorically in the dark, out of sight of the law.

Black markets flourish particularly when governments place restrictions on the production or the selling of goods and services that come into conflict with market demands. These markets prosper, then, when state restrictions are heavy. Typical examples are the Prohibition Era in the UNITED STATES, when organized crime groups took advantage of the lucrative opportunities in the resulting black market in banned alcohol production and sales, or rationing especially during wars or famine. In many countries today, a "war on drugs" has created a similar effect for goods such as marijuana. Black markets are normally present in any type of economy as for some it is common wisdom that laws are made only to be broken.

The direct result of the increase in government restrictions is the rising of black market prices for the controlled goods, because legal restrictions represent a decrease in supply. According to the theory of SUPPLY and DEMAND, a decrease in supply, making the product more difficult or impossible to find, will increase PRICES. Similarly, increased enforcement of restrictions will increase prices for the same reason. However, products acquired illegally can also be less expensive than legal market prices, because the supplier did not have to sustain the normal costs of production and taxation (this is the case, for example, of bootlegged cigarettes).

Underground markets are vast and represent an important sector of national economies. The size of the black market in a particular country at a particular time also reflects the size and effectiveness of the bureaucratic machinery the government mobilizes to catch people who violate its economic regulations and the severity of the punishments that are regularly inflicted on those who get caught. Thus it was surely no accident that the regulated economic institutions of Nazi GERMANY, Soviet RUSSIA, eastern Europe and communist CHINA coexisted in symbiosis with gigantic regulatory and secret police apparatuses, extensive informer networks, crowded prison systems featuring thousands of slave labor camps, and frequent imposition of the death penalty for so-called "economic crimes."

The paradox was of course that members of the communist party who were officially fighting the black market were actually its first clients. Through the black market they could obtain services and commodities unavailable on the legal market. It was surely no accident that even the first very tentative and partial actions by the various communist regimes to abolish or restrain many of their more extreme "police-state" practices during the last decades of the 20th century soon resulted in an enormous expansion of black market activity, despite the fact that these governments were also just beginning to loosen up their control of the economy at the same time. In ESTONIA underground dealings are accountable for the 39 percent of the gross domestic product and the figures rise up to 45 percent for Russia and peak to the 51 percent for Ukraine. Underground markets represent the largest section of the domestic products of dictatorial regimes in developing countries: 65 percent in Bolivia and up to 76 percent in NIGERIA, just to limit the example to the most apparent cases.

The currency used for these illegal transactions is the U.S. dollar. This phenomenon started in the late 1960s and in the 1970s and climaxed in the 1990s when analysts calculated that about $20 billion in U.S. currency was shipped to foreign countries every year and that three-quarters of the total $100 bills circulated outside the United States. This wide circulation of American currency has proved a bonus for the American economy and figures show that, in 2000 alone, the U.S. Treasury earned approximately $32.7 billion in interest from foreign circulation of its banknotes. Some market analysts suspect that the 1996 redesign of the $100 bill was due to the creation of an extremely convincing fake from Middle-Eastern forgers, which was undermining the real bill in unofficial operations. It is anticipated that the new 500-euro note will be just as popular with smugglers and drug-dealers and for this reasons countries such as Portugal have already banned it.

Black markets are not simply endemic to dictatorial regimes or to countries where the state's interventions in the national economies are extensive. At the beginning of the 21st century, in European democracies shadow economies range from an estimated 12 percent in Britain to a 27 percent peak in ITALY, nourished by years of high unemployment, high tax rates, illegal immigration and widespread suspicion of governmental policies and politicians. In the United States, government efforts to regulate the economy have historically been minimal and the American commitment to the general ideal of free enterprise is usually considered as the strongest in the more industrialized Western countries. Nevertheless, several large examples of the black market can be easily found also in the United States. For example, the U.S. government has been extremely aggressive in its attempts to regulate and control economic activities during times of perceived national crisis, especially during wartime. World War II rationing and price controls were accompanied by extensive black market activity involving illegal dealings in meat, sugar, automobile parts and gasoline, penicillin and other regulated commodities, as well as common evasion of rent controls.

Even in relatively normal times, however, there are important areas of black market activity in the U.S. economy. According to Eric Schlosser, underground dealings covers 10 percent or more of the whole national market and, since the last three decades of the 20th century, has represented a parallel economy with its own secretive and well-hidden structure, its labor demand, prices and set of commodities. The American black market feeds on a queer mix of Puritanism and American's reckless faith in the ideal of a free market. For example, Americans consume more marijuana but also imprison more people due to marijuana-related crimes than the rest of the world. American laws guarantee maximum freedom to Californian agricultural employers so that migrant workers have become mainly illegal immigrants from MEXICO. This is a clear instance of how "the growing reliance on illegals has far-reaching implications beyond the underground, affecting wages, working conditions and even the practice of democracy in the rest of society."

As Schlosser has pointed out, the division between an underground and an over-ground market should be challenged: the shadow economy is inextricably linked to the mainstream. Striking parallels can be drawn between the two: both tycoons and gangsters rise and fall, new technology shapes both markets, government intervention can reinvigorate black markets as well as mainstream ones, big business learns and profits from the underground. "The lines separating them are fluid, not permanently fixed. One cannot be understood without regard to the other," Schlosser concludes.

BIBLIOGRAPHY. Peter Lilley, *Dirty Dealing: The Untold Truth About Global Money Laundering* (Kogan Page, 2001); Eric Schlosser, *Reefer Madness: Sex, Drugs and Cheap Labor in the American Black Market* (Houghton Mifflin, 2003); R.T. Taylor, *Wages of Crime: Black Markets, Illegal Finance, and the Underground Economy* (Cornell University Press, 2002).

LUCA PRONO, PH.D.
UNIVERSITY OF NOTTINGHAM, ENGLAND

BNP Paribas

THE FEBRUARY, 2003, issue of *Fortune* magazine listed this powerful financial services group as number seven among the world's banks and financial institutions. Created through a successful merger in the 1990s, BNP Paribas has solid roots around the world. In fact, analysts have cited it as the most profitable bank in continental Europe currently formulating an active presence in the United States. As well, it holds a leading position in Asia and is rated one of the top-ranking financial institutions in most of the 85 countries where it does business. But, because it is Paris-based, three quarters of its 85,000 employees work in geographic Europe, many within its 2,200 retail-focused branches in FRANCE.

The company is comprised of three core businesses: corporate and investment banking, retail banking, and private banking (which includes asset management, securities services and insurance). A franchise, BNP Paribas Capital, spearheads the private equity business, offering a comprehensive range of property-related products and services.

Continuing a growth strategy for the North American continent, BNP Paribas in the United States now owns BancWest, First Hawaiian Bank and, most recently, United California Bank. In 2001, net banking income rose 7.3 percent and operating income 11 percent. Revenues are at $55 billion with 18.2 percent return on equity and a cost/income ratio of 62.7 percent, one of the lowest in Europe.

BNP Paribas credits its success to its obsessive adherence to "Three Commitments." These are: To give first priority to customer satisfaction and to constantly improve customer relations and products; to put value-creation at the heart of shareowner options; and to ensure stimulating career-management and share-ownership programs for its employees. Commitments aside, BNP Paribas ranked as the 44th largest company in the world in 2002.

BIBLIOGRAPHY. BNP Paribas, "Investor Relations," www.bnpparibas.com; "Global 500: World Largest Companies," *Fortune* (July, 2002); "Fortune 500 corporate profile," www.fortune.com; *Hoover's Handbook*, "BNP Paribas," www.hoovers.com.

JOSEPH GERINGER
SYED B. HUSSAIN, PH.D.
UNIVERSITY OF WISCONSIN, OSHKOSH

board of directors

ACTING AS A GROUP, a board of directors collectively governs a corporation. The number of directors is set forth in a corporation's articles of incorporation, or the corporate bylaws, and may be subject to statutory limitations. Most directors serve for a term of one year, but many state statutes allow directors to serve for more than one year or stagger their terms.

Shareholders of the company elect the members who serve on the board. A director may be removed for cause, that is, for failing to perform a required duty. Generally, there is no statutory requirement concerning a director's qualifications. A few states do impose a minimum age or residency requirement. The articles of incorporation or the bylaws specify the amount of compensation a director shall receive.

Basically, a director has three major duties: the duty of care; the duty of loyalty; and, the duty of obedience. The duty of care dictates that the director uses such care that a reasonably prudent person would exercise under such circumstances. The duty of loyalty requires the director to act in a fiduciary manner. That is, the director must put the interest of the corporation and the shareholders ahead of her own. The duty of obedience requires directors, subject to law, to abide by the organization's mission and purposes as expressed in both the bylaws and articles of incorporation.

In addition to the above duties, a director must abide by any duties that may be imposed under statutory laws and court decisions. Directors are bound by civil rights laws that prohibit discrimination based upon gender, disability, religion or age. A director's failure to comply with these laws may expose her to personal liability. Recent corporate scandals, such as ENRON, and WORLDCOM, have caused lawmakers to evaluate the responsibility and accountability of directors.

Directors do have certain rights: They have the right to notice of all meetings, and the right to participate in them. The directors have the right to access to all corporate books and records, so as to allow them to undertake their duties properly. Such a right is absolute, and cannot be restricted in any manner.

The board of directors is responsible for certain management decisions. These include: the declaration and payment of dividends; the appointment and removal of officers; financial decisions such as the issuance of authorized shares of stock or bonds; and making major corporate policy decisions.

BIBLIOGRAPHY. R.L. Miller and G.A. Jentz, *Business Law Today* (South-Western, 2000); L. Stegink, "A Look at the Legalities," *Association Management* (v.55/1, 2003); Charles N. Waldo, *Boards of Directors: Their Changing Roles, Structure, and Information Needs* (Quorum Books, 1985).

MARK E. MOTLUCK, J.D.
ANDERSON UNIVERSITY

Boeing

IN 1903, THE WRIGHT BROTHERS MADE their first flight in Kitty Hawk, North Carolina. A few years later, William Boeing, an engineer, became entranced by aviation, and together with another engineer, began to develop an airplane. Boeing was founded in 1916 in Seattle, Washington, and grew to be the world's largest aircraft manufacturer, helped by significant government investment in the (military aircraft) industry before and during WORLD WAR II. Boeing has dominated the U.S. market since World War II, and indeed, by 1967, there were just two other rivals, McDonnell Douglas (MD) and, to a lesser degree, Lockheed Martin.

Douglas was incorporated in 1920, McDonnell in 1939, and the two firms merged to form MD in 1967. Although the firm dominated the early civil-aircraft industry, by 1991, MD was the United States' leading military-aircraft contractor, but was no longer a key player in civil aircraft. This was essentially due to its failure to devote sufficiently high RESEARCH AND DEVELOPMENT (R&D) to develop high quality civil airplanes. After MD faced serious financial difficulties in the 1990s, and as defense spending slowed significantly, Boeing acquired MD in 1997, after intense scrutiny by both the United States and European ANTITRUST commissions.

Boeing's biggest increase in market share came with the jet age, beginning in 1959. Boeing's first jet, the 707, successfully commercialized the technology developed with an earlier-awarded U.S. government military contract. In 1967, Boeing introduced the 737, and followed this with its most successful plane, the 747, in 1970. The 747 was an innovation that nearly bankrupted the firm, mainly due to the (unexpectedly) high R&D costs of $1 billion that were necessary to bring the plane to market, as well as a steep learning curve and significant production economies of scale. By 1990, however, its manufacturing capacity stood at 430 planes per year (approximately 70 percent of global demand at that time), and in 1994, Boeing held a 57 percent global market share, with a virtual monopoly in the long-range niche with the 747, and a major presence in all other ranges. The aircraft industry was often the largest net contributor to the U.S. balance of trade, and Boeing the largest U.S. exporter.

Since the mid 1980s, Airbus (a European consortium from GERMANY, FRANCE, the UNITED KINGDOM, and SPAIN, that was formed through the aid of EUROPEAN UNION subsidies) has emerged as a significant industry player. Airbus began life in the virtually untapped short- to medium-range market, but now competes against Boeing directly in the long-range market, and by 1994, had achieved a 28 percent global market share. In 1996, Airbus booked close to 50 percent of the world's new orders, and delivered almost one-third of the global output of civil aircraft.

There have been various trade disputes since the inception of Airbus, due to the large R&D subsidies, which Boeing and the U.S. government claim have violated the GENERAL AGREEMENT ON TARIFFS AND TRADE (GATT, now the WORLD TRADE ORGANIZATION). In 1992, these disputes were believed to be settled when Boeing and Airbus signed a bilateral agreement that limited the EU's direct R&D subsidies, and also the U.S. government's indirect aid (via military contracts).

After the 1997 merger with McDonnell Douglas, shareholders did not see the synergies that were expected and, in fact, Boeing recorded its worst performance for 50 years in 1997. This was mainly due to losses in civil aircraft arising from the phasing out of MD's airplanes, the relative neglect by Boeing's own management of their civil business in order to focus on expanding the military side, escalating production costs and inefficiencies, as well as the increasing competition from Airbus.

As the crisis deepened, Boeing attempted to return to profitability in 1998 by changing top management, reorganizing the two major product groups and introducing radical cost-cutting measures, including cutting R&D expenditure. In addition, Boeing chose not to invest in designing a new plane to compete with Airbus' new super-jumbo jet, the A380, but instead to focus on short-haul flights. Boeing also relocated their headquarters from Seattle to Chicago.

By 2002, Boeing had improved its performance. Boeing's revenues were $54.1 billion, 53 percent from civil aircraft and 47 percent from the military sector; net earnings were $2.3 billion, R&D expenditure was $1.6 billion, and 166,800 people were employed worldwide. Boeing's commercial aircraft include the 737, 747, 767 and the 777; its military aircraft include the F/A-18 Hornet strike fighter, and the F-15 Eagle bomber.

BIBLIOGRAPHY. "Collision Course in Commercial Aircraft: Boeing-Airbus-McDonnell Douglas," Harvard Business School (1991); I. Cohen, *The Boeing Company: the Merger with McDonnell Douglas* (San Jose State University Press, 1999); "Inside Boeing's Big Move," *Harvard Business Review* (2001); www.boeing.com.

CATHERINE MATRAVES
ALBION COLLEGE

Böhm-Bawerk, Eugen von (1851-1914)

ALONG WITH CARL MENGER and Friedrich von Weiser, Eugen von Böhm-Bawerk made up the original AUSTRIAN SCHOOL of economics. Böhm-Bawerk's particular contribution was in the area of CAPITAL and interest theory.

One of the major strands in the theoretical explanation of interest is that interest is paid because of the ordinary predominance of positive time preference. This is widely accepted among economists due to the influence of Irving FISHER, whose interest theory is, to a great extent, a translation of Böhm-Bawerk's idea into mathematical language.

Böhm-Bawerk's interest theory can be stated succinctly: Interest is an *agio*, a premium paid in an intertemporal exchange. Interest is normally positive because positive time preference usually predominates. To have positive time preference is to prefer obtaining something sooner rather than later.

For example, were your professor to bring a basket of sandwiches to class, and offer to give one to anyone who would promise to give in return two identical sandwiches next week, some people would probably agree to this. They would do it because they are hungry and they want the sandwich now. The extra sandwich would be interest. People pay interest because they want things now.

It is fairly easy to understand interest paid on a consumer loan as resulting from positive time preference. Böhm-Bawerk extended this idea to cover two cases in which the connection might not be so apparent. First, the net income that accrues from renting the services of a durable good is an *agio*. The price of a videotape is equal to the discounted value of the stream of services the tape is expected to provide. If one buys the tape at this price, then rents the services, the income received will be equal to the undiscounted total value of the stream of services. The difference between the two is interest. Buying the tape today and renting its services is an intertemporal exchange. Second, capitalist undertakings, in general, involve the transformation of things such as raw materials and labor into consumer goods. Since production takes time, this transformation can be thought of as another intertemporal exchange, and the capitalist's profit as interest.

Unfortunately, Böhm-Bawerk is better known for a widely dismissed idea about capital than for his seminal contribution to interest theory.

One of the reasons for positive time preference is "the technical superiority of present over future goods." This results from the benefits of "roundaboutness" in production. Spending time making a boat or a net is a roundabout way of catching a fish. Generally, deliberately chosen roundabout methods are superior. The more roundabout the method, the more capital goods that will exist, such as partially completed boats or nets, raw materials, and tools.

Böhm-Bawerk tried to use the "average period of production," defined as the average elapsed time between the expenditure of productive powers and the emergence of the finished product, to indicate the capital intensity of a process. This is what many people came to think of as "Austrian capital theory." The average period of production was used by some economists in the first half of the 20th century, but did not have much life after that.

BIBLIOGRAPHY. Eugen von Böhm-Bawerk, *Capital and Interest: Three Volumes in One* (Libertarian Press, 1959); Irving Fisher, *The Theory of Interest* (Kelley and Millman, 1930); Joseph A. Schumpeter, *History of Economic Analysis* (Oxford University Press, 1954): Henry Spiegel, *The Growth of Economic Thought* (Duke University Press, 1991).

SAMUEL C. WESTON, PH.D.
UNIVERSITY OF DALLAS

bond

A BOND IS A NEGOTIABLE contract that evidences debt and usually has a maturity of greater than five years. The issuer of a bond makes periodic, usually fixed, payments according to a predetermined schedule to the bondholder, and agrees to repay the principal amount at the maturity of the instrument. Bonds are usually issued in a standardized format, in physical form or book entry, with a contract that specifies all relevant terms and dates. Bondholders have claims that are senior to those of equity stakeholders in a company.

Bonds will usually have a series of key or common features. Principal value is the denomination or value of a bond. For trading purposes this is usually expressed as a percentage. Maturity or redemption is the date on which principal repayment occurs. A coupon is the interest payment amount. The coupon is usually quoted as an annual percentage of nominal value, and occurs on pre-determined dates as specified in the bond contract. Bond-call provisions set out the terms on which a bond issuer has the right to redeem a bond issue prior to maturity. This early redemption may usually only occur after a specific date and at a pre-determined price or yield. Bond-put provisions specify the holder's right to seek early redemption of a bond issue prior to maturity. Amortization also means that the bond is partially redeemed prior to maturity. Amortization can occur in several forms. A serial bond allows for either partial repayment of the principal amount or the retirement of a portion of the issue prior to the maturity of the bond. A sinking fund requires the issuer to repurchase part of the issue prior to maturity, while a purchase fund allows the issuer to repurchase part of the issue prior to maturity. A bond is usually put-able only on fixed dates and at predetermined yields or prices. A convertible bond gives bondholders the right to convert the bond issue into another security, often the common stock of the issuer.

Bond issues can be either secured or unsecured. A secured bond is collateralized by an asset or pool of assets pledged against the obligation by the issuer. The most common forms of secured bonds are asset-backed or mortgage-backed bonds. For an unsecured bond the issuer has only a general obligation. Consequently, secured bonds have prior claims over unsecured bonds with respect to certain assets in the case of default. This prior claim is a form of ranking, or seniority of a specific bond over other bonds of the same issuer. Unsecured bonds rank alongside general creditors, but above junior bonds whose claim is deferred to the claims of other bonds of a similar class. The claim of subordinated bonds is further deferred according to both class and repayment conditions.

Bond issues are governed by contracts, in which the above features are set out if applicable. These contracts are often called indentures or trust deeds and specify the obligations of both the bond issue and the bondholder. Often the trust deed will also detail a trustee who shall act for the interests of bondholders. This contract will also specify any covenants that may govern a particular issue. Covenants are terms and conditions that are intended to protect bondholders and can be affirmative or negative. While negative covenants require a bonds issuer to not take certain actions, affirmative covenants require issuers to take certain actions. A negative pledge means that a bond issuer has agreed not to issue any further debt that has priority over that issue. A breach of covenants can often be considered an event of default.

The price action of a bond can be described either in terms of percent nominal value or in terms of yield. Yield is usually cited as an annual percentage, and can be quoted as yield to maturity, yield to call, or yield to put. The yield calculates the return to the investor by taking the present value of the sum of future interest payments plus the present value of any future premium or discount and dividing by the purchase price of the bond. As this calculation shows, yield and price have a negative relationship: as the purchase price goes up, the yield must go down.

Bond yields are usually higher for those bonds that carry a greater risk of default. This risk is analyzed by credit-rating agencies such as Moody's, Standard and Poor's, and Fitch, who then publish credit ratings that act as standardized classifications of a company's comparative financial strength. This credit-worthiness is also usually evidenced by the price action, or yield of an issuer's bonds. Those issuers who carry a greater risk of default must pay a greater credit spread (a higher yield) in order to attract investors. Credit spreads are usually quoted as a basis point spread over

the domestic government bond spread, or with reference to the risk free rate.

Certain government DEBT, such as with the UNITED STATES, has customarily been considered risk-free. The risk-free rate is the rate of interest that one can earn without the risk of default. Default occurs when an issuer fails to make interest payments or principal repayments, or fails to meet other requirements of the specific bond contract. Bondholders' rights in default are determined by this contract or indenture, as well as the relevant local regulatory and legal environment.

Bonds can be issued by many different entities, including governments, government agencies, municipalities or regions and corporations. Government or municipal debt can often provide tax benefits (such as interest earned tax-free to holders). Corporate debt can also provide tax benefits, but to the corporation itself (such as interest payment deductibility). In all these forms, bonds can trade in the securities market.

BIBLIOGRAPHY. *Banking Terminology* (American Bankers Association, 1989); Peter Noles and Nicholas Terry, *The Handbook of International Financial Terms* (Oxford University Press, 1999); David W. Pearce, ed., *The MIT Dictionary of Modern Economics* (MIT Press, 1996); John Eatwell, Murray Milgate, Peter Newman, eds., *The New Palgrave: A Dictionary of Economics* (Macmillan, 1987).

KIRSTIN HILL
MERRILL LYNCH & COMPANY

Bosnia-Herzegovina

LOCATED IN THE NORTHWESTERN part of the Balkan Peninsula, Bosnia-Herzegovina has Croatia to the north, Serbia to the east, and Montenegro to the south. Bosnia-Herzegovina, often called Bosnia for the sake of simplicity, in the Middle Ages was the location of the kingdoms or principalities of Bosnia and Herzegovina.

In the mid-20th century, it was one of the six constituent republics (along with Serbia, Croatia, Slovenia, Montenegro, and Macedonia) of the Socialist Federal Republic of Yugoslavia. In April 1992, Bosnia declared its independence, which was recognized almost immediately by the UNITED STATES and other European countries and admitted soon after as a full member of the UNITED NATIONS.

In 1463, the Turkish Ottoman Empire took control of the region in its attempts to expand northward into Europe. Under Ottoman rule, many Bosnians, particularly wealthy elites who sought to maintain their properties and power, converted to Islam. The spread of Islamic culture and outlook also was influential in Bosnia. The result today is a religious and cultural mix. Most Bosnians speak Bosnian (Serbo-Croatian) and are Slavic in race but adhere to three different faiths. Bosnian Muslims (also called Bosniaks) make up approximately 40 percent of the population. Bosnian Serbs (who are Orthodox Christian) are about 31 percent and Bosnian Croats (who are Catholic Christian) are about 15 percent of the country's population.

This mix reveals one of the enduring characteristics of Bosnia: It is a border region that has never been ruled consistently or completely by any group, empire, or ideology. Unlike other parts of Yugoslavia, being a Bosnian refers to a region, not a nationality or ideology. The religious and cultural mix of Bosnians has caused them widespread and intense suffering in the 1990s as nationalist Serbs and Croats sought to carve out regions of Bosnia to create larger nation-states for themselves through the terror and carnage of warfare and "ethnic cleansing." In 1995, after years of terrible bloodshed, the United States and United Nations established and enforced, through the Dayton Accords, a military presence and a parliamentary democracy that precariously seeks to build a multi-ethnic nation-state. Bosnia and Herzegovnina consists of two areas, the Federation of Bosnia and Herzegovina (mainly Muslim and Croat, and divided into ten cantons) and the Republika Srpska (mainly Serb).

The country, with a population estimated at nearly 4 million, had a GROSS DOMESTIC PRODUCT (GDP) of $7 billion in 2001.

BIBLIOGRAPHY. Barbara Jelavich, *History of the Balkans* (Cambridge University Press, 1983); L.S. Stavrianos, *The Balkans since 1453* (Holt, Rinehart and Winston, 1958); Noel Malcolm, *Bosnia: A Short History* (New York University Press, 1994); Misha Glenny, *The Fall of Yugoslavia: The Third Balkan War* (Penguin Books, 1994); *CIA World Factbook* (2002).

GEORGE KOSAR
BRANDEIS UNIVERSITY

bourse

IN OLD FRENCH, a bourse is a purse or sack, whose likeness was used as a symbol for the meeting place of merchants in medieval Flanders. The term is commonly used to designate the formal stock markets of continental Europe, especially the exchange in 19th-century Paris. The Paris stock exchange was not like any other, as unique as the history of FRANCE.

Beginning in the late Middle Ages, Parisian merchants congregated on a bridge which is now named for their activities, the Pont-au-change. The sale of stock was not widespread, however, until the arrival of a Scottish rogue, John Law, in the early 18th century. Law convinced thousands of Frenchmen, including the regent Duke of Orleans, to purchase stock in his Mississippi Company. Law's charisma boosted the status of stockbrokers, who formed an official corporation in 1724. Law's company failed in spectacular fashion and many prominent members of French society lost their fortunes overnight. Because of this, the regent was forced to resign and the French became very concerned with regulating financial speculation of any kind, especially the sale of stock and they took actions to regulate the exchanges.

The number of officially licensed brokers (called *Agents de change*) was limited to 60, a restriction that remained in force throughout most of the 20th century. Only these 60 agents could legally buy and sell securities in France. To obtain such a desirable position, an applicant had to get approval from the government, then purchase his position (usually at a price beyond the reach of an individual; partners were usually required), and finally to proffer a substantial deposit, to be held by the government as security for his activities. If the new agent should succeed, he had to routinely supply full accounts of every transaction made to a board designed to review transactions. Though they were appointed for life, agents were forbidden to buy any stock for themselves and their income was derived strictly from commissions. The Company of Agents was directly accountable for losses incurred by any of its members. These stringent measures may seem strangely uncompetitive from the modern viewpoint, but they were quite effective in restoring faith in French finance.

Though some contemporary critics found the system of official brokers old-fashioned or medieval, modern theorists do not. In the bourse, officials used an auction system to set stock prices at a level where supply equaled demand. A particular security was traded at that set price for the remainder of the session, a practice devised to minimize speculative activities. Economists John Maynard KEYNES and Leon WALRUS both used this example in their models of ideal price formation and defense of perfect competition

The monopoly of the agents was briefly rescinded during the FRENCH REVOLUTION, but restored by Napoleon to help refinance French debt. Because of their close relationship with the government, the agents became major handlers of government securities, especially foreign securities, in the 19th century. Until 1914, more than half of the transactions of the bourse involved foreign countries and total foreign investment topped $14 million. While these operations were normally profitable, the French would be the chief victims of the repudiation of debt that followed the RUSSIAN REVOLUTION.

The other main source of French investment in the 19th century was railroad stock, but these transactions were not usually handled by the agents. Outside of the official business done at the parquet (a raised circular platform inside the bourse), a number of unofficial agents did their business outside, on the steps. Because of this, they were referred to as *Coulisse* (those waiting in the wings) though they preferred the term "free market." The *Coulisse* handled railroad stock because they represented the speculative element in French finance, which was forbidden to the agents. By 1900, over 500 firms maintained this shadowy existence. There was nearly constant tension between the two groups and each tried to eliminate the other. Analysts believe that the two complemented each other in practice and efforts at elimination were blocked by the French voters.

In the end, the *Coulisse* won out and the Company of Agents was dissolved in 1988. Without the agents, the bourse lost many of its unique features. In 2000, the stock markets of Amsterdam, Brussels, and Paris combined to form Euronext.

BIBLIOGRAPHY. George R. Gibson, *The Stock Exchanges of London, Paris, and New York: A Comparison* (1889); William Parker, *The Paris Bourse and French Finance: with Reference to Organized Speculation in New York* (Columbia University Press, 1967); George V. Taylor, "The Paris Bourse on the Eve of the Revolution, 1781–1789," *The American Historical Review* (July 1962); Donald A. Walker, "A Factual Account of the Functioning of the Paris Bourse," *European Journal of Economic Thought* (Summer, 2001).

LAURA CRUZ
WESTERN CAROLINA UNIVERSITY

BP (British Petroleum)

BRITISH PETROLEUM (originally called the Anglo-Persian Oil Company) owes its origins to William Knox D'Arcy, who was convinced that there were large oil deposits in IRAN (then Persia). After making the oil discovery, BP was formed in 1909, and was fully privatized in 1987, when the British government sold its 51 percent stake, acquired for strategic reasons during WORLD WAR I. BP has major oil-exploration facilities in Alaska, the Gulf of Mexico, COLOMBIA, and the North Sea, with current production activities in 22 countries. BP is vertically integrated, that is, BP is present in the exploration and production of crude oil and natural gas, refining, marketing, and the petrochemical industry.

In the 1990s, BP undertook significant restructuring to improve efficiency, similar to many of its major rivals. BP and Amoco (incorporated in 1889, formerly Stan-dard Oil, Indiana) completed their $53 billion merger on December 31, 1998. BP Amoco went on to acquire ARCO (founded in 1866 as the Atlantic Petroleum Storage Company) and Burmah Castrol in 2000, and Veba Oil (Germany) in 2002.

In 2001, BP was the second largest petroleum refining company in the world, and ranked fourth overall on *Fortune* magazine's Global 500 list of the largest companies in the world, with proved oil reserves of 7.8 billion barrels. BP has 115,250 employees, 16.4 percent in the UK, and 37.8 percent in the United States. BP earned revenues of $178.7 billion in 2002, operating 29,200 service stations worldwide, with 15,000 in the United States alone. Of total sales, refining and marketing accounted for 68.5 percent, oil exploration for 4 percent, gas and other renewables for 20.2 percent, and chemicals for 7 percent.

An exciting new growth opportunity for BP is the construction of the BTC pipeline, which will transport oil in the (formerly Soviet controlled) Caspian Basin. Over the next years, BP aims to develop new activities to replace and expand current reserves, as well as strengthening its capabilities in refining, marketing, and petrochemical manufacturing.

BIBLIOGRAPHY. www.bp.com; K. Cool, J. Reuer, I. Montgomery and F. Gee, "BP-Mobil and the Restructuring of the Oil Refining Industry," *INSEAD* (1999); "Global 500: World Largest Companies, " *Fortune* (July, 2002).

CATHERINE MATRAVES
ALBION COLLEGE

Brazil

LATIN AMERICA'S LARGEST and most populous economy, Brazil is a mid-income developing country. Brazil's territory is larger than the contiguous United States and well endowed with natural resources; most of its soil is arable and rich in minerals.

The country's abundance of natural resources was nevertheless virtually ignored by the rest of world until 1530, when PORTUGAL, 30 years after first arriving in the area, started exploring Brazil's stock of brazilwood. The extraction of brazilwood did not last long, however. With the lack of proper care in the exploration process, before the 16th century was over the country's stock of brazilwood was virtually depleted.

Simultaneously, Portugal's interest shifted to the production of sugarcane in the northeastern part of Brazil. The production of sugar turned out to be a very profitable activity from the second half of the 16th century until around 1750, with the country holding the post of world's largest producer for several decades. This status was nonetheless lost in the second half of the 17th century, when the Dutch colonies in the Caribbean began to produce sugar more efficiently and of better quality than Brazil's.

The downturn in the profitability of sugar production characterizes a long period of economic stagnation in Brazil. The country's economy reinvigorated only by the end of the 17th century, with the emergence of the so-called gold cycle, which took place mainly in the southeastern state of Minas Gerais.

The extraction of gold, especially during the peak years, was by all criteria very substantial as a proportion of Brazil's economy, as a support of Portugal's declining economy, and even as a significant contributor to Europe's inflation. Moreover, and in spite of the deep decline in gold production from the mid-18th century on, the gold cycle had important structural consequences for Brazil. By fostering the development of urban agglomerations in the southeastern part of the country, it induced demand for goods and services that were supplied mainly by northeastern and southern producers, thus promoting the country's economic integration. The extraction of gold also stimulated the first significant flow of European immigration to Brazil.

On the political side, Brazil obtained its independence from Portugal in 1822, largely as a result of the Napoleonic Wars, which forced Portugal's king to move to Brazil in 1807, taking with him the official capital of Portugal's empire.

As an independent country, Brazil was ruled as a monarchy until 1889, when it became republican. During that period, and for at least 40 more years, the country's economy relied mainly on agriculture, where the production of coffee played (by far) the leading role: By the end of the 19th century, coffee accounted for more than half of Brazil's EXPORTS. The coffee boom in Brazil induced significant immigration flows from countries such as ITALY, SPAIN, GERMANY, and JAPAN.

It was only after the world economic crisis of the 1930s that Brazil's economy started to diversify and industrialize. The industrialization process was oriented toward "import substitution," with support for domestic industries and restrictions on manufactured imports as the rule. Industrialization was sought through public direct investments focused on "heavy" industrial sectors such as energy and steel, and with the use of multiple instruments to induce private investment in targeted industrial sectors. The latter included production subsidies, import restrictions, subsidized credit, and foreign-exchange controls. There were also circumstances when policies to attract foreign direct investment were promoted, but those were relatively short-lived, taking place especially during the Kubitscheck administration (1956–60).

Interestingly, the orientation in the control of the economy varied little until the early 1990s, in spite of sweeping periodical overturns in Brazil's political scenario. Ruled as an oligarchic republic in the first 30 years of the 20th century, Brazil was governed by only one person, Getúlio Vargas, for the subsequent 15 years under three distinct political regimes. Democracy was re-established after WORLD WAR II, but only to succumb again in 1964, when the military took control for the ensuing 21 years. Ironically, although the military coup was motivated mainly by economic problems, the conduct of the economy did not change much after 1964. In fact, the military ruling only amplified the tendency of enlarging the government and handpicking private sectors to support.

As a result of the interventionist policies of the state, by 1985, the government held direct or indirect control of a large part of the Brazilian economy. State-controlled sectors ranged from telecommunications and electricity to steel and oil. By contrast, the private sector was largely inactive and dependent on the government's incentives.

The interventionist strategy did, however, create a diversified industry. It also generated substantial growth during some periods, in particular throughout the Kubitscheck administration and for most of the 1970s. But growth plummeted after 1980 and has not yet (by 2003) recovered significantly since then.

A key element behind the dismal growth in the last two decades has undoubtedly been the recurrent public deficits, with resulting high internal and external debts. The public deficits reflected, to a large extent, the industrialization strategy and the government's historical disregard of inflation, which plagued Brazil from the late 1950s to the mid-1990s. In fact, the Brazilians' ability to cope with price instability has been remarkable: after more than two decades of double-digit inflation, the population still managed to adjust to inflation of three to four digits for yet another decade.

Many changes have occurred since 1990, however. Democracy has been fully re-established and the country has become substantially more market-oriented and open. This was the result of a set of liberal reforms that included a far-reaching privatization program and significant trade liberalization, at the unilateral and the regional levels, with Argentina, Paraguay, and Uruguay.

Moreover, the Real Plan in 1994 represented the first successful stabilization plan after a sequence of failed heterodox attempts to control inflation. Despite severe balance of payments restrictions from 1995 to the early 2000s, faced by most developing countries, the Real Plan has been by all accounts successful in eliminating chronic inflation.

Although it is hard to overstate the benefits of low inflation, in Brazil the most important consequence has probably been on income distribution, as the drastic reduction of the inflationary tax has helped especially the poorest in the country. Nevertheless, although alleviated with the end of high inflation, income inequality remains one of the most pressing issues in Brazil.

BIBLIOGRAPHY. Marcelo P. Abreu, org., *A Ordem do Progresso—Cem anos de política econômica republicana: 1889–1989* (Campus, 1989); E. Bradford Burns, *A History of Brazil* (Columbia University Press, 1980); Instituto Brasileiro de Geografia e Estatistica, www.ibge.gov.br; Ronald M. Schneider, *Order and Progress* (Westview Press, 1991); Roberto C. Simonsen, *História Econômica do Brasil: 1500–1820* (Companhia Editora Nacional, 1937).

EMANUEL ORNELAS, PH.D.
UNIVERSITY OF GEORGIA

Bretton Woods

THE BRETTON WOODS SYSTEM refers to the international monetary agreement negotiated in Bretton Woods, New Hampshire in July 1944. The agreement implemented an international fixed-exchange rate system tying the U.S. dollar to gold and, other currencies to the DOLLAR. This system functioned until March 1973, when it was replaced with a system of floating exchange rates for the major industrialized nations. The Bretton Woods agreement also established the INTERNATIONAL MONETARY FUND (IMF) and the WORLD BANK, two important financial institutions that continue to operate despite the demise of the exchange-rate system adopted at Bretton Woods.

The international GOLD STANDARD (1870–1914) fostered price stability and provided a mechanism to prevent nations from running chronic trade imbalances. As a fixed exchange-rate system, the gold standard enjoyed the predictability merchants and governments desired (since the value of one currency in terms of another was "fixed"), but necessitated active central bank intervention to preserve convertibility of currencies into gold. This intervention frequently required manipulating interest rates, a practice that often conflicted with other economic goals.

WORLD WAR I placed the gold standard on hold. Despite efforts to restore the gold standard after the war, the Great DEPRESSION and WORLD WAR II forced nations to again suspend gold convertibility. This left the international monetary system in chaos. Many observers viewed the system of floating exchange rates as a source of destabilizing speculation. There was also a growing awareness that national governments were no longer willing to sacrifice domestic employment goals to protect fixed exchange rates. Consequently, the Bretton Woods conference participants wanted to construct a post-war monetary system that resembled the gold standard but also accommodated newly recognized government responsibilities for fostering full employment.

The Bretton Woods agreement sought to address trade imbalances through a mechanism that wouldn't require recessionary policies, such as raising interest rates. This mechanism was to be achieved through a combination of "adjustable pegs," capital controls, and IMF lending. "Adjustable pegs" acknowledged the occasional need for a fixed exchange rate to be adjusted (through either a devaluation or a revaluation) because of a "fundamental disequilibrium." Though the term "fundamental disequilibrium" was never actually defined, it was generally understood to apply to a situation where permanent changes in trade conditions required modifying an existing exchange rate. As indicated, the Bretton Woods agreement also created the IMF, an institution designed to lend foreign currencies to nations facing trade imbalances. Finally, the agreement permitted government restrictions on international capital flows as a means to control speculative activity.

As World War II drew to a close, the war-torn nations of Europe needed U.S. exports to assist with rebuilding their economies, but they lacked strong manufacturing sectors to produce trade-able goods. The result was a chronic dollar shortage, only partially alleviated by the $13 billion dollar foreign aid package known as the MARSHALL PLAN implemented by the U.S. government in 1948. Marshall Plan assistance helped with the dollar shortage, but European powers struggled nonetheless, and many were forced to devalue their currencies in 1949. Interestingly, it is argued pressure from the U.S. government kept the IMF from intervening to assist Marshall Plan recipients with payments problems associated with trade imbalances, presumably to enhance U.S. leverage with those nations. In any event, by the late 1950s the rebuilding process had advanced sufficiently to permit European nations to restore currency convertibility, an important goal of the Bretton Woods agreement.

By 1960, the dollar shortage had vanished, European nations had built sufficient currency reserves, and policymakers began to worry about the long-term viability of a system based on gold-backed U.S. dollars. As the global dollar shortage turned into a dollar glut, a series of measures were implemented to keep the system solvent. These measures started as early as 1961 and persisted through the creation of two-tiered gold markets and "Special Drawing Rights" in 1968. Despite these efforts the United States continued to lose gold reserves and the long-term viability of the system grew increasingly problematic.

To further complicate matters, the post-war rebuilding process dramatically improved the competitiveness of European and Japanese economies, undermining the dominance of U.S. exports. This erosion, coupled with ambitious (and expensive) U.S. political and military agendas (as well as accelerating inflation in the United States) shifted U.S. trade surpluses to trade deficits by the end of the 1960s and further exacerbated the global excess of U.S. dollars.

By 1970, the situation had reached crisis proportions. U.S. gold reserves had fallen from $22.7 billion in 1951 to $11.8 billion. Dwindling reserves and rising U.S. trade deficits combined to create a situation that was not sustainable. As a result, U.S. President Richard NIXON "closed the gold window" in August 1971, declaring that the United States would no longer back U.S. dollars with gold reserves at the rate of $35 per ounce. Though viewed as a temporary solution until a devaluation of the U.S. dollar could be negotiated, this drastic action spelled the beginning of the end for the Bretton Woods system. Although a devaluation of the dollar was implemented later that year, it proved to only be a temporary solution. In early 1973, another crisis emerged, and by March of that year the currencies of major industrial nations were floating (within limits) against the dollar. This system of market-based exchange rates has remained in place ever since.

BIBLIOGRAPHY. Fred L. Block, *The Origins of International Economic Disorder* (University of California Press, 1977); Barry Eichengreen, *Globalizing Capital: A History of the International Monetary System* (Princeton University Press, 1996); Robert Guttmann, *How Credit-Money Shapes the Economy: The United States in a Global System* (M.E. Sharpe, 1994); Paul R. Krugman and Maurice Obstfeld, *International Economics: Theory and Policy* (Addison-Wesley, 1997).

PATRICK DOLENC, PH.D.
KEENE STATE COLLEGE

bribery

GENERALLY DEFINED as money or favor, a bribe is given or promised in order to influence the judgment or conduct of a person in a position of trust. Transparency International, an international non-governmental organization devoted to combating national corruption, defines bribery in terms of behavior on the part of officials in the public sector, whether politicians or civil servants, in which they improperly and unlawfully enrich themselves or those close to them by the misuse of the power entrusted to them.

Thus, here bribery is expressed as the misuse of public power for private profit and is a significant aspect of a broader social, political, and economic ill:

CORRUPTION. In 1997, the Organization for Economic Co-Operation and Development (OECD) broadened its definition of bribery to include international business transactions. Specifically, the OECD Convention on Combating Bribery of Foreign Public Officials in International Business Transactions defines bribery as a criminal offence whereby a person intentionally offers, promises, or gives any pecuniary or other advantage, whether directly or through intermediaries, to a foreign public official to obtain or retain business or other improper advantage in the conduct of international business. This broad definition explicitly recognizes that both parties, the public servant receiving bribe and the person giving the bribe, are equally guilty. It criminalizes bribery for everyone involved in the act of bribery: transnational companies, as well as the foreign civil servants.

From an economic and capitalist point of view, a bribe is a rent or personal profit collected by a public servant who is holding a monopolistic position in a public agency. The primary economic cost of bribery is misallocation of resources because it distorts competition and channels resources to areas where they are not used in the most efficient and productive manner.

On the other hand, according to the "efficient grease" hypothesis, bribery could be perceived as a way to go around the bureaucratic red tape, reducing the cost of regulation and hence eliminating delays. Therefore, it could actually improve economic efficiency. However, the argument that bribery could raise efficiency is shortsighted because, in the long run, the persistence of bribery would inevitably lead to an increase in bureaucratic regulation to collect bribes. This proliferation would at one point become regressive enough to lower economic efficiency significantly.

Other economic costs of bribery include its adverse effects on investment, economic growth, and economic inequality. Because bribery can influence government contracts, licenses, permits, legal outcomes, and benefits, it raises uncertainty and risk. It might therefore divert investment funds to speculative use, lowering investment and growth. It might even shift these funds into the underground economy. Bribery and corruption may decrease the quality and availability of public goods and services, such as education and health care, limiting the productivity and income potential of economically disadvantaged groups.

Bribery is often regarded as a characteristic phenomenon of developing countries. It is argued that factors such as culture, regressive political regimes, high inflation, low salaries for civil servants, and lack of economic freedom are causes of bribery in such countries. Recently, however, events in the UNITED STATES and Europe have shown that bribery and corruption are common to all political and economic systems.

At the same time, however, it is well documented that free market systems and democracy affect the quality of governance institutions and act as a deterrent to bribery and corruption. An effective way to deter bribery is the development of institutions that foster accountability and transparency in the public sector, and that have strong legislative and judicial systems with severe penalty for bribery.

BIBLIOGRAPHY. J. Cartier-Bresson, "Economics of Corruption." *OECD Observer* (v.221/222, 2000); D. Kaufmann and Shang-Jin Wei, "Does 'Grease Money' Speed Up the Wheels of Commerce?" *NBER Working Paper: 7093* (National Bureau of Economic Research, 1999); "Helping Countries Combat Corruption: A World Bank Strategy" (The World Bank, 1997), www.transparency.org.

M. ODEKON
SKIDMORE COLLEGE

Buchanan, James (1791–1868)

THE 15TH PRESIDENT of the United States, James Buchanan was born in Mercersburg, Pennsylvania. After graduating from Dickinson College in 1809, he studied law and was admitted to the Bar in 1812.

Buchanan entered politics after returning from the WAR OF 1812. He served in the U.S. House of Representatives and Senate, and had a diplomatic career as President Andrew JACKSON's minister to Russia, President James POLK's secretary of state, and President Franklin PIERCE's minister to England.

As minister to the UNITED KINGDOM, Buchanan wrote the Ostend Manifesto, stating the United States would be justified in annexing Cuba through military force. The document's publication embarrassed the Pierce administration and enraged Northerners, as they perceived the Manifesto as a Southern effort to expand the power of slave owners.

Buchanan unsuccessfully sought the Democratic presidential nomination in 1844, 1848, and 1852. He was nominated in 1856, primarily because his absence from the country during the controversial Kansas-Nebraska Act and his reputation as a compromiser made him more acceptable than President Pierce or others. Buchanan won the election, primarily based on Southern support.

President Buchanan hoped to rise above politics by announcing at his inauguration that he would not seek a second term. However, this only weakened his position as both sides saw him as a lame duck from the beginning.

Buchanan's Cabinet included no anti-slavery Democrats. He urged support for the Supreme Court's 1857 decision in *Dred Scott v. Sanford*, which held that the government could not restrict slavery in any territories. Buchanan also supported the Kansas pro-slavery faction's application for statehood.

As *Dred Scott* and "Bleeding Kansas" enraged the North, abolitionist John Brown ignited Southern tempers. In 1859, Brown raided Harper's Ferry, Virginia, with the hope of starting a slave rebellion. Although the raid was quickly quelled, it rekindled Southern fears of a slave revolt.

By 1857, U.S. banks had heavily invested in railroads and western land. With increased uncertainty about the future of the west after the *Dred Scott* decision, land values fell dramatically. The subsequent failure of the Ohio Insurance Company in New York raised concerns that escalated when an uninsured shipment of more than 16 tons of gold from California was lost at sea, leaving bankers without sufficient specie to meet demand. First New York banks, but later banks nationwide, experienced panic runs and failures. The subsequent RECESSION led to deficit spending, tripling the national debt by the end of Buchanan's term. Because the recession particularly hit Northern manufacturers, some historians speculate the recession showed how Northern economic interests were in direct conflict with Southern interests, thus influencing the decision of Southern states to secede.

A divided Democratic party nominated two candidates for president in 1860. Northerners supported Senator Stephen Douglas, while Buchanan and the Southerners backed Vice President John Breckenridge. As a result, Republican Abraham LINCOLN won the divided election.

After Lincoln's election, but before he took office, Southern states seceded and formed the Confederacy. Buchanan did nothing to stop them. He even allowed his Southern secretary of war to ship arms to the South where the Confederate Army would take control of them. However, when Buchanan refused to abandon Fort Sumter in Charleston harbor, the South's attack on that fort began the AMERICAN CIVIL WAR.

Buchanan seemed relieved to leave the presidency. He supported Lincoln and the Union during the war although he opposed emancipation on the grounds it was unconstitutional. Despite his support, Buchanan was seen as a Southern sympathizer and as the president who let the nation fall into Civil War. Buchanan spent most of his final years trying to justify his actions as president.

BIBLIOGRAPHY. Charles W. Calomiris and Larry Schweikart, "The Panic of 1857: Origins, Transmission, and Containment," *Journal of Economic History* (v.51/4, 1991); James Huston, *The Panic of 1857 and the Coming of the Civil War* (Louisiana State University Press, 1987); Nathan Miller, *Start-*

Spangled Men (Scribner, 1998); Elbert Smith, *The Presidency of James Buchanan* (University Press of Kansas, 1975).

MICHAEL J. TROY, J.D.
THOMAS D. JEITSCHKO, PH.D.
MICHIGAN STATE UNIVERSITY

Buchanan, James M. (1919–)

JAMES BUCHANAN WAS awarded the 1986 Nobel Prize in Economics for "for his development of the contractual and constitutional bases for the theory of economic and political decision-making." His 1962 book *The Calculus of Consent* written with Gordon Tullock, bridged a gap between economics and politics, by initiating a research field—public choice—that encompasses the economic analysis of political decision-making.

Public finance, as taught in the 1950s, assumed a social welfare function that needed to be maximized by the government as if by a benevolent dictator. This, according to Buchanan, trivialized economics as mathematical maximization exercises based on a suspect assumption, an aggregate measure of social welfare, and took economics away from its political economic roots. Policies based on this premise often have costly unintended consequences for both economic WELFARE and democratic institutions.

Buchanan, a student of Frank KNIGHT, offered an alternative perspective, which has come to be known as neo-institutionalism that is entwined with public choice, law and economics, and the economics of property rights. The central focus of this perspective is rooted in Adam SMITH's concept of mutually beneficial exchanges. Efficiency in voluntary exchange transactions is realized because markets allow an institutional framework for individuals to engage in mutually beneficial behavior. The modern political process did not allow mutually beneficent behavior between the public and its government (principle-agent problem). Buchanan created a political model that was based on the assumption that the principle agents, politicians and bureaucrats, acted like everyone else, in their own interests, and not in the interests of the public. As such, both adverse selection and MORAL HAZARD would be present in the political class. Buchanan thought that a cultural conservatism could temper the self-interest of the agent, but that in its absence the agent's self-interest would be toward bigger government budgets or to please the special-interest groups that could offer rewards with post-government private sector employment. The result would be a perception that the provision of public services doesn't serve the public's interests.

Although politicians and bureaucrats can be noble, it doesn't take many of the other kind to cause a cynical perception of government. When combined with the observation that regularly scheduled elections do not provide any real electoral sanctions, the public would have even less incentive to monitor the agents. Buchanan saw this as a threat to democratic government.

Influenced by the Swedish economist Knut Wicksell, Buchanan believed that to improve politics, one had to improve the rules and the structure. It isn't the agents' fault, given the rules of the modern political experience with democracy. It's the rules that need adjustment. Although a libertarian in political orientation, he also saw that individuals have a perceived importance of personal involvement in the collective process. He argued that the rule of unanimity was the counterpart to voluntary market exchange. To avoid the consequences of the Hobbesian state of anarchy, and its costs, cooperative behavior is sought out through rules. Buchanan's work will look for rules that are based on unanimity and result in mutual gain from social cooperation. For small homogeneous populations, unanimity is reached and a social contract can be established relatively easily. However, he realized that social contracts must be kept up to date and will need periodic adjustments. He was aware that changing the status quo is not a free good. For larger heterogeneous groups, unanimity is costlier and needs to be weighted against the benefits of social cooperation. Buchanan argued for a geographic decentralization of the political process that would allow for the devolution of the decision-making process with unanimity of consent attained more easily.

Buchanan's rules need to be set out under a veil of uncertainty. Although he would be troubled with an outcome espoused by social democrats, a good rule would not preclude that result. The key condition is that the rule be freely agreed upon unanimously, *ex ante*. Buchanan calls on fellow economists to seek out the rules that would improve the institutional environment for democracy. He sees this as the principal moral responsibility of economists.

BIBLIOGRAPHY. James Buchanan and Gordon Tullock, *The Calculus of Consent: Logical Foundations of Constitutional Democracy* (University of Michigan Pres, 1962); James Buchanan, *Cost and Choice* (Libert Fund, 1969), *The Demand and Supply of Public Goods* (Libert Fund, 1968), *Freedom in Constitutional Contract* (Texas A&M University Press, 1977); James Buchanan and Robert P. Tollison, *The Limits of Liberty* (University of Chicago Press, 1975); David Reisman, *The Political Economy of James Buchanan* (Texas A&M University Press, 1990).

HARRY KYPRAIOS, PH.D.
ROLLINS COLLEGE

Burke, Edmund (1729–97)

AN ILLUSTRIOUS STATESMAN, parliamentarian political thinker active in British public debates after 1765, Edmund Burke is remembered primarily as England's most outspoken opponent of the FRENCH REVOLUTION.

His responses to this fundamental political challenge in his most famous work, *Reflections on the Revolution in France* (1790) produced arguments about the ideal quality of social change that lie at the basis of conservative political thought in the West since the French Revolution. Born in Ireland, Burke entered Parliament in 1765 as the secretary to a Whig minister, the Marquis of Rockingham, and served subsequently himself as minister representing the pocket borough of Wendover. In Parliament, Burke became known for his pragmatist and liberal views on FREE TRADE, the management of colonies, and opposition to national budget deficits.

He opposed British colonial policy in North America. Burke was a contemporary and friend of Adam SMITH, and evidence suggests that while Burke originally arrived at his economic views due to his education at the University of Dublin, and so independently of Smith, the two thinkers appreciated and influenced each other's subsequent work. The most important assumption of Burke's thought is his emphasis on the support of traditional order and the maintenance of social stability, two concepts that underlay all of his works.

This preoccupation has been related by various authors to Burke's loyalty to British hierarchical society, his inheritance of Aristotelian ideas and natural law thinking, his conviction that civilized society was the prerequisite for successful commerce (a contradiction to the views of the Scottish political economists, that commerce led to civilized society), or his view that the origin of government lay in its prerogative to protect property. On a political level, Burke argued that social change should occur slowly and organically, according to the inherited constitution of a country, and that tradition, rather than metaphysical speculation, should govern the structure and content of politics.

Although Burke's economic attitudes can be read throughout his works and seen to underlie his complaints about the French Revolution (he thought, for instance, that the debt crisis that provoked the threatened government bankruptcy of 1789 could have been avoided if the government had been prevented from financing its debt in this way), his most explicit economic text is *Thoughts and Details on Economic Scarcity* (1795). In it, he equated the laws of commerce with natural and divine law, and coined the phrase "bite the hand that feeds them" in an argument against government food support for the poor. This text is frequently used to support an understanding of Burke as a supporter of an unrestrained free-market economy, the interpretation of Burke's political economy adopted by utilitarians and most common until recent decades, against which Karl MARX reacted sharply in *Capital*. The text, however, should not be separated from its context. Intended as a persuasive memorandum to British Prime Minister Pitt in response to the Speenhamland famine, it was published only in 1800 after his death and is specifically a response to local circumstances. In 1795, after repeated famines, justices of the peace subsidized wages of workers whose earnings fell below subsistence, thereby negatively impacting the local wage market for both laborers and employers.

The text should be read as an argument against government wage supports, not a justification of allowing the hungry to starve, for Burke himself supported private charitable efforts both in print and in person. This apparent disjunction might be attributed to a general philosophical emphasis in Burke's thought on prudence and pragmatism.

Recent interpretations, particularly that of Francis Canavan, have turned away from reading Burke as an unmitigated supporter of LAISSEZ-FAIRE capitalism and focused on his notions of common good deriving from property, as an outgrowth of natural law.

BIBLIOGRAPHY. Edmund Burke, "Excerpt from Thoughts and Details on Economic Scarcity," www.swan.ac.uk; Edmund Burke, *The Portable Edmund Burke* (Penguin Putnam, 1989); Francis Canavan, *The Political Economy of Edmund Burke: The Role of Property in His Thought* (Fordham University Press, 1990); C.B. MacPherson, *Burke* (Hill & Wang, 1980); J.G.A. Pocock, "The Political Economy of Burke's Analysis of the French Revolution," *Historical Journal* (v.25, 1982).

SUSAN R. BOETTCHER, PH.D.
UNIVERSITY OF TEXAS, AUSTIN

Bush, George H.W. (1924–)

THE 41ST PRESIDENT of the United States, George Herbert Walker Bush was born in Milton, Massachusetts. His father was a wealthy investment banker and a senator from Connecticut. Bush grew up in Greenwich, Connecticut, where he attended the Country Day School and later Phillips Academy in Andover, Massachusetts.

Bush enlisted in the U.S. Navy at the age of 18 and was, for a time, the Navy's youngest pilot. He served in the Pacific theater of WORLD WAR II and flew 58 combat missions, once shot down and then rescued by a submarine.

After the war, Bush attended Yale University and graduated in three years with a Bachelor of Arts in economics. He decided not to join his father's banking firm but to move to Texas with his wife and children to work for an oil-supply company. In 1953, he co-founded the Zapata Petroleum Corporation and, in 1954, became president of its subsidiary, the Zapata Off-Shore Company. He served as president of Zapata until 1964, and chairman until 1966, until he entered politics.

Bush first ran for public office in 1964 and was defeated. He had won the Republican nomination for the U.S. Senate but lost in the general election. In 1966, he ran for a seat in the House of Representatives and won. He was re-elected in 1968. In 1970, Bush ran again for the Senate and once again lost. After this defeat, President Richard NIXON, who appreciated the fact that Bush had given up a safe House seat to run for the Senate, appointed him to the position of Permanent Representative of the United States to the UNITED NATIONS.

By most accounts, Bush was an effective spokesman for the United States even though he had been criticized for having little foreign-policy experience. In 1973, President Nixon asked Bush to become chairman of the Republican National Committee just before the Watergate scandal broke. As the scandal progressed, revealing criminal activity in the highest offices of the White House, Bush defended Nixon until it became apparent the president was lying.

At that time, August 1974, Bush wrote to Nixon asking him to resign. Bush's letter was just one of many that Nixon had received, but along with Congressional and media pressure, Nixon's leadership was untenable; he resigned. The new president, Gerald FORD, asked Bush to head the U.S. Liaison Office in the People's Republic of CHINA. Bush remained in that post for 14 months.

At the end of 1975, Ford asked Bush to return home and take on the assignment of director of the Central Intelligence Agency. The Agency was reeling from Watergate-era revelations and Bush played a large role in lifting morale and preventing further damage to the Agency. After Ford lost the 1976 election, Bush returned to private life in Texas. In 1979, he entered the race for the 1980 presidential nomination, a field dominated by Ronald REAGAN. Bush, though winning the Iowa caucuses, did not do well in the primaries and withdrew before the convention. Reagan did receive the nomination and asked Bush to be his running mate. The Republicans carried 44 states and were sworn in on January 20, 1981.

A vice president's real importance derives from responsibilities given to him by the president. Bush traveled to more than 60 countries and maintained an office in the White House. Bush headed taskforces on crime, terrorism, and drug smuggling. Reagan and Bush were re-nominated in 1984 and won 49 states in the November voting.

Speculation was rife during Reagan's second term about what Bush knew of the Iran-Contra Affair; the selling of arms to Iran in exchange for the release of U.S. hostages held in the Middle East. Bush explained he had attended several key meetings but he denied knowledge of the deal.

Defying history, Bush won the 1988 presidential race. He was only the second vice-president in American history to move from the vice-presidency to the presidency directly (Martin VAN BUREN in 1837 was the first). Bush won 40 states and 53.4 percent of the popular vote, and was inaugurated on January 20, 1989.

The Democrats were in control of both Houses of Congress and as a result the president often took middle-of-the-road positions on issues. In 1990, Bush abandoned his "Read my lips, no new taxes" campaign pledge and acknowledged that new or increased taxes were necessary. This upset many Republican conservatives and his popularity ratings fell. Bush was able to fill two Supreme Court vacancies by appointing David Souter in 1990 and Clarence Thomas in 1991.

The president received strong support for his handling of foreign affairs. Due to his diplomatic experience, he was able to play a key role in advancing U.S. foreign policy. A series of summits was held with Soviet President Mikhail Gorbachev resulting in the signing of treaties on arms reductions, and the eventual dissolution of the Soviet state into numerous independent countries, including RUSSIA.

Bush quickly and officially recognized the new states and met with Boris Yeltsin (the new president of Russia) several times, resulting in an agreement to make substantial cuts in nuclear weapons. In addition, during the Bush administration, his policies militarily removed Manuel Noriega from power in Panama, helped to belatedly speed the dismantling of apartheid in SOUTH AFRICA, and played a key role in the defeat of the Sandinistas in Nicaragua.

In August, 1990, Iraq invaded Kuwait and the resolution of this crisis has been cited by historians as Bush's finest hour as president. He was able to put together an international coalition to expel the Iraqis from Kuwait. In a ground war that lasted just 100 hours, U.S. and allied forces drove the Iraqis from Kuwait. Bush did receive criticism for ordering a cease-fire before the Iraqi president, Saddam Hussein, was ousted. Historians point out Bush was constrained by resolutions passed not only by the U.S. Congress but also by the United Nations. But this inability to remove Hussein resurfaced in the administration of George W. BUSH, son of President George H.W. Bush.

After the Persian Gulf War, the president's popularity soared and it appeared he would be easily re-elected to a second term. However, with the U.S. economy mired in slow growth and recession after the war, Bush seemed unable to apply the success he enjoyed in foreign policy to economic affairs.

By the time of the Republican Convention, Bush's popularity had fallen dramatically on continued bad economic news. He received the nomination but left the convention with a divided party. Bush's Democratic opponent, Bill CLINTON ran his campaign on economic issues, even focusing his campaign staff with the slogan, "It's the economy, stupid!" and won the election of 1992.

BIBLIOGRAPHY. George W.H. Bush, www.infoplease.com; George H.W. Bush, www.americanpresident.org; Bob Woodward, *Shadow: Five Presidents and the Legacy of Watergate* (Simon & Schuster, 1999); David Gergen, *Eyewitness to Power* (Simon & Schuster, 2000); Bruce W. Jentleson, *With Friends Like These: Reagan, Bush, and Saddam, 1982–1990* (W.W. Norton, 1994); Michael Duffy, *Marching in Place: The Status Quo Presidency of George Bush* (Simon & Schuster, 1992); Michael Gordon and Bernard E. Trainor, *The Generals' War* (Little, Brown, 1995).

LINDA L. PETROU, PH.D.
HIGH POINT UNIVERSITY

Bush, George W. (1946–)

THE 43RD PRESIDENT of the United States, George W. Bush was born in New Haven, Connecticut, the oldest son of George H.W. BUSH, the 41st president. When Bush was two, his family moved to Texas, where he spent his early childhood. He attended Phillips Academy and Yale University, graduating in 1968 with a degree in history. Bush then joined the Texas Air National Guard and took two years of flight training.

Bush, or "W" as many referred to him to distinguish him from his father, entered Harvard Business School and received a Master of Business Administration degree in 1975. Returning to Texas, he established an oil and gas business, and met and married his wife, Laura.

Bush ran for the U.S. Congress as a representative from Texas in 1978 but was defeated. In the 1980s, he put his oil business aside to work on his father's presidential campaign as both an advisor and a speechwriter. After the elder Bush won, "W" put together a group of investors and purchased the Texas Rangers baseball team.

Bush decided to go into politics relatively late in life, saying he lacked a focus until he reached his forties. In 1994, at age 48, he ran against a popular Democratic incumbent Texas governor, Ann Richards. During the campaign, she mocked Bush as intellectually vacuous, but her obvious contempt for the Republican candidate backfired and Bush defeated her. He ran for re-election as governor in 1998 and won. The strong re-election, and the obvious import of the family name, brought Bush to the forefront for the Republican nomination for president in 2000.

Initially, the field of candidates was large but Bush was able to attract major party and donor support early on, which demoralized the rest of the field and a number of the candidates dropped out. It was expected that he would coast to the nomination but no one counted on the broad appeal of Senator John McCain, a VIETNAM WAR hero and national leader for campaign finance reform. It became a bitter and increasingly personal fight, but in the end Bush won the Republican nomination.

Facing Democratic opponent and Vice-President Al Gore, Bush clearly benefited from the public's desire for change after eight years of the CLINTON-Gore administration. Bush narrowly won the electoral college vote though he lost the popular vote to Gore in the 2000 election, one of the most controversial in U.S. history. The vote in Florida was so close it triggered a recount in certain counties. Bush was declared the winner and Gore challenged the results. After two months of national anguish over whom the country had truly elected, the entire matter was resolved by the U.S. Supreme Court, which ruled in favor of Bush.

The Bush administration faced several problems right from the start. One was the closeness of the election and the feeling in some quarters that Bush was not the truly elected president; and secondly, the Senate and House were closely divided along partisan lines. Bush's economic policy was predicated on tax cuts, especially since the nation faced its largest budget surplus in history after the roaring economic growth of the 1990s.

But within a few months of his election, Bush faced an economic recession: The nation's economy was in the doldrums and the federal budget surplus was dwindling. Bush's popularity was declining and he was becoming the butt of jokes on late-night television shows. Then, on the morning of September 11, 2001, terrorists struck the World Trade Center and the Pentagon and the entire world woke up to a new reality.

The terrorist attack not only shocked the public, it had a major impact on the U.S. and thus, the world economy. The NEW YORK STOCK EXCHANGE was shut down for a number of days due to its proximity to the attack site in New York City. The American consumer, numb with shock, did not fly on airlines, did not buy goods, and promptly dumped securities and stocks as the exchanges plummeted. In the subsequent months, demonstrably showing just how important consumerism is to a capitalist economy, Bush and other leaders implored the American public to fight terrorism by going out and buying something.

As evidence suggested the terrorist attack originated with Islamic fundamentalists based in Afghanistan, Bush ordered U.S. air strikes against military installations and terrorist training camps in that country. With his straight-forward manner, Bush was able to calm the country and put together an international coalition to fight terrorism. The public rallied behind Bush and any debate about who was the truly elected president quickly faded.

Focusing on the War on Terrorism and a renewed military action against IRAQ, in 2002 and early 2003, Bush had high marks for national defense but the economy remained in poor condition, still struggling to recover from the effects of the terrorist attack and recession. Unemployment rose steadily, job creation remained at all-time lows, state and federal budgets slid into deficits, and it seemed the collective economy held its breath, waiting to see what would happen next.

BIBLIOGRAPHY. "George W. Bush,"www.infoplease.com; "George W. Bush," www.amerianpresident.org; Bob Woodward, *Shadow: Five Presidents and the Legacy of Watergate* (Simon & Schuster, 1999); David Gergen, *Eyewitness to Power* (Simon & Schuster, 2000); David Kaplan, *The Accidental President* (Morrow, 2001); Fred Barnes, "The Emerging 9/11 Majority," *The Weekly Standard* (November 19, 2002).

LINDA L. PETROU, PH.D.
HIGH POINT UNIVERSITY

business cycles

SINCE 1820, THE U.S. ECONOMY has exhibited tremendous growth, as calculated by changes in real GROSS DOMESTIC PRODUCT (GDP). Real GDP is a measure of total output produced by an economy in one year, so that when it grows there are more goods and services of all sorts available within the economy. In fact, real GDP has increased 3.6 percent per year, on average, for this entire time, starting at $12.4 billion (measured in 1990 dollars—all prices have been statistically adjusted to 1990 levels) in 1820 and rising to approximately $7,916 billion (again, in constant 1990 dollars) in 2002.

Looking at this upward trend alone, however, one does not see that there were many short-term fluctuations, where the economy would actually contract, and only then increase after some period of time. These short-term fluctuations of real GDP, around the long-run trend, are known as business cycles. To be more precise, a business cycle can be defined in the following way: First, a capitalist economy will experience increasing levels of real GDP. This is known as an expansion,

one phase of the business cycle. At some point, however, the economy will reach a peak, after which real GDP will then decline, going into what economists call a contraction, the other phase of the business cycle. In a viable economy, a contraction will, in turn, end with the economy reaching a trough, after which the economy will once again expand. This cycle of expansion-peak-contraction-trough-expansion repeats itself over and over again throughout the history of a capitalist economy.

Anatomy of a Business Cycle

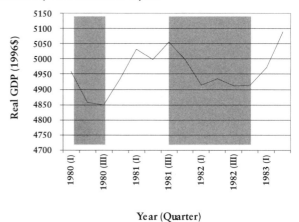

An example of a business cycle is shown in the figure above. The ups and downs of the economy are clearly seen, with the shaded areas being contractions (as determined by the National Bureau of Economic Research). The first cycle shown begins with a peak in the first quarter of 1980. The economy then contracted for six months, bottoming out in the third quarter of 1980. This economic downturn coincided with the re-election campaign of President Jimmy CARTER, who, in large part because of this bad economic news, lost the election to Ronald REAGAN. The economy then expanded for exactly one year, reaching a peak in the third quarter of 1981. This ends the first business cycle shown in the figure. The beginning of the next business cycle ushered in extremely hard times for the U.S. economy. This contraction lasted for 16 months, the longest and deepest downturn to date (2003) since the DEPRESSION of the 1930s. The economy finally started a recovery in the fourth quarter of 1982, the beginning of which is shown in the figure.

Business cycles and panics. Business cycles are very irregular. There is no set duration to any of the phases, and correspondingly, there is no specific duration that the entire cycle lasts. For example, since the AMERICAN CIVIL WAR, there have been 29 complete business cycles in the United States. The shortest one was only 17 months (August, 1918 to January, 1920), with its expansion lasting 10 months, while the longest lasted more than 10 years (July, 1990 to March, 2001). Clearly the length of business cycles varies considerably.

Although we cannot specify with any precision the duration of business cycles, there is a particular relationship between the two phases. Since the U.S. economy has grown considerably over the past 150 years, expansions tend to be longer than contractions (the former averaged 38 months compared to 18 months for the latter, since the Civil War), even though both vary quite a lot in duration. The longest contraction, from October 1873 to March 1879, was only about half the length of the longest expansion.

Business cycles also appear to be characteristic of capitalism. We have seen that they exist in the United States, but they also exist in any capitalist economy. In the early 1930s, for example, every major capitalist economy in the world experienced contraction, but by the end of that decade all saw their real GDPs rising once again. This (irregular) expanding and contracting of an economy seems to be unavoidable within the capitalist framework.

Throughout history, economists have seemed to be ambivalent about what to call the different phases of the business cycle. The contractionary phase, in particular, has had many different appellations over the years. Originally known as panics, they became crises by the beginning of the 20th century. The term panic seemed to indicate a dire situation, not simply a normal manifestation of a well-functioning economy, and so it had to go. It didn't take long, however, for the term crisis to become problematic as well. So economists started to describe economic downturns as merely "depressions," using a word that seemed to offer more solace to those experiencing it. After a while, this word too began to seem, well, too depressing, causing economic commentators to finally stop using these psychological terms with negative connotations, and adopt the pleasingly neutral term, RECESSION. This is what is now most widely used as the descriptive term for a contraction, although some economists go even further, and try to put a positive spin on negative growth, by using such terms as "rolling readjustment" or "growth correction," explains economist John Kenneth GALBRAITH. Marxists, on the other hand, still use the term crisis to describe a contraction. Not having any desire to make capitalism look good, they continue to use this term as an apt description of a shrinking economy.

As for expansions, there have not been so many terms, perhaps because no one has ever seen the need to soften the blow of what is essentially a positive economic event. Variously referred to as a boom or a recovery, depending on the speed of economic growth, this phase of the business cycle is trumpeted as the success of an economy, something to be celebrated, rather than hushed-up or neutralized as is done for a contraction.

In terms of measurement, it is not always clear when a recession or an expansion begins or ends. Since a business cycle is defined as expansion-peak-contraction-trough, whose duration is measured peak to peak (or trough to trough), the determination of peaks (the end of an expansion) and troughs (the end of a contraction) is quite important. We defined a business cycle above as simply the ups and downs of real GDP. Corresponding to this understanding, a recession would be seen as six or more consecutive months of falling real GDP. This is what is used as a rule of thumb by most commentators on the economy.

However, a more complicated procedure is used by the National Bureau of Economic Research (the source of the business cycle statistics cited above). In these quasi-official statistics, "a recession is a period of significant decline in total output, income, employment, and trade, usually lasting from six months to a year, and marked by widespread contractions in many sectors of the economy." Note that a declining real GDP is only part of this definition. This means that our definition of a business cycle is a simplification, albeit one highlighting the most important aspect of the issue.

The effects of business cycles. The most well known business cycle in U.S. history began in August 1929 and ended in May 1937. With a couple of years added (extending the end to 1939), this period of economic difficulties is known as the Great Depression. While technically only 56 out of the approximately 120 months were during contractions, the economy during this entire period was faltering. Certainly, in terms of high unemployment and declining real GDP, the U.S. economy was never so dysfunctional. The unemployment rate averaged 18.4 percent, reaching over 25 percent at times, while real GDP fell 27 percent, bottoming out in 1933, and didn't reach its pre-Depression level until 1936. For many, the Great Depression seemed to be the death knell of capitalism. This is the negative side of the business cycle.

By definition a recession entails a declining real GDP. This is not good because it means that individuals, on average, will be able to consume fewer goods and services, thus lowering their material standard of living. With the assumption that everyone always wants more, this can only be a bad situation. This, however, is not the worst of it. When real GDP declines it does not affect everyone equally. Some people still continue to gain, others stay about the same, and others lose. Among those that lose, some lose a little and some lose a lot. In particular, those who become unemployed suffer the most. Without jobs, they earn no money, and can consume far fewer goods and services than before; their material standard of living inevitably declines precipitously. Rising unemployment is the worst part of a recession.

On the other hand, there is an upside to business cycles. Once the economy reaches a trough at the end of a recession, real GDP begins to rise, employment begins to recover, and most things economic look brighter. For example, during the expansion of the Bill CLINTON administration years, the longest one in U.S. history, the economy seemed to be booming. Real GDP rose 3.5 percent per year, the unemployment rate averaged 4 percent, and the stock market experienced its largest increase in history. Certainly, in many ways, the U.S. economy was healthy and prosperous. Expansions, as the counterpart to contractions, are the positive side of the business cycle.

Fortunately, in the United States, business cycles have diminished in severity. Since WORLD WAR II, there have been 10 cycles, with expansions averaging 57 months and contractions averaging only 10 months. In the most severe recession during this time (July 1981 to November 1982), output fell only 2.9 percent, and unemployment reached a maximum of 11 percent. In contrast, in the years between the Civil War and World War II there were 19 cycles, with expansions averaging 28 months and contractions averaging 22 months. In the most severe contraction during this time, the Great Depression, output fell 27 percent, and unemployment reaching over 25 percent. With output falling farther and longer, and unemployment reaching much higher levels, pre-World War II recessions were both more frequent and more severe than those of the past 60 years. Expansions are now twice as long as they previously were, and contractions average one-half of their former duration, so that the balance between the two has improved significantly. Capitalism, perhaps, is not as brutal as before.

INFLATION, defined as an increase in the average price level, has been a constant in the United States since the Great Depression. In all but three of the 70 years since 1932, prices have increased, and the last time that the United States experienced deflation (prices on average decreasing) was 1954. Thus, throughout the various business cycles of the post-World War II period, prices have continued to rise, both during contractions and expansions.

This structural inflation is unrelated to the business cycle. There is, however, a component of inflation that is related to the business cycle. During expansions, prices rise more quickly than during contractions. As an expansion takes hold, labor costs tend to rise, leading to an increase in prices charged by businesses (inflation). Then, once the economy reaches its peak, rising labor costs ease up, and there is less pressure on firms to increase their prices.

Thus, during expansions, inflation tends to rise, and during contractions inflation tends to fall. This cyclical inflation rises and falls with economic activity, around a long-term structural inflationary trend (which itself rises and falls).

Theories and policies of business cycles. Business cycles appear to be an inevitable part of capitalism. Throughout the history of capitalism, business cycles have come and gone, just as surely as waves have continually pounded our coastal shorelines. It may be too much to say that these cycles have pulverized economies just as the waves have reduced rock and stone to sand, but some of the contractions that we have seen have surely brought much suffering to the populations of capitalist economies. While expansions indicate a vibrant economy, where more and more goods and services are being produced, contractions indicate an economy that is failing to deliver as much as it can to consumers. With output down and unemployment up, recessions are an economic problem and generally seen as something to be avoided.

Given the harm done by economic contractions, for the last 70 years economists have attempted to see how recessions could be eliminated or at least mitigated. John Maynard KEYNES, perhaps the most famous economist of the 20th century, weighed-in with his thoughts on this matter in the 1930s. Writing during the depths of the Great Depression, he argued that economic downturns were caused by a lack of total (aggregate) demand. All of the purchasers in the economy—consumers, businesses, and the government—were simply not buying enough goods and services for the economy to be going ahead full steam. Firms, not needing to produce so much (because sales were slower), would cut back on production, causing real GDP to fall and unemployment to rise, in other words causing a recession. Could anything be done to get the economy back on track?

Keynes' prescription for the ailing economy (remember, at that time, capitalist economies worldwide were going through their worst Depression in history) was for the government to increase aggregate demand, either through reducing taxes or increasing government spending, thereby pumping the economy back up to good times. If only the government would take charge by manipulating aggregate demand, the Depression would soon be over. This method of manipulating aggregate demand is known as countercyclical FISCAL POLICY, because it was expressly designed to counter the business cycle, more particularly, to soften the hardships of contractions and to end recessions.

This policy passed its first test with flying colors during World War II. As the U.S. government increased its wartime spending at the end of the 1930s and the beginning of the 1940s, the Great Depression ended and the U.S. economy experienced phenomenal growth (actually doubling in size from 1939–44) and historically low levels of unemployment. In recent years, however, there has been some grumbling from economists as to the efficacy of fiscal policy.

A somewhat different view of recessions is taken by other economists. While agreeing that they create suffering in the economy (primarily because of increased unemployment), these economists emphasize the necessity of recessions for the overall health of capitalism. Expansions, as they gain steam, tend to raise labor costs (the primary cost for most firms), which, in turn, uncomfortably squeeze the profits of firms. A recession is then needed in order to repress wages so that in the future profits can get back to more normal levels. A recession is seen as a necessary cost of capitalism, or as a needed "correction" to an overheated economy. Ironically, this view is both Marxist (which sees it as an indictment of capitalism) and conservative (in agreement with many businessmen who explicitly see recessions as good for the economy).

The history of the U.S. economy shows that business cycles are here to stay. Try as they might, economists have been unable to eliminate recessions completely. While some success has been achieved in ameliorating the worst aspects of recessions, they still haunt the economy at least once every decade. Whether seen as a necessary correction to an over-exuberant economy, or as a social problem that needs to be minimized as much as possible by governmental action, recessions and their corresponding business cycles are an integral part of any capitalist economy.

BIBLIOGRAPHY. Samuel Bowles and Richard Edwards, *Understanding Capitalism* (Harper & Row, 1985); Bureau of Economic Analysis, www.bea.doc.gov (2003); Bureau of Economic Analysis, *Survey of Current Business* (v.82/8); Bureau of Labor Statistics www.bls.gov (2002); John Kenneth Galbraith, *Money: Whence It Came, Where It Went* (Houghton Mifflin, 1975); Angus Maddison, *Monitoring the World Economy 1820–1992* (Development Centre of the Organization for Economic Co-operation and Development, 1995); National Bureau of Economic Research, www.nber.org; U.S. Bureau of the Census, *Historical Statistics of the United States, Colonial Times to 1970* (U.S. Bureau of the Census, 1975).

PAUL A. SWANSON
WILLIAM PATERSON UNIVERSITY

C

Cambodia

THE KINGDOM OF CAMBODIA is located in the southwestern part of the Indochina peninsula. It has borders with THAILAND on the north and west, Laos on the northeast, VIETNAM on the east and southeast, and the Gulf of Thailand on the west. With an area of 181,040 square kilometers, Cambodia is about the size of the state of Missouri. More than 90 percent of its people are Khmer; they believe in Theravada, a branch of Buddhism emphasizing the doctrine of elders. Ethnic minority groups include Chams (who believe in the Islamic faith), Khmer Loeu, Vietnamese, and Chinese.

The Khmer people have been living in today's Cambodia for thousands of years. The first Khmer kingdom was established in the first century C.E. The golden age of Khmer civilization, however, was the period between the 9th and 13th centuries, when the kingdom of Kambuja, from which Cambodia is derived, ruled the land.

In 1863, FRANCE made Cambodia a protectorate. During WORLD WAR II, the Nazi-controlled French Vichy colonial government collaborated with the Japanese in Cambodia. After the war, King Norodom Sihanouk negotiated his country's independence from France, which had returned to reassert colonial control. In 1953, Cambodia obtained independence. Sihanouk then formed his own party, the People's Socialist Community, and made Cambodia a constitutional monarchy. In foreign policy, Cambodia adopted neutrality and NON-ALIGNMENT.

Sihanouk's government faced political challenges at home. In 1970, Lon Nol, prime minister and a military general, staged a successful coup against Sihanouk. The new government under Lon Nol was not popular among the majority of people, who remained loyal to Sihanouk. A broad alliance between Sihanouk and the Kampuchean Communist Party (KCP, also known as Khmer Rouge) was formed against the Lon Nol regime. In 1975, the Khmer Rouge forces drove Lon Nol into exile and the Democratic Kampuchea was established under KCP's leader Pol Pot. The Khmer Rouge adopted radical and brutal policies in the 1970s, killing hundreds of thousands of people and drove many others to flee the country as refugees.

In 1978, Vietnam invaded Cambodia and installed a puppet regime in Phnom Penh, the capital. Different factions, including the Khmer Rouge, organized a resistance movement under the leadership of Sihanouk. Vietnam finally withdrew its troops from Cambodia and, in 1993, UNITED NATIONS-sponsored elections restored relative stability to the country. In 2001, Cambodia's GROSS DOMESTIC PRODUCT (GDP) was $18.7 billion with tourism as the fastest-growing part of the economy. Foreign investment is still weary of political instability but the country's economic climate is improving with the aid of international organizations.

BIBLIOGRAPHY. Martin F. Herz, *A Short History of Cambodia from the Days of Angkor to the Present* (Praeger, 1958); David P. Chandler, *The Tragedy of Cambodia: Politics, War, and Revolution since 1945* (Yale University Press, 1991); Madhavi Kuckreja, *Prince Norodom Sihanouk* (Chelsea, 1990); *CIA World Factbook* (2002).

SHEHONG CHEN, PH.D.
UNIVERSITY OF MASSACHUSETTS, LOWELL

Canada

FRENCH EXPLORER Jacques Cartier (1491–1557) was the first mandated sailor to write in his numerous diaries the description of his journeys through what was called New France (Canada's six eastern provinces, including Québec) in 1534–35. Like many other explorers, Cartier was looking for a passage to reach India; instead, he discovered what would become France's biggest colony. Québec City, Canada's oldest urban center, was founded in 1608 by Samuel de Champlain. But endless conflicts between FRANCE and England that lasted long in Europe were later transposed to Canada.

After two centuries of prosperous French regime, frequent cooperation with natives and many attacks from England, Canada was invaded by the British army in 1755 and 1759; its immense territory (that included the Mississippi River Valley with many later states between the Great Lakes and Louisiana) became part of the British Empire in 1763. French-speaking populations from Acadie (the Canadian province later renamed Nova Scotia) were deported to Louisiana by the British Army in 1755.

According to scholars, the French-speaking population was still a majority in Canada until the mid-19th century. Since then, the province of Québec (today one quarter of Canada's population and the largest provincial territory) is the only province to remain with a francophone majority, many of them fluent in Canada's both official languages, English and French.

Considering those cultural and linguistic reasons, Québec has always been a distinct society compared to the rest of Canada. Since 1867, francophone populations have constantly been diminishing, assimilated into English in all other Canadian provinces, therefore Québecers feel their French language has to be protected by special provincial laws, something the federal government has failed to do. Because of these cultural, historical, and economic reasons, almost half of the population of Québec strongly feels their province should become an independent country. Two referendums were voted on (1980 and 1995) in which the people of Québec chose to give a last chance to the Canadian federation. As American scholar Marc Levine has explained, this political issue is crucial in order to understand traditional anglophones' attitude towards Québec's place in Canada. Also, Québec's aspirations for an independent, democratic country are sometimes given as an excuse for any Canadian problem or weakness.

Canada is a large and contrasted country, the second largest country in the world, and a little bigger than its southern neighbor, the UNITED STATES, covering almost 10 million square kilometers. Its population of more than 30 million is among the most highly educated in the world. With a GROSS DOMESTIC PRODUCT (GDP) of $923 billion (2002) and a per capita purchasing power of $29,400, Canada has been, by far, the United States' main commercial partner and economic ally for centuries. Both countries share the longest unprotected border in the world. Canada is a member of the organization of top economies in the world who participate in the G8 SUMMIT.

Historically, Canada has always been seen by Europeans as a privileged place for trade. Because Catholics were not allowed to eat meat during many periods of the year (Lent, Advent, Fridays), Basque and French fishermen sailed around Newfoundland to find rich reserves of cod. One of Canada's oldest companies, the Hudson Bay Company, was created for fur trading with natives and exportation of furs to Europe. The Hudson Bay Company, founded in 1670, is North America's oldest commercial enterprise still operating (today, under the name The Bay). At some point, before Canadian confederation (1867), almost half of Canada's territory was conceded to the Hudson Bay Company.

The Canadian confederation was the beginning of modern Canada, first with four founding provinces (Québec, Ontario, New Brunswick, and Nova Scotia), then with 10 provinces since 1949 (Newfoundland was the last to join). Ethnic and class tensions between anglophones and francophones, which could somewhat be compared with black-white relations in the United States, have been punctuated by class and constitutional conflicts since 1763.

Since 1982, all political parties in Québec have refused to sign Canada's new constitution; this means that the province of Québec is ruled every day by a constitution that was rejected by all successive provincial governments, leaders and parties, which is unusual, to say the least, in a Democratic federation. People outside Canada often get only one side of this issue if they rely on anglophone Canadian media, which are far from objective, as journalist Normand Lester and university scholar Kenneth McRoberts have explained in best-selling books.

Canada is too often considered as only a resource-rich country with its economy reduced to basic products (grains and fisheries) and utilities such as gold, minerals, wood, oil, gas and energy. Most people don't know much about the Canadian biotechnologies and high-tech research centers concentrated in Québec and Ontario. Important Canadian companies include Nortel Networks (the world's largest manufacturer of telecommunications and internet systems) and its rival JDS Uniphase, Alcan Aluminium, INCO (the world's most important producer of nickel), Bell Canada Enterprises (telephone and telecommunications), Québécor World (the largest printing company in the world), and Bombardier (aircraft and rail transportation equipment). Compared to the hundreds of financial institutions in the United States, Canada only has seven banks. The oldest of these, the Bank of Montréal, already issued coins and paper money in the 19th century. In Québec, most people prefer credit unions to banks; they are named (in French) *caisses populaires*.

The Canadian dollar's value has often fluctuated in the past decades. It was sometimes worth more than the

U.S. dollar, during the 1960s and also in 1976. At the beginning of 2003, it was worth around 65 U.S. cents, an historic low. This is why global economic strategist Sherry Cooper describes Canada as "The Fallen Global Growth Leader" in her book, *The Cooper Files* (1999).

Although not perfect, the Canadian HEALTH care system has a strong, enviable reputation: all Canadian citizens may see a doctor or go to the hospital for free. This also means that social costs are assumed by the provincial governments, which have to rely on higher income taxes. Some Canadian provinces, such as Québec, also offer free medical drug prescriptions.

The Canada-U.S. Free Trade Agreement created a free trade zone in 1989. In a traditional suspicion toward the United States, many Canadian provinces opposed that agreement, but Québec was strongly in favor from the beginning. The North Atlantic Free Trade Agreement (NAFTA) was launched in January 1994, with the goal of fostering greater economic growth in Canada, the United States, and MEXICO by removing barriers to trade and investment among the three nations. Though commercial conflicts fester now and then (the U.S. surtax on Canadian wood; a series of American branches and factories closing in Canada to reopen in Mexico), free trade is still presented as a way of constructing closer commercial relations between the neighbors. Although government measuring practices and methods of managing labor have changed during the 1990s, unemployment remains Canada's main challenge for the 21st century.

BIBLIOGRAPHY. Sherry Cooper, *The Cooper Files* (Key Porter Books, 1999); Jacques Lacoursière, Jean Provencher and Denis Vaugeois, Canada-Québec, *Synthèse historique, 1534–2000* (Septentrion, 2000); Normand Lester, *The Black Book of English Canada* (McClelland & Stewart, 2002); Marc V. Levine, *The Reconquest of Montreal: Language Policy and Social Change in a Bilingual City* (Temple University Press, Conflicts in Urban and Regional Development Series, 1990); Kenneth McRoberts. *Misconceiving Canada: The Struggle for National Unity* (Oxford University Press, 1997); Jean-Francois Lisée, "Invest in Quebec's Uniqueness," *Inroads* (v.10, 2001).

YVES LABERGE, PH.D.
INSTITUT QUÉBÉCOIS DES
HAUTES ÉTUDES INTERNATIONALES

capital

THE PLACE OF CAPITAL as an economic resource is of extreme importance. In economic theory, defining capital is not easy because of its nature. Capital GOODS are produced by humans, and therefore differ from the original factors of production, LABOR, and LAND. Capital is used in the means of production and is distinguished from consumer goods in that it is an intermediate product. Capital may be financial, physical, or human. Financial capital has to do with the value of physical capital or capital goods. Capital goods are usually divided into durable and non-durable types. Most early writers on the subject focused on circulating, or nondurable capital.

The economic analysis of capital did not begin until tools and machines became more widely used in production. Thus, writers did not examine capital as a factor of production essentially until the 18th century. These early writers saw capital as advancements to workers made necessary to provide food and other necessities from the beginning of the agricultural season to the harvest and the sale of the goods. The PHYSIOCRATS, in their view of the economy as a circular flow, envisioned capital in this vein. This view of capital achieved its peak in the wages fund doctrine of the 19th century.

Theories of capital. Adam SMITH borrowed much his theory of capital from the Physiocrats and A.J.R. TURGOT. Smith's view of fixed capital focused on its ability to contribute to the productivity of labor. Labor in Smith's view, as he makes clear in the opening chapter of his *Wealth of Nations* on the division of labor, is the engine of economic progress. Smith also argued that some capital is productive and some unproductive. Capital as advancements to servants, for example, is unproductive. Smith's influence on economic writings of the 19th century on capital was enormous and consequently we cannot speak of the development of capital theory without Smith. Fixed capital would not receive its due until long after.

Smith's influence did not stop there. Although he was not the first to formulate a labor theory of value, his acceptance and presentation of it sealed its fate for 19th-century economists. Smith's famous exposition of how capital first comes to play a role in "rude and original state of society" was simple and convincing. As a follower, albeit a critical one, David RICARDO plays a crucial role here in the labor theory of value. Ricardo defined capital as "that part of the wealth of a country which is employed in production, and cost of food, clothing, tools, raw materials, machinery, etc., necessary to give effect to labor." Capital is merely another kind of labor in a labor theory of value. It is embodied labor. This would lead to many difficulties, theoretical and technical, that would occupy and distract some of the best minds in economics throughout the century.

It was Karl MARX, however, who, extending Ricardo's labor theory of value, squarely put capital goods into the forefront of economic analysis. Marx viewed capital as a stock of goods and in the form of an aggregated value. Capital goods are owned by capitalists and as such exist only in such a society. Capitalists accumulate these goods in order to exploit workers and increase their surplus. Along with Marx's emphasis on capital, came the controversies that would surround the concept for the following century.

The greatest contribution in capital theory is, perhaps, from the AUSTRIAN SCHOOL. The leading figure in the Austrian theory of capital, Eugen von BÖHM-BAWERK, elaborated the principle of "roundaboutness." That is, capitalistic methods of production tend to be roundabout or indirect. The most direct way to get a pint of blueberries, for example, is to go into the woods and pick the blueberries. A more roundabout way is to plant some seeds, tend to the plants, and then to pick the blueberries. Böhm-Bawerk followed in the grand tradition of Austrian economics in incorporating the element of time into the notion of capital. It is easy to see in this example that the period of production is lengthened by the planting of the seeds and then tending to the plants. We can then think of an average period of production.

In this process of making production more roundabout, original factors of production, land, and labor are converted and stored into capital, which is later used to make consumer goods. The capital inputs are thus encapsulated within the production of a consumer good for some average period. Böhm-Bawerk recognized the heterogeneous nature of capital and allowed for this in his model. The heterogeneity of capital goods meant that the stock of capital cannot be aggregated. Hence, capital goods are simply valued by a theory of imputation that considers the present value of the capital goods in the production process. Capital and the period of production are measured in MONEY terms (although one may assume that money is neutral in this process). The calculation of the average period of production proved to be too difficult and confusing for Böhm-Bawerk and his theory suffered accordingly. Böhm-Bawerk's theory is, at heart, an extension of the classical theory because it relies on advances as the basis of capital.

The writer Knut Wicksell, who would broaden and give greater substance to the Austrian theory of capital, tried to meld Böhm-Bawerk's theory with that of Leon WALRAS. Walras' approach was to treat a capital good like any other good. It is the cost of production that determines the prices of capital goods. In a general EQUILIBRIUM, capital goods are valued in the same way as are consumer goods. The demand for capital goods are demands by firms that sell products, that in turn, have their own demands. The demand for capital goods are, therefore, derived demands. In a general equilibrium system, all prices and values are determined simultaneously. Wicksell accepted Böhm-Bawerk's average period of production asserting that a lengthening of this, that is, more roundaboutness, leads to a greater output of

consumer goods. The original factors of production become dated quantities in Wicksell's analysis and are integrated into his general equilibrium analysis.

Capital controversies. One of the controversies generated by Wicksell's analysis is what is known in the literature as the Wicksell Effect. In a general equilibrium system, the value of capital goods is derived from the costs of production of the original factors of production. Although he accepted the average period of production as a measure of the amount of capital in the economy, it would not do as a relative measure. Higher wages mean a higher cost of production for capital goods. But this rise in the value of capital goods means a fall in the rate of interest. The real Wicksell Effect means a change in technique at various rates of interest. The Wicksell Effect is simply the change in the value of capital due to a change in the rate of interest (and the change may be negative or positive). Wicksell had unwittingly set the stage for the famous Cambridge Controversy over capital switching.

In the 1950s and early 1960s, the question of a production function based on an aggregate quantity of capital was called into question by Joan ROBINSON (1953) and other Cambridge University economists and would especially be sparked by a book by Pierro SRAFFA, *The Production of Commodities by Means of Commodities* (1960). This was the genesis of the legendary Cambridge Controversy. The central issue involved aggregating heterogeneous capital goods into a production function. This issue actually goes back to Wicksell who, while using the average period of production (a measure of actual capital) used capital values in comparing capital and other factors of production (which is necessary in aggregate production functions).

When there is a single homogenous capital good, however, aggregate production functions can be used without apology, save one: the possibility of reswitching. It can be shown that the same technique can be profitable at two different INTEREST RATES. That is, when the interest rate changes, if technique A is initially used at interest rate r_0, and technique B at a lower interest rate r_1 is used, then at the lower interest rate r_2, the economy reswitches to technique A. Without a unique relationship between the rate of interest and the amount of capital, the interest rate cannot be used as a determinate factor in capital demand.

Separating the rate of interest from the demand for capital would destroy the theoretical construct of capital. Around 1907, Irving FISHER, in his theory of interest, avoided this problem by avoiding macroeconomic formulations. This microeconomic approach steers clear of the problems presented by a heterogeneous amount of capital goods condensed into a homogeneous globule for an aggregate production function. The interest rate is simply a theoretical construct when it comes to physical capital and should be used only when considering capital values.

Now, the rate of interest plays a significant role in the determination of the capital stock. Wicksell, Ricardo, and others have all based their theory of capital directly on a theory of interest and the two are inseparable despite the Cambridge Controversy. Wicksell sought to reconcile a theory of saving (based on waiting) and the demand for capital. Wicksell used both short-run and long-run dynamics in showing how the interest rate affects SAVING and investment. In the short-run, the money rate of interest could deviate from the natural rate of interest (a long-term interest rate determined by supply and demand for saving). This would set in motion price changes that would provide what Wicksell saw as the missing link in quantity theories of money, namely the dynamics by which a change in the quantity of money (or equivalently in a credit economy, the bank rate) brings about a change in the price level. The inflationary spiral that a lower bank rate brings with it is important in understanding the link between the rate of interest and the prices of goods. If the bank rate remains stationary or is slow to move while the natural rate changes—a change in the demand and supply of saving and capital—the dynamics of the price changes will likewise occur.

From Wicksell, John Maynard KEYNES (1936) developed a theory of capital still widely accepted today. Keynes's theory is founded on the marginal efficiency of capital, which determines the demand for capital. Keynes clearly took the neoclassical approach to capital. The marginal efficiency of capital is assumed to be diminishing because of expected diminishing returns on future investments. The intersection of the marginal efficiency of capital and the supply of saving then determine the rate of interest. Keynes is very like Fisher in this regard, except that his analysis is geared more toward macroeconomics.

While there are many theories of capital and the issue is still unresolved today, it is unlikely that any formulation of an aggregate of capital goods will ever make it into an aggregate production function. This is true also for labor, however. It seems that heterogeneous capital goods can be used only in a general equilibrium analysis unless one is willing to accept that peculiarities such as reswitching might occur, although this seems to be empirically unimportant. The Austrian attempt of the treatment of time as a factor in capital theory, however, seems to be a lasting aspect of capital theory.

BIBLIOGRAPHY. E. von Böhm-Bawerk, *The Positive Theory of Capital* (Macmillan, 1891); I. Fisher, *The Nature of Capital and Income* (Macmillan, 1906); I. Fisher, *The Rate of Interest* (Macmillan, 1907); J.R. Hicks, *Value and Capital* (Macmillan, 1939); W.S. Jevons, *The Theory of Political Economy* (Kelley and Millman, 1957); J.M. Keynes, *The General Theory of Employment, Interest and Money* (Harcourt, Brace, 1936); K. Marx, *Capital: A Critique of Political Economy* (1867, Lawrence and Wisehart, 1969–72); J. Robinson, "The Production Function and the Theory of Capital," *Review of Economic Studies* (v.21/2, 1953); P. Saffra, *Production of Commodities by Means of Commodities: Prelude to a Critique of Economic Theory* (Cambridge University Press, 1960); P. Samuelson, "Paradoxes in Capital Theory: A Symposium, A Summing Up," *Quarterly Journal of Economics* (November 1966); A. Smith, *The Wealth of Nations* (Modern Library, 1937); K. Wicksell, *Lectures on Political Economy* (A.M. Kelley, 1967).

ZELJAN SCHUSTER, PH.D.
UNIVERSITY OF NEW HAVEN

capital accumulation

CAPITAL REFERS TO all materials that are necessary for the production of commodities. It consists of the stock of raw materials and partly finished GOODS, tools, machinery, and equipment. Pursuit of profits, in capitalism, is the driving force of capital accumulation.

Among the most important defining features of capitalism is the private ownership of capital (means of production) that is at the basis of its class system—a capitalist class that owns and controls the means of production, and a working class that does not own or control a substantial portion of the means of production, and relies mainly on the ability to work. Two of the most important sources of capital accumulation in the history of capitalist development are:

1. agricultural revolution and the enclosure movement

2. increased commerce and market expansion.

Adam SMITH undertook the examination of the accumulation of capital "stock" in Book II of *The Wealth of Nations*. He asserts that when the division of labor has thoroughly been introduced, a person's own labor can satisfy little of her wants and needs. Furthermore, distribution and exchange would also take time. Therefore, it is necessary to store up sufficient supplies to carry them through these periods. Accumulation of stock is, therefore, the prerequisite to the division of labor. Once the capital is sufficiently accumulated and we move from an independent commodity-producing setting into a capitalist one, according to Smith, capital becomes a property that yields its owner a flow of income, in the form of profits. Under these circumstances, the accumulation of capital becomes the principal source of economic progress, and profits become the source of new capital. He believed that the original accumulation was the result of abstinence by entrepreneurs.

In his endeavors to discover the source of profits, David RICARDO introduced his theory of rent and the law of diminishing returns to land cultivation. With prices determined by the labor theory of value, he specified economic agents as classes of landowners, workers, and capitalists. Ricardo shows that the size of profits is determined residually by the extent of cultivation on land and the historically determined real wage. Given profits, capital accumulation and labor-demand growth are deduced. Population is regulated by the funds that are to employ it, and increases or diminishes with the increase or diminution of capital.

Capital accumulation would increase population and require more land, of less and less quality, to be brought under cultivation. Therefore, according to Ricardo's theory, as the economy continued to grow profits would eventually be squeezed out by rents and WAGES. As this process continued, Ricardo argued, a "stationary state" would be reached where capitalists make near-zero profits and no further accumulation would occur. Ricardo suggested that technical progress and foreign trade would sustain accumulation.

In his endeavors to discover the laws of motion of capitalism, Karl MARX examined the capital accumulation process in detail in volumes II and III of *Capital*. As with the classical economists, Marx also believed that pursuit of profits is the driving force of capitalist accumulation. He contended that competition forces capitalist firms to invest in new technology to reduce costs and raise their profits. The new technology would yield the individual capitalist higher profits at the expense of other capitalists as its composition of capital rises. However, employing the new labor saving technique reduces the value content of the commodity by reducing the labor time socially necessary for its production. Over time as other capitalist firms adopt the new technique to remain competitive, the profit advantage would disappear. Capitalist firms as a whole will find themselves with a higher composition of capital (capital to labor ratio) and consequently a lower profit rate at a constant rate of surplus value. Marx's theory of the falling rate of profit predicts that the drive to capital accumulation would lead to the breakdown of capitalism.

BIBLIOGRAPHY. Maurice Dobb, *Theories of Value and Distribution Since Adam Smith: Ideology and Economic Theory* (Cambridge University Press, 1989). E.K. Hunt, *History of Economic Thought: A Critical Perspective* (HarperCollins, 1992); Karl Marx, *Capital: A Critique of Political Economy* (International Publishers, 1967); David Ricardo, *The Principles of Political Economy and Taxation* (Penguin, 1962); Isaac Rubin, *A History of Economic Thought* (Ink Links Publishers, 1979); Adam Smith, *An Inquiry into the Nature and Causes of The Wealth of Nations* (Modern Library Edition, 1965).

HAMID AZARI-RAD, PH.D.
STATE UNIVERSITY OF NEW YORK, NEW PALTZ

capitalism, ancient

ECONOMICS AND TRADE are as old as humanity itself and can be traced all the way back to the Stone Age. The real beginnings of business organization, though, can be traced to the four cradles of civilization in ancient IRAQ, EGYPT, the Indus Valley, and Shang CHINA. These economies of the ancient world would be considered mixed economies. They included both primitive local markets in foodstuffs and tools and long-distance trade organized initially by the "public sectors" of temple and palace.

The oldest civilization arose in Sumer during the Copper Age between 4000 B.C.E. and 3500 B.C.E. The Old Kingdom of Egypt was formed around 3100 B.C.E.; that of the Indus around 2600 B.C.E., and China followed not long after 1800 B.C.E. Ancient Iraq, though, was destined to become the most dynamic and the true cradle of prototype capitalist enterprise.

Sumer: the first urban/industrial revolution. The river network of the Tigris and Euphrates permitted Eridu, Uruk, Kish, Ur, and other Sumerian cities to each have independent access to foreign trade. In Mesopotamia, Uruk's public temples initially dominated its economy, which set the stage for the full flourishing prototype capitalism after 3100 B.C.E. when a few clever coppersmiths began to fashion tools and artifacts from bronze. These allowed peasants to grow enough food to support a growing city population that could earn a living in trade and manufacturing.

After 3000 B.C.E., the royal palaces of god-kings like Enmerkar and Gilgamesh rose to create a new public economic centre. Both temple and palace employed a manager—a Sumerian *damgar* or Semitic *tamkaru*. The *damgar* would travel long distances trading on behalf of the royal interest. Other activities included extensive private trading networks between the Tigris and Euphrates, independent grain and poultry farmers, and private real estate deals in the city of Lagash.

From 3000 to approximately 500 B.C.E., trade and commerce would flourish in the Near East on the model perfected in ancient Sumer. This might be called the *tamkarum* or the temple/palace model of capitalism. During the pre-urban Uruk period and toward the early part of the urban revolution, Sumerian temple clergy handled banking and social welfare functions. Its rulers sought to alleviate unemployment and other stresses of a new urban society through temple- and palace-building and other public works.

By 2600–2500 B.C.E., the Fertile Crescent was covered with a network of city-states each averaging about 20,000 inhabitants. One of the most prosperous was the Semitic kingdom of Ebla. Now known as Syria, Ebla boasted the most balanced and prosperous economy of the time. It was history's first liberal society with a constitution that let it make treaties in the name of Ebla itself. These treaties show a remarkably advanced comprehension of business law, international taxation, and territorial jurisdiction.

According to Ebla's discoverer Giovanni Pettinato, Eblaite *tamkaru* signify the first recorded real capitalists. Though there was still much state control, Ebla's economic system was more open to private enterprise than Egypt or Sumer. "The great novelty of Ebla," writes Pettinato, "lies precisely in the fact that in it coexist in a perfect symbiosis the public and private economy." Its economy stimulated by temple, palace, productivity, and hard currency, Ebla suffered little inflation. Its silver and gold became the basis for a Near Eastern trading system where Eblaite merchants coordinated the flow of goods from Egypt, Cyprus, Sumer, and Elam.

The city-states of Syria/Mesopotamia soon began to battle for hegemony in which Ebla lost out to more militaristic states such as Kish. The region exploded in a series of ferocious wars. The need for copper and tin to equip chariots, axes, swords, spears, daggers, shields, and arrows further stimulated commercial development. These metals were not found in Sumer so they were obtained through trading networks able to absorb the risks involved in long-distance trade. Timber and stone were also imported. Thus, Sumer, by 2600 B.C.E., became the core of a known-world economy stretching from Egypt to the Indus Valley. This international economy was already working on the principles of the resource- and market-seeking behavior characteristic of modern multinational enterprises.

The Mesopotamian economy reached its peak at the end of the Early Bronze Age (2250–1800 B.C.E.) with the Semitic king, Sargon of Akkad, who created the first world empire. This permitted, and even stimulated, the expansion of known-world international trade. Private *tamkaru* now truly began to flourish in Mesopotamia, although long-distance trade remained in temple/palace hands. Sargon's own records mention such far-flung locations as Bahrein, Baluchistan, and India.

After the demise of Sargon's empire, private enterprise became more significant in Mesopotamia. Smaller boats now plied the Persian Gulf as trading voyages had to be self-financed in the absence of public subsidies. International trade was now managed by an early chamber of commerce called the *karum*, which was granted authority to regulate commerce and governmental duties the public sector could no longer sustain.

Private merchants now traded from Iraq into the Gulf—especially from Ur. While Ur did not have a stock exchange, people speculated on future profits from the copper trade. Ea-Nasir financed trading expeditions that sailed to Bahrein and back, assembling investors in some of the first limited partnerships and joint ventures. Hundreds of small investors in Ur involved their money as well. Ea-Nasir thus managed the first mutual fund on the expectation of big future earnings in copper. The first mutual fund, though, ended in the first recorded crash when Ur's King Rim-Sin suddenly declared all loans null and void.

Around this time, the ancient Assyrians took a considerable step toward the multinational company. The kings Ilushuma (1962–1942 B.C.E.) and Erishum (1941–1902 B.C.E.) left the financing of international trade commerce to private merchants. To gain access to the valuable mines and keep trade in Assyrian hands, the merchants set up permanent Anatolian and Babylonian establishments. After approximately 1950 B.C.E., a network of Assyrian *karu* operated in Syria and all over what is now eastern and central TURKEY. Its head colony was in Kanesh, over 600 miles from Ashur.

The northern and central parts of Kanesh were occupied by a self-contained community of Assyrians with home offices. Ashur-based Assyrian firms shipped Babylonian grain and textiles within their own privately owned networks to Kanesh, Syria, and Asia Minor. The best known was the House of Ashur-Imitti, which "fashioned a highly organized commercial enterprise, an international import-export business in the fullest sense." Could this be history's first recorded multinational enterprise? By strict definition, probably not, since the establishments abroad did not engage in production. However, taking a broader definition of the proto-multinational and observing that these were privately owned companies operating permanent branch offices, then yes, a very considerable step toward the multinational was indeed taken.

Phoenicia. The *tamkarum* model became intercontinental when it was applied in the city-states of Lebanon and Syria. This strip of land was inhabited by debt-ridden Canaanite farmers who became dependent laborers in a feudal system. Shipbuilding and manufacturing became the most profitable means of economic survival. Seaborne Canaanites, known to the Greeks as Phoenicians, became the classic middlemen of the Late Bronze and the Iron Age. Craftsmen—many self-employed—manufactured goods from imported bronze and ivory. Royal and private traders then shipped them abroad by caravan or sailing ship.

The royal throne was the driving force behind Phoenician capitalism. Since the Phoenician city-states had limited agricultural resources, prince-kings (especially of Tyre) saw economic salvation in the capitalization of the strongest assets—a highly skilled population, timber for shipbuilding, and access to both the Mediterranean and the overland routes of Asia. The *Ras Sharma* text from Ugarit reveals a strong governmental role in the economy as well. Most of the economy was under the direct management of the royal vizier and his harbor master. Beneath them, the major nobles and princes also took part in commerce. Phoenician merchants and guilds organized joint ventures to finance trading expeditions to Egypt, the Hittite realm, Crete, or Babylonia. Copper, lumber, shipbuilding, and wheat were designated as the monopolies of crown merchants.

The Phoenician naval model was perfected by the rulers and merchants of Tyre after 1000 B.C.E. A royal trading alliance between Hiram of Phoenicia and Solomon of Israel meant vast profits and royalties, which were invested in temples, palaces, public works, shipyards, and vessels. After King Itobaal seized the Tyrian throne around 900 B.C.E., Israel was split into two kingdoms: Israel and Judah. Itobaal united Tyre and Sidon and continued to trade with Israel.

The final phase of Tyrian commerce, from 840–538 B.C.E. was truly intercontinental. The kings of Tyre erected a line of permanent establishments across the Mediterranean and Mesopotamia. The powerful Assyrian empire conquered the Near East but left Tyre independent. Assyrian demand for hard currency, garments, and metals provided Tyre's merchants with a vast new market. Tyre's managers began to expand their trade across the Mediterranean.

In SPAIN, Tyrian colonists purchased huge quantities of silver ore mined from southwestern Spain. Some was floated downriver to Cadiz while the rest was sent overland being processed en route. The Spanish operation stimulated further economic activity in southern Spain, Africa, Sicily, and Sardinia. By 650 B.C.E. the Tyrian viziers and their merchants were operating the most impressive trading organization in antiquity.

Greece. The economies of ancient Greece and Italy began to grow in synergy with the Tyrian after 1000 B.C.E. Greece adopted the iron technology of Cyprus that brought about an Aegean market revolution led by the large island of Euboea. With few good roads or big cities and no centralized power, the rural Greek world was quite conducive to independent enterprise. Before 1000 B.C.E., Greek traders began trading as far as Sardinia and Spain. Spreading outward from Cyprus, the knowledge of iron-working aided the development of a new economic individualism.

A trail of Egyptian amulets leading from North Syria through Greece to Italy points to the existence of an 8th-century B.C.E. trading network in which Greeks were involved. Greeks operated as private individuals and small-scale enterprises. Merchants operated as independent agents, buying on a contractual basis, bringing iron, goods, and profits back to Greece.

The new agricultural prosperity of cash crops such as wine and olive oil, combined with the development of iron tools and weapons strengthened the city-state or *polis* as the basic unit of Greek life. Business values began to challenge the dominant agrarian ones, though they never fully replaced them.

Rome. While the Greeks perfected the first democratic free-market culture, the Romans would modify that culture, universalize it, and apply it to big and small business. Starting as an outpost in central Italy, Rome slowly emerged from obscurity to conquer first Italy, then Carthage, and finally most of the Hellenistic kingdoms. Rome's constant wars stimulated the growth of a powerful business culture. Roman entrepreneurs formed huge partnerships called *publicani*, which bid on the open market for large food, uniforms, weapons and construction projects.

Roman firms were internalized—a further step toward multinational enterprise. Roman partners came together to execute a contract, and then disband. They were lean and mean in adapting to different markets with little permanent staff. Some of them may arguably be seen as the first real "multinational" conglomerates, and the first recorded limited liability corporations. *Publicani* often pooled the resources of as many as twenty *socii* who could be considered shareholders and the board of directors. The *magistii* wielded executive power and supervised the company's *decuria* or divisions.

In 27 B.C.E., *Princeps* Augustus Caesar officially ushered in the Roman Empire. No other economy would come as close to global proportions until the voyages of Vasco Da Gama and Christopher Columbus. Europe, Africa, and the Near East became one vast market whose hub lay in Rome. The Roman Empire was the first EUROPEAN UNION, integrated by a common currency (*denarius*), law, and infrastructure.

Roman emperors rejected the strict mercantilist policies of the Near East. Ports such as Puteoli and Ostia were open to all trade. After 100 C.E., these cities began to host branch offices of associations based outside Italy. Gaul and Spain exported food to Greece; Asia exported marble to Italy; grain flowed from Egypt and Libya to Latin Europe. Clay and metal industries among others became very important, and many of these even pioneered in an early form of mass production. The closest Roman counterparts to a modern multinational operated in the marble industry of Asia Minor. Building programs in the western part of the empire provided a huge market for Bithynian marble.

The first "world" economy. Rome's economic expansion went all the way to INDIA. Through Indian middlemen, Roman managers reached markets in southeast Asia and China. Roman agents lived on Indian soil, allowing them to upstage Arab traders. Roman ships left ports in Egypt on the Red Sea every July to arrive in India by fall. Returning to Egypt late in the year via the northeast monsoon, they came with huge shipments of Indian spices and Chinese silk. Shipping such bulk cargoes once a year could only be afforded by large Roman firms able to raise the money and hire the overseas agents.

The effect of this GLOBALIZATION on the Roman economy was noted even by the Emperor Tiberius himself, who worried that Rome's ladies were transferring its wealth to foreigners. The elder Pliny claimed that imports from Arabia, China, and India were costing Rome a huge annual trade deficit. Exaggerated or not, these remarks show the existence of the first known-world economy stretching from Spain to Africa to India to VIETNAM to China.

The memory of this exotic trade would continue to entice Europeans for hundreds of years after the Roman world economy collapsed. After establishing the business culture that is the closest to both the American and modern European model, Rome eventually declined through inflation, corruption, and loss of markets.

BIBLIOGRAPHY. Lionel Casson, "Ancient Naval Technology and the Route to India," *Rome and India, The Ancient Sea Trade* (University of Wisconsin Press, 1991); B.S.J. Isserlin, *The Israelites* (Thames and Hudson, 1998); Samuel Kramer, *The Sumerians, Their History, Culture and Character* (University of Chicago Press, 1963); Amélie Kuhrt, *The Ancient Near East, c. 3000–330* (Routledge, 1995); M.T. Larsen, "The Tradition of Empire in Mesopotamia," *Power and Propaganda: a Symposium on Ancient Empires* (Akademisk Forlag, 1979); M.T. Larsen, *The Old Assyrian City-State and Its Colonies* (Akademisk Forlag, 1976); W.F. Leemans, *The Old Babylonian Merchant* (E.J. Brill, 1950); W.F. Leemans, *Foreign Trade in the Old Babylonian Period* (E.J. Brill, 1960). E. Linder, "Ugarit, A Canaanite Thalassocracy," *Ugarit in Retrospect: Fifty Years of Ugarit and Ugaritic* (Eisenbrauns, 1981); Thomas R. Martin, *Ancient Greece, From Prehistoric to Hellenistic Times* (Yale University Press, 1996); Karl Moore and David C. Lewis, *Birth of the Multinational, 2000 Years of Ancient Business History from Ashur to Augustus* (Copenhagen Business School Press, 1999); Karl Moore and David C. Lewis *Foundations of Corporate Empire: Is History Repeating Itself?* (Prentice-Hall, 2000); Robin Osborne, *Greece in the Making, 1200–479* B.C.E. (Routledge, 1996); John K. Papadopoulos, "Phantom Euboeans," *Journal of Mediterranean Archaeology* (v.10/2, 1997); Giovanni Pettinato, *The Archives of Ebla: An Empire Inscribed in Clay* (Doubleday, 1981); J.N. Postgate, *Early Mesopotamia: Society and Economy at the Dawn of History* (Routledge, 1992); David W. Tandy, *Warriors into Traders: The Power of the Market in Early Greece* (University of California Press, 1997); K.R. Veenhof, *Aspects of Assyrian Trade and its Terminology* (Free University, 1972).

KARL MOORE, PH.D.
MCGILL UNIVERSITY

DAVID LEWIS, PH.D.
CITRUS COLLEGE

capitalism, political

POLITICAL CAPITALISM IS a private-property market system shaped by special-interest government intervention. Regulation, subsidies, and tax-code provisions are less reformer-driven than business-driven. This is to say, most interventions are not the result of government authorities acting on general impulse about the public good but are sponsored, or at least shaped, by the directly affected businesses and their sponsored organizations.

The growth and modernization of the U.S. economy has created greater transparency and competition than was evident in the business-dominated politics of the past. Interventions can now result from the successful lobbying by representatives of the environment, labor, minorities, taxpayers, consumers, religions, gun owners, military, and others. These competing elites, the most powerful of which is still business, create what in the aggregate is political capitalism, also known as corporatism. This "ism" is closely linked to modern American capitalism.

There are two avenues to business success under the profit/loss system. The free market means is where entrepreneurs provide a good or service in an open market that is voluntarily patronized by consumers. The political means is where a governmental restriction or favor provides the margin of success beyond what consumer preference alone would provide. Market entrepreneurship is the way of capitalism; political entrepreneurship is the way of political capitalism.

Business interests, including labor, welcome competition for the things they buy (to minimize costs) far more than for things they sell. They may profess support for free enterprise in general but not in their particular area. Competition disparaged as "unbridled," "cutthroat," "excessive," or "unfair" can be the clarion call for constraints placed on open markets.

Historian Gabriel Kolko defined political capitalism as "the utilization of political outlets to attain conditions of stability, predictability, and security—to attain rationalization—in the economy." Much of the intervention that historians have documented was for business by business to "allow corporations to function in a predictable and secure environment permitting reasonable profits over the long run."

MERCANTILISM in Adam SMITH's day was a prominent form of political capitalism. Under this doctrine, the wealth of nations was perceived to result from the inflow of monetary species (gold primarily) from international trade. Business and political elites worked together to restrict competition from imported products to reserve home markets for home products and keep specie at home. Smith and other free-trade proponents argued that the wealth of nations resulted from capital accumulation and a global division of labor, not protectionism.

For much of the 19th and 20th centuries, American capitalism was business capitalism. Major interventions into the economy such as the Interstate Commerce Act (1887), public utility regulation, wartime planning, and 1930s NEW DEAL planning were driven more by the desires of big business than any other constituency. Business participation in foreign policy decision-making, explains economist Joseph Stromberg, coupled "domestic intervention (corporatism) with overseas intervention (empire)."

The following constraints on rivalry have characterized political capitalism, particularly from the mid-19th century until today:

Import restrictions. A tariff or quota on foreign goods can raise prices and increase market share for domestic industry.

Price supports. A price floor, such as for an agricultural product, allows a firm or firms to have greater and more predictable revenue.

Grant protection. A government permit, franchise, or license to enter into a line of commerce reduces the number of competitors to advantage the established firm(s). Under "natural monopoly" public-utility regulation, franchise protection is accompanied by rate regulation (the "regulatory covenant").

Loan guarantees. Taxpayer-backed obligations can reduce or eliminate risky business investments such as those undertaken in a developing country.

Antitrust laws. The spectrum of laws against charging more, the same, or less than one's rivals, called "monopolistic," "collusive," or "predatory" pricing respectively, have resulted in many more private than government antitrust lawsuits.

Subsidies. Grants for research and development are made in areas considered to be in the public good, such as non-polluting energy technologies.

Quality standards. A minimum standard can advantage firms at the high end of the quality range at the expense of lower-end competitors.

Virtually all of these interventions, intentionally and sometimes not, alter the production of goods and services compared to what would exist from consumer demand alone.

Political capitalism is closer to capitalism than SOCIALISM since private property and profit/loss accounting are at work, and major interventions such as price and allocation controls are the exception. Political capitalism is also different from macroeconomic planning of the so-called mixed economy. Activist fiscal and monetary policy are broader policies than those enacted by particular firms or industries, although the major institutions of intervention (for one, the Federal Reserve Bank) can be established and influenced by national business organizations such as the U.S. Chamber of Commerce.

Political capitalism is the unplanned, opportunistic result of transient interest-group coalitions and temporary political majorities. It is not the work of a central plan in part or whole, although elements of central planning can co-exist and, indeed, inspire dispersed special-interest politicking.

"Follow the money" has led many historians studying political capitalism from effect to cause, from intention to result. In an economic system where the use of the political means is accepted and common, the entrepreneur weighs whether the benefits of government lobbying are greater than the costs *ex ante*. If so, a firm or trade association is likely to pursue government favor. Such decisions to proceed often prevail over the interests of the less organized opposition since the benefits are concentrated to the involved firm(s) and the cost is spread out (and small) over all taxpayers and/or consumers. But this disparity has closed over time as taxpayer, consumer, and other "common good" groups have been formed to lobby alongside other interests.

Political capitalism has aroused strong criticism. Marxists and socialists seek a more "democratic" economic system in place of what is seen as an inherent link between political influence and capitalism. Libertarians see the "political" as the problem, identifying business as not only the friend but also the foe of capitalism, to support LAISSEZ-FAIRE. Defenders of political capitalism view competing elites as democracy in action.

BIBLIOGRAPHY. Robert Bradley, *Oil, Gas, and Government: The U.S. Experience* (Rowman & Littlefield, 1996); Stephen Breyer and Paul MacAvoy, "Regulation and Deregulation," *The New Palgrave: A Dictionary of Economics* (Palgrave, 1998); Gabriel Kolko, *The Triumph of Conservatism: A Reinterpretation of American History, 1900–1916* (The Free Press, 1963); Murray Rothbard, "Left and Right: The Prospects for Liberty," *Egalitarianism as a Revolt against Nature and Other Essays* (Libertarian Press, 1974); Joseph Stromberg, "The Role of State Monopoly Capitalism in the American Empire," *Journal of Libertarian Studies* (v.15/3,

2001); Howard Wiarda, *Corporatism and Comparative Politics: The Other Great "Ism"* (M.E. Sharpe, 1997).

ROBERT L. BRADLEY, JR.
INSTITUTE FOR ENERGY RESEARCH

Carnegie, Andrew (1835–1919)

THE PRE-EMINENT SYMBOL of America's Gilded Age, Andrew Carnegie was the most powerful capitalist of the last quarter of the 19th century. Born in Dunfermline, Scotland, Carnegie died in Lenox, Massachusetts.

After emigrating to the UNITED STATES with his family in 1848, Carnegie worked as a telegrapher before joining the administrative staff of the Pennsylvania Railroad, where he was named a vice president at the age of 24. After amassing a fortune through his investments, Carnegie formed the Carnegie Steel Company in 1872. His vertical integration of the company—buying up raw materials and transportation facilities to control the entire process of steel-making—as well as his lucrative, and sometimes illegal, arrangements with other steel producers and railroads made Carnegie's company the largest manufacturer in the world by 1890. Stung by criticism over his company's use of lethal force to end a strike at Homestead, Pennsylvania in 1892, Carnegie attempted to rehabilitate his reputation by practicing the "Gospel of Wealth," giving away a substantial part of his fortune before he died.

Carnegie was the older of two sons born to William and Margaret (Morrison) Carnegie. The family emigrated to Pittsburgh, Pennsylvania, in 1848 after William Carnegie, a linen weaver, found he could not compete with the new, mechanized power looms that were just beginning to dominate the textile industry. Fascinated by technology, Andrew Carnegie worked in a telegraph office as a 13-year-old; four years later, he joined the staff of the Pennsylvania Railroad as a telegrapher and secretary.

Despite his lack of formal education, Carnegie rose quickly through the ranks of the railroad. Demonstrating his financial acumen with a series of profitable investments in railroads, sleeping cars, oil, and telegraph systems, Carnegie was a wealthy man by the time he was 30 years old. He founded his first company, the Keystone Bridge Company, in April 1865. With orders coming in to rebuild the country after the Civil War, Carnegie needed a regular supply of iron for his bridge-building enterprise. Accordingly, he soon established an iron company, the Union Iron Mills.

With his bridge- and iron-making companies, Carnegie demonstrated two of the strategies that transformed the American industrial sector in the latter half of the 19th century: investment in technological innovation and vertical integration of the industrial process. Carnegie did not hesitate to invest in new manufacturing processes that would improve efficiency and output, and he was always on the lookout to bring more steps of the production process under his control, buying up everything from the raw materials needed to make iron to the transportation facilities needed to ship his product.

Carnegie also did not hesitate to engage in secret—and illegal—kickback arrangements with railroads to get cheaper shipping rates for his product. When the Duquesne Works developed an innovation to the steel-making process in 1889 that gave it an advantage over other steel producers, Carnegie sent a libelous letter to all of the railroads claiming that the new process produced inferior steel rails. Carnegie's tactic nearly forced his competitor out of business and he quickly bought it up at a bargain price; he then began producing steel with the same process that he had claimed was inferior.

Carnegie reached the pinnacle of his career as the steel baron of the Gilded Age. He entered the steel business by combining a series of holdings in 1872 to form what would eventually become the Carnegie Steel Company.

An important supplier of steel rails for the nation's railroads and steel beams for the construction of skyscrapers and other buildings, the company was one of the most profitable of its era and ranked as the largest manufacturing entity in the world. By the turn of the century, after buying up many of his rivals and driving several others out of business, Carnegie could essentially dictate the price of steel in the United States.

As Carnegie reached the height of his success, he began to articulate a theory of philanthropy that he hoped other wealthy industrialists and financiers would follow. In *The Gospel of Wealth and Other Timely Essays*, published in 1889, Carnegie expressed his sense of duty "To set an example of modest, unostentatious living, shunning display or extravagance . . . the man of wealth thus becoming the mere trustee and agent for his poorer brethren, bringing to their service his superior wisdom, experience, and ability to administer, doing for them better than they would or could do for themselves." Carnegie implemented the "Gospel of Wealth" by donating money to build libraries throughout the United States and endowing several universities and cultural institutions.

Although he was widely praised for his philanthropic endeavors, Carnegie's reputation did not fully recover from one of the bloodiest confrontations in American labor history, which occurred at his Homestead steel works in western Pennsylvania. Refusing to sign a contract with the Amalgamated Association of Steel and Iron Workers in June 1892, Carnegie ordered his partner, Henry Clay FRICK, to break the ensuing strike and reopen the works while he left for a vacation in Scotland. Frick employed Pinkerton agents to forcibly reopen the plant, which touched off a bloody battle on July 5–6, 1892. Nine strikers and seven Pinkerton agents were killed and the strike was eventually broken. From that point on, Carnegie had achieved complete mastery of his labor force, which worked in continuous 12-hour shifts, seven days a week.

After the Battle of Homestead, Carnegie was equally reviled and revered; his company, however, was an undisputed success. With revenues of $40 million in 1900, it alone produced more steel than the entire nation of Great Britain. The following year Carnegie sold his steel holdings to financier J.P. MORGAN, who reportedly paid a small sum for the company. Morgan then combined eight other steel companies to form U.S. STEEL, which became the first corporation valued at over $1 billion.

Andrew Carnegie died on August 11, 1919, at his summer home in Lenox, Massachusetts. He was survived by his wife, the former Louise Whitfield, whom he married in 1887, and their only child, Margaret. At the time of his death, it was estimated that Carnegie had given away all but $30 million of his $400 million fortune.

Some of his contemporaries pointed to Carnegie's life as an example of the opportunities available to talented, hardworking immigrants to the United States. Others noted his less-than-ethical business practices and ruthlessness in dealing with his competitors and his work force as examples of the dangers of America's rugged individualism during the Gilded Age.

Carnegie doubtless transformed the corporate landscape of the industrial world by emphasizing relentless technological innovation and corporate control of each step in the manufacturing process. His harsh tactics against labor organizations, however, tarnished his reputation as an all-American success story.

BIBLIOGRAPHY. Andrew Carnegie, *The Autobiography of Andrew Carnegie* (1920; reprint, Northeastern University Press, 1986); Maury Klein, *The Change Makers: From Carnegie to Gates, How the Great Entrepreneurs Transformed Ideas into Industries* (Henry Holt and Co., 2003); Paul Krause, *The Battle for Homestead, 1880–1892* (University of Pittsburgh Press, 1992); Richard Krooth, *A Century of Passing: Carnegie, Steel, and the Fate of Homestead* (University Press of America, 2002); Harold C. Livesay, *Andrew Carnegie and the Rise of Big Business* (1975; reprint, Addison-Wesley Publishing, 1997); Thomas J. Misa, *A Nation of Steel: The Making of Modern America, 1865–1925* (Johns Hopkins University Press, 1995); William Serrin, *Homestead: The Glory and Tragedy of an American Steel Town* (Times Books, 1992); Abigail Van Slyck, *Free to All: Carnegie Libraries and American Culture, 1890–1920* (University of Chicago Press, 1996); Kenneth Warren, *Triumphant Capitalism: Henry Clay Frick and the Industrial Transformation of America* (University of Pittsburgh Press, 1996).

TIMOTHY G. BORDEN, PH.D.
INDEPENDENT SCHOLAR

carrying capacity

ACCORDING TO ITS historical evolution and field of application, the concept of carrying capacity has been defined in very many ways. Generally speaking, it addresses the upper limits of a certain system allowing, at the same time for continued existence of that system without any significant damage.

Thus, biophysical carrying capacity expresses the "maximal population size that could be sustained biophysically under given technological capabilities," whereas social-carrying capacity specifies "the maxima that could be sustained under various social systems," according to articles in *Ecological Economics*. In tourism, for example, carrying capacity is conceived as "a maximum number of visitors that can be tolerated without irreversible or unacceptable deterioration of the physical environment without considerably diminishing user satisfaction." Finally, human-carrying capacity has been redefined "as the maximum rates of resource-harvesting and waste-generation (the maximum load) that can be sustained indefinitely without progressively impairing the productivity and functional integrity of relevant ecosystems wherever the latter may be located."

The concept of carrying capacity dates back to Thomas MALTHUS' population theory stating that population growth will always entail food shortage under the assumption that population increases exponentially, whereas food production can only be increased linearly. During the last decades, the concept of carrying capacity has gained a broader perspective and is being more widely discussed, in particular with respect to a growing awareness of the upper limits of population, economy, and ecosystems. It is thus applied in several fields including biology, demography, applied and human ecology, agriculture and tourism. "The main contribution of carrying capacity in applied and human ecology is as a political concept generally highlighting that exponential growth, and thus environmental pressures have to be curbed," explain Irmy Seidl and Clem Tisdell.

The ecological footprint, originally co-developed by Wiliam E. Rees, has been suggested as an indicator of biophysical limits and sustainability, being defined as "the corresponding area of productive land and aquatic ecosystems required to produce the resources used, and to assimilate the wastes produced, by a defined population at a specific material standard of living, wherever on Earth that land may be located." Strengths and weaknesses of this indicator are differently perceived, as well as over- and underestimated. One strength consists in the conversion of typically complex resource use patterns to a single number—the equivalent land area required—and thus, allows for a ranking of the ecological impact of nations. The ranking reveals that out of 52 countries accounting for 80 percent of the world's population, only 10 are living below the world's carrying capacity limit of 1.7 hectares per citizen, including, for example, EGYPT (1.2 ha/capita), INDIA (0.8), the PHILIPPINES (1.4), and PAKISTAN (0.8). Due to resource-intensive production and consumption patterns, however, most of the developed countries show ecological footprints that exceed available capacities.

This implies that, at present, most industrialized nations are running massive unaccounted ecological deficits with the rest of the planet, thus living at the expense of underdeveloped nations. The question of intergenerational and interregional equity will thus remain one of the most challenging tasks to be tackled by politicians in the near future.

The ecological footprint concept has been further developed by including international trade, as well as a sustainability criterion in order to assess regional contributions to global sustainability. It could be shown that "most of global sustainability growth can be attributed to western Europe, Asia and Japan, particularly through high savings ratios," whereas the United States "has made a very small net contribution to the growth in global sustainability," according to ecological economists John L.R. Roops and others.

In some areas, the concept of carrying capacity has been successfully implemented (e.g., in hunting and tourism areas), notably in the Okawango Delta, Botswana, where the daily number of tourists is limited, or in some European mountain stations setting a cap for the number of people allowed in the skiing arena. In other areas, such as agriculture, research argues that global or regional carrying capacity limits have been reached, and current economic models used by the WORLD BANK need to be modified to take account of biophysical limits. It has been further stated by Jonathan M. Harris and Scott Kennedy that "a supply-side strategy of increased production has led to serious problems of soil degradation and water overdraft, as well as other ecosystem stresses. This implies that demand-side issues of population policy and efficiency in consumption are crucial to the development of a sustainable agricultural system." Nevertheless, on a global scale, more efforts will have to be made to reconcile economic development, population growth, and ecosystems' carrying capacity.

BIBLIOGRAPHY. Irmy Seidl and Clem A. Tisdell, "Carrying Capacity Reconsidered: from Malthus' Population Theory to Cultural Carrying Capacity," *Ecological Economics* (v.31/3, 1999); William E. Rees, "Revisiting Carrying Capacity: Area-Based Indicators of Sustainability," *Population and Environment: A Journal of Interdisciplinary Studies* (v.17/3, 1996); Robert Constanza, "The Dynamics of the Ecological Footprint Concept," *Ecological Economics* (v.32/3, 2000); www.ecouncil.ac.cr; John L.R. Roops, Giles Atkinson, et al., "International Trade and the Sustainability Footprint: A Practical Criterion for its Assessment," *Ecological Economics* (v.28/1, 1999); Jonathan M. Harris and Scott Kennedy, "Carrying Capacity in Agriculture: Global and Regional Issues," *Ecological Economics* (v.29/3, 1999).

URSULA A. VAVRIK, PH.D.
UNIVERSITY OF ECONOMICS, VIENNA, AUSTRIA

cartel

AN ASSOCIATION OF FIRMS, a cartel explicitly agrees to coordinate its activities. A cartel that includes all firms in a market is in effect a monopolist (i.e., if a cartel includes all firms in a market then the cartel problem is identical to that of a monopolist, and the resulting market outcome with respect to price and quantity will be the pure MONOPOLY outcome).

Hence, in general, one can define a cartel as a formal price-fixing agreement among firms. During the 1880s a cartel of U.S. RAILROADS operated openly as the Joint Executive Committee. The Joint Executive Committee allocated market shares rather than the actual quantities shipped. While each member railroad was allowed to set their individual fares, the Joint Executive Committee reported weekly accounts so that each individual railroad had information regarding the total amount transported. Because total demand fluctuated, each member's market share depended on both the fares charged by all the members of the cartel, and the demand fluctuations. Hence, fixing the market share of each member can be viewed as price-fixing under demand uncertainty.

These kinds of horizontal price-fixing agreements, or more generally, cartels were a common phenomenon of American industries. The cartel agreements were not restricted to formal price-fixing agreements but also included sales quotas, exclusive sales arrangements, geographical market division, customer allocation, and the imposition of penalties for infractions. In 1890, the Sherman Act declared cartels illegal in the United States. The Sherman Act implicitly prohibits the formation of cartels. Section 1 of the Sherman Act prohibits "every contract, combination . . . or conspiracy in restraint of trade . . ." This vague language means that collective efforts to increase price, reduce output, prevent entry, exclude actual competitors, and a host of other business practices that are aimed at restraining competition are illegal.

However, the Sherman Act did not imply the end of legal cartels since most European countries did not have any systematic cartel legislation prior to World War II. Up to 1939, there were at least 70 international cartels operating in over 40 industries. All of these cartels were legal and had written cartel contracts. On average, these cartels lasted slightly more than five years before they broke up. About 83 percent of the cartels had 10 or fewer firms, 64 percent had five or fewer members, and 39 percent had three or less members, while 74 percent of the cartels each had a world market share of over 50 percent.

OPEC. Thus, as with U.S. cartels before the Sherman Act, these international cartels involved relatively few firms with large market shares. In the early 2000s, the best-known cartel still operating is the ORGANIZATION OF PETROLEUM EXPORTING COUNTRIES (OPEC), a legal cartel of oil-producing countries that attempts to set the prices for crude oil by agreeing on production quantities for its member countries. Looking at the history of cartels a number of questions arise, such as: Why do cartels form? What factors cause some cartels to break up even without government intervention? What are the welfare effects of cartels?

The answer to the first question is simple. In a competitive market each firm, maximizing its own profit, considers only the effect that its output decision has on its profit, ignoring the effects that the output level it produces has on the profit of all other firms in the market. Thus, firms in a competitive market produce a greater level of output then firms that are part of a cartel. In theory, a cartel can achieve monopoly profits simply by maximizing the joint profit of its member firms. Since the pure monopoly profit is as least as great as any other feasible level of profit for the same market, all members of a cartel will be able to enjoy higher profit levels than under competition, assuming that the monopoly profit is divided appropriately among the cartel members. Hence, firms who recognize their mutual interdependence have a profit incentive to reach a cartel agreement as long as the profit, that each firm can obtain when acting according to the cartel agreement, is higher than when they act as competitors.

However, reaching a cartel agreement, which is acceptable to all members, is only the beginning of the process. Cartel stability becomes a crucial issue. The mere fact that the cartel price is above the perfectly competitive price and that, for the cartel members, marginal revenue exceeds marginal cost gives each cartel member an incentive to cheat. In fact, the more successful the cartel is in raising the price above the competitive price, the greater is the incentive for members of the cartel to cheat on the cartel agreement.

Because incentives to cheat are strong, a cartel, in order to be stable, must be able to detect increases in output above the agreed-upon output levels, or secret price cuts by one or more of its members in case of a price-setting cartel. Of course, detection by itself is not sufficient to prevent cheating. The cartel must also be able to punish its members who deviate from the cartel agreement. In an attempt to deter cheating virtually any punishment can be threatened. However, it is crucial that the threatened punishment is a credible punishment. For example, the cartel may announce that it detects cheating by a member, all other cartel members will cut their price below average cost, or increase output so that the resulting market price is below average cost, until the cheater is forced to leave the market.

However, such a threat is not credible, since it would not be the best response once cheating has been detected. The problem here is that the punisher gets punished as well as the cheater, and given a choice the punisher would probably not go through with the punishment. Threats can, however, be made credible via pre-commitment. There is a large body of literature discussing the conditions that facilitate the formation and stability of cartels.

Regarding the formation of cartels, it is necessary that a cartel is, indeed, able to raise the market price. In addition, formation is more likely if there are low organizational costs, and in the case of illegal cartels, the expectation of severe punishment is low. Regarding the stability or enforcement of a cartel agreement, it is necessary that cheating can be detected. In general, cheating will be easier to detect the fewer the number of firms in a cartel, the less prices fluctuate independently, the easier it is to observe prices and the more homogeneous the product sold by the cartel members.

The less prevailing these conditions are in a particular market, the more likely it is that a cartel will break up after a relatively short time period. Empirical evidence regarding formation and stability of cartels directly supports these theoretical assertions. Econometric tests have shown that most cartels, or price-fixing agreements, involve 10 or fewer firms that produced a relatively homogeneous product. Regarding the stability or lifetime of cartels, there is empirical evidence that supports the theoretical arguments put forward above. What are the welfare effects of a successful cartel? The cartel price will be above marginal cost, consequently, there will be a loss in consumer surplus and total surplus, or welfare. Hence, consumers and society will be worse off, while the cartel members will be better off due to a transfer of surplus from the consumers to the member firms of the cartel.

A number of empirical studies have tried to estimate the loss in welfare, also called deadweight loss. Most studies conclude that the deadweight loss is relatively small. However, these studies neglect the role of transfer and employment effects of cartels. Few would argue that the possible large transfer of wealth from consumers to the cartel firms is negligible from a welfare point of view. In addition, employment effects may also be important; the decreased cartel output leaves some workers unemployed, who may not, in the short run, find employment alternatives in the competitive sectors of the economy.

It is for these reasons that governments in many countries have adopted a hostile position regarding the formation of cartels, as is the case in the United States. In fact, one can argue that one of the major achievements of U.S. ANTITRUST laws and enforcement has been the elimination of formal cartels. However, one has to realize that cartel behavior may also rise from non-cooperative behavior (i.e., collusion does not have to be formal and explicit). So-called tacit collusion, which results in the cartel outcome, may well be the result of repeated interaction between rival firms.

Hence, with the exception of a few international cartels such as OPEC, formal cartels have been successfully eliminated, yet cartel behavior still remains.

BIBLIOGRAPHY. R.D. Blair and D.L. Kaserman, *Antitrust Economics* (Irvin, 1985); D. W. Carlton and J.M. Perloff, *Modern Industrial Organization* (Addison-Wesley, 1999); A. Jacquemin and M.E. Slade, *Cartels, Collusion, and Horizontal Merger*, R. Schmalensee and R.D. Willig, eds., *The Handbook of Industrial Organization* (v.1, North Holland, 1989); R.A. Posner, *Antitrust Law* (The University of Chicago Press, 1976); W.G. Shepherd, *Public Policy toward Business* (Irvin, 1985); G. Stigler, "A Theory of Oligopoly," *Journal of Political Economy* (1964); G. Stigler, *The Organization of Industry* (University of Chicago Press, 1968).

KLAUS G. BECKER, PH.D.
TEXAS TECH UNIVERSITY

Carter, Jimmy (1924–)

BORN IN PLAINS, GEORGIA, Jimmy Carter became the 39th president of the UNITED STATES in 1976. He received an appointment to the U.S. Naval Academy at Annapolis and graduated in 1946. Beginning naval service on battleships, two years later Carter was accepted for submarine duty, and eventually became one of a small group of officers working on the nuclear submarine program.

Carter studied nuclear physics at Union College in New York and served on the crew of the nuclear submarine *Sea Wolf*. In 1953, after the death of his father, he resigned from the Navy and returned to Plains to take over the family farm. He started a fertilizer business, increased his landholdings, and acquired a cotton gin, a peanut-shelling plant, a farm-supply operation, and warehouses.

Carter began his public career as chairman of the local school board and, in 1962, ran for a new state senatorial district. He served two terms, then ran for governor of Georgia in 1970. Departing from the racially segregationist legacy of previous governors, Carter pointedly called for an end to racial discrimination in his 1971 gubernatorial inauguration. During his term as governor, Carter appointed increased numbers of African-Americans to state boards and agencies; reorganized state government; and abolished some 300 offices, boards, and commissions. He instituted zero-based budgeting and the passage of a "sunshine law" to open government meetings to the public.

Carter started his run for U.S. president as soon as his gubernatorial term expired in January 1975. The country was still recovering from the Watergate scandals and the resignation of Richard NIXON, and Carter correctly perceived the country wanted a candidate who was not associated with Watergate, the VIETNAM WAR, or Washington, D.C.

Carter campaigned by promising never to lie to the people and to institute a government that was decent, compassionate, and responsible. Going to some extreme in personal honesty during the campaign, Carter even admitted he sometimes looked upon women with "lust in his heart," as he told *Playboy* magazine. Carter narrowly defeated Gerald FORD, and immediately after his inauguration he took symbolic actions to demonstrate his disdain for what he considered to be the imperial presidency: He walked to the White House, sold the presidential yacht, and eliminated other ceremonial trappings of the presidency.

Carter was best known for establishing human rights as a tenet of American foreign policy, frequently criticizing nations that violated basic human rights. One of his first challenges involved the U.S. role in Panama and he successfully concluded the negotiations to turn the canal over to Panama in 1999. Carter's greatest foreign policy success involved the Middle East.

In 1978, Carter invited ISRAEL's Prime Minister Menachem Begin and EGYPT's President Anwar Sadat to the presidential retreat at Camp David to discuss and to reach a peace agreement, successfully signing the accord in 1979. Carter also hoped to continue the policy of detente with the SOVIET UNION. He signed the SALT II treaty with the Soviets, which limited the deployment of nuclear missiles, but it was never ratified by the U.S. Senate, due to the Soviet invasion of AFGHANISTAN in 1979. After the invasion, it was clear the Senate would take no action on SALT II. In retaliation for the Soviet invasion, Carter ordered a boycott by U.S. athletes of the 1980 Moscow Summer Olympic Games.

Carter continued to expand American contacts with China that had begun under Nixon. In January 1979, he granted formal diplomatic recognition to the communist Peoples' Republic of China, but in doing so, he had to withdraw formal recognition of capitalist Taiwan as the official Chinese nation.

But one event overshadows the historical perspective of the Carter administration: the Iranian Hostage Crisis. By early 1979, internal opposition to the shah (king) of IRAN had become so virulent that he was forced to flee and turn over power. Shortly after his abdication, the leading Islamic cleric, Ayatollah Khomeini, returned from exile in Paris and seized the reigns of power. The shah, now in Mexico, was dying of cancer, and Carter allowed him entry to the United States for medical treatment. Previous U.S. support for the shah had already enraged Islamic fundamentalists in Iran, but Carter's action was the last straw.

In November 1979, rioting university students and fundamentalists overran the U.S. embassy in Iran's capital, Teheran, and seized the American embassy personnel. After months of fruitless negotiations to free the hostages, Carter, in an agonizing decision, approved a poorly planned secret military mission to free the hostages. The mission ended in an embarrassing public failure as two U.S. helicopters collided over the Iranian desert.

This military failure seemed to reinforce the widespread belief that Carter was a president who could not get things done. For the rest of his administration, Carter was focused on finding ways to free the hostages; they were finally freed as President Ronald REAGAN was giving his Inaugural Address in January 1981.

Carter had inherited an economy that was slowly emerging from recession; however, during his tenure in office, the economy worsened. The annual inflation rate went from 4.8 percent in 1976 to 12 percent in 1980; federal deficits in 1979 totaled $27.7 billion and for 1980, $59 billion; unemployment leveled off in 1980 at 7.7 percent. The increasingly depressing economic indicators only further fostered a despairing view of Carter's presidency.

Carter did have some success in awakening Americans to their dependence on Arab oil. After the 1970s OIL embargo by the ORGANIZATION OF PETROLEUM EXPORTING COUNTRIES (OPEC), Carter advanced a long-term program designed to solve the energy problem by proposing limits on imported oil; instituting a gradual price decontrol on domestically produced oil; imposing a stringent program of conservation; and encouraging the development of alternate energy sources.

By July 1980, Carter's approval rating stood at 21 percent, and Senator Edward Kennedy challenged him for the Democratic nomination. While Kennedy was not successful, the challenge required Carter to spend precious energy and time campaigning against Kennedy. Carter received the Democratic nomination, but left the convention with a divided party and a low standing in the polls.

Meanwhile, the Republican candidate, Ronald Reagan, asked the question: "Are you better off today than you were four years ago?" Americans said no and overwhelmingly voted for Reagan in November 1980; he received 489 electoral votes to Carter's 49.

After leaving the White House, Carter returned to Georgia where he established the Carter Presidential Center, devoted to democratic and human-rights issues, at Emory University. Rehabilitating his public reputation over the subsequent decades, Carter acted as a diplomat-at-large, facilitating peace agreements at various hotspots around the globe. He also helped to found Habitat for Humanity, an organization working to provide houses for underprivileged people. For his Camp David peace accord between Egypt and Israel and other efforts, Carter was awarded the 2002 Nobel Peace Prize.

Always considered highly intelligent and moral, Carter nevertheless presided over a period of "malaise," or sickness, in the history of American capitalism.

BIBLIOGRAPHY. "Jimmy Carter," www.infoplease.com; Bob Woodward, *Shadow: Five Presidents and the Legacy of Watergate* (Simon & Schuster, 1999); David Gergen, *Eyewitness to Power* (Simon & Schuster, 2000); G. Barry Golson, ed., *The Playboy Interview* (Wideview Books, 1981); Jimmy Carter, *Why Not the Best?* (Broadman Press, 1975); William L. Miller, *Yankee from Georgia: The Emergence of Jimmy Carter* (Times Books, 1978); Pierre Salinger, *America Held Hostage: The Secret Negotiations* (Doubleday, 1981).

LINDA L. PETROU, PH.D.
HIGH POINT UNIVERSITY

cash flow

"CASH IS KING" is a favored proclamation of market analysts and entrepreneurs. Cash, in that sense, refers not to that physical green substance we all treasure, but to cash receipts minus disbursements from a given asset or operation for a specified period.

Cash flow, for all intents and purposes, is the transfer of money in and out of a given operation. After all, it is the cash inflows and outflows that determine the solvency of a business.

In the strict accounting sense, cash flow is assessed in a company's statement of cash flows, wherein the analyst starts from accrual basis net income, adds non-cash (or "paper only") charges, such as depreciation or amortization, subtracts or adds changes in asset and liability accounts, then adds or subtracts payments and receipts related to investing and financing, and arrives at a cash basis net income. The end result of a cash flow statement is to emphasize the change in cash and cash equivalents for the year.

There are various components of an enterprise that affect cash flow, such as inventory, accounts receivable, accounts payable, and investment and financing activities undertaken by the enterprise. By performing a cash flow analysis on these components, business managers are able to more easily identify potential cash flow problems and find ways to improve it.

Cash flow is meant to capture all real cash outlays of the present, and analyzing this in detail helps an ENTREPRENEUR to determine the ability of his business to generate cash from its current operations. While cash flow is not a fashionable point of focus among the majority of business media, to financial professionals it is generally a valuable indicator of a company's immediate financial health and its ability to stay solvent.

Austrian economist Ludwig von MISES explained that both economic actors and entrepreneurs take specific actions and make choices that allow them to more accurately cope with an uncertain future and improve their state of satisfaction. On balance, entrepreneurs wish to alleviate business uncertainties as painlessly as possible. Typical uncertainties that an entrepreneur faces are expected costs, risk, return, and earning power.

A business enterprise succeeds in generating earning power when it uses cash to generate more cash. Earning power, in turn, increases an enterprise's monetary wealth so that it may pass on this wealth to its owners, and this denotes a healthy cash flow. The passing of wealth may be to a single proprietor or a series of partners, or in the case of the corporation, it may be shareholders.

This brings us to another aspect of the value of cash flow, and that is providing information to outside users such as investors or creditors. Both investors and creditors rely on healthy cash flows of an enterprise to which they have committed funds, because clearly, the motive for committing funds is to earn a favorable rate of return from the investment, whether the funds were exchanged for a percentage of ownership and dividends, or for an interest-bearing loan.

Whereas solvency issues and growing-concern problems can be hidden beneath vigorous revenues and satisfactory profits, the financial reporting of cash flows allows prospective investors, creditors, and business partners to assess the viability of the enterprise to meet their wealth-increasing objectives.

Cash flows are essential in this respect because cash-flow information can always be derived from accrual information, whereas the opposite is not true. However, there has been a long-standing battle on whether accounting principles should emphasize cash flows and de-emphasize income, or whether income is indeed the more valuable tool for measuring the results of enter-prise operations. In 1971, the Accounting Principles Board (APB) underscored the importance of income as the primary measurement in its Opinion No. 19, and they were followed by a similar position taken by the SECURITIES AND EXCHANGE COMMISSION (SEC) in 1973.

Certainly, there are other ways in which cash flows are useful in a capitalist system. Cash-flow ratios are used to measure performance factors within the firm. A cash flow-to-assets ratio assesses the ability of the assets on hand to generate operating cash flows, and a cash flows-to-sales ratio gauges how well sales are generating cash flows.

Nevertheless, difficulties in presenting accurate cash flows are at hand in a time of market volatility. With the deceleration of financial markets in the early 2000s, arrival of RECESSION, and the focus on stock price levels, corporations have become more dependent on the immediate appearances presented by revenue and profit numbers because of the modern media's fixation on short-term presentations, as opposed to long-term prospects. Therefore, accounting principles, overall, are stretched to allow for more tolerant accounting policies and procedures.

In early 2003, Tyco International, amid a looming liquidity crisis, decided to consider changing its standards for calculating cash flow because the company was under a backlash from investors for excluding certain types of cash outlays that would seriously hinder its earnings outlook. The company had been excluding the expenses of buying customer accounts from independent dealers in its ADT security alarm business, and this, in turn, glossed over some otherwise apparent cash problems within the company. By March 2003, Tyco had filed a lawsuit against its own CHIEF FINANCIAL OFFICER.

In fact, how companies adhere to overall accounting principles was under heavy fire by regulatory agencies, financial analysts, the media, and the general public. In an era of competition-heavy industries and mega-corporate bankruptcies and failures, companies are constantly looking for ways to edge out a competitor in order to look more attractive to Wall Street analysts and potential investors. Cash flow is just one of the many new measurements of financial performance that is gaining ground in terms of significance. Cash is, indeed, king.

BIBLIOGRAPHY. Joel G. Siegel and Jae K. Shim, *Barron's Business Guide: Dictionary of Accounting Terms* (Barrons, 2000); Robert N. Anthony, *Tell It Like It Was: A Conceptual Framework for Financial Accounting* (Irwin, 1983); Jan R. Williams, Keith G. Stanga, and William W. Holder, *Intermediate Accounting* (Dryden Press, 1995); Ludwig von Mises, *Human Action* (Mises Institute, 1949); "Tyco Likely to Alter Free Cash Flow Definition-WSJ," *Forbes* (2002).

KAREN DE COSTER
WALSH COLLEGE

central banks

A CENTRAL BANK IS the most powerful financial institution in a nation's economy, charged with critical monetary and financial responsibilities. Central banks issue currency, serve the banking needs of the national government, maintain foreign exchange reserves, support the banking system (including serving as a clearinghouse for bank drafts and as a "lender of last resort"), and perhaps most importantly, protect the value of the currency through monetary policy.

Examples of central banks include the FEDERAL RESERVE (UNITED STATES), the BANK OF ENGLAND (UNITED KINGDOM), the BANK OF JAPAN (JAPAN), and the recently created EUROPEAN CENTRAL BANK (EUROPEAN UNION).

Though some of these institutions have functioned for centuries (the Bank of England was established in 1694), their current roles and responsibilities are very different than those envisioned when they were initially created. As capitalism has evolved, the central bank has shifted its responsibilities to meet the changing monetary needs of the system.

In earlier times, our modern conception of a central bank as a stabilizing institution did not yet exist. Instead, the early central banks were established to meet the borrowing needs of national governments and existed mostly as private, profit-making institutions. Whether the central bank competed alongside other banks or precluded their emergence because of its monopoly power, the central bank was not viewed as an institution responsible for supporting nor monitoring other banks.

Modern banking operates on a principle known as "fractional reserve banking." Under this system banks accept currency deposits and make loans. Because banks use some of the deposited money for lending activities, they do not hold all the currency they receive. Consequently, the total amount of money in circulation is greater than the total amount of currency. This system functions effectively as long as depositors do not wish to withdraw all the funds at the same time. If such a situation occurs, the system experiences a "bank run" (when the rush to acquire currency happens at one institution) or a "bank panic" (when the currency mania infects many banks at the same time). In these situations banks desperately need access to additional currency to calm the fears of depositors.

Because bank runs have the potential to turn into bank panics, individual banks are understandably reluctant to part with currency reserves to assist other banks in trouble (not to mention a conflict of interest in assisting a competitor bank). As a consequence of repeated 19th-century bank panics, central banks took on the "lender of last resort" function. In this capacity, the central bank stands prepared to provide emergency currency reserves to any bank that faces a run. Although this role was not understood nor embraced when central banks competed with private banks, by the early 20th century this role was well established and central banks had emerged as banking "leaders" rather than competitors.

In the heyday of the international GOLD STANDARD (1870–1914), central banks, where they existed (experts identify only 18 such institutions in 1900), were responsible for maintaining the convertibility of a nation's currency into gold. Under normal conditions, this responsibility limited the issuance of currency. In times of war, financing government debt took precedence (generally requiring central banks to issue additional currency) and convertibility was suspended.

When the international gold standard was suspended at the outbreak of WORLD WAR I, the convertibility constraint disappeared. Despite several attempts to restore the gold standard and modified versions of the gold standard (including the BRETTON WOODS system that lasted into the early 1970s), monetary policy was forever changed in 1914.

During the early 20th century, central banks discovered the power of MONETARY POLICY and have been exercising this power to influence macroeconomic events ever since. Monetary policy refers to the manipulation of the money supply and interest rates to achieve macroeconomic objectives. Central banks typically have a variety of tools at their disposal to conduct monetary policy including: altering the interest rate banks pay when they borrow from the central bank (known as the discount rate in the United States and the bank rate in Great Britain); changing reserve requirements (i.e., the portion of bank depositors' funds that banks must hold in liquid reserves); and engaging in "open market operations" (i.e., buying or selling bonds to alter the amount of cash reserves in the banking system).

Monetary policy objectives generally focus on price stability (i.e., restricting inflation), unemployment, or economic growth. Experience has shown that these objectives often conflict with one another and therefore must be prioritized. Although the Great DEPRESSION of the 1930s raised awareness of prolonged unemployment as a concern, central banks have historically emphasized maintaining their currency's value, a role most compatible with the price stability objective.

No central bank today can ignore the needs and perceptions of financial markets. With stock market volatility the norm and global capital flows at historic highs, public statements made by central banks often invoke strong market reactions. With the power to calm public concerns or induce fear merely through a press conference, central banks have inherited additional power. Consequently, central banking in the 21st century extends beyond the realm of banking and monetary policy and necessarily encompasses the entire financial sector.

Two long-standing controversies deserve attention. For nearly 200 years economists have debated the merits of operating under precise rules (e.g., the gold standard) versus empowering central banks to exercise greater discretionary power. Though the current consensus favors an active role for the central bank, this controversy persists.

A second issue questions the degree of independence central banks should enjoy. Recent studies suggest greater freedom from political pressures results in greater central-bank success against inflation. Granting such freedom is controversial because the stakes are so high. Anti-inflation policies often extract high costs on non-financial sectors of the economy, and some have argued that these choices require the open discussion and debate we've come to expect in a democratic society.

Regardless of how these particular debates unfold, there can be no mistake that central banks have proven to be indispensable institutions in a capitalist economy.

BIBLIOGRAPHY. F. Capie, C. Goodhart, S. Fischer, and N. Schnadt, *The Future of Central Banking: The Tercentenary Symposium of the Bank of England* (Cambridge University Press, 1994); Robert A. Degen, *The American Monetary System: A Concise Survey of its Evolution Since 1896* (Lexington Books, 1987); Barry Eichengreen, *Globalizing Capital: A History of the International Monetary System* (Princeton University Press, 1996); William Greider, *Secrets of the Temple: How the Federal Reserve Runs the Country* (Simon & Schuster, 1987); C. Holtfrerich, J.Reis, and G. Toniolo, eds., *The Emergence of Modern Central Banking from 1918 to the Present* (Ashgate, 1999); Michael G. Rukstad, *Macroeconomic Decision Making in the World Economy* (The Dryden Press, 1992).

PATRICK DOLENC, PH.D.
KEENE STATE COLLEGE

ChevronTexaco

FORMED BY THE 2001 merger of OIL giants Texaco and Chevron, the company is involved in all aspects of petroleum production including exploration, drilling, refining, distribution, and retailing, as well as energy technology and petrochemicals. The company has operations in over 180 countries.

With 2001 revenues exceeding $100 billion, ChevronTexaco is one of the five largest oil companies in the world and the second largest headquartered in the UNITED STATES. The merger completed 65 years of cooperation between the two companies that started with the formation in 1936 of CalTex, a joint venture uniting the companies' marketing and production facilities in the eastern hemisphere.

Texaco was founded as the Texas Fuel Company by "Buckskin Joe" Cullinan and Arnold Schlaet in 1901 in Beaumont, Texas. After huge oil discoveries in south Texas in 1903 saved the company from bankruptcy, the company became involved in refining and retailing. The company expanded and officially changed its name to Texaco in 1959.

Texaco acquired Getty Oil for $10 billion in 1984, doubling its oil and natural gas reserves. The purchase led to an extended legal battle with Houston-based Pennzoil, which also claimed an intent to purchase Getty. A series of court rulings unfavorable to Texaco led the company to file for bankruptcy in 1987. With company assets in excess of $35 billion at the time of filing, the bankruptcy was the nation's largest to that point and remains one of the 10 largest in U.S. history. Texaco ultimately paid a $3 billion settlement to Pennzoil. After emerging from bankruptcy, Texaco was involved in one of the more prominent racial discrimination lawsuits of the 1990s. In 1996, Texaco settled charges of bias with 1,500 current and former African-American employees for $176 million.

Chevron was founded in 1879 as the Pacific Coast Oil Company following oil discoveries in southern California. The company merged with John D. ROCKEFELLER'S STANDARD OIL COMPANY in 1900 and changed its name to Standard Oil Company (California). In 1911, in *Standard Oil of New Jersey v. United States,* the Supreme Court ordered the breakup of the Standard Oil Company and Standard Oil (California) again became an independent company. The company began using a "chevron" emblem in 1931 and eventually adopted the logo as its corporate name in 1984. Chevron purchased Gulf Oil in 1984 for $13.2 billion in what was the largest corporate merger up to that time in order to save that company from corporate raiders.

Fortune magazine ranked ChevronTexaco as the 14th largest company in the world in 2002.

BIBLIOGRAPHY. M. Economides, et al., *The Color of Oil: The History, the Money and the Politics of the World's Biggest Business* (Round Oak, 2000); www.chevrontexaco.com; Thomas Petzinger, Jr., *Oil & Honor: The Texaco-Pennzoil Wars* (Putnam, 1987); Bari-Ellen Roberts, Jack E. White, *Roberts vs. Texaco: A True Story of Race and Corporate America* (Avon Books, 1999); Alfred Chandler, *Scale and Scope: The Dynamics of Industrial Capitalism* (Belknap Press, 1990); Global 500, *Fortune* (July 2002).

VICTOR MATHESON, PH.D.
WILLIAMS COLLEGE

Chicago Board of Trade

FOUNDED IN 1848, the Chicago Board of Trade (CBOT) is the world's oldest and largest futures and future-options exchange. It began modestly, trading only agricultural commodities, but has significantly grown in both absolute and relative terms over the years; it now also trades financial contracts and options on futures contracts, and has become one of the great capitalistic institutions in America.

A futures exchange differs from a STOCK EXCHANGE in that contracts are bought and sold in a futures exchange, while stocks are bought and sold in a stock exchange. Futures contracts are standardized with respect to quantity, quality, delivery time, and location but variable with respect to the price of a commodity that is established or "discovered" on the trading floor of the exchange. These contracts are referred to as "futures" since they stipulate an intent to accept (buy) or deliver (sell) an agreed quantity of a commodity at a future date.

Futures differ from options in that a futures contract obliges both a payment and a delivery, whereas an option contract provides a right to buy or sell rather than an obligation to buy and sell. These types of markets facilitate and enhance commodity trade and financial transactions since they bring together buyers and sellers; provide information; act as a clearinghouse between buyers and sellers; and can appreciably reduce levels of risk, risks that would otherwise increase cost and dissuade transactions between buyers and sellers.

It is no accident that this exchange developed in Chicago. The Midwestern city's crucial location relative to the Great Lakes gave it a natural transportation system that endowed it with distinct advantages as an emerging commercial center. Canals and railroads augmented these inherent cost advantages and from the mid-19th century onward the economic expansion of Chicago was unprecedented.

Comparative advantages in storage and freight rates, along with the distributive effects of the AMERICAN CIVIL WAR and other public policies and political unions inexorably linked the economic and financial development of New York City and Chicago. As an early hub of financial and commercial activity, it was predictable that New York would emerge as a financial center with a concentration of banks, underwriters, and insurance companies, stock and bond exchanges. Given its proximity to western lands, raw materials, and agricultural resources it was reasonable for Chicago to emerge as the center of trade in agricultural and LAND-based commodities. Chicago was ideally situated to utilize its hinterland markets, the forests and woodlands to its north and east and the prairies to its south and west. Internationally, the Crimean War (1853–56) disrupted world grain trade and as the demand for American grain rose, large shipments of wheat flowed through Chicago's markets. By the mid-1850s, Chicago was the world's leading grain and lumber market. Grains and flour, lumber, and hogs and other animal products were the initial commodities traded but, more important, Chicago's position as the nation's leading interior commercial center was enhanced by the formation and operation of the Chicago Board of Trade. Markets are significant, not merely because they assist in the exchange of commodities but they also help establish the institutional conditions that are the basis of modern economies. In 1859, the Illinois Legislature chartered the Board and granted it authority over the appointment of inspectors, for the certification of standards of quality and consistency, and to establish arbitration procedures.

Within just a few years, the grading system first adopted by the Chicago Board of Trade in 1856 became the standard for the world's grain markets. Once commodities could be effectively categorized by grade, such as various types of wheat, they could be more easily stored in grain elevators, and could be more efficiently shipped and distributed through a central market like Chicago. Buyers and sellers could now effectively trade commodities by the exchange of contracts and the use of receipts rather than the archaic methods of buyers inspecting and bidding on piles of grain in the street or based on samples brought to the trading floor. It was no longer necessary to match individual buyers and sellers and this resulted in fewer risks that lowered costs and encouraged more expansion.

Given the time lag from planting to harvesting, there are obvious reasons for farmers to hedge their risks and to be interested in a futures market, and thus the Chicago Board of Trade was a likely place to see the development of futures and options. But hedgers are not the only traders in a futures market; there are also speculators. Whereas hedgers are trying to shed risk, speculators hope to profit by the assumption of risk in a futures market. Futures were exchanged on the Chicago Board of Trade as early as the 1850s and had become a regular feature by the 1860s.

By the 1870s, the value of trade in futures greatly exceeded the monetary value of grain as a commodity. Futures contracts are also bought and sold multiple times before a delivery date and as such provide price-change protection. By trading in the price of grain as well as the commodity of grain the market allowed for diversification of risks and was more financially sophisticated. It also explains why the Chicago Board of Trade remains the world's pre-eminent grain and commodity trader long after Chicago had ceased to be a stacker of wheat and hog-butcher to the world.

Over the years, futures have been developed in a wide variety of commodities and financial instruments, including U.S. Treasury bond futures, U.S. Treasury Yield Curve Spread futures, and options on stocks. Futures contracts are even bought and sold on such things as air pollution and health insurance. The development of a futures market was a notable financial and economic innovation and has had a lasting and profound effect on capitalism.

BIBLIOGRAPHY. William Cronon, *Nature's Metropolis: Chicago and the Great West* (W.W. Norton, 1991); William G. Ferris, *The Grain Traders: The Story of the Chicago Board of Trade* (Michigan State University Press, 1988); Jonathan Lurie, *The Chicago Board of Trade 1859–1905: The Dynamics of Self-Regulation* (University of Illinois Press, 1979); Donald L. Miller, *City of the Century: The Epic of Chicago and the Making of America* (Touchstone, 1996).

TIMOTHY E. SULLIVAN, PH.D.
TOWSON UNIVERSITY

Chicago School

THE CHICAGO SCHOOL of economics describes a number of economists and theories that have been produced or influenced by the economics department of the University of Chicago. What is known as the First School of Chicago began in 1920 under the leadership of Frank KNIGHT and Jacob Viner. The Chicago School is most closely associated with conservative economic theory that promotes a free market with full competition and an emphasis on laissez-faire government nonintervention. The tendency of the Chicago school has been to question, analyze, and rebel against accepted theory and practice, and the school has a reputation for promoting cooperation among economists in all fields.

The influence of the Chicago School has been documented through nine Nobel Prizes in economics: Friedrich von HAYEK in 1974, Milton FRIEDMAN in 1976, Theodore SCHULTZ in 1979, George STIGLER in 1982, Merton MILLER in 1990, Ronald COASE in 1991, Gary BECKER in 1992, Robert FOGEL in 1993, and Robert LUCAS in 1995.

In the 1940s, the range of the economics department was expanded by the addition of agricultural and mathematical economists. While Chicago economists had some impact on government decision-making before the 1960s, it was Friedman's departure from traditional Chicago thinking that began the period of overt government influence. Under Friedman's influence, the Chicago School adopted the theory of MONETARISM, maintaining that controlling the money supply would provide inflation controls and result in stable economic growth. Therefore, all past government actions to con-

trol the economy were useless. For example, cutting interest rates and unemployment only provided temporary remedies. Friedman's political-economic model has been used in decision-making in Great Britain, ISRAEL, Latin American, and IRAN. In the United States, monetarist influences convinced the FEDERAL RESERVE to announce in 1979 that it would place more emphasis on controlling the money supply than on other methods of fiscal control. The policy was abandoned, however, in 1982 because of the "unusual behavior of money growth." Reaganomics and the deregulation of the 1980s remains the most substantial tribute to the economic theories of the Chicago School of Economics.

The Reagan landslide in 1984 seemed to suggest the unqualified success of the theories of the Chicago School of economics, particularly those of Friedman. However, the national debt was over $2 trillion, and the United States had a trade deficit of over $15 billion a month. As candidate George H.W. BUSH said in the 1980 election, "voodoo economics" comes with a price. On October 19, 1987, which came to be known as Black Monday, the stock market took a nosedive. It was a signal for greater economic woes ahead. Even though Bush won the 1988 election, the stage was set for a Democratic election in 1992. Friedman contended that Reagan's worst mistake was choosing Bush as his running mate in 1980. Friedman also maintained that the reason Reaganomics did not totally achieve its goals was that Reagan never went far enough in implementing deregulation.

Not everyone accepts the theories of the Chicago School of economics. Paul SAMUELSON, a Chicago graduate and a classmate of Friedman's argued that the Chicago theories they studied had already failed. Unlike Friedman, Samuelson endorsed liberal economic views, influencing generations of economic students with his popular textbook *Economics*. Samuelson and Friedman have carried on a public argument for years, going so far as to write competing columns for *Newsweek* and co-authoring a book on the responsibility of government. Philanthropist George Soros, who personally funded efforts to end socialism, accused laissez-faire capitalism of being a threat to democracy because of its disinclination to prepare for the realities of a new world order.

Robert Kuttner, coeditor of *An American Prospect*, argues that the financial aspect at the beginning of the 21st century has much in common with the outlook of the 1930s during the Great Depression. The collapse of investor confidence, the lack of government regulations, and corruption within the financial community have created problems that Kuttner believes Chicago School economics cannot solve. He contends that a major problem with the free market is that it cannot police itself. Writer Steve Kangas offers a scathing critique of the Chicago School of economics, maintaining that most economists today are "New Keynesians" rather than advocates of the Chicago School.

BIBLIOGRAPHY. "Chicago School," cepa.newschool.edu; , *The Fourth Great Awakening and the Future of Egalitarianism* (University of Chicago Press, 2000); Robert L. Formaini, "Frank H. Knight: Origins of the Chicago School of Economics," *Economic Insights* (Federal Reserve Bank of Dallas, 2002); Milton Friedman and Paul A. Samuelson, *Milton Friedman and Paul A. Samuelson Discuss the Economic Responsibility of Government* (Texas A & M University Press, 1980); Steve Kangas, "Myth: The Chicago School of Economics Is A Leader in the Field," www.huppi.com; Robert Kuttner, "Today's Markets Need A Whole New Set of Rules," *Business Week* (July 29, 2002); Robert Leeson, *The Eclipse of Keynesianism: The Political Economy of the Chicago Counter-Revolution* (Palgrave, 2000).

ELIZABETH PURDY, PH.D.
INDEPENDENT SCHOLAR

chief executive officer

HEADING ALL OPERATIONS and decision-making within a firm, the chief executive officer (CEO) is at the top of the corporate hierarchy, though there could be a president of the corporation, who would technically out rank the CEO. In a publicly held firm, however, the CEO is an agent of the stockholders of a corporation. Shareholders are the owners of the firm, but are unable to run the company, so they need an employee or CEO to oversee the operations of the firm.

Monitoring the CEO can become a problem. For that reason, a BOARD OF DIRECTORS will normally be appointed by the stockholders to oversee the CEO. Traditionally, the CEO is not involved with day-to-day operations as much as he or she is involved with the overall strategy or vision of the firm. More than any other person in the company, it is the CEO who converts challenges into profit opportunities. As part of the strategic plan, the CEO must allocate resources among various divisions within the firm. He or she is ultimately responsible for mergers and acquisitions. The CEO uses his or her knowledge of finance, marketing, globalization, and technology to facilitate corporate strategy. The CEO must use interpersonal skills and knowledge of incentives and corporate culture to motivate employees to follow through on strategy. Not only does the CEO need to be a strategist, but Wall Street seems to favor CEOs who have strong capabilities in raising the value of the company stock. At times, this requirement is met with missionary zeal when "selling" the company to the stock analysts.

It is important to recognize that the job duties that are attached to any job title can vary significantly from firm to firm. The CEO's job is normally very similar to the president of the firm and many firms have only one or the other. In firms with both a president and a CEO, the CEO's job description may by similar to a chief of operations (COO). Only rarely would a firm have all three. The CEO's job description is, however, different from the CHIEF FINANCIAL OFFICER who is responsible for accounting management, including financial reporting and fraud protection, management of the debt-to-equity ratio, and budgeting.

Occasionally, a CEO's salary becomes a public issue. Stockholders and reporters sometimes question whether or not CEOs deserve multimillion dollar salaries and incentive compensation or bonuses. However, many boards of directors feel that high pay for CEOs serves two functions; the first is that it is very difficult to monitor a CEO's work, and the second is to motivate upper-middle management.

Neither the board of directors nor the stockholders can easily monitor the CEO all of the time, so it is relatively easy for a CEO to shirk his or her responsibility at the margin. If the board of directors or shareholders detect shirking on the part of the CEO, he or she will be fired and his or her next best job offer will have a much lower salary. Thus, the thinking goes, by offering high salaries, CEOs become reticent to lose their jobs, thus increasing the cost of shirking.

High salaries also serve as an incentive for vice presidents. By the time managers become vice presidents, they realize that the chance of promotion is becoming exceedingly small. While the CEO is directly supervising vice presidents, and doing so much more closely than the board of directors can monitor the CEO, there is still an opportunity to shirk. A very high salary for the CEO forces the vice presidents into a tournament where one of them will make tremendous amounts of money, thus encouraging all vice presidents to exert maximum output.

It should be noted that these are the theoretical reasons for high CEO pay. In practice, boards of directors are not very independent. Often they are made up of people who were recommended by the CEO or who are themselves CEOs in other firms, with little or no incentive to closely monitor top management. Empirical research has found that the less independent the board is, the more the CEO makes. Furthermore, high CEO salary may not encourage maximum effort by vice presidents because shareholders can just as often pick an external candidate to be the next CEO. [Editor's Note: By the early 2000s, additional concerns have arisen about whether high-salaried CEOs should have their compensation tied directly to the performance of their respective companies.]

BIBLIOGRAPHY. John E. Garren, "Executive Compensation and Principal-Agent Theory," *Journal of Political Economy* (v.102, 1994); Donald C. Hambrick and Sydney Finkelstein, "The Effects of Ownership Structure on Conditions at the Top: The Case of CEO Pay Raises" *Strategic Management Journal* (v.16/3, 1995); Michael C. Jensen and Kevin J. Murphy, "Performance Pay and Top-Management Incentives" *The Journal of Political Economy* (v.98/2, 1990); Michael C. Jensen and Kevin J. Murphy, "CEO Incentives: It's Not How Much You Pay, but How," *Harvard Business Review* (v.68, 1990); Michael C. Jensen, and Kevin J. Murphy, "Performance Pay and Top-Management Incentives," *Journal of Political Economy* (v.98, 1990).

DAVID MITCHELL
GEORGE MASON UNIVERSITY

chief financial officer

THE CHIEF FINANCIAL OFFICER (CFO) is typically the executive officer in charge of all financial matters within a business or organization. Exact duties and titles may differ within firms. In larger firms, the CFO may oversee both the treasurer and the controller. In smaller firms the CFO will often also perform duties of the treasurer and controller. Overall, the CFO is responsible for questions relating to capital budgeting, capital structure, net working capital, accounting, and tax planning. The CFO may also be called the vice president of finance. Typically, she will report directly to the president or CHIEF EXECUTIVE OFFICER (CEO) and make direct reports to the BOARD OF DIRECTORS.

Specifically, the CFO oversees capital budgeting decisions or decisions relating to the purchase or lease of fixed or long-term assets. She oversees analysis of capital structure or decisions relating to the way that the firm finances projects, whether through debt or equity. Net working capital analysis refers to the ways that firm manages cash accounts, collects payments, pays suppliers, and deals with inventory. She performs detailed profitability analyses and sales and profitability forecasts, oversees the monthly financial close, including preparation of full financial statements in accordance with GENERALLY ACCEPTED ACCOUNTING PRINCIPLES (GAAP).

Developing, implementing, and managing appropriate financial-planning and control procedures are also part of the CFO's responsibilities. Often in larger firms these tasks are assigned to the controller, with the CFO acting as the final approver. She directs preparation of budgets, reviews budget proposals, and prepares necessary supporting documentation and justification including those documents that must be filed with the SECURITIES AND EXCHANGE COMMISSION (SEC) or other regulatory agency. The CFO manages the day-to-day activities within the accounting, finance, tax, and pension fund departments while helping to establish a financial team with other senior managers in the organization.

The CFO needs to have more than just financial analysis skills. She manages a large number of skilled professionals, so she needs to be able to direct other professionals and employees. She needs leadership abilities. In a publicly traded firm, she also needs to be able to deal with Wall Street analysts, not only answering their questions but also selling them on the value of the stock. The increased load of information, whether it be purely financial data or reporting requirements for the SEC, has also required CFOs to have strong information-technology backgrounds.

As an integral member of senior management, the CFO is also responsible for helping with strategy decisions. This is an increasingly important part of the job description, and as such, it requires a broad knowledge of the company and the industry in addition to the technical financial knowledge required for the position. One strategic aspect of the CFO's position is to implement a set of financial incentives and methods for measuring employee performance.

For a long time when CFOs worried about fraud and accountability, they worried about suppliers, customers, and employees defrauding the company. Currently, there is much more emphasis on senior management defrauding stockholders and even employees. Fraudulent accounting practices, such as those used by ENRON, have shifted the spotlight. Legislation, such as the Sarbanes-Oxley bill, has lowered the standard of proof that investigators will need in order to prosecute and convict corporate officers of misdeeds. The Department of Justice, the Federal Bureau of Investigation, and the SEC can bring criminal charges (and have done so) against executives who participate in fraud, or who should have known that fraud was occurring.

BIBLIOGRAPHY. Mark E. Haskins and Benjamin R. Makela, *The CFO Handbook* (McGraw-Hill, 1996); Price Waterhouse Financial & Cost Management Team, *CFO: Architect of the Corporation's Future* (John Wiley & Sons, 1997).

DAVID MITCHELL
GEORGE MASON UNIVERSITY

Chile

CHILE WAS UNATTRACTIVE to the first configuration of international capitalism, MERCANTILISM. The long and thin mountainous coastal Latin American country lacked gold, silver, and docile indigenous peoples useful for cheap labor. However, with the INDUSTRIAL

REVOLUTION, the abundant copper and steel resources attracted investors.

Nominally independent since 1810, Chile's official independence began with the rest of Latin America in the 1820s. Although dominated by *caudillos* and dictators, liberal constitutions, stability and a social contract gradually evolved, making the state especially receptive to democracy in the late 19th century. There was no military coup in Chile from the early 1930s through 1973, making it one of the very few stable and democratic polities of turbulent Latin America. In 1970, a socialist, Salvador Allende who was unsuccessful in three previous elections, won a plurality of popular votes and endorsement of the Chilean Congress to become president. His most important campaign promise was to use Chilean resources to benefit Chileans. Thus, Allende's first actions as president were to nationalize foreign corporations, which in the case of Anaconda and Kennicott copper had turned an $80 million investment into a $4 billion return for the North American owners. He also established redistributive policies and price controls. These proved very distressing to international capital.

Henry Kissinger, U.S. Secretary of State at the time, was quoted, "I don't see why we need to stand by and watch a country go communist because of the irresponsibility of its own people." The ambassador to Chile, Edward Korry, said, "Not a nut or a bolt [will] be allowed to reach Chile under Allende." Capital starvation from international organizations under U.S. pressure, assassinations of Chilean nationalist generals, and support for pro-business factions that orchestrated a number of strikes to bring the country to a standstill, set the stage for a coup and the alleged suicide of Allende on September 11, 1973. After the takeover by a military junta, the commander of Chilean armed forces, Augusto Pinochet was appointed president beginning nearly two decades of military rule. U.S.-based multinational companies reopened, labor discipline was renewed (often by brutal repression of unions), and foreign investors were encouraged by very favorable terms.

Since that time, the class analysis of Chile's role and governance in the world, has demonstrated consistently contradictory interpretations. Some Chilean elite and members of the international financial community, suggest that Pinochet's police state, advised by University of Chicago economists, provided labor peace, rid the country of the communist plague, brought stability, and created the environment to make Chile an exemplar neo-liberal society in Latin America. To the rich and middle classes, the human rights abuses of the Pinochet regime were greatly exaggerated. However, for nationalists, unionists and human rights activists, the brutal dictatorship between 1973 and 1990 was the equivalent of dark ages, with massive repression and thousands of extra-judicial killings, privatization at the expense of the Chilean people, and management for the benefit of international capital.

Despite attempts to gain immunity from prosecution, the Pinochet regime began to face criticism and growing unrest in the late 1980s. The military stayed in the background or returned to posts in the civilian-elected governments. While Pinochet, who had named himself Senator for Life, was on a medical visit to Britain in 1998, he was arrested and held by a Spanish judge for crimes against humanity. That act of international conscience, brought the human rights community back to life in Chile, and although Pinochet was never jailed, he is no longer part of public conversation.

There is substantial criticism of Chile's privatized Social Security system, and little praise in Chile for the neo-liberal economic model. However, many Western economists think that Chile's economy makes it a logical target for expansion of the NORTH AMERICA FREE TRADE AGREEMENT (NAFTA), an option that was apparently negotiated in January 2003, behind closed doors. Chile had a GROSS DOMESTIC PRODUCT (GDP) of $153 billion in 2001, with a per capita purchasing power of $10,000.

BIBLIOGRAPHY. Seymour Hersch, *The Price of Power: Kissinger in the Nixon White House* (Summit Books, 1983); Lucy Komisar, "Kissinger Encouraged Chile's Brutal Repression, New Documents Show," *Albion Monitor*, www.monitor.net; K.H. Silvert, *Chile: Yesterday and Today* (Holt, Rinehart and Winston, 1965).

CHARLES WEED, PH.D.
KEENE STATE COLLEGE

China

THE LARGEST COUNTRY in east Asia, China borders NORTH KOREA, RUSSIA, Mongolia, Kazakhstan, Kyrgyzstan, Tajikstan, AFGHANISTAN, PAKISTAN, INDIA, Nepal, Bhutan, Burma, Laos, and VIETNAM. China has a long coastline of 11,250 miles. Starting from the east coast, China's vast land of 3,720,000 square miles rises gradually westward.

The highest point of the world, Mount Qomolangma or Mount Everest, is located on the border between China and Nepal. About one-third of its land contains plains and basins, while mountains, plateaus, and deserts comprise the other two-thirds. The two famous rivers are the Yellow River and the Yangzi River and its major lakes include Poyang Lake, Dongting Lake, and Qinghai Lake. Most of China is in the temperate and subtropical zones, with four distinctive seasons. Its most southern part reaches into the tropical zone. Monsoon climate of much rain and humidity dominates most of China's eastern part. While its northwest has dry climate, it is cold on the Tibetan and Qinghai plateaus.

The Chinese nation is made of 56 nationalities or ethnic groups. While Han people make up more than 90 percent of the population, its major minority ethnic groups such as Mongolians, Tibetans, Weiwuers (Uygurs), Zhuangs, and Miaos number in millions. Many of the minority ethnic groups observe their own customs, have their own religions and customs, and speak their own languages.

Archaeological findings show that anthropoid ape and early humans lived in today's China millions of years ago. About half a million years ago, Beijing man (*Sinanthropus pekinensis*) used fire and created tools outside Beijing, today's capital of China. According to archaeological findings, around 4,000 years ago people were already carving inscriptions on bones or tortoise shells. These inscriptions are the beginnings of the Chinese written characters.

Confucianism is the most important school of thought supporting Chinese culture. Kongfuzi, or Confucius, from whom Confucianism derives, lived from 551 B.C.E. to 479 B.C.E. Confucius was among the many great thinkers of the time period; most of his ideas are in *The Analects*, a recording of conversations he had with his students. Confucius focused on social order and believed humanity was the highest code of moral conduct. To achieve humanity, man should "subdue one's self and return to propriety." Confucius was an educator; his students spread and developed his ideas into Confucianism. Most rulers in dynastic China promoted Confucianism.

Also important to Chinese culture and thought are Taoism and Buddhism. Taoism theorizes that the universe is a unity of opposites such as *yin* and *yang*. Because this is the most essential law of the universe, human beings should understand and obey it, according to Taoism. Buddhism was introduced into China about 2,000 years ago. Many dynastic rulers promoted it; some forbade it. Buddhism has experienced expansion and transformation in China. Its principal idea of escaping from all sufferings in life to achieve nirvana has attracted many Chinese believers since its introduction into China.

Early societies. China's long history underwent primitive and SLAVERY societies and in 211 B.C.E., it became a unified feudal system under Qin Shihuang, Qin the Beginning Emperor. Under Emperor Qin, China started a system of prefectures and counties for administrative purposes and standardized currency, weights and measures, gauges, and the written characters. The feudal society, ruled by an emperor and dominated by feudal lords and landlords, survived in China for more than

The Great Wall of China, built to stop invaders, runs 6,700 kilometers east to west across five provinces.

2,000 years. Feudal dynasties were usually overthrown by peasant uprisings and powers shifted from one emperor to another. Major dynasties include Qin, Han, Sui, Tang, Song, Yuan, Ming, and Qing.

The early Chinese civilization made many contributions to mankind. Chinese people invented the compass, paper-making, block printing, and gunpowder. The Great Wall, which was built to defend China from invaders, is one of the greatest man-made projects in the world. The Grand Canal, which is 1,120 miles long, remains the world's longest man-made water transportation route.

China was a self-sufficient agricultural country throughout its feudal period. Although trade with other countries, especially trade on the famous Silk Road, was developed very early, foreign trade and domestic commerce did not play a significant role in China's economic life.

The arrival of European capitalists. In the 18th and particularly the 19th century, capitalists from Europe and America arrived in China to exploit its market and raw materials. In 1839, having made opium trade illegal, the Chinese Emperor sent Commissioner Lin Zexu to Guangzhou, where most of the opium entered, to stop the illegal opium trade. Lin destroyed the opium that was already inside China. Britain, the main opium trader, launched a war on China.

The defeated China was forced by Britain to sign the Nanjing Treaty in 1842. According to the Treaty and a supplementary Treaty of the Bogue signed in 1843,

China had to open five seaports to British trade, pay for the destroyed opium as well as Britain's military expenses for the war, and award HONG KONG to Britain. Further China had to compromise on its sovereignty by allowing extraterritorial rights for British subjects (exemption from Chinese laws), stationing of British troops, and permitting British control of the rates of import and export duties. After the Nanjing Treaty, the rest of Europe, RUSSIA, the UNITED STATES, and Japan obtained similar treaties. By the end of the 19th century, China was carved into many spheres of influence controlled by various foreign powers.

Defeat at the hands of Western imperialism led to the Hundred-Days Reform. Kang Youwei, a Confucian scholar, and other reform-minded Chinese intellectuals succeeded in persuading the Emperor to carry out a comprehensive reform. In a hundred days from June to September 1898, Emperor Guang Xu issued reform edicts including restructuring government institutions, changing criteria in civil service exams, establishing modern schools, promoting new ways for economic development, and encouraging international cultural exchanges. The reform met with tremendous opposition from officials in the central and provincial administrations. It was finally suppressed by the Empress Dowager Ci Xi when she put the Emperor under house arrest, executed some of the reform leaders, and took control of the government.

Groundwork of communism. The failure of the reform movement and the continued worsening of conditions opened ways for more radical changes. The Revolution of 1911 led by Sun Yat-sen ended the Qing dynasty. Sun Yat-sen, who had received Western education, established the Republic of China and ended the centuries-long monarchical system. Burdened by external encroachment and internal strife, the republic did not bring peace or prosperity to Chinese people or make China a strong country. In 1915, Japan made the notorious Twenty-One Demands, which, if accepted totally, would have made China Japan's protectorate. In 1916, Yuan Shikai, president of the republic, attempted to restore a monarchical system, which led to a civil war. After Yuan died in 1916, power fell into the hands of warlords and China verged on national disintegration. In 1919, the western powers at the Paris Peace Conference confirmed Japan's claim over GERMANY's former holdings in China's Shandong Province.

Intellectuals in China started to look internally and externally for answers to their nation's problems. The result was the New Culture Movement. Leaders of the movement proposed reforms in the Chinese written language in order to make it more accessible to ordinary people and called upon young people to rebel against the old and rotten elements of Chinese society and choose fresh and practical elements, such as democracy and science, from other cultures and societies.

The New Culture Movement received tremendous impetus on May 4, 1919, when students in Beijing demonstrated against the Paris Peace Conference's decision concerning Shandong. After that, the initiative became known as the May Fourth Movement, regarded by some scholars as the "Chinese Enlightenment" because it aroused patriotism and mobilized ordinary people to participate in politics concerning the future of China.

The intense patriotism aroused by the May Fourth Movement and the awakening of ordinary people paved the way for the rise of the Chinese Communist Party (CCP). On July 1, 1921, a dozen intellectuals, all of whom were active participants in the New Culture and May Fourth Movements, representing some 50 communities throughout China, met in Shanghai and officially founded the party. The party based its theory on Marxism and looked to Vladimir LENIN's successful revolution in Russia as a practical example. Its immediate goals included ending warlord control and imperialist oppression and creating a true, independent republic in China.

In 1922, Sun Yat-sen's Guomindang (GMD) and the CCP joined together in a revolution against the warlord government. In 1925, Yat-sen died. When the revolution was about to succeed, Chiang Kai-shek, commander of the GMD forces, staged a coup against the CCP in mid-1927, killing its members and sympathizers. By 1928, Chiang had defeated the warlords and his party, the GMD, became the ruling party in China. The CCP was driven underground and to the rural areas. In the rural, mountainous regions of southern China, the CCP relied on the support of poor peasants, organized its own army, the Red Army, to resist Chiang's effort to exterminate it, and carried out land reforms in the areas it occupied. In order to escape from Chiang's encirclement and extermination campaigns and to organize people in north China in a resistance movement against Japanese aggression, the CCP and its Red Army made the famous Long March from 1934 to 1936. The war between the central government, led by Chiang, and the CCP lasted a decade.

In 1937, Japan, which had occupied China's northeast for six years, launched a full-fledged war against China. After having focused on exterminating the CCP while tolerating Japanese aggression, Chiang Kai-shek finally began to resist the invasion. His government recognized CCP's legal status. The CCP Army fought against Japanese troops and liberated large occupied areas, while the larger government forces confronted Japanese advances.

The CCP and its army had grown a great deal during the war. In 1945, The CCP had a membership of 1,200,000 and an armed force of 900,000. In the same year, Mao Zedong, chairman of the CCP, delivered a speech proposing a coalition government in China. This coalition government, Mao said, should allow equal representation from all parties and factions and should lead the Chinese people in winning the war against Japan and then in building an "independent, free, democratic, unified, and strong" China.

After Japan surrendered, Chiang Kai-shek and Mao met to talk about forming a post-war government. Even during the talks, government forces attacked CCP forces. Chiang's military superiority of five-to-one over the CCP at the time made him believe that he could easily get rid of the communists.

The Chinese Civil War. A civil war broke out in China in 1946. The CCP and its army, now called the People's Liberation Army, took deep roots among peasants, carried out land reforms in the areas they controlled, and, with its platform for a new China, won wide support. The government, on the other hand, refused any social and political reforms, mismanaged an economy that was running wild with inflation and destroying the livelihood of millions, and was infested with wide-scale corruption. The government used murders and random arrests for suppression. By 1949, the CCP had won the war on the mainland. Chiang Kai-shek and his followers retreated to the island of TAIWAN.

Mao Zedong declared the founding of the People's Republic of China (PRC) on October 1, 1949. Land reform was carried out in the countryside, materializing the ideal of land to the tiller. Lack of farming tools such as draft animals and ploughs prompted peasants to organize mutual aid groups in order to share farm tools. Such organization was encouraged by the government and, by the end of 1957, the rural areas had become collective entities in which peasants worked and shared harvests together.

In urban areas, at first, the state made investments into private enterprises and shared profits and losses. Such joint ownership guaranteed state income, fair WAGES and benefits for WORKERS, and promoted interests of business owners. But from 1956 on, the state bought out private businesses and paid owners annual fixed dividends based on the shares they owned at the time of the purchase.

The CCP's success in China met with military encirclement, political containment, and economic blockade from the United States and some of its allies. The United States regarded Chiang's regime on Taiwan as the legitimate government representing all China until the 1970s. China and the SOVIET UNION were allies in the 1950s but communist ideological disputes developed. In the late 1960s, China and the Soviet Union sporadically confronted each other. China followed and promoted the Five Principles of Peaceful Coexistence and established diplomatic relations with countries around the world.

In 1958, in order to push for fast industrialization and economic development, the CCP launched the Great Leap Forward, a program aimed at extremely high goals. Peasants were organized into communes, huge dining rooms were set up to save human resources from individual cooking, and primitive furnaces were put up to produce steel. Huge amounts of material and human resources were wasted. Officials at various levels inflated reports of yields. Although such radical programs did not last very long, the result, coupled with three years (1959–61) of natural disasters of droughts and floods, was widespread starvation and famine.

Revolution and reform. In 1966, Mao launched the Cultural Revolution. This was a mass campaign aimed at getting rid of all party officials who had supported capitalist development and at eradicating "non-proletarian ideology" in society. Violent conflicts erupted among different political factions. Party officials at all levels, managers and supervisors, former landowners, former business owners, and intellectuals were targets of the mass campaign.

Existing government operations at all levels were destroyed and new ones were put into place; large numbers of innocent people were tortured and persecuted in various ways; and some people with ambitions and hungry for power occupied government positions. Mao was deified and regarded as the embodiment of truth. Anybody who spoke out against him or his policies was criticized or condemned. The massive accusation and condemnation and factional violence subsided after the first few years, but the repressive atmosphere continued until 1976.

The Cultural Revolution caused economic stagnation and popular discontent. Mao died in 1976. The Revolution came to an end when the radicals in the Party Central Committee, known as the Gang of Four, were arrested. In 1978, the CCP introduced a comprehensive program of reforms. In rural areas, a contract system gradually replaced the collective system. Under the contract system, farmers signed contracts with local governments, managed the land themselves, assumed full responsibility for profits or losses, and, of course, paid taxes to the state.

The system tremendously increased the efficiency of agricultural production, benefiting the farmer as well as the state. In urban areas, four special economic zones along the southeast coast were established at the beginning of the reforms. In these zones, market economy was practiced and foreign investments were welcomed. The market economy was successful in the four zones and has now been adopted in the entire country.

In today's China, there are state-owned businesses, private businesses, businesses jointly owned by Chinese and foreign capitalists, businesses owned solely by foreign capitalists, and businesses owned by shareholders.

Since the beginning of the economic reforms, China's GROSS DOMESTIC PRODUCT (GDP) has been growing at an average annual rate of more than 9 percent, one of the fastest growing countries in the world. In 2001, its total GDP was $6 trillion. China's economy is the sixth largest in the world. Yet, with a population of 1.28 billion in 2001, China's GDP per person is only about $900, making it still one of the developing countries in the world.

By the late 1980s, widespread abuse of reform policies by party and government officials led to demands for more political reforms, culminating in the 1989 Tiananmen Square demonstrations that were finally suppressed by the government.

The political process is becoming somewhat more open. Efforts are being made to strengthen and improve the legal system. According to China's Constitution, the CCP is the ruling party. Citizens in China elect representatives, who form people's congresses at the city, the county, the province, and the national levels. These people's congresses, in turn, make laws and elect and dismiss government officials. At the local level, residents directly elect and dismiss officials of village and town governments.

In 1997 and 1999, China respectively recovered its sovereign control over Hong Kong and Macao, territories previously controlled by Britain and Portugal, respectively. According to China's Basic Laws, Hong Kong and Macao are special administrative regions, which continue to practice capitalism. China is a member of the UNITED NATIONS Security Council and has recently joined the WORLD TRADE ORGANIZATION.

BIBLIOGRAPHY. William E. Soothill, trans., *The Analects* (Oxford University Press, 1937); James Legge, trans., *The Texts of Taoism* (Dover Publications, 1962); Jacques Gernet, *A History of Chinese Civilization*, trans. J.R. Foster (Cambridge University Press, 1986); Immanuel C. Y. Hsu, *The Rise of Modern China* (Oxford University Press, 2000); John K. Fairbank, *The Great Chinese Revolution, 1800–1985* (Harper & Row, 1986); Vera Schwarcz, *The Chinese Enlightenment: Intellectuals and the Legacy of the May Fourth Movement of 1919* (University of California Press, 1986); Edgar Snow, *Red Star Over China*, (Grove Press, 1968); William Overholt, *The Rise of China: How Economic Reform Is Creating a New Superpower* (W.W. Norton, 1994).

SHEHONG CHEN, PH.D.
UNIVERSITY OF MASSACHUSETTS, LOWELL

China National Petroleum

THE CHINA NATIONAL Petroleum Corporation (CNPC) is the People's Republic of China's (PRC) largest OIL concern, with 1.5 million employees. It focuses on the exploration and production of oil and gas, controlling all oil and gas fields, refineries, and petrochemical enterprises in 12 provinces, autonomous regions, and municipalities in northern and western China.

Ranked as the 81st largest company in the world by *Fortune* magazine, CNPC reported revenues of $41.5 billion in 2001. Originating in the early days of the founding of communist China, CNPC's roots can be traced to a 1950 Sino-Soviet agreement to develop Xinjiang's Dushanzi Oil Mines and the creation of the Ministry of Petroleum Industry (MOPI) in 1955.

The CNPC replaced MOPI in 1988, pursuant to the PRC's efforts to organize the petroleum industry and attract capital and technology through cooperative ventures with foreign companies. The CNPC's global search for oil began in the 1990s, when it acquired oilfield rights in THAILAND, CANADA, Papua New Guinea, the Muglad Basin, VENEZUELA, and Kazakhstan, expanding in 1999 with the completion of its first long-distance pipeline linking the Muglad oil field to Port Sudan.

In 2000, PetroChina, CNPC's main subsidiary, was listed on the New York and Hong Kong stock markets; however, controversy over human rights and environmental violations in the Sudan and Tibet led to disappointing results.

BIBLIOGRAPHY. *China Petroleum Industry* (China Petroleum Information Institute, 1996); Paul McDonald and Jareer Elass, "China National Petroleum Corporation" (Energy Intelligence Group, 1999); Steven Hamelin, *Petroleum Finance Week* (v.8/3, 2000).

CRISTINA ZACCARINI, PH.D.
ADELPHI UNIVERSITY

Citigroup

CITIGROUP IS A FINANCIAL services company operating in over 100 countries. Its formation in 1998 through the merger of Citibank, Traveler's Insurance Group, and the investment bank Salomon Smith Barney combined commercial, insurance and investment services, a watershed in the history of the U.S. banking industry.

Founded in 1812, the City Bank of New York began as an agent in the trade of cotton, sugar, metals, and coal. Reorganized in 1865 as the National City Bank of New York, the bank performed certain official functions, such as distribution of the national currency and sales of government bonds while it continued to provide credit to merchants. By 1894, the National City Bank had $30 million in assets, the largest bank in the UNITED STATES.

From 1897–1933 the bank expanded in two dimensions. First, National City pioneered the creation of a network of foreign subsidiaries. Passage of the FEDERAL RESERVE Act (1913), opening of National City branches throughout Latin America (1914), and acquisition of the International Banking Corporation (1915) all helped to make the National City Bank the leading organizer of U.S. capital investment in Latin America and Asia. As a result, by 1919 the bank had over $1 billion in assets. Second, National City Bank expanded its services, moving from its main business of commercial banking into personal banking and investment services. This effort to diversify from a commercial bank into an integrated financial services company met resistance from government regulators. In 1933, the Glass-Steagall Act radically restructured the U.S. banking industry, separating commercial banking from investment services and insurance.

From 1933–1998, the two themes of overseas expansion and product diversification dominated the bank's activities. By 1975, foreign loans represented two-thirds of the bank's overall business. The bank continuously sought to avoid the restrictions of Glass-Steagall, and in 1974 created Citicorp, a non-banking holding company. Citibank also introduced certificates of deposit in 1961 and automated teller machines in the 1970s to secure customers and to help fund its ever-larger portfolio of loans.

After the repeal of the Glass-Steagall Act in 1999, the push for diversification culminated in the merger of Citibank with Travelers' Insurance Group and Salomon Smith Barney, creating the first integrated financial services company in modern U.S. banking history. In 2002, Citigroup ranked as the 11th largest company in the world with $112 billion in revenue.

BIBLIOGRAPHY. Harold van Cleveland, *Citibank, 1812–1970* (Harvard University Press, 1985); David Leinsdorf, *Citibank: Ralph Nader's Study Group Report on First National City Bank* (Center for Responsive Law, 1974): Lisa Mirabile, ed., *International Directory of Company Histories* (St. James Press, 1990); www.citigroup.com; "Global 500: World's Largest Companies," *Fortune* (July 2002).

JONATHAN SCHRAG
HARVARD UNIVERSITY

The Citicorp building is one of Manhattan's skyline icons of business and capitalism.

Clark, John Bates (1847–1938)

J.B. CLARK WAS arguably the first American economist to gain an international reputation, due in large part to his debate with Eugen von BÖHM-BAWERK over the nature of capital and interest. Clark exerted a profound influence on modern microeconomics by his unification of the theories of production and distribution, and by his rigorous analysis of static equilibria. He taught at Carleton University (where one of his students was Thorstein VEBLEN) and Smith and Amherst Colleges before settling in for a long career at Columbia University.

Prior to Clark's writings, John Stuart MILL had insisted that production and distribution were two distinct spheres. Whereas production was determined by technological factors similar to laws of nature, after things were produced they could be distributed however people chose. Understanding how this happened required one to study laws, customs, and institutions.

In *The Distribution of Wealth*, Clark used marginal productivity to show in EQUILIBRIUM, under competitive conditions, the value of marginal product of the last unit of LABOR hired. By analogy the same is true for rent, the payment for the productive services of CAPITAL. Clark saw LAND as a form of capital. Thus the payments to land, labor, and capital were determined by the value of their marginal productivity, or distribution and production were part of the same theory. Clark's analysis remains the backbone of the theory of factor demands found in most introductory and intermediate MICROECONOMICS texts.

Clark thought this finding exonerated capitalism from the charge of exploitation, since it showed that workers were paid exactly the value of what they produced. For this reason, Clark acquired a long-standing reputation as an apologist for capitalism.

Clark and Böhm-Bawerk had a 20-year debate centered on the nature of capital. Clark insisted that a distinction must be made between "pure" capital and capital goods, and that both concepts belonged in economic analysis. Pure capital is a permanent fund of value. Capital goods have finite lives. Pure capital is perfectly mobile. For example, the capital that used to be invested in the New England whale industry was later embodied in the textile mills. Böhm-Bawerk called Clark's pure capital a "mystical conception" and an "elegant abstraction."

Clark's pure capital appears to have been a stylized representation of the normal business practice of maintaining the value of capital. Whatever the justification, making capital permanent was necessary for capital to take a place in a static equilibrium model. There can be no equilibrium when capital is changing. Having banished time from his model, Clark, in a flat contradiction of Böhm-Bawerk, denied that time had anything to do with interest.

More profoundly, Clark challenged one of the premises that had been the basis of capital theory: Rather than being needed to provide advances required by the interval between the application of labor and its result, capital served to *synchronize* production so that labor was in fact paid out of current output.

The Clark *vs.* Böhm-Bawerk debate was never satisfactorily resolved, erupting again in the 1930s. Related issues were part of arguments raging between economists in Cambridge, England, and Cambridge, Massachusetts, in the 1950s and 1960s.

BIBLIOGRAPHY. J.B. Clark, *The Distribution of Wealth* (Augustus M. Kelley, 1965); Mark Perlman, *The Character of Economic Thought, Economic Characters, and Economic Institutions* (University of Michigan Press, 1996); Samuel Weston, *Editing Economics: Essays in Honour of Mark Perlman* (Routledge, 2002).

SAMUEL C. WESTON, PH.D.
UNIVERSITY OF DALLAS

class structure

MOST PEOPLE VIEW economic class as defined by income and wealth levels. According to this way of thinking, there are lower, middle, and upper classes, or alternatively, the poor, the middle class, and the rich. Members of these economic classes do not necessarily have any functional economic interests in common, but rather have lifestyles and material interests in common.

The three classes differ first by the annual incomes of their members. In the UNITED STATES there is an official federal government poverty level that can be used as the line between the poor and the (lower) middle class. In 2003, this level was set at $18,400 for a family of four. This means that any member of a family whose annual income was less than $18,400 was living in poverty, and thus was a member of the lower class (poor). Demarcating the middle class is not so easy. Certainly, the lower income limit would be $18,400, but what the upper limit would be is unclear. Some people would put it at $200,000, some people at $500,000, some even higher. Given that there is no generally accepted definition of the maximum income for the middle class, the range for the upper limit is quite large. At some income level, however, the upper class (rich) begins. As for the upper boundary for this class, the sky is the limit.

The second difference between the classes is net wealth, defined as the value of the total assets held by a household minus their debts. What is interesting to note about wealth is that a significant proportion (18 percent) of households have no wealth. Those with no wealth would include the poor, as well as the lower end of the middle class. The rest of the middle class would have minimal to fairly high levels of wealth, perhaps up to $900,000. Wealth really begins to accumulate, however, with the rich (after all, they are considered wealthy). As with income, the upper boundary for wealth is fantastical; for a single family it is in the billions of dollars.

When class is viewed in this tripartite fashion, the middle class is by far the largest of the three in the contemporary United States. Those classified as poor are about 13 percent of the population, while those who are rich constitute about 1 percent or 2 percent, depending on where the upper income limit for the middle class is set. That leaves about 85 percent of the population who would be considered middle class. By this standard, the United States is quite homogeneous by class.

In political economy, economic class is looked at in a different way. Rather than relating to income or wealth, a class is defined by its ownership, or lack thereof, of the means of production. The means of production are defined as the tools, machinery, buildings and all other non-human material with which labor works to produce output. In a capitalist economic system these means of production are privately owned; they are (primarily) not owned by the government. There is a connection between this conception of class and our first conception, since there is a correlation between class as now defined and income and wealth levels. Members of the owning class will, on average, be significantly richer than members of the non-owning class. Certainly there are exceptions to this, with some non-owners being quite wealthy, and some owners not having all that much, but the difference between the average material standards of living of the two classes is large and noticeable.

Those who own the means of production constitute the capitalist class. Through their ownership they are able to control production, as well as control workers, those who do not own the means of production. This latter group, the working class (proletariat), owning nothing but their ability to work must labor for capitalists in order to survive. Since they do not own anything with which to produce, workers must sell their ability to work to someone else—the capitalist—and subject themselves to the discipline of the production process.

These two classes—the working class and the capitalists—are considered in political economy to be the two major classes within capitalism. Each exists only as a counterpart to the other. By defining class in relation to the ownership of the means of production, it can be seen that the two classes are fundamentally antagonistic. Capitalists will want workers to produce as much as possible and as cheaply as possible. Workers, on the other hand, will resist being driven too hard, and will want to be paid as much as possible. Thus, there is an inherent conflict between the two classes over control of the production process and over distribution of income.

Divisions within class divisions. In addition to the basic division between classes, there also exist divisions within each class. For example, within the capitalist class there may be conflicts that arise between financial institutions, which lend money, and industrial capitalists who use this borrowed money for production—the former would want to receive high interest payments, while the latter would want interest payments to be low. Similarly, within the working class, interests may differ between skilled and unskilled workers, or between workers and managers. Thus, within the overall division of society into two classes, there is a further division of the classes into various parts.

It is the essence of class that society is not seen as a collection of atomized individuals. Their group identification—in this case defined by their ownership relation to the means of production—influences and informs their interactions in society. They will differ as individuals, of course, but they will have important similarities as workers or capitalists, especially with regard to their economic relations in society.

In addition to class, other social groups can be identified as well. For example, individuals may be members of gender, racial, ethnic, and religious groups that are important to their identity as social beings. While these intersect with class in a complex way, and may influence how class is experienced, it is important to note that they are distinct from, and have a different economic status than, class. All of these social formations combine into a complex social structure in which individuals come together in overlapping groups, acting not as isolated economic agents, but as members of various social groups.

Economic class is considered important in political economy because it is thought that economic interests primarily lie with this particular grouping. Because of this shared economic consciousness, strong political-economic bonds should be formed in opposition to the other class: class "distinguish[es] the groups whose antagonisms define the basic historical processes," explains Leszek Kolakowski. Or, as Karl MARX and Friedrich ENGELS put it in a famous passage from the *Communist Manifesto*, "The history of all hitherto existing society is the history of class struggles," or the dynamics of the class struggle are the basis for determining social change.

We have identified only two classes in the discussion above. In advanced capitalism (such as the United States), however, there appears to be a large group between capitalists and workers. This group would include, among others, the intelligentsia, managers, teachers, entertainers, and engineers. Some economists believe that this group constitutes a new class because they are in economic opposition to both of the other two classes. Since they are WAGE workers, selling their ability to work to capitalists, this middle class would have economic interests opposed to capitalists, and since they control and manage workers, they would also have a fundamental antagonism to workers. While acknowledging the existence of this middle stratum, other economists would see this group as occupying a

The upper levels of the middle class can enjoy leisure activities out of reach for the lower-middle class.

contradictory class position, not really a class, but sometimes aligning with workers, and sometimes aligning with capitalists. Whether a separate class or not, due to its large size, this middle stratum plays a significant role in the class structure of advanced capitalist economies.

One further comment on the possibility of a third class, or the possibility of shifting class alliances, is in order. In recent decades, there has been a tremendous upsurge in stock ownership throughout the entire population of the United States. In a legal sense this makes all of these people (partial) owners of the means of production, and thus, by the definition used above, capitalists. Legal ownership, however, does not constitute control over the means of production (i.e., economic ownership): This widespread diffusion of stock ownership does not imply widespread diffusion of any sort of control of the production process itself. Thus, owners of relatively small amounts of stock (who are the vast majority of stockholders) would have little reason to be economically aligned with capitalists, so that stock ownership would not change their class alliance. Similarly, holders of large amounts of stock, who would therefore wish to see profits maximized, and hence would have reason to be aligned with the capitalist class, would not see their class position change, as they would be wealthy, and have large stock portfolios, precisely because they were capitalists. Stock ownership, as it exists in the United States, does not appear to alter the dynamics, or the structure, of class.

Political economy sees economic class as one of the most important divisions within society affecting the historical development of the economy. The class structure of capitalism is both simple, consisting of only two (or three) classes, and complex, with numerous divisions within the classes interacting with each other and with the other classes, as well as with all of the other non-class societal divisions. The nature of the class struggle, along with the struggles of the other non-class groups, will determine, in large part, the future of capitalist economies.

BIBLIOGRAPHY. Tom Bottomore, ed., *A Dictionary of Marxist Thought* (Harvard University Press, 1983); Samuel Bowles and Richard Edwards, *Understanding Capitalism* (Harper & Row, 1985); Leszek Kolakowski, *Main Currents of Marxism* (Oxford University Press, 1978); Karl Marx and Frederick Engels, *Manifesto of the Communist Party* (Foreign Languages Press, 1965); Pat Walker, ed., *Between Labor and Capital* (South End Press, 1979); U.S. Department of Health and Human Services, "The 2003 HHS Poverty Guidelines," aspe.os.dhhs.gov (2003).

PAUL A. SWANSON
WILLIAM PATERSON UNIVERSITY

Clay, Henry (1777–1852)

ONE OF THE MOST ubiquitous political figures of the early 19th century, Henry Clay was born in Hanover County, Virginia. His political career, stretching nearly five decades, included positions as U.S. Senator, U.S. Representative, Speaker of the U.S. House of Representatives, and Secretary of State. In addition, he made five unsuccessful bids for the presidency (1824, 1832, 1840, 1844 and 1848) and was the guiding force behind the Whig party, and the author of the American System, a program of economic nationalism. An experienced politico and highly skilled orator, he orchestrated the era's most important compromises over the increasingly volatile issue of slavery.

When Missouri applied for statehood in 1819 as a slave state, it threatened to upset the balance of free and slave states in Congress and sparked an enormous controversy. Clay was instrumental in resolving the crisis, guiding two bills through Congress that allowed the entrance of Missouri as a slave state and Maine as a free state and divided the rest of the territory acquired in the Louisiana Purchase (1803) into slave and free sections. On the issue of slavery, Clay was ambivalent; though he owned a few dozen slaves in his lifetime, he believed slavery was evil and advocated the gradual emancipation and overseas colonization of American slaves. Clay's intense commitment to order, stability, and consensus placed him in a centrist position throughout the sectional wars of the antebellum years and earned him the nickname, the Great Compromiser.

This same commitment underscored his belief that economic progress should be supported and supervised by a strong and activist federal government. His nationalism grew out of his support for the WAR OF 1812, and by the 1820s had crystallized into an entire program designed to integrate the American economy into one whole instead of sectional parts, to encourage American manufactures, and to wean the young nation off of foreign trade. The American System included protective tariffs, internal improvements, slowed western expansion, and a new Bank of the United States.

It was around this latter issue, in particular, that the second party system coalesced in the 1820s and 1830s. While Jacksonian Democrats opposed the Bank's re-charter and viewed it as an emblem of economic privilege, greed, and debt, Clay saw the Bank as an insurer of sound currency and an instrument of economic stability and development. Clay vigorously opposed Andrew JACKSON's policies, and those of his successor, Martin VAN BUREN; likewise, Democrats did all in their power to defeat the American System at every turn. Congress passed very few of Clay's measures, and western expansion soon eclipsed the American System as the focus of political interest.

Clay's last starring role, perhaps the one that made him most famous, was as author of the Compromise of

1850. The MEXICAN-AMERICAN WAR (1846–48) added vast new territory to the United States' holdings, re-igniting the debate over slavery's extension. When California applied for admission into the Union as a free state, debate gave way to open sectional conflict. Clay was in favor of the territory's admission, but not at the expense of political instability and potential war. The Great Compromiser introduced an Omnibus Bill that attached to California's entrance concessions to Southerners: a new Fugitive Slave Law; the resolution of a border dispute between New Mexico and Texas in favor of the latter; and the passage of no further restrictions on slavery in the Mexican Cession. The compromise included an additional measure to appease Northerners, the banning of the interstate slave trade in the District of Columbia. The bill pitted Clay against his fellow Whig, President Zachary TAYLOR, who opposed it on matters of expediency. But when Taylor died unexpectedly July 9, 1850, Clay and his allies were able to win passage of the measures. The Compromise of 1850 averted war for the time being, but did not prevent it.

Clay died less than two years later from tuberculosis. His last congressional action was to introduce an internal improvements bill, which, like his American System as a whole, did not pass. Despite his political defeats, Clay died a revered American statesman who helped shape and define the politics and economic policy of his era and his Whig party.

BIBLIOGRAPHY. George Dangerfield, *The Awakening of American Nationalism, 1815–1828* (Waveland Press, 1994); Daniel Walker Howe, *The Political Culture of the American Whigs* (University of Chicago Press, 1979); David M. Potter, *The Impending Crisis, 1848–1861* (HarperCollins, 1963); Robert V. Remini, *Henry Clay: Statesman for the Union* (W.W. Norton, 1991); Glyndon G. Van Deusen, *The Jacksonian Era, 1828–1848* (Waveland Press, 1959).

HOLLY A. BERKLEY, PH.D.
HARDIN-SIMMONS UNIVERSITY

Cleaver, Harry M., Jr. (1944–)

BORN IN OHIO, Harry M. Cleaver received a B.A. in economics from Antioch College in 1967 and a Ph.D. in economics from Stanford University in 1975. He taught at the Université de Sherbrooke in Québec, Canada (1971–74) and the New School for Social Research in New York City (1974–76). Cleaver's Marxist perspectives in economics brought him to the University of Texas, Austin, in 1976.

Cleaver is a self-taught Marxist who, dissatisfied with the answers provided by mainstream economics, sought alternative theoretical frameworks to study social issues. He identifies himself as a member of the autonomist Marxist tradition alongside Antonio Negri, Mario Tronti, George Caffentzis, Silvia Federici, and C.L.R. James. This tradition places the working class, broadly defined to include non-WAGES sectors such as peasants, students, the unemployed, and housewives, at the center of capitalist development. The self-activity of the working class is identified as the basis of capitalist development and crisis, the origin of accumulation as well as its point of disruption, resulting in the centrality of class conflict for the analysis of capitalism.

A common thread in Cleaver's work has been the use of Marxist theory to analyze mainstream economic theory and policy in order to inform and strengthen social struggles. Evidence of this begins with his doctoral thesis on the Green Revolution, where his application of Marxist categories of analysis reveal new agricultural technologies as a weapon wielded against peasant struggles in developing nations. He later extended his analysis to other technologies, supply-side economics, and the international debt crisis.

Cleaver's most important contribution to Marxist theory is his analysis of Chapter 1 of Karl MARX's *Capital*, presented at length in his book *Reading "Capital" Politically*. His interpretation of the labor theory of value reveals capitalism as a system of social control through the endless imposition of work. Armed with this insight, he proceeds to conduct a political reading of *Capital* and capitalism, bringing to life abstract Marxist concepts in the analysis of contemporary class conflicts. Cleaver's method shows that no matter how much capitalist relations of production have changed since *Capital* was written, Marxist categories of analysis have retained their relevance for the study of contemporary issues.

Cleaver has also been an active participant in numerous social struggles since his early involvement in the civil rights and the anti-Vietnam war movements. A self-styled activist, he was a pioneer in the use of the internet to compile and disseminate information about the struggle of the landless Mayan peasants in Chiapas, Mexico.

BIBLIOGRAPHY. Harry Cleaver, *Reading "Capital" Politically* (University of Texas Press, 1979); Harry Cleaver, www.eco.utexas.edu.

LEOPOLDO RODRÍGUEZ-BOETSCH
PORTLAND STATE UNIVERSITY

Cleveland, Grover (1837–1908)

CONSIDERED BY MANY historians to be the greatest president between Abraham LINCOLN and Theodore ROO-

SEVELT, Cleveland was also the first Democratic president since the Reconstruction and the only president to serve non-consecutive terms. Although best remembered for his independence and integrity, his two administrations were also times of political, social, and economic turmoil.

Born at Caldwell, New Jersey, the fifth of nine children of a Presbyterian minister, his family was of limited means. After his father's death, life became even more difficult, and Cleveland abandoned his dream of a college education. With the help of an uncle, he obtained a position studying law in a Buffalo, New York firm and was admitted to the Bar in 1859. After becoming active in the Democratic Party in a decidedly Republican Buffalo, he won election as Erie County Sheriff in 1870, a position in which he first gained his reputation for honesty by fighting petty corruption. After one term, he returned to private practice. His image of integrity was strengthened after being elected mayor of Buffalo in 1881, and the following year he won the governorship. Once again, he opposed corruption by standing up to the Tammany Hall Democratic machine.

In 1884, the Democrats nominated Cleveland for the presidency. The campaign was one of the most bitter in U.S. history. The Republican nominee, James G. Blaine, was accused of accepting bribes while in Congress, and Cleveland took responsibility for fathering a child out of wedlock. Cleveland won a close contest with 219 electoral votes to Blaine's 182. The popular vote was even closer. Cleveland garnered 4,874,621 votes to Blaine's 4,848,936.

As president, Cleveland continued his stand against graft and the spoils system. He expanded civil service protection, and continually vetoed what he considered special-interest legislation despite the political costs. He even vetoed a bill to provide modest aid to farmers suffering from the drought of 1887, and dared to veto a measure that would provide disability payments, even for disabilities unrelated to military services, to Union Army veterans.

He also vetoed hundreds of private pensions bills for veterans. His use of the veto power and a vigorous foreign policy reinvigorated the presidency, an office eclipsed by Congress since Lincoln's death. He further exposed and prosecuted those responsible for corrupt sales of government lands in the West, and supported federal arbitration of labor disputes. Although winning the popular vote for re-election in 1888, he lost the electoral vote to Republican Benjamin Harrison. Nevertheless, four years later he defeated Harrison to become the only president to serve two non-consecutive terms, and thus is considered the 22nd and 24th president.

During his more difficult second term, Cleveland continued his conservative policies centered on a limited view of government involvement in the economy, especially when regulating business activities. But his conservatism did not mean he always supported the corporate agenda. He called for low tariffs in the belief that protectionism unfairly favored business at the expense of consumers, and, during his first term, signed into law the Interstate Commerce Act of 1887 to address rate-setting abuses by railroads. Yet he was even more stringent in standing up to organized labor and sent troops to Chicago to crush the violent Pullman strike of 1894 over the objections of Illinois' governor.

The devastating Depression of 1893 and his controversial move to avert a monetary crisis, by having the government borrow $62 million in gold from a syndicate controlled by the widely hated J.P. MORGAN, damaged Cleveland's popularity. His support of low tariffs and the gold standard, his handling of the Pullman strike, and his refusal to support his party's pro-silver nominee, William Jennings Bryan, also helped to divide the Democrats and elect Republican William McKinley in 1896. After leaving the presidency in March 1897, Cleveland retired to Princeton, New Jersey, and served actively as a trustee of Princeton University.

BIBLIOGRAPHY. Paul H. Jeffers, *An Honest President: The Life and Presidencies of Grover Cleveland* (HarperCollins, 2000); Robert McElroy, *Grover Cleveland: The Man and the Statesman* (Princeton University Press, 1923); Allan Nevins, *Grover Cleveland: A Study in Courage* (American Political Biography, 1933).

RUSSELL FOWLER, J.D.
UNIVERSITY OF TENNESSEE, CHATTANOOGA

Clinton, William Jefferson (1946–)

BORN WILLIAM JEFFERSON Blythe IV in Hope, Arkansas, Bill Clinton became the 42nd president of the UNITED STATES. His father was killed in an automobile accident before he was born and his mother eventually married Roger Clinton, adopting the new family name.

Clinton met President John F. KENNEDY in Washington, D.C., on a Boys' Nation trip and he was inspired to go into politics. He earned a B.S. degree in international affairs in 1968 at Georgetown University and received a Rhodes scholarship to attend Oxford University between 1968–70. He then attended Yale Law School. Clinton taught at the University of Arkansas from 1974–76. He was elected state attorney general in 1976 and, in 1979, became the nation's youngest governor at 33. Defeated for re-election in 1980, he was nonetheless re-elected governor a few years later, and then ran for U.S. president in 1992.

Clinton was described by political analysts as "the most gifted American politician since Franklin Delano ROOSEVELT, in every respect: intelligence, policy, knowledge, political skill, capacity to relate to the American people." A study in contradictions, Clinton was also the first directly elected American president to be impeached and almost convicted.

Clinton presided over a period of extraordinary prosperity, yet left office with a widespread sense of squandered opportunities, particularly in HEALTH-care reform and social-insurance reform. He rebuilt a national Democratic Party to be competitive in presidential elections and, yet, he saw Democratic fortunes decline at every other level of political office. Clinton moved the Democratic Party to the center on crime, on welfare, on fiscal responsibility. He made paying down the national debt a tool of progressive policy. Clinton pushed through two deficit-reduction packages that led to improved interest rates, budget surpluses, and economic growth. He also lobbied Congress in 1993 to pass the North American Free Trade Act (NAFTA), which opened up new markets for American products and enabled Mexico to explore modern solutions for its old-world economy.

Clinton's 1993 transition into the White House was chaotic and his early years as president were disorganized. According to his critics, he ran most of his presidency based on polls; even to determine where he would go on summer vacation in 1996. The White House did not become organized until Leon Panetta became chief of staff. Some political pundits referred to this period as "when the grown-ups took charge."

Clinton's enduring legacy is likely to be the economic boom that began shortly before he took office in 1992. During his eight years in the White House, the economy expanded by 50 percent in real terms and by the end of the era the United States had a GROSS NATIONAL PRODUCT (GDP) equal to one quarter of the entire world economic output. The UNEMPLOYMENT rate dropped by half to 4 percent, a 40-year low, while the economy created some 15 million jobs. The stock market grew even faster, by more than three times, creating thousands of millionaires among middle-class stockholders. Clinton had decided early in his administration that debt reduction, not tax cuts, was the best way to preserve economic growth.

This economic policy set the scene for a series of confrontations between Clinton and Congress over what spending should be cut to reach a balanced budget. There were two government shutdowns when agreement could not be reached on the budget, one lasting nearly six weeks.

The U.S. trade deficit, the gap between the goods the United States sells to the rest of the world, and the amount it buys, ballooned during the Clinton administration. Clinton sanctioned a limited intervention in for-eign currency markets, first to save the YEN from a catastrophic decline, and second, and less effectively, to try and boost the value of the EURO, the single currency for Europe. Interest-rate cuts in 1998 also helped stabilize the world financial system and prevented the ASIAN FINANCIAL CRISIS from spilling over into a global catastrophe, but at the cost of increasing imports to the United States even further.

Against strong opposition from within his own party, Clinton pushed through NAFTA in 1995. However, in doing so, he sidelined agreements incorporating labor and environmental standards. He was never able to gain "fast track" authority from Congress, which would have given him the authority to negotiate further trade deals without Congressional approval. His plans for a Latin American free-trade zone faltered. He did negotiate an agreement with CHINA in 1999 that cleared the way for its membership in the WORLD TRADE ORGANIZATION (WTO) and managed to persuade Congress to back that deal, encouraging the world's most populous country to continue its path of economic reform and integration in the world economy.

However, at the Seattle WTO meeting Clinton, against the advice of his own trade negotiators, urged the inclusion of labor-standards issues in the trade talks, alienating many third-world delegates. The talks then dissolved into acrimonious failure, with all sides blaming the United States for inadequate preparation and succumbing to domestic political pressure. As well, a number of nagging disputes over beef, bananas, aircraft subsidies, and tax breaks continued to cause friction between the United States and the EUROPEAN UNION (EU) during the late 1990s.

Clinton came into office with little experience and interest in foreign affairs, despite his undergraduate degree. In the beginning, he made serious missteps especially in Somalia, Rwanda, and Haiti. But he recovered and created a new policy that he called the "doctrine of enlargement." This policy embraced free trade, multilateral peacekeeping efforts, and international alliances, in addition to a commitment to intervention in world-crisis situations when it was practical and morally defensible. This policy also promoted and extended basic human and civil rights. One of the main foreign policy demands on Clinton came from the numerous civil and ethnic wars in Eastern Europe, especially the Balkans. He left behind a new approach to the world based on intervention in the interests of humanity rather than for profits.

Despite Clinton's economic leadership, many historians believe his presidency undermined the office of the president. His impeachment, extramarital affairs, and his easy way with the truth fundamentally eroded the chief executive's symbolic powers as the leader of the nation. His presidency was involved in scandals, and round after round of financial and moral investigations.

Unfortunately, no historical mention of Clinton will be complete without briefly discussing his affair with intern Monica Lewinsky, which led to his impeachment and near-dismissal from office. The president had an affair with Lewinsky, lied about it to the American public and under oath, was impeached but not convicted, and then apologized to the American public for his inappropriate behavior. Most Americans believed Clinton was guilty of lying to the nation and he received low marks for character and honesty. A majority of Americans wanted him to be censured and condemned for his conduct but not convicted of impeachment and removed from office.

The question to be answered by future historians is how could a man with so many gifts end up, in the words of Hamilton Jordan, Jimmy CARTER's former chief of staff, as a grifter (a term used in the Great DEPRESSION to describe fast-talking con artists).

Yet, from a purely economic and capitalist perspective, Clinton's presidency may go unmatched for decades to come in economic growth, stock valuations, and the general welfare of U.S. citizens.

BIBLIOGRAPHY. "Bill Clinton," www.infoplease.com; Bob Woodward, *Shadow: Five Presidents and the Legacy of Watergate* (Simon & Schuster, 1999); David Gergen, *Eyewitness to Power* (Simon & Schuster, 2000); Hamilton Jordan, "The First Grifters," *The Wall Street Journal* (25 February 2001); George Stephanopoulos, *All Too Human, A Political Education* (Little, Brown, 1999); William Hyland, *Clinton's World: Remaking American Foreign Policy* (Praeger, 1999).

LINDA L. PETROU, PH.D.
HIGH POINT UNIVERSITY

Coase, Ronald H. (1910–)

BRITISH-BORN RONALD COASE was awarded the 1991 Nobel Prize in Economics for his discovery and clarification of the significance of transaction costs and property rights for the institutional structure and functioning of the economy. According to the Nobel citation, "Coase's achievements have provided legal science, economic history and organizational theory with powerful impulses . . ."

Coase was known throughout the London suburb of Willesden as the most intellectual child in the community. "My main interest was always academic," Coase wrote. "I was an only child but although often alone, never lonely." He was a thinker and one of his favorite hobbies, playing chess, afforded him many pondering hours.

His earliest memories of Kilburn Grammar School include his erudite geography teacher, Charles Thurston, who introduced him to Wegener's hypothesis and, on field outings, to the wonders of the Royal Geographic Society. When called on to choose a college preparatory curriculum, he found torn between subjects. Science and chemistry fascinated him, but the requirement of a mathematics adjunct did not. Recalling, Coates explained, "I switched to the only other degree for which it was possible to study at Kilburn, one in commerce."

Coase was accepted to the London School of Economics in 1929. Majoring in commerce, he managed to fall under the tutelage of the celebrated Arnold Plant, previously of Cape Town University, South Africa. Professor Plant's series of lectures on business administration changed his views of economics. To Coase, he emphasized the value of "the invisible hand"—that is, how a competitive economic system could be coordinated by the pricing system.

From 1931–32, Coase studied abroad, having earned a Cassell Traveling Scholarship. In the United States he visited major manufacturing plants, such as GENERAL MOTORS, to understand how American business was structured and industries organized. Coase came away with a new concept of economic analysis, transaction costs, and an explanation as to *why* firms exist.

The lessons learned in America provided him with a focus, a beginning of a new concept for an economic structure, the nature of which he would continue to work on and finally publish in 1937 under the title, *The Nature of the Firm*.

In the meantime, he taught at the Dundee School of Economics (1932–34), at the University of Liverpool (1934–35), then at the London School of Economics, with which he would be associated through 1951. Coase's career was interrupted in 1939 when the UNITED KINGDOM entered WORLD WAR II. He served as a statistician for both the Forestry Commission and the British War Cabinet.

Accepting a position as professor at the University of Buffalo, New York, Coase immigrated to America in 1951. Eight years later, he joined the economics department at the University of Virginia. There he remained until 1964 when he took over editorship of the University of Chicago's *Journal of Law and Economics*. Coase retired in 1982.

BIBLIOGRAPHY. *Essays on Economics and Economists* (R.H. Coase, University of Chicago Press, 1995); Ronald H. Coase Autobiography, www.nobel.se; Ronald H. Coase Biography, University of Chicago Law School online newsletter, www.law.uchicago.edu.

JOSEPH GERINGER
SYED B. HUSSAIN, PH.D.
UNIVERSITY OF WISCONSIN, OSHKOSH

Colbert, Jean-Baptiste (1619–83)

MINISTER OF FINANCE under FRANCE's King Louis XIV for more than 20 years (1661–83), Jean-Baptiste Colbert is remembered as one of the greatest practitioners of mercantilist policy, and his influence was so extensive that the French coined the term *colbertisme* (or Colbertism), which is virtually synonymous with MERCANTILISM as that word is used in other languages.

Despite his modest origins, Colbert rose to this position of great power through hard work, attention to detail, and perhaps some unscrupulous means. Though King Louis provided the symbolic head, it was Colbert who was almost exclusively responsible for France's nationalistic policymaking and its implementation during this period. His historical renown is derived from his ambitious, but largely unsuccessful attempts to direct the French economy.

Colbert's objective was to systematize the state management of the economy that had begun under his predecessors. Under his administration, almost every aspect of economic production came under government control.

Colbert was successful in raising the state's revenues significantly, but he could never extract sufficient revenue to finance both the expenses of an extravagant court and of the king's perpetual warfare. Much of the blame could also be assigned to the system of taxation itself, which placed the main burden of TAXES on the rural population. Most noblemen, clerics, and office holders could claim exemption from the direct tax, and landowners were able to lessen their burden by reducing the valuations on their holdings.

Colbert could be described as a bullionist who favored expanded exports, reduced imports, and strict prohibitions on the outflow of bullion from the country. Because he believed that one nation could become richer only at the expense of another, he viewed commerce as an unending and bitter struggle among nations for economic advantage. Colbert encouraged the expansion of manufacture by means of subsidies. High protective tariffs and a system of prohibitions were designed to secure a favorable balance of trade and to make France economically self-sufficient.

Government regulation of business was also an important feature of Colbertism. This meant a network of detailed regulations for the manufacture of literally hundreds of products to attain quality control and to protect the good reputation for French luxury goods in foreign markets. Since these regulations were often resisted and evaded, enforcement became a costly undertaking and ultimately inhibited technological progress. Colbert was also responsible for laws that allowed aristocrats to engage in commerce without losing their status and privileges, and numerous decrees restricting the conduct of merchants.

Like many other mercantilists, Colbert desired to build and maintain an overseas empire. During the first half of the 17th century, the French had established colonies in CANADA, the West Indies, and INDIA, but had not given them much support. Colbert regarded the colonies as desirable outlets for French goods and as sources of raw materials. Though he sought to expand these efforts, he effectively smothered the colonies with an excess of paternalistic regulations. He also created monopolistic joint-stock companies to carry on trade with the East and West Indies, but these initiatives were largely public rather than private ventures and did not enjoy the successes of their Dutch and English counterparts.

Many of Colbert's efforts to facilitate internal trade were also unsuccessful, due largely to the feudal provincialism and tradition that still remained a strong influence in France. The internal customs barriers and taxes on the movement of goods, which Colbert opposed, were not abolished until the French Revolution of 1789. Even his attempts to establish a uniform system of weights and measures were thwarted. He did, however, exploit the remnants of the feudal system of compulsory labor of peasants to improve the transportation infrastructure internally. The more than 15,000 miles of road that were resurfaced under this system expedited internal travel, but made Colbert thoroughly unpopular among the peasants. He also was responsible for improving ports and building canals.

Despite the attempts that Colbert made to strengthen the French economy, the fiscal drains he encountered were overwhelming, and the economy did not flourish under his extreme mercantilist practices. The government's emphasis on manufacture, its relative neglect of agriculture, and the inability of the fiscal system to generate sufficient revenue continued to plague the French economy for many years.

BIBLIOGRAPHY. Stanley L. Brue, *The Evolution of Economic Thought* (South-Western, 1994); Rondo Cameron and Larry Neal, *A Concise Economic History of the World, From Paleolithic Times to the Present* (Oxford University Press, 2003); Frank Neff, *Economic Doctrines* (1950).

ELEANOR T. VON ENDE, PH.D.
TEXAS TECH UNIVERSITY

Colombia

THE REPUBLIC OF COLOMBIA is bordered by PANAMA and the Caribbean Sea to the north, VENEZUELA and BRAZIL to the east, PERU and Ecuador to the south, and the Pacific Ocean to the west. Bogotá is the capital.

In 2002, Colombia's population was approximately 41 million. Almost 60 percent of the population is *mestizos* (mixed European and Native Indian descent), with 20 percent being white, 14 percent mulatto, and the rest black, black-Amerindian, and Amerindian. Spanish is the official language, but the 1991 constitution recognized the languages of ethnic groups and provided for bilingual education. The population is largely concentrated in the interior Andean region and more than one-third of the population lives in Colombia's six largest urban areas. Colombia has a high-rate of emigration, especially to the UNITED STATES and oil-rich Venezuela. There is a high rate of internal movement from rural to urban areas, due in part to the search for better wages and living conditions, and to rural violence linked to the drug trade.

From the conquest and settlement of Colombia by Europeans in 1525 through World War II, when conservatives took control of the government and instituted reprisals against liberals, to the 1960s, when Marxist guerilla groups began to appear, Colombia has had a volatile history. But, since the mid-1970s, Colombia's economic power has developed as it became a major supplier in the international illegal drug market.

The drug leaders used their early profits from marijuana to diversify into cocaine trafficking. As the drug cartels became more powerful, they began to use terror as a means to increase their bargaining position with the government. In the 1990s, the government began a series of economic reforms that were in line with the neoliberal mood sweeping through Latin America. But drug-trade violence also reached new heights in the 1990s despite paramilitary forces uniting under the auspices of the United Self-Defense Groups of Colombia. In 1998, Colombia's economy entered its worst recession since the 1930s. In 2000, the United States approved an aid program that would supply military assistance to help control the drug trade.

Colombia is the leading producer of mild coffee and is second to Brazil in total annual volume of coffee produced. In the mid-1990s, coffee growers experienced a drastic drop in coffee earnings due in part to high production costs and low global prices.

Colombia is rich in mineral resources, chief among them coal, gold, and petroleum. In the 1990s, petroleum passed coffee as Colombia's largest source of foreign income.

Industry accounts for more than one-quarter of Colombia's GROSS DOMESTIC PRODUCT (GDP), services more than half, and agriculture slightly less than 20 percent. Small-scale enterprises carry out the majority of Colombia's industrial activity. Colombia's currency is the Colombian peso (COP). The Bank of the Republic operates the government's emerald, mint, and salt monopolies, and is the sole bank of issue. There are ap-

proximately 30 commercial banking institutions, several partially foreign-owned.

Colombia's exports are valued at approximately $12.3 billion annually and its imports at $12.7 billion; partners include the United States, the EUROPEAN UNION (EU), and the Andean Community of Nations.

Colombia's illegal drug trade is a major economic contributor—trade balances can be made positive even though they were negative for legitimate goods; drug dealers spend money to grow their businesses, which can benefit Colombians more than the legitimate economy does. Despite government initiatives, the drug trade remains a key factor in Colombia's economy.

BIBLIOGRAPHY. David Bushnell, *The Making of Modern Colombia: A Nation in Spite of Itself* (University of California Press, 1993); Robert H. Davis, *Historical Dictionary of Colombia* (Scarecrow Press, 1993); Harvey F. Kline, *State Building and Conflict Resolution in Colombia, 1986–1994* (University of Alabama Press, 2002); *CIA World Factbook* (2002).

S.J. RUBEL, J.D.
NEW YORK CITY

colonialism

COLONIALISM IS THE control by one power over a dependent area or people. In recent centuries, it was associated with political control by European states over people of other races inhabiting lands separated by the seas from Europe. Salient features of colonialism include: domination by an alien minority; assertions of racial and cultural superiority; economic exploitation; and reshaping of the colonized society.

The age of modern colonialism began around 1500, following circumnavigation of Africa (1488) and discovery of the Americas (1492). Through discovery, conquest, and settlement, the leading European powers of the time (PORTUGAL, SPAIN, the NETHERLANDS, FRANCE, and the UNITED KINGDOM) expanded and colonized most of the world.

The post-WORLD WAR II period spelled the demise of colonialism. Between 1945 and 1975 most European colonies gained independence and became formally sovereign states. As a foundational phenomenon of the modern age, colonialism shaped both the colonizing and colonized societies, and has left lasting impressions on the political, economic, and cultural forms of these societies.

Colonial expansion. Colonialism and the emergence of nation-states in Europe were contemporaneous. Portugal led the way, expanding westward to BRAZIL and eastward to the Indian Ocean. It enjoyed a monopoly of trade in these regions until other European states moved in. Spain first occupied the larger West Indian islands, and later, fueled by the gold and silver of MEXICO, established a colonial empire stretching from CHILE to California.

The rise of the Dutch as the leading European naval and commercial power in the 16th century resulted from their control of the spice islands of Asia (now INDONESIA). The Dutch East India Company was chartered in 1602 and controlled European trade with Asia for many years. The French began with New France (CANADA), founded Québec in 1608, and later established colonies in Africa and Asia. England established 13 colonies (1607–1732) on the Atlantic coast of North America. The defeat of Spain in 1713, and the successful conclusion of the French and Indian War in 1763 gained for England all of North America east of the Mississippi River. The British EAST INDIA COMPANY, chartered in 1600, led the colonization of INDIA starting with the conquest of Bengal in 1757. AUSTRALIA and the Caribbean were colonized soon after.

The Napoleonic Wars slowed Portugal and Spain's colonial growth. Due to French occupation of the two countries in 1807, Portugal and Spain were unable to effectively deal with nationalist movements and civil wars in their South American colonies. By 1825, Brazil gained independence from Portugal and Spain's American colonial empire was reduced to CUBA and Puerto Rico.

During the late 19th and early 20th centuries, new colonial powers emerged: GERMANY, the UNITED STATES, BELGIUM, RUSSIA, ITALY, and JAPAN. Russia expanded over land, as did the United States, eliminating and displacing indigenous inhabitants and cultures. Russia occupied Siberia, the Caucasus region, and East Asia as far south as the Korean peninsula. The United States expanded west of the Mississippi and following the defeat of Mexico (1848) consolidated its control up to the Pacific coast. The United States also took possession of Spain's colonies in the Caribbean, South Pacific, and the PHILIPPINES following the SPANISH-AMERICAN WAR (1898). The partitioning of CHINA by European powers began with the Opium wars waged by England to force China to accept exports of opium from colonial India. After these concessions were secured by the Treaty of Nanjing (1842), the United States, France, and Russia secured similar economic concessions from China. Japan started its colonial expansion with control of the Korean peninsula and northeastern China.

The European "scramble for Africa" unfolded between 1880–1900. The French colonized ALGERIA and the British took control of EGYPT. Sub-Saharan Africa was divided between Britain, France, Germany, and Belgium. Britain assumed control over SOUTH AFRICA following the Boer War (1899–1902). After WORLD WAR I, Britain and France took over Middle Eastern countries that were formally a part of the Turkish Empire.

Colonialism reached its highest point at the eve of World War I. Competition for colonies among the European powers was one of the causes of the war. During the inter-war period, forces opposed to colonialism grew in strength. Emerging nationalist movements in the colonies and the RUSSIAN REVOLUTION (1917) produced a worldwide movement against colonialism. Costs of containing nationalist movements, spread of ideas hostile to racism and colonial domination, comparative weakening of European powers, and changes in the global economic system, rendered continuation of colonial rule increasingly untenable.

World War II, caused in no small measure by competition for colonies, accelerated these processes. The UNITED NATIONS Charter (1945) contained an implicit endorsement of decolonization, and following the war decolonization unfolded rapidly. India and PAKISTAN gained independence in 1947 and Britain's colonies in Africa followed suit in the late 1950s. Decolonization of French colonies was accompanied by prolonged wars of liberation in Indochina and North Africa. Belgium, the Netherlands, and Portugal were forced to give up their colonial possessions during the 1960s and 1970s.

Capitalism and colonialism. Colonialism served vital though varied roles in the economic growth of modern Europe, particularly in the transition to and consolidation of capitalism. During the mercantilist era, gold bullion appropriated from the colonies helped fill the coffers of European powers. Colonial products were often paid for in exported manufactures, thus saving foreign exchange. Colonial trade and investments in the colonies helped in the transition to capitalism by furnishing an avenue for large-scale capital investments and formation of joint stock companies.

Colonialism helped inaugurate two enduring features of capitalism: that it is a global system of production and that it can help maintain pre-capitalist modes of production in subordinate roles. Slaves and indentured labor from the colonies supplied labor power for colonial plantations and extractive enterprises. Raw materials from the colonies freed European powers from dependence on European supplies that were more expensive and could be cut off during wars. Colonies provided favorable and stable markets for European exports, and thus helped employment in European industries. Colonies were prevented from developing competing industries and different sectors of their economies were disengaged from one another and linked with needs of the economies of colonizing powers. As investments at home became less profitable due to the rise of monopolies and declining profitability of marginal lands, colonies furnished an attractive outlet for investment of CAPITAL. Settler colonies of North America and Australia provided opportunities for European emigration, virgin lands, and capacity to absorb investments. Colonies were essential as markets for the SURPLUS production of European industries, thus helping mitigate the negative effects of the boom and bust cycles of capitalism. By serving as an engine of the INDUSTRIAL REVOLUTION and profitability in Europe, colonialism served as an insurance against social strife and unrest that may have resulted from absence of economic growth.

Modern Europe sees itself as the product of the Enlightenment, with the attending ideals of reason, freedom, liberty, equality, and the rule of law. Modernity of Europe is, however, coterminous with its colonial expansion and imperial rule, marked by conquest, subjugation, and even genocide. In an age when exercise of political power was increasingly linked with rights of citizens, and good government was recognized as intimately linked with self-government, colonialism rested upon the repudiation of these linkages. How were these two contradictory strands reconciled? It was the modern construction of race that facilitated the establishment and consolidation of colonialism, a relationship of domination and subordination. Faced with the contradictions between ideals of the Enlightenment and colonialism, hegemonic forces in Europe fashioned strategies of exclusion, grounded in a racial dichotomy between human and sub-human, or civilized and savage. This triggered the mutually constitutive role of colonialism and modern Europe. Many foundational constructs of modernity—reason, man, progress, the nation—were developed in contrast with a racialized "non-Europe," with the latter posited as pre-modern, not fully human, irrational, and outside history.

The age of colonialism also saw the consolidation of a unilinear, progressive, teleological, and Eurocentric history as the dominant mode of experiencing time and being. In this history, others' present is seen as Europe's past and Europe's present is posited as others' future. In this construction, nations attain maturity only when a people are fully conscious of themselves as subjects of unilinear and progressive history, and it is only such nations that realize freedom. Those placed outside this history have no claims or rights and may rightfully be subjugated even if to bring them into the stream of the Eurocentric history.

White man's burden. Colonialism, in this frame, is seen as an indispensable instrument the "civilizing mission" of Europe, the "white man's burden"—the project of forcing the otherwise incapable savage along the road to enlightenment and freedom. Modern racism, by fixing upon race as the repository of those attributes that enable or prevent evolution toward civilization, wrote the

legitimating script for colonialism. Modern evolutionary racism consolidated the double binary of fair/dark and civilized/savage by positing the anatomical investigations of Europeans and Africans as establishing the top and bottom of a progressive series of races with differential mental endowments and civilizational achievements. With the diagnosis accomplished, prescription quickly followed: backward races were to be civilized under the discipline and "paternal despotism" of superior races. Modern construction of race thus bridged the Enlightenment with colonialism.

Colonialism and the attendant modern construction of race also furnished the scaffolding for many foundational constructs of modernity. Modern theories of the state based on consent of the governed rest upon a distinction between an original "social contract" and a precontractual "state of nature," with the latter identified with the state of affairs of the colonized people before colonization. The grounds of modern secular law rest on a posited distinction between civilized and savage norms and practices.

The very self-identity of modern Europe took shape in counter-distinction with the non-European other. Many modern academic disciplines, organizational models, institutions of governance and discipline, and cultural practices are a product of the colonial encounter. For example, the science of fingerprinting developed in colonial Bengal to facilitate revenue collection and law enforcement. What is today taken as the canonical curriculum of English literature was developed in the British colonies as part of training regime for colonial administrators. Green tea from Asia was roasted before shipment to Europe to protect it for mold induced by the long ocean voyage; today black tea is consumed all over the world.

Colonialism reconstituted colonized societies in many lasting forms. Many vibrant and growing indigenous economies were destroyed and denuded of wealth. Primary, secondary, and tertiary sectors of colonized economies were disjointed and separately linked with the economies of colonizing states. The coexistence of capitalism with pre-capitalist modes of production in the colonies retarded the prospects of a comprehensive transition to capitalism for post-colonial economies.

Hybrid legal systems were set in place distorting or destroying indigenous normative frameworks. As existing or newly established cities, usually close to a port, served as the nerve centers of colonial political and economic activities, the economic and cultural gulf between rural and urban areas widened substantially. Client classes were created to serve the colonial authorities as middlemen in political and economic fields, thus creating lasting internal fractures in colonized societies. Colonial rule was based on coercion not consent, and colonial political institutions were designed accordingly. Consequently, the state apparatuses bequeathed by colonialism to post-colonial states are conducive to centralized authoritarian control and resistant to demands for representation and civil rights. Colonial powers demarcated their possessions without any regard for cultural, linguistic, or religious homogeneity of their colonial subjects. The straight lines running across the map of Africa are a good example of this phenomenon. As a result, many post-colonial states have territorial boundaries that do not comport to any reasonable divisions of identity, ethnicity, language, or religion; instability, social strife, and civil wars often follow. Colonialism did indeed serve as a vehicle of transmission of modern ideas, frameworks, technologies, and modes of life across the globe. The structure and history of colonialism, however, remains stamped on the modernity thus transmitted. Post-colonial modernity remains partial and fractured, whereby its promise remains trumped by its burdens.

In a few, but vitally important places, colonialism was not followed by de-colonization but by the establishment of colonial-settler states. Australia, Canada, ISRAEL, NEW ZEALAND, and the United States fall in this category.

Colonialism is the relationship of domination and subordination between the West and the Rest that lasted for nearly 400 years. Economic exploitation, alien and authoritarian political control, and assertions of cultural superiority were its hallmarks. The modern construction of hierarchy of races facilitated and legitimated this un-equal relationship. Colonialism helped shape many defining features of modernity and capitalism, and has left deep imprints on both the colonized and colonizing societies.

BIBLIOGRAPHY. Samir Amin, *Imperialism and Unequal Development* (Monthly Review Press, 1977); Asad Talal, *Anthropology and the Colonial Encounter* (Ithaca Press, 1973); Ernst Cassirer, *Philosophy of the Enlightenment* (Becon Press, 1951); Johannes Fabian, *Time and the Other: How Anthropology Makes Its Object* (Columbia University Press, 1983); Peter Fitzpatrick, *Modernism and the Grounds of Law* (Cambridge University Press, 2001); Stephen Gould, *The Mismeasure of Man* (W.W. Norton, 1981); Ranajit Guha, *Dominance Without Hegemony: History and Power in Colonial India* (Harvard University Press, 1997); Eric Hobsbawm and Terence Ranger, eds., *The Invention of Tradition* (Cambridge University Press, 1983); Edward Said, *Orientalism* (Routledge, 1978); Robert Young, *White Mythologies: Writing History and the West* (Routledge, 1995).

TAYYAB MAHMUD, PH.D., J.D.
CLEVELAND-MARSHALL COLLEGE OF LAW

commodity

see GOODS, PRODUCT, SERVICES, OIL, LAND, LABOR.

communication

COMMUNICATION CAN BE seen as an evolving concept. According to historians Asa Briggs and Peter Burke (2002), the definition of communication has changed considerably in just a few decades, during the second half of the 20th century. Comparing two definitions of that same word in two editions of the same dictionary shows how current conceptions of communication have been significantly modified, adding a stronger degree of technical awareness and more sensibility towards recent conceptions of how people communicate at a distance. In the conclusion of their book titled *A Social History of the Media, From Gutenberg to the Internet*, Briggs and Burke oppose two very different quotes separated by only 17 years:

In 1955, the *Oxford English Dictionary* defined "communication," the first of a related cluster of words to change its usage, as 1) "the action of communicating, now rarely of material things and 2) the imparting, conveying or exchange of ideas, knowledge etc. whether by speech or writing or signs." By the time that a 1972 Supplement to the *Dictionary* appeared, however, communication was described as "the science or process of conveying information, especially by means of electronic or mechanical techniques."

Briggs and Burke conclude from this shift that "the difference was enormous."

Since about half a century ago, it is not so much objects and merchandise that travel (although transportation still exists, of course). We are much more aware of the fact that ideas, images, sounds, bits, and networks can also carry a great deal of information, in just a few seconds; another kind of merchandise, namely messages, data, information, and signals, that can be produced, negotiated, bought, sold, exchanged, transformed, even stolen. Communication has become more virtual, but still has a cost, plus value, and can therefore be traded as any material GOODS that you could actually touch with your hands. Communicating, which means transmitting that information, also has a price, as sending any parcel through the mail, because satellites and networks rely on high technology. Among the new media, the internet is the most fascinating example of that recent mutation.

Since a complete history of communication would cover many books we will only highlight a few economic and social aspects about the ways people communicate today. We will concentrate on two aspects regarding media economics: first, the media as an actor or catalyst in the global economy and then, the media conglomerates as examples of a capitalistic tendency to concentrate OWNERSHIP.

Satellite and cell phone towers have become ubiquitous in our age of communications.

For many persons, the media have first been considered as a tool, a commodity, a practical technical device to enhance communication between persons that are physically separated or very far away. The telephone played that role from the end of 19th century; the mail service did the same since ages ago. The usefulness of the telephone has been proven since; it is still recognized as a public service and therefore regulated by governmental institutions in most countries. This explains why in some countries (CANADA, UNITED STATES), many local phone calls made from home are packaged as flat rates (except for some cellular phones), while in most European countries, every local phone call must be paid by the user, even at home, minute by minute, on every monthly bill. These are examples of different conceptions of the same fundamental public service, depending on telephone companies' rules. Until the 1990s, in countries such as Canada and FRANCE, telephone companies were monopolistic corporations regulated by the state. By breaking the MONOPOLY, the number of employees and profits were reduced, basic rates increased to cover higher advertising costs and

higher wages for Board members. In this move, only costs for long distance calls were reduced.

Mass communication and advertising. The telephone is a perfect example of a device used to keep in touch two persons interacting together at a distance. But some other kind of media allow a few individuals to reach very large audiences; we talk about mass communication and mass media. Among those are books and the press, newspapers, magazines, but also motion pictures, radio, television, the latter two also known as electronic media.

From an economic perspective, the way the media are financed explains why they seem to be cheap for the consumer. For instance, when you buy a newspaper or a magazine in any newsstand, you just don't pay only for the paper and printing, but also for the whole chain of workers, merchandising, and services that have together built the pages that you read. In fact, the paper in itself is worth much less than the newsstand price. The retail price of that newspaper would be rather much higher if the press industry couldn't rely on another vital source of revenues: advertising. Publicity is now the heartbeat of most media. Newspapers, radio and television stations, and most major web servers depend highly on advertising. There are of course exceptions, depending on countries. Small community radio stations and public television have other sources of financing, such as donations, grants, governmental help; in some other cases in community networks, many employees volunteer their time and energy. Other corporations, such as the U.S. Public Broadcasting System, mix both systems.

Advertising in the public sphere. From telemarketing to ads on the radio, publicity is almost everywhere, even unusual newer places, such as museums, on public television and radio, in doctor's offices, on subway platform, and on restaurant menus. Even doctors propagate selected brand names from pharmaceutical companies (on posters in their waiting rooms ad offices, or on prescription pads). Schools are no exceptions anymore; colleges affiliate with their exclusive partner drink. In the United States, big arenas do not have a famous local name anymore, but rather a brand label: the Pepsi Coliseum, the Molson Centre, etc. Many industries benefited from an idealized, bigger-than-life image created by advertising in the 1950s. We observe the automobile industry (with happy, fast, and powerful drivers), the cigarette recognition (the "cool" smokers), or the happy, decent beer-drinkers and high-class liquor consumer. Publicity or advertising helps to sell and to give legitimacy.

Newspapers and magazines are subdivided into thematic sections, but everything that goes into these sections (as well as everything that is left out because of a lack of space) is selected by a handful of persons. Their criteria are to include what they consider as important matters (or those they believe their readers might find relevant) and to include breaking news that their competitors would cover as well, because no publisher would want to find he or she is behind the curve. In Roger Rosenblatt's *Consuming Desires*, the editorial atmosphere is put this way: "The pervasive emphasis on what's hot and what's not makes for an atmosphere frantic with anxiety."

One of the consequences of the dependency toward advertising in the media industry is that most newspapers might tend to pay more attention to their advertisers. For instance, according to that logic, a book critic who receives a free review copy of a recent novel might give more visibility to it. Small weekly newspapers or free magazines (those that you find for free at the door of your local supermarket) often depend exclusively on advertising and conceive as a tacit rule that companies must first advertise their products (either movies, books, shows, restaurants) in order to get attention in a review, that would serve as a recognition and exposure in the public sphere (that can be seen as a kind of advertising). Those who can't afford or those who don't want to pay for advertising might be given less attention or less space in those pages. Some magazines even buy their visibility in selected book stores' shop-windows. What you see easily in the showcase or near the cash register at the supermarket is not necessarily the best or the most important magazine; in some cases it is just the one that had enough money to buy the best chosen space with the best visibility.

The problem is many people rely on the media to select for them what to choose and buy, be it books, records, food, restaurants, etc. If many critics are sometimes guided by their announcers, their judgments might be influenced by the choices that were made for them. Other critics or commentators feel no pressure from their advertisers, but they see that other critics have largely covered a new show, a new movie, and they wouldn't want to be the last to talk about it. Some critics will even talk about a forthcoming movie that they haven't seen but that was rumored as excellent, just to prove they are aware of its existence. There is a kind of a similar competition among reporters who want to be the first to "discover" a new phenomena, fashion, trend, or tendency in any field.

The average citizen is not unaware of these subjective phenomena, but how can you and I know about something going on (a product, an event, something alternate or just out of mainstream culture) if it hasn't been publicized? It is always possible for us to know, one way or another, but you will have to do more research in order to find about it. The easiest way would be just to open your eyes and watch, but what we see first is mainstream mass culture. Major networks, be it national newspapers or large TV networks, don't talk much about local, regional, or alternate events, unless they are of a national interest. For instance, we don't see much about foreign movies—even celebrated ones—in local newspapers, especially in the United States.

More and more, people tend to respond to publicity, not necessarily by buying immediately almost everything that is publicized, but just by being aware that this product, that movie, this book, that program exists. And when time comes to choose between products, one brand will inevitably be the one we have heard about, the one we've seen before. To paraphrase Andrew Wernick, all discourse is so saturated with the rhetorical devices of promotion that, in our public lives and perhaps increasingly in our private lives, we are unable to think and act outside of a promotional frame of reference.

With no doubt, advertising is the first step toward the consuming framework in our modern societies. According to Don Slater, "advertising is generally understood as paradigmatic of modern consumer capitalism." In 1961, Raymond Williams wrote that 20th century capitalism could not exist without devices "for organizing and ensuring the market." The main device is advertising communication: "Modern advertising, taking on its distinctive features in just this economic phase, is one of the most important of these devices, and it is perfectly true to say that modern capitalism could not function without it."

The cost of watching free TV. The equivocal question about the costs of watching television is quite interesting. Apart from the electricity and the cost of buying the TV set, watching (broadcast, non-cable) TV seems to be costless. Not really. As we know, television stations get financing from advertisers, but these companies that buy publicity and air time use a part of their revenues in order to afford the advertising expenses. This sum is included in their products' price. As a consequence, you always pay, directly or not, for the advertisement that you see in the media. But we keep in mind the illusion that television is for free. In a book titled *Understanding Popular Culture*, John Fiske argues that "the economic function of a television program is not complete once it has been sold, for in its moment of consumption it changes to become a producer, and what it produces is an audience, which is then sold to advertisers."

Audiences are groups of people who attend any kind of a show, film presentation, conference or concert, or watch a program on television, or listen to the radio. Some people often imagine the audience (for a film, a book, a TV program) as a natural consequence of the program's contents, qualities, and effective potential to attract viewers. The truth is, no matter how good their products are, producers and publishers try to promote and offer everything they have to sell; distributors selecting products are first motivated by the commercial

The rise and dominance of global media affects how we communicate individually—and what we talk about.

potential and not by quality. This is a consequence of the mass marketing of commodities and culture. What Thomas Guback writes about the American motion pictures industry is also true for other media conglomerates dominated by U.S. corporations: "Consumers, of course, are at liberty to select from what is on the market. But the shape of this market, including its range of alternatives, is the result of conscious efforts to structure it and keep competitors in their place."

You may freely watch any program as long as you want; watching television is easy, at every hour, from almost anywhere. You can concentrate on a single station, select your favorite programs, change to another TV station, skip the ads. But it is very difficult for "ordinary people" to go on TV, to be on the other side of the camera, even for contests, quiz and game shows, where thousands of persons send in their names. The media is a privileged place. If you want people in the media to know that you will do a presentation, a conference, a show, that you organize an event, that you have just published a book, you might get a little attention from programs produced by the local stations, since their mission is to talk about what is going on around the regional community; but in many cases it is difficult to get a major presence in the media, especially national media, because too many persons have things to say or to publicize, and air time is in demand and costly.

Even politicians try to get more and more time on television (except if they are implied in a scandal), and unless they have something very important to tell, they usually won't get as much air time as they want. This explains why a candidate has to pay in order to get her message into the media, for instance by advertising that message or idea. When a new TV show or series is planned, producers often worry about potential advertisers; they hope that the biggest possible audience will watch the program and therefore beat the other networks' numbers. Advertising rates are currently adjusted accordingly to the total number of viewers by portions of 15 minutes. Producers, broadcasters, and television stations try to reach a larger audience and therefore prefer to air general content and mass culture instead of art, high culture, and more "serious" matters.

There are those who have access to the media, and also those the media look after, such as stars, celebrities, pop artists, cult icons, and popular idols. There has been a true celebrity culture since the 1920s, and as commodities, the most famous personalities have their own price, since they can attract large audiences and more viewers. According to Thomas O'Guinn, "One of the undeniable hallmarks of American consumer culture is a fascination with celebrity." For instance, among the data collected by O'Guinn, we learn that more than three million American read *People*, more than a million are members of at least one fan club. Fan cultures (with fans trading collectors items, collectables, photos, videotapes; the perfect example would be the Elvis Presley cult in Memphis) have to be understood as a means of "touching greatness."

The media concentration issue. We can't ignore the fact that even though the media corporations want less regulation from governments, especially about ownership and concentration, there is a constant tendency toward this trend. In terms of media economics, capitalist enterprises are allowed to exist as long as they avoid the extreme limit of the monopolistic control of news, ideas, and opinions. In other terms, those who control the means of communication must be numerous, and that number is, of course, discussed and negotiated over and over.

The circulation of all opinions and ideologies can be possible only if we avoid a system where a majority can only hear the voices of the few. Since the logical, profitable, efficient way of managing media enterprises seems to be the widest audience for a single message, public and independent regulation of the media propriety becomes vital. In this area, states cannot just let the market control itself, mainly because the actual rules already comfort the strongest players inside their already dominant position. As Benjamin Compaine wrote, "The mass communications industry is unique in the American private enterprise system because it deals in the particularly sensitive commodities of ideas, information, thought and opinion."

Juliet Schor and Douglas Holt go further: "Now, a handful of mega-conglomerates have taken over all the major media. Profitability and reproducing the political legitimacy of the system have become the dominant criteria for cultural production." But concentration has become a natural move toward growth for major media enterprises, either on a vertical (owning more companies from different media) or horizontal perspective (buying more corporations in a same field, and by doing so, reducing competition), such as proven by the AOL TIME WARNER merger in 2000. Vertical integration in the media industry means that the six biggest multi-media conglomerates (SONY, Universal, Paramount, Warner, Disney, Fox) will intensify their activities in similar or complementary fields, thus raising their collective power, control, and profits, "by spending millions to acquire interests in movie theater chains, cable television systems, over-the-air television stations, TV networks and home video operations such as Bluckbuster Video," Compaine explains.

History has shown that unique voices characterize most totalitarian societies; plurality of ideas and sources are proven to be the essence of free media. The problem is, concentration in the media might have advantages from an economic perspective, but at some level this trend couldn't be tolerated in any democratic society. In economic terms, the artificial compromise or disguise to mask a monopolistic control of an economic sector is known as an OLIGOPOLY. This system allows a handful of corporations, whose interests are common, to control a whole sector in one country or more. There are no laws against this structure of conglomerates, even though the consequences are that oligopolies operate very much alike a monopoly *per se*. In his authoritative and comprehensive analysis on media ownership in the United States, Douglas Gomery states that the current situation in the American media industry is almost a *de facto* monopoly, except that it is made with a few players and not just one. Gomery writes, "A handful of firms dominate in an oligopoly, the most heralded example being the longtime three (now more) television networks. But there are other oligopolies, including the five major music record labels, the six commanding major Hollywood studios and the 10 major book publishers. If there is a ownership pattern that best categorizes the mass media industries, it is one where sellers are few in number."

BIBLIOGRAPHY. Eric Barnouw, ed., *International Encyclopedia of Communications* (University of Pennsylvania Press, 1989); Asa Briggs and Peter Burke, *A Social History of the Media, From Gutenberg to the Internet* (Polity Press, 2002); Benjamin M. Compaine and Douglas Gomery, *Who Owns the Media: Competition and Concentration in the Mass Media Industry* (Erlbaum Associates, 2000); Paul du Gay and Michael Pryke, eds., *Cultural Economy* (Sage Publications, 2002); Thomas Guback, "Non-Market Factors in the International Distribution of American Films," *Current Research in Film: Audiences, Economics, and Law* (Ablex, 1985); Martyn J. Lee, ed., *The Consumer Society Reader* (Blackwell, 2000); Sally R. Munt, ed., *Technospaces: Inside the New Media* (Continuum, 2001); Roger Rosenblatt, ed., *Consuming Desires* (Island Press and Shearwaater Books, 1999); Janet Wasko, *Understanding Disney: The Manufacture of Fantasy* (Blackwell, 2001); Raymond Williams, "Advertising: The Magic System," *The Cultural Studies Reader* (Routledge, 1999).

YVES LABERGE, PH.D.
INSTITUT QUÉBÉCOIS DES
HAUTES ÉTUDES INTERNATIONALES

company

A COMPANY IS AN ASSOCIATION of persons or of capital organized for the purpose of carrying on a commercial, industrial, or similar enterprise. The primary advantage of a company structure (of some legal types) is that it has its own juridical personality independent of its owners or shareholders. Companies are often considered the very backbone of capitalism; and yet they raise questions about their necessity in an economic system founded rather on markets than on organizations. The origin of companies then concerns two issues: how companies have come into being; and why companies have come into being.

History. The known history of several cultures involves developed institutions that may be called "companies." In a wide sense, any organized barter or trade that is not simply carried out on an ad hoc basis involves companies. Commerce along the ancient trade routes was maintained by trading companies. In Europe, they are rooted in the Greek *etairia*, a mercantile association, and in the institutions of *collegium* (or *corpus*) and *societas* under Roman law. European companies developed primarily from mediaeval institutions such as guilds, cooperatives, municipalities, monasteries, universities, and the *commenda* (or *collegantia*), a commercial joint enterprise limiting the liability of investors and endowed with its own legal personality.

Two mediaeval organizations that prospered for a long period of time were the Hanseatic League, based in Lübeck, and the Merchant Adventurers Company of London. The Hanseatic League was an association of German towns that, from major trading posts in Bruges, London, Bergen, and Novgorod, developed trade in much of northern Europe. The Hansa coordinated and distributed capital, goods, and skills throughout its domain and was engaged in many activities such as sheep rearing in England, iron production in SWEDEN, and agriculture in POLAND. The Merchant Adventurers were a group of British wool and cloth merchants who were granted special trading privileges and enjoyed extensive control over trade and commerce between northern FRANCE and DENMARK.

In the 14th century, Italian banking firms began to dominate international commerce. There were an estimated 150 Italian financial companies engaged in exchange, lending, and investment business throughout Europe, perhaps the most prominent among them being the Medici family of Florence. Two of the dominant multinational companies of the 16th century were those of the Fugger family in Augsburg and the Muscovy Company of Russia. By 1525, the Fuggers owned the wealthiest company in Europe, controlling mines from HUNGARY and SPAIN to CHILE, maintaining a string of trading depots or chain stores in all the great cities of central and western Europe, and dealing in all forms of finance (including the lending of money to kings, emperors, and popes). The Muscovy Company was an English group that had received permission from the czar to trade in Russia, and for decades dominated commerce in eastern Europe.

Different countries developed various legal types of companies, forms of sole proprietorships, partnerships, and corporations being known both in civil law and common law jurisdictions. For the development of capitalism, the most important of these was the (public or private) corporation. In the 17th and 18th centuries, two types of corporations developed: state-sponsored trading companies set up to support the colonial trading systems of European governments; and companies with the goal of promoting colonization and land development, particularly in the eastern UNITED STATES and CANADA. The British EAST INDIA COMPANY, founded in 1600 under a Royal charter, and the Dutch East India Company (*Verenigde Oostindische Compagnie*), chartered in 1602 by the States-General of the Netherlands, were early prototypes of public-trading corporations with a multitude of shareholders, monopolists under government control, and exercising sovereign authority on behalf of the state. The Hudson Bay Company, incorporated in England in 1670 to seek a Northwest Passage through Canada to the Pacific and to trade with the lands of northern Canada, was a major protagonist in the economic and political history of Canada (and still exists today as a retail chain). Colonization companies in North America comprised the Virginia Company of London, the Massachusetts Bay Company, the New Sweden Company, and the Company of New France.

The common trait of all early companies that achieved commercial prominence in Europe and America is their dependence on state privileges and protection under a mercantilist economic system. Based on a franchise, they were closer to the form of the modern public corporation than to that of a private business. With the rapid development of commerce in the 17th century and the INDUSTRIAL REVOLUTION in the 18th century, the corporation became the ideal way to run a large enterprise, combining centralized control and direction with moderate investments by a potentially unlimited number of people. The emergence of companies of the modern type occurred over the first two-thirds of the 19th century, during the "Second Industrial Revolution," and in some countries as late as in the 20th century. These companies are founded on private entrepreneurship, on the right to engage in business enterprise, and on a "divorce between ownership and control."

The development of large corporations was necessitated by the spread of new capital-intensive technologies of production and transportation. In particular, the construction of RAILROADS in Europe and America required large sums of capital that could be secured only through the corporate form, and efficient transportation in turn contributed to the expansion of steel and coal industries organized as corporations. Concurrently with these developments in industrializing economies, the various legal traditions became consolidated and were codified into modern company law.

Economic rationale. The second question is why companies have developed at all. In economies founded on a division of labor, producers specialize on their comparative advantages and exchange what they produce for what they want from among the produced goods of others. Even if intermediaries become necessary, one may argue, the price system alone would allocate goods and services without the necessity of companies arising. In a classic paper, Ronald COASE provided an answer to this question by showing that markets are costly to use. Allocation by the price system alone implies costs of searching for appropriate suppliers, and subsequently costs of negotiating and concluding a separate contract for each exchange transaction.

The total cost of transacting consists not only of the cost of goods and services themselves but also of the "marketing costs" of finding and engaging buyers and vendors. Market participants may reduce what has later become known as their transaction cost by using only one contract instead of several, and by concluding longer-term contracts. This is tantamount to substituting the firm for the market, and such substitution will occur if the cost of managing and organizing is smaller than that of transacting. This applies also to the cost of inputs, where producers are faced with a "make or buy" decision, the choice of producing every input factor themselves or buying it from other, more specialized, producers on the market. Vertical integration will come about if the cost of managing the production of the input is less than the cost of transacting to buy it. Thus, Coase described the role of companies in capitalism as being "islands of conscious power in this ocean of unconscious co-operation like lumps of butter coagulating in a pail of buttermilk."

This explanation of the spontaneous origin of companies has been the starting point for much economic work toward a general theory of the firm. Several current approaches in economics and management theory such as institutional economics, transaction cost economics, principal-agent theory, evolutionary economics, and the resource-based theory of the firm have incorporated the cost-reducing and efficiency-enhancing nature of companies in a capitalist system.

BIBLIOGRAPHY. Mark Casson, *The Firm and the Market* (University of Chicago Press, 1987); Alfred D. Chandler, *Scale and Scope: The Dynamics of Industrial Capitalism* (Belknap Press, 1990); Ronald H. Coase, "The Nature of the Firm," *Economica* (v.4, 1937); Ronald H. Coase, *The Firm, the Market, and the Law* (University of Chicago Press, 1988); Richard N. Langlois and Paul L. Robertson, *Firms, Markets, and Economic Change* (Routledge, 1995); Edith T. Penrose, *The Theory of the Growth of the Firm* (Oxford University Press, 1959); Oliver E. Williamson, *The Economic Institutions of Capitalism* (Free Press, 1985); Oliver E. Williamson and Sidney G. Winter, eds., *The Nature of the Firm: Origins, Evolution, and Development* (Oxford University Press, 1993).

WOLFGANG GRASSL, PH.D.
HILLSDALE COLLEGE

comparative advantage

THE PRINCIPLE OF COMPARATIVE advantage asserts that any country can gain from trade by specializing in producing and exporting the good or GOODS that it produces relatively efficiently. This principle, expounded by David RICARDO in the early 1800s in his *Principles of Political Economy and Taxation*, is the most frequently used argument in favor of FREE TRADE.

Adam SMITH, in *The Wealth of Nations*, had in the late 1700s used the LABOR theory of value to assert the principle of absolute advantage. In a free MARKET, each good will be produced and exported by the country that can produce it using the least number of labor hours. Included in these hours are not just the labor used directly in producing the good, but also the labor hours embodied in the portion of the tools, equipment, and raw materials that is used up in the production process.

Ricardo's insight was remarkable. Even if a country was not the most efficient producer of any good, it would still be *comparatively* efficient in producing at least one good, and could still therefore gain from trade. An example shows how this works.

Suppose that in a given year England can produce a yard of cloth using 4 hours of labor and a bottle of wine using 6 hours of labor. Suppose also that Portugal can produce a yard of cloth using 2 hours of labor, and a bottle of wine using 1 hour. Portugal is clearly the most efficient producer of both cloth and wine. But let us see why England is *relatively* more efficient at producing cloth, and Portugal at producing wine, creating the possibility for them both to gain from trade.

England has two methods of getting wine: produce it using local labor, or buy it from Portugal. What is the tradeoff between wine and cloth in each method? By producing wine locally, England gets each bottle of wine at a cost of 6 hours of labor, which means that (6 hours)/(4 hours) = 1.5 fewer yards of cloth are produced, assuming full employment. So a bottle of wine "costs" 1.5 yards of cloth by this method. Now if England can instead import a bottle of wine from Portugal at a lower cost than 1.5 yards of cloth per bottle of wine, then England is better off putting its labor into cloth and importing wine from Portugal.

But is Portugal willing to sell a bottle of wine to England at a cost of less than 1.5 yards of cloth? Yes. Portugal reasons similarly: in producing a bottle of wine, it uses up 1 hour of labor, which means giving up the half yard of cloth it could have produced in that time. So the cost of a bottle of wine is half a yard of cloth. Portugal would be happy to export wine if England is willing to pay Portugal more than half a yard of cloth for a bottle of wine. And as we already know, this is so: England is happy to pay not only 0.5 yards of cloth, but any price up to 1.5 yards of cloth.

The price will therefore actually settle somewhere between 0.5 and 1.5 yards of cloth per bottle of wine, and both countries will be willing to trade. Both will be better off by doing so, because—as is not hard to show—both will be able to consume during a year a combination of wine and cloth which is larger than it could produce on its own. We say that Portugal has a comparative advantage in wine and England has a comparative advantage in cloth.

But is comparative advantage a good guide to trade policy? Is a poor country always better off adopting free trade and producing the goods in which it has a comparative advantage? Advocates of free trade tend to say yes. Critics, however, cite Alexander Hamilton's argument in favor of protecting infant industry, and point out that the United States and Britain developed under protectionist policies, only later lowering trade barriers.

After all, the comparative advantage model is a static model: it takes as given the state of a country's natural resources, technology, skills, intermediate goods and capital equipment at a moment in time, and says that opening up trade will bring gains. This may be true, but it may also be possible to achieve greater gains by deliberately changing a country's comparative advantage. In fact, once a country has opened up trade, the one-time gain due to comparative advantage is used up. From there on out, the contribution of trade to growth depends in large part on how rapidly export demand is growing for the particular good a country happens to export.

A government may seek to pursue *dynamic comparative advantage* by developing production of goods for which demand is rising rapidly. For example, as incomes rise, the demand for food tends to rise more slowly, so it is wise to shift toward producing manufactured goods, such as electronic equipment for which demand is growing. Credit can be subsidized to targeted sectors, policies can be designed aimed at acquiring new technology cheaply, and infant industry can be protected, as JAPAN, South KOREA, and TAIWAN did with great success in the 1970s and 1980s.

BIBLIOGRAPHY. Richard E. Caves, Jeffrey A. Frankel and Ronald W. Jones, *World Trade and Payments* (Addison-Wesley, 2002); David Ricardo, *Principles of Political Economy and Taxation* (Dent, 1973); Graham Dunkley, *The Free Trade Adventure* (Zed, 1997).

MEHRENE LARUDEE, PH.D.
UNIVERSITY OF KANSAS

competition

PROPONENTS OF CAPITALISM often seem to go against common sense. They maintain that left entirely to their own devices, profit-maximizing businesses will charge reasonable prices to consumers, maintain product quality, pay workers according to their productivity, and constantly strive to do even better. But if business only cares about the bottom line, why not charge consumers exorbitant prices for junk, and pay all workers their bare subsistence?

The answer is competition. A business that gives consumers a bad deal soon has no consumers left. They take their patronage elsewhere. An employer who pays productive workers less than they are worth faces the same dilemma. A rival employer will "steal" these workers by offering them a raise. Why bother to maintain product quality? Because cutting corners is penny-wise, pound-foolish: You save on production costs, but sacrifice your firm's reputation.

Once you look at the economy through the lens of competition, the whole picture changes. To the untrained eye, greedy businesses "take advantage" of consumers and workers. Due to competition, however, the road to profit is lined with good intentions: To succeed, you must give your customers and employees a better deal than anyone else.

It is easiest to see the impact of competition in markets with thousands of small firms. Economists call this "perfect competition." The wheat market is a classic example. If one farmer charged more than the prevailing price, all his customers would switch to one of the thousands of alternative suppliers. Under perfect competition, firms produce until the product price equals the marginal cost of production. Moreover, competition ensures that firms produce at the minimum average cost in the long run. Any firm with higher costs will be undercut. It is an elementary economic theorem that perfect competition's triple equality of price, marginal cost, and average cost maximizes society's gains to trade; it is, in economists' jargon, "fully efficient."

This conclusion is easily misinterpreted. It does not mean that *only* perfect competition is fully efficient. Perfect competition is a sufficient condition for efficiency, not a necessary one. It is important to bear this in mind because in most industries, perfect competition will not naturally arise, and would be disastrous to impose. Perfect competition normally exists only if the minimum efficient scale—the smallest quantity a firm can produce at the minimum average cost—is small relative to industry demand. If minimum efficient scale is large relative to industry demand, in contrast, only a few firms can survive; a small firm would have enormous average costs and be undercut by larger rivals.

Fortunately, it is entirely possible for market performance to be as good with few firms as with many. Indeed, two genuine competitors may be enough. Imagine that two firms with identical and constant marginal costs supply the same product. The firm with the lower price wins the whole market; if they offer the same price, each gets half. Competition still induces each firm to price at marginal cost. Why? If the firms initially ask for $1.00 above marginal cost, each firm could steal all of its competitor's business by cutting its price by one penny. Like an auction, price slashing continues until price and marginal cost are equal.

What if the minimum efficient scale is so large that only one firm can survive? Surely competition breaks down? Not necessarily. As long as there is potential competition, a single firm may act like a perfect competitor. As long as other equally able firms would enter the market if it became profitable, the incumbent firm cannot raise prices above the competitive level. Note, though, that in this case competition drives price down to average cost, but not marginal cost. Given fixed costs, a firm that sets price equal to marginal cost would lose money.

Illegal competition. When does competition not work? The simplest and most empirically relevant answer is when a government makes competition illegal. In agriculture, governments have long strived to hold prices above the free-market level. The sector would be perfectly competitive in the absence of REGULATION, but many deem this outcome politically intolerable. Restrictions on international trade, such as tariffs, have the same effect for domestic firms. Licensing and related regulations have kept prices above free-market levels in airlines, trucking, railroads, and other industries.

The intensity of government restrictions on competition varies. In the post–WORLD WAR II era, restrictions were especially draconian in the Third World. Under the rubric of "import substitution industrialization," many less-developed nations cut themselves off from world markets with strict TARIFFS and QUOTAS. Internal policy allowed handpicked firms to receive strict monopoly privileges. Such policies are in retreat, but remain a heavy burden for developing countries.

Public opinion and ANTITRUST laws tend to overlook monopolies created by the government. Instead, they focus on firms' alleged ability to hold prices above average costs even though it is perfectly legal to compete against them. There is a simple, common, and relatively harmless way to achieve this: be the best. If the lowest-cost firm can produce shoes for $10 per pair, and the second-lowest requires $12, then the former can safely charge $1.99 more than its own marginal cost. While this is not perfectly efficient, the problem is mild. Indeed, punishing industry leaders for being the best ultimately hurts consumers by reducing firms' incentive to leapfrog over the current industry leader.

There are two other commonly cited paths to free-market monopoly: collusion and predation. The idea of collusion is that the firms in an industry stop competing with each other. This might be achieved through merger or monopoly, a formal cartel arrangement, or an informal "gentlemen's agreement." Under U.S. antitrust laws, these are all either illegal or heavily regulated.

When it was legal, collusion was still easier said than done. Even if the number of firms is small, it is hard to get all of them to sign a CARTEL agreement, and even harder to actually honor it. As the number of firms rises, the creation of viable voluntary cartels soon becomes practically impossible. Regardless of industry concentration, though, the most fundamental check on collusion is new entry. Once all of the firms currently in the industry raise prices, what happens when outsiders notice their inordinately high profits? Existing firms could invite them to join the cartel, but then the cartel has to share its monopoly profits with anyone and everyone. But if new firms are not admitted, they will undercut the cartel and ruin the arrangement.

What about predation? The idea is to condition your price on the behavior of other firms. You threaten to give the product away until you are the only firm left; once consumers have no other choice, you raise prices to recoup your initial losses. But predation, even more than

collusion, is easier said than done, and there are few good examples even before the existence of ANTITRUST laws. The hitch is that the predator loses far more money than the prey. If the predator begins with a 90 percent market share, it loses at least $9 for every $1 than its rivals lose. It is not enough for the predator to have slightly "deeper pockets" to outlast the prey; in this example, their pockets need to be at least nine times as deep. Other factors amplify the predator's troubles: Rivals can temporarily shut down; consumers may stock up when prices are low, making it hard to recoup the losses; successful predators may attract the attention of large-scale entrants with even deeper pockets than their own.

In sum, competition is a robust mechanism for reconciling individual greed and the public welfare. The key is not the number of firms in a given industry, but whether competition is legally permissible. More firms may reduce the probability of collusion, but that is unlikely to happen anyway. "Trust-busting" and other artificial efforts to reduce concentration tend to backfire. Industries are concentrated because the minimum efficient scale is large. Nevertheless, many economists believe governments can do much to strengthen competition: They can repeal the panoply of policies designed to curtail it.

[Editor's Note: Most mainstream economists seem to be of the view that at least a few, not just one or two firms in the market, are necessary for competition to function effectively. This view is supported by significant statistical evidence. Hence, the justification for the trust-busting role of the government, in addition to the need for government intervention in cases of market failure occasioned by EXTERNALITIES, public goods, concerns of equity, etc.]

BIBLIOGRAPHY. William Baumol, "Contestable Markets: An Uprising in the Theory of Industry Structure," *American Economic Review* (1982); Robert Bork, *The Antitrust Paradox: A Policy At War With Itself* (Basic Books, 1978); Harold Demsetz, "Barriers to Entry" *American Economic Review* (1982); David Friedman, *The Machinery of Freedom: Guide to a Radical Capitalism* (Open Court, 1979); Murray Rothbard, *Power and Market: Government and the Economy* (Sheed Andrews and McMeel, 1977); Jean Tirole, *The Theory of Industrial Organization* (MIT Press, 1988).

BRYAN CAPLAN
GEORGE MASON UNIVERSITY

competitive economics

THE ROLE OF COMPETITION in economics is vital toward understanding the entire process of production and the evolution of society. COMPETITION is the force that ensures progress and growth. The Malthusian theory of population growth is fueled by competition as much as evolution is determined by natural selection. It is competition that is responsible for this push forward in market economies. Yet the idea of competition in economics has always been controversial and often misleading. The idea of perfect competition, for instance, is wrought with such logic that it is virtually unrealistic in most respects. But the idea of realism is another story. Nonetheless, perfect competition has served as a useful tool of analysis, almost so much so that it drew economists, perhaps unwittingly, into seeing it as *the model* of competition even so far as to exclude dynamic rivalry among economic agents. This is the problem with neoclassical forms of theories, their neglect of time as an element.

The concept of competition in economics is as crucial as that of opportunity cost. Competition is a fact of life central in capitalist or market economies. Without competition markets would not exist. Competition takes place on many levels of economic society, that between persons within a firm, among firms, groups of firms, etc. Competition also takes place on other aspects of life other than what would think of as economic such as in card or board games, sports, video games, etc. and indeed may take place within an individual as a struggle within a person's conscience or psyche (Macbeth, for example). In biology, competition takes place among the individuals of a species, between species, etc. Quite simply, competition is an unavoidable fundamental fact of life. There are several conceptions of competition including the classical, neoclassical, Austrian, Marxian, and Darwinian theories in economics.

The classical theory gained a foothold in Adam SMITH's economics and would be practically unchanged in its basic format until the end of the 19th century (although writers such as Antoine Cournot were already discussing other forms of competition in the first half of the 19th century). Smith saw competition among firms as one firm's striving to obtain scarce resources, then competing with one another in selling its outputs. Smith did not, as some later economists would assert, conceive of competition as either perfect or as a general equilibrium.

The writer to whom the notion of perfect competition may be attributed is Cournot. He used mathematics to study what we call today market structure. Cournot is famous for his theory of OLIGOPOLY, especially that of a duopoly. While Cournot did define monopoly and how a monopoly prices—use analysis took marginal costs explicitly into account—he also discussed the effect that the number of firms had on price (and how the number would come to be one of the defining characteristics of market structure and competition). Cournot's

influence on British economists would have to wait until Alfred MARSHALL's *Principles* in 1890.

Perfect competition is the theoretical base from which all neoclassical theories of competition stem. Cournot's analysis uses the basic definition of profit as revenue minus cost. By applying calculus one arrives at the first order condition for profit maximization, namely marginal cost equals marginal revenue. As the number firms grows larger, price approaches marginal cost. In another mathematical treatment, F.Y. Edgeworth defined the condition for competitive equilibrium, and his analysis also depended on the number of competitors in the market. Number of firms in the market would be the defining characteristic of neoclassical competition theory.

The crowning achievement, or rather most elegant and comprehensive—at least to that date—of perfect competition appeared in Frank KNIGHT's (1921) *Risk, Uncertainty and Profit*. Knight clearly outlined all the textbook assumptions necessary for perfect competition. The assumptions include perfect knowledge, free mobility of resources, large number of firms, a homogeneous product, and free entry and exit. These rather restrictive assumptions meant that no real world industry would fit the mold.

The Austrian concept of competition concentrates on the rivalry aspect and almost wholly excludes any notion of perfect competition. Perfect competition in the Austrian version is used solely as a benchmark. Austrian economists are concerned with processes in real time. Equilibrium is a useful idea as a benchmark, but not as a description of real world competition. Especially unacceptable is the assumption of perfect knowledge. As Friedrich von HAYEK (1945) was to make clear, knowledge is costly, and depends on place and time. To assume prefect knowledge is negate any notion of competition in real time.

The Schumpeterian (Joseph SCHUMPETER) concept of competition, while associated with the AUSTRIAN SCHOOL, gives center stage to the entrepreneur as a disequilibrating cause in economic development. The entrepreneur is a driving force in competition, at least at the industry level. The entrepreneur initiates, and keeps the engine of change and competition in perpetual motion. The entrepreneur introduces new techniques, products, markets, etc. and carries out innovation. In biological evolution, this is the role played by mutations in natural selection. While Schumpeter, however, might deny any strong analogy between economic and biological evolution, he did provide the analytical framework for a theory of economic evolution.

Hayek contributed one of the more important Austrian tenets in the economics of competition. Competition according to Hayek is very much a matter of place and time. Knowledge is the key to understanding competition among the many agents in the economic world. As Hayek put it, "The economic problem of society is mainly one of rapid adaptation to changes in the particular circumstances of time and place, it would seem to follow that the ultimate decisions must be left to the people who are familiar with these circumstances, who know directly of the relevant changes and of the resources immediately available to meet them." Hayek would adopt the invisible hand paradigm in the guise of what he called spontaneous order.

The invisible hand is an organizer of economic activity and promoter of competition that brings about socially desirable results. The competition among individuals, firms, etc, produces goods that are desired by consumers and at the lowest cost. None of the agents involved intends these results but because of competition, these results are obtained. The invisible hand is similar to an organizing force whereby the actions of millions of individuals in competition with one another brings about socially desirable consequences none had intended.

Darwinian competitive economics. The natural selection metaphor in economics came into the forefront with Armen Alchian's (1950) seminal contribution. His idea was simply to apply Darwinian natural selection to competition among firms. Firms are selected on the basis of the rules they put into operation and the actions they take based on these rules. The firms that use the better rules are selected in competitive environment. Those that do not, do not survive. It does not matter whether these firms know what rules are best; it is simply a matter of outcome as the firms adopting the best rules will be the profit maximizers. Alchian's theory neglects any role of intention. It does not matter about purposeful behavior, just as in Darwinian selection; teleology plays no role.

The fact that intentions were downplayed in Alchian's theory led to a debate among economists about the acceptability of the natural selection paradigm in competitive economics. Alchian's selection process can be criticized on many levels, not least is that it is a one-step process instead of a cumulative process. The debate brought to light the all-important second part of the cumulative process, retention of the better rules. Firms, like organisms that are selected must have memory—genes, of course, play this role in natural selection.

Milton FRIEDMAN's celebrated essay on economic methodology undoubtedly brought the "assumptions don't matter" practice into competition theory—the unrealistic assumptions of perfect competition do not matter so long as the results of the theory are accurately predictive of behavior among firms in the real world. The important result in Friedman's theory is that firms act "as if" they are maximizing.

Competition in economics has almost always been, even since the day of Smith, bound up in efficiency. Perfect competition again comes into play as the standard market structure by which all others are judged. In perfect competition, economic welfare is maximized (notwithstanding a rigorous explanation and proof of competitive equilibrium). Resources are allocated to their highest and best uses, and in the product markets, price is equal to marginal cost. With PARETO OPTIMALITY efficiency, it is impossible to improve upon this competitive equilibrium. Monopoly—one price monopoly that is— would then give the furthest deviance from perfect competition and therefore bring about the largest welfare loss.

BIBLIOGRAPHY. A.A. Alchian, "Uncertainty, Evolution and Economic Theory," *Journal of Political Economy* (1950); A.A. Cournot, *Research into the Mathematical Principles of the Theory of Wealth* (Macmillan, 1838); M. Friedman, *Essays in Positive Economics* (University of Chicago Press, 1953); F.A. Hayek, "The Use of Knowledge in Society," *American Economic Review* (1945); F. Knight, *Risk, Uncertainty and Profit* (Houghton, Mifflin, 1921); P. McNulty, "A Note on the History of Perfect Competition," *Journal of Political Economy* (1967); A. Marshall, *Principles of Economics* (Macmillan, 1890); J.A. Schumpeter, *The Theory of Economic Development* (Harvard University Press, 1934).

ZELJAN SCHUSTER, PH.D.
UNIVERSITY OF NEW HAVEN

computer

A COMPUTER IS A DEVICE that takes data (input), processes it, and returns information (output) to the user. The development of computer technology has vastly increased worker productivity and opened up new opportunities for business.

Computers consist of hardware, which includes all the physical parts of the computer, and software, which includes all instructions that tell the computer how to operate. Hardware includes items such as computer chips, disk drives, modems, monitors, and cooling fans. Software consists of programs, which are sets of instructions written by human beings in specialized programming languages. The programming-language text of a program is called source code.

Though the details of computer technology are complex, the essential idea is simple: the on-off switch. All modern computers are essentially elaborations of this one simple idea. Computers contain billions of microscopic on-off switches in the electronic chips that serve as their brains and memories.

Any simple on-off switch, such as a light switch or a car ignition, can represent information by being on or off. The state of the switch, on or off, gives an instruction to a room light or to your car that it should be on or off. When you put millions or billions of on-off switches in sequence, the sequences can represent more complex information in what is called binary code. In computer binary code, each on-off switch is called a bit (for "binary digit"). Eight bits, which can represent a letter or number, are called a byte.

All modern computer programs work by using the computer's brain, called its processor or central processing unit (CPU), to read and manipulate bytes of data in the computer's memory, called either read-only memory (ROM) or random-access memory (RAM). The computer then sends the processed information to another device, such as a disk drive for storage, a monitor for viewing, a printer for printing, or a modem for sending to another computer over the internet.

Early computers. The earliest computer bearing any resemblance to modern computers was the "difference engine," conceived and partially built by British mathematician Charles Babbage in 1822. Another early computer was the slide rule, invented by Edmund Gunter in 1623 and used for mathematical calculations (including those for the first American moon landings) until Hewlett-Packard introduced the first personal-sized electronic calculators in 1972.

During WORLD WAR II, the first computers able to re-use software ("stored-program" computers) were developed in the U.S. Navy by Lt. (later Admiral) Grace Murray Hopper and at the University of Pennsylvania under John Mauchly. In these early non-electronic computers, software was programmed by manually setting mechanical switches inside the computer. The term "bug," meaning a software malfunction, was coined by Hopper

The advent of the computer has vastly increased worker productivity in almost all facets of the U.S. economy.

when she tested a prototype computer on a ship at sea. When her program failed to work, she opened the case and found a moth wedged between two switches: the first computer bug.

Hopper's and Mauchly's efforts came to fruition in 1946 with the development of ENIAC, the closest ancestor of modern computers.

Hopper and Mauchly were later involved in the development of programming languages such as Fortran (Formula Translating Language) and Cobol (Common Business-Oriented Language). Other programming languages developed in the coming years were Pascal, Basic, C, C++, and specialty languages such as Jovial and Lisp.

Business computers. The first commercial computer was the BINAC, built by computer pioneers J. Presper Eckert and John Mauchly, who formed their own company to build business computers. Their company was bought by Remington Rand, under which they developed UNIVAC, the first general-purpose business computer. Another early business computer was the Lyons Electronic Office, built in 1951 by the Lyons Tea Co. in England.

International Business Machines (IBM) started in 1884 as the Hollerith Tabulating Machine Co. and built its first stored-program computer in 1948. In the 1960s, IBM's System 360/370 computers—called "mainframes" because of their enormous size—dominated the computer industry.

During the 1960s, software was developed by the computer manufacturers and was sold with their hardware. An ANTITRUST decision in 1969 forced IBM to unbundle software from hardware and sell it separately: that was the beginning of the software industry. Even then, most specific-purpose software ("application software") was developed by users who traded it for programs developed by other users. The process was facilitated by a small but important firm, International Computer Programs (ICP), which published catalogs of software available for trade or purchase.

Personal computing. The first personal computer was the Altair 8800, introduced in 1975 and sold via mail-order to hobbyists who assembled the computer themselves. At about the same time, Xerox's Palo Alto Research Center was developing a personal computer called the Xerox Star, with an icon-based screen display that would later inspire the Apple Macintosh, IBM's OS/2, and Microsoft Windows. Also in 1975, Microsoft co-founder Bill GATES dropped out of Harvard to develop an Altair 8800 version of the Basic programming language, which was Microsoft Corp.'s first product. In 1976, Dan Bricklin and Bob Frankston, students at Harvard and MIT respectively, developed VisiCalc, the first spreadsheet program for personal computers.

Personal computers became widely popular with the 1978 introduction of the Apple II, which many users bought to run VisiCalc. The Apple II was the first personal computer to be used mainly by non-hobbyists. In 1981, Apple introduced the Lisa, a $10,000 model whose icon-based screen and "mouse" pointing device were inspired by the Xerox Star and, in turn, inspired later icon-based systems. Also that year, IBM introduced the IBM PC, with the same 8088 processor as the Altair 8088, 64K of RAM, and one diskette drive.

Apple and IBM approached the personal computer market in dramatically different ways. Apple believed that personal computers were the wave of the future and, thus, chose to keep tight ownership and control of its technology. IBM, however, regarded personal computers as unimportant compared to sales of its hugely profitable mainframe computers. IBM expected that demand for PCs would be about 50,000 per year and that it would be a low-profit item. Thus, IBM designed its PC with off-the-shelf parts and a non-proprietary architecture that anyone could copy. The eventual result was that "IBM-compatible" PCs from non-IBM manufacturers became cheaper and more popular than Apple computers.

For the PC operating system, IBM first went to Digital Research Inc. in California, whose CP/M operating system ran most non-Apple personal computers. However, industry legend has it that Gary Kildall, Digital Research's CEO, kept the IBM executives waiting until they left in a huff. They then went to Bellevue, Washington, and hired Microsoft to do the job. Microsoft, in turn, went to Seattle Computer Products, which had developed an operating system called Q-DOS (Quick and Dirty Operating System). Microsoft bought Q-DOS and modified it to create the first version of PC-DOS.

In the 1980s, personal computers became more powerful and began to eclipse the older "big iron" mainframes. In 1983, Apple introduced the Macintosh, a smaller, cheaper version of the Lisa, with the same mouse and icon-based screen interface. A year later, Microsoft began development of Microsoft Windows, early versions of which were too slow and crash-prone to be useful. Windows awaited the development of more powerful personal computers to become popular.

PC software continued to be the main reason for buying PCs. VisiCalc was a top seller until 1984, when it was crushed by Lotus 1-2-3, the dominant PC spreadsheet program of the 1980s. VisiCalc's revenues plummeted from $40 million in 1983, before the introduction of Lotus 1-2-3, to a paltry $600,000 in 1984 after Lotus 1-2-3.

WordStar, WordPerfect, and a distant also-ran called Microsoft Word were the most popular word PC processing programs. Ashton-Tate's dBASE was the most popular database program, along with runners-up such as R:Base, Paradox, and various "dBASE-compatible" programs such as Clipper and dBXL.

Meanwhile, IBM belatedly realized the importance of the PC market and extended its alliance with Microsoft to develop a Macintosh-like operating system for the PC. The operating system, OS/2, would be jointly marketed by IBM and Microsoft.

After OS/2's introduction in 1987, Microsoft urged other software firms to focus their development efforts on moving their programs to OS/2. At the same time, Microsoft continued to develop Windows, which would in the 1990s displace both PC-DOS and OS/2 in the marketplace. Other software vendors later complained that Microsoft, which lacked a single number-one application software product under PC-DOS, dominated every category in the 1990s via its control of Microsoft Windows.

Partly as a reaction against Microsoft's heavy-handed tactics, the late 1990s saw the development of "open source" software, freely distributed programs whose program code was open for inspection and improvement by users. Also in the 1990s, the U.S. government filed an antitrust suit against Microsoft, alleging abuse of its Windows monopoly. Early in the George W. BUSH administration, however, the government settled the suit on terms favorable to Microsoft.

The internet. Developed in the late 1960s by the Defense Advanced Research Projects Agency (DARPA), the internet was originally designed as a communication tool for the Defense Department. By the 1980s, however, people in universities and business were using the internet as well. Outside those contexts, individuals could also get limited internet access by purchasing accounts on Compuserve, GEnie, and other online services, as well as email-only accounts from firms such as MCI Mail.

For individuals, full internet access was hard to get and harder to use. It required knowledge of both internet commands and the Unix operating system, which ran on most computers connected to the internet. For those reasons, home users seldom wanted full internet access, though firms such as Delphi sold subscriptions for a fee.

That picture changed in 1993 with the development of the World Wide Web, a graphic, icon-based interface that made it unnecessary to learn complex commands to use the Internet. Both businesses and individuals suddenly found it easy to access computers on the other side of the world—to get information, coordinate business activities, or to make purchases. The World Wide Web has been credited with creating a "new economy" of permanently higher productivity in the 1990s. Though enthusiasm for the Web led to unrealistic hopes that were deflated in the recession of

2001–03, the Web and personal computing will continue to influence economies and nations for the foreseeable future.

BIBLIOGRAPHY. Dieter von Jezierski, *Slide Rules: A Journey Through Three Centuries* (Astragal Press, 2000); Scott McCartney, *ENIAC: The Triumphs and Tragedies of the World's First Computer* (Walker & Co., 1991); Paul E. Ceruzzi, *A History of Modern Computing* (MIT Press, 2000); Louis V. Gerstner, *Who Says Elephants Can't Dance? Inside IBM's Historic Turnaround* (HarperBusiness, 2002); Tim Berners-Lee et al., *Weaving the Web: The Original Design and Ultimate Destiny of the World Wide Web* (HarperBusiness, 2000).

SCOTT PALMER, PH.D.
RGMS ECONOMICS

Conference of Montréal

THE CONFERENCE OF MONTRÉAL is an annual forum of the Americas on the international economy that has met in Montréal, Québec, CANADA, each spring since its founding in 1994.

The Conference of Montréal brings together members of the international business community, public sector, universities, international institutions, and civil society. It focuses on issues of GLOBALIZATION and has sought to bring new ideas and understanding on such themes as innovation in an uncertain world; creating a hemispheric free-trade zone encompassing all countries in the Americas; how to do business with Africa and the Middle East; and how to do business with the EUROPEAN UNION (EU). Its speakers have included heads of state and leaders of international organizations such as the Inter-American Development Bank, the Organization for Economic Cooperation and Development, the North Atlantic Treaty Organization, and Doctors without Borders.

The Conference was founded in 1994 by Gil Remillard, who was then the Québec Minister of Justice and Minister of State for Canadian Intergovernmental Affairs. Remillard organized the Conference under the auspices of the Institut international d'études administratives de Montréal, with the support of the governments of Canada and the province of Québec.

The themes of the 1999 Conference, economic integration, free trade, cultural nationalism and the enormous disparities in wealth and income, inspired a PBS documentary "The Americas in the 21st Century" that was aired in both the UNITED STATES and Latin America. The 2000 Conference addressed issues confronted by Western companies and governments doing business with Africa and the Middle East. The 2001 Conference focused primarily on Western hemispheric economic integration. In 2002 and 2003, Conference themes included the effects of globalization and economic development on international security, public health, agriculture, the environment, small business, and corporate governance.

In November 2002, the Conference formed a partnership with the Organization for Economic Cooperation and Development (OECD), an international organization based in Paris, France, which holds a similar forum. The OECD Forum began in 1999 and gave business leaders, labor leaders and other members of civil society the opportunity to discuss important economic issues with government ministers and members of international organizations. The two organizations now cooperate in the organization of their international forums. They work together on program development, identification of speakers and issues, and promoting the visibility of both forums.

The Conference of Montréal has not gone unnoticed by opponents of globalization who view the conference as an additional hobnobbing opportunity for the transnational financial elite. Protests of the conference have been staged by such organizations as "Collectif d'actions non-violentes autonomes" and various progressive and anarchist networks.

BIBLIOGRAPHY. www.conferencedemontreal.com; www.montreal.indymedia.org.

LINDA DYNAN, PH.D.
INDEPENDENT SCHOLAR

conglomerate

A CONGLOMERATE IS A FORM of combining companies in unrelated businesses. Companies can gain MARKET power through internal growth. However, merging with other companies is a much faster and more effective way to gain market power. Usually, large corporations spread beyond a single market. Multi-markets operation is a strategy for growth. These firms typically spread by conglomerate diversification as well as vertical integration (operating at different stages of production) and multinational operation.

In a conglomerate merger an automaker might buy a financial institution. Conglomerate mergers raise two main concerns. First, concentration of assets in the top companies has grown substantially. The data show that the share of the top 200 has almost doubled since 1910. This trend has concerned many economists, policymakers and the FEDERAL TRADE COMMISSION (FTC) as the giant corporations might "ultimately take over the country." However, in many instances of conglomerate mergers the effective competition has risen. When Du Pont purchased Conoco (an OIL company), or when Philip Morris (a cigarette company) bought General Foods, despite the fact that the concentration of assets increased, the degree of competition in the related industries seemed to rise. In addition, the data do not account for foreign competition.

The second objection to conglomerate mergers concerns the economic validity of the mergers. Many ask what does meatpacking have to do with airplane business or typewriters with birth-control pills? Recent merger of news organization with companies remotely related to journalism which have profit interests in aviation, financial services, hazardous waste materials and nuclear power, has become the subject of a great deal of debate. Many observers have expressed concern about the effect of these mergers on freedom of press.

Conglomerates are more likely to wage a predatory price war against specialist firms, or may refrain from competing vigorously with their allies, entering into tacit collusion to respect each other's sphere of influence, or promote their sale of products through reciprocal purchase of their customers' products. In actual merger cases predatory pricing and reciprocal dealing have been attacked. Three main varieties of conglomerate mergers are market extension mergers, product line extension mergers, and "pure" conglomerate mergers, which have no link with prior operations. All three types have been challenged under the Celler-Kefauver Act. One of the major objections to conglomerate mergers has been that such mergers can eliminate or reduce potential competition. This precedent was established in a case against Pacific Northwest Pipeline Corporation (1964). The principle of potential competition has been applied in many cases.

Another major challenge to conglomerate mergers was in cases of Reynolds Metal Company (1962). Reynolds was the nation's leading aluminum foil producer. The Federal Trade Commission raised the concern about the ability of the company to practice predatory pricing to drive out a small independent firm specialized in florist foil wrapping paper—the power of the "deep pocket." This view was also applied in the case against Procter & Gamble's acquisition of the Clorox Company.

Reciprocal purchase arrangements and its effect on potential competition was raised in another leading case concerning the Gentry, Inc. a specialist in manufacturing of dehydrated onion and garlic, owned by Consolidated Foods Corporation (1965). The record shows that the company brought reciprocal buying pressures on its suppliers, especially those making soup and related products that had the Consolidated Foods' brand name for distribution. Gentry's market share in onion and garlic rose from 32–35 percent in the next ten years. The Supreme Court ordered the firm to divest and separate itself from Gentry. This basis of their decision was the probable effect of the merger in the future.

In the case of conglomerate mergers, the courts have taken prospective cost savings into account. In the case of the Procter & Gamble (1967), the Supreme Court's view was that it could actually harm competition. The cost saving in that case was expected to be in adverting, which could have been used to deter potential entry.

The 1968 Merger Guidelines view was concerned with market structure and preservation of competition. It stated that "within the over-all schemes of the Department's antitrust enforcement activities, the primary role of the Section 7 of the Clayton Act enforcement is to preserve and promote market structures conducive to competition." Market structure was the focus of the guidelines because the individual firms tend to be controlled by the structure in their markets, principally the number of firms in their industry. Usually, when a few firms account for a large share of the market, the barriers to entry are high, price competition is discouraged; inefficient methods of production or excessive promotional advertising are commonly found.

At the time, the Department of Justice regarded two categories of conglomerate mergers as having "sufficiently identifiable anticompetitive effects . . ." They were mainly concerned with two types of mergers: mergers involving firms that could enter the market on their own; and mergers with potential for favoring a major customer over others.

The decade of 1980s brought a new chapter in American antitrust policy. The dismissal of the case against IBM and the revision of the guidelines was the beginning of a new chapter in regulation of business. The emphasis shifted to efficiency: "If big is efficient, big is good."

Globalization of the world's economy has led to a concerted effort to coordinate laws governing competition. Currently, the rules of competition are determined by more than 100 national and regional governments. The Department of Justice and the European Union Commission for Competition are collaborating to develop standards for multi-jurisdictional coordination of their laws for competition and their enforcement.

BIBLIOGRAPHY. Columbia Journalism Forum, "The Real Dangers of Conglomerate Control," *Columbia Journalism Review* (March-April 1997); Charles A. James, *Antitrust in the Early 21st Century: Core Values and Convergence* (Department of Justice, 2002); Douglas E. Geer, *Industrial Organization and Policy* (Macmillan, 1991); F.M. Scherer, *Industrial Market Structure and Economic Performance* (Rand McNally,

1970); Paul A. Samuelson and William D. Nordhaus, *Microeconomics* (McGraw-Hill, 2000); 1968 Merger Guidelines (Department of Justice, 1968).

SIMIN MOZAYENI, PH.D.
STATE UNIVERSITY OF NEW YORK, NEW PALTZ

conservatism

A SYSTEM OF THOUGHT, conservatism has a philosophical core that centers upon upholding traditional values, social arrangements, government, and economic structures. Conservatives have, over the past few centuries, held varying opinions about the role of government in the economy and the value of democracy. Conservatives have been linked by a suspicion of change in a modernizing world and the urge to preserve traditional institutions.

Historians typically find the origins of conservatism during the 17th and 18th centuries in Europe and America. The 17th-century philosopher Thomas Hobbes, author of *Leviathan*, argued that government is necessary to provide order that is typically lacking among humans subject to the consequences of original sin. For Hobbes, "all men in the state of nature have a desire and will to hurt" because they are all seeking the same thing, which usually the strongest acquires. The solution, Hobbes believed, was that the English should "confer all their power and strength upon one man, or upon one assembly of men, onto one will: which is as much as to say, to appoint one man, or assembly of men, to bear their person."

A century later the English philosopher Edmund Burke, reacting to the astonishing changes brought about by the FRENCH REVOLUTION, sought in his writings the stability of past tradition and absolute, unchanging values. Revolution is about utter change, chaos, ideas and institutions never before seen. Burke attacked the ideological program of the French revolutionaries, who worked to destroy the hierarchy of church and state and the aristocratic belief in human inequality. Burke was shocked by the revolutionary program to create a secular state, to abandon divine providence, to substitute traditional morality with humanistic values, and to embrace modern capitalism and all of its implications. Burke feared the impact of LAISSEZ-FAIRE economics and the rejection of landed property as the traditional basis of society, economy, and government.

American conservatism. Leading conservatives in America at the time of the American and French Revolutions included John ADAMS and Alexander HAMILTON. Adams and Hamilton were leaders of the Federalist political faction that strongly advocated the adoption of the Constitution of the United States. These American conservatives were heavily influenced by the writings of Thomas Hobbes. Adams and Hamilton did not go as far as Hobbes, defending the English monarchy, but they accepted Hobbes' pessimistic assessment of human nature, and assumed that government must impose order upon its people.

They applauded the Constitution for circumscribing the liberties of the American citizen within the structure of an orderly, rational government. American conservatives feared the disruptive consequences of the AMERICAN REVOLUTION, and sought to prevent anarchy and chaos by the overwhelming influence of the "best men," the economic, social, and cultural elite. Adams, for example, believed not in an aristocracy of birth (as did Burke) but in an aristocracy of talent and merit. This "natural aristocracy" represented the very few in America who should inevitably supervise the liberties of the majority. Such was the reasoning behind the Electoral College in the American presidential election process; it would mediate the popular vote with the influence of the elite electors. Hamilton, the first secretary of state, advocated an economic program that made the federal government very influential in the credit and banking structures of the United States. He encouraged the government to promote manufacturing, international trade, policies favoring the rich, and investment in the American economy.

The forces of modernization—the INDUSTRIAL REVOLUTION, new technologies, and the emerging dominance of scientific thinking—forced conservatives during the 19th century to reassess their ideas and policies. Conservative programs of continued government involvement in the U.S. economy during the antebellum period, such as Henry Clay's American System, gave way in the post–AMERICAN CIVIL WAR era to a conservatism that embraced laissez-faire economics. Republicans advocated limited government involvement in the economy, and opposition to labor and trade unions and other reforms that would impede unlimited economic progress. They advocated economic policies that supported the wealthy, big business, and manufacturing interests, which in turn would benefit the entire economy, and all Americans, rich and poor.

The maintenance of the GOLD STANDARD, that is, a limited money supply, which supported creditors over debtors, brought opposition to the Republican administrations of, for example, William MCKINLEY, from liberal reform groups such as the Populists. Industrialists, such as Andrew CARNEGIE, spoke for the majority of conservatives in *The Gospel of Wealth*, arguing that competition dominates economic and social existence; those who compete the best also thrive the best. Social Darwinists, such as William Graham SUMNER, applied the implications of Darwin's theories of natural selection and survival of the fittest to humans: inequality is the natural state of things; the poor serve a purpose—performing the drudgery of human labor—just as the rich serve a purpose—directing the application of labor to the infrastructure of society.

20th-century conservatism. In the early part of the 20th century, American conservatives, such as Irving Babbitt and Paul Elmer More, who led an intellectual movement called the New Humanism, feared the rise of the masses, the typical American and his rude habits and uncultured jargon, and the anti-intellectualism in American life. The New Humanists believed modern society was under attack from the new ideologies of pragmatism, naturalism, behaviorism, and liberalism. Babbitt, More, and other New Humanists believed in the moral presence of decorum and order existing within the human soul, which by cultivation and intuition can be accessed—but only a very few can do so. The New Humanists were not alone in responding with concern that the post–WORLD WAR I era would bring new democratic, liberal forces to the world. The "Roaring 20s" in America included a conservative reaction to the war in the forms of Prohibition, the Red Scare, the rise of religious fundamentalism, and the Republican administrations of Warren HARDING, Calvin COOLIDGE, and Herbert HOOVER.

Late 19th-century and early 20th-century American conservatives were clearly influenced by their European counterparts. In 1889, German intellectual Ferdinand Tonnies penned *Community and Association*, in which he decried the impact of modernization upon a traditional society. Artificial associations replaced the organic institutions of family and community. Close-knit society and orderly class structure were giving way to a new middle class and working class with completely different moral assumptions, economic concerns, and social habits. Max Weber, Emile Durkheim, and Auguste Comte examined past societies to question the validity of modern change upon medieval, communitarian institutions.

Conservatism after WORLD WAR II has been of two types. First, there was the intellectual conservatism of thinkers such as Russell Kirk, author of *The Conservative Mind* (1953). Kirk's brand of conservative thought was similar to that of 19th-century conservatives in his focus on absolute truth and morality, elitism, and opposition to modern relativism and secularism. Added to the postwar uncertainty was the triad of tragedies for conservatives in 1949 and 1950: the SOVIET UNION's acquisition of the atomic bomb, the fall of China to communism, and the attack of communist North KOREA against South KOREA. Anxiety about communism led to fears of espionage and the emergence of Joseph McCarthy to public attention in the United States. Many American conservatives rallied around McCarthy and his ideas of anti-communism and anti-liberalism—in short, opposition to anything that appeared un-American. Such was the mentality, liberals contend, that William Buckley promulgated in starting the *National Review* magazine in the 1950s.

The second expression of postwar conservatism has been represented by the Republican Party. Barry Goldwater, who unsuccessfully ran for president in 1964 against Lyndon B. JOHNSON, became the spokesman for a new political conservatism embracing the economic principles of laissez-faire. Goldwater, author of *The Conscience of a Conservative* (1960), argued for a vastly reduced federal government and deregulation of economic and social policies in favor of turning power over to state and local governments. Conservatives, according to Goldwater, opposed the rights of LABOR, the fight for civil rights, and government intervention into the economy. He supported individual freedoms and the sanctity of private property. He saw the federal government as having a limited role, involving itself in maintaining public order and involvement in foreign affairs. Goldwater's stance on the Cold War and the spread of communism in Europe, Asia, and Africa was that of a "hawk," believing in aggressive military and economic containment, and confronting the Soviet Union and its communist satellites with a vast superiority of nuclear weapons.

Although Goldwater lost to Johnson, his ideals found new life during the Republican administrations of Richard NIXON and Ronald REAGAN. Both Nixon and Reagan endorsed Goldwater's run for president, and both gained important influence in supporting a lost cause. Nixon rode his conservative reputation to the White House in 1968, while Reagan became a leading conservative spokesman and governor of California. As a two-term president from 1981–89, Reagan was the unquestionable leader of the conservative movement.

At the beginning of the new millennium, conservatism is still an important political philosophy focusing on government restraint, the free market, individual freedoms, sanctity of private property, and strong defense of American values both at home and abroad.

BIBLIOGRAPHY. Ronald Lora, Conservative Minds in America (Rand McNally, 1979); Allen Guttmann, The Conservative Tradition in America (Oxford University Press, 1967); John P. Diggins, Up from Communism: Conservative Odysseys in American Intellectual History (Harper & Row, 1975); David J. Hoeveler, Jr., *The New Humanism: A Critique of Modern America, 1900–1940* (University of Virginia Press, 1977); F.J.E. Woodbridge, *Hobbes Selections* (Scribner's, 1930).

RUSSELL LAWSON
BACONE COLLEGE

consumer

TO CONSIDER THE CITIZEN as a consumer is not just another way to conceive the markets as groups of individuals seen as potential users and buyers. The consumer may be seen as any person, adult or minor, who uses goods and services, but who also has to manage a personal budget as well as affording credit and debts. In the 1990s, social scientist George Ritzer, among others, has theorized about the constant temptation of consuming that seems to be stronger than ever, talking about new phenomena such as the credit-card culture and the addiction to debt that many American consumers have to face.

Is there a real need for assessing the consumer behavior knowledge? Academic literature on consumer studies has burgeoned in the last two decades. Most recent research concentrates on many topics, even though behaviorist approaches are not the only ones referred to. Relationships between producers and consumers can take many forms and are not limited to just plain transactions. One key word to understand consumption issues and consumer dynamics is influence. Consumers' decisions can be influenced in various ways (by advertising, other customers' comments and choices, statistics, a sampler, a demonstration in a store); but these buyers and users can as well influence other potential consumers in their choices and could even bias producers, retailers, and corporations with their suggestions, complaints, or even organized boycotts.

Since we consume more of a wider variety of commodities, ranging from HEALTH care to entertainment, from news to body treatments, we need to be aware of the many strategies involved in the construction of needs, fashion, commodities, images, and distinctive symbolic meanings. From time to time, consumers try new products and new brands they have heard about, but they are not necessarily satisfied with all these changes. Others hesitate, are reluctant to make the move. Whenever advertising can incite a change in the consumer's habits, there must be a reward in the new product in terms of quality, price, design or availability. But as we have all experienced at least once, it is not always the case. As Douglas Holt and Juliet Schor rightly point it, "if corporations created needs, particularly in insidious ways, they could hardly be credited for meeting them."

The American way of life. In 1950, an American retail analyst named Victor Lebow wrote the following comments about the constant need to have consumers buying and consuming more and more, in order to get a wealthy economy and prosperity; his reflexions from more than half a century ago could serve as well as a definition, or at least an elementary explanation of the consumer society: "Our enormously productive economy demands that we make consumption our way of life, that we convert the buying and use of goods into rituals, that we seek our spiritual satisfaction, our ego satisfaction, in consumption. We need things consumed, burned up, worn out, replaced, and discarded at an ever-increasing rate." But, if what is usually labeled as the American way of life first appeared in the United States, the phenomenon is not anymore limited to North America and it often seems to be a desirable standard for some populations in non-Western countries.

German philosopher Karl MARX wrote about what he called the "fetishism of the world of commodities." As Marx explains, commodities are not sold according to the real efforts asked of the workers; there is a value added to these nonessential objects because of their social meaning, but the worker who builds them isn't paid for that extra portion of the value.

In the early 1970s, French sociologist Jean Baudrillard criticized Marx's approach and theorized the concept of the consumer society, saying that in common urban spaces of the late 20th and early 21st centuries, we don't interact anymore with persons, but mainly with objects (commodities made to be consumed) and messages (such as advertisements). Steven Connor has summarized Baudrillard's thoughts: "Consumer society is not based on scarcity but on overproduction. Where there are no agreed or demonstrable needs for a product, such needs must be actively stimulated by means of advertising and marketing strategies."

Fashion dynamics and new trends in society are not spontaneous popular responses from a majority of individuals who are *en vogue*. In an article, Christopher Hackley explains that advertising agencies that build corporate images and visions related to brands and labels play a decisive role in the production of consumer culture. The case of the fashion movement created by the Sony Walkman in the early 1990s remains a clear example. It is not just that brands have to correspond to a respectable reputation, but many consumers now rely only on companies' images and reputations in their choices of what they will buy.

In his provocative book published in 1991, *Promotional Culture*, Andrew Wernick explains that promotion has become so important that most consumers only react and respond to widely advertised products or novelties, ignoring other products, ideas, concepts that are not as widely advertised. "All discourse is so saturated with the rhetorical devices of promotion that, in our public lives and perhaps increasingly in our private lives, we are unable to think and act outside of a promotional frame of reference."

The consumer culture. In modern countries, shopping centers and malls are built to be the consumer's paradise. No temperature extremes, no day or night, no time (no clocks), no problem with parking availability and limits (as opposed to downtown stores surrounded by parking meters), therefore the consumer can concentrate on browsing, choosing, and buying at his or her own rhythm. Apart from those activities, one can also do something else than going into stores or boutiques, such as eating in restaurants, or watching a movie in a multiplex. There are even small artificial indoor parks, with trees, fountains and benches, where you can sit and rest, as in any happy city. Baudrillard identifies the modern drugstore (or the new shopping malls) as the "synthesis of profusion and calculation."

According to Don Slater, "The central aspects of consumer culture—such as needs, choice, identity, status, alienation, objects, culture—have been debated within modern theories, from those of earlier thinkers such as Marx and Georg Simmel." But it would be wrong to see all consumers as blind, unconscious slaves of a system that sees them as idiots. In her article, "Consumerism and its Contradictions," Mica Nava states that "Consumers are not cultural dopes, but active, critical users of mass culture; consumption practices cannot be derived from or reduced to a mirror of production; consumer practice is far more than just economic activity: it is also about dreams and consolation, communication and confrontation, image and identity."

During the 1990s, a new kind of consumer appeared, mainly in some Anglophone countries, nicknamed the Green Consumer. For ages, there were always people (individuals and consumer groups) who were concerned with environmental problems related to massive consumption, and thus reacted in different ways: looking for natural products without artificial additives, asking for bags, boxes and packaging made from recycled materials, or avoiding clothes made with polyester and nylon. There recently has been more positive response from industry and some multinational corporations that provide alternate products conceived according to their environmental and ethical choices.

Corporations are often seen as immutable, unalterable institutions, so monolithic, powerful, and prosperous that they can just ignore those few buyers who ask for changes and exceptions. But, as John Elkington, Julie Hailes, and Joel Makower have explained in their 1988 book, *The Green Consumer*, "The marketplace is not a democracy; you don't need a majority opinion to make change." This is true for consumers who ask for more environment friendly products, or recycled packaging. The three authors argue that only 10 percent of the customers are enough to force a change or to create a new line, a new "green" product. Letters, petitions, calls to customer service are frequent ways to express opinions. Corporations can be aware of any change about customer's satisfaction. When a change occurs, the other competitors often feel they have to follow the new trend.

The consumer confidence index. Although consuming often relies on emotions and desires, there are regular data about the state of mind of American consumers. In the United States, the quantitative measure of consumer optimism toward the national economy is called the Consumer Confidence Index. Created in 1985, this indicator was arbitrarily set at 100 and is now adjusted every month according to the results of a survey of almost 5,000 U.S. households. Randomly chosen families are asked about their opinion of present and future perceptions of the economy, as well as their saving plans and their possible spending. Even though it is highly subjective and related to a current state of mind, the release of every Consumer Confidence Index has a strong influence on stock exchanges, whether it is optimistic or pessimist.

Even in our everyday lives, some of our daily work at home is now replaced by someone else's work. Some people don't buy food to be cooked by themselves anymore; they rather buy frozen cooked dinners that can be rapidly heated. Therefore, they pay somebody to cook for them. In the same way, most employees at work buy their cups of coffee instead of preparing them. As Douglas Holt and Juliet Schor explain, "less and less of daily life is produced at home; more and more of what we consume is commodified, i.e., produced for sale on the market." But even in the best of worlds, growth and prosperity do have limits. The ever-growing expansion of consuming might drive negative side effects, such as consuming addiction, indebtedness, fraud, invasion of privacy, rationalization, dehumanization, and homogenization stemming from increasing Americanization, according to Ritzer. As Zygmunt Bauman explains, "Poverty is no longer defined by unemployment but by being an 'incomplete consumer.'" One question remains: Is consuming a means to an end, or an end in itself?

BIBLIOGRAPHY. Jean Baudrillard, *The Consumer Society: Myths and Structures* (Sage Publications, 1998); Zygmunt Bauman, *Work, Consumerism and the New Poor* (Open University Press, 1998); Howard Becker, *Outsiders: Studies in the Sociology of Deviance* (The Free Press, 1963); Pierre Bourdieu, *Distinction: A Social Critique of the Judgement of Taste* (Harvard University Press, 1990); Steven Connor, "Cultural Sociology and Cultural Sciences," *The Blackwell Companion of Social Theory* (Blackwell, 2000); Paul du Gay, Stuart Hall, Linda Janes, Hugh Mackay, and Keith Negus, *Doing Cultural Studies: The Story of the Sony Walkman* (Sage Publications, 1997); Aland Durning, *How Much Is Enough?* (W.W. Norton, 1992); Douglas Holt and Juliet Schor, eds., *The Consumer Society Reader* (The New Press, 2000); Don Slater, "Consumer Culture and Modernity," *Polity* (1998); Christopher Hackley, "The Panoptic Role of Advertising Agencies in the Production of Consumer Culture," *Consumption, Markets and Culture* (v.5/3, 2002).

YVES LABERGE, PH.D.
INSTITUT QUÉBÉCOIS DES
HAUTES ÉTUDES INTERNATIONALES

consumer behavior

THE KEY QUESTIONS concerning consumer behavior are what determines it, and is it rational? Do innate personal characteristics factor into consumer behavior or does our environment alone shape it? Do consumers respond to changes in the economic environment sensibly, or do they err systematically?

As a general proposition, human behavior aims toward attaining more desired states of affairs. Rational consumers demand commodities when they recognize causal connections between the characteristics of these commodities and the increase of their well-being. Since these goods increase consumer welfare, they have value in use.

In terms of specific motivations, we need not assume anything in particular from the outset. We can assume altruistic, selfish, or malevolent motivations within the same general framework. Each consumer ranks different uses for GOODS from most to least preferred. If consumers have some quantity of a good, such as water, they will use it to satisfy their most urgent wants first. They might use water for drinking first, then washing perhaps, and after this want gets satisfied; they might use water for irrigation to raise food. As the satisfaction from drinking additional ounces of water declines relative to using water for washing or gardening, consumers will move toward these alternative uses for water.

Generally, consumers will get less satisfaction from consuming additional amounts of a good, relative to other goods. Economists call this diminishing marginal substitution. If a consumer has 200 gallons of water to use for a day, but only a few bits of food, she will value additional food more than water. Conversely, someone with 50 pounds of food for a day, but only a few ounces of water will likely place a very high value on additional water, relative to additional food. Since the marginal value that consumers get from goods changes in accordance with the relative amounts and uses that consumers have, the allocation of goods changes behavior

SCARCITY of goods implies the need for allocating goods according to alternative uses. Each consumer spends money on a good, so long as the amount of satisfaction that they expect from that good exceeds the amount of satisfaction that they expect from their next most desired good. Ideally, consumers equate the marginal utility of the last dollar spent on each good that they buy. Since water exists in great supply, consumers apply it to uses that have relatively low marginal use values. Some scarce items, like diamonds, are less essential to life than water, but have high exchange values because competition directs them to uses where they have the highest value at the margin. This connection between market prices and marginal-use values is important because it implies that consumer behavior directs market activity.

Incomes and market prices set limits on consumer behavior by prohibiting certain options. Consumers bargain over goods, given their incomes and the prices sellers offer. Consumers initially face different combinations of goods and potential prices that they can buy with their incomes. As actual prices form, consumer options narrow to combinations of different goods and actual prices that they can afford. As prices adjust, the combinations of goods that consumers can afford changes, as do the combinations of goods that consumers find most desirable

The law of demand. As the price of a good falls, money spent on a given amount of that good buys less of other goods. A lower price for a good, relative to other goods, means that consumers give up less by buying more of the cheaper good. Such a change in exchange values implies that the value in use per dollar spent on the cheaper good has increased. This is the law of demand.

We can illustrate this law by examining how changes in available supply affect price and market exchange. If wine becomes scarcer, then entrepreneurs who sell it are now in a position to charge a higher price for it. As the price of wine increases, consumers must give up larger amounts of other goods to get it. By requiring greater sacrifices for those who buy wine, market prices prompt consumers to conserve it. Since a higher price for wine increases the amount of other goods that consumers could buy for the money they spend on this good, they will substitute more of other goods for the good whose price has risen. This substitution effect is central to the law of demand. As the price of one good goes up relative to other goods, consumers will look for substitutes for it, and the demand for that good will fall.

It is important to note that the law of demand pertains primarily to the effect that changes in relative prices have on goods. Economist John HICKS distinguished between substitution and income effects of changes in prices. Reduced (increased) prices increase (reduce) the purchasing power of consumer income. Increased income usually means that people will want to buy more of all goods. There are some goods, called inferior goods, that people will buy less of when they have more income. But consumers buy more of most goods as their income increases. Since consumers can buy more goods in total after prices fall, price reductions increase the demand for most goods.

It is changes in relative prices that cause consumers to substitute cheaper goods for more expensive ones. A large income effect for an inferior good might overwhelm the substitution effect of a price change. Nevertheless, once we adjust for income effects, we find that the law of demand holds for all goods.

In a competitive market, consumers bargain with entrepreneurs until all parties involved agree to exchange prices that align their expected marginal use values. Once consumers have arrived at this point, trading will move resources to their most highly valued uses.

Since exchange values, or market prices, derive from consumer demand, factors of production (i.e., CAPITAL, LAND, and LABOR) derive their value from consumer goods. Increased demand for any particular good will increase the demand for labor and capital used in producing it. So, consumer behavior drives wage formation and other factor pricing.

Consumers and capital. Consumer behavior determines the rate and pattern of CAPITAL ACCUMULATION. All savings are really nothing more than deferred consumption. Consumers postpone some present consumption to increase their future consumption. Since they earn interest on income that they save, consumers have an incentive to postpone their consumption, according to the rate at which they discount future consumption. When consumers discount future consumption heavily, they save relatively little of their income.

Entrepreneurs borrow savings to earn profit. The interest they get charged deducts from their profits, so high interest rates (i.e., high discount rates by consumers) cause entrepreneurs to invest in smaller and shorter-term projects. Inter-temporal consumer behavior thus determines investment and the capital structure of industry. When consumers decide what to consume and when to consume it, they shape the capital structure of industry itself.

Some criticize the marginal utility approach to understanding consumer behavior for being unrealistic. Marginal value supposedly fails because it takes a static and teleological view of human nature. It ignores cultural and historical influences on behavior. It "conceives of man as a lightning calculator of pleasures and pains, who oscillates like a homogeneous globule of desire of happiness under the impulse of stimuli that shift him about the area, but leave him intact," said economist Thorstein VEBLEN. Do real consumers think and act as this theory implies?

It might seem that MARGINAL ANALYSIS indicates that consumer behavior always changes gradually. This is obviously not the way people act. Sometimes market demand shifts very suddenly. Economist Kelvin Lancaster developed an explanation for this kind of behavior. Consumers buy goods with characteristics that satisfy their wants. Goods often have several characteristics and consumers compare both the bundle of characteristics in similar goods and their prices. So, consumers may continue to buy a particular good as its price increases, but at some point, they will switch entirely to another good with a better combination of characteristics and price. Since Lancaster considered multiple elements to consumer choice, he was able to show how consumer behavior can appear disjointed but still derive from marginal valuations.

The generality of the law of demand becomes even more apparent when one considers how markets impose rationality on people who seek to act otherwise. Even if consumers try to buy more products at higher prices, the fact that prices place some options out of reach will still push consumers toward acting as if they were rational.

Factors other than price. Some consumers might emulate the actions of other consumers. Alternatively, consumers might dissimilate themselves from others. Consumers may also buy products simply to flaunt their wealth. It is certainly true that these factors sometimes affect some consumer behavior. Consumers can take multiple factors into account when making their decisions. The status element of certain goods amounts to a different type of use value to consumers, over which they will trade on relevant perceived margins. The incorporation of status into consumer motivations enriches our understanding of consumer behavior, but does not invalidate marginal concepts.

Economists typically assume that consumers behave according to innate preferences for goods. John Kenneth GALBRAITH objected to this because most consumer demands derive from the processes that produce goods, rather than from innate preferences. It is obvious that the only natural wants that emerge from within consumers are for food, shelter, and intercourse. Consumers are not born with the desires to see operas, wear designer clothes, or to hear a symphony. Galbraith concludes from this that the private wants that remain unsatisfied in society do not matter, and that we should instead devote more resources to meritorious public projects.

Economist Friedrich von HAYEK countered Galbraith's claim by pointing out that the mere fact that "processes that satisfy some wants create wants" does not imply that they are less important than public spending programs. Nearly all goods in modern society depend upon the social environment, including those which constitute mankind's greatest cultural achievements. Some of the things that consumers spend their money on might seem odd to others. Some may find opera boring or professional wrestling crude, but each has his own preferences, and the mere fact that we are not born with the want for these things does not make them unimportant. Nor does it imply that consumers cannot introspect to see how these things improve their personal well being, at the margin.

Economists at the University of Chicago and Harvard University argued over how advertising affects consumer behavior by focusing on how it affects prices. The Harvard hypothesis claimed that advertising changes consumer preferences so that demand increases, so more (less) advertising should produce higher (lower) prices. The Chicago hypothesis claimed that advertising informs consumers about alternatives in market. This means that advertising might increase demand initially by informing consumers about new products, but more (less) advertising will generally reduce (increase) prices by intensifying competition between entrepreneurs.

Some empirical studies have tended to support the Chicago hypothesis, but not in every instance. Thus, it would seem that advertising usually informs consumers, as well as influencing their behavior.

Consumer behavior sometimes changes with experience. There are some goods that we appreciate more, the more we consume them. Consumers will have an underlying preference for some activities, but will often indulge in them more over time. One explanation for this behavior is that consumer preferences might change over time. Alternatively, we might consider how changes in our abilities might change observed consumer demand. For instance, we may appreciate playing tennis more as we improve our tennis skills.

Consumers sometimes become addicted to certain products. We can think of addictive goods as goods that a consumer's current satisfaction from consuming depends upon the volume of past consumption. It might seem that prices have little effect on the demand for addictive goods, but this is not necessarily true. Permanent price increases may have little affect on the demand of current addicts. However, such price increases may deter potential addicts from experimenting with addictive products.

The full price of consumer behavior. When considering how consumers behave we must consider the full price that consumers pay for goods. Consumers pay not only in terms of the alternative goods that they could have spent their money on, but also in terms of the value of the time they spend acquiring goods. Consumers will search for alternative goods, and for prices for particular goods, up to the point where the marginal cost of time spent searching equals the expected marginal benefit from additional search. Consumers also account for risk in their consumption. If some types of consumption entail physical danger or a legal penalty, these factors add to the total price of a good.

Legal penalties against drug use, prostitution, or gambling increase the full price that consumers pay for those goods. If these penalties apply to sellers, marginal sellers will drop out of the market for these goods. This will raise the (black) market price and reduce demand. If penalties apply to consumers, they will factor this into their decisions, along with the cost of forgone consumption alternatives. Of course, these penalties do not eliminate consumer demand. Increased costs will reduce demand at the margin, and leave consumer behavior off of the margin unaffected.

One interesting aspect of this notion that full costs affect consumer behavior is the Alchian-Allen effect. Economists Armen Alchian and William Allen demonstrated that transportation costs increase the demand for high-quality goods. Since higher quality goods have a higher price, the adding of shipping costs to high quality goods lowers their relative price. If good apples cost 10 cents, average apples cost 5 cents and shipping each apple costs 5 cents, there is a difference between the relative prices of apples in the places where they are grown and the places they are shipped. Locally, the relative price is 10/5, or 4/2. Otherwise, the relative price is 15/10, or 3/2. Since shipping costs reduce the relative price of high quality goods, these goods will constitute a large portion of exported goods. It might seem to be the case that people buy expensive foreign goods in order to seem elite or superior. There is, however, a sound reason in price theory to explain why high-quality goods tend to get exported more so than others.

Economists tend to take consumer preferences as given. There are good reasons for this. Since personal consumer decisions depend upon unobservable satisfactions, we have no practical way of weighing one consumer's satisfaction against any others. Prices enable consumers to compare different alternatives, in terms of what others will trade with them. Some economists praise or object to particular types of consumer behavior. We might then consider if some particular goods are inherently meritorious or undesirable. If there are merit (or demerit) goods, then people will buy too few (too many) in efficient private markets. This implies a need for subsidies (or taxes or prohibitions) to ensure a proper level of supply in the market for these goods.

There are certainly some goods that some consumers see as meritorious or objectionable. The problem in using government intervention to alter consumer behavior, with respect to such goods, is in determining which consumer preferences are correct. Drinkers may see little or nothing wrong with alcohol. Members of temperance leagues obviously disagree. The prohibition of alcohol in the United States took place largely in response to claims that alcohol consumption is inherently undesirable.

While it may be true that alcohol consumption leads to undesirable behavior, the prohibition of alcohol (or any drug) will likely lead to the consumption of its harder form. By applying the logic of the Alchian-Allen affect, we can see that legal penalties for the sale or consumption of alcohol consumption reduce the relative price of hard liquor. If we add the costs of criminal sanctions to all alcoholic beverages, the price of expensive hard liquors will fall relative to cheaper drinks. Some may stop drinking due to prohibition, but those who do not will probably switch to harder liquor.

There is some disagreement over what determines consumer behavior. It is clearly the case that outside influences, such as prices, advertising, fads, and technology matter to consumer behavior. Some claim that consumers are born with innate preferences that derive from genetics. People have certain desires, dislikes, and fears because these traits enhance their ability to survive, as in Darwinian natural selection. Skills and culture surely enter into consumer behavior, but this does not mean that people lack innate preferences.

There is also disagreement over the rationality of consumer behavior. Some consumer behavior may seem odd to others. Though, in the strict economic sense, we sometimes have trouble making sense out of the decisions that others make, there are serious problems with forming a rational basis for directing economic activity by some means other than private consumer choice. The incentives inherent to private markets penalize error and reward learning. Consumer behavior shapes the outcomes of market processes, but the market process itself causes consumers to behave more rationally.

BIBLIOGRAPHY. Armen Alchian, *University Economics* (Wadsworth Publishing, 1971); Gary S. Becker, "Irrational Behavior and Economic Theory," *The Journal of Political Economy* (v.70/1, 1962); Gary S. Becker and Kevin M. Murphy, "A Theory of Rational Addiction," *The Journal of Political Economy* (v.96/4, 1988); Lee Benham, "The Affect of Advertising on the Price of Eyeglasses," *The Journal of Law and Economics* (v.15, 1972); Thomas E. Borcherding and Eugene Silberberg, "Shipping the Good Apples Out: The Alchian and Allen Theorem Reconsidered," *The Journal of Political Economy* (v.86/1, 1978); John Kenneth Galbraith, *The Affluent Society* (1969, Houghton Mifflin, 1998); Friedrich Hayek, "The Non Sequitur of the Dependence Effect," *Southern Journal of Economics* (v.27, 1961); Kelvin J. Lancaster, "A New Approach to Consumer Theory," *The Journal of Political Economy* (v.74/2, 1966); H. Liebenstein, "Bandwagon, Snob, and Veblen Effects in the Theory of Consumers' Demand," *The Quarterly Journal of Economics* (v.64/2, 1950); Carl Menger, *Principles of Economics* (1871, Libertarian Press, 1974); Ludwig von Mises, *Human Action: A Treatise on Economics* (1949, The Mises Institute, 1998); Thorsetin Veblen, "Why Is Economics Not an Evolutionary Science?" *The Quarterly Journal of Economics*, (v.12/4, 1898).

D.W. MacKenzie
George Mason University

contagion

THE REPUBLICAN SENATOR Dick Armey's most famous axiom in the field of political economy is "the market is rational and the government is dumb." After all, isn't it obvious that the best aggregate decisions will be reached by people taking them based on their individual knowledge and interest?

Consider the STOCK MARKET. Thousands of investors risk their money (which means they will be really careful) on shares or derivatives, after weighing whether that security is worth more than its current price, or less. After all of them sell and buy at a furious pace, we could reasonably expect the resulting price at a given moment to be close to its "real" one, in which all the "fundamental" information is included.

This is a powerful argument, and it was notably deployed by authors such as Friedrich von HAYEK in the 1930s against those arguing for a centralized economy (where Armey's "dumb government" would be charged with allocating production decisions).

But this argument of the market as an optimal price calculator takes for granted that people make up their minds in isolation, without regard for other participants in the market, and working upon the locally available information on the real value of the asset. What if buyers and sellers took very much into account what they think others think about the value of an asset? Wouldn't you buy something if you guessed other people would be desperate to buy it at some point, even if you thought it was essentially worthless? Say, first issues of (what you think is) a lousy comic, or ENRON shares in 2000. This is why the British economist John Maynard KEYNES compared finance to beauty contests once organized by newspapers, in which readers are asked to guess which girls will be voted the prettiest by the aggregate readership of the paper. So you're now trying to guess what other people are guessing all of us will guess.

But if the beauty-contest view of the market does provide an insight, serious problems arise for the central institution of capitalism. Investors could make poor and hasty judgments of what "the crowd" is bound to think of a particular event (some research in fact contends we are very poor judges of aggregate behavior). Imagine that a CEO sells stock of his own firm, and we believe that could be construed by other investors as an omen of an imminent fall in the price of those shares. Note that we ourselves might not think this is the case; we could even privately know that the CEO, say, needs cash for funding his charitable foundation, but the corporation is as healthy as ever.

No matter: we would immediately call our broker with a sell order. If many investors thought the same, and did the same, and as a consequence the price of the stock did come tumbling down, we would see it as a sure sign of the generalized mistrust of the market, and frantically shed all remaining shares like a stampeding herd. Fear is contagious. A "strong buy" would thus change to "strong sell" without any change in the fundamental situation of the underlying assets.

Take that to a country level. Suppose that a country is close to default on its INTERNATIONAL MONETARY FUND (IMF) loans, and that you own bonds of a neighboring country. You might think that the economy of this other country is sound enough to withstand without a flinch the crisis across the border. But you fear other less sanguine bondholders are bound to release theirs, and the price will accordingly decline. So you sell immediately, hoping to outdo them, they sell—hoping to outdo everyone else—and the price does go down.

All investors fear an epidemic of fear, they all sell in what is in fact an epidemic of fear, and thus a country, or an entire region of the world, is ruined. This scenario of financial contagion probably caused, at least in part, immense suffering in east Asia and Latin America in recent years, and the Great DEPRESSION of the 1930s.

Where we stand regarding the potential for contagion-based economic and financial behavior, and the social suffering associated to it, is quite relevant for a range of political choices. In terms of what the world financial institutions should be, for example, it has been argued that we need to lessen the ability of "hot money," investments and disinvestments that take place at literally lighting speed (thanks to electronic markets), to fly out of a country, and therefore for economic shocks to be catching. That could be implemented by means of a small tax, discussed in early 2003, which would kick in when shares or bonds are sold, adding some "friction" to virtual hot money.

BIBLIOGRAPHY. Franklin Allen and Douglas Gale, "Financial Contagion," *Journal of Political Economy* (v.108/1, 2000); Stijn Claessens and Kristin J. Forbes, eds., *International Financial Contagion* (MIT Press, 2001); John Duffy and Rosemarie Nagel, "On the robustness of behavior in experimental 'beauty contest' games," *Economic Journal* (v.107/445, 1997); J.M. Keynes, *The General Theory of Employment, Interest and Money* (Prometheus Books, 1997).

EMILIO LUQUE, PH.D.
UNED UNIVERSITY, SPAIN

contract

CONTRACTS ARE AGREEMENTS between two parties whereby each of them gives up something to the other, in return for receiving something from the first person. Perhaps the best pictorial image of a contract ever depicted was that old Norman Rockwell picture featuring two delivery men eating a pie holding a bottle of milk; in the background are shown two trucks: one for milk and one for pies. What happened before this scenario took place? Obviously, the pie man swapped one of his products for that of the milkman.

Contracts of this sort, and this is the paradigm case, are guarantors of mutual benefits to both parties, at least in the *ex ante* sense of expectations. Before this contract was consummated, the pie man was probably saying to himself something like, "Here I sit with hundreds of pies, and not a drop of milk to drink." We know, also, that the milkman valued the pie he received more than the milk he had to give up. They both gained from this exchange; we can infer this since they agreed to swap. It must be that each of them preferred what he received to what he gave up, otherwise they would scarcely have agreed to the exchange.

On the other hand speculation about motives is always risky. Who knows; the milkman might have hated pies, and only entered into this contract in order to curry favor with the pie man. Maybe he wanted to date his daughter. We cannot know his motive; we can only know that there is something about the pie that he liked more than his bottle of milk, and vice versa for his trading partner.

It might be that one or both of them will come to regret the trade at a future time, even in the absence of any fraud or underhanded dealing, simply due to a later change in tastes. Or, possibly, each will learn he is allergic to the product of the other. Therefore, there is no iron-clad guarantee that such contracts will benefit both parties in the *ex post* sense. However, this is usually the case, especially for repeat purchases. It is the rare consumer who will regret, after the fact, the purchase of a pie, bottle of milk, newspaper, pen, or paper.

So far we have been considering a barter contract, where one good is exchanged for another. But this is only one of many possibilities. Other alternatives include sale, where money is traded for a good or service; or a WAGE contract, where money is again on one side of the equation, and labor hours on the other. Another is a rental contract, in which a car, or an apartment, or a lawn mower is leased to a tenant, for a given fee. Then there is the rental of money, or borrowing, where interest payments are made in return. But all of them, without exception, have the necessary characteristic that (at least in the *ex ante* sense, and most usually in the *ex post* sense as well) that they are mutually beneficial to both contracting parties.

Suppose, now, that some outside authority abrogates a contract. Can this possibly enhance the economic welfare of either of the parties (in the *ex ante* sense)? It cannot possibly do so, even if the motivation for this intervention is unimpeachable (remember, the road to hell is paved with good intentions).

Let us consider a few alternatives. Maybe the government is Marxist, and thinks that all commercial contracts are "exploitative." With the milk-pie trade prohibited by law, each party will have to keep his own supply of goods, and they will not be able to rearrange property titles among themselves as they had wished. Obviously, each will suffer as a result of this inability to arrange for and consummate their contract.

Or suppose that the state determines that one pie for one bottle of milk is not a "fair" price, and forbids trade at any other pie-milk price. Can we any longer deduce mutual benefit? We cannot. The pie man was willing to give up one unit of his product to obtain a unit of the other, but not three of his. The trade no longer takes place, to the regret of both parties. Now suppose that the government *compels* the two men to trade with each other on the basis of one pie for one bottle of milk. Here, no longer can we *deduce* mutual benefit from trade, for it was not, in this context, made on a voluntary basis. For all we know as outside observers, one of these men did *not* value the possession of the other more highly than what he gave up.

One last complication. We must distinguish between a contract and a promise. The two resemble one another, but in the former case, consideration is given, and not in the latter. Suppose that the pie milk contract stipulates that the following will take place: first in time, at noon, the pie is to be given to the milkman; second in time, at 12:01 P.M., the milk is to be given to the pie man. But now posit that the milkman reneges on the deal; that is, he accepts the pie at noon, but when 12:01 P.M. rolls around, he refuses to give any milk in return to the pie man. If he does this, he is guilty of theft—the pie that he took. This is the "consideration" that the pie man gave him at noon, which the milkman stole. Failure to abide by a contract constitutes theft of the consideration.

Now suppose that on day 1 a man promises to marry a woman; and on day 2 he reneges, and refuses to go through with this plan. Has he stolen anything from her? He has not. He may have hurt her far more than the loss of a pie, but, nonetheless, no theft has occurred. This, then, is a promise, not a contract.

Let us sum up so far. In this simple case we have shown that contracts are necessarily beneficial in the *ex ante* sense, and that there is a strong presumption to this effect in the *ex post* sense. We now consider real world cases in which government has abrogated contracts, and examine whether these conclusions can still be sustained.

[Editor's Note: Contracts between "non-equals" may be problematic, perhaps non-voluntary as in the case of a WORKER who faces the choice of working for a low wage given the alternative of starving.]

The minimum wage law. This legislation stipulates that no wages may be paid below a certain level. As of the time of this writing (early 2003), the federal cut-off point between legal and illegal wages is $5.15 per hour (the states vary in this regard). This means that a contract stating, for example, that A will pay B $4.00 per hour for the latter's labor services would not only be null and void, but could land both parties in jail.

Actually, it is unlikely that the employee would end up in the hoosegow, since he is seen by those who promulgated this law as the victim. The employer, in sharp contrast, is in danger of such a punishment merely for engaging in a mutually agreed upon contract, since he is looked upon as the exploiter. Why? This is due to the fact that the average citizen is woefully ignorant of economics, and thinks that this law in point of fact serves as a sort of floor below which wages will not be allowed to fall: raise this "floor" and wages will rise. Since people paid at this rate are among the most unskilled, and hence poorest in society, it is not difficult to explain the popularity of this law.

However, some economists believe this scenario is entirely misbegotten. The correct interpretation, they point out, is that minimum wages are more like a high-jump bar, and only those with skills of greater value than stipulated by this law will be able to "jump over" the barrier, and remain employed. Those who cannot catapult over this level will be consigned to unemployment. Why, after all, do employers want to hire employees? They do so because of the revenue forthcoming from the latter. But suppose the addition to the bottom line of a person is $4.00 per hour (i.e., that is his productivity) and that the law stipulates that such a worker must be paid $5.15, then it is clear that the firm will lose $1.15 every hour he is on the shop floor. If the minimum wage were raised to $1,000 an hour, then it would be crystal clear that no one would be hired in the entire economy apart from movie stars, top professional athletes, and other very highly productive superstars. But the logic is inexorable, and applies, as well, to the more modest end of the productivity pyramid.

To return to our insights regarding the mutual benefits of contracts, all contracts, we can see that as long as the unskilled worker agrees to take the $4.00 per hour job, it is, in his own estimation, the best option open to him; it is certainly better than unemployment.

Who, then, does benefit from such legislation? Paradoxically, it is the highly skilled, typically unionized worker. For, when organized labor demands a wage increase, the natural tendency of the firm is to attempt to substitute, at the margin, unskilled labor for it. However, some economists believe minimum-wage law effectively unemploys all those to whom the business might turn in an attempt to wrest itself free from union domination. It is thus no accident that organized labor is the most outspoken advocate of this unemployment law for the poor.

Unconscionability. The lawsuit *Williams v. Walker-Thomas Furniture Co.* (United States Court of Appeals, District of Columbia Circuit, 1965, 350 F.2d 445) is the classic case of the doctrine of "unconscionability" being used to overturn voluntary contracts. This firm operated in a poor part of town, and sold its wares on the installment plan. However, the contract stipulated that unless all goods purchased from this store were paid in full, the buyer would own none of them, and they could all be repossessed in case of non-payment for everything. A numerical example will make this clear. A plaintiff could purchase a couch for $500, and pay, in installments, $450 of this. Then he could buy a lamp for $200, and render $150 of that amount in this manner. He has now disbursed a total of $600 ($450 + $150) and yet, if he fails to pony up the remaining $100 ($500 + $200 = $700 – $600 = $100) of what he owes, he can keep none of these possessions, and must return all of them to the repo man.

This sounds pretty harsh. And it was upon the basis of the court's view of fairness that they overturned this contract, even though it was agreed upon by both parties, on the ground that it was "unconscionable," and thus against the so-called "public interest."

Yet, if there were vast amounts of money to be made in this business, more competitors would have flocked in, and the terms of trade would have tilted in favor of the purchaser. The reason this did not occur is that the buyers in this neighborhood were poor risks. They had a higher rate of reneging on their contracts than other people. The only way the furniture company could remain in business, other than with this installment-plan contract, would have been to either charge higher prices, or raise interest rates for the outstanding loans. Yet, if they did the former they might have been accused of "discrimination," and if the latter then "usury."

Blocked from recouping their losses in any way, firms of this sort could not operate at all. Hence, the people in this neighborhood, "thanks" to a dissolution of their contracts, would be left with fewer stores, and, in the extreme, with no stores at all. This example constitutes yet further evidence of the beneficial effects of contracts to all parties, even those ostensibly hurt by them.

Lochner v. New York. Lochner is a law case in which a contract to work more than 60 hours a week was upheld by the court, despite the fact that many people thought this unfair to the worker (U.S. Supreme Court No. 292, April 17, 1905). This case is sometimes thought of as the high-water mark in favor of contracts, in that the court upheld a voluntary agreement between two consenting adults, namely the baker and his employer. It was no such thing. Rather, it rested on the weak-reed majority argument that "There is no demonstrable causal link between labor hours of a baker and the quality of his product or his own health."

But suppose this link could be demonstrated. Then, presumably, the majority would have voted the other way, with the minority, and suppressed the contract. However, based on our insights regarding contract, this would have been a mistake. For suppose baking for such long hours was personally injurious. It is a violation of the baker's rights to override his decision to trade some of his health for additional money. Prohibiting such arrangements on these grounds would imply that we ban boxing, hang gliding, fatty foods, cigarettes, auto racing, etc. Suppose, now, that the quality of baked goods would decline with such long hours. Would the court be justified in banning the contract on those grounds? Not at all. Not unless, that is, it would also be proper to prohibit day-old bread, or anything but the most ornate, high-quality baked goods. Obviously, if the quality of the product falls, so must its price. Do not consumers have the right to prefer a cheaper, but inferior product?

BIBLIOGRAPHY. Walter Block, "Paternalism in Agricultural Labor Contracts in the U.S. South: Implications for the Growth of the Welfare State," *Unisinos: Perspectiva Economica* (v.35/112, 2000); Steven N.S. Cheung, "The Contractual Nature of the Firm," *Journal of Law and Economics* (v.26, 1983); Hans-Hermann Hoppe, et al., "Against Fiduciary Media," *Quarterly Journal of Austrian Economics*, (v.1/1, 1998).

WALTER BLOCK, PH.D.
LOYOLA UNIVERSITY, NEW ORLEANS

Coolidge, Calvin (1872–1933)

THE 30TH PRESIDENT of the UNITED STATES, Calvin Coolidge was born in Plymouth, Vermont. After graduating from Amherst College, he was admitted to the Bar and became involved in Massachusetts politics. Coolidge was soon elected to the state legislature, eventually becoming president of the senate. By 1918, he was elected governor of Massachusetts, and as governor he reached national fame through his resolute handling of the Boston police strike. During the strike Coolidge proclaimed, "There is no right to strike against the public safety by anybody, anywhere, any time."

In the wake of the RUSSIAN REVOLUTION and the subsequent public debate over workers' rights and workers' role in society, this statement put Coolidge on the national political stage and, in part as a consequence of this, he was chosen as Warren G. HARDING's vice president on the Republican ticket in the 1920 presidential election.

Upon Harding's sudden death in 1923 Coolidge became president. His removal of officials and his support for prosecution of wrongdoers quickly brought the corruption scandals of the Harding administration to an end. In 1924, Coolidge was elected to a full term. After announcing that, despite his popularity, he would not seek re-election in 1928, the Republican Party nominated Herbert C. HOOVER, who succeeded Coolidge in 1929—just a few months before the STOCK MARKET crash and the subsequent Great DEPRESSION.

Coolidge's philosophy of government was decidedly pro-business. Indeed, it was Coolidge who once exclaimed, "The business of America is business." His view of the fiscal responsibility of government is well-captured by a contemporaneous maxim on the principle of good government by C.N. Fay, vice president of the National Association of Manufacturers: "Least Government, with its companion principle of Least Taxation." Coolidge maintained a philosophy that taxes and government spending should be lower, and that regulatory activity should be minimal. This philosophy of "constructive economy" was meant to bring about greater individual freedom that would translate into entrepreneurial and innovative creativity, ultimately benefiting all members of society.

With substantial input from Andrew MELLON, secretary of the Treasury, the tax rates were decreased from the high rates enacted during WORLD WAR I and some TAXES were abolished altogether. The maximum tax rate on individual income was reduced from a high of 77 percent to 25 percent, and the so-called "excess-profit" taxes were repealed. A reduction in government spending caused the federal budget to decline from $5.1 billion in 1921 to $3.1 billion in 1929. Moreover, under Coolidge, regulatory agencies were frequently led and staffed by representatives of the very industries that they were to oversee, indeed, in some instances he appointed vocal critics of agencies to head those same agencies.

In 1926, Coolidge supported and signed into law the Railway Labor Act (RLA). The RLA guaranteed railway workers the right to form UNIONS, but also reduced the danger of crippling RAILROAD strikes by setting up a mediation board that handled all labor disputes. It is one of the oldest labor laws still in use, and has since been extended to cover AIRLINES.

Economic growth was rapid during the Coolidge years. The era witnessed the advent of mass production and consumerism and became known as the Roaring Twenties. The unemployment rate dropped from 11.7 percent in 1921 through a low of 1.8 percent in 1926 to 3.2 percent in 1929.

While there has been some debate about how much of this prosperity was caused by a rebound from the end of WORLD WAR I and how much was facilitated, if not caused, by the policies pursued by Coolidge, there is no dispute that the prosperity was not universal. One group who did not share in the prosperity was farmers.

From around the turn of the century, the agricultural sector experienced a boom that lasted through World War I. Farmers anticipated a continued increase in farm incomes throughout the 1920s. However, the post-war depression that hit the country in 1920 affected farmers particularly hard as they had invested large sums of money in land that quickly depreciated in value. Twice the U.S. Congress passed bills giving price supports to farmers. But both times, following the advice of his Secretary of Commerce Herbert Hoover, and his belief in free markets, Coolidge vetoed the bills.

For a long time the Coolidge administration and its policies of constructive economy have been viewed with skepticism, due to the Great Depression following Coolidge's term in office. Indeed, Coolidge was unaware of the impending economic collapse, stating in his final State of the Union message in December 1928 that one could "anticipate the future with optimism." However, such analysis is somewhat anti-historical and unjustified. Not only were the underlying dynamics that led to the Great Depression not understood at the time, it is still altogether unclear that Coolidge realistically could have anticipated and averted the Great Depression. In any event, the causes of the Great Depression are to a large extent found in failed monetary policies rather than the fiscal and regulatory policies that Coolidge championed.

Coolidge's ideas of constructive economy once again became very popular with President Ronald REAGAN, renamed "supply-side economics." In fact, Mellon, just like the supply-sider Arthur Laffer years later, had made the argument that reduced tax rates would lead to higher tax revenue due to the economic growth they induce economy-wide. However, a big difference between the Coolidge years and the subsequent Reagan years is that under Coolidge spending (in particular defense spending) was reduced, whereas under Reagan spending (in particular defense spending) escalated, leading to budget surpluses in the 1920s and deficits in the 1980s.

BIBLIOGRAPHY. W. Elliot Brownlee, *Dynamics of Ascent: A History of the American Economy* (Random House, 1978); Calvin Coolidge, *The Autobiography of Calvin Coolidge* (Charles E. Tuttle, 1931); Jonathan Hughes and Louis P. Cain, *American Economic History* (Addison-Wesley, 1998); Robert R. Keller, "Supply-Side Economic Policies during the Coolidge-Mellon Era," *Journal of Economic Issues* (v.16/3, 1982); Robert Sobel, *Coolidge: An American Enigma* (Regnery, 1998).

MICHAEL J. TROY, J.D.
THOMAS D. JEITSCHKO, PH.D.
MICHIGAN STATE UNIVERSITY

Cooper, Peter (1791–1883)

AN INVENTOR, INDUSTRIALIST and philanthropist, Peter Cooper made his fortune during America's transition from agriculture to industry. He founded the Cooper Union School for the Advancement of Science and Art in 1859, a New York City tuition-free school.

Born in New York City, Cooper's father and grandfathers fought for American independence. He obtained no formal education and, as a child, Cooper worked with his hat-maker father. Then he tried his hand at brewing and brick making, and was also apprenticed to a coach maker.

At 21, Cooper found employment on Long Island making cloth-shearing machines. He purchased the sole right to make such machines in New York State, but after the War of 1812, business declined and Cooper turned to furniture making, then owned a grocery store. His financial success began when he invested in a glue factory—a move that led to the serendipitous discovery, with the assistance of his wife Sarah Bedell, of Jell-O.

In 1828, Cooper founded the Canton Iron Works in Baltimore, securing his enormous wealth. Two years later he built "Tom Thumb," the first steam RAILROAD locomotive built in America for the Baltimore and Ohio Railroad.

Cooper sold the Baltimore iron works and built a rolling mill in New York, moving it to New Jersey by 1845 as the Trenton Iron Company. In 1854, the first wrought-iron structural beams were made at Trenton, and similar beams from this factory can be found in the dome of the United States Capitol building. The Bessemer process (a technique for converting pig iron to steel) was used for the first time in America at the New Jersey company. Cooper was awarded the Bessemer Gold Medal from the Iron and Steel Institute of Great Britain in 1879 for his advancements in the steel industry.

During the 1850s, Cooper became principal investor and president of the New York–based Newfoundland & London Telegraph Company, financing the Atlantic Cable project of Cyrus Field when banks refused. He was also president of the North American Telegraph Company that controlled more than half the telegraph lines in the country.

As a civic leader of New York City, Cooper was elected alderman and was instrumental in initiating the public school system. In 1875, Cooper became associated with the Greenback Party that gained support from southern and western farmers who were concerned with high railroad rates, deflationary currency, and falling farm prices.

Cooper was the Greenback Party's 1876 presidential nominee against Rutherford HAYES and Samuel Tilden. Although receiving very few votes, the party still managed to send 15 representatives to Congress

In later years, Cooper published *The Political and Financial Opinions of Peter Cooper, with an Autobiography of His Early Life* (1877) and *Ideas for a Science of Good Government, in Addresses, Letters and Articles on a Strictly National Currency, Tariff and Civil Service* (1883).

BIBLIOGRAPHY. Cooper Union, www.cooper.edu; Miriam Gurko, *The Life and Times of Peter Cooper* (Thomas Y. Crowell Company, 1959); Edward Mack, *Peter Cooper: Citizen of New York* (Duell, Sloan and Pearce, 1949).

LINDA DYNAN, PH.D.
INDEPENDENT SCHOLAR

corruption

CORRUPTION IS TYPICALLY defined within the realm of capitalism as the misuse of government office for private gains. But many examples do not fit this definition; for example, insider trading is a more common form of corruption that does not involve a government office. The concept of corruption is thus a value-loaded term that receives different definitions. Political scientist Arnold Heidenheimer has defined terms such as black, gray, or white corruption. In his view, whether an act is corrupt depends on what the majority of people think of it. Black corruption means there is a majority of individuals who condemn the act. Gray corruption means some individuals would condemn the act, but some others would not; there seems to be no consensus. White corruption means there is a majority of people who do not want the action to be condemned.

Essential characteristics of corruption are: First, two parties or more act in mutual agreement; second, their action violates the law; third, they illegally benefit from the decision; and finally they try to conceal their behavior.

Corruption exists in all countries at various levels of society. We can, however, distinguish between three main forms of corruption:

1. Small corruption is also known as petty corruption. It can be found in situations where an agent bribes a custom officer to avoid merchandise taxes.

2. Large bureaucratic corruption can be found when a company bribes a top government official to get a contract.

3. Large political corruption can be found when interest groups bribe congressmen to pass a law.

Petty corruption occurs when officials (mostly low-level government officials) use their offices for private gains.

Typically, the official is put in charge of managing government resources, such as budgets and tax revenues. If the official is, for example, obligated to issue trade licenses and erects some barriers, he induces license applicants to bribe him. The official thus engages in an act of corruption. Petty corruption can take two distinct forms: First, when an official derives illegal private gains from services or contracts that are provided according to the rule; second, the official might derive gains from contracts he is prohibited from providing, as they are mostly against the rule.

Corruption takes place at all levels, from low-level to high-level government officials. When major political figures, or high-level government officials, are involved it is called "grand corruption." Grand corruption includes the last two descriptions mentioned above (large bureaucratic and political corruptions). This type of corruption can impact the country's budget and growth prospects, and includes major transfers of property rights, major contracts, concessions, privatization of major public firms, and the formulation of laws.

Sources of corruption. Most studies on the sources of corruption are quantitative; corruption data are now developed by various organizations such as Transparency International (TI). The data generally range from 0 (most corrupt) to 5 or 10 (least corrupt) and represent the perception of these organizations about the level of corruption in a given country. There are actually some survey data on the true levels of bribery (i.e., the amount paid by firms to officials in developing countries) but are not yet released to the public.

Some economists have argued that we should expect more corruption in countries with large governments, as defined by the share of government spending in the GROSS DOMESTIC PRODUCT (GDP). An increase in the size of the government raises the probability of having more red tape, regulations, and bureaucratic delays. When the data are closely examined, the positive relationship between size and corruption is not borne out. In fact, there seems to be an inverse relationship between these two variables: Corruption seems to be concentrated in countries with low levels of government expenditures.

Further study of the data has shown that countries where citizens are free to hold property and operate a business display low levels of corruption. This freedom may mean less harassment from government officials and therefore fewer bribes asked. The degree of political freedom is also an important source of corruption. Political systems consisting of a unique ruling party, or repressed opposition parties, tend to breed corruption; government officials working with the unique ruling party can engage in immoral behaviors such as bribe-seeking without facing a major penalty.

Less COMPETITION in an economy tends to be another source of corruption. When governments erect trade restrictions, it creates an opportunity for rent-seeking activities. For example, if a government imposes quotas on foreign goods only a few selected foreign firms will be granted access to the domestic market. Government officials in charge of the quota licenses have complete discretion over which firms to select, giving rise to the opportunity for grand corruption.

Corruption is also associated with low wages in the government sector. In many developing countries, wages are so low that they barely cover basic subsistence needs. Civil servants in these societies supplement their income through bribes. Typical examples include police officers stopping buses on the road to ask for "tips." In these countries, the level of illiteracy is so high that the masses can be easily exploited by the civil servants who, relatively speaking, appear to be "highly" educated.

Finally, economists have argued that sociological factors and the degree of ethno-linguistic fractionalization can be sources of corruption: Officials tend to grant favors to people from the same ethnic group.

Consequences of corruption. Corruption has serious consequences in the economy. Recent research indicates that corruption has a detrimental effect on investment and is associated with a significant fall in the investment rate. The effect of corruption on economic GROWTH tends to be mixed at a theoretical level.

Some economists believe that corruption can speed up economic growth (the revisionist view) while others (the moralists) believe that it is harmful to growth. The revisionist view argues that corruption might not be inconsistent with economic growth and development for two main reasons: First, bribes act as a piece-rate for government employees (i.e., bureaucrats work harder when "paid" directly), and second, bribes enable investors to avoid cumbersome bureaucratic processes and delays. We should then expect a positive link between corruption and economic growth, and the relationship should be stronger in countries with heavy bureaucratic regulations.

At the other extreme, the moralists argue that corruption slows growth. An investor can bribe several public officials and still face the possibility that none of them has the power to allow the project to proceed.

Empirically, most studies have found that corruption lowers the rate of growth of an economy. Some economists have found that, though corruption lowers investment, it fosters the latter in countries with heavy bureaucratic delays. (To the extent that investment is associated with economic growth, this finding will imply that corruption fosters economic growth in some developing countries.) However, they also point out that the empirical evidence seems to suggest that the revisionist view is not necessarily a robust finding either.

Another consequence of corruption involves the allocation of resources in an economy. When corruption is prevalent, talented individuals tend to migrate toward jobs offering them the opportunities for rent-seeking. Since these jobs are not necessarily the ones that make best use of their talents, corruption is said to introduce allocative inefficiencies into an economy. For example, in many developing countries, intelligent citizens who have completed their studies abroad in a given field return to their native countries and take jobs with the government in areas that have nothing to do with their education. These jobs simply offer them an opportunity for bribery.

High levels of corruption within a country lead to political instability. When citizens are frustrated because of grand corruption, their government is likely to be overthrown. Political instability itself can both be a source and consequence of corruption. It can be a source since government officials in unstable countries, facing a high probability of being overthrown, are more likely to engage in corrupt behavior to amass as much as possible before the inevitable change of regime. In a sense, corruption and instability can create a virtuous circle, whereby corruption leads to instability which itself creates more corruption.

Corruption also leads to distortion in the allocation of government expenditure. Corrupt government officials will tend to prefer those expenditures whose amounts are difficult to determine. For example, expenditure on such projects as bridges offer an opportunity for corruption since a bridge's value is hard to determine. The empirical literature also suggests corruption causes a decline in public expenditure on education and health. Further, corruption exacerbates social inequities in a country: It redistributes resources from the public to corrupt individuals. In many developing countries with high levels of corruption, the poor are made even poorer by government officials continually engaged in petty and grand corruption.

Finally, corruption may lead to the ineffectiveness of aid flowing from developed to developing nations. Corrupt officials in developing countries can divert funds earmarked for productive projects into unproductive ones.

Fighting corruption. How can a country fight or control corruption? Three main initiatives can be directed to deter corruption.

First, a country can increase its information-gathering to detect corruption by promoting transparencies at all sectors of the government and at the corporate level, and identifying individuals whose lifestyle is more lavish than it should be. A country can also give increased independence and power to auditing agencies so they can conduct better audits of targeted individuals. Government reformers can establish where corruption is the most harmful to its economy, and where it can be fought in the most efficient way. That is, a country should not waste valuable resources fighting all corruption prevalent in the economy, but should concentrate its efforts mostly on the most harmful.

Second, a country can increase the risk and costs, raising the penalty of corruption. This can be achieved by linking the penalty to the size of the bribe; as the bribe or expected profit rises, so does the size of the penalty. The penalty can include firing, jail times, and freezing bank accounts. Raising the risks and costs of corruption can also take the form of rewarding honest and decent employees through the implementation of progressive pay schemes. Since developing countries are also heavily indebted, raising the salary of government officials will probably mean reducing the size of the civil service. The regulatory environment that induces the firms to bribe should be carefully studied. Regulatory laws can be simplified in many developing countries; if regulations are too complicated, businesses are induced to circumvent them by bribing officials.

Third, a country can welcome the international community in the fight against corruption. Multilateral organizations such as the WORLD BANK and the INTERNATIONAL MONETARY FUND (IMF) can be of great help. These institutions have now (somewhat) linked financial assistance to the overall level of corruption. Aid can be interrupted if a country is too corrupt.

The international business community must also engage in strategic planning, coordinate transnational approaches, support anticorruption initiatives, and insist on good governance. Corruption is not only limited to developing economies; the multibillion-dollar bailout of failed savings and loan associations in the United States in the late 1980s is a striking example of corruption in a developed country. More recent examples include the collapse of big corporations such as ENRON and WORLDCOM. Anticorruption measures must include a system of checks and balances, effective law enforcement, and education programs. The media and the non-governmental organizations (NGOs) must also have a voice in the fight against corruption.

BIBLIOGRAPHY. Susan Rose-Ackerman, *Corruption: A Study in Political Economy* (Academic Press, Inc., 1978); Kimberly Ann Elliott, *Corruption and the Global Economy* (Institute for International Economics, 1997); World Bank Staff, *Governance: The World Bank's Experience* (World Bank, 1994).

ARSÈNE A. AKA, PH.D.
CATHOLIC UNIVERSITY OF AMERICA

cost accounting

ENTERPRISE PROFITABILITY is the sum and substance of a free market. Cost analysis, including the assignment of costs to particular products and services, is a precursor to managing entrepreneurial profits.

Cost accounting, overall, is perhaps the most valuable tool for the ENTREPRENEUR for making business decisions in a capitalist economy. It is the non-reporting variant of accounting that takes into account only the internal decisions necessary for the day-to-day operations and management of business profitability.

To improve profit-seeking activities, the entrepreneur must have a means by which to develop strategies for competitive advantage, and this is brought about by allocating costs to particular goods or services within a complex environment of changing market conditions. Cost accounting takes into effect all costs of production, and additionally, it focuses on an organization's acquisition and consumption of resources.

The methodology behind cost accounting is ever changing, and it becomes more critical in this era of increasing competition, economies of scale, and shrinking profit margins. Modern concepts of importance to the business decision maker include cost-volume-profit analytics that examine the effects of costs on overall revenue performance and bottom-line profitability; activity-based costing, which has a fundamental focus on activities as cost objects and uses the cost of these activities to assign costs to products, services, and customers; and relevance decision models, which take into effect qualitative factors in deciding expected profitability among varying courses of action. Such methodologies furnish timely information in the aggregate or in detail, and are concerned with profit, of course; but just as important, profits are more narrowly correlated to various divisions, lines, territories, customers, outsourcing decisions, and resource replacement evaluations.

Implicit in the economic concept of cost is the notion of sacrificing time, money, or other resources, in order to commit to the production of goods or services. After all, resources are scarce, and it is necessary to approach the use of scarce items with as much verifiable information as can be obtained. Cost accounting methodology therefore takes into account all perceived costs, including opportunity costs. Opportunity costs are the forgone benefits of the next best alternative when any scarce resource is used for one purpose over another.

The use of qualitative measures is what sets cost accounting apart from financial accounting, which is only concerned with the external reporting of historical information to outside users. The cost accountant therefore analyzes a basic economic problem revolving around scare resources: to what end do scarce resources get devoted, and what ends are sacrificed?

This combination of quantitative and qualitative analytics is unique in that it enables that which is perhaps the most significant pillar of capitalism, and that is economic calculation. Economic calculation necessarily depends on cost determinations, hence making cost accounting an essential apparatus for the individual entrepreneur as well as the competitive market force as a whole. Without cost accounting analysis, and thus the use of relevant information with the purpose of influencing strategies on resource use and production, the free market would not prosper, and instead, would be reduced to a state of disarray.

BIBLIOGRAPHY. W.T. Baxter and Sidney Davidson, *Studies in Accounting Theory* (John Wiley & Sons, 1962); Robert N. Anthony, *Tell It Like It Was: A Conceptual Framework for Financial Accounting* (Irwin, 1983); Charles T. Horngren, George Foster, and Srikant M. Datar, *Cost Accounting: A Managerial Emphasis* (Prentice Hall, 1997); Thomas C. Taylor, "Current Developments in Cost Accounting and the Dynamics of Economic Calculation," *The Quarterly Journal of Austrian Economics* (v.3/2).

KAREN DE COSTER
WALSH COLLEGE

cost of information

THE VALUE OF INFORMATION measured as the price one would be willing to pay for perfect information, or alternatively the expense incurred by an individual with imperfect information is termed by economists as cost of information.

Information and decision-making. A fundamental assumption of the classical model of economics is the existence of perfect information. Basic demand and supply analysis, as taught in most introductory economics courses, is constructed around this assumption. Consequently, the inner workings of the market mechanism are based on the philosophy that buyers and sellers have access to equal information. The conclusion that the market equilibrium represents an optimal solution in which neither a surplus nor shortage exists implicitly assumes that the EQUILIBRIUM was arrived at with full information.

Based on current information, quantity demanded and quantity supplied are equal (i.e., consumers are willing to purchase, for example, 100 boxes for $10 per box while firms are willing to produce 100 boxes for the same price). Both production and spending decisions in this case are based on the information sets available to consumers and firms at the time of exchange. Should a consumer or producer's information set change, he would most likely cease to be satisfied with the market equilibrium (i.e., he would no longer be willing to purchase, in the case of the consumer, or provide, in the case of the producer, 100 boxes for a price of $10 per box). Note that many economic models have been modified to allow for imperfect information, but that does not change the fundamental assumption of classical economists and the relationship this has to market outcomes.

For consumers, a lack of information may result in individuals paying "too much" or "too little" for a particular product. Consequently, the equilibrium quantity in a market economy may be artificially high or low (i.e., higher or lower than it would have been had consumers had access to more and better information). For example, consumers above may have been willing to purchase 100 boxes for $20 per box or perhaps 200 boxes for $10 apiece had they known that these boxes were top quality and contained features that were not available on other boxes in the market. Alternatively, consumers would have been extremely angry had they discovered they paid $10 for boxes that were of poor quality. Had consumers known the boxes were of such poor quality, they would have been willing to pay at most $4 per box or would have purchased no more than 20 boxes for a price of $10.

Imperfect information like this causes consumers to over- or under-pay and distorts the market equilibrium. Producers are not immune from the dangers of imperfect information either. If, for example, information regarding costs of production are not exactly known, a company may charge too much (reducing quantity demanded and profits) or too little (causing profits to fall because prices are not high enough to cover costs). Without perfect information an equilibrium outcome considered efficient might not be efficient at all. Had producers and consumers had access to full information, quantity demanded and quantity supplied would not have been equal at the "equilibrium" price. In fact, the "equilibrium" price would not be an equilibrium price at all.

Information problems. Information is a key component of decision-making and as such is a principal part of a market-oriented system. CONSUMER choice, production decisions, portfolio diversification, and numerous other decisions made every day in a capitalist system depend on the availability of information. Lack of information may, at best, delay decision-making and consequently exchange or, at worst, put a stop to exchange altogether if individuals feel they do not have enough reliable information to make maximizing decisions.

Capitalism relies on well-functioning markets. Market participation depends on information. Hence, the success of capitalism rests largely on the availability of perfect information for all market participants.

Despite the benefits of perfect information (e.g., maximum market participation, truly efficient market equilibria, etc.), numerous instances of imperfect information exist in market systems. One example of imperfect information frequently encountered is the problem of adverse selection, a situation in which sellers know precisely what kind of item they plan to provide buyers (e.g., whether the item is top quality or not) but buyers, on the other hand, have limited information about the quality of the product and hence are not quite sure how "good" the product is that they are about to buy.

George AKERLOF brilliantly and simply illustrated the problem of adverse selection in his famous work, "The Market for 'Lemons': Qualitative Uncertainty and the Market Mechanism." According to Akerlof, markets (in this case, the market for used cars) will operate efficiently only as long as both buyers and sellers have perfect information about the item to be exchanged (in this case, a used car). In other words, as long as buyers and sellers have access to full information, both good cars and lemons will sell and the market for used cars will clear. Buyers, presented with a lemon (i.e., a car of lower quality that most likely will require additional funds to repair), will know that they are being given a lemon and will offer sellers a relatively low price for the lemon. Knowing that they are selling a lemon that is not very valuable, sellers will accept the buyers' low offer, and all of the lemons will be sold. Likewise, presented with a top-quality car, buyers will offer sellers top dollar for the good cars. Sellers will accept, and all of the good cars will be sold. The result is an efficient market in which all cars, lemons and top-quality cars, sell (i.e., the quantity demanded equals quantity supplied), neither buyers nor sellers will have over- or under-paid for products purchased and equilibrium is achieved. This situation in which buyers and sellers have perfect information, however, is atypical.

Sellers generally have more and better information about the quality of goods and services for sale than buyers. In the case of the used car market, buyers, unsure about the quality of the car presented to them, will offer to pay sellers an "average" price that is based on, among other things, the probability that the car is a lemon. The average price proposed by buyers typically falls somewhere in between the sellers' valuation of a lemon and a top-quality car. Because good cars are worth more to sellers than the average price offered by buyers, only lemons will sell. The market will not clear and might possibly cease to function at all once buyers learn that they are overpaying for lemons. The problem of adverse selection is a common problem in virtually all markets and poses a particular danger in financial markets where buyers are receiving slips of paper rather than commodities.

Another information problem encountered in market economies is MORAL HAZARD, a situation in which buyers cannot observe the behavior of sellers after an exchange has taken place. This is a particular problem in service markets (including the labor market) and financial markets where buyers are not buying an item with some sort of intrinsic value. In the case of LABOR, the full value is not realized at the time of purchase but is obtained piecemeal over time as the worker performs the task for which he was employed.

Buyers in financial markets receive securities, slips of paper that gain or lose value depending on the future performance of the company. Whether a buyer has paid too much, too little, or just the right price will depend on the behavior of the seller after the initial transaction has taken place. The principal-agent problem is a classic example of moral hazard when it occurs in the equity market. The costs incurred as a result of the principal-agent problem are referred to as agency costs. The moral hazard problem implies that sellers, once they have obtained money from buyers, may perform poorly or behave in such a way that the value of the good or service purchased rapidly depreciates. Buyers, wary of such behavior, will be less likely to pay sellers top dollar for their wares if they will be willing to buy them at all. Moral hazard and adverse selection problems, should they become severe, may lead to market inefficiencies and under extreme circumstances may cause markets to stop functioning altogether.

Market for information. The fact that buyers and sellers stand to incur substantial costs due to lack of information means that buyers and sellers would (under certain circumstances) be willing to pay for information. There is, in other words, a market for information, and like any market it will be driven by the forces of demand and supply. As the demand for information increases so too will the price that individuals are willing to pay for information. If one assumes that the marginal cost of providing information remains relatively constant, the high demand for information will make the private production and sale of information profitable and hence one would expect to see firms enter the information market.

Evidence of such a market can be found by the existence of periodicals like *Consumer Reports*, a magazine sold with information regarding typical consumer products like cars, refrigerators, etc., *Moody's*, a collection of bond ratings, and *Standard and Poor's*, a publication that provides information about publicly traded corporations. The fact that individuals hire stockbrokers and accountants, for example, is further evidence that people are willing to pay for information. It is, on the other hand, no surprise that companies have not gone into the business of publishing comprehensive analyses regarding candy bars. Consumers would be unlikely to pay for this information presumably because they do not feel they would be harmed by a lack of information when choosing an afternoon snack or if they would, it would

not be serious enough to warrant paying for additional information.

The availability of information will depend on how profitable it is to provide information. High demand means increased revenues and, as a result, encourages the production of additional information. Total revenues and total profits may not necessarily rise with increased demand, however, due to the free-rider problem, the situation in which consumers who have not paid for the information have access to, and hence are able to benefit from, the information. The existence of the free-rider problem makes the production of information less profitable and explains why so few companies are in the business of providing information despite the high demand for it.

Rapid changes in technology, particularly television and the internet, has significantly reduced the cost of providing information and consequently made the free-rider problem less of an issue to profit-maximizing firms that are able to make up for lost revenues by providing information for negligible costs. As a result, the supply of information has been increasing at an unprecedented rate. Unfortunately, more information is better only if it is reliable and consumers have the know-how to process it properly. As long as there is uncertainty about the accuracy of information or some question of how to interpret the information once it has been obtained, individuals will be willing to pay for top-quality data and markets for information will continue to exist.

BIBLIOGRAPHY. George Akerlof, "The Market for 'Lemons': Qualitative Uncertainty and the Market Mechanism," *Quarterly Journal of Economics* (1970); William J. Baumol and Alan S. Blinder, *Economics: Principles and Policy* (South-Western, 2002); Frederic S. Mishkin, *The Economics of Money, Banking, and Financial Markets* (Addison-Wesley, 2002); Martin J. Osborne and Ariel Rubinstein, *A Course in Game Theory* (MIT Press, 1994); Louis Phlips, *Economics of Imperfect Information* (Cambridge University Press, 1989).

KRISTIN KUCSMA, PH.D.
SETON HALL UNIVERSITY

cost, theory of

KNOWLEDGE OF THE THEORY of cost is essential for a variety of reasons. In economic theory, many of the predictions regarding the behavior of firms are based on concepts such as profit, marginal cost, variable cost, fixed cost, and sunk cost. Without knowledge of these cost concepts one cannot empirically test these predictions or even understand them. In addition, every firm needs to know what it costs to produce its goods and/or services if it is to make rational business decisions. Profit maximization, the objective of most firms, requires cost minimization.

The cost function is a mapping from the input prices and the level of production to the total cost of producing. The cost function is therefore a technological relationship that can be derived from the firm's production function—showing the minimum private cost of producing various levels of output assuming that the input prices are held constant.

It is important to realize that economic costs differ from accounting costs since the former includes both explicit and implicit costs. Explicit costs are the actual out-of-pocket expenditures of the firm. Implicit costs are the value of the inputs owned and used by the firm. Thus, the notion of economic costs is that of an opportunity cost. Opportunity costs, or economic costs, will always be greater than (or equal to) accounting costs. To illustrate the difference between economic and accounting costs (or opportunity cost and explicit costs) consider the following example: Suppose you were one of the lucky ones who was able to buy a ticket to the NCAA Men's Final Four Basketball tournament. Suppose you had to pay $150 for the ticket. Attending the Final Four would require additional expenses for travel, lodging, meals, souvenirs, etc. Suppose these expenses total $1000.

Hence your accounting costs of attending the Final Four would be $1150. However, the economic or opportunity costs would be much higher. Since Final Four tickets are usually highly sought after by fans of the competing teams it is reasonable to assume that you could sell your ticket for more than the face value of $150 that you paid. Suppose that you were able to sell your ticket for $850. Hence, by attending the Final Four you would forego the $850, which you would get from selling your ticket. An economist includes these implicit costs, and the opportunity cost of attending the Final Four would be $2000: the explicit costs of $1150 plus the implicit cost of $850.

Cost theory also distinguishes between short-run and long-run costs as well as avoidable and unavoidable costs. The short run for a firm is defined as a time period for which at least one of the firm's inputs is fixed, whereas in the long run all of the inputs the firm uses are variable. The existence of a fixed input in the short run gives rise to a fixed cost. This is the part of the firm's total costs, which does not depend upon the level of output produced by the firm. Hence, the total short-run cost of the firm can be divided into fixed costs and variable costs. Variable cost is the sum of the cost minimizing quantities of the variable inputs multiplied by their prices; fixed cost is the sum of the quantities of the fixed inputs multiplied by their prices; and total cost is the sum of variable cost and fixed cost ($TC = VC + F$).

Given the total costs one can define four other cost concepts: average total cost (ATC), average variable cost (AVC), average fixed costs (AFC), and marginal costs (MC). If we let Q denote the output level of the firm, then $ATC = TC/Q$, $AVC = VC/Q$, $AFC = F/Q$. Since $TC = VC + F$, $ATC = AVC + AFC$.

Of course, since the fixed costs do not depend upon the level of output, AFC is decreasing as the firm increases output. Given the standard economic assumptions, i.e., positive input prices and positive marginal products for all inputs, variable cost and total cost increase as output increases. At what rate these costs increase—and therefore whether AVC and ATC are increasing, constant, or decreasing—depends upon the technology the firm has access to. Marginal cost is defined as the change in total cost resulting from a unit change in output, since by definition fixed costs do not change as output changes, marginal cost is, of course, also equal to the change in variable cost resulting from a unit change in output.

It is important to realize that the firm's short-run output decision is determined by the firm's marginal cost and the demand condition it faces (i.e., fixed costs do not affect the firm's output decision in the short run).

In the long run, all inputs of the firm are variable, hence there are no fixed costs and total costs are equal to variable costs. There is an important relationship between the firm's short-run average total cost and long-run average total cost (LAC): The firm's long-run average cost curve is the lower envelope of the firm's short-run average cost curves for various levels of the fixed input, $LAC = TC/Q$ where TC stands for the firm's long-run total cost. In addition, long-run marginal cost is defined as the change in long-run total cost resulting from a unit change in output.

Another important cost concept is that of sunk costs. Sunk costs are defined as unavoidable costs (i.e., costs that the firm cannot recover even if it ceases to exist). If, for example, an airline bought a plane for $20 million, used it for 5 years and the economic depreciation is $8 million but is only able to sell the plane as it goes out of business for $10 million, then the sunk cost associated with the plane would be $2 million. Note that fixed costs do not have to be sunk costs and sunk costs do not have to be fixed costs.

BIBLIOGRAPHY. William J. Baumol, John C. Panzar, and Robert D. Willig, *Contestable Markets and the Theory of Industry Structure* (Harcourt Brace Jovanovich, 1982); Dennis W. Carlton and Jeffrey M. Perloff, *Modern Industrial Organization* (Addison-Wesley, 1999); Robin Bade and Michael Parkin, *Foundations of Microeconomics* (Addison-Wesley, 2002); Ronald W. Shephard, *Cost and Production Functions* (Springer-Verlag, 1981).

KLAUS G. BECKER, PH.D.
TEXAS TECH UNIVERSITY

Council of Economic Advisors

AN AGENCY WITHIN the Executive Office of the President of the UNITED STATES, the Council of Economic Advisors is composed of three members appointed by the president and confirmed by the U.S. Senate. The president designates one member as chairman and another as vice chairman. The chairman of the Council also serves on the National Economic Council that was created by Executive Order in 1993. To be a member of the Council, a person must be exceptionally qualified to analyze and interpret economic developments. Many members of the Council have been economists, teaching and researching at major universities, although other members have come from business, finance, and other sectors.

The Council of Economic Advisors was created in the Employment Act of 1946. Many members of Congress and the public were concerned that the end of WORLD WAR II could lead to another DEPRESSION and economic stagnation in the United States. Creation of the Council was part of a broader attempt to give the president more power to coordinate economic policy and to introduce long-range planning. The Council originally concentrated on macroeconomic issues, although it later also began to address microeconomic problems.

The Employment Act of 1946, as amended by the Full Employment and Balanced Growth Act of 1978, declared various policy goals for the federal government that the Council is charged with furthering. The Employment Act, as amended, calls for full opportunities for employment for all individuals, a reduced rate of inflation, coordination of federal policies and programs, expansion of private employment, a balanced federal budget, and expansion of the private sector. It is also federal policy to promote free enterprise, balanced growth, an improved international trade balance, and reasonable price stability. It is noteworthy that these goals can and often are inconsistent, requiring tradeoffs in legislation.

The philosophical approach of the Council of Economic Advisors toward government regulation of the economy has varied over time. This approach is consistent with changes in the federal government and American society toward government interference with business and the economy. Early approaches of the Council tended toward large and frequent intervention in the economy, while recent approaches have been friendlier toward free markets and government de-regulation.

The Council has a number of statutory duties. First, it assists in the preparation of the president's annual economic report. This economic report describes the current state of the U.S. and world economy, and then makes broad recommendations for changes in economic policy. The report can be used as a basis for the introduction of specific legislation in Congress and well as action in the executive branch.

Second, the Council gathers timely and authoritative information on economic developments and trends. It then analyzes this information with a view to submit to the president studies relating to these developments and trends.

Third, it analyzes the programs of the federal government in light of Congressional policy on the economy. The purpose is to discover whether federal programs contribute to the overall economic goals of the Employment Act of 1946.

Fourth, it makes recommendations to the president on national economic policies to foster free enterprise, avoid economic fluctuations, and maintain full employment, production, and purchasing power. Fifth, it makes recommendations to the president on economic policy and legislation as requested by the president. Finally, it makes an annual report to the resident which becomes part of the president's economic report.

The Council of Economic Advisors also prepares and publishes *Economic Indicators* for the Joint Committee of the U.S. States Congress. *Economic Indicators* appears monthly and contains important statistical information on the national and international economies. It addresses the following topic areas: domestic output, income and spending; employment, unemployment and wages; production and business activity; prices; money, credit and security markets; federal finances; and, international statistics.

Members of the Council of Economic Advisors have made major contributions in economics and public policy outside their membership on the Council. Many have been academics who published major advances in various disciplines such as economics and finance. Two former chairmen of the commission (Alan GREENSPAN and Arthur Burns) went on to become chairmen of the Board of Governors of the Federal Reserve System. Another, Janet L. Yellen, was appointed as a member of this same Board of Governors. Still another member of the Council, Joseph STIGLITZ was awarded the Nobel Prize in Economics in 2001.

BIBLIOGRAPHY. Erwin Hargrove, *The President and the Council of Economic Advisors: Interviews with CEA Chairman* (Westview Press, 1984); Joseph Ford and C. O'Donnell, "The Evolution of the Council of Economic Advisors," ww.nssa.us/nssajrnl; Council of Economic Advisors, www.whitehouse.gov/cea.

DAVID PAAS, PH.D.
HILLSDALE COLLEGE

credit

A TRANSACTION IN WHICH resources are obtained in a present time while they are paid for in the future is based on credit. The future payment generally includes compensation in excess of the original value of the resource, that is, interest. Credit, and its opposite DEBT, are operations which involve lending. By giving a credit, a lender finances the expenditures of a borrower against future repayment. Accepting credit is simply an equivalent to going into debt.

While the credit extension and debt creation are almost as old as human interaction, the volume and complexity of credit transactions have grown exponentially with the emergence of capitalism. Credit transaction emerges whenever capital is used and savings are required. Thus, credit enables producers to close the gap between PRODUCTION and sales of GOODS and services. Similarly, it allows consumers to purchase goods and services at present time and pay for those services from their future income.

The credit instruments address the ways in which credit can be extended. The most commonly used instruments of credit are the acceptance, bill of exchange, letter of credit, and promissory note. The instruments are often negotiable and traded in money markets.

Generally there are three types of credit. The first type is consumer credit, a short-term loan extended to the public for the purchase of specific goods and services. The principal economic function of consumer credit is to move consumers' consumption of goods and services forward in time. The main types of consumer credit are non-installment credit and installment credit. Non-installment credit is to be repaid in a lump sum. Installment credit, which is a prevalent form, represents all consumer credit that is scheduled to be repaid in two or more installments.

The second type of credit is trade credit. This is a credit extended by a trader or producer to other business firms through the terms, which allow payment at some time in the future. It may be extended by material suppliers to manufacturers, or by manufacturers to wholesalers or retailers. While the explicit charge for the credit through the charge accounts and/or bill of exchange is possible, the implicit charge in the form of a discount for an early payment is more common. An individual firm or business can be both a giver and taker of this type of credit. Trade credit is a principal channel through which credit flows across various sectors of economy and is one of the pillars of the financial system.

The third type of credit is bank credit. This type involves lending by the banking institutions through bank advances, overdrafts, discounting bills or purchasing securities. Overdrafts are primarily used in the UNITED KINGDOM. The system of overdraft allows a borrower to draw checks beyond the credit balance in his account, but not over the pre-set limit. The borrower is obliged to pay interest on daily amounts by which his account is overdrawn. Based on the assessment of borrowers'

credit worthiness, a bank may require a collateral security for the credit. The term, securities, is used for income yielding financial assets. There are two main types of securities, fixed-interest and variable-interest securities. Fixed-interest securities include debentures, preference shares, stocks, and BONDS, including all government securities. Variable-interest securities include ordinary shares. The securities are saleable, and they may be redeemable (fixed-interest) or irredeemable (variable-interest) quotable or unquotable.

Credit plays an important role in MACROECONOMICS, especially in money supply theory. In the aggregate models of the financial sector of an economy, credit markets and credit creation are analyzed via their relation to money markets and money creation and price level. These models clarify the role of CENTRAL BANK policies in controlling money supply and price level.

BIBLIOGRAPHY. Graham Bannock, R.E. Baxter, and Evan Davis, *The Penguin Dictionary of Economics* (Penguin Books, 1998); John Eatwell, Murray Milgate, and Peter Newman, eds., *The New Palgrave A Dictionary of Economics* (Stockton Press, 1991); Irving Fisher, *The Theory of Interest* (Macmillan, 1930); LeRoy Miller, et al., *Money, Banking, and Financial Markets* (South-Western, 2003); D. Patinkin, *Money, Interest and Prices* (Harper & Row, 1956); D.W. Pearce, *The MIT Dictionary of Modern Economics* (MIT Press, 1992).

ZELJAN SCHUSTER, PH.D.
UNIVERSITY OF NEW HAVEN

Credit Suisse Group

CREDIT SUISSE BEGAN as a commercial bank in 1856, at a time when SWITZERLAND was first embracing the INDUSTRIAL REVOLUTION. In 2003, Credit Suisse Group was the second-largest financial services firm in Switzerland, behind rival Union Bank of Switzerland (UBS).

In 1856, Alfred Escher, a young Zurich political figure from a prominent local family, was making slow progress in his talks with foreign banks about ways to finance a proposed northeastern railway, so he decided to set up an independent bank in Zurich. Between 1856 and the outbreak of WORLD WAR I, Credit Suisse continued financing the country's RAILROAD system, and began financing the electrification of the country. The bank helped develop the Swiss monetary system and, by the end of the Franco-Prussian War in 1871, Credit Suisse was the largest bank in Switzerland.

With the outbreak of World War I, foreign investment stopped completely. Investors in hostile countries returned Swiss securities. Credit Suisse played a crucial role in placing them on the Swiss market while defending the interests of investors abroad.

During WORLD WAR II, Credit Suisse extended huge amounts of credit to Swiss authorities who were owed more than SFr 1.7 billion by Germany by the end of the war.

After the end of the war, Credit Suisse again took up issuing paper for foreign debtors.

During the 1960s the bank set up a business arrangement with White Weld, a leading American investment bank in Europe, which would eventually establish Credit Suisse's leading role in the eurobond-issuing market and would ultimately lead to its relationship with the American investment bank First Boston (CSFB).

The bank also experienced a major scandal in 1977 when authorities began investigating a fraudulent banking and foreign-exchange trading scheme at the company's Chiasso branch involving more than $1.2 billion. Meanwhile the company was tainted by mid-1980s charges of laundering drug money from Turkey and Bulgaria.

The stock market crash of 1987 hit CSFB and First Boston particularly hard. CSFB lost an estimated $15 million on a 1987 debt swap with Italy. First Boston meanwhile suffered large losses from bad bridge loans for mergers and acquisitions. In 1990, Credit Suisse bailed out the still troubled First Boston by agreeing to pump $300 million in equity into the firm, increasing Credit Suisse's stake to 60 percent and making the Swiss bank the first foreigner to own a Wall Street investment bank.

Acquisitions and new growth areas were major themes of the 1990s for Credit Suisse. In April 1990, Credit Suisse acquired Bank Leu, Switzerland's fifth largest bank. This was the first hostile takeover in Swiss banking. In addition to private banking, Credit Suisse added another operating unit to its organization chart when it entered the insurance business by establishing CS Life Insurance. Credit Suisse expanded its insurance operations by purchasing Winterthur Insurance in August 1997.

In 1996, Credit Suisse turned its attention away from Switzerland, and the group decided to become a truly international banking and financial services power that happened to be based in Switzerland and had some core businesses there.

About the same time the company was being restructured, its activities, and those of other "Big Three" Swiss banks during World War II, were being re-examined with resulting negative publicity. Reports of the banks' financial dealings with Nazi Germany were published, and Jewish groups pushed for the reclamation of money that had been placed into Swiss bank accounts before World War II by victims of the Holocaust. The Swiss banks reluctantly published lists of people who owned dormant accounts that had been opened before 1945. In early 1997, the Big Three banks agreed to set up a SFr 100 million (US $70 million) humanitarian fund for the victims of the Holocaust.

BIBLIOGRAPHY. "Credit Suisse Restructures," *Banker* (August, 1996); Johanna McGeary, "Echoes of the Holocaust," *Time* (February 24, 1997); *125th Anniversary of Credit Suisse: An Historical Survey* (Credit Suisse, 1981).

MICHAEL MCGREGOR
FANNIE MAE

Cromwell, Oliver (1599–1658)

BRITISH SOLDIER, LAWYER, and statesman who rose to power at the head of a pro-Parliamentary army during the First English Civil War (1640–46), Oliver Cromwell headed the faction opposed to King Charles I during the Second English Civil War (1647–49), supported the regicide (1649) and after 1653 headed the British government as Lord Protector until his death.

Cromwell was educated at Cambridge and the Inns of Court. During the 1630s, he suffered a spiritual crisis of unknown origin that spawned a conversion experience from which he emerged a committed Puritan. He represented Cambridge in the Parliaments of 1639 and 1640, during which he became attached to the anti-royal faction or "Roundheads." Cromwell gained his initial military experience in a minor skirmish in 1642, when he seized the silver of the Cambridge colleges that had planned to sell it to support the king's forces in the First Civil War. He rose to military prominence as the leader of the victorious cavalry at the battle Marston Moor (1644), where after routing the royal armies, he showed his socially radical side by promoting soldiers solely on the basis of merit and was roundly criticized for it by his (noble) superiors.

In 1645, Cromwell helped to engineer the Self-Denying Ordinance, which prevented sitting ministers from serving in the army (but did not apply to him); the effect was to remove the nobility from military command. The Parliament was now represented on the field by the New Model Army, now cleansed of the nobility and filled with socially radical elements that Cromwell encouraged, such as Anabaptists, Levellers, and Diggers. Levellers were primarily pamphleteers and supporters of more radical democracy than the Parliament; Diggers incorporated early utopian socialist views into their mix of religious conviction and politics. Although Cromwell supported the Levellers in their dispute with Parliament in 1647, he never favored universal suffrage and appears to have used the threat of the army to purge those moderate parliamentarians considering a settlement with the king. After their expulsion (Pride's Purge, 1648), Cromwell sympathized with the remaining "Rump" Parliament, and suppressed Leveller mutinies in 1649, after which Parliament made him Lord-General.

He was responsible for the brutal massacres of Catholics at Drogheda and Royalists at Wexford. After defeating the Scots and royalist forces at Dunbar and Preston, Cromwell turned the army toward London, where he expelled the Rump Parliament, which he felt was too slow in instituting social reform, and instituted more agreeable and radical replacements. After suppressing Royalist revolts, he refused the office of king when it was offered, and was succeeded by his son when he died in 1658. By 1660, Parliament had restored Charles II to the English throne in the wake of severe chaos.

A gifted military strategist and man of acute political skills, Cromwell has defied characterization and the fundamental nature of his motivation has been contested practically since his death. Although he was a moderate supporter of economic and political reform, his intense Puritan sentiments are the best key to his actions. His initial support of parliamentarians and Levellers, which ended in the purge of both groups, has been seen as the result of political opportunism by those who argue that Cromwell supported the Levellers only long enough to keep them in the army, but sacrificed them as soon as his push to power was achieved. Little evidence suggests that he was other than a moderate bourgeois liberal. He consented reluctantly, on the basis of his commitment to thorough-going but not complete freedom of the press, to publication of James Harrington's *Oceana* (1656), a tract that argued that political power was based on land ownership and that the government should act to prevent the accumulation of large portions of land.

At the same time he revised the charter of the English EAST INDIA COMPANY in 1657 to permit the accumulation of capital. He was one of few to argue for re-admission of Jews to England. Still, Parliamentarians such as Slingsby Bethel were stronger supporters of lowering trade barriers than Cromwell, and he was frequently criticized by these men for the shortsightedness of his expensive foreign policy's effects on the economy. While he considered the development of foreign trading partners desirable, in part to prevent a royal restoration, his approval of the Navigation Act of 1651, which granted to English ships a monopoly on goods carried into English ports, provoked a war with the Dutch. Cromwell has been characterized as a bourgeois liberal traitor to the movement he had helped to foment. Views of Cromwell are inevitably tied up with preferences for particular explanations of the origins of the English Civil War.

BIBLIOGRAPHY. British Civil Wars, Commonwealth, and Proctorate, 1638-1660, www.skyhook.co.uk/civwar/index; J.C. Davis, *Oliver Cromwell* (Oxford University Press, 2001); Peter Gaunt, *Oliver Cromwell* (Blackwell, 1996); Christopher Hill, *God's Englishman: Oliver Cromwell and the English Revolution* (Harper & Row, 1970).

SUSAN R. BOETTCHER, PH.D.
UNIVERSITY OF TEXAS, AUSTIN

Cuba

THE REPUBLIC OF CUBA is located south of the Tropic of Cancer at the entrance to the Gulf of Mexico. The nearest countries are Haiti to the east, Jamaica to the south, and the UNITED STATES to the north. Havana is the capital.

In 2002, the population of Cuba was approximately 11.2 million, with approximately 50 percent mulatto, 33 percent white and largely of Spanish descent, 10 percent black, and one percent Chinese. Almost the entire population is native-born and more than three-quarters can be classified as urban. The national language is Spanish. Cuba's declining birth rate and increase in emigration has led to a sharp decrease in its rate of population growth.

Prior to SPAIN's exploration of Cuba, the native population was made up of the Ciboney, Guanahatabey, and the Taino. In 1492, Christopher Columbus discovered Cuba and in 1511, Spain began permanent settlements. The Spaniards used the island as a staging ground for its explorations of Florida, the Gulf Coast, and MEXICO's Yucatan peninsula. Due to mistreatment, disease, and emigration the native population became almost extinct and, by the middle of the 1500s, the Spaniards were forced to depend on the importation of African slaves to staff their expeditions, mining operations, and plantations.

By the mid-1800s, Cuba's sugar industry was the most mechanized in the world and accounted for almost one-third of the world's sugar. In 1895, war broke out between Cuba and Spain, and in 1898, the United States declared war on Spain. In 1899, Spain signed a peace protocol ending the war, as well as Spanish rule over Cuba. An American military government ruled Cuba until May 20, 1902, when the Cuban republic was formally instituted. The Cuban constitution, adopted in 1901, incorporated the provisions of the Platt Amendment, legislation that established conditions for United States intervention in Cuba, and gave the United States the authority to oversee Cuba's international commitments, economy, and internal affairs and to establish a naval station at Guantanamo Bay.

Under United States occupation, Cuba's income from the sugar industry was augmented by enormous growth in the tourism industry. While foreign interests controlled the economy—owning about three-quarters of the arable land, 90 percent of the essential services, and 40 percent of the sugar production—most Cubans were unemployed or under-employed.

Led by Fidel Castro, the 26th of July Movement took control of Cuba on January 1, 1959. The new regime modeled itself after the Soviet-bloc socialist countries and nationalized approximately $1 billion in U.S. property and businesses. In response, the United States imposed a trade embargo and, in January 1961, completely broke off diplomatic relations with Cuba. In April 1961, the United States unsuccessfully tried to invade Cuba at the Bay of Pigs. Relations with Cuba worsened even further in 1962, when the United States discovered Soviet-supplied missiles in Cuba. The United States imposed a naval blockade and after several days of negotiations, during which the threat of nuclear war seemed a distinct possibility, the SOVIET UNION agreed to dismantle and remove the missiles.

During the Castro regime's early years, hundreds of thousands of educated and wealthy Cubans emigrated to Spain, the United States, and other countries. These years were also marred by an inability to diversify the economic base, and by Castro's desire to export his ideological revolution. By the 1980s, Cuba began to provide aid to several African, Latin American, and Caribbean nations. In 1987, the United States and Cuba agreed to allow for the annual emigration of 20,000 Cubans to the United States. And, though there were additional improvements in Cuban-United States relations, the embargo has remained basically in force. In 1995, Cuba participated in forming the Association of Caribbean States (ACS), a free-trade organization.

From 1960, when Castro re-established full diplomatic relations with the Soviet Union, until the Soviet Union's dissolution in 1991, the Soviet Union was Cuba's main trading partner and source of economic aid and military support. The Soviet Union bought the majority of Cuba's sugar crop, usually at a price above the free market, and supplied aid that totaled several billion dollars annually. The dissolution of the Soviet Union in 1991 adversely affected Cuba's already troubled economy with the loss of essential commercial, economic, and military support that amounted to $4 to $6 billion annually. The effect was severe enough that Castro had to declare a "special period in peacetime" of food rationing, public services reductions, and energy conservation.

Prior to the Castro revolution, almost 300,000 tourists, predominantly from the United States, visited Cuba annually. However, by the early 1970s tourism had decreased dramatically. Since the 1980s it has begun to make a slight comeback.

In 1960, all Cuban banks were nationalized and, since 1966, the state has operated the banking system via the National Bank of Cuba. Cuba has no stock exchanges. All prices are centrally administered, and the national economic plans determine the allocation of investments. Cuba's monetary unit is the peso and its rate is officially linked to the U.S. DOLLAR. Due to Cuba's planned economy, inflation is negligible. Since 1982, Cuba has allowed foreign investment, but so far it has failed to attract substantial amounts.

Cuba's labor force is approximately 4.3 million, about half in services, one quarter each in agriculture and industry. Almost 80 percent of workers are employed by the state. Cuba's exports in 2002 were valued at approximately $1.7 billion annually and its imports at $4.9 billion. Exports include coffee, tobacco, nickel, sugar, and medical products. Imports include petroleum, consumer goods, food, machinery, and transport equipment. Its export/import partners include RUSSIA, CANADA, the NETHERLANDS, Spain, VENEZUELA, and ITALY.

In recent years, reforms have been undertaken to increase enterprise efficiency, alleviate shortages, and to stem excess liquidity. The average standard of living is still below that of the early 1990s. In 2001, damage from Hurricane Michelle, high oil prices, and recessions in key export markets hampered economic growth. Since the September 11, 2001 terrorist attacks in the United States, tourism has declined. In 2002, the peso was depreciated by approximately 30 percent and Cuba was aiming for economic growth of three percent.

Despite its difficulty with the United States, Cuba has achieved a high level of literacy, a low level of infant mortality, and an extensive network of educational and medical services.

BIBLIOGRAPHY. Barry Levine, *The New Cuban Presence in the Caribbean* (Westview Press, 1983); Ana Julia Jatar-Hausmann, *The Cuban Way: Capitalism, Communism and Confrontation* (Kumarian Press, 1999); Max Azicri, *Cuba Today and Tomorrow: Reinventing Socialism* (University Press of Florida, 2001); *CIA World Factbook* (2002).

S.J. RUBEL, J.D.
NEW YORK CITY

currency

GOING BY A DICTIONARY definition, currency is the notes and coins that serve currently as a medium of exchange in a country (i.e., currency is MONEY that facilitates buying and selling transactions in a market economy).

Coins, for example pennies, nickels, dimes, quarters, 50-cent pieces, and dollar coins, in the United States form a small (less than 5 percent) fraction of total money

A nation's currency, its coins and notes, is usually controlled by the country's central bank and its monetary policy.

supply of the nation. Coins are minted and issued under the supervision of the U.S. Treasury Department. Historically, coins contained sufficient value in metal that represented the purchasing power of the particular coin. This is no longer the case. The value of coins does not depend on their metal content anymore. Instead they are generally accepted in exchange transactions because the government has declared them to be legal tender (i.e., they must be accepted for all debts, public and private).

Notes or paper money on the other hand are the larger portion of currency and money supply. Historical origins of bank notes reside in the 16th and 17th centuries. European goldsmiths issuing receipts for gold deposited them for safekeeping. The modern-day banking practices are an extension of the activities of goldsmiths who began lending money based on these gold deposits for a fee (today's INTEREST RATE charged to the borrower) and their deposit receipts, as well as the bank-notes they issued, came to be used as money. These days such notes are issued in the United States by the FEDERAL RESERVE banks (and the CENTRAL BANKS in other countries). These notes, formally the Federal Reserve notes, printed under government supervision and distributed to the regional Federal Reserve banks are also legal tender: Each such note carries a statement printed up front: "This note is legal tender for all debts, public and private." That is to say that these notes are to be accepted by law as money in the payment of any and all debts incurred.

A store of value. Currency as money serves the purpose of being a store of value, which means that it can be held and later used for future purchases. Also, it serves as a standard of value (i.e., it is used to measure and compare the market values—prices of different goods and services). However, currency is not all the money a modern economy has. As already mentioned it is a small fraction of the total money supply—the rest is mostly represented by the demand deposits in the commercial banking system, the accounts that permit direct payments on demand to third parties with a check.

There is a common perception that the amount of currency in circulation is reflective of the amount of gold available to back the issuance of such currency. The impression persists because of historical evolution of money in general and currency in particular. The goldsmiths' receipts-turned-money began with an exact equivalence to the gold deposits at hand. However, the issuance of notes by the goldsmith was constrained only by the probability of a deposit of gold being withdrawn by the original depositor. If, at any given time, only a specific fraction of gold was being claimed and withdrawn from the goldsmith's vault, only that fraction was required to be kept on hand. The rest could be loaned out either as specie, or, more likely, in the form of bank notes issued by the goldsmith.

This is the basis of modern fractional reserve banking. But how much currency notes to issue at any given time? The so-called banking school theorists have argued that the demand for currency in a free market would be matched by a corresponding supply through the expansion of deposits regulated by the price of money (i.e., the rate of interest). The currency school proponents, on the other hand, claimed that this mechanism may not be sufficiently sensitive to take into account the effect of balance of payments (i.e., the net result of transactions in the international trade arena)

Hence the necessity of a non-market regulating mechanism, such as the guarantee of actual convertibility into gold. U.S. currency was, until the 1930s, convertible into gold, and until the 1960s, it was partially backed by gold. Since then, the currency—or the rest of money supply for that matter—is not backed by gold at all. The monetary authorities are free to change the note issue as required by the contingencies of monetary policy. The note issues are thus entirely fiduciary in nature (i.e., issued in response to financial considerations and based on trust in the economy alone—the power of the myth, so to speak).

Currency exchange. This leads to exploring the value of currency and its availability as part of monetary and economic policy measures, both domestically and internationally. Since all sovereign nations tend to have their own national currencies, there must be some rate of exchange between different currencies for international trade transactions. If an American tourist has dollars and wants to purchase French wine denominated in price in euros, it is necessary to be able to convert the euro-denominated price into dollars, that is an EX-CHANGE RATE between euro and dollars. The intuitive exchange rate should be based on what is called purchasing power parity. This implies that if a basket of goods sells at $1 dollar in the United States and the same basket sells for 3 euros in France, then a dollar should be equated with three euros—the equivalence in purchasing power.

As eminently sensible as this equivalence is, it suffers from several theoretical and practical weaknesses. First, not all goods and services are internationally traded. Therefore, their corresponding demand/supply conditions are not reflected in the international market. Second, not all currencies are created equal. Some represent hegemonic, strong, and established economies, others are connected to weak, less-developed and uncertain economic arrangements. This is captured in the nomenclature of hard currencies: those with a persistently high demand in the foreign-exchange market like the DOLLAR; and soft currencies, those with declining and uncertain demand like the peso. Generally speaking, countries that suffer deficits in international trade—exporting less and importing more value—have respective currencies that tend to be soft or likely to lose value in response to a lower demand abroad for their goods, which is equivalent to having lower demand for their currency.

On the other hand, countries that have a balance of payment surplus in their account—exports being higher in value than imports—are likely to have hard currencies. And then there is a special category called a reserve currency. This is an institutional arrangement in which governments and other international agencies are willing to hold a particular currency as part of their foreign exchange reserves. The expressed requisites for such a status are:

1. maintenance and stability of value in relation to other currencies

2. convertibility into other currencies

3. representation of a large, open economy that has a significant share of international trade.

The dollar and the pound sterling have historically served this function. It means that a large proportion of international trade is conducted through the medium of these currencies. This, in turn, lends a banking advantage to the respective economy represented by these currencies—for which reason the status is jealously guarded as an expression of hegemonic political endeavor as well as economic benefit.

In a free market context, the value of a currency (i.e., the exchange value of one country's money unit in terms of another country's money unit) tends to fluctuate like all other market prices in response to the changes in demand and supply conditions. If a country experiences persistent balance of payments deficit, its currency is likely to lose value in exchange. This market phenomenon is called depreciation. The converse happens with a balance of payments surplus and is known as currency appreciation. However, at times governments in their attempts to promote exports reduce the foreign exchange value of their currency as a policy measure—to make their goods appear cheaper to foreign buyers because of cheaper currency. This is termed devaluation. The reverse of this policy—a much rarer phenomenon for obvious reasons—is called revaluation.

On occasion, and for a short period of time, these policies of devaluation and revaluation may work especially if other countries do not retaliate in kind. After all, the benefit thus garnered by one country comes at the expense of the other countries. Retaliation is a likely response, thus neutralizing any differential advantage. However, this demonstrates the role of foreign-exchange determination in the execution of domestic monetary and fiscal policies. By devaluation, a prospect of increased exports is anticipated, which, in turn, can lead to higher domestic production and employment as well as address the deficit in balance of payments.

Conversely, a revaluation can help alleviate domestic inflationary pressures, at least in theory. The downside of

The U.S. Treasury in Washington, D.C., supervises the minting of coins and printing of notes in the United States.

this kind of policy manipulation is that the domestic currency loses its stability in the foreign-exchange market. This increases uncertainty and risk for entrepreneurs on the one hand, and opens up political space for undue interference in economic policy making on the other. Many less-developed countries find themselves in this dilemma of poorly managed foreign exchange and currency policies leading to severe detrimental economic consequences. In response, economic managers have come up with some currency stabilization schemes. The two main options, both highly controversial, are a currency board or "dollarization."

In the case of a currency-board regime, the monetary authority pegs its currency to an anchor currency at a fixed exchange rate and issues coins and notes only to the extent that can be converted into the anchor currency. The anchor currency, likely the dollar or pound sterling, is supposed to be not only relatively stable, but also internationally acceptable. Gold could possibly be used in lieu of the anchor currency as well for the well-documented characteristics of this metal serving as money. Clearly this implies that the currency board must have sufficient reserves of either gold or the anchor currency to provide 100 percent coverage to its issuance of coins and notes. This might be problematic by itself, but in addition it also means that the monetary authority has no policy discretion available to respond to macroeconomic conditions that could change over time.

The other option is outright dollarization. This entails buying dollars to use as legal tender instead of the local currency, in part or whole. Again, the strain of acquisition of dollars in exchange for sufficient foreign reserves, and the straitjacket of no monetary policy discretion to address domestic economic contingencies in return for a stable currency, makes this a rather mixed blessing. Several Latin American countries—beset with the problem of political interference in policy-making of central banks—have attempted to work with these new schemes with at best mixed results.

BIBLIOGRAPHY. S. Edwards, "The Determinants of Choice Between Fixed and Flexible Exchange Regimes" (NBER Working paper #5756, 1996); R. Nurkse, *The Interwar Currency Experience: Lessons From the Period* (United Nations, 1944); F. Weaver, *Economic Literacy* (Roman & Littlefield, 2002).

SYED B. HUSSAIN, PH.D.
UNIVERSITY OF WISCONSIN, OSHKOSH

Czech Republic

FOR 300 YEARS THE Hapsburg Empire ruled the Czechs until they combined with the Slovak Federal Republic. After WORLD WAR I, the independent country of Czechoslovakia was formed, but by the end of WORLD WAR II it fell under the Soviet Union's sphere of influence.

The Communist Party seized power in 1946 and instituted a Soviet-style socialist regime. In 1968, during a period of liberalization known as the Prague Spring, the government adopted a policy of "socialism with a human face." This did not last long, and the Soviets invaded and retook control.

In 1989, the Civil Forum movement began which, along with the dissolution of the Soviet empire, led to the nonviolent "Velvet Revolution" and the eventual end of the Czechoslovakian state. In 1993, the Czech Republic and the Republic of Slovakia were founded. Since then, the Czech Republic has become one of the most developed and industrialized economies in Eastern Europe. The Czech Republic is a member of the UNITED NATIONS and the North Atlantic Treaty Organization, and expects to join the EUROPEAN UNION (EU) officially in 2004.

With a population of 10.2 million people in 2001, the Czech Republic had a GROSS DOMESTIC PRODUCT (GDP) of $147.9 billion.

BIBLIOGRAPHY. The Department of State Background Note, www.state.gov; *CIA World Factbook* (2002); Michael G. Roskin, *The Rebirth of East Europe* (Prentice Hall, 2002); Karen Dawisha, *The Kremlin and the Prague Spring* (University of California Press, 1984).

LINDA L. PETROU, PH.D.
HIGH POINT UNIVERSITY

D

Dai-ichi Mutual Life Insurance Company

SINCE ITS INCEPTION just over a century ago, in 1902, Dai-ichi Mutual Life has tried to live up to its name: "Dai-ichi" in Japanese means "first," and to date the company has driven itself to stay at or near the top ranking of not only Japanese insurance companies, but also worldwide. One of Japan's foremost insurers, the firm has gained recognition and esteem in the industry, culminating in its winning the Japan Quality Award for 2001, Japan's answer to America's Malcolm Baldridge Award in recognition of competitiveness, quality, and productivity.

Dai-ichi, based in Tokyo, sells individual and group life insurance, as well as individual and group pension products. Through partnerships, it also provides non-life insurance, such as automobile and fire, as well as strategic products such as asset management and risk management.

Its 40,000 sales representatives are guided by their employer's demand to conduct business "with the greatest regard for the needs and views of customers." Accordingly, Dai-ichi's pursuit of its three major goals—customer satisfaction, profitability, and cost effectiveness—led to structural reform in 2002. The restructuring was the company's latest step in following through with, what it calls, a "Lifelong Plan Concept." Translated, it means to address the changing needs of customers through each and every stage of their lives with quality planning, products, and service.

Despite social and cultural transformation throughout the industry, Dai-ichi Chairman Takahide Sakurai and President Tomijiro Morita recognize the importance of strengthening their company's products and services. To ensure that their Lifelong Plan extends to all those who require it, they have formed alliances with companies such as MIZUHO Holdings, Sompo Japan, and AFLAC (the U.S. company well-known for its duck commercials in the early 2000s) the largest foreign insurer in Japan.

Dai-ichi Mutual Life Insurance Company ranked as the 76th largest company in the world in 2002 on *Fortune* magazine's Global 500 list, with revenue exceeding $43 billion.

BIBLIOGRAPHY. *Plunkett's Health Care Industry Almanac 2003* (Plunkett Research, Ltd., 2002); "Global 500: World's Largest Companies," *Fortune* (July, 2002); Dai-ichi Mutual Life Insurance Company, www.dai-ichi.co.jp.

JOSEPH GERINGER
SYED B. HUSSAIN, PH.D.
UNIVERSITY OF WISCONSIN, OSHKOSH

DaimlerChrysler

FORMED FROM A merger of Daimler-Benz AG and Chrysler Corporation in November, 1998, Daimler-Chrysler is today one of the largest automotive manufacturers in the world. With nearly 375,000 employees worldwide and manufacturing plants in 37 countries, the company generated revenues just over $136 billion in 2001, selling nearly four million passenger vehicles and nearly half a million commercial vehicles. Ranging from passenger cars such as Mercedes to Jeep, with at least eight commercial lines of vehicles, DaimlerChrysler enjoys a global presence, selling its products in over 200 countries. It has also diversified itself beyond vehicle production, offering financial and other services through DaimlerChrysler Services.

According to the company, its global strategy revolves around four concerns: global presence, strong brands, broad product range, and technology leadership. Technology has been a heightened focus since the merger, with DaimlerChrysler employing 28,000 people worldwide in research and development alone. The company secures some 2,000 patents annually. Some recent technological advancements have included development of fuel-cell technology, and DaimlerChrysler has announced the introduction of a fleet of fuel-cell vehicles to be tested worldwide. This technology relies on the reaction between oxygen and hydrogen to produce energy, and the result is a vehicle that produces little to no emissions, hence it's environmentally friendly and has enhanced efficiency.

DaimlerChrysler prides itself on its commitment to diversity: The corporation offers a minority dealer development program that trains qualified ethnic minorities, making them eligible for general manager positions in dealerships. In existence since 1983 as part of Chrysler, most of the program's participants have gone on to become dealers. One goal of the program continues to be to increase the number of minority-owned dealerships. Supporting this goal is an association for such individuals, the DaimlerChrysler Minority Dealer Association.

BIBLIOGRAPHY. "Global 500: World Largest Companies," *Fortune* (July 2002); DaimlerChrysler, *Driving the Future: Annual Report 2000* and *Answers for Questions to Come: Annual Report 2001*, www.daimlerchrysler.com.

AUDREY D. KLINE, PH.D.
UNIVERSITY OF LOUISVILLE

De Gaulle, Charles (1890–1970)

CHARLES DE GAULLE served as president of FRANCE from 1945–46 and from 1958–69. Before WORLD WAR II, he gained the reputation as a military innovator, based upon a prescient text of 1934 that had criticized the French Army's antiquated weaponry and its reliance on outdated strategies, which he believed would be of little use in a modern war. At that time De Gaulle was associated with the far-right political-military group *Action Française*, but this was little remembered as compared with his critique of France's military elite and his decision to move to exile in Britain following the Fall of France in 1940.

De Gaulle's Free French resistance movement, based in London, gave him great political and national credi-

bility, and in the latter years of the war he managed, with British support and the acquiescence of key resistors in France, to unify much of the French resistance into a single force. In 1944 it was "De Gaulle's Resistance," as well as the British and the Americans, who were seen to liberate France.

De Gaulle was an obvious choice as postwar leader of France, not least to himself and to the British and Americans who could stomach De Gaulle more than they could a possible communist government. De Gaulle led an interim government of unity as a successor to the collaborationist Vichy regime, with the aim of developing a technocratic administration, which would cut across the party and ideological lines that had conventionally split French politics. His abrasive personality led to rather limited success in this aim of recasting French political culture, though De Gaulle was once again called to power in 1958 when the politicians of the Fourth Republic found themselves unable to deal with crises at home and a bloody war of independence in the French colony of Algeria. De Gaulle demonstrated his essential pragmatism in leading the French withdrawal from Algeria, and his sense of *gloire* in initiating a Fifth French Republic in which much greater power was invested in the presidency.

In all areas of politics De Gaulle aimed for reform based on a very personal set of beliefs about France, its culture, and the French weaknesses he had identified in the interwar period. Just as De Gaulle wished to create a French political culture that went beyond parties, he envisaged a new kind of French economic arrangement that lay somewhere between capitalism and socialism, combining the best aspects of those systems, while abandoning their faults and their partisan qualities. De Gaulle's economic Third Way was rather vaguely defined using the ideas of association and participation, but there is no doubt that it formed a cornerstone of his political beliefs. He acknowledged the potential for wealth creation in capitalism, but his analysis of its human consequences was almost Marxian: "But, however, the ownership, the management, the profits of enterprises in the capitalist system belong only to capital. And so those who do not possess it find themselves in a sort of state of alienation inside the very activity to which they contribute. No, capitalism, from the point of view of humanity does not offer a satisfactory solution."

Such a critique was partly based on social Catholic ideas, and De Gaulle's aim was to recreate the Revolutionary notion of *Fraternité* through his schemes of participation, which in practice meant the establishment of worker representation in firms (1945), the development of social security schemes (1945), and guaranteed profit-sharing for workers (1965). During his time in office, De Gaulle's economic ideas were regarded with some skepticism by both allies (his own political colleagues) and by opponents (leftist political parties, employers groups, trade unions), but in retrospect his advocacy of a French capitalism that combined state-directed technocratic growth and a recognition of the alienation of workers in capitalist society, seems a rather elegant French solution to the challenges of the modern economic world.

While De Gaulle's symbolic policy of participation was decisively rejected by the French people in a 1969 referendum (shortly after which he left power, and then died), he could point to his role in the successful rebuilding of the French economy after World War II, and in particular the development of high-technology industries and the entry of France into closer economic union with its European partners.

BIBLIOGRAPHY. Charles G. Cogan, *Charles De Gaulle: A Brief Biography with Documents* (Bedford/St. Martin's, 1996); Daniel J. Mahoney, *De Gaulle: Statesmanship, Grandeur and Modern Democracy* (Praeger, 2000); Charles Williams, *The Last Great Frenchman: A Life of General De Gaulle* (John Wiley & Sons, 1993); Philip Thody, *The Fifth French Republic: Presidents, Politics and Personalities* (Routledge, 1998).

WILLIAM GALLOIS, PH.D.
AMERICAN UNIVERSITY OF SHARJAH

In his 1959 book, *The Theory of Value*, Debreu proposed a more general equilibrium theory, using mathematical tools such as set theory and topology to prove his theorems. Though some economists cite a lack of real-world application for some of Debreu's theories, others say Debreu's work, even as pure theory, is helpful to any analysis of economic reality.

In early 2003, Debreu was a professor of economics and mathematics at the University of California, Berkeley, and had received honorary degrees from the universities of Bonn and Lausanne. He has also served as president of the Econometric Society and as a fellow of the American Association for the Advancement of Science. And, though Debreu became a naturalized U.S. citizen in 1975, his native France awarded him the honor of Chevalier of the French Legion of Honor in 1976.

BIBLIOGRAPHY. Gerard Debreu, *Theory of Value: An Axiomatic Analysis of Economic Equilibrium* (Yale University Press, 1971); Gerard Debreu Autobiography, www.nobel.se; David R. Henderson, *The Concise Encyclopedia of Economics* (Liberty Fund, 2002); Gerard Debreu and Kenneth Arrow, "Existence of a Competitive Equilibrium for a Competitive Economy," *Econometrica* (v.22/3, 1954).

SYED B. HUSSAIN, PH.D.
UNIVERSITY OF WISCONSIN, OSHKOSH

Debreu, Gerard (1921–)

AWARDED THE Nobel Prize in Economics in 1983, Gerard Debreu was cited by the Nobel Committee for "having incorporated new analytic methods into economic theory and for his rigorous reformulation of the theory of general equilibrium."

Born in Calais, FRANCE, Debreu studied mathematics at the College of the City of Calais until 1939 and the start of WORLD WAR II. In the first few years of the war, he attended regional universities until making his way to École Normale Supérieure in Paris, under German occupation. Despite the war, Debreu describes his years in Paris as extraordinary and teeming with an intense intellectual atmosphere.

By 1948, Debreu had shifted his focus to economics; he obtained a Rockefeller Fellowship and visited several American universities, including Harvard and Columbia, and the universities of Chicago and Oslo. While at Chicago, Debreu was offered a research position at the Cowles Commission for Research in Economics.

Debreu's contributions are in the field of general EQUILIBRIUM, explorations of whether and how each market reaches equilibrium. Writing with Kenneth ARROW, Debreu published the 1954 article "Existence of a Competitive Equilibrium for a Competitive Economy," proving that, under fairly unrestrictive assumptions, prices exist that bring markets into equilibrium.

Gerard Debreu, using mathematical tools, explored how competitive markets reach equilibrium.

debt

IN ITS SIMPLEST sense, debt is a liability for the borrower who promises to make future payments to the lender. It constitutes an agreement between the lender and borrower regarding the exchange of funds, or resources. The borrower obtains the privilege to use the resources, and in turn compensates the lender with future payments. Such agreements can be informal contracts that are enforced by community and social institutions, or can be formal contracts that are enforced by legal institutions.

The economic basis of debt is the mismatch between the resources and needs of the individual parties involved. A debt contract matches a borrower, who is in need of or "short" of current resources, but commands or is "long" in future resources, and a lender, who is currently long, and thus sufficiently patient. Indeed, debt can be viewed as an exchange or trading of funds over time. The lender sacrifices current use of these funds in exchange for financial return. The return is usually referred to as the rate of interest, that also measures the cost of borrowing. For example, a high-school graduate, who wishes to obtain college education and improve her future earnings may lack the funds to pay the tuition. A loan (or student debt) with a certain interest rate allows the student to access education, and improve her skills. This effectively enables the student to transfer some of her future income to today. Similarly, firms may borrow against their future sales and profits, and governments may borrow against their future tax revenues.

Debt involves risks both for the lender and borrower. The lender transfers the funds and waits for future payments, that may never materialize, say, because the student never finishes college, or the firm goes bankrupt. This is the default risk for the lender. To cover some of these risks, lenders may request that a certain amount of collateral be posted by the borrower. Collateral is typically a physical asset that is the property of the borrower, and can be liquidated by the lender in the event of a default. The borrower, on the other hand, faces a risk due to uncertain future income and ability to pay back the debt and the interest. The college student, for instance, is usually uncertain about returns to education, and, similarly, firms are uncertain about future demand.

Debt contracts stipulate the amounts and frequency of future payments (typically over a specified period of time). The final payment date is known as the maturity. The yield to maturity is the constant interest rate that makes the price of a debt contract equal to the present value of its payments. Outstanding debts differ in terms of their maturity; a short-term debt matures within one year, whereas a long-term debt has a maturity of ten or more years. Medium-term debt falls in between.

Debt instruments. There are different types of instruments that can be used to issue debt. One of the most common debt instruments is a BOND, issued primarily by governments and corporations, and traded in exchanges. New issues are sold in the primary market to initial buyers. Previously issued bonds are then traded in the secondary market. The existence of an active secondary market makes bonds attractive, because it gives the bondholders the ability to liquidate their savings held in bonds before the maturity date.

Short-term debt instruments are traded in the money market. These instruments include short-term bonds (bills), negotiable bank certificates of deposit (only large denominations), commercial paper, and repurchase agreements. Long-term debt instruments are traded in the capital market. These instruments include long-term government and corporate bonds (bonds), residential, commercial, and farm mortgages, and commercial and consumer loans.

Borrowers are typically rated according to the default risk they carry. A default risk-free borrower commands a much lower interest rate than a risky borrower. The interest rate differential (spread) between the interest rates on bonds with and without default risk is called the risk premium. For instance, governments of developing and emerging market economies frequently issue bonds in international markets (in foreign currencies), and pay sometimes very hefty risk premiums.

The spread between the short- and long-term bonds with identical default risk is called the term structure of interest rates. This spread contains valuable information about the financial markets' expectations of future interest rates. For instance, when the spread is negative (short rates below the long rates), the short-term future interest rate is expected to increase. For this very reason bond markets are closely watched by analysts and economists.

Government debt. Two aspects of debt have attracted considerable attention: national and international debt. The analysis of national (government) debt concerns the causes and consequences of indebtedness of a government both to its citizens and foreign nationals, and that of international debt concerns the indebtedness of a nation vis-à-vis the rest of the world. We consider them in turn.

A government budget over a period (typically, measured by a fiscal year) consists of revenues (mostly taxes) and expenditures. If expenditures exceed revenues, the government budget is said to be in deficit. Government debt is the past deficits that have accumulated over time. In a given fiscal year government deficits will have to be financed through new borrowing. This new borrowing is then added on to the existing debt. Most of this debt is securitized in government bonds. Government expenditures thus usually have two components: government spending on goods and services, and interest payments on outstanding debt. The difference between government revenues and spending on goods and services is called the primary deficit (or surplus).

Although some of the short term financing of government expenditures is due to a mismatch between the timing of the receipt of revenues (collection of taxes) and outlays (salaries and wages, and transfers), government deficits typically arise due to national emergencies, fluctuations in the government revenues, and spending over the business cycle, and government's desire to smooth taxes. National emergencies include wars and natural disasters, which are temporary events. Under such circumstances government expenditures tend to increase and revenues may decline. Similarly, during economic recessions transfer payments to the economically disadvantaged tend to increase, because of rising unemployment, and tax revenues tend to decline, because of declining economic activity. In either case, the government can finance the primary deficit either by borrowing or by higher taxes or both.

The choice between raising taxes in the current period versus debt financing has been a topic of debate among economists and policy makers. In both cases, the government sector lays a claim on current resources that are otherwise available to the private sector. This transfer of resources appears transparent in the case of current taxes, but is sometimes underappreciated in the case of government debt. Indeed, by issuing bonds, the government simply postpones taxing its citizens, and thus the choice between debt financing versus current taxes can be viewed as a choice between current versus future taxes. After all, the only source of revenue available to governments to pay down their debt is levying taxes.

The notion of viewing government debt as future taxes has an important intellectual tradition in economics. One particular interpretation of this viewpoint is known as the Ricardian equivalence, which states that for the private sector decisions the precise form of financing government deficits (taxes versus bonds) should not matter. This influential viewpoint was originally developed by David RICARDO, and was resurrected by Robert J. Barro. One of the implications of this proposition is that the private sector's savings decisions mirror those of the government's. For instance, according to the equivalence proposition, if the government decides to reduce taxes today, without reducing its expenditures, the private sector would increase its current savings, because it would (correctly) anticipate higher future taxes.

Whether such equivalence results hold in reality or not is intensely debated in economics. While empirical evidence in support of the Ricardian equivalence may be weak (or at best inconclusive), most governments seem to exhibit preferences for bond financing over taxes for events that are evidently transitory. For instance, during the WORLD WAR II, the governments of Allied forces ran considerable deficits, most of which were financed through bonds. As a consequence, the financial costs of the war were spread over several generations of taxpayers, by way of relatively higher taxes. Such a choice is described as preference for tax smoothing, because this form of financing does not require significant fluctuations in the tax rate.

Government debt is a special case of sovereign debt, which has been in existence for more than 500 years. Philip II of Spain (1556–98) borrowed from the Genoese-led cartel of lenders to finance his war in Flanders and pay for his armies in the Low Countries. Partial default and debt repudiation are also as old as the sovereign debt itself. Philip II, for instance, suspended interest payments and tried to renegotiate the debt more than twice. In all the cases, the Genoese-led cartel responded by suspending further deliveries, and inflicted substantial damage on the ability of Philip II to supply provisions to his armies. This example also demonstrates that default is costly for the borrower, because the reputation effects restrict, or even eliminate, its ability to access future credit.

Default and debt renegotiation. Partial default and debt renegotiations have also been a recurrent theme, at least since the announcement by the Mexican government in August, 1982, that it was temporarily suspending interest payments on its outstanding foreign currency denominated debt. This announcement unleashed a period of economic turmoil and uncertainty, known as the international debt crisis. The causes of the debt crisis included rapid expansion of lending by international banks to emerging markets at relatively favorable interest rates. Coupled with the increased demand for funds by developing countries, as their economies were growing at a relatively rapid pace, these countries quickly accumulated large amounts of foreign debt. Both the governments and the private sector borrowed extensively. While part of this debt was used for productive investments and infrastructure, most of the foreign borrowing was channeled into private consumption. At the beginning of the 1980s the combination of slow economic growth worldwide and high interest rates culminated in excessive debt burden on developing countries and ultimately in the crisis.

The consequences of the debt crisis were far-reaching. The flow of foreign credit into the developing countries came to a sudden halt, and most indebted countries were forced to reduce their foreign-debt obligations over the 1980s. In most cases, the inability to borrow from abroad led to domestic financial crises, negative economic growth, and reduced social spending. While some of the countries affected by the debt crisis have since regained access to international credit and financial markets, the social and economic consequences of the debt crisis partly lingered for decades, especially for the group of heavily indebted poor countries. Their access to international credit has been limited because of their heavy debt burden. However, there have been debt relief or debt forgiveness initiatives targeted for these countries, since they already represent some of the poorest nations.

BIBLIOGRAPHY. Robert J. Barro, "Are Government Bonds Net Wealth?" *Journal of Political Economy*, (v.87, 1974); Robert J. Barro, "The Ricardian Approach to Budget Deficits," *Journal of Economic Perspectives* (v.3, 1989); B. Douglas Bernheim, "A Neoclassical Perspective on Budget Deficits," *Journal of Economic Perspectives* (v.3, 1989); John Y. Campbell, "Some Lessons from the Yield Curve," *Journal of Economic Perspectives* (v.9, 1995); James Conklin, "The Theory of Sovereign Debt and Spain under Philip II," *Journal of Political Economy*, (v.106, 1998); Robert Devlin, *Debt and Crisis in Latin America: The Supply Side of the Story* (Princeton University Press, 1989); Robert Eisner, "Budget Deficits: Rhetoric and Reality," *Journal of Economic Perspectives* (v.3, 1989); David Ricardo, *On the Principles of Political Economy and Taxation* (Cambridge University Press, 1951); Frederic S. Mishkin, *The Economics of Money, Banking, and Financial Markets* (HarperCollins, 1995); World Bank, *Debt Initiative for Heavily Indebted Poor Countries*, www.worldbank.org.

TALAN IŞCAN
DALHOUSIE UNIVERSITY

demand

THE TOTAL AMOUNT of a good that a consumer is willing and able to purchase at various prices, with all other things (income, preferences, etc.) held constant, is commonly known as demand. One must be careful to distinguish the demand for a product from the quantity demanded, where the latter refers to the total amount of output that a consumer is willing and able to buy at one specific PRICE.

The concept of demand is of critical importance in a market-oriented economy and helps answer one of the most fundamental economic questions, namely what will be produced with scarce resources? Demand essentially tells us what consumers are willing and able to buy while the quantity demanded tells us how much of a particular product consumers are willing and able to purchase at a particular price.

Existence of demand for a product indicates that consumers expect to receive a certain level of satisfaction from (i.e., are interested in) that product regardless

of the product's price. This does not, however, mean that consumers will purchase any amount of the item. Such confusion often arises when one uses demand and quantity demanded interchangeably; this highlights the importance of differentiating between the two. Individuals interested in a particular item may choose not to purchase the product if they feel they would not receive enough satisfaction to justify payment of the prevailing price of the item. In this case, the quantity demanded would be equal to zero despite the fact that there is a demand for the product. Alternatively, the absence of demand indicates that consumers expect to receive no satisfaction from and hence have no interest in a particular product regardless of price. It is not possible for quantity demanded to exist if demand is zero.

Demand plays a significant role in a capitalist system as it serves as a signal of how consumers wish to see scarce resources allocated. One can think of demand as a voting mechanism whereby consumers communicate to firms what they would like to see firms produce. As economic agents free to pursue their own self-interest, firms may entertain or ignore consumer demand. As we examine below, changes in demand are, in fact, extremely effective methods of communication as they provide profit-maximizing firms with the proper incentives to allocate resources according to consumer wants.

Deriving demand. Individual demand can be constructed using two common techniques: utility theory and indifference curve analysis. According to utility theory, an individual will decide whether or not he wants to buy an item and, if so, how much of the item he wants by considering the amount of utility or satisfaction that he will receive from the item. Assuming an individual is interested in a particular product, he will choose how much to consume by comparing the marginal utility, defined as the extra satisfaction provided by one more unit of consumption, to the product's price.

Because it measures the change in total satisfaction that an individual will experience should he consume one more unit of output, the marginal utility can be interpreted as an individual's valuation of the additional unit (i.e., a measure of how much an individual would be willing to pay for one more unit of output). An individual then will continue to purchase additional units of output only as long as the marginal utility is greater than or equal to the product's price (i.e., as long as the amount a consumer is willing to pay exceeds the actual price of the product). It is important to note that this discussion of utility is simplified and assumes individuals are consuming just one item at a time. By applying utility theory and varying the price of a product we can determine how much output an individual would choose to consume at various prices and hence generate an individual's demand. The outcome of utility analysis is a schedule of an individual's quantity demanded at various prices. One can think of this demand schedule as a contingency plan of how much output a consumer would be expected to buy depending on the actual price of the product.

It is important to remember that demand does not tell us how much output an individual will purchase but merely indicates whether a consumer is interested in a particular product or not. The graphical illustration of this schedule results in an individual's demand curve. Total market demand for a product can then be constructed by adding up individual demands or, in the case of the demand curve, by horizontally summing individual demand curves.

Utility theory provides valuable insight into those factors likely to contribute to changes in demand. Because the demand for a product is the collection of price-quantity demanded pairs, changes in a product's price will have no effect on overall demand but will lead only to a change in the quantity demanded and a movement along a fixed demand curve. A change in demand refers to a situation in which an individual chooses to consume more units at any given price (in the case of an increase in demand) and fewer units at any given price (in the case of a decrease in demand).

In other words, if consumers become more interested in a particular product regardless of price, demand will increase. When consumers become less interested in a product regardless of that product's price, demand will fall. Utility theory predicts then that only changes in the utility associated with a particular product will lead to changes in demand. Utility or the satisfaction derived from consumption is a function of how much an individual wants or needs a product and may be influenced by a myriad of factors including individual preferences, quality of the commodity, style, weather, age, tastes, gender, geographic location, advertisements, prices of related commodities, etc. Changes in any one of these factors will make an individual more or less interested in a product regardless of price and consequently will lead to changes in demand.

Another approach to understanding demand involves the use of indifference curve analysis. Indifference curve analysis and utility theory are not unrelated. The former is in fact a graphical representation of the latter. However, the two may be considered as alternative routes by which one may arrive at a better understanding of demand. Indifference curve analysis, like utility theory, emphasizes the importance of satisfaction in consumer decision-making. An individual's satisfaction and preferences are represented by a map of his indifference curves and explain, in part, how much of a particular item he will choose to purchase at various prices.

Indifference curve analysis deviates from utility theory by highlighting the role that an individual's budget plays in the decision making process. An individual's budget will depend on his income as well as the prices of the commodities he is interested in buying. His budget is thus a reflection of all the possible combinations of output that this individual could afford to purchase. Which one of these combinations an individual will choose to purchase will depend on his personal preferences and will ultimately determine the quantity demanded of the products in question. Assuming consumers are rational agents, they will attempt to achieve the greatest level of satisfaction that is possible within their budget. In most cases, the bundle chosen by an individual (i.e., the quantity demanded of output) will occur at the point at which one of the indifference curves is tangent to the budget. Indifference curve analysis then predicts that changes in an individual's budget or preferences will lead to changes in demand.

Changes in a product's price would be expected to alter an individual's budget and consequently the quantity demanded of that product. By varying the price of the product, the demand for a particular product can be derived. Changes in income and prices of other commodities would also affect the budget and consequently would be expected to influence consumption patterns even in the absence of a change in the price of the product in question. Hence, changes in income and prices of other commodities would be expected to lead to changes in demand as an individual would choose to consume more or less of an item at any given price.

Changes in the shape of the indifference curve brought about by changes in preferences would also be expected to lead to changes in demand. Factors influencing consumer preferences include, but are certainly not limited to, quality, style, weather, age, tastes, advertisement, etc.

The significance of demand in MICROECONOMICS is obvious as it, along with SUPPLY, directly influences prices, and in so doing determines the allocation of resources in a capitalist economy. An increase in demand indicates that consumers would choose to purchase more of a commodity at any given price. In other words, consumers either want or need the product more than they did previously regardless of price. Consequently, an increase in demand means a product has become more valuable to consumers and implies, therefore, that consumers will be willing to pay a higher price for the product. Higher prices will lead to a reallocation of resources toward the production of items desired by consumers. It is important to note that this reallocation occurs not because most firms are interested in maximizing consumer satisfaction (at least not explicitly) but because they see an opportunity to increase profits through the increase in price. Conversely, a decrease in demand suggests consumers do not want or need a product as much as they once did. Thus, with a decrease in demand a product becomes less valuable to consumers who will no longer pay as high a price for the product.

Thus, in a market economy, demand plays a significant role in determining which products are produced and which are not. The concept of demand also plays an important role in MACROECONOMICS. Aggregate demand, an extension of market demand, is used in macroeconomics to explain fluctuations in, among other things, general economic activity, unemployment, inflation and GROSS DOMESTIC PRODUCT (GDP).

BIBLIOGRAPHY. William J. Baumol and Alan S. Blinder, *Economics: Principles and Policy* (South-Western, 2002); John Creedy, *Demand and Exchange in Economic Analysis: A History from Cournot to Marshall* (Edward Elgar, 1992); Steven E. Landsburg, *Price Theory and Applications* (South-Western, 2001); Arthur O'Sullivan and Steven M. Sheffrin, *Microeconomics: Principles and Tools* (Prentice Hall, 2003); Leon G. Schiffman and Leslie Kanuk, *Consumer Behavior* (Prentice Hall, 1999); Michael R. Solomon, *Consumer Behavior: Buying, Having and Being* (Prentice Hall, 2002).

KRISTIN KUCSMA, PH.D.
SETON HALL UNIVERSITY

democracy

THE IDEA OF DEMOCRACY, like the idea of capitalism, promises much, though the reality always falls short. The promise is of wide participation in government, free and open competition among diverse groups, and self-determination. Democracy offers the vision of individuals working together to achieve their own particular goals, using similar means to accomplish collectively individual wealth and freedom. History offers few examples of really successful democracies, success being defined as actual structures of government and society that make concrete the image that the word democracy conjures up. Democracy, like liberty, freedom, and equality, is elusive, visualized in the mind as dreams never quite fulfilled. That these concepts, democracy, liberty, freedom, equality, are linked to capitalism implies that capitalism itself is more image than reality.

The word "democracy" is a combination of two classical Greek words from the 5th century B.C.E. The Greek *deme* was a tribe in ancient Athens; there were 10 such tribes that comprised the city-state, or *polis*, of Athens. The *demos* were therefore the people of the ten tribes. The Greek word *kratos* implies power, strength, control—the attributes of government. Demos joined with kratos means to give the people the power, hence the English word democracy, the rule of the people.

Democracy and capitalism. The linkage between democracy and markets is seen from the beginning, at the creation of the concept of democracy around 500 B.C.E. At that time, Athens had experienced centuries of government by kings (rule by one), by the aristocracy (rule of the best men), and by tyrants, which came to mean oppressive rule. But under the leadership of Cleisthenes, the Greeks adopted a form of government that developed from the interchange of goods and ideas at the marketplace. Here the citizens of Athens met in assembly to vote on proposals offered by speakers at the rostrum. The Council of 500, composed of 50 citizens selected by lot from each of the ten tribes, typically set the agenda for the assembly. The assembly of citizens passed legislation by acclamation, and in time by secret ballot. Athenian citizenship was restricted to adult men; women had little power in Athenian society. Slavery was practiced at Athens as well. Hence the majority of people living at Athens did not exercise power—they were disenfranchised. However, it was remarkable that among the male citizens there was no property qualification for voting, nor even for addressing the assembly.

Another clear example of the relationship between democracy and capitalism comes from the period of the later Middle Ages and early Renaissance in European history. Medieval FEUDALISM was the antithesis of democratic society and government. The Medieval manor, in which serfs worked the land of an aristocrat and warrior, the Lord who was the sole authority and judge, was a closed system of few rights, fewer opportunities, and no government participation on the part of the landed serfs. As long as the Medieval economy was primitive, relying on agriculture and barter, lacking widespread surpluses, having few of the components and resources for trade, serfs had no outlet, no way to change their condition. After 1000 A.D., various technological improvements in agriculture led to increased surpluses and generated wealth, trade, markets, and eventually market centers—villages, then small cities. This generation of a very limited capitalism provided the serf with the alternative to lifelong service on the medieval manor. Market centers were places of diversity and transition, where one could blend in, be anonymous, and start a new life. Trade has always raised the potential for newness, growth, and opportunity.

The commercial revolution after 1100 C.E. and continuing into the early modern period represented the replacement of feudal with urban structures. The organic, static, unequal, monarchal, aristocratic feudal society gave way to the independent, free and equal, republican and democratic European towns and cities. These towns were incorporated, that is, the residents joined together into a common self-governing cause where each person had certain rights and responsibilities incumbent upon citizenship. Such an open environment encouraged the self-made man and woman, who, in turn, knew that without towns, their freedoms, open markets, and mobility, such opportunity for personal success would be limited.

The Renaissance (1300–1600) focused on the individual, which was further supported by the Protestant Reformation of the 16th and 17th centuries, encouraged active men and women who worked for their city and state, their God, and themselves. One sees this personal capitalistic urge in the early colonists of America. Men such as Captain John Smith in Virginia and John Winthrop in Massachusetts worked for the good of the state of England, their own community of colonists, the development of their respective religious beliefs, and their own fortunes.

American democracy and capitalism. The historian of early America sees clearly the wedding of democracy to capitalism in the example of Benjamin FRANKLIN (1706–90), the great entrepreneur and democrat of the 18th century. Franklin's *Autobiography* is the story of a self-made man in the open society of early America. Franklin listed those characteristics that made him a success: temperance, silence, order, resolution, frugality, industry, sincerity, justice, moderation, cleanliness, tranquility, chastity, humility.

These were the same characteristics that made Franklin a successful diplomat, statesman, revolutionary, and political thinker. Franklin helped write the *Declaration of Independence*, agreeing with Thomas JEFFERSON that "all men are created equal." He served as the first Postmaster General, guaranteeing open communications in a free society. Franklin was one of the few American statesmen who could see the advantages of a government that provided order and security as well as freedom of movement, speech, belief, and work.

Most of the founders of the American republic, it is true, were less supportive of democracy, fearing the disorder and possible anarchy of a people who exercised influence over the government without control. This was the theme of James MADISON's famous *Federalist Paper 10*, in which he argued against a democracy that would yield a tyranny of the majority, supporting instead a republican government of important, if controlled, freedoms. Madison, who wrote the draft of the U.S. Constitution, was joined by Alexander HAMILTON in rejecting the first government of the United States, the Articles of Confederation, which allowed too many freedoms to states, localities, and individuals—for example freedom to determine the rules of interstate and international commerce. Under the Constitution, Congress has the power to regulate interstate and international commerce, which to some was an undue restriction imposed on the capitalistic inclinations of early Americans.

Jefferson was one of the great liberal intellectuals of the 18th century, yet was part of the system of slavery in the American south. One of the strongest advocates of free trade in the early republic, Jefferson was heavily influenced by the thinking of John LOCKE, the English philosopher who argued that humans are naturally good, free, and equal; that government is not a requirement, rather a choice; that humans choose to join together into voluntary association, giving up some of their rights and freedoms for the overall goal of mutual survival and prosperity. Jefferson once told his friend John ADAMS, when both were in retirement reflecting upon the past, that the AMERICAN REVOLUTION was unfinished, and would continue uncompleted for generations to come, only reaching finality when freedom became "intuitive," and Americans could exercise true self-government. Jefferson's image of a pure democracy existing in the future depended in part on free trade.

Democracy and free trade. Free trade, throughout American history, has been the perceived foundation of American, and world, democracy. Free trade means trade without restrictions, without the encumbrances of tariffs, quotas, embargo, and other means to hamper trade. The principle of free trade eschews using trade as a means of political policy, or using trade as an incentive in diplomacy. The foundations of the ideology of free trade emerged during the 18th-century Enlightenment. Adam SMITH, for example, in *The Wealth of Nations* (1776) argued against the control of trade as practiced by the British imperial system of MERCANTILISM. Smith applied liberal ideas to the economy. He argued that self-interest drives the economy and society. Benevolent altruism is not the stuff of capitalism, nor of democracy.

The American experience of having colonial trade controlled by the Navigation Acts and other forms of British mercantilism spurred American thinkers such as Jefferson to develop similar principles of American free trade. Jefferson believed that free trade would be an agent of the spread of the American system of self-government throughout a world that engaged in constant aggression and warfare, the origins of which often occurred because of trade restrictions. Free trade was the principle of the open mind and open society informed by reason and liberty rather than the narrow-minded, closed system of trade restrictions.

Free trade has been considered the agent of democracy, and has been one of the primary cornerstones of American diplomacy. Right from the beginning, presidents have generally refused to engage in trade wars and restrictions. Americans responded to the wars between England and France of the late 18th and early 19th centuries with proclamations of neutrality and free trade. Jefferson's embargo of 1808 was an exception, and a failure—it completely contradicted Jefferson's own principles. The MONROE Doctrine of 1823 was issued in part to promote free trade throughout the western hemisphere. Free trade was the cornerstone of Woodrow WILSON's post-WORLD WAR I plans and Franklin ROOSEVELT's post-WORLD WAR II plans. More recently, American political leaders supported such free trade programs as the North American Free Trade Agreement (NAFTA).

Alexis de Tocqueville, in *Democracy in America*, observed about 19th-century American society that the typical American, without pretense to birth or social rank, engaged in lifelong entrepreneurship. The American commoner was restless, hardworking, always seeking something, especially a satisfactory amount of wealth, which was always just out of reach. Such characteristics formed the backbone not only of American capitalism but of American democracy as well. The aggressiveness of the American in business spilled over to local assemblies, state legislatures, and courthouses. Ideas of American justice, morality, and law had a pragmatic, business-like approach. The American democracy, like American business, involved controversy rather than conciliation, anger and argument rather than acceptance and apathy. Even in the 20th century, in the wake of World War I and World War II, when traditional values were being challenged everywhere, and democracy was under attack from the left and the right, it was diversity rather than sameness, relativism rather than absolutism, that strengthened American democracy.

After centuries of development, democracy is still the rule of the people. The people, however, rarely act in unison, rarely agree, but it is in disagreement and disunity that democracy thrives. American democracy is based on pluralism. If America ever becomes uniform, predictable, and at one with itself, it might still be an American society, but it will not be American democracy.

BIBLIOGRAPHY. Edward A. Purcell, Jr., *The Crisis of Democratic Theory: Scientific Naturalism & the Problem of Value* (University Press of Kentucky, 19730; Robert L. Heilbroner, *The Worldly Philosophers: the Lives, Times, and Ideas of the Great Economic Thinkers* (Time Inc., 1962); Alexis de Toqueville, *Democracy in America* (Knopf, 1980); John Locke, *Treatise of Civil Government* (Irvington Publishers, 1979); Benjamin Franklin, *Autobiography* (Dover, 1996); Richard Reeves, *American Journey: Traveling with Tocqueville in Search of Democracy in America* (Simon & Schuster, 1982).

RUSSELL LAWSON
BACONE COLLEGE

Denison, Edward (1915–)

EDWARD DENISON'S contributions to economics lie in the area of national income accounting and growth accounting. His work has pioneered techniques for estimating the contributions of various factors to aggregate economic growth, measured in a variety of ways, including total output, output per labor hour, and output per unit of input (combined labor and capital). Denison's work has enhanced our measurement and understanding of economic growth and has informed growth policy.

Born in Omaha, Nebraska, Denison graduated from Oberlin College in 1936 and earned his Ph.D. from Brown University in 1941. From 1941–62, he worked in the Office of Business Economics in the U.S. Department of Commerce, and became its assistant director. From 1962 through 1978, he worked as a Senior Fellow at the Brookings Institution. In 1978, he returned to the Department of Commerce as associate director of national accounts.

Denison's early work (1962, 1974) measures the contributions of LABOR, CAPITAL, TECHNOLOGY and other factors of growth in the U.S. economy. His estimates employ the residual method, whereby growth not accounted for by labor, capital and other specific sources is attributed to "advances in knowledge," his term for technical advance. He found technical advance and increases in education to be the two primary sources of growth in output per worker over the period. His finding spurred development in the areas of education and technology policy.

In a related book (1967), Denison altered his approach to compare the relative role of capital, labor, technology, education, and other factors in explaining differences in growth rates among eight western European countries and the United States. Denison's work here represents the first significant contribution in the area of comparative growth analysis. Other significant work includes an analysis of Japan's relatively strong productivity performance (1976), contributions to the slowdown in productivity growth during the 1970s (1979, 1985), and analysis of rates of growth of industry productivity (1989). In addition, Denison contributed significantly to developing and improving modern national income and product accounting conducted by the Bureau of Economic Analysis of the U.S. Department of Commerce.

Denison's growth accounting has augmented our understanding of the dynamics of capitalist economies, generating a foundation for forecasters, policy makers, and employers and others concerned about the path of economic growth.

BIBLIOGRAPHY. Edward Denison, *The Sources of Economic Growth and the Alternatives before Us* (Committee for Economic Development, 1962); Edward Denison, *Why Growth Rates Differ; Postwar Experience in Nine Western Countries* (Brookings Institution, 1967); Edward Denison, *Accounting for U.S. Economic Growth 1929–1969* (Brookings Institution, 1974); Edward Denison, *How Japan's Economy Grew so Fast:*

the Sources of Postwar Expansion (Brookings Institution, 1976); Edward Denison, *Estimates of Productivity Growth by Industry: an Evaluation and an Alternative* (Brookings Institution, 1989).

WILLIAM D. FERGUSON
GRINNELL COLLEGE

Denmark

THE KINGDOM OF DENMARK is located in western Europe, occupying the peninsula of Jutland and an archipelago of 400-plus islands. Copenhagen is the capital. The population of Denmark is approximately 5.3 million and approximately 85 percent live in urban areas. Danish is the official language and English is the predominant second language. The net population growth has remained stagnant for many years.

Once home to Viking raiders and subsequently a north European power, Denmark is now involved in the political and economic integration of Europe. Since the mid-20th century, Denmark has faced a series of economic problems including a negative balance of payments and a tight labor market. In the 1980s, the government was forced to implement austerity measures. In the 1990s, the economy improved and unemployment shrank. However, the country struggled with the status of immigrants and the desire to maintain its social welfare programs, while decreasing the taxes needed to support them. In 1992, Denmark removed itself from participation in the European Union's Maastricht Treaty. In 1993, Denmark joined the EUROPEAN UNION (EU), but only after it negotiated exemptions from certain of the treaty's provisions. In 2000, Denmark, rejected use of the euro currency.

Industry accounts for about one-quarter of Denmark's GROSS DOMESTIC PRODUCT (GDP), services approximately 70 percent, and agriculture the remainder. Denmark's industries include clothing, food processing, furniture, machinery, metal production, and textiles. Denmark's currency is the Danish krone (DKK) and is pegged to the euro. The National Bank of Denmark is the bank of issue. All banks are under government supervision and must have public representation on their boards.

Denmark's labor force is approximately 2.9 million, with about 80 percent working in services, 17 percent in industry, and the remainder in agriculture. Women make up almost half of the workforce. The majority of skilled workers, technicians, and handicraft workers belong to unions.

In 2002, Denmark's exports were valued at approximately $56.3 billion annually and its imports at $47.9 billion. Its leading exports are chemicals, dairy products, furniture, ships, and windmills. Denmark's leading imports include consumer goods, grain, machinery and equipment, and raw materials. Since the mid-1960s, West Germany (and later GERMANY) has been Denmark's leading export/import partner. Other partners include the UNITED KINGDOM, FRANCE, the NETHERLANDS, SWEDEN, and the UNITED STATES.

Denmark's economic objectives include streamlining government bureaucracy and further privatization of state assets. Given the sluggishness of the global economy in the early 2000s, Denmark's economic growth may be moderate.

BIBLIOGRAPHY. Stewart Oakley, *A Short History of Denmark* (International Thomson Publishing, 1973); Palle Lauring, *Denmark a History* (Nordic Books, 1984); W. Glyn Jones, *Denmark: A Modern History* (Routledge, 1986); *CIA World Factbook* (2002).

S.J. RUBEL, J.D.
INDEPENDENT SCHOLAR

dependency theory

THE DEPENDENCY THEORY attempts to provide a comprehensive explanation to the phenomena of the simultaneous existence of highly developed, capitalist countries on the one hand, and underdeveloped, poor capitalist countries on the other, in the world today.

The concept was first articulated cohesively by Paul A. Baran in *The Political Economy of Growth* (1957), and Andre Gunder Frank in *Capitalism and Underdevelopment in Latin America*, (1967) and *Latin America: Underdevelopment or Revolution* (1969). These seminal works inspired a number of studies in the 1970s, a good representative collection of which appear in *The Political Economy of Development and Underdevelopment*, edited by Charles K. Wilber (1973). In late 1970s and 1980s, a number of modifications, additions, and deletions were made to this theory in light of the criticism, mainly from Marxist perspective that the original version had attracted. These critics' central point was that the theory did not incorporate the role of classes and class-conflict within its structure. Some of the major contributions to the New Dependency Theory were: James Petras (*Critical Perspectives on Imperialism and Social Class*, 1978); Guillermo O'Donnell (*Bureaucratic Authoritarianism: Argentina, 1966–1973, In Comparative Perspective*, 1988); Fernando H. Cardoso (*Dependency and Development in Latin America*, 1979); Peter Evans (*Dependent Development: The Alliance of Multinational, State and Local Capital in Brazil*, 1979).

The dependency theory emerged as a critique of the failed Import Substitution Industrialization strategy devised by the U.N. Economic Commission for Latin America (ECLA) for the economic development of Latin American countries after World War II. As Alvin So (1990) writes:

> . . . Many populist regimes in Latin America tried out the ECLA developmental strategy of protectionism and industrialization through import substitution in the 1950s, and many Latin American researchers had high hopes for a trend towards economic growth, welfare, and democracy. However, the brief expansion in the 1950s quickly turned into economic stagnation. In the early 1960s, Latin America was plagued by unemployment, inflation, currency devaluation, declining terms of trade, and other economic problems.

The two main contributions of the early dependency perspective were:

1. It pointed to the indispensability of incorporating the history of colonial domination and the particular division of labor imposed on the colonized countries into the analytical framework

2. It highlighted the role of unequal exchange relations between developed capitalist countries and underdeveloped countries as a factor that contributes significantly to stagnation in the latter.

However, the early dependency theory suffered from at least three major shortcomings. These were:

1. It theorized core-periphery relations at a very high level of abstraction, meaning that it treated all underdeveloped countries as essentially similar, overlooking the possibility of analyzing and understanding separate societies differently on the basis of their particular external and internal factors

2. It looked at underdevelopment almost exclusively as an economic phenomena

3. It inevitably relegated the possibility of development of an underdeveloped country to the rather impossible imperative that it sever all ties with the capitalist core and international markets dominated by its business groups.

These shortcomings were addressed by latter researchers within this paradigm mentioned above. Altogether, these authors expanded the dependency perspective along three different dimensions. First, following Cardoso's historical-structural method, dependency literature started paying much greater attention to the specific historical circumstances in which different countries become de-

pendent, and the particular nature of each dependency relationship. The discussion deepened from the level of general and abstract analysis of the relationships between core and periphery to the specific and concrete analysis of the dependency linkage of different Third World countries with the core.

While early dependency theorists had mainly focused on the effects of external relationships of dependent countries, characterized at first by the distortions and deformities created in them by European colonial exploitation, and later, by the system of unequal exchange, the new dependency studies, while not ignoring these dimensions, mainly focused on the internal socio-political conditions within peripheral countries that make the continuation of dependency relationship possible. In other words, it focused on the "internalization of external interests." In doing so, these authors have given primary attention to the class basis of various political regimes and the role of the state. A summary synopsis of their argument would go something like this: There are three dominant actors in the context of dependent countries. These are the bureaucratic-technocratic state that is "relatively autonomous" from the control of national dominant classes; the indigenous bourgeoisie; and the transnational corporations (TNC) of the core countries.

The interests of these three forces come together in certain specific areas, namely, in creating social and political stability; in keeping wage increases in check; in orienting industrial manufacturing for production for export markets; in gaining access to the international markets for traditional products produced by the peripheral country; and in development of a modern communications and energy infrastructure. These common interests provide the context and basis of the formation of a "triple alliance" between the state, national bourgeoisie, and the TNCs. But it is an uneasy and limited alliance in which each party tries to maximize its interests and which can only be sustained given certain favorable circumstances, most important of which is an expanding international market.

The latter dependency theorists reshaped the original argument of this school considerably but without violating its basic premises. In this regard, two important points must be noted here. First, contrary to the early dependency theories which postulated that the domination of foreign corporations in the national economy precludes any possibility of development, the latter theorists advanced the idea of conceptualizing the existing socio-economic processes in terms of associated dependent development. Doing so accounted for the contradictory nature of development in peripheral countries under political and economic conditions that are established by the core countries.

This accounts for the phenomenon of dynamic economic expansion that some Third World countries experienced in the 1970s, that not only resulted in the growth of the internal market, but which also re-molded their economies in certain basic ways in accordance with the imperatives of world capitalist system. The development that did take place was limited, lopsided, disintegrated, and only the classes associated with the triple alliance regime benefited from it, while the majority of the people were left outside this narrow circle of beneficiaries.

Notwithstanding the changes that have occurred in many peripheral capitalist countries in the 1980s, the analytical framework of the dependency perspective is still quite useful in explaining the internal and external contexts and imperatives of government policies. However, certain limitations of this perspective still remain and it is necessary to overcome these in order to construct a theoretical framework with greater explanatory powers. Thus, while the new dependency perspective successfully focuses on the class alliances to explain the internal developments, it nevertheless lacks a cohesive and dynamic explanation of the underlying mechanisms and structures that produce the structural conditions of peripheral capitalism. The new dependency perspective also lacks the conceptual power to bring into purview and analyze the phenomena and tendencies that exist or unfold outside the real external links of a particular peripheral country, but nevertheless affect it due to the articulation and manifestation of capitalism on the international scale.

BIBLIOGRAPHY. Colin Leys, *The Rise and Fall of Development Theory* (Indiana University Press, 1996); Gilbert Rist, *The History of Development: From Western Origins to Global Faith* (Zed Books, 1997); Ronald H. Chilcote, ed., *The Political Economy of Imperialism* (Rowman and Littlefield, 2000); F.H. Cardoso and Enzo Falleto, *Dependency and Development in Latin America* (University of California Press, 1979); P.B. Evans, *Dependent Development: The Alliance of Multinational, State, and Local Capital in Brazil* (Princeton University Press, 1979); J.F. Petras, *Latin America in the Time of Cholera: Electoral Politics, Market Economics, and Permanent Crisis* (Routledge, 1992).

AURANGZEB SYED, PH.D.
NORTHERN MICHIGAN UNIVERSITY

depreciation

THE DECLINE IN value of an asset spread over its economic life is termed depreciation. Depreciation covers deterioration from use, age, and exposure to elements. Since the consumption of CAPITAL is considered as cost of production, the allowance for depreciation is always made before net PROFIT is calculated. The rationale of keeping these costs is to measure current income accurately and to prevent decreasing the value of the overall assets of business.

Depreciation can be measured only at the end of the economic life of an asset, so companies are required to estimate both the total amount of depreciation and the asset life. The annual depreciation allowance is determined by allocating historic cost less residual value over the service life. The annual depreciation provisions are typically calculated by one of two methods. The first is the "straight line method" where the annual amount of depreciation is calculated by subtracting the estimated disposable residual value (scrap) from the original cost of the asset and then by dividing that amount by the number of years of its expected life. The second method is the "declining balance method" where the actual depreciation expense is set as a constant proportion of the value of the asset. Since the value of the asset declines over time so does the annual absolute amount of depreciation.

The peculiar problem is the time of high inflation when the replacement cost of any asset may be considerably higher then historic cost. In these circumstances, the method of replacement-cost depreciation is used. This method implies periodic revaluation of assets and the adjustment of depreciation rates.

Depreciation is accepted as an allowance against profits for tax purposes. However, depreciation has to be calculated according to certain rules and those rules often differ from the depreciation charged by a business firm in its accounts.

The decline of value of an asset may also come from obsolescence, the loss of usefulness due to availability of modern and more efficient types of goods serving the same purpose. Obsolescence, however, is not an equivalent to depreciation, since the changes in value of an asset coming from obsolescence are rapid, and the life of the asset is written off over a very short period.

Another definition of depreciation is the decline in value of one currency in terms of gold or other currencies. The currency depreciation occurs under the flexible, or floating exchange-rate arrangements when there is a shortage of demand for currency and/or excess of supply of currency.

BIBLIOGRAPHY. David G. Luenberger, *Investment Science* (Oxford University Press, 1997); Earl A. Saliers , *Principles of Depreciation: Dimensions of Accounting Theory and Practice Series* (Ayer, 1981).

ZELJAN SCHUSTER, PH.D.
UNIVERSITY OF NEW HAVEN

depression

GROWTH IS A COMMON FEATURE of modern economies. However, economic growth is an irregular phenomenon. The recurring variations in the aggregate economic activity are known as BUSINESS CYCLES. The modern economic theory makes a distinction among several types of business cycles. Kitchin cycles (named after Joseph Kitchin) were the movements caused by the changes in the level of inventories with the average duration of 24–40 months. Trade cycle, or Juglar cycle, with the duration of approximately seven years, were typical in the European economies in the course of the 19th century. The longer Kuznets cycles (Simon KUZNETS) last between 20–25 years and indicate alternate phases of European and American long-term investment.

While a portion of the economic and business literature refers to depression as the bottom phase of a business cycle, economists in general, were reluctant to term the trough phase of these cycles as depression. Contraction, downturn, and RECESSION were more widely used terms to denote the phase of the business cycle characterized with the drop in economic activity.

The more suitable usage for the term depression is to describe periods of severe and prolonged periods of economic decline usually on a broader international scale. The typical examples of depression were the period following Napoleonic wars, the Great Depressions of 1873–96 and of the 1930s, as well as the period following the first OIL shock in 1973.

While outside of the traditional business cycle, depression as a recurring phenomenon warranted theoretical explanation. The first attempt of theoretical clarification was provided by the Dutch Marxist, J. van Gelderlen (1913). However, the major theory was developed by Russian economist N.D. Kondratiev (1922), who analyzed the price movement in major Western economies over the course of two centuries. Kondratiev identified two depression periods (from 1810–17 to 1844–51 and from 1870–75 to 1890–96) during which a significant decrease in price level as well as in the production of coal and iron, and in agriculture occurred. According to him, during the depression periods, new technologies were developed, and technological innovations spurred the increase in economic activity. The upswing phase of Kondratiev long cycles were characterized by the rapid rise in gold production, wars, and revolutions.

Joseph SCHUMPETER incorporated the Kondratiev scheme into his concept of cyclical development of modern capitalism. Schumpeter assumed that the Kondratiev long investment cycle incorporates six Juglars, and the depression phase contains three Juglars. The depression periods started with a major crisis, high unemployment rates, and overall decrease in economic activity, especially in the agricultural sector. Similar to Kondratiev, Schumpeter also emphasized that the driving force of investment booms and expansions are major innovations such as railways, electricity, and steel.

Walt W. Rostow offered a Keynesian version of long cycles in economic development. He identified three depression periods that lasted from 1815 to 1848, 1873 to 1896, and from 1920 to 1936. The depression periods were characterized by falling prices, particularly agricultural prices, falling interest rates and low profits. The principal cause of economic crisis and prolonged downturn in economic activity (or depression) Rostow found in declining employment opportunities for capital, or in the excess of savings, due to the lack of profitable capital investment.

The attempt to associate major technological breakthroughs and/or their absence with recurrent periods of depression and economic prosperity regained its popularity during the prolonged crisis of the 1970s. Gerhard Mensch, Christopher Freeman, Ernest Mandel, and Robert Boyer advanced various explanations of how depressions can be averted by the rapid and broad introduction of new technologies.

Despite their appeal, the cyclical theories did not succeed in establishing a coherent explanation of the regular recurrence of economic depressions. Thus, the answer to the question whether the depressions are an intrinsic and salient feature of world capitalist development, or whether they are a product of a juxtaposition of circumstances, still remains open.

The viable alternative to the cyclical theories is to observe each of the depression periods as a unique and separate historical event. Thus the depression of 1873–96 should be viewed and analyzed separately from the depression of the 1930s. Economists vary in their explanations for the major causes of depression. The Keynesian approach focused on insufficient demand for goods and services and emphasized the role of government in creating a new purchasing power. Milton FRIEDMAN and other monetarists stressed the key role of money supply. According to Friedman, the downturn of economic activity was greatly aggravated by repetitive reductions in quantity of money. Consequently, a controlled monetary expansion is a secure way out of depression.

Keynesian and monetarist evaluations of causes and cures of the crises in the 1970s are diametrically opposed. Modern policymakers use prescriptions by both approaches in order to alleviate prolonged periods of depressed economic activity; in other words, they employ deficit spending in stimulating demand and attempt to control the quantity of money in the system via central bank (FEDERAL RESERVE) policies.

The modern history of depression in the world economy started with the Great Depression of 1873–96. The beginning of the depression was preceded by the collapse of the expansive boom in the capital goods industries (1871–73). The slump in economic activity was especially pronounced in Great Britain. The slowdown affected financial markets the most. These were upset by the default of the overseas borrowers, low profitability of investment in domestic economies, and the French war indemnity to Germany. However, the depression was less visible in real terms. While unemployment existed in the late 1870s and the mid-1880s, it was mild by the standards of the 20th century. The decline of GROSS NATIONAL PRODUCT (GNP) was moderate, and the sharp declines in profits affected only the grain farmers in agriculture. The depression affected the profit earners, and financiers the most, while the standard of living of the rest of population went up.

The depression of the 1930s, also known as the Great Depression, brought about financial crashes, the collapse in the real world production and trade, and unprecedented unemployment. The NEW YORK STOCK EXCHANGE crash in the fall of 1929 marked the beginning of the share collapse and was followed by series of financial disasters in Austria, Germany, Great Britain, and the United States. The fall in INTEREST RATES and profits was accompanied by unprecedented unemployment and decline in output and real national income. The unemployment affected 15–30 percent of the population in many countries; from 1929–33 the GROSS DOMESTIC PRODUCT (GDP) in the United States dropped by 30 percent and in Germany by 16 percent.

The drastic oil price rises by the ORGANIZATION OF PETROLEUM EXPORTING COUNTRIES (OPEC) in 1973–74 and in 1979, and the floating of the dollar marked the beginning of the depression of the 1970s. This depression was characterized by the stagnation in economic activity and increase in the overall price level, or so called "stagflation," an entirely new economic phenomenon.

BIBLIOGRAPHY. Graham Bannock, R.E. Baxter, and Evan Davis, *The Penguin Dictionary of Economics* (Penguin Books, 1998); K. Brunner, ed., *The Great Depression Revisited* (Nijhoff, 1981); John Eatwell, Murray Milgate, and Peter Newman, eds., *The New Palgrave: A Dictionary of Economics* (Stockton Press, 1991); M. Friedman and A. Schwartz, *A Monetary History of the United States* (Princeton University Press, 1963); G. Haberler, *Prosperity and Depression* (Harvard University Press, 1958); C.P. Kindleberger, *The World in Depression, 1929-1939* (University of California Press, 1973); N.D. Kondratieff, "The Long Waves in Economic Life," *The Review of Economic Statistics* (November, 1935); E. Mandel, *Late Capitalism* (New Left Books, 1975); D.W. Pearce, *The MIT Dictionary of Modern Economics* (MIT Press, 1992); W.W. Rostow, *The World Economy: History and Prospect* (Texas University Press, 1978); S.B. Saul, *The Myth of the Great Depression* (Macmillan, 1969); J.A. Schumpeter, *Business Cycles* (McGraw-Hill, 1939); P. Temin, *Did Monetary Forces Cause the Great Depression?* (W.W. Norton, 1976).

ZELJAN SCHUSTER, PH.D.
UNIVERSITY OF NEW HAVEN

derivative

A SECURITY WHOSE payoff depends on, or derives from, the value of another asset is referred to as a derivative, or a "contingent claim." The most common types of derivatives are options, futures, and swaps.

An option is a security that gives its holder the right, but not the obligation, to buy or sell another asset ("the underlying asset"). The lack of an obligation implies that the holder's loss from an option is limited to the price paid for it. The underlying asset may be common stock, bonds, stock indices, commodities, foreign currency or even other derivatives such as futures contracts or swaps.

The option contract specifies the price at which the asset may be bought or sold (the "exercise price" or the "strike price"), as well as the time over which the option contract is valid and may be exercised (the "maturity period"). A call option on a company's stock, for example, gives the holder the right to buy one or more shares (the underlying asset) in the company at a fixed price, not later than a certain date. Employee stock options, that are granted to the employees of a firm, enabling them to purchase company stock, fall under this category. A put option gives the holder a corresponding right to sell the underlying asset.

European style options may be exercised only at maturity, while American style options may be exercised prior to maturity as well. An option is said to be In the Money (ITM), if its exercise would lead to a positive payoff to the holder, such as when the strike price of a call option is lower than the current market price of the underlying asset. Similarly, an option is Out of the Money (OTM) if its exercise would lead to a negative payoff, and is At the Money (ATM) if its exercise would lead to a zero payoff. An option's value, also referred to as the "Option Premium," consists of two parts:

1. The intrinsic value, which is the payoff from immediate exercise for ITM options and zero for ATM and OTM options

2. The time value, which represents the potential future increase in value of the option from beneficial movements in the price of the underlying asset within the time left for expiration.

In 1973, Fischer Black and Myron Scholes, and Robert Merton independently, developed the first formula for determining the value of an option. The Black-Scholes formula has since been refined and expanded to become the most widely used option pricing technique.

Standardized option contracts trade on several exchanges, such as the Chicago Board Options Exchange, the Chicago Mercantile Exchange, the AMERICAN STOCK

EXCHANGE, and the Philadelphia Stock Exchange. These options have standardized contract sizes, exercise prices and expiration dates. Such standardization facilitates trading, by increasing liquidity and lowering trading costs. There also exists an Over the Counter (OTC) market for options, where the terms of the option contract may be tailored to meet the requirements of the transacting parties. However, the trading costs associated with such non-standard options are higher.

The rapid pace of financial innovation in the last two decades has led to the creation of many customized options with peculiar features. Such "exotic options" include the Average Rate or Asian Options whose payoffs depend on the average price of the underlying asset over a specified period; Knock-out or Barrier Options, whose payoff depends on whether the underlying asset price did or did not cross a specified barrier; Compound Options, which are options on options; Swap Options, which are options to enter into swap contracts at a later date; and Chooser Options, which allow the holder to choose at a later date whether the option is to be a call or a put option.

Forward contracts are contracts to buy or sell an asset at a specified price on a later date. Unlike options, such contracts carry an obligation on the part of the holder to go through with the purchase or sale of the underlying asset even if this would lead to a loss. Forward contracts are most frequently entered into in the OTC market for foreign currency. For example, a firm that anticipates a need for foreign currency to pay for imports may enter into a forward contract to purchase foreign currency on the expected date of payment for the imports.

Futures contracts are standardized versions of forward contracts that are traded on exchanges. A person who buys a futures contract on a commodity thus agrees to purchase a specified amount of the commodity at a fixed price (the "futures price") at a certain date in the future. Like options, futures contracts are traded on a variety of underlying assets such as commodities, metals, energy, foreign currencies, stock indices and bonds. An important feature of futures markets is the leverage inherent in these transactions: the initial outlay (called the "initial margin") required from a person purchasing a futures contract may be as low as 5 percent of the value of the contract. Another feature distinguishing futures trading is the practice of "marking to market." This refers to the process of daily settling of profits and losses (depending on the closing futures price) on all traders' positions.

Swaps are contracts involving the simultaneous purchase and sale of two securities. In currency swaps, the two securities are designated in different currencies. Thus, the swap will bind the parties to exchange fixed amounts of two currencies at regular intervals over the maturity of the swap. In interest rate swaps, the two securities may be two bonds, one paying a fixed interest rate and the other, a floating rate. Thus, the swap will bind one party to exchange a fixed cash flow for a variable cash flow at fixed intervals over the maturity of the swap.

All these derivatives are widely used by firms to hedge various kinds of risk that they are exposed to in the course of their activities.

BIBLIOGRAPHY. Zvi Bodie, Alex Kane and Alan J. Marcus, *Investments* (McGraw-Hill); Fisher Black and Myron Scholes, "The Pricing of Options and Corporate Liabilities," *Journal of Political Economy* (v.81, 1973); Robert C. Merton, "Theory of Rational Option Pricing," *Bell Journal of Economics and Management Science* (v.4, 1973); Chicago Board Options Exchange, www.cboe.com; Philadelphia Stock Exchange, www.phlx.com.

NARAYANAN SUBRAMANIAN, PH.D.
BRANDEIS UNIVERSITY

DeSoto, Hernando (1942–)

BORN IN LIMA, PERU, Hernando DeSoto studied economics in Switzerland, founded the Institute of Liberty and Democracy (ILD) in Lima, and was responsible for a series of legal and economic reforms in PERU.

The research of the ILD showed that despite the opportunity of entrepreneurship, the poor could not join Lima's formal market economy because of extensive government regulations and bureaucratic hurdles, such as application processes and fees for licenses and permits. In *The Other Path: The Economic Answer to Terrorism* (1989), DeSoto argued that the only effective way of overcoming the insurgent Maoist group, known as the Shining Path, was by incorporating the urban informal sector into the formal market economy by legitimizing the economic activities of the so-called "informals." Subsequently, DeSoto became an advisor to various presidents of Peru as well as abroad, including Haiti. He achieved international claim with his book *Mystery of Capital: Why Capitalism Triumphs in the West and Fails Everywhere Else* (2000). This book focuses on the effects of government bureaucracy and, more importantly, on the lack of formal property rights in Peru and other developing countries. DeSoto argues that this lack of legal OWNERSHIP of property in shantytowns and in squatter camps and townships prevents the poor from accessing formal credit markets.

Thus, the poor are blocked from an important means of raising the necessary financial capital for small entrepreneurs in capitalist economies. If poor entrepreneurs could lawfully show their property and their other assets as collateral, and could therefore finance their economic activities, they would be part of the formal market economy and contribute to economic growth and development through the accumulation of wealth. According to DeSoto, the existing potential for wealth and capital accumulation in developing countries can only be realized if laws are reformed to free the capital.

BIBLIOGRAPHY. Hernando DeSoto, *The Mystery of Capital: Why Capitalism Triumphs in the West and Fails Everywhere Else* (Basic Books, 2000); Hernando DeSoto, *The Other Path: The Economic Answer to Terrorism* (HarperCollins, 1989): The Institute for Liberty and Democracy, www.ild.org.pe.

M. ODEKON
SKIDMORE COLLEGE

Deutsche Bank

THE DEUTSCHE BANK (German Bank) is one of the world's leading international financial institutions. Of the bank's 84,500 employees 37,400 are employed in GERMANY, 22,200 in other European countries, 18,600 in North and South America, and the remaining 6,300 throughout the Asian-Pacific region.

The Deutsche Bank has about 12 million clients throughout 75 countries. Services Deutsche Bank provides include asset management and wealth management for private and business clients, corporate investments, global transaction banking, global corporate finance, and global equities. The 520,000 shareholders of the German Bank are as diversified as the services it offers, 50 percent of the shares are held outside Germany and corporate investors hold 80 percent of the shares.

Founded in 1870 in Berlin, the Deutsche Bank opened its first foreign branch office in 1873 in London. After WORLD WAR II, the Deutsche Bank closed its offices in Berlin and the Soviet military zone. In the British and U.S. military zones, the German Bank was broken up into 10 independent institutions. In 1957, these banking institutions were allowed to merge into the Deutsche Bank AG, with its headquarters in Frankfurt am Main. From 1970–2002 the German Bank established branch offices in Moscow, London, Tokyo, Paris, and New York and engaged in a number of successful take-over bids in Europe as well as the United States.

In 2001, the shares of the German Bank were for the first time traded at the NEW YORK STOCK EXCHANGE.

BIBLIOGRAPHY. www.deutsche-bank.de; Deutsche Bank, *Die Deutsche Bank in Zahlen* (Deutsche Bank, 2003); Deutsche Bank, *Die Deutsche Bank im Ueberblick,* presse.deutsche-bank.de (2003).

KLAUS G. BECKER, PH.D.
TEXAS TECH UNIVERSITY

Deutsche Telecom

DEUTSCHE TELECOM (Deutsche Telekom AG), with a 2002 operating income of about $40 billion, is the world's fourth largest and Europe's largest telecom carrier.

Deutsche Telecom supplies a large range of telecommunication services such as telephone, high-speed internet, data transmission, and mobile communications to more than 100 million customers worldwide. In addition, with approximately 5 million subscribers, Deutsche Telecom has also become Europe's largest internet service provider (ISP).

Deutsche Telecom operates in over 65 countries and has subsidiaries and offices in Tokyo, London, Brussels, Moscow, Kiev, New York, Washington, Chicago, Atlanta, San Francisco, Toronto, Singapore, Hong Kong, New Delhi, and Beijing. Deutsche Telecom's U.S. subsidiary is Voice Stream (T-Mobile USA).

As of December 2001, Deutsche Telecom had 257,000 employees worldwide, one-third of whom were employed outside Germany. In 2001, Deutsche Telecom had a capital stock of approximately $10.5 billion. About 25 percent of Deutsche Telecom's revenue was generated in foreign markets. Deutsche Telecom is listed on stock exchanges in GERMANY as well as the UNITED STATES and JAPAN. In 2002, *Fortune* magazine listed Deutsche Telecom as the 75th largest company in the world.

BIBLIOGRAPHY. Deutsche Telecom, www.telekom.de; "Global 500: World's Largest Companies," *Fortune* (July 2002); Guenter Knieps, *Wettbewerb in Netzen* (Mohr Siebeck, 1996).

KLAUS G. BECKER, PH.D.
TEXAS TECH UNIVERSITY

discount

THE TERM DISCOUNT refers to the practice of treating money today as more valuable than an identical sum at a future date. For instance, given the choice between receiving $1000 today or $1000 in one year's time, the rational choice is to take the money today. In order to make meaningful comparisons between two monetary sums separated across time, we therefore use the tool of "discounting." This tool not only allows us to compare monetary amounts in different times, but it also simplifies the task of comparing monetary amounts that are qualitatively different (perhaps due to risk).

Several reasons explain why money has different values at different points in time. Positive interest rates are one important reason for the difference. Positive interest rates guarantee identical sums will always be preferred in the present rather than in the future (hence, we "discount" the future). For instance, money received today can be placed in a savings account (or used to purchase a certificate of deposit) for the time interval in question and will increase in magnitude simply as a result of earning interest.

Economists have a range of theories to explain interest rates, some of which use the concept of time preference, or the idea that present consumption is preferred to future consumption. Positive interest rates and time preference seem intimately connected, but it is possible to identify reasons for preferring present consumption without using interest rates as an explanation. Uncertainty about the future is one explanation. Without knowing whether you will be alive to enjoy future consumption, your bias may very well be to enjoy consumption today. Opportunity cost also helps explain positive time preference. Access to a financial sum today provides more possibilities than postponing access. The notion of savings as a sacrifice is directly connected to this concept of opportunity cost.

With an understanding of why future amounts should be discounted, the next question is, "How?" Discounting involves four variables: an interest rate, a time period, a current monetary amount, and a future monetary amount. If any three of these four variables can be identified, the fourth value can be found using the following formula:

Present Value $*$ (1 + interest rate)^{time} = Future Value

For example, $100 today invested at a 10 percent interest rate would be worth $121 in two year's time (earning $10 in interest in the first year and $11 in interest in the second year). Alternatively, we can say that $121 two years from now is the equivalent to $100 today if we use an interest rate of 10 percent to make the comparison. These results can be verified by applying the discount formula provided: $100 * (1 + 0.10)^2 = 121$.

Notice that the formula for discounting incorporates time as an exponent due to the nature of "compounding." In our example, the $10 in interest earned the first year also earns interest in year two. It is this "interest on interest" that requires treating time in an exponential fashion.

Discounting is also used to conduct cost-benefit analyses where time separates the relevant costs from the benefits. For instance, if you needed to replace your hot water heater and had to choose between a relatively cheaper electric hot water heater or a more expensive solar heater, but recognized that the solar heater would generate a series of lower utility expenses during its lifetime, discounting would be necessary to compare future savings to current costs. Such a process is essential when comparing financial sums spread out over time, but not as straightforward as it may seem. For instance, in the mid-20th century the UNITED STATES and CANADA explored constructing a tidal power project between the two countries. Despite using identical cost and benefit estimates, they reached different conclusions because they each selected a different interest rate for conducting the calculation. Similar examples can be found in a variety of settings.

Historically the practice of discounting has also been used to compare monetary amounts with qualitative differences. For instance, if I made identical loans to Jane and John and Jane is more likely to repay the debt, then it would be irrational to treat the loans as identical sums if we wished to establish a "market value" for each loan. Based on this difference in risk, we would agree that John's loan should be discounted more than Jane's if I sold it to you (this assumes we both have the necessary information to evaluate each loan's risk).

In a similar fashion, 19th-century merchants and banks in the United States discounted banknotes issued at distant locations (prior to the AMERICAN CIVIL WAR, individual banks issued their own currencies known as banknotes). Because banknotes from distant locations were more difficult to exchange for specie (gold or silver), they represented a greater risk for the merchant or bank accepting them (similar to cashing an out-of-state check today). In each of these instances the greater risk can be quantified by discounting.

BIBLIOGRAPHY. Mark Blaug, *Economic Theory in Retrospect* (Cambridge University Press, 1985); Meir Kohn, *Money, Banking, and Financial Markets* (The Dryden Press, 1991); Frederic S. Mishkin, *The Economics of Money, Banking, and Financial Markets* (Addison-Wesley, 1997); Tom Tietenberg, *Environmental and Natural Resource Economics* (Addison-Wesley, 2000).

PATRICK DOLENC, PH.D.
KEENE STATE COLLEGE

discount rate

DEFINED BY the FEDERAL RESERVE system, the discount rate is "the interest rate charged to commercial banks and other depository institutions on loans they receive from their regional Federal Reserve Bank's lending facility—the discount window." Loans made by the

Federal Reserve to depository institutions are referred to as discount loans.

Upon the founding of the Federal Reserve system in 1913, commercial banks that chose to join the system (member banks) were granted the privilege of acquiring funds, when necessary, from the Fed. After a series of financial panics in the late 1800s that peaked with the panic of 1907, many Americans became increasingly concerned about the lack of a steadfast lender of last resort, an institution that would stand ready, willing, and able to provide liquidity to the financial system in times of trouble.

Runs on some of the largest trust companies in the UNITED STATES, including the Knickerbocker Trust Company, precipitated the panic of 1907, which might have had calamitous results on the economy had it not been for the assistance of George Cortelyou, secretary of the treasury, and renowned financier J.P. MORGAN. By organizing money pools of $25 million one day and $10 million the next, Morgan ultimately engineered a bailout package that contained the runs and brought the panic to an end. There was no doubt that Morgan's plan had worked but there was some skepticism about his motives as well as concern about the wisdom of allowing the entire financial system to become so dependent on a private organization

By establishing a central bank for the United States, the Federal Reserve Act provided a lender of last resort whose main objective was that of preserving the stability of the banking system, not maximizing profit. Also, with access to potentially unlimited funds, the newly created Fed could assure an elastic currency, something that even the country's largest financiers like Morgan could not guarantee.

During the Fed's early years, the discount rate was a key monetary policy tool. A substantial portion of bank reserves, as much as 82 percent in 1921, was provided by the Fed through the discount window. By providing discount loans, the Fed could increase liquidity in the banking system thus driving down interest rates to encourage more spending. Likewise, the Fed could attempt to slow down the economy if need be by raising the discount rate which would, in turn, tighten credit markets driving up interest rates discouraging spending. Changes in the discount rate continued to have a significant impact on reserves in the decades immediately following 1921, but have since become a lesser monetary policy tool in the United States. Open market operations have replaced discount policy as the chief instrument of monetary policy.

The discount window is no longer available exclusively to member banks of the Fed but, as a result of the Monetary Control Act of 1980, is now accessible to all depository institutions in the U.S. Federal Reserve District Banks generally offer three types of discount window credit to depository institutions: adjustment credit, extended credit, and seasonal credit. Emergency credit is available, according to Section 13 of the Federal Reserve Act, to "individuals, partnerships and corporations under 'unusual and exigent' circumstances." Such loans, however, have not been granted since the 1930s. Typically overnight or weekend loans, adjustment credit loans are extended to institutions in need of funds to meet temporary liquidity problems arising from changes in the market value of the institution's assets and liabilities. The interest rate charged on adjustment credit is set below market interest rates (hence the name, the discount rate). Borrowers, however, are expected to exhaust all reasonably available alternative sources of funds before seeking the less expensive adjustment credit from the Fed.

Depository institutions that require funds on a recurring basis during particular times of the year (e.g., banks in agricultural or seasonal resort communities) may apply to the Fed for seasonal credit. Before 1990, banks paid the same interest rate on seasonal credit as they did on adjustment credit. In early 1990, however, the Fed established a market-related rate for seasonal credit as well as extended credit that remains outstanding for more than 30 days. Depository institutions in need of liquidity due to "exceptional circumstances" may receive extended credit from the Fed. Exceptional circumstances include changing money-market conditions as well as troubled banks in danger of failing.

The rate that is commonly referred to as the discount rate is the rate charged by the Federal Reserve system for adjustment credit. In the early stages of the Fed's history, each Federal Reserve District Bank set its own discount rate. Consequently, it was not unusual to see discount rates vary across regions. The discount rate presently is established by each Reserve Bank's board of directors, reviewed and approved by the Board of Governors of the Federal Reserve System. As a result, the discount rate is constant for depository institutions across the United States.

BIBLIOGRAPHY. Board of Governors of the Federal Reserve System, *The Federal Reserve System: Purposes & Functions* (1994); Milton Friedman and Anna Schwarz, *A Monetary History of the United States, 1867–1960* (Princeton University Press, 1963); Eugene N. White, "The Political Economy of Banking Regulation, 1864–1933," *Journal of Economic History* (March 1982).

KRISTIN KUCSMA, PH.D.
SETON HALL UNIVERSITY

Disraeli, Benjamin (1804–81)

POLITICIAN AND NOVELIST, scion of a well-to-do Jewish family of Venetian origins, Benjamin Disraeli was born in London and baptized as an Anglican at the age of 13. As a young man, he wrote several moderately successful novels dealing with contemporary English social problems before aiming for a career in politics.

Having failed to secure election to the House of Commons as a Whig, he switched party allegiance and became member of parliament for Maidstone in the Tory interest in 1837. A man of few fixed principles, Disraeli helped to split his own party in 1846 when he led the opposition against Prime Minister Sir Robert Peel's repeal of agricultural tariffs, largely out of pique at having been overlooked by Peel for governmental office. His tenure as Chancellor of the Exchequer in three subsequent Tory administrations (1852; 1858–59; 1866–68) was unremarkable, with the notable exception of his stewardship through Parliament of the Second Reform Act. This measure, which doubled the size of the British electorate, represented Disraeli's attempt to outflank the Whigs by fastening to the Tory Party the landed aristocracy at one end of the social spectrum, and the better-off members of the working class at the other. Although in the long term this strategy was to prove highly successful, it was insufficient to prevent the fall of a short-lived administration headed by Disraeli himself in 1868. During the next six years in opposition, the Tories refined their appeal to the newly enfranchised electorate. In the general election campaign of 1874, Disraeli offered a potent combination of inexpensive but popular measures to improve the conditions of the working class and a more aggressive stance in foreign and imperial affairs. The result was a comfortable Tory victory, the party's first in more than thirty years and an achievement for which Disraeli could legitimately claim the credit.

Disraeli's second term in office started well in both domestic and overseas affairs. Guided by his able Home Secretary, Richard Asheton Cross, the prime minister oversaw the passage of a series of acts to improve public health, limit the maximum length of the working day, and extend the legal rights of employees. In imperial policy, Disraeli scored a distinct coup when he arranged in 1875 for the purchase by the British government of a controlling interest in the SUEZ COMPANY, thereby securing control over a vital trade route to the East Indian colonies and paving the way for an eventual de facto protectorate over EGYPT. The passage of the Royal Titles Act conferring upon Queen Victoria the title of Empress of India the following year was also a popular measure. The seal appeared to be set on Disraeli's reputation as a statesman when, ennobled as the first Earl of Beaconsfield, he assembled an international coalition at the Congress of Berlin in 1878 to check Russian expansion in the Balkans and protect the interests of Britain's traditional ally in the region, the Ottoman Empire.

Disraeli's star began to wane, however, during the last two years of his premiership. Wars in Zululand (Africa) and Afghanistan in 1879, in each case precipitated by over-enthusiastic imperial proconsuls, led to humiliating military reverses at Isandhlwana and Kabul. Although the tide of battle was quickly turned in both countries by the arrival of British reinforcements, many Britons regarded the conflicts as the result of a reckless and increasingly expensive Disraelian imperial policy. Disraeli's support of the Ottoman Empire was tarnished by Turkish atrocities against Bulgarian Christians, an issue upon which his great political rival, William Ewart Gladstone, campaigned effectively. In home affairs, too, the government seemed bereft of new ideas after its legislative spurt of the mid-1870s.

Lastly, Disraeli's indifference to near-famine conditions in parts of Ireland, for whose people he felt undisguised contempt, contributed to the rise of the militant Irish National Land League in 1879 and the outbreak of the somewhat melodramatically named "Land War." The Tories' heavy defeat in the general election of 1880 was thus hardly to be wondered at; that it came as a surprise to Beaconsfield himself was an indication of how far he had lost touch with the circumstances of the time.

Historians remain divided on the significance of Disraeli's achievements. To some he was a political chameleon, discarding policies and even party allegiance whenever they proved inconvenient. Others credit him with devising a winning formula for the Tory Party and paving the way for British Conservatism's future successes. Without question, however, he was the most charismatic politician of his age, whose parliamentary skills and mastery of the attention-seizing gesture would be emulated, though hardly equaled, by a host of imitators in British public life.

BIBLIOGRAPHY. P. Adelman, *Gladstone, Disraeli and Later Victorian Politics* (Longman, 1970); R. Blake, *Disraeli* (Eyre & Spottiswoode, 1968); P. Smith, *Disraelian Conservatism* (Routledge & Kegan Paul, 1967); M. Swartz, *The Politics of British Foreign Policy in the Era of Gladstone and Disraeli* (St Martin's Press, 1985); S. Weintraub, *Disraeli: A Biography* (Hamish Hamilton, 1993).

R.M. DOUGLAS, PH.D.
COLGATE UNIVERSITY

distribution

SUPPLY AND DEMAND are considered as the two major forces that can make prices fluctuate in free markets. Distribution is the way to make sure a company's products are made available to all potential consumers, not only when they order them specifically, but also whenever they browse to compare items and labels, in a store, a supermarket, in a catalog or on the internet. For instance, over half a century ago, most people living in northern countries could only find oranges at Christmas time and therefore those rare fruits were given as gifts for the New Year's Eve. SCARCITY contributed then to their value as much as their taste. Today, oranges and more exotic fruits are commonly available all year long in North America and are imported from different countries, according to availability, contractual partnerships, prices and harvest seasons. Diversified distribution networks make these fragile fruits available to new foreign markets for longer periods.

Distribution is the vital link between the producer and the consumer, from the factory to the retailer, that gives any kind of a product a concrete existence and visibility, among many brands or labels. For almost any type of merchandise and commodity, there are either general or distinctive labels: those advertised novelties of all types and standard products that are to be found almost anywhere, as opposed to the hard-to-find non-mainstream things that are so distinctive (the selected imports) or high-quality products (from deluxe foods, imported French wines and cheese, to entertainment systems that are of a high fidelity and quality). These distinctive categories can in part explain why there are general retailers (such as Wal-Mart, Sears) and specialized stores for about every kind of a product.

For marketers, penetration is a way to measure how efficient a distribution strategy is, in a targeted market or area. For instance, a penetration of 25% means a product is available in a quarter of all possible related stores in an area.

Foreign products. It is always interesting to observe how different markets can change when you travel in foreign countries. In other contexts, the label landscape (i.e., what is currently offered to consumers in their local outlets) looks different in any supermarket or retail store abroad, because supplies and habits are not exactly the same. For decades, young American tourists traveling in France packed jars of peanut butter in their bags, because they were told by the first editions of the travel guide *Let's Go Europe* that there was no peanut butter in French stores and *supermarchés*. Things have changed since then, but this old rumor shows how a lack of distribution makes a somewhere popular product unavailable in a whole region or even a country.

Those tourists might remember the Renault, Citroën or Talbot cars that they saw or drove in Europe, and ask why these automobiles can't be found in North America as easily as a Ford, Chevrolet, Jeep, or even the German Volkswagen. One might say it is because most car buyers prefer the conventional U.S. types of cars; but from a socio-economic perspective, research proves that consumers might have the power to select the most convenient product to them, but they can only choose from what is currently being offered to them. "Availability" is

more decisive, more determinative than a rather subjective and elusive concept such as "consumer preference."

Usually, imports are harder to find compared to national products. Sometimes, a strange paradox that appears in various situations makes foreign products more easily available than local ones. For instance, in the food industry, Icelandic and French lamb are considered as the best in the world for their naturally salted taste, but imported Australian and New Zealand lamb is less expensive and much easier to find in many Western countries, even in French or in Canadian supermarkets, although they are two countries that produce these animals at a large scale. In this case, imports from a far-away continent are offered to consumers at a lower price and local producers of the same merchandize sometimes have hard time finding local retailers who accept to buy their products.

Coke or Pepsi? On campuses and high schools, in recent years, big corporations have special agreements that give them exclusive visibility in cafeterias and vending machines. In arenas, public schools, colleges and university campuses, Pepsi or Coke becomes the "official" and exclusive drink on limited premises. These aggressive distribution strategies could be compared to a kind of monopolistic aim, because competitors are selected, chosen or excluded, and then ruled by institutions to be adopted or banned from a private area. But as a response, competing corporations prefer to reach the best possible deals with renewed key partners instead of battling, one competitor against another, in court. Above market competition, at an international scale, there are special exclusive distribution agreements, that are politically negotiated between countries and serve as an almost permanent protection against competitors.

One example is the famous Pepsi agreement, that President Richard Nixon made with Soviet Union government in the early 1970s, that allowed Pepsi to dominate the exclusive Russian market for 20 years. Coke responded soon after with a similar effort in China.

Direct sales. Corporations such as Avon (beauty products), Time-Life (books and CDs), as well as some Disney divisions (publishing) have created a large network of retailers in many countries, using direct-marketing and other approaches to reach customers in other places than common retail stores. For instance, Avon's salespeople meet you at home; publisher Readers' Digest sell subscriptions for its magazine mostly through mail and other telemarketing strategies; now, both corporations now use the internet to promote and show their products that are usually not available in stores.

Another alternative to retail sales is the underground economy. On a much darker side, there have always been parallel distribution networks when official channels could not be used, often for legal reasons. For instance,

The complexity and power of distribution can make foreign fish, for example, easy to find in local markets.

during national Prohibition in the United States, many illegal networks were created to import alcohol into the country (notably from Canada). Other underground networks exist today to import and distribute cigarettes, pornography, banned drugs, or other illegal substances. Counterfeiting and illegal copies of copyrighted materials (CDs, DVDs, electronic games, books) can also be included in these lucrative black markets.

The never ending circle. Usually, most stores tend not to keep products that are not sold within a year, sometimes if not sold in days. For commercial reasons and because of the lack of space, an item not sold within a specific period can sometimes be returned to its distributor for credit. Following that logic, only the best-selling products remain in stores, but not always the best quality. For instance, classic books and films are not instant best-sellers but durable, long-time true values. As publisher André Schiffrin explains, "serious work that may take time to find its audience, whether in the classroom or in paperback, and ambitious work by new authors, become harder and harder to publish."

This trend leads to the blockbuster strategy, which represents the worst of mass culture, in popular literature, music, videos, etc. The success (evaluated only in terms of profits) of the blockbuster strategy is always evaluated in terms of sales and return, visibility, and not artistic quality. Many people read the book or saw that new film, but did they really like it? Bad or good, films are judged at the box office. There is a step-by-step strategy for distributing movies in different ways: movie theaters, pay-per-view TV, cable television stations (such as Time-Warner's HBO), videoclubs, television, DVD, etc.

In many countries, movies presented on most television stations are rented by the TV networks from film distributors through a method of block-booking. This means, in order to get permission to rent one or two titles, they have to air some ten other films (of lesser quality, mostly produced by Hollywood majors) without having the possibility to choose them. By forcing TV stations to buy products none would select otherwise, film distributors can find an easy way to make sure all their less-appealing movies will be profitable. This explains why Hollywood films get more market share in most countries. "Indeed, worldwide distribution has been the basis of Hollywood's power," media analyst Douglas Gomery writes n *Who Owns the Media?*. This is why there are so few foreign movies on U.S. big television networks, compared to Canada or other European countries.

Sometimes distribution means slightly changing a product's nature or appearance. In countries such as Italy, many TV stations let the movie run while they present advertising spots or even cut movies that seem too long. Movies can be cut or abridged, but advertising is the untouchable element for private television stations.

Globalization and cultural hegemony. In the best of worlds, one could imagine globalization as the ideal way of fairly sharing products, programs, entertainment, arts, culture, from all countries to all countries However, the plain reality is that globalization means increasing dominant positions by breaking borders and protecting measures through free-trade agreements and other measures. In terms of media domination, the U.S. power is made on a successful capitalist strategy, and not for the quality of its contents. As film expert Toby Miller asks, "Is Hollywood really giving the people of the world what they want, or does it operate via a brutal form of monopoly-capitalist business practice?"

One of the main problems related to mass culture is that "massification" of commodities and cultural products does not mean more diversity, but rather more of the same style, contents, patterns, ideological schemes. Some believe that books and movies are not seen anymore as culture but rather just as plain commodities that are potentially lucrative. But the recent UNESCO Universal Declaration on Cultural Diversity Paris, 2002) stipulates (in its Article 8) that "Cultural goods and services which, as vectors of identity, values and meaning, must not be treated as mere commodities or consumer goods." Canada and European countries adopted this new paradigm of cultural diversity, meaning that one country's cultural landscape should be represented by works (art, music, movies) from different nations, foreign languages, and cultures from abroad. As a strategic response, some multi-ethnic countries may try to pretend that they already conform to the model of cultural diversity, only because their population is a mixture of people from many ethnic origins. Cultures and films should be free to circulate anywhere, but some travel more easily than others, and some others never go out of their national borders.

This conflict about the media control and cultural domination by the United States is not recent. Since 1980, UNESCO's efforts promoted another conception of world communication that would allow Third World countries to export more of their cultural products without being overwhelmed by the rich nations' mass culture. In terms of distribution, the media industry ranks among the most lucrative, but also remains the most debated and highly controversial.

BIBLIOGRAPHY. Benjamin M. Compaine and Douglas Gomery *Who Owns the Media: Competition and Concentration in the Mass Media Industry*, (Lawrence Erlbaum Associates, 2000); Douglas Holt and Juliet Schor, eds., *The Consumer Society Reader* (The New Press, 2000); Lawrence Glickman, ed., *Consumer Society in American History: A Reader* (Cornell University Press, 1999); Alain Labrousse, *Dictionnaire géopolitique des drogues. La drogue dans 134 pays. Productions, trafics, conflits, usages* (De Boeck Université, 2002); Martyn J. Lee, *The Consumer Society Reader* (Blackwell, 2000); Toby Miller, et al., *Global Hollywood* (British Film Institute, 2001); André Schiffrin, "When We Devoured Books," Roger Rosenblatt, ed., *Consuming Desires: Consumption, Culture, and the Pursuit of Happiness* (Island Press, 1999); UNESCO, *UNESCO Universal Declaration on Cultural Diversity* (UNESCO Press, 2002).

YVES LABERGE, PH.D.
INSTITUT QUÉBÉCOIS DES
HAUTES ÉTUDES INTERNATIONALES

dollar

AT THE DAWN OF THE new millennium, the dollar is the imperial currency in every sense of the word. It bears the signature of the largest economy to date. Supported as it is by the most productive labor force in the world, provisioned with the best technological infrastructure, and endowed with an enormous resource base to draw on, the dollar today is the symbol of not only U.S. economic might but its political prowess. No wonder it is both admired and envied.

It was toward the end of the 18th century that, faced with the choice of owing England a debt of monetary survival or creating its own money, the U.S. Congress opted for the latter authorizing the issuance of the dollar as the unit of American currency. But it is the 20th century—also dubbed as the American Century by many commentators—that saw the dollar become the currency of international acceptance, or some would say, of universal dominance. Today, a traveler can pay a taxi driver in Moscow or a waiter in Jakarta in dollars without having to make any explanations. The taxi drivers and the waiters, among others, are only too happy to receive their payment in dollars. The dollar represents the universal convertibility and acceptance, a stable and predictable value, a prized asset. But to fully appreciate the logic and circumstance of this meteoric rise to prominence, it is useful to recall that this position of status was occupied by the British pound sterling for a whole era in which, as they used to say, "The sun never sets on the British empire."

Even though the British flag flew triumphantly over seas and continents for many decades, the U.S. population surpassed that of England in the 1870s, U.S. economic production outpaced that of England in the 1880s, and the U.S. share of world trade overtook that of England around the 1920s. Just before WORLD WAR I, the United States developed a vast industrial infrastructure, which allowed enormous economies of scale through mass production techniques. The war weakened, if not outright ruined, the productive capacity of European powers. The U.S. economy was strengthened even further in relative terms as "the arsenal of democracy." The interwar (between the two world wars) period proved to be rather unstable and chaotic in terms of international transactions and therefore currency valuations.

However, any lingering doubts about the ascendancy of the dollar were clearly set aside after WORLD WAR II. Most of Europe lay in ruins while the United States, both economically and politically, grew even stronger. The productive capacity of America got a big fillip by supplying war material of all sorts. Capital intensity of production increased dramatically. Productivity of the work force improved significantly. The gold reserves accumulated to massive proportions. And the demand for U.S.-produced goods appeared to be limitless. All these and other factors provided the backdrop for the dollar becoming the anchor currency when a post-World War II international monetary system was being fashioned.

At the BRETTON WOODS conference in 1944, it was agreed that the value of dollar would be tied to the price of gold (at \$35/oz of gold) and that all other currencies would be pegged to the dollar in their relative value in a fixed-exchange regime of an international monetary system. The dollar obviously had arrived as a reserve currency par excellence in more ways than one. It was agreed that the burden of adjustment, when necessary, would be on the currency other than the dollar. If a country experienced a balance of payments deficit, its currency weakens and depreciates. But in a fixed exchange rate of the Bretton Woods type, this can be allowed only as an exception in response to some extenuating circumstance of fundamental economic change. Otherwise the fixed peg will have to be maintained. This is possible if the issuing country (e.g., Brazil) can buy its own currency with its foreign reserves to prop up its currency value, or if another country with appreciating currency (e.g., the United States) can purchase the weakening currency. The Bretton Woods system laid the burden squarely on the other country—in this case Brazil. But there is a limit to foreign reserves held by a country, hence a limit to how long it is possible to artificially prop up a currency.

Another option would be for the deficit country (say Brazil) to institute contractionary economic policy or for the surplus country (say the United States) to have an expansionary policy. Again, the adjustment responsibility was assigned to countries like Brazil. Consequently, the Bretton Woods fixed exchange system could not bear the burden of this one-sided adjustment for very long and had to be essentially abandoned. It may be mentioned here that a balance of payments deficits for a reserve currency does not pose the same problem. It is the demand for the reserve currency itself—its role in mediating international transactions—that compensates for the deficit and allows the country (like the United States) to enjoy a higher standard of living than would be possible as commensurate with their productions.

Euro-dollars and petro-dollars. The demand for the dollar, which in turn is demand for U.S. goods and U.S. bonds, increased dramatically in the post–World War II period. A whole phenomenon of a Euro-dollar market (dollar-denominated securities traded outside the United States) appeared and the United States was ready to supply it. Later on, the similar phenomenon of petro-dollars surfaced in response to the enormous cash accumulated by petroleum exporting countries for which the United States was quite happy to serve as the reserve currency supplier. The economic advantage to America was obvious: The United States supplied the currency in return for goods such as petroleum. The recipients of dollars bought U.S. securities, thus returning the proceeds as investment in the

Despite its rise and fall in value compared to other currencies, the dollar remains the premier reserve currency.

United States. The U.S. economy could not go wrong in such a scenario. But this was too good to last forever.

The economic dominance of the United States and the pre-eminence of the dollar struck a sour note with the misadventure of the VIETNAM WAR. The internal compulsion of fighting a war on poverty and external requirement of supplying personnel and equipment for battle led to an endemic inflationary pressure. The value of he dollar depreciated. By this time, enormous pools of Euro-dollars—later to be supplemented by petro-dollars—had been supplied in the market.

There was pressure to cash dollars for gold at $35/oz. However, the price of gold had increased dramatically as the trust in the dollar turned a bit shaky. The United States did not have enough gold to cash the outstanding issues of dollars. It would have to buy it from the Soviet Union or South Africa—the two big gold producers. America would have to absorb a huge loss buying gold at much higher price and selling it at $35/oz—a real bargain for dollar holders.

On the political side, the United States did not want to allow windfall profits for governments it did not quite approve of. President Richard NIXON, in an evening's television address, informed the world of dollar holders that the United States would no longer honor the peg of dollar-to-gold (at $35/oz) and this saved the economy many billions of dollars of loss it would have had to incur otherwise. The fact that the United States could get away with going off the gold standard, without too much bother from other nations, is a testimony to the hegemonic power of the United States and the resultant staying power of dollar as the reserve currency.

Despite a few bumps in the road here and there, the dollar continues to be the premier reserve currency. It is still the anchor currency for stabilizing the currencies of less developed countries. Either because of inconsistent economic policies or undue political interference in policy-making, when the currency of a country loses value and stability they tend to peg their currency to the dollar at a fixed exchange rate. This eliminates the discretion from monetary authorities in return for a possibility of stabilization. Other countries have experimented with outright "dollar-ization"—in part or in whole. This requires that the country should purchase dollars with their foreign reserves and use the dollar as legal tender. Again, this is a huge cost, first in terms of having to procure dollars and then of being locked in a straightjacket of no monetary policy discretion to respond to domestic economic contingencies.

Clearly, the dollar gains in stature and value and the U.S. economy gains goods and services and investment in return—a pretty good deal for the United States overall.

The rise of the euro. In the early 2000s, the dollar faced some competition from the EURO—the official currency of the EUROPEAN UNION (EU). Since the European Union is objectively a serious competitor both in its size of combined population and combined economic output in relation to the United States, the euro was already a respectable contender—despite its teething difficulties. The 2003 significant rise in the value of euro vis-à-vis the dollar was noted all around—for its economic as well as political import. Some have even suggested that the tiff between the United States and its European allies over the Iraq War may have something to do with this dollar-euro competition. It was rumored that some of the Iraqi petroleum cash deposits were intended to become petro-euros rather than petro-dollars, thus dampening the demand for dollars with its attendant negative economic consequences for the United States. However, it is clear that the European Union is not quite ready for currency leadership, especially in the face of U.S. military muscle.

The clearest manifestation of the premier status of the dollar as reserve currency is that foreigners who produce goods for U.S. markets and earn dollars in profit have a great incentive to invest these profits in U.S. securities—the best way for them to keep their wealth safe (from their workers) and profitable in guaranteed returns from U.S. securities. For the United States, it is easy to return the favor. America accumulates a large balance of payment deficits, living a higher standard of consumption than would be warranted by domestic production, and still keeps the dollar in good standing—healthy and strong.

BIBLIOGRAPHY. R. Carbaugh, *International Economics* (Southwestern, 2002); J. Morrell, *The Future of the dollar and World Reserve System* (Butterworths, 1981); F. Weaver, *Economic Literacy* (Roman & Littlefield, 2002).

SYED B. HUSSAIN, PH.D.
UNIVERSITY OF WISCONSIN, OSHKOSH

Dow Jones

IN 1882, THREE young journalists left their jobs at Kiernan News Agency and established Dow, Jones and Company, as it was then known. Charles Henry Dow (1851–1902), Edward Jones (1856–1920), and Charles Milford Bergstresser (1852–1905) were well qualified since their place of employment, popularly known as Kiernen's Corner, was the center of the financial scene of the day and stood where the NEW YORK STOCK EXCHANGE (NYSE) is now located. When Bergstresser joined Dow and Jones, he chose to be added as "and Company."

Their first publication was the *Customer's Afternoon Letter,* called a "flimsie" because of the paper on which it was printed. It was hand-written and personally delivered daily to subscribers. By 1885, Dow Jones was doing its

own printing, and the flimsie developed into the WALL STREET JOURNAL, which was published for the first time on July 8, 1899. The four-page paper cost 2 cents per copy and $5 a year. Its stated purpose was "to give fully and fairly the daily news attending the fluctuation in prices of stocks, bonds, and some classes of commodities." Each of the three partners brought special talents to the development of the company. Dow loved collecting financial facts and was always looking for better ways to get them out to investors. Jones, on the other hand, was best at managing and editing the newspaper. Bergstresser had people skills, and enjoyed personal contacts with business leaders and the financial community. The first issue of the *Wall Street Journal* identified Henry Dow's market concepts, which later became known as the Dow Theory.

Dow Jones has traditionally been determined to keep up with the technology of the day, so the Dow Jones News Service was added in 1897 to bring news and stock quotes quickly, using telegraph wires. In 1899, Jones sold his shares to his partners and left the company. Dow remained with Dow Jones until he died in 1902. After Dow's death, Clarence Barron (1855–1928) purchased the company for $130,000; he then modernized the printing process and added new staff. By 1920, the circulation had risen to 20,000. In 1942, the *Wall Street Journal* began publishing multiple business editions to better serve the country's financial needs; and by 1960, the circulation of the *Wall Street Journal* had swelled to over 500,000. Barney Kilgore (1908-67) who took over in 1941 has been credited with turning Dow Jones into a modern-day giant. Electronic services were added as access to the internet became commonplace, and information and stock data can be transmitted around the globe in seconds.

On May 9, 1921, *Barron's National Business and Financial Weekly* began publication at a cost of 20 cents a copy and $100 for a year's subscription. The journal had an elite list of subscribers made up of company presidents, chairs of various boards, directors, owners, and partners. The slogan was "For Those Who Read for Profit," and it included financial articles, analysis, and reviews. In addition to *Barron's National Business and Financial Weekly,* Dow Jones publishes *Smart Money,* and the *Wall Street Journal* is published in various versions around the world. The company also owns a number of local newspapers and several television stations.

The Dow Jones Index. The Dow Jones Index started with only 11 stocks, and nine of these were RAILROAD stocks since railroads were the most influential market sector. The two industrials were Pacific Mail Steamship and Western Union. By 1885, the list had grown to 14 as the St. Paul Railroad was deleted and four other railroads added. The average over the next few years tended to be consistent, rarely varying over 40 points because railroad stocks grew steadily, and the economic system was stable. By October

4, 1915, the number of stocks had risen to 20: American Beet Sugar, American Can, American Car and Foundry, American Locomotive, American Smelting, American Sugar, AT&T, Anaconda Copper, Baldwin Locomotive, Central Leather, GENERAL ELECTRIC, Goodrich, Republic Iron and Steel, Studebaker, Texas Company, U.S. Rubber, U.S. STEEL, Utah Copper, Westinghouse, and Western Union. The changes reflected the decline of railroads and the presence of new technologies such as electricity and automobiles. Changes were made only eight times in this list. On October 1, 1928, the list increased to 30 stocks.

At the beginning of the 21st century, the Dow is made up of 30 "blue chip" stocks that serve as a sample of the stock market as a whole. Changes are still rare. For example, in 1997, Woolworth, Westinghouse, Texaco, and Bethlehem Steel were replaced with HEWLETT-PACKARD, Johnson and Johnson, Traveler Group Inc., and WAL-MART. In January 27, 2003, the 30-stock list included: 3M, Alcoa, Altria Group, American Express, AT&T, BOEING, Caterpillar, CITIGROUP, Coca-Cola, DuPont, Eastman Kodak, EXXON MOBIL, General Electric, GENERAL MOTORS, Hewlett-Packard, HOME DEPOT, Honeywell, Intel, International Business Machines, International Paper, J.P. MORGAN CHASE, Johnson and Johnson, McDonald's, Merck and Company, PROCTER & GAMBLE, SBC COMMUNICATIONS, United Technology, Wal-Mart, and Walt Disney Company. The changes indicate trends in society as a whole, such as the growth of technology and the move toward one-place shopping and convenience. When most people think of the stock market, they think about Dow Jones and the New York Stock Exchange, but it actually includes thousands of companies whose stock is traded every day, as well as a number of other stock exchanges. Other indexes are also published, such as STANDARD AND POOR'S and the *New York Times*.

The stability of the stock market affects other elements in the economic system. For example, a company might decide whether or not to add to its holdings based on the Dow Jones Industrial Average (DJIA), which was first published in 1896. Editors of the *Wall Street Journal* continue to choose the stocks, and the index is used around the world to identify trends in the stock market. In its early days, the average was derived by the simple formula of adding the points (with each point equal to one dollar) and dividing the total by the number of stocks included in the average. As the stock market grew and became more complex, the formula for DJIA was changed to reflect mergers and stock splits and other such factors. In order to maintain a stable market, the stock market occasionally suspends operations. Rule 80B of the NYSE mandates that the market be shut down for an hour if the average drops below 10 percent by 2 P.M. from the previous day's closing amount. If it drops more than 20 percent by 1 P.M., the NYSE closes for two hours; and if it drops more than 30 percent at any time, the NYSE closes for the entire day.

The Dow, as it is commonly known, explains the behaviors of a single stock, a group of stocks, and the stock market in general. When stocks are up, investors are more active, and the public feels more secure. When stocks go down, the reverse is true. Tracking the DJIA over time provides an indicator of the health of the economic system. The DJIA is followed closely because more than half of the adults in the United States own at least some shares of stock.

BIBLIOGRAPHY. "About Dow Jones," www.dowjones.com; "Dow Jones Averages," www.djindexes.com; James K. Glassman and Kevin A. Hassett, *Dow 36,000: The New Strategy for Profiting from the Coming Rise in the Stock Market* (Random House, 1999); James Madoff and Andrew Harless, *The Indebted Society* (Little, Brown, and Company, 1996); Jerry M. Rosenberg, *Inside The Wall Street Journal: The History of Dow Jones and Company and America's Most Influential Newspaper* (Macmillan, 1982); Robert J. Shiller, *Irrational Exuberance* (Princeton University Press, 2000); Richard J. Stillman. *Dow Jones Industrial Average: History and Role in An Investment Strategy* (Dow Jones-Irwin, 1986).

ELIZABETH PURDY, PH.D.
INDEPENDENT SCHOLAR

drugs

DRUGS, OR PHARMACEUTICALS, are inputs to the production of health. The market for pharmaceuticals is particularly interesting because of the many complexities that differentiate it from a free, perfectly competitive market. On the demand side, consumers of pharmaceuticals are constrained by government regulation and the purchase of pharmaceuticals is generally subsidized by health insurance. On the supply side, producers often act as monopolists under patent protection, engage in intensive research and development, and operate under strict government regulation.

In most developed countries, governments require a physician prescription for the purchase of certain pharmaceuticals. Pharmaceuticals that can be obtained without a prescription are called over-the-counter drugs.

When deciding whether to purchase prescribed pharmaceuticals, consumers weigh the anticipated benefits of the drug with its out-of-pocket cost. Because health insurance generally subsidizes the purchase of pharmaceuticals, the out-of-pocket cost to the consumer is typically far less than full price. As a result, consumers tend to consume more pharmaceuticals than would be socially optimal. If pharmaceuticals were available at zero out-of-pocket cost to consumers, they would use them if they offered any benefit at all. To prevent this expensive outcome, insurers typically only cover expenditures on pharmaceuticals above a specific deductible paid by the insured and/or the price of the drug above a specific co-payment on each prescription. Co-payments are typically set lower for generic, inexpensive drugs than for patent-protected name-brand ones. INSURANCE companies may also impose annual limits on reimbursements for spending on pharmaceuticals. In each case, the existence of some out-of-pocket cost is a disincentive for the insured to consume additional pharmaceuticals and limits MORAL HAZARD on the part of the insured.

Information is a public good; once created, information can be circulated at zero cost and its dissemination is difficult for its creator to restrict. For this reason, information, like other public goods, tends to be underprovided by free markets. Governments use two methods to encourage research and development (which is the creation of information) on pharmaceuticals.

First, basic research in this sector is subsidized by government agencies such as the U.S. National Institutes of Health. Second, governments issue patents on pharmaceuticals. The PATENT guarantees that the patent holder has a monopoly on production of that drug for a specified period of time; firms can invest heavily into producing new drugs with the confidence that their discoveries cannot be immediately copied by competitors.

Policymakers must balance the interest of encouraging innovation by guaranteeing a long period of patent protection with the interest of guaranteeing consumers access to inexpensive pharmaceuticals. After the expiration of a pharmaceutical patent, competitors are free to introduce generic equivalents to the previously patented drug. The added competition to this previously monopolistic market lowers prices and increases the quantity of the drug transacted. Generic manufacturers may seek to earn profits by differentiating theirs from other versions. The original patent holder may seek to price discriminate among consumers by continuing to sell its name-brand version at a high price (to exploit brand loyalty and name recognition) while simultaneously selling a generic version at a low price to compete with the new entrants.

Patents and regulation. Pharmaceutical firms respond to the profits possible through patent protection, and commit one of the highest fractions of revenues of any industry to RESEARCH AND DEVELOPMENT (R&D). While R&D costs are high, the profitability of drugs is highly variable. Only three-tenths of new drugs earn enough to cover the costs of production, distribution, and marketing. Thus, pharmaceutical companies use monopoly profits on a few blockbuster drugs to cover the costs of developing the vast majority of drugs that prove to be unprofitable.

It is not uncommon for pharmaceutical firms to charge high prices for the most efficacious drugs; this is the result of the firm's monopoly power combined with a

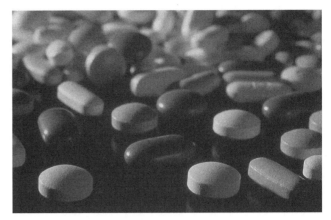

Drugs, or pharmaceuticals, are often first introduced as a patent-protected monopoly.

price elasticity of demand that is highly inelastic. Price elasticity of demand is inelastic because some patients are willing to pay virtually anything for drugs that will save their lives or reduce their pain, and also because patients face so little of the total cost thanks to health insurance coverage of pharmaceuticals. For these reasons, the price of each dose of a patented medicine may be set a hundred times higher than its marginal cost of production.

The ability of manufacturers to exploit a monopoly position on patented drugs is, in some cases, limited by powerful forces on the demand side; for example, in the United States, health maintenance organizations have negotiated discounts from pharmaceutical firms after threatening to refuse to cover their products. Monopoly power is also limited by competition from firms producing drugs that, though chemically distinct, are in the same therapeutic class and can therefore serve as substitutes.

Governments of many industrialized and developing countries regulate prices or profits in pharmaceuticals. In this regard, the United States may be the least regulatory developed country; as a result, many studies have found that pharmaceutical prices are higher in the United States than abroad. This price disparity has led to periodic calls by U.S. consumers and insurers for price regulation of pharmaceuticals. To some extent, even if regulated, the prices of drugs need to be kept high to keep pharmaceutical firms solvent; pharmaceutical manufacturers cover their losses on the vast majority of unsuccessful drugs by earning high profits on the few successful ones.

Still, lightly populated and developing countries often free-ride, in a relative sense, in this market by imposing strict price controls or refusing to enforce patents on pharmaceuticals, confident that their actions will not be enough to dissuade pharmaceutical firms from continuing to innovate. Despite widespread regulation, pharmaceutical manufacturing has consistently ranked as one of the most profitable industries. The debate over price regulation of pharmaceuticals is a reflection of the societal tradeoff between cheap medicine for consumers in the present day and encouraging research and development by producers to improve the set of medicines available to consumers in the future.

Varying price regulation explains some, but not all, of the variation in prices of pharmaceuticals across countries. Like any monopolist that perceives differing price elasticities of demand among its buyers, pharmaceutical firms try to maximize profits by price discriminating across countries. Research also suggests that part of the cross-national price differential is due to differences in expected lawsuit damages. Such price differences across nations represent an arbitrage opportunity, but many governments ban such trade in pharmaceuticals.

Governments regulate the drugs that pharmaceutical firms are allowed to sell. Government regulators typically seek proof that new drugs are both safe and efficacious; a process that involves multiple phases of clinical testing, and years to complete. Here, too, policymakers face a tradeoff. They must balance the interest of guaranteeing that all drugs are safe and effective against the interest of giving patients immediate access to newly developed drugs. This can be rephrased in the terminology of statistics as striking a balance between the risk of Type I and Type II error; Type I error is the mistake of approving an unsafe or ineffective drug, and Type II error is the mistake of withholding from the market a safe and effective drug.

If bureaucratic decision-makers are more concerned about avoiding the public embarrassment of Type I error than they are about the largely unpublicized deaths that result from Type II error, then fewer drugs will be approved, or drug approval will take longer, than is socially optimal. The difficulty of choosing the right balance between these priorities was illustrated by the public debate in the United States in the early years of the AIDS epidemic, when little treatment for HIV existed, and it was predicted that newly developed treatments would take years to move through the approval process before becoming available to HIV-positive patients.

Traditionally, pharmaceutical firms marketed their products in a process called "detailing;" manufacturer's representatives visited individual doctors, providing information and offering enticements for the physicians to prescribe drugs produced by the firm. Pharmaceutical advertisements were limited to medical journals. In recent years, marketing in the pharmaceutical industry has taken the form of direct-to-consumer advertising. Critics, including some physicians, allege that such advertising represents demand inducement. Some insurers have tried to counter direct-to-consumer marketing with requirements that pharmacists substitute preferred drugs on the insurer's formulary for more expensive equivalent drugs.

As the number and efficacy of pharmaceuticals has increased, they are increasingly substituted for labor in the production of health. For example, in the 1960s, treat-ment of depression was overwhelmingly labor-intensive: psychotherapists would engage patients in psychotherapy one-on-one. With the development of antidepressants, the production of mental health has become overwhelmingly pharmaceuticals-intensive. Similar substitutions of pharmaceuticals for labor in the production of health have occurred throughout the health care industry.

BIBLIOGRAPHY. Henry G. Grabowski, "R&D Costs and Returns to New Drugs in the 1990s," unpublished manuscript (2002); Henry G. Grabowski and J. M. Vernon, "Returns on New Drug Interactions in the 1980s," *Journal of Health Economics* (1994); F.M. Scherer, "The Pharmaceutical Industry," *Handbook of Health Economics* (2000); Henry G. Grabowski and J. M. Vernon, "Brand Loyalty, Entry, and Price Competition in Pharmaceuticals After the 1984 Drug Act," *Journal of Law and Economics* (1992); Patricia M. Danzon and Li-Wei Chao, "Cross-National Price Differences for Pharmaceuticals: How Large and Why?" *Journal of Health Economics* (2000); Ernst R. Berndt, "Pharmaceuticals in U. S. Health Care: Determinants of Quantity and Price," *Journal of Economic Perspectives* (2002).

JOHN CAWLEY, PH.D.
CORNELL UNIVERSITY

Duke Energy

DUKE ENERGY IS ONE of the largest ENERGY companies in the world, with sales of $59 billion in 2001. From its beginnings in 1904 in South Carolina, the core business of Duke Energy has been the provision of energy services, offering generation, transmission, and management of electricity and natural gas around the world. Duke Power, a subsidiary, is the second largest investor-owned electric utility in the United States. Other subsidiaries provide telecommunications, financial services, and real estate development services.

Duke Energy enjoys a strong reputation in the electricity utility industry, a strong balance sheet, and adaptability in the recently deregulated energy market. In the early 2000s, allegations had arisen, however, that the company manipulated the California wholesale electricity market by withholding power from its California plants.

BIBLIOGRAPHY. California Public Utilities Commission, *Report on Wholesale Electric Generation Investigation* (2002); Duke Energy, *Duke Energy's History* (2002); Energy Information Administration, *100 Largest Utility Net Generation* (2000); Jeffrey Resnick, "Reputation Matters," *Platt's Energy Business & Technology* (July/August 2002).

JAMES PRIEGER, PH.D.
UNIVERSITY OF CALIFORNIA, DAVIS

Dutch West India Company

FOUNDED IN 1621 by the States General of the NETHERLANDS, the West-Indische Compagnie (WIC) was chartered to manage Dutch trade and state-sponsored piracy along the west coast of Africa and the coastline of North and South America. Like its counterpart in Asia, the Vereinigde Ost-Indische Compagnie (VOC), the Dutch West India Company came into existence as an extension of 16th-century Dutch maritime exploration and commerce; these organizations exercised considerable power and independence in orchestrating Dutch overseas activity in the early modern world.

Early Dutch activity in the New World mirrored the politics of continental Europe, where the Dutch were engaged in the Eighty Years' War against SPAIN for their political and economic autonomy. Since this ongoing conflict played havoc with European trade routes, the Dutch, by the end of the 16th century, had begun looking elsewhere for imports. They launched what privateering operations they could against the treasure ships of the Spanish Main.

The Dutch West India Company was overseen by a board of directors appointed by the Dutch States-General, who granted the board virtually autonomous power over administration within its territories, stopping only at prohibiting it from declaring war of its own accord. In addition to its ongoing mandates to expand Dutch trade and carry out economic piracy against the Spanish, the WIC had by the early 17th century expanded into the management of commercial colonies in the Western Hemisphere, and became involved in running the Dutch slave trade with Africa.

In the 1620s, the WIC founded several North American colonies, including Fort Orange (Albany, New York), Fort Good Hope (Hartford, Connecticut), and Fort Amsterdam (New York City). Beginning in 1624, WIC ships seized part of northeastern BRAZIL from the Portuguese. One of the more colorful agents of the WIC, Piet Heyn, captured a Spanish treasure fleet in 1628; the WIC funneled the proceeds into further expansion throughout the New World. Its activities reached their height in the 1630s and1640s, when its main bases of operation were located in New Amsterdam, Curaçao, and Pernambuco.

The West India Company never, however, achieved the long-standing success of its eastern counterpart. Expansion beyond early gains grew expensive with increasing competition. The company then sought to only maintain and defend what it had, but even this proved impossible over time. By the middle 17th century, it had suffered a number of setbacks and defeats, losing the Brazil colony to the Portuguese in 1654 and New Netherland to the English in 1664. The company was reorganized in 1674, after which it gave up the goal of territorial acquisition and focused almost exclusively on the African slave trade, making additional profit running contraband goods to English colonies in North America. After the invasion of the Netherlands by French armies in 1794, control of the company passed briefly to the puppet state known as the Batavian Republic before the WIC was dissolved in 1798.

BIBLIOGRAPHY. Van Cleaf Bachman, *Peltries or Plantations: The Economic Policies of the Dutch West India Company in New Netherland, 1623–1639* (Johns Hopkins University Press, 1969); Cornelius Goslinga, *The Dutch in the Caribbean and on the Wild Coast, 1580–1680* (University of Florida Press, 1971); A.M. Rutten, *Dutch Transatlantic Medicine Trade in the Eighteenth Century under the Cover of the West India Company* (Erasmus, 2000); Willie F. Page, *The Dutch Triangle: The Netherlands and the Atlantic Slave Trade, 1621–1664* (Garland, 1997).

CHARLES ROBINSON, PH.D.
BRANDEIS UNIVERSITY

Dynegy

DYNEGY IS ONE OF the largest ENERGY companies in the UNITED STATES with assets worth $25 billion in 2001. Unlike many other large players in the energy industry, Dynegy did not begin as a regulated utility. The company was founded in 1984 as the Natural Gas Clearinghouse, which was created to take advantage of opportunities in the about-to-be deregulated gas market. The core business of Dynegy today is the provision of energy services, offering generation, transmission, marketing, and management of natural gas and electricity around North America. Illinois Power, a subsidiary since 2000, is a regulated electric and gas energy delivery company located in Decatur.

Another subsidiary provides telecommunications services. Dynegy is generally admired in the energy industry for its innovation, talented employees, sound management, and financial soundness. In the early 2000s, allegations had arisen, however, that the company manipulated the California wholesale electricity market by withholding power from its California plants.

BIBLIOGRAPHY. California Public Utilities Commission, *Report on Wholesale Electric Generation Investigation* (2002); Dynegy, *Dynegy Fact Sheet* (2002); Energy Information Administration, *100 Largest Utility Net Generation* (2000).

JAMES PRIEGER, PH.D.
UNIVERSITY OF CALIFORNIA, DAVIS

E

E.ON Energie

HEADQUARTERED IN Munich, GERMANY, E.ON Energie is one of the largest investor-owned service utilities in continental Europe. It supplies electricity, gas, and water to some 25 million customers across Germany and a dozen more countries, among them RUSSIA, AUSTRIA, the Baltics, and SWITZERLAND. Continuing to invest in subsidiaries and affiliates, company forecasters in early 2003 look to a doubling in all types of sales within the next five years.

Fast becoming a global player, E.ON came to fruition in June, 2000, with its merger of two decades-old industrial companies, VEBA and VIAG. It currently operates via 80 subsidiaries and affiliates in which it owns large-stake holdings, including the recent addition of the Sydkraft Power Station in Sweden, acquired May, 2000. Of its three types of power plants—conventional, nuclear and those that run on renewable energy—they combine to produce a capacity of 34,000 mw.

Since the VEBA and VIAG merger, the consolidated E.ON has boosted electricity sales volumes by nearly 50 percent, a tremendous rise. In terms of gas and water, the acquisition of German-based corporations, HEIN GAS and Gelsenwasser, has greatly increased output in both industries.

Fortune's edition of July 22, 2002, reported E.ON's latest fiscal year figures as follows: revenues, $66 billion; profits, $2 billion; assets, $88 billion; and stockholders' equity, $22 billion.

BIBLIOGRAPHY. "Global 500: The World's Largest Companies," *Fortune* (July 2002); "E.ON History," www.eon.com.

SYED B. HUSSAIN, PH.D.
UNIVERSITY OF WISCONSIN, OSHKOSH

East India Company, British

IN 1599, A GROUP OF influential English merchants had established a joint stock of £30,000 with the purpose of voyaging to the "Est Indies and other ilandes and cuntries therabouts." They requested the monarch to grant them permission for this purpose and so was founded the English East India Company by a royal charter signed by Queen Elizabeth I in December, 1600. The new company was granted a monopoly on all English trade east of the Cape of Good Hope, Africa. It was rather pretentiously titled *The Governor and Company of Merchants of London Trading into the East Indies* and was composed of 218 members.

There were several reasons why the English crown saw it fit at that moment to launch a company of this nature. There was a need to diversify English trade, especially to find new markets for English woolen cloth after the loss of some of their traditional markets in continental Europe. The English also wished to gain more control over trade in general in Asia. The new route around the Cape of Good Hope opened up immense possibilities of trading with Asia and the English feared being out-maneuvered by the Dutch and the French. The English Crown and the merchants agreed upon the chartering of a company to deal specifically with Asia as a means to bolster overseas trade.

It was by no means smooth sailing for the newly formed company in its initial days. Indeed, there were hardly any indications in these opening years of the tremendous influence and power that this company would wield in the next two decades. It faced bitter competition from its European rivals, the Dutch and the Portuguese, and at home the fact of its monopoly brought them hostility from other English merchants.

Within the next 40 years, however, the East India Company had built up a network of factories all over southern Asia. It had become by this time the largest trading company, commanding a capital of nearly £3 million. It was also a formidable force within England itself. Most of the investors of the company were wealthy merchants who held important government offices thus instituting the interests of the company firmly into English politics.

Spice was the primary trading enticement that Asia offered the company. Pepper, significantly known as "black gold" in Europe, had been available around the Mediterranean area for a while. The company was anxious to purchase at source in order to increase their profits. Pepper was grown all along the southwestern coastal area of India, and Java, Sumatra and other southeastern Asian islands were home to rare varieties of spice.

There was a dangerous problem at the root of the English trade with Asia. While Asia had to offer an immense variety of products that Europe coveted, the reverse was far from true. The pride of the English market, woolen cloth, had no place in the warm climate of south and southeastern Asia. From the very outset, English merchants were unable to sell European products to the Indies and they were also almost solely dependent on the pepper and spice trade.

Two solutions emerged for the above problem. The first, certainly the less desirable, was arrived at due more to necessity than choice. Since there was nothing Europe could offer Asia as barter, the only way the company could pay for its imports was in cash. Silver fetched a high price in Asia and hence the standard practice for the East India Company became the export of bullion from England to pay for its Asian trade. This was a source of constant anxiety and much deliberation among scholars, merchants, and state officials. The export of treasures across national borders was not the most popular activity of the East India Company and made it the target of ceaseless popular criticism.

The second alternative for the company's trading choices was the development of what came to be known as the "country trade." The company discovered that the spices procured from one part of Asia could be bartered for goods from another part. The company thus began to use their ships to carry goods for other Asian merchants and as a result locked the entire region, from the Red Sea to Japan, into a complex network of interdependent trading units.

The popular assumption about the trajectory of the company is that it started out exclusively as a trading company and only reluctantly assumed the mantle of governance in India. Recent scholars have persuasively disproved such claims and have shown that force was "an implicit part" of Europe's trade with Asia. Control over Indian revenues was a lasting solution to the drain-ing of bullion from England and this could only be secured by force. Protecting trading interests from rival European powers as well as from indigenous rulers could prompt the most astute of merchants to become the most fearless of warriors.

The victory of the English in the Seven Years' War (1756–63) in Europe was decisive in reordering the priorities of the East India Company. Competition with the French East India Company had reached a peak and between 1744 and 1761 there were a series of battles between the two rival companies to establish hegemony on Indian soil. The final impetus to the English side came, when in 1757, the English general Robert Clive won a critical victory over the ruler of Bengal. By 1765, the English had secured the right of civil administration in Bengal and its neighboring provinces, thus giving them power over nearly 20 million people and control over revenues worth £3 million. This revenue was used to buy Bengal goods resold at immense profit overseas, and also to fund the conquest of other parts of India.

The rise of the fortunes, profits, and dividends of the East India Company was marked by a contradictory fall in its popularity in the home country. Tales of corruption, degeneration, and bribery filtered into the popular press about the lifestyles of the company officials.

In reality, the monopoly of the company was slowly emerging as a threat to the newly emergent class of industrial capitalists in England. They were in need of their own markets to sell cheap manufactured goods and the trading privileges of the East India Company was a major barrier in their way. Thus emerged in this period a strident rhetoric in favor of "free trade" against company monopoly.

The first major loss of power in the company occurred in 1773 with the passing of the Regulating Act. The company was then at the verge of bankruptcy and appealed to the Parliament for financial aid. While the Crown agreed to a loan, it used the opportunity to establish control over the company. The Regulating Act established some guidelines for rule in India and also banned private trade by company agents.

It was not the end of woes for the company. By 1784, it was once again heavily in debt and this time Parliament established a Board of Control that would preside directly over the company's directors. This arrangement, arrived at by the India Bill of 1784, split the governing of British India between the company and the British government.

The loss of power in the company over its territories and the eventual take-over by the Crown was a gradual but steady process. In 1813, the company was stripped of its trading monopoly and trade was opened up to all English merchants by a licensing system overseen by the court of directors. In 1833, the company ceased all its trading activities and fell back strictly to a role of governing the vast territories that it had acquired in the Indian subcontinent.

The final blow to the company came with the mutiny of the Indian soldiers in 1857 that cost the British government £50 million to quell. The India Bill that officially handed control over to the Crown was passed in August, 1858. Queen Victoria was declared the Empress of India in an ostentatious ceremony in 1858 and the merchant-adventurers, having played their part in the colonial project, now yielded place to the industrialists and the civil servants.

BIBLIOGRAPHY. K.N. Chaudhuri, *The Trading World of Asia and the English East India Company* (Cambridge University Press, 1978). Antony Wild, *The East India Company: Trade and Conquest from 1600* (Lyons Press, 2000); Anthony Farrington, *Trading Places: The East India Company and Asia 1600–1834* (British Library, 2002).

TITHI BHATTACHARYA, PH.D.
PURDUE UNIVERSITY

econometrics

ECONOMETRICS IS THE STATISTICAL method used to measure the effect one variable, and a group of variables have on one another. It is the main tool used in economics, finance, and business to untangle real-world empirical data. In the pure sciences, a controlled experiment can be set up to test the effect of one variable on the outcome. This controlled experiment keeps everything constant, except for one variable, so that any change in the outcome can be attributed to that variable. In business and capitalism, however, the laboratory is the economy, and the researcher cannot change variables in the economy independently just to see what happens. Instead, econometrics must separate out effects of a number of variables all moving at the same time.

Simple regression model. The basic form of estimation of the relationship between two variables in a simple regression model is:

$$y = \alpha + \beta x + \varepsilon$$

The simple regression model put a form on the relationship as a line that best describes how that data falls. y is the dependent variable that is being explained. x is the independent variable (also called explanatory variable) whose value is used to explain the dependent variable. α and β are the parameters of the relationship. α is the constant which give the average level of y if x is zero. β

is the slope coefficient that tells how much a one unit change in x changes y. If β is positive, then an increase in x is associated with an increase in y, that is there is a positive relationship between x and y. If β is negative, then an increase in x is associated with a decrease in y, that is there is an inverse relationship between x and y. If β is zero, there is no relationship between x and y. ε is the error term (also called the residual) that is the unexplainable, random component of y since no real-world process can be completely explained.

Estimation. The most common method of estimating the parameters of a regression model is Ordinary Least Squares (OLS). OLS calculates the estimates a and b for the parameters α and β which minimize the sum of squared residuals for a given set of data. For each observed value of y, the estimated error associated with that value is y – a – b x. In this way, the estimated regression line passes through the actual data with the least squared error. By squaring the errors, this implicitly penalizes the estimate more for large errors than small errors. Squaring the errors also penalizes the estimate equally for positive and negative errors. The errors that remain after finding the estimated OLS regression line then can be used to determine the accuracy of the estimates since large errors indicate that the regression line does not fit the data well.

Multiple regression model. The only difference between a simple regression and a multiple regression is that in a multiple regression model more than one independent variable is used to explain the dependent variable:

$$y = \alpha + \beta_1 x + \beta_2 x + \beta_3 x + \ldots + \beta_k x + \varepsilon$$

A common concern with multiple regressions is *multicollinearity*. Multicollinearity is a problem when there are high correlations between two or more independent variables. When this occurs, OLS estimation is not as precise since the effect of each variable cannot be separated. A sign of multicollinearity is when the model seems to predict well, but no one variable has a significant coefficient (see statistical significance below). More precision can be gained by increasing the size of the dataset, transforming the variables into ratios or logs, or simply by dropping a highly correlated variable.

Determining the fit of the model. R^2 (pronounced "are squared") is one measure for how well the regression model fits the data. R^2 is calculated by taking the Total Sum of Squares (TSS), which is the total variation in the dependent variable around its mean without estimating the regression [$TSS = \Sigma(y - \mu_y)^2$ where μ_y is the average of y], and compared it to the errors explained by the regression:

$$R^2 = 1 - ESS/TSS$$

where ESS is the sum of the squared errors. R^2 can range between 0 and 1. The higher the value of R^2, the better the fit of the model.

One drawback of R^2 is that it does not give an objective answer to the question "Is this a good model?" The F statistic performs a test of the null hypothesis that the estimated regression does no better than a simple average:

$$F = \frac{R^2/(k\text{-}1)}{(1\text{-}R^2)/(n\text{-}k)}$$

If the calculated F value is greater than the critical value found by computer software (such as SAS or Excel) or found in statistical tables of the F distribution, then one can reject the null hypothesis that the independent variables provide no explanation of the dependent variables. The alternative is that at least one variable is statistically significant.

Statistical significance. To determine if the effect of a single independent variable is statistically significant, the t statistic is used. The t statistic tests the null hypothesis that the slope parameter associated with a particular independent variable is equal to zero (2 tail test) or is greater than or less than zero (1 tail test). If the coefficient is zero, then changes in that variable do not affect the dependent variable.

The t statistic is a standardized statistic, meaning that it takes the estimate of that parameter, b, and divides it by its standard error, σ_b (pronounced sigma). Calculation of σ_b is detailed in the references below. If the calculated t statistic is either above the upper critical value or below the lower critical value, then the null hypothesis is rejected and the coefficient is statistically significant. The alternative is that the variable does have an effect.

Properties of a good estimator. For any statistical estimate, there are some desirable properties. If an estimator is unbiased, then its expected value is the true parameter value. This means that even though an estimate will never be exact, on average it measures the true value. The next desirable property is to have an efficient estimator. An efficient estimator gets as close to the true parameter as possible (i.e., it has the lowest dispersion around its mean as measured by its standard error). Finally, an estimator should be consistent, meaning that as the sample size increases the estimate converges on the true parameter value.

The OLS estimator is said to be the Best Linear Unbiased Estimator (BLUE) since it is unbiased, consistent, and has the lowest standard error of any other estimate using a linear regression model. The OLS estimate is only BLUE, however, if it does not break the assumptions listed below:

1. The linear model must be appropriate, and the correct variables must be included. The linearity of the model forces each variable to have the same level of effect on the dependent variable for all ranges. This may not be appropriate in cases where an effect starts out strong, and then fades away. Taking the log of variables, or including squared independent variables to allow for decreasing or increasing effects can compensate for some non-linearity.

2. The expected value of the error term is equal to zero. This assumption ensures that the average of the predicted value of the dependent variable (a + b x) is equal to the average of the observed dependent variable. If this assumption is violated and the error has a non-zero average, then the constant will not be unbiased.

3. The independent variables are not random and are not perfectly collinear. If independent variables cannot be considered as given, then the estimate of the parameter may be biased due to simultaneous equations. Simultaneous equations is the situation where x effects y, but y also effects x. OLS cannot separate out the effect of x on y, instead some type of instrumental variable estimation must be used. Perfect collinearity indicates that there is a redundant variable since two or more variables move exactly together.

4. Error terms have the same volatility and are not correlated with each other. If errors have differing volatility (known as heteroscedasticity) then some observations are more precise than others. OLS does not use this information. While it is still unbiased, OLS is not efficient in the presence of heteroscedasticity. If errors are correlated, as is common with time-series data (known as autocorrelation), one time period can help predict another time period. With both heteroscedasticity and autocorrelation, Weighted Least Squares provides a more efficient estimate by using the additional information to weight the sum of squared errors.

5. There must be more data points than parameters to be estimated. Degrees of freedom (defined as the number of data points less the number of estimates) greater than zero ensures that there are enough observations to mathematically be able to solve for the unknowns. Furthermore, if degrees of freedom are less than thirty, then statistical tests lose power, and in some cases can not be used at all.

Business applications of econometrics. Theories abound in finance and management that point to better investing techniques, or more efficient organization of the firm. Econometrics is the process of putting these theories to the test. Some areas have more data than others, which in some part determines the statistical techniques used. For example, stock market data can be obtained daily, hourly, or by the second, so stock market researchers have thousands of data points. This means that sophisticated time series techniques can be used, and the data can be partitioned into separate datasets to test for robustness. Event studies are common in stock research to determine the market reaction to certain announcements and can be timed rather precisely when coordinated with electronic news services. Data for emerging market macroeconomic variables, on the other hand, are released yearly, or quarterly at best. This data set also rarely goes back more than 20–30 years and is often of suspect quality.

In some areas, econometrics has become so commonplace that practitioners may not even realize that regressions are producing the numbers. Altman's Z-score measures the probability that a company will not default. Certain financial variables of a firm increase the likelihood of a firm staying in business, such as liquid assets, liabilities, and market value. A type of regression analysis was used by Altman (1968) to find the proper effect of each factor. These weightings are still being used over three decades later.

Another area where regression analysis is routine is in the calculation of beta for the Capital Asset Pricing Model (CAPM). Beta measures the reaction of excess returns (return minus the risk-free rate) of a stock to fluctuations in the excess returns of a market portfolio. This is accomplished by running a regression with the excess returns of the stock as the dependent variable, and the excess returns of the market as the independent variable. Beta is the estimated slope coefficient. The higher the estimated beta, the higher the risk premium that is required according to CAPM.

The pervasiveness of regression analysis has also meant that statistical computer programs to estimate regression parameters are more accessible even for very large datasets. Some common statistical packages are SAS, STATA, SPSS, EVIEWS, and GAUSS, but regression add-ins also come bundled with many spreadsheet programs such as Excel, Lotus, and QuattroPro.

BIBLIOGRAPHY. Edward Altman, "Financial Ratios, Discriminant Analysis and the Prediction of Corporate Bankruptcy" *The Journal of Finance* (v. 23/4, 1968); John Y. Campbell, Andrew W. Lo, and A. Craig MacKinlay, *The Econometrics of Financial Markets* (Princeton University Press, 1996). Greene, William, *Econometric Analysis* (Prentice Hall, 2003); Damodar Gujarati, Basic Econometrics (McGraw-Hill, 2003); Dominick Salvatore and Derrick Reagle, *Schaum's Outline of Theory and Problems of Statistics and Econometrics* (McGraw-Hill, 2001).

DERRICK REAGLE, PH.D.
FORDHAM UNIVERSITY

economic indicators

DATA AND OTHER STATISTICAL measurements are the economic indicators used by economists, financial analysts, and public policy-makers to assess current, prior, and future economic events.

Indicators, and their reputed explanatory and predictive abilities, can be related to either general economic conditions as measured by a region's GROSS DOMESTIC PRODUCT (GDP) or to particular sectors of the economy, such as manufacturing, households, or labor. Levels of production, patterns of spending or consumption, investment and savings, employment, inflation, exchange rates, and the rate of economic growth are just a few of the economic events that are analyzed, and that can be correlated to a number of assorted indicators.

Many of these indicators are generally accepted in practice and by a majority of economists but since there are alternative economic theories there are also alternative economic indicators used by analysts with opposing explanations for economic events. Indicators can be used to evaluate current economic conditions or to forecast future conditions and are often used to literally indicate or signal changes in business or economic activity relative to the BUSINESS CYCLE. Business cycles are defined as the recurrent, alternating but non-periodic phases of expansions and contractions in a region's business or economic activity, and one business cycle can be defined as the length of time from one peak or trough to the next peak or trough.

The fluctuations in the business cycle are commonly referred to as periods of economic recovery, expansion or prosperity, recession or depression. Given the complex structure of modern economies, it is not surprising that fluctuations in business and economic activity persist. But accurately predicting, or even confirming, the precise shifting points—the peaks and the troughs in the business cycle—can be problematic.

Generally there are three types of indicators that are of particular interest to policy-makers and analysts: leading, coincident, and lagging indicators. Leading indicators are those indicators that tend to move in anticipation of turning points or changes in general economic conditions or the business cycle. That is to say, a variable that consistently reaches its peak or its trough prior to the peak or trough in the business cycle can be reliably used to forecast an upcoming high or low point in the business cycle. Business confidence and anticipated profits, interest rates, changes in the money supply, building permits, housing starts, and automobile sales are examples of leading economic indicators.

Coincident indicators are those indicators that tend to move with, or within a month or so of, the turning points or changes in the general business cycle. Thus a variable that consistently reaches its peak or its trough at about the same time as the peak or trough in the general business cycle can be used to monitor the high and low points in the business cycle. Industrial production, unemployment data, real weekly earnings, and the number of hours worked are examples of coincident economic indicators.

Lagging indicators are those indicators that tend to move after the turning points or changes in general economic conditions or the business cycle have occurred. These variables tend to consistently arrive at their peaks or their troughs only after the business cycle has already reached its peak or trough and, as such, these variables can be used to either confirm prior movements in general economic conditions, or these can be seen as resulting from those prior events or activities. Manufacturing capacity utilization, job vacancies and the duration of unemployment, order backlogs, productivity, and the average prime rate charged by commercial banks are examples of lagging economic indicators.

Normally, leading indicators are a sign of business expectations or commitments while coincident indicators describe current economic conditions, and lagging indicators bear out how production costs and economic conditions have changed. Unfortunately, the lead or lag time between the change in an indicator and the corresponding change the direction of an economic condition can also vary from one business cycle to another, so the use of indicators to form reliable forecasts remains less than an exact science.

Even though there are about 20 commonly accepted indicators used in leading composite indexes of indicators, there are literally dozens of indicators that could be used by economists, financial and public-policy analysts to evaluate current and future economic trends. And since economic analysis and forecasting is less than an exact science, there are some disagreements about the classification and effectiveness of some indicators.

Indicators are also re-evaluated over time to consider whether or not an indicator remains a useful estimator or indicator of economic activity. In addition, given that economic indicators are measured variables, there are bound to be variations in the estimated values of the statistics and the indicators themselves will likely be revised as additional information becomes available.

Despite these drawbacks, economic indicators can reveal relative changes in economic conditions. One method for increasing the probability of correctly estimating changes in economic conditions is to employ more than one indicator. For practical reasons, indicators are used in clusters to approximate the end of a period of expansion or the end of a contraction phase.

Since the precise timing of the end of one phase and the beginning of the next phase in a business cycle can be difficult to identify, making use of a number of economic or social indicators increases the likelihood of positioning the specific turning points in the business cycle and for assessing relative strengths or weaknesses in an economy.

BIBLIOGRAPHY. A.F. Burns and W.C. Mitchell, *Measuring Business Cycles* (National Bureau of Economic Resources, 1946); Norman Frumkin, *Guide to Economic Indicators* (M.E. Sharpe, 2000); *Guide to Economic Indicators: Making Sense of Economics* (The Economist, 1997); R. Mark Rogers, *Handbook of Key Economic Indicators* (McGraw-Hill, 1998).

TIMOTHY E. SULLIVAN, PH.D.
TOWSON UNIVERSITY

economic theory, classical

CLASSICAL ECONOMIC THEORY, which began in the 19th century and continued into the early part of the 20th century, evolved from the philosophies of British classical liberals such as Thomas Hobbes (1588-1679) and John LOCKE (1632-1704). Hobbes and Locke articulated the notion that individuals sign a contract with government to receive only those services that they cannot provide themselves. While Hobbes believed that a contract once made could not be broken, Locke argued that government had a responsibility to the individuals who created the government. Because individuals, in Locke's view, were born with inalienable rights that no government could take away, citizens retained the innate right of rebellion. Locke's inalienable rights were the right to life, liberty, and the right to own property.

Classical economists used Locke's inherent right to own property as the core of capitalism. Locke contended that each individual owns the results of his or her property. Because Locke believed that rational individuals were able to govern themselves, classical liberals endorsed the concept of laissez-faire, or limited, government.

Classical economists translated these theories to mean that government's main economic responsibility to individuals was to leave the market alone to become self-regulating. They endorsed the classical liberal idea of the three basic functions of government: domestic protection, national security, and public works. Since human nature dictated that self-interested individuals would try to grab as much of the limited resources as possible, classical economists believed that the public good would be served by allowing unfettered market competition to check innate greed. Individual economic liberty and the contention that each individual was best able to determine his or her own best interests meant that each person was free to choose how goods were accumulated, and to identify the kinds and amount of goods and profits needed to guarantee individual happiness.

Adam Smith (1723-1790). A product of the Scottish Enlightenment, Adam SMITH is known as the father of classical economic theory. In 1776, the same year that the American colonies declared their independence from Great Britain, Smith's *An Inquiry into the Nature and Causes of the Wealth of Nations* called for independence from the economic theories and practices of the mercantilists who used the British government to pursue individual wealth. Smith originated the idea that an "invisible hand" regulates the economy as long as government foregoes unnecessary regulations on free trade. Although the idea of the invisible hand is Smith's most often cited contribution to classical economic theory, he only used the term three times in his writings. Unlike the mercantilists, Smith believed that the "wealth of nations" could be found in the ordinary people who produced goods for the market rather than in the industrialists who controlled production. He argued that the market has a built-in equilibrium. Wages, according to Smith, rose or fell according to the demand for labor. Smith saw specialization, or division of labor, as a major element of an efficient market.

Jean-Baptiste Say (1767-1832). The French liberal school of thought was heavily influenced by the economic theories of Jean-Baptiste Say who after reading *An Inquiry into the Nature and Causes of the Wealth of Nations* called Smith's work a "confused assemblage" of economic principles. While technically considered classical economists, the French liberal school rejected some of its core beliefs. Say's *Treatise of Political Economy,* published in 1803, contributed what became known as SAY'S LAW to the understanding of economics, maintaining that overproduction was an economic impossibility because demand would always rise to meet production. According to Say, each product produces a return in wages, interest rates, profits, or rents that enables individuals to acquire desired or necessary products. Say believed that whenever income dropped, prices fell accordingly. Excess profits and savings, in his view, were simply reinvested in the economy to ensure a certain level of spending

Thomas Malthus (1798-1820). Thomas MALTHUS rejected Say's Law out of hand. Malthus, often identified as anti-classical, argued that a natural process weeded out those not strong enough to survive. Since the food supply was essential to survival, the population decreased when food became scarce. If wages rose beyond subsistence level, population also rose. However, since wages tended to settle at subsistence level, population would be curtailed as the cycle repeated itself. Malthus was dramatically opposed to any kind of government interference that improved the lives of the poor and interfered with nature's cycle of elimination by poverty, disease, and death.

Jeremy Bentham (1748-1832). Jeremy BENTHAM is considered the founder of the utilitarian school of thought, also known as "philosophical radicalism." Bentham advocated the theory that the guiding principle of government should be the "greatest happiness for the greatest number." Individuals, according to utilitarian thought, sought to maximize pleasure and minimize pain. Utility, as might be expected, is the essential element of utilitarianism, and the goal of utility is to ensure happiness. In 1776, Bentham published *A Fragment on Government: Being An Examination of What Is Delivered, on the Subject of Government in General in the Introduction of Sir William Blackstone's Commentaries,* which attacked *Blackstone's Commentaries on the Laws of England,* the cornerstone of the English legal system. Bentham argued that Blackstone's conservative stance served as an obstacle to the passage of new and more responsive legislation.

David Ricardo (1772-1823). In *Principles of Political Economy and Taxation,* published in 1817, David RICARDO developed and refined Smith's theories into a more organized explanation of classical economics. Like Smith, Ricardo has had a lasting influence on economic theory. Ricardo contended that the value of a good is derived from the labor required to produce it. His "iron law of wages" maintained that wages tend to stabilize around the subsistence level; therefore, raising wages increases prices, which cycles the worker back toward subsistence. Ricardo also developed the idea of comparative advantage in which each country produced only what was most efficient and profitable, then traded with other countries who were doing the same thing. In this way, each country received the greatest advantage from international trade.

John Stuart Mill (1806-1873). John Stuart MILL articulated and synthesized the ideas of classical liberal economics. After its publication in 1848, Mill's *Principles of Political Economy* became the standard textbook on economics. The individual was important to Mill, and he believed that the classical system of economics was unjust but capable of improving. As a liberal, Mill was optimistic enough to believe that as capitalism evolved, individuals would be better served. He eventually rejected his earlier endorsement of the wage-funds theory that identified a fixed amount of revenue to be allocated among all workers. Like his father James Mill, John Start Mill had an enormous capacity for social justice. He was the first major political philosopher to consciously include women in his ideas.

BIBLIOGRAPHY. Chip Cariappa, "The Political Origins of Neoclassical Economics," www.eco.utexas.edu; "The Classicals," cepa.newschool.edu; John Kenneth Galbraith, *Economics in Perspective* (Houghton Mifflin, 1987); Thomas J. Hailstones, *Basic Economics* (Doubleday, 1969); Robert Heilbroner and Lester C. Thurow, *Economics Explained* (Simon & Schuster, 1982).

ELIZABETH PURDY, PH.D.
INDEPENDENT SCHOLAR

economic theory, Marxian

WHAT IS THE SUBSTANCE of value that makes commodities exchangeable? The answer to this question lies at the core of the economic theory in determining relative prices. Attributing value to the labor content, or to utility—the subjective value placed on the commodity based on pleasure derived—have led to the development of the two major schools of thought: 1) classical school and Marxian economics based on the labor theory of value, and 2) the neoclassical school based on the utility theory of value. Both of these schools are rooted in Adam SMITH's magnum opus, the *Wealth of Nations*. The labor theory of value culminated in the works of David RICARDO and Karl MARX and the utility theory of value culminated in the marginalist revolution of Léon WALRAS, William Stanley JEVONS, and Carl MENGER.

Marx had published his ideas on political economy on various occasions, however, Marxian economic theory was started with the publication of Volume I of *Capital*. Volumes II and III of *Capital* were published after his death based on his notes, by his lifelong friend, Friedrich ENGELS. As the subtitle of the volumes indicate—*A Critique of Political Economy*—Marxian economics attempted to critically assess and extend the classical political economy as a serious scientific inquiry, and did not address writings of other economists that Marx considered to be "vulgar." A distinguishing characteristic of Marxian economics is its interpretation of the labor theory of value that emphasizes the social character of production in the historically specific conditions of capitalism.

In Volume I of *Capital,* Marx made the simplifying assumption that prices were proportional to values. He then proceeded to develop his theory of exploitation by focusing on the labor process, clarifying the social relations underlying production, and showing the general nature of capital. Under capitalism, in this view, as the result of historical developments the ownership and control of the means of production—raw materials, tools, and machinery—had become separated form workers who applied their labor power to them in the production process. Capitalists, through ownership and control of the means of production extracted more work from laborers than was necessary to produce the laborers' means of subsistence (value of labor power). Thus, the total value of a commodity (W) is expressed as

$$W = c + v + s$$

where, c is constant capital (value of means of production), v is variable capital (value of labor power) and s is the surplus value. The ratio s/v is referred to as the rate of surplus value or the rate of exploitation. Thus, Marx's theory of exploitation asserts that extraction of

surplus value through the control of the labor process created capitalist profits through the institution of private property. Industrial production by introduction of assembly lines or implementation of systems of scientific management increases the control over the labor process and the extraction of surplus value. Harry Braverman's (1974) detailed account of the process of deskilling of labor in the 20th century, and extension of capitalist control over the labor process is one of the major works in this area.

In Volume III of *Capital,* when considering the aggregate capital, Marx had to tackle the problem encountered by Smith and Ricardo earlier: the inconsistency between the labor theory of value and equalized rates of profit prevailing in competitive markets. This is the source of the famous "transformation problem" which has preoccupied both critics and proponents of Marxian economics to date. In aggregate the rate of profit r is defined as the ratio of surplus value to capital advanced—sum of constant and variable capital.

$$r = \frac{s}{c + v} = \frac{\dfrac{s}{v}}{\dfrac{c}{v} + 1}$$

Note that given the organic composition of capital c/v (capital to labor ratio) there is a direct relationship between the rate of profit and the rate of exploitation s/v. Furthermore, given the rate of profit, the expression for value of the commodity can be rewritten as:

$$W = c + v + s = c + v + r(c + v) = p$$

Where p is the price of production—long-run equilibrium price attained from equalized rates of profits in the long run. In aggregate, with equalized rate of profit (and constant rate of surplus value), prices of production would not correspond to total values. Hence, to transform values to the prices of production, the composition of capital must vary. Marx demonstrated that given the constant rate of profit and varying organic compositions of capital, prices would be higher than the labor content for firms with higher than average composition of capital, and lower for firms with lower than average composition of capital. Thus, surplus value would leak from the latter firms to former ones. However, as critics pointed out, while Marx transformed the output prices, he did not transform the prices of the inputs to production, and they are themselves, products of labor. A number of solutions have been presented to the transformation problem based on various interpretations of Marxian labor theory of value.

In Volumes II and III of *Capital,* Marx examined the capital accumulation process to discover the "laws of motion" of capitalism. Marx contends that competition between capitalist firms forces them to invest in new technology to save on labor costs and increase profits. The new technology yields the employing firm higher profits at the expense of other capitalists since their composition of capital rises. However, employing the new technique lowers the value content of the commodity by reducing the labor time socially necessary for its production. Other capitalist firms would soon have to adopt the new technique to remain competitive. When this process is complete, the surplus value would no longer be transferred between firms and the profit advantage disappears. However, capitalist firms as a whole will find themselves with a higher composition of capital, and as shown in the profit equation, this lowers profits at a constant rate of exploitation. Marx's theory of the falling rate of profit is at the core of his theory of crisis and breakdown of capitalism. Other theories of crisis fall into two groups: 1) underconsumptionist, and 2) disproportionality theories.

The underconsumptionist theories suggest that since workers only receive a fraction of the value they create as wages, their consumption demand always falls short of the value produced, leaving an excess supply on the market.

The disproportionality theories focus on Marx's dynamic analysis of accumulation and argue that disproportional growth between various interdependent sectors of economy would result in breakdown. As with other schools of thought, lively debate on these issues abounds as the frontier of knowledge is advanced.

BIBLIOGRAPHY. Harry Braverman, *Labor and Monopoly Capital* (Monthly Review Press, 1974); George Catephores, *An Introduction to Marxist Economic,* (New York University Press, 1989); Duncan K. Foley, *Understanding Capital: Marx's Economic Theory* (Harvard University press, 1986); E.K. Hunt, *History of Economic Thought: A Critical Perspective* (HarperCollins, 1992); Karl Marx, *Capital: A Critique of Political Economy,* Volumes I, II, and III (International Publishers, 1967); David Ricardo, *The Principles of Political Economy and Taxation* (Penguin, 1962).

HAMID AZARI-RAD, PH.D.
STATE UNIVERSITY OF NEW YORK, NEW PALTZ

economic theory, neoclassical

NEOCLASSICAL ECONOMICS is the name often given to the dominant variety of MICROECONOMICS taught for most of the 20th century and into the early 21st. In the UNITED STATES, it is so prevalent that it is possible to get a bachelor's degree and never know that one was studying neoclassical economics. It is often presented simply as "economics." Economists outside of the mainstream are more acutely aware of such economics being neoclassical. When someone uses this term, it could refer to at least three overlapping things. This is because the mainstream is not all that precisely defined, and it is always changing. The label "neoclassical" could refer to: a structure of thought, a method of approaching economic analysis, or a historical legacy.

Structure of thought. Sometimes neoclassical economics refers to a large-scale conception of the economy, represented by a structure of thought. Due to resources being scarce, every society must somehow decide what to produce, by what means to produce it, and who gets it. In the neoclassical world these questions are largely answered through markets. The amounts of hamburgers, loaves of bread, blue jeans, and so on are the quantities demanded and supplied at market-clearing prices. The methods of producing these things are the ones that minimize cost to the profit-maximizing producers, thus minimizing the cost to society. The payments to productive resources are themselves determined in markets by the supply and demand for their services. The people who are willing and able to pay for the products get them. This depends on personal preferences and on incomes, which are largely determined by the prices of productive services.

Market prices play a crucial role in the neoclassical account. This is why introductory courses quickly get to SUPPLY and DEMAND. Market prices act as indicators of the relative degree of SCARCITY of things; while at the same time providing incentives to act appropriately according to such scarcity. Suppose oats become more desirable after a report that they reduce cholesterol. This causes increased demand, which results in rising oat prices. This higher price signals that oats have become scarcer. The higher price will give an incentive for farmers to plant more oats, while simultaneously providing a reason for users of oats to be more frugal with them. Both of these behaviors are suitable in the face of the increased scarcity of something. Contrary behavior, growing fewer oats and/or using them profligately, if widespread would threaten the viability of society. Resource allocation through a market system can thus be viewed as being regulated by feedback from prices.

Neoclassical economists have attempted to represent this system abstractly with general EQUILIBRIUM models. General equilibrium occurs when all markets in the economy are simultaneously in equilibrium. By contrast the supply and demand models that students encounter in introductory courses are partial equilibrium models. In partial equilibrium models incomes and prices of related goods must be assumed constant in order for the supply and demand curves to hold steady.

In general equilibrium all prices are variables. It is still unresolved whether general equilibrium models are powerful tools of thinking or intellectual curiosities. One thing they do is to make explicit how complex an economy is. A simple model of exchange (no production) with 1,000 individuals selling 1,000 goods has 1,000,999 equations and variables. This strongly suggests that a fundamental difficulty in replacing the market system with some form of central control is the likely impossibility of being able to gather, process, interpret, and act upon all the information needed. Another result of general equilibrium analysis is the invisible hand theorem. This states that every competitive equilibrium is Pareto optimal, and that every Pareto optimum can be realized by a competitive equilibrium. PARETO OPTIMALITY is a state in which no one can be made better off without making at least one person worse off. This is an abstract version of Adam SMITH's idea that people pursuing their own interests will produce a desirable social outcome.

Method. Neoclassical economics is also a method of doing economics. Although virtually every modern economist has been exposed to general equilibrium analysis, many, due to specialized professional interests or more practical inclinations, spend very little time working with or thinking about it. Yet they would still be called neoclassical economists by virtue of the methods they use.

The distinguishing feature of the neoclassical method is the search for and analysis of equilibria that result from arbitrage. Arbitrage is a process in which the existence of an opportunity for a net gain (the benefits of an action outweigh the costs) results in behavior that causes that opportunity to disappear. Arbitrage is the reason supermarket checkout lines tend to be the same length. If people see a short line they move to it. This lengthens the short line while shortening the longer lines. When all the lines are equal there is no incentive to change lines. In equilibrium all the lines are equal.

Characterizing individuals as rational optimizers provides the particular content of neoclassical arbitrage. As consumers, people want to maximize utility, or find the most desirable bundle of goods, subject to their limited budgets. As suppliers they want to maximize their profits. People are assumed to be economically rational in that they do not take actions that are contrary to the achievement of their goals, whatever these may be.

The widespread use of mathematical optimization tools in the second half of the 20th century caused the emphasis to shift from the process resulting in equilibrium to the equilibrium itself. The various arbitrage stories describing the process leading to equilibrium are now largely relegated to introductory courses. However, even if time and space constraints prevent the arbitrage story from being told, it implicitly underlies all neoclassical equilibria.

The reason behind the search for and analysis of equilibria is to explain social phenomena in terms of the rational decisions of economizing individuals. This methodological individualism is another distinguishing characteristic of neoclassical economics, although this is held in common with Austrian economics.

MACROECONOMICS does not generally follow methodological individualism, and thus is not strictly speaking neoclassical. Macroeconomics grows directly out of John Maynard KEYNES' *General Theory of Employment, Interest, and Money.* Keynes did not reject neoclassical economics, but he thought it was inadequate for analyzing his problem, the national level of employment. Specifically, Keynes thought that it was misleading to view employment as the outcome of a national labor market seen as a big supply and demand diagram. Keynes instead asserted that the national level of employment was a function of the national product that, in turn, depended on the level of investment, the marginal propensity to consume, the interest rate, and the money market. In Keynes' theory the fundamental units of analysis are accounting categories derived from the national accounts, not economizing individuals. Many economists have been dissatisfied with the Keynesian approach. This has resulted in attempts to provide micro-foundations for macroeconomics.

Historical legacy. Neoclassical economics is a result of the evolution of economic thought. The name "neoclassical" suggests that it is a revival of classical economics. This is accurate in some ways, but not in others.

The name "classical" is usually given to the economists, mostly British, of the two or three generations following Adam Smith. David RICARDO, Thomas Robert MALTHUS, James Mill, Nassau SENIOR, John Stuart MILL, and sometimes Karl MARX are considered classical economists. These economists refined and extended Smith's work, and applied it to the problems of their time. In most ways, classical economics is closely related to Smith's economics.

Smith gave us the idea that the economy is a complex system regulated by feedback from prices. This system produces desirable results, such as increased productivity of labor through specialization and the coordination of production with consumer desires, from individuals following their own interests. In numerous places in *The Wealth of Nations,* Smith employs arbitrage as an explanatory principle.

The overall emphasis of Smith and of the classical economists is on economic growth and development. Population growth and the accumulation of capital are major topics, closely woven together, for economists from Smith through Marx. Growing capital is the basis for high wages with Smith. It leads to low interest, the end of new accumulation, and thus the end of rising wages and growing population in John Stuart Mill's stationary state. It causes falling profits, concentration of OWNERSHIP, and attempts at increased exploitation of workers, all leading to the self-destruction of capitalism for Marx.

The biggest event in the transition from classical to neoclassical economics was the marginal revolution. This refers to the appearance of the marginal utility theory of W.S. JEVONS, Carl MENGER, and Léon WALRAS in the early 1870s, and marginal productivity, introduced by J.B. CLARK, Alfred MARSHALL, and Knut Wicksell in the 1890s. The eventual absorption of these innovations added much flavor to the style of economics now called neoclassical.

Marginal utility had a dual impact. It provided the basis for a subjective theory of value, in contrast to the cost-based backward-looking classical theory. This was Menger's emphasis. It also, in the hands of Jevons and Walras, ushered in the use of mathematics.

Utility had a prior history in British ethical and political philosophy. It was notably formalized and put at the center of the scheme developed by Jeremy BENTHAM. Bentham's radical step was to reduce all pleasure- and pain-producing capacity to a single dimension: utility. Not only could this be conceived of for an individual; but also individual utilities could be summed up to arrive at an operable concept of the common good, the greatest good for the greatest number.

Jevons, trying to practice economics as a natural science, took Bentham's utility and expressed it as a mathematical function of the quantity of a good possessed. He distinguished the total utility from the marginal utility, which is the particular addition to total utility of the last unit of the good acquired, or, the rate of change in total utility caused by an incremental increase of the good. Treating marginal utility as the rate of change of total utility makes it equivalent to the first derivative of the total utility function.

Twenty years later marginal productivity, a formal generalization of the classical Law of Diminishing Returns, allowed a new approach to factor demands. This resulted in a unified theory of production and distribution, as opposed to Mill's insistence that these were two separate spheres.

During the last 30 years or so of the 19th century the Ricardo-Mill orthodoxy and the "psychological school" (i.e., marginal utility theorists), debated the question of the cause of value. Marshall largely put these disputes to rest. He used a subjectively determined demand and a "real cost"-based supply curve to solve the problem of value. In the process, Marshall put supply and demand analysis, of the sort that is familiar to any modern student, at the center of economics. Marshall made numerous analytic contributions to modern economics, including elasticity, returns to scale, short- and long-run analysis, and the distinction between fixed and variable cost. If one were

forced to attribute neoclassical economics to any single writer, Marshall would have to be the first choice.

In the 1930s, neoclassical economics changed to the result we almost see today. Joan ROBINSON and Edward Chamberlin contributed the theory of imperfect competition. Robinson's account included the analysis of monopoly profit maximization using the marginal revenue curve. John HICKS used ordinal indifference curves to derive the demand curve, borrowing a technique developed earlier by Irving FISHER and Vilfredo Pareto. John von Neumann and Oskar Morgenstern published a book on GAME THEORY in the 1930s, which, along with John NASH's equilibrium (1950), paved the way for one of the few introductions of new material to undergraduate microeconomic theory after the 1930s.

Apart from substantive theory, the biggest development in the second half of the 20th century was shift to mathematics as the preferred mode of expression. While this can be traced back to A.A. Cournot in the 1830s, the big push came with Paul SAMUELSON's *Foundations of Economic Analysis*.

Critics of neoclassical economics. Neoclassical economics has been under continual attack since its formative years. One dimension to these attacks is political/normative. Cambridge Keynesians, Institutionalists, and Marxians are usually less enthusiastic about the market system than are neoclassicals. Austrians are more so. It is important to note that knowledge of someone's motive for arguing a certain way is irrelevant in judging his argument. The fact that somebody wants something to be true doesn't make it untrue. However it is rare in economics for an argument to be decisively resolved, usually because of ambiguities concerning interpretation of the evidence. This leaves considerable room for argument. While the critics generally attack the structure or method of neoclassical economics, it would be misleading to ignore the political/normative alignments that flavor the controversies.

Led by the group that helped Keynes write *The General Theory*, Cambridge Keynesians questioned the use of comparative statics to represent a dynamic world. Their discovery of "reswitching" suggested the possibility of a flaw in the neoclassical model of income distribution, that depended on a negative relationship between factor pieces and the amounts demanded of these factors by firms. Pierro SRAFFA's *Production of Commodities by Means of Commodities* (1960) proposed an alternative abstract conception of the economy in which the distribution of income determined prices rather than the other way around.

Thorstein VEBLEN coined the term "neoclassical." The connection that he saw between the marginalists and classical economists was the determinate, teleological nature of their price theory, which Veblen attributed to outdated metaphysical presuppositions. Veblen proposed to replace this with an open-ended evolutionary approach to economics. In addition, Veblen and other Institutionalists have criticized neoclassical economics for overemphasizing pecuniary calculation, which is one aspect of human behavior, and therefore only a partial explanation of how society functions.

In the Marxist scheme, consciousness is the product of the epoch. Economists and other social philosophers are part of the "supporting superstructure" that props up the system of social relations based ultimately on the mode of production. The neoclassical conception of the economy takes for granted the existence of private property rights, without which there could be no markets. Marx saw private property rights as a defining characteristic of the specifically capitalist epoch, making possible exploitation and accumulation. He envisaged a future without private property.

Most neoclassical textbooks present scarcity as the fundamental cause of the economics problem. They also assert that opportunity cost is the concept of cost relevant to economic decisions. These are the Austrians' contributions. Yet Austrians remain outside the mainstream for a number of reasons. From the Austrian standpoint, neoclassical economics did not fully absorb the notion of subjective value, thanks to Marshall's scissors. Austrians are not comfortable with the emphasis on equilibrium, as opposed to the market process. The abstract model of perfect competition distorts actual competition. Many Austrians reject the use of mathematics to represent economic thinking. Some reject the use of statistics to test theories.

Neoclassical economics, as practiced and taught for most of the 20th century, became a theory of static resource allocation. Capital and population are treated as given parameters. It is not that neoclassical economists are uninterested in growth and development; rather, in the formal theory the mathematical methods ushered in by the marginal revolution resulted in a truncation of the subject matter to fit the available methods. A question for the future is whether economics will be driven by its methods or by its subject matter.

Insiders and outsiders have long questioned the adequacy of comparative static to represent a dynamic world. In *Capitalism, Socialism, and Democracy*, Joseph SCHUMPETER contrasted the standard neoclassical conclusion that monopoly is harmful to consumers with the empirical observation that the great increase in the average standard of living occurred precisely with the concentration of ownership in industry. His point was that it is highly misleading to judge the performance of an economic system with static models.

Representing dynamic phenomena is difficult. It can be done, in ways, with differential equations. This makes economics inaccessible to 98 percent of the population. Inexpensive powerful computers may offer help. Uri Wilensky at the Center for Connected Learning and Computer-Based Modeling offers numerous examples of complex dynamic phenomena (some economic) that can be represented rather simply using object-oriented programming environments.

The basic logic of arbitrage is compelling. Even when the lines do not seem strongly to equalize, such as where three lanes of high speed traffic empty into twelve tollbooths, the explanation that comes most readily to mind is obstacles to arbitrage. Scientific explanation has generally consisted of explaining a lot with a little, finding unity in diversity. It is possible that apart from arbitrage resulting from the rational pursuit of self-interest, there are no big explanatory principles in the economic realm.

BIBLIOGRAPHY. G.C. Harcourt, *Some Cambridge Controversies in the Theory of Capital* (Cambridge University Press, 1972); W.S. Jevons, *Theory of Political Economy* (Augustus M. Kelley, 1965); Alfred Marshall, *Principles of Economics* (Porcupine Press, 1920); Deirdre McCloskey, "Economics Science: A Search Through the Hyperspace of Assumptions?" *Methodus* (v.3/1, 1991); Henry Spiegel, *The Growth of Economic Thought* (Duke University Press, 1991).

SAMUEL WESTON, PH.D.
UNIVERSITY OF DALLAS

economies of scale

IN THE THEORY OF PRODUCTION, the word "scale" refers to a long-run situation where all inputs of the firm are variable. If one asks the question: what happens to output if all inputs are doubled? There would be three possible answers: Output doubles, output more than doubles, and output increases but less than doubles.

If output doubles, the firm's technology is said to exhibit constant returns to scale; if output more than doubles the firm's technology exhibits increasing returns to scale; and it exhibits decreasing returns to scale if output increases by less than twice the original level.

In general, constant returns to scale refers to a technology where output changes by the same proportion as inputs. Increasing returns to scale refers to the case where output changes by a larger proportion than inputs, and decreasing returns to scale refers to a technology for which output changes by a smaller proportion than inputs.

Constant returns to scale are easily explained. One would expect that two workers, who are equally skilled and use identical capital (machines) would be able to produce twice as much as one worker using one unit of capital. However, increasing or decreasing returns to scale are also possible. The explanation most often given for the existence of increasing returns to scale is that, as the scale of production increases, the firm is able to exploit technological advantages of mass production. As the scale of production increases, division and specialization of the inputs can take place. For example, each worker can be assigned to perform a specific task rather than multiple ones in the production process. Hence, workers can become more efficient in the single task they perform resulting in higher productivity and increasing returns to scale.

Some physical properties of capital (machinery, equipment) can also lead to increasing returns to scale. Doubling the diameter of a water or natural-gas pipeline more than doubles the flow of water or natural gas. Doubling the weight of a ship, for example an oil tanker, more that doubles the capacity of the ship (this explains why oil tankers are always as large as technically possible).

Decreasing returns to scale are usually associated with managerial diseconomies. As the scale of production increases it becomes more difficult to manage the firm efficiently and coordinate the various activities of the firm. Assuming that the firm faces fixed input prices for all of its inputs, constant returns to scale means that the per-unit cost (average cost) of output remains unchanged as output is increased.

Increasing returns to scale implies that the per-unit cost decreases as output increases, and decreasing returns to scale would result in increased per-unit cost as output increases. Hence, economies of scale determine the slope of the long-run average cost curve of the firm. The long-run average cost curve will be decreasing if there are increasing returns to scale, constant if there are constant returns to scale, and increasing if there are decreasing returns to scale. It is not uncommon that the forces for increasing and decreasing returns to scale operate together, implying that a firm's technology may exhibit increasing returns to scale for some output levels and constant or decreasing returns to scale for others.

Empirical studies indicate that, in many manufacturing industries in the UNITED STATES, the long-run average cost curve is approximately U-shaped with a flat bottom over a large range of output levels, indicating that in most industries, economies of scale are relatively quickly exhausted, and constant returns to scale or near constant returns to scale prevail over a large range of output levels. Of course, firms would not consistently produce an output level at which decreasing returns to scale are present. The output level, or the output levels, at which the long-run average cost curve reaches a minimum is called the minimum efficient scale. The smaller the minimum efficient scale relative to the size of the

market, the larger the number of firms that can operate efficiently in the industry.

Empirical findings indicate many industries are characterized by a flat bottom, long-run average cost curve. This provides, therefore, an explanation of why, in a number of industries, relatively small firms are able to coexist with large firms. If, for example, the minimum efficient scale is 10 percent of the size of the market, and the long-run average cost curve has a flat bottom up to 80 percent of the size of the market, then any number of firms between 2 and 10 would be efficient. Both constant returns to scale and decreasing returns to scale are consistent with COMPETITION.

However, if we seek everywhere increasing returns to scale, or increasing returns to scale at the relevant output level, then efficiency requires production by a single firm. Industries for which this is the case are called natural monopolies. Public utilities are often cited as examples of natural monopolies.

BIBLIOGRAPHY. Dennis W. Carlton and Jeffrey M. Perloff, *Modern Industrial Organization* (Addison-Wesley, 1999); Donald A. Hay and Derek J. Morris, *Industrial Economics and Organization* (Oxford University Press, 1991); F.M. Scherer, *Industrial Market Structure and Performance* (Rand McNally, 1980).

KLAUS G. BECKER, PH.D.
TEXAS TECH UNIVERSITY

Economist, The

ONE OF THE MORE INFLUENTIAL periodicals of the modern era, *The Economist* has for more than 150 years combined financial and statistical information with outspoken political commentary and advocacy. It is especially notable for the consistency of its editorial stance, which has been characterized by admirers as an unwavering commitment to the telling of uncomfortable truths, and by critics as tirelessness in the defense of the interests of the wealthy and powerful. Most would agree, though, that *The Economist* (along with a few other periodicals) is a steadfast advocate of capitalism, albeit in many guises, over the decades.

The Economist was launched in August, 1843, by James Wilson, a Quaker hat-maker from Scotland. Its purpose was to promote the classical free-trade doctrines of Adam SMITH, David RICARDO, Jean-Baptiste Say and Thomas Tooke, and more particularly to campaign against the agricultural tariffs, or Corn Laws, whose abolition had become the object of a middle-class LAISSEZ-FAIRE crusade in the early 1840s. Although the infant *Economist* remained formally independent of the Anti-

Corn Law League, the nationwide pressure group whose mouthpiece it effectively became, its survival during its earliest years was made possible only by subventions from the League. Paradoxically, the repeal of the Corn Laws in 1846 and the consequent dissolution of the Anti-Corn Law League the following year helped to secure *The Economist*'s future: with the discontinuance of the League's own house organ, Wilson's magazine stood alone as the most prominent free-trade journal in circulation. From mid-century, its financial future was no longer in doubt.

So successful did *The Economist* become that it helped launch the political career of its founder. The vehemence of its defense of laissez-faire principles, demonstrated most notably in its opposition to the extension of state aid to the starving people of Ireland during the catastrophic famine of 1845–51, brought Wilson to the attention of the leaders of the Whig Party. In 1847, through the intervention of his patron and financial supporter, the third Earl of Radnor, Wilson was elected as a member of Parliament—ironically, in light of his editorial fulminations against electoral corruption, for the borough of Westbury. Beyond his unsuccessful campaigns against railway regulation (it was, he contended, no part of the government's duty to prevent competing railway companies from constructing as many lines between the same two points as they wished) and the act revising the charter of the Bank of England, Wilson left little mark either as a parliamentary performer or during his tenure as financial secretary to the Treasury.

Wilson's political career, on the other hand, had a definite and deleterious impact upon *The Economist*. Criticized during its first years for following too faithfully the line of the Anti-Corn Law League, it now became little more than a vehicle for promoting the interests of Wilson and his colleagues in the Whig Party. (An unhealthily intimate relationship could also be discerned in the opposite sense, one example being the appointment of *The Economist*'s assistant editor, William Greg, to a lucrative government sinecure.) The journal was elevated above mere partisan propaganda, however, by the caliber of its writers, most notably the idiosyncratic socialist Thomas HODGSKIN, the youthful Herbert SPENCER, and above all the effervescent, opinionated and eminently quotable banker Walter Bagehot, who became Wilson's son-in-law in 1858 and, following the former's death two years later, *The Economist*'s editor.

Bagehot's 16-year stewardship of the paper has often been considered *The Economist*'s golden age. Broad in his interests, the new editor elevated the journal from a partisan organ to the status of required reading for the business community, both in Britain and overseas. His own contributions, while often ill-informed or naïve—he wrote trenchantly in support of the Confederacy during the AMERICAN CIVIL WAR, and

against the extension of the franchise to the potentially "dangerous" artisan classes at home—were never dull. His death in 1877 deprived *The Economist* of much of its sparkle, though the tendency toward conservatism in a political as well as an ideological sense, which had been evident during his stint in the editor's chair, became more pronounced under his successors.

The Economist's rightward tilt reached its greatest extent in the last quarter of the 19th century. Always deeply marked by Victorian hibernophobia and critical of most efforts to conciliate the "Celtic" Irish rather than coerce them into obedience, *The Economist* broke publicly with the liberal prime minister, William Gladstone, over his support for local autonomy, or Home Rule, in Ireland. By the turn of the century, the journal had become the firm advocate of a policy of imperial domination tempered by parsimony; the denial of the parliamentary vote to women; and the reversal of Irish land reform. Fortunately for both *The Economist*'s credibility and its marketability, this drift toward *Diehardism avant la lettre* was arrested under the editorship of F.W. Hirst, who took up the reins in 1907. An unsuccessful liberal parliamentary candidate, Hirst shared some of his predecessors' prejudices, most notably over the issue of women's suffrage; but his expansion of the staff and his recruitment of a group of talented young writers helped to reverse *The Economist*'s incipient ossification, and ensured that in the future it would not stray too far from the central ground of British politics.

The outbreak of WORLD WAR I, indeed, found *The Economist* uncharacteristically occupying a position normally associated with the Left. Opposed both to the conflict itself, in which he could see no valid issue justifying British involvement, and to the undermining of cherished civil liberties by wartime emergency regulations, Hirst used the columns of his paper to conduct an outspoken campaign against the introduction, for the first time in British history, of compulsory military service. Such views were increasingly out of step with public opinion; and in 1916, Hirst was compelled to resign by the Board of Trustees, composed of James Wilson's descendants, in whose hands overall direction of the journal lay. Thenceforward, *The Economist*'s opinions on the war remained entirely conventional, although upon the defeat of Germany it distinguished itself by criticizing the economic provisions of the Treaty of Versailles and speaking warmly of John Maynard KEYNES' *Economic Consequences of the Peace*.

Between the world wars, *The Economist* was transformed from a family trust to a modern journal run on commercial lines. In 1926, a limited-liability company, The Economist Newspaper Ltd., was set up to purchase the title from the Wilson family on behalf of a consortium of business, media, and political interests. An independent board of notables was created to ensure the paper's editorial independence. Almost as important to its continued viability, however, had been the recruitment five years earlier of Walter (subsequently Lord) Layton as editor. The most distinguished holder of the position since Walter Bagehot, Layton came to *The Economist* with an impressive background in academic, governmental, and political life. Under his direction, The Economist Intelligence Branch (subsequently renamed The Economist Intelligence Unit) was launched, to provide expert statistical and financial information to individuals and businesses. Other innovations included the publication of detailed country and subject supplements; a redesigned layout including the use of color; and the upgrading of the journal's statistical section.

Layton's international reputation—before taking over the editorship, he had held an important position on the staff of the League of Nations—enhanced *The Economist*'s standing overseas; and although the circulation figures were not notably enhanced as a result, the journal came to be regarded abroad—in much the same manner as *The Times*—as reflecting the outlook of the British policy-making elite. In these years, *The Economist* became a truly international journal, half of each issue being sold outside the UNITED KINGDOM.

Notwithstanding the galaxy of journalistic talent Layton was able to attract—most conspicuous among whom were Arnold Toynbee, Aylmer Vallance, Harry Hodson and Douglas Jay—the 1930s cannot be said to have been *The Economist*'s finest hour. Although the readability of the paper was vastly improved in these years, its editor's consciousness that he was presiding over what was now regarded as a national institution meant that there was little place for adventurousness or iconoclasm in its columns. During one of the most turbulent and dangerous eras in British history, readers of *The Economist* more often than not were presented with little more than cleverly written expressions of conventional wisdom. Particularly unfortunate, all the more so in light of the general excellence of its reportage, was its response to the rise of National Socialist GERMANY. While the journal's editorial line was consistently anti-Nazi, and often insightful as to the dangers Fascist expansionism posed to the democracies of Europe, it lacked the courage of its own convictions. Thus, while correctly identifying the Rhineland crisis as presenting "the choice between a risk of war now, at our time, and a certainty of war later, at Herr Hitler's time" (March 14, 1936), it contrived to find a third way between these uncomfortable alternatives with an appeal to Hitler to voluntarily withdraw his troops. Nor were *The Economist*'s readers assisted in forming a correct appreciation of the seriousness of the Nazi threat by its frequent assertions that Hitler's departures from orthodox free-trade principles were certain to result in the eventual collapse of the German economy. The paper's grim verdict on the aftermath of the Munich debacle—"We are starting on a desperate effort to ensure by arms a safety which a little courage and a little foresight at any time in these tragic years would have protected from all danger" (October 15, 1938) was double-edged: it could itself have been accused of having exhibited the latter but not the former.

Layton's replacement in 1938 by 30-year-old Geoffrey Crowther completed the process of modernization that had been under way since Hirst's time. Obliged by the exigencies of wartime to give up many of its male staffers to military or government service, *The Economist,* for the first time, admitted a significant cadre of women to its inner circles. The distinguished economist Barbara Ward (subsequently Baroness Jackson) served as foreign editor; others who wrote regularly included Margaret Cruikshank and Margaret Stewart. (To this day, a higher proportion of women is to be found among *The Economist*'s staff than among its readership.) Under Crowther, too, the modern *Economist* acquired its characteristic tone of witty and astringent self-assurance, that to some readers has seemed to smack of the arrogant and cocksure. In part, this was the consequence of a recruitment policy oriented increasingly toward the hiring of recent graduates of the ancient universities rather than professional journalists. As one of their number, Sarah Hogg, has observed, "not the least of *The Economist*'s successful peculiarities has been the magisterial tone sounded by generations of thirtysomethings." But the journal's retention of the Victorian convention of not disclosing the identity of contributors also lent its coverage of events an Olympian quality, which the not-infrequent failure of its predictions to materialize did little to diminish.

Since the 1960s, *The Economist* has striven to extend its global reach. It has experienced mixed success. An attempt in 1967 to launch a Spanish-language edition aimed at Latin America proved a costly failure. The production of a series of confidential briefing papers, entitled *Foreign Reports*, also dates from this time, although as Ruth Dudley Edwards notes, the new offshoot had to surmount "a period when it looked rather like a propaganda sheet for the CIA." Partly through ideological conviction, and partly with one eye upon the crucial North American market, the post-World War II *Economist* has, in fact, been generally supportive of the foreign policy of successive U.S. governments. It was one of the few British journals of opinion to support the United States throughout the VIETNAM WAR, and also firmly backed the campaign against left-wing guerrillas in Nicaragua and El Salvador in the early 1980s; Operation Desert Storm in 1991; and military action to deprive Iraq of weapons of mass destruction in 2002-03. Its Cold Warrior credentials have, however, occasionally been dented—most embarrassingly by its employment of the notorious Soviet spy H.A.R. "Kim" Philby as Middle East correspondent in the early 1960s.

At the turn of the century, *The Economist* is as much a mid-Atlantic periodical as a British one. With weekly sales of 700,000 (80 percent outside the UK), the journal has never been more widely read. This unprecedented commercial success ought not necessarily to be taken as evidence of a corresponding growth in influence, especially as its focus has become more diffuse, both geographically and thematically. No longer a significant publisher of statistical data, which is readily available from other sources, *The Economist* is valued by its international readership largely for its synopses of complex current issues. Nonetheless, the journal has never been content merely to publish compilations of useful information: as a "three-decker pulpit" for the broadcasting of free-market principles, it has remained true to the missionary ideals of its founder.

BIBLIOGRAPHY. A. Burnet, *The Economist: America 1843–1993* (Economist Books, 1993); G. Crowther, ed., *The Economist: A Centenary Volume* (Oxford University Press, 1943); R.D. Edwards, *The Pursuit of Reason: The Economist 1843–1993* (Hamish Hamilton, 1993); S. Koss, *The Rise and Fall of the Political Press in Britain* (University of North Carolina Press, 1984).

R.M. Douglas
Colgate University

Edison, Thomas Alva (1847–1931)

A PROLIFIC AMERICAN INVENTOR who established the foundation for modern communications, Thomas Edison was born in Milan, Ohio, and died in Orange, New Jersey.

Edison changed the way that people live and work by improving or inventing a host of devices including the stock ticker, telegraph, telephone, electric light, electric pen, motion picture, phonograph, and storage battery. As much of an entrepreneur and industrialist as a man of science, he focused on products that were readily marketable.

Edison began life as the last child of a middle-class family. His father was a shopkeeper and land speculator. His mother, a former schoolteacher, taught her youngest at home when the inquisitive boy proved unable to adjust to the rote learning style of the local school. Typical for the day, his formal education ended at 12 when he took a job with the railroad. Edison used his free time to conduct experiments, read extensively, and showed an entrepreneurial spirit at an early age when he organized a sales force of other boys to sell produce and newspapers. Excited by the opportunity to use scientific machinery, Edison accepted a job as a telegraph operator in 1862.

The telegraph would introduce Edison to the powers of electricity. A telegraph sent messages by translating letters into short or long breaks in the flow of an electrical current. Although in demand for his ability to receive high-speed messages, Edison was not a particularly good employee. He roamed around the country in search of work as employer after employer fired him for unauthorized experimentation with the office equipment and occasional careless disregard for his telegraph duties. Edison's experiences with the telegraph sparked his scientific curiosity and opened the door to broader inquiries about electricity and electromagnetism.

In 1869, Edison became a full-time inventor. To succeed, he needed to combine business acumen with inventive skills as he discovered with his very first device. Edison developed the electrographic vote recorder to instantly log a yea or nay by means of a button. He thought that elected officials would be eager to buy it, then discovered that no one wanted it. In the future, Edison would locate a market before devoting resources to an invention. His next product, the 1869 stock ticker would improve on the current version by printing the letters of the alphabet as well as figures. It became a reliable moneymaker because of high demand.

Edison emerged as a successful inventor and manufacturer by combining finance, management, and marketing skills with technological improvements, new designs, and new products. He settled in New Jersey, in large part because the environs offered inexpensive land and easy access to the massive test market and commercial network of New York City. Journalists from New York were always welcome in Edison's laboratory for the free publicity that they provided, while venture capitalists from the city would supply funds for experimentation, testing, and development thereby dividing the risk of product launching.

Once Edison established his process of invention, he developed new products at an astonishing rate. As he famously stated, he aimed to produce a minor invention every ten days and a big creation every six months. In 1872, he received 38 patents just for new models or new parts of his stock ticker. In 1873, he earned an additional 25 patents, including several for wholly original inventions. Edison eventually held 1,093 patents, the largest number issued to one person by the U.S. Patent Office. Many of these inventions made their way into the marketplace.

The danger in being so prolific lay in Edison's inability to fully develop all of his inventions. The 1877 electric pen, which later developed into the mimeograph machine, was sold to another businessman because Edison lacked the time to effectively market and fully develop it. He observed radio waves in his lab, but failed to pursue this basis of the electronics industry because of the pressure of creating of other products.

By the 1870s, Edison had become a major industrialist. Most of his products were aimed at the business sector because large companies demanded high efficiency and could afford the capital expense of Edison's goods. When Edison discovered recorded sound and began to envision products that capitalized on the discovery, he did not consider the entertainment possibilities of the phonograph. This 1877 invention would be sold as an office and educational aid. Although the phonograph had a home use, Edison believed that the best profits could be found in other markets. He would always focus on volume sales.

Edison located his Menlo Park (1876–81) and West Orange (1887–1957) laboratories in New Jersey as the largest private laboratories in the world, where he could work on several projects at once, thereby ensuring momentum and thinly spreading the risk of failure. The Wizard of Menlo Park, as Edison become known, focused his research efforts on products with the potential for immediate impact. This strategy would lead Edison to his most famous accomplishment: providing electric power to all of New York City.

Edison decided to enter the business of electric lighting because he could deliver good service at competitive rates to areas of dense population. The development of a commercially practical incandescent lighting system, including the lamp, electric generator, and distribution system, proved enormously complex. The completion of the project in 1881 brought Edison worldwide acclaim as well as a profitable new line.

At the start of the 20th century, Edison increasingly preferred to maintain market share rather than develop new inventions. His last major creation was a 1910 storage battery aimed to power automobiles. With Edison's methods superseded by the systematized operations of firms like Bell Laboratories, his company entered a period of decline.

Edison contributed to the material progress of the world by creating products of enduring utility. As an inventor who became a major industrialist through superb management and marketing skills, he established a model for future industrial laboratories.

BIBLIOGRAPHY. Matthew Josephson, *Edison: A Biography* (John Wiley & Sons, 1992); Thomas P. Hughes, *Thomas Edison: Professional Inventor* (HMSO, 1976); David W. Hutchings, *Edison at Work: The Thomas A. Edison Laboratory at West Orange, New Jersey* (Hastings House, 1969); Martin V. Melosi, *Thomas A. Edison and the Modernization of America* (Addison-Wesley, 1990); A.J. Millard, *Edison and the Business of Invention* (1990); William S. Pretzer, ed., *Working at Inventing: Thomas Edison and the Menlo Park Experience* (Edison Institute, 1989); Robert Silverberg, *Light for the World: Edison and the Power Industry* (1967).

CARYN E. NEUMANN, PH.D.
OHIO STATE UNIVERSITY

education

THE ACQUISITION OF knowledge and skills, education is considered by many to be an important determinant of worker productivity, standards of living, and long-term economic growth. Economists treat the decision to purchase an education as an investment decision rather than a consumption decision because the benefits of education are long-lasting and usually result in greater productivity and improved earnings.

An investment in education is referred to as an investment in human capital. As with any investment decision, the benefits must be weighed against the costs to determine if the investment is worthwhile. Education produces a stream of future expected benefits in the form of enhanced earnings; in theory these future benefits can be estimated and put into present value terms. The costs of education include both the explicit costs such as tuition and books and the implicit costs resulting from sacrificed earnings while in school. To the extent that a potential student expects to earn more as a result of graduating from college, for example, such an investment makes sense as long as the present value of the future dollars the student expects to earn (in excess of what would have been earned without the degree) exceed the present value of the cost of education. Of course, some pursue knowledge for it's own sake, without regard to monetary payoff, so the investment model does not completely explain the decision-making process, only the pecuniary aspects.

Education of the labor force. Adam SMITH labeled education the principal cause of the various talents observable in men, and went on to explain how different talents command different wages. Modern ECONOMETRIC models developed to explain wage differentials show that an important reason for these differentials is educational attainment. That is, with other things constant, a person with many years of schooling earns a higher wage than a person with few years of schooling. Herbert Stein and Murray Foss find that "the increased education of the labor force has been an important source of growth in output since at least the early part of the 20th century."

The synthesis of education and technology continues to increase worker productivity into the 21st century.

They report that the percentage of the labor force between the ages of 25 and 64 who had not obtained a high school diploma fell from 38 percent in 1969 to only 11 percent in 1993, while the percentage of the same group who had obtained a college degree rose from 14 percent in 1969 to 27 percent in 1993. This remarkable increase in educational attainment went hand in hand with increases in worker productivity and, according to the Bureau of Labor Statistics, about one-sixth of the increase in output per hour was due to increased educational attainment.

The most common belief among researchers appears to be that a more-educated worker can perform better, can perform more jobs, and is more capable of taking advantage of the best job opportunities, hence the observed relationship between educational attainment and output. Challenging the assumption that education necessarily causes workers to be more productive, A. Michael SPENCE developed signaling theory, the notion that employers use educational attainment as a signal of the individual's inherent ability. The reasoning behind this theory is that each person possesses abilities, but in order to demonstrate these abilities to potential employers, the person must acquire educational credentials. Employers then screen applicants according to educational attainment, proceeding under the assumption that a person with the right skill set for the job will have been able to, for example, graduate from college. According to this theory, educational attainment enables a person to prove the abilities they already possessed, leading to a good match in the job market.

The major criticism of this model is that formal schooling is a very expensive method of signaling productivity, so it would be in everyone's best interest to find a cheaper method, such as pre-employment testing. In a study involving 1,300 FORD MOTOR COMPANY employees, D.A. Wise finds that schooling affects career salary growth, implying that educational attainment is more than just an initial signal used for the hiring process.

Investing in education. The widely-held belief that investing in education will pay off in terms of higher lifetime earnings explains why many individuals choose to invest in education, but why does society make such a substantial investment in education? In many modern societies, some amount of education is both mandatory and free, in the sense that the costs are covered by taxpayers. Higher education is also heavily subsidized, so that for many students the biggest cost of attending college is the opportunity cost, or the earnings foregone during those years when the bulk of the student's time is devoted to study rather than earning an income. To some, public support of education is a method of improving the efficiency of a market economy by correcting an externality or market failure. To others, subsidizing education is justified on equity grounds rather than on efficiency grounds. Giving each person the opportunity to acquire an education promotes a more equitable distribution of income in this view.

Consumption of a good provides benefits directly to the consumer, but in some cases, consumption of a good can provide benefits to others. When non-consumers benefit, the good is said to generate positive external benefits and is used as an example of a positive or beneficial externality or spillover benefit. If there are spillover benefits, then the marginal social benefit of consuming an additional unit of the good exceeds the marginal private benefit. A free-market equilibrium is achieved when the marginal private benefit of consuming one more unit of the good equals the marginal cost of providing one more unit of the good. The free market equilibrium quantity is considered inefficiently low when there are positive external benefits because the marginal social benefit exceeds the marginal cost at the free market equilibrium quantity.

From society's perspective, it is efficient to continue providing and consuming the good up to the point where the marginal social benefit equals the marginal cost, but this efficient amount will likely not be reached without some government interference in free markets. In this framework, there is a potential efficiency gain if government subsidizes education enough to move the quantity of education consumed from the free-market equilibrium quantity to the socially efficient quantity. Harvey S. Rosen points out that we do far more than merely subsidizing education in order to achieve a socially efficient outcome when we make public education both free and compulsory. Thus, the explanation for public education is probably based partly on efficiency and partly on equity considerations. Many hold an egalitarian view that each person is entitled to a good education.

Because we invest so much in education, both as individuals and as a society, we are naturally very interested in knowing whether and how much increased expenditure on education leads to an improved educational outcome. This relationship is very difficult to test because it is hard to measure educational outcome. Studies have attempted to do so using test scores, attendance records, dropout rates, or continuation rates to higher levels of schooling, and labor market outcomes. Eric Hanushek surveyed hundreds of attempts to estimate the relationship between educational inputs and outcomes, concluding that there is virtually no relationship between expenditure on inputs and the quality of education. The research indicates that, although clearly some schools and teachers are more effective than others, we cannot predict which will be most effective based on cost or level of expenditure. For example, experienced teachers generally earn more than inexperienced teachers, but there is little or no correlation between years of teacher experience and test scores. Thus, we may be spending more to retain experienced teachers, but having a more experienced teacher cannot by itself guarantee that a student will achieve a higher score on a skills-based test.

If greater expenditure on education fails to produce higher test scores, most people will nevertheless support additional public expenditure on education provided it results in improved earnings. James HECKMAN estimates that a 10 percent increase in educational expenditure raises earnings by about 1 or 2 percent. It is up to society to determine whether this payoff justifies increased expenditure. Heckman also finds that educational investments made in early childhood improve later performance by children from low-income families, suggesting that the larger issue may not be how much we spend on education, but how we allocate our education dollars.

Support for public expenditure on education is weakened by such well-publicized facts as falling SAT scores since the 1960s, despite increased expenditure per pupil from $3,796 (in 1998 dollars) in 1970 to $6,576 (in 1998 dollars) in 1990, according to the U.S. Census Bureau. There is a growing perception that public schools are less effective than private schools, that spending more on public schools will have little or no payoff, and that a drastic change in how we provide public education is needed. These perceptions have led many to consider a major reform involving private school vouchers, following a plan proposed by Milton FRIEDMAN in 1962.

Private and public education. The general idea behind a voucher plan is to place the money provided by government to pay for education in the hands of families rather than using these dollars to directly pay the costs of providing a public education. Education subsidies in the form of vouchers can be used by families to purchase the best education available, so a family need not simply accept the education provided by the nearest public school. Allowing families to make the choice could force schools to compete with one another to attract students, resulting in competition-induced improvements in overall quality. There are many concerns about how such a system could be managed to, for example, avoid discrimination, guarantee that teachers have acceptable credentials, avoid a constitutional conflict if education vouchers are used to pay tuition at religious schools, and ensure that families have sufficient information to make good choices.

Thomas J. Nechyba cites the well-known argument that a private-school voucher plan, by promoting choice and introducing greater competition among schools, could improve the quality of education. His model supports the belief that the quality of public school education will decline as high-ability students move into private schools, and it is as yet unknown whether the competition-induced increases in performance by public schools can offset this decline. A great deal of additional research is needed to resolve these issues; without more evidence it is unlikely that political support for education vouchers will grow.

In the extreme, a voucher system could completely eliminate the distinction between a public school and a private school, essentially turning all schools into private schools competing for education vouchers and private money. The critical issue concerns just how much of an improvement in quality we could expect if we made such a radical change in our method of subsidizing education. Critics of education vouchers argue that it would be virtually impossible to return to the present system of public education if we made such a radical change and then decided we were not happy with the results.

There are a large number of issues yet to be resolved in the field of education. Many of these are addressed by Jack L. Nelson, Kenneth Carlson, and Stuart Palonsky. Should spending taxpayer dollars on education be different in different school districts? Many states have enacted measures to equalize school finance, often under court order to do so. How should we approach the issue of integration, which continues to be a concern despite the fact that segregation levels are at their lowest point since roughly 1920, according to the 2000 census? Should schools focus on teaching the basics, or should the goal be to develop critical thinking skills? Standardized tests are administered to students with increasing frequency, often affecting funding, and seem to focus more on skills assessment now than on memorization of facts. Should there be a national curriculum, or should local government decide what constitutes knowledge for their students? Should schools educate for technological competence? Should business have more influence on schools to ensure that students are taught employable skills and work values? Should gifted students be identified and separated from the mainstream, leaving other students feeling ordinary? The Montessori philosophy holds that each student should be treated as a gifted student with unlimited potential and many parents have begun to protest the segregation of a select few students into gifted classes.

There are many issues involving education that may never be resolved to everyone's satisfaction. As time goes on, there is perhaps much more that each child needs to be taught in order to succeed, and there is so much information at our fingertips that the prospect of internalizing even small bits of the sum of human knowledge can be daunting. There is little doubt that education will continue to be a primary determinant of productivity, living standards, and economic growth, so we all have a vital interest in solving the problems that now exist and preparing to solve the problems of the future.

BIBLIOGRAPHY. Adam Smith, *The Wealth of Nations* (Modern Library, 1994); Milton Friedman, *Capitalism and Freedom* (University of Chicago Press, 1962); A.M. Spence, *Job Market Signaling* (Quarterly Journal of Economics, 1973); D.A. Wise, *Academic Achievement and Job Performance* (American Economic Review, 1975); Jack L. Nelson, Kenneth Carlson, and Stuart Polonsky, *Critical Issues in Education: A Dialectic Approach* (McGraw-Hill, 1993); Morgan Reynolds, *Economics of Labor* (South-Western College Publishing, 1995); Herbert Stein and Murray Foss, *The New Illustrated Guide to the American Economy* (The AEI Press, 1995); Eric Hanushek, "Measuring Investment in Education," *Journal of Economic Perspectives* (1996); James Heckman, "Policies to Foster Human Capital" (NBER Working Paper No. 7288, 1999); Thomas J. Nechyba, "Mobility, Targeting, and Private-School Vouchers," *American Economic Review* (2000); Harvey S. Rosen, *Public Finance* (McGraw-Hill, 2000).

SUSAN DADRES
SOUTHERN METHODIST UNIVERSITY

Egypt

ONE OF THE OLDEST cornucopias of civilization, Egypt has, for many years, reflected an economy based on internal and external upheavals, and its place in a growing commercial world. The current economy is no exception. In the wake of overtaxed resources and stressed personal incomes, the government has worked to structure economic reform and maintain an ongoing investment to keep its place in the global marketplace.

At the turn of the second millennium, Egypt, long considered a poor country, has displayed stable economic growth. The bureaucracy has slimmed somewhat while activities in the agricultural, textile, and mining arenas continue to dominate the country's industry. The government at Cairo has managed to weaken inflation, slash budget deficits, and strategically strengthen its foreign reserve power.

Still, there are remaining problems to dampen an altogether optimistic outlook for the first decade of the 2000s. For one, lower foreign-exchange earnings since the 1990s trimmed the monetary value of the Egyptian pound, and have caused periodic dollar shortages.

The overpopulation factor, still growing, cannot be ignored. (2002 estimates discover a populace of more than 70 million.) As well, tourism—a main economic commodity that was just beginning to show appreciation despite the area's political and religious bloodletting—has once again fallen, this time plummeting after terrorist-incited international events, such as an attack on tourists in Luxor near the famous Pyramids (October 1997) and a surprise attack on American soil by Islamic fundamentalists (September 2001).

Agriculture remains a strong component of Egypt's economy. Manufacturing, too, continues to roll on a stable plan, being controlled by a public sector that also runs most of the heavy-industry environment. Trade and investment have been partially liberalized, along with the relaxation of certain price controls and reduced subsidies. Construction, mandatory services of a non-financial genre, and internal marketing are largely private. Output of Egypt's GROSS NATIONAL PRODUCT (GNP) is, therefore, climbing at a rate that places Egypt second among the Arab countries, just behind SAUDI ARABIA.

Examining composition by economic factor, recent figures released (2001) state that agriculture comprises 14 percent; manufacturing/industry some 30 percent, and services the final 56 percent of the country's economy.

Import and export both remain busy and have harvested relationships with other countries. Import of commodities from GERMANY, ITALY, FRANCE, the UNITED STATES, Asia and the Middle East coincides with an equally rapid exportation of commodities to ITALY, GERMANY, the UNITED KINGDOM, the United States, Middle East and Asia. Growth rate of the GROSS DOMESTIC PRODUCT (GDP) is 2.5 percent with a per capita purchasing power parity of $3,700.

In AGRICULTURE, an industry that brings in about 18 percent of the GNP, major crops are cotton, wheat, maize and rice, other outputs being sugarcane, corn, barley, millet, onions, figs and potatoes. Forty percent of Egypt's population is engaged in farming; most of the farming takes place in a highly cultivated area of 2.5 million hectares, or 6 million acres, within the fertile

Nile River Valley and Nile Delta. The Aswan High Dam, which has controlled the flow of the Nile waters to keep the soil rich, is largely responsible for the fertility garnered. Lately, certain new farms, large and small, are being developed elsewhere to yield produce. More and more farms, especially the larger ones, are beginning to produce livestock—specifically, cows, chickens, and water buffaloes.

Egypt's mining industry shows no signs of slowing. Principal minerals are iron, salt, phosphates, gypsum, manganese, limestone and gold. Cairo, in the northeast of the country, and Alexandria, in the northwest, are the main industrial centers. Processing plants in Port Said and along the Nile produce chemicals, fertilizers, clothing, and construction materials.

Petroleum and natural gas (most of it derived from the northeast part of the country in the Gulf of Suez area) account for 7 percent of the GDP (according to fiscal year 2000 estimates). Crude oil channeled primarily from the Gulf of Suez and the western desert earned $16 per barrel, some $2.6 billion in the year 2000. With some decline in production, 2001 figures indicate a minor decrease.

Output of natural gas is on the increase, however. With its partner, the kingdom of Jordan, Egypt planned on a June, 2003, completion of the Eastern Gas Company to export natural gas to Jordan.

BIBLIOGRAPHY. Mahmoud A.T. Elkhafif, *The Egyptian Economy: A Modeling Approach* (Praeger Publishers, 1996); "Egypt," *CIA World Factbook* (2003); *Encyclopaedia of the Orient*, www.bowdoin.edu.

JOSEPH GERINGER
SYED B. HUSSAIN, PH.D.
UNIVERSITY OF WISCONSIN, OSHKOSH

Eisenhower, Dwight D. (1890–1969)

EVEN BEFORE BECOMING president, Dwight David Eisenhower was one of the most important world figures, having led the Allied forces to victory in Europe in WORLD WAR II. Some historians concluded that he was an uninvolved occupant of the White House, but recently declassified documents establish that he was very much in control of his administration, and his ranking by historians has risen accordingly.

Ike, a nickname he obtained as a child, was born at Denison, Texas, the third son of hardworking Mennonite parents. The following year, the family moved to his beloved Abilene, Kansas, where he experienced an idyl-lic small-town childhood among sturdy mid-western farmers and shopkeepers.

Admitted to West Point in 1911, he was successful at football until sidelined by a knee injury. He graduated in 1915 and won recognition for his wartime training skills during WORLD WAR I. In the 1920s, he served in the Panama Canal Zone before graduating first in his class from the prestigious Army War College in 1926, and went to France to prepare a study of the World War I battlefields, there gaining invaluable knowledge of the European terrain. In the 1930s, he joined the staff of the flamboyant General Douglas MACARTHUR in Washington and the Philippines. He was promoted to colonel and then major general in the early 1940s. At the start of World War II, he demonstrated superior organizational and war strategy skill as assistant chief of staff under army Chief of Staff George C. Marshall.

In June 1942, Eisenhower was named commander of American forces in Europe and thereafter placed in command of the Allies' offensive in North Africa. By June 6, 1944, he was Supreme Commander of the Allied expeditionary force landing at Normandy. During his planning and execution of the D-Day invasion, he showed political finesse in keeping his generals of various nations united in strategic purpose. "Ike" swiftly became a household word and America's greatest military hero of the war. After the liberation of Europe, as chief of staff, he directed the military occupation of GERMANY and demobilization, and then retired from the army as a five-star general in 1948. After a brief tenure as president of Columbia University, he agreed to assume supreme command of NATO forces at the request of President Harry TRUMAN in 1950.

As early as 1948, leaders from both major parties tired to induce Eisenhower to run for the presidency under their banner. Even Truman made an effort on behalf of the Democrats, but Ike determined that he was a Republican. He thought the Democrats too weak in containing international communism and agreed with the Republicans' traditional view of limited government. He also wanted to save the GOP from its isolationist wing. Furthermore, the Republican Party had lost five consecutive presidential elections, causing some to fear for the viability of the two-party system.

After outmaneuvering conservative Senator Robert Taft, he was nominated on the first ballot at the Republican National Convention. With his popularity, larger-than-life persona, the slogan "I like Ike," and effective use of the new medium of television, Eisenhower and his running mate, Richard NIXON, defeated the cerebral Democratic nominee Adlai Stevenson with 442 electoral votes to 89. Four years later, he would trounce Stevenson again with an electoral total of 457 to 73.

Throughout the 1950s, as polls repeatedly indicated, the president, and government in general, enjoyed especially high levels of trust. Elvis Presley and Ike became the positive and popular personifications of the era. This popularity resulted partly from Eisenhower's reassuring, fatherly presence in the nervous, early years of the Cold War. Nevertheless, his personal popularity did not translate into Republican victories in congressional races. The Democrats took control of Congress in 1954, holding it for the rest of his presidency and beyond. Yet despite divided government, Eisenhower's domestic and economic achievements were substantial.

Although an economic conservative, who signed three balanced budgets, Eisenhower was a pragmatist in domestic matters. Therefore, even though favoring private enterprise involvement over solely government-run government projects, he accepted Franklin ROOSEVELT's NEW DEAL programs as here to stay.

However, he demanded efficiency and military-style responsiveness and accountability from officials and agencies. On the legislative front, be obtained pro-business tax reform, was the first president to give air and water pollution serious attention, expanded social security and unemployment coverage, passed a school building program, and created the federal interstate highway system, an unprecedented and massive construction project of incalculable and perpetual benefit for the economy. During his administration, American productivity increased almost 25 percent, family income went up 15 percent, credit was easily obtainable, and consumer spending was heavy. Hence, the president's chief economic concern was not economic growth, but keeping inflation in check. Like Franklin Roosevelt, he preferred to deal with cyclical business downturns with economic stimulus measures.

Although criticized by some historians for not placing civil rights high on his agenda, in 1954, he decisively sent federal troops to Little Rock, Arkansas, to enforce court-ordered desegregation of public schools. In 1957, he approved the first civil rights measure to be passed by Congress in 82 years and secured adoption of the Civil Rights Act of 1960, that provided for sanctions against officials who hindered the registration and voting of African-Americans. Although faulted for not openly confronting Joseph McCarthy, a demagogic Wisconsin senator leading a witch-hunt against communism in America, Eisenhower correctly predicted that McCarthy would self-destruct, and worked behind the scenes to discredit the senator. He eventually directed executive branch officials not to cooperate with McCarthy's congressional investigations.

Under Eisenhower, the United States aggressively promoted democracy and capitalism around the world, both overtly and covertly. He increased civil and military foreign aid, actively participated in the UNITED NATIONS, worked to prevent nuclear proliferation, and traveled the world extensively. He ended the fighting in Korea, and strove to reach arms control agreements with the SOVIET UNION, until his efforts at détente were derailed in 1960 by the downing of an American U-2 spy plane over Soviet territory. Eisenhower boldly forced a ceasefire during the Suez crisis, resulting in preservation of Egyptian nationalization of the canal. Although keeping a strong defense, as he left the presidency, he warned Americans of the dangers of "unwarranted influence, whether sought or unsought, by the military-industrial complex."

Eisenhower retired to Gettysburg, Pennsylvania, with his wife Mamie. After a long history of heart problems, he died and was laid to rest in a chapel next to his boyhood home in Abilene. Justice William O. Douglas wrote: "His smile and simple frontier approach to complex problems made him as American as apple pie."

BIBLIOGRAPHY. Stephen E. Ambrose, *Eisenhower: Soldier and President* (Touchstone, 1990); Stephen E. Ambrose, *The Supreme Commander: The War Years of General Dwight D. Eisenhower* (University Press of Mississippi, 1970); Blanche Cook, *The Declassified Eisenhower* (Viking, 1981); Dwight D. Eisenhower, *Crusade in Europe* (Johns Hopkins University Press, 1967); Dwight D. Eisenhower, *Mandate for Change* (Johns Hopkins University Press, 1963); Robert H. Ferrell, *The Eisenhower Diaries* (Johns Hopkins University Press, 1981).

RUSSELL FOWLER, J.D.
UNIVERSITY OF TENNESSEE, CHATTANOOGA

El Paso Corporation

RANKED NUMBER 17 on the 2002 Fortune 500 list of the largest global companies, the El Paso Corporation was North America's leading provider of natural gas and related services.

The company was founded in 1928 by Houston attorney Paul Kayser to supply fuel to El Paso, Texas. Initially, El Paso Natural Gas (as the company was then known) concentrated on natural gas delivery via pipelines until 1947, when their customer base ranged from California to West Virginia. After expanding into hydrocarbon production and oil refinery, El Paso Corporation focused on fuel transportation in the 1980s and aggressively pursued partnerships with and acquisitions of competing natural gas corporations in 1996. Also during this time, El Paso largely concentrated on energy trading, both domestically and overseas.

2002 was a troubled year for the El Paso Corporation. After El Paso's stock collapsed, dropping in value from $45 to $7 per share, the company was sued by Oscar Wyatt, founder of the 2000 El Paso-acquired oil company Coastal Corp. Among Wyatt's suit claims are that El Paso artificially inflated its revenues with bogus energy trades. El Paso was also under investigation by the SECURITIES & EXCHANGE COMMISSION (SEC), the Federal Energy Regulatory Commission, and a federal grand jury for illegal business practices in 2002–03.

BIBLIOGRAPHY. *El Paso Corporation*, www.epenergy.com; "Global 500: World's Largest Companies, *Fortune* (July, 2002) ; "El Paso Corp.'s Past, Present Face Off," (Knight-Ridder Tribune Business News); Carol J. Loomis, "El Paso's Murky Magic," *Fortune* (July, 2002).

MIKE S. DuBose
BOWLING GREEN STATE UNIVERSITY

employee benefits

IN MODERN MARKET ECONOMIES the total compensation that workers receive often significantly exceeds their wage or salary payments. This additional compensation is generally called "fringe benefits." In the UNITED STATES, fringe benefit payments largely consist of four kinds of benefits. One important category is government-mandated benefits such as Social Security, unemployment payments, and workers' compensation for on-the-job injuries. In addition, fringe benefits include a range of private benefit categories, the three most important being retirement plans, insurance (medical, dental, life), and paid time off from work (vacations, holidays, sick leave).

These four general categories each represent between 6.1 percent and 6.5 percent of total worker compensation. Today, the average yearly cost of fringe benefits to employers is approximately $15,000 per person that represents roughly 27 percent of total wage and salary compensation in the United States. The proportion of fringe benefits relative to total compensation varies greatly across industries and occupations. For example, the fringe benefit proportion is larger in high-paying relative to low-paying industries, in goods-producing relative to service industries, and blue-collar relative to white-collar occupations.

In any discussion of worker compensation a basic question that arises is why do workers choose to take part of their compensation in the form of fringe benefits instead of a direct cash payment? Should not a rational worker prefer a cash payment of a dollar that can be spent as the worker sees fit rather than a dollar of, say, health insurance? The answer is that fringe benefits are the result of certain institutional features in the economy, in the American context the most important being the tax treatment of fringe benefit payments. Specifi-

cally, workers reap large tax advantages from fringe benefits because fringe-benefit payments are entirely untaxed.

Fringe benefits in lieu of wage payments also offer significant gains to employers. First, firms benefit because some employer tax liabilities rise with higher wage and salary payments. For example, every dollar saved in wages lowers an employer's Social Security taxes by 7.65 cents. In addition, fringe benefits such as private pensions and health insurance help induce workers to stay with a firm, thus reducing employee turnover costs. Finally, employers generally receive lower rates on employee benefits such as health or life insurance due to scale economies.

Causes of fringe-benefit growth. Since WORLD WAR II, fringe benefits have increased significantly. In 1929, they represented less than 3 percent of total compensation, by 2003 they represented approximately 27 percent. The basic economic force driving this growth has been the growing tax advantages of fringe-benefit payments to both employees and employers. To begin, high inflation rates increasingly pushed wage earners into higher and higher tax brackets. For example, in 1961 only 10

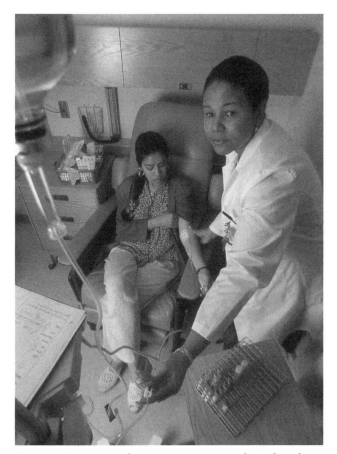

For most Americans, the most important employee benefit (or fringe benefit) is employer-sponsored health insurance.

percent of taxpayers were in a tax bracket exceeding 22 percent but by 1979, this increased to more than 35 percent of taxpayers. Moreover, the Social Security payroll tax increased from 4 percent in 1955 to 15.3 percent by 1990. Finally, the costs to recruit and train new workers have risen steadily over time. All of the above factors have lowered the cost of fringe benefits to both employers and employees, and induced them to opt for a larger fraction of total compensation in the form of fringe-benefit payments.

The growing significance of fringe benefits has increasingly linked these benefits to important labor-market outcomes. During the 20th century, a dramatic change in U.S. labor supply occurred. The average workweek declined from approximately 53 hours in 1900, essentially a six-day workweek of nine hours per day, to approximately 38 hours by 1970. Most of the decline, however, occurred between 1900 and 1945 with a much slower decline in the postwar period. One likely explanation involves the large increase in fringe benefits in the form of paid time off for vacations, illness, and holidays. In brief, the apparent slowdown in the growth of leisure time may simply be a statistical artifact arising from the increasing gap between the number of paid hours of work and the actual hours of work. Specifically, before 1940 paid vacations and holidays were largely unheard of whereas by 1977, the average American worker enjoyed nine paid holidays and almost two weeks of paid vacation.

An even more fundamental economic question involving fringe benefits concerns one of the central tenets of neoclassical ECONOMIC THEORY. According to the neoclassical theory of distribution, the factors of production in a capitalist economy receive income payments equal to their (marginal) productivity. With respect to labor, neoclassical theory asserts that wages, meaning total labor compensation, will equal labor productivity. Or, in a dynamic context, the increases in worker productivity will result in proportionate increases in (inflation-adjusted) wages.

In recent years, however, many journalistic reports have appeared claiming that wages for American workers increasingly fail to correspond to worker productivity. For example, one widespread report in the popular press stated that between 1982 and 1995 worker productivity had increased over 21 percent, while wages (adjusted for inflation) had risen only 7.4 percent. Such comparisons are often seriously misleading for several reasons. First, sometimes an unrepresentative base year is used. Second, an accurate measure of real, or inflation-adjusted wages, requires use of an appropriate price index. A third key deficiency of many wage-productivity comparisons is the failure to account for fringe benefits as part of total labor compensation. Popular writers generally cite data on direct wage payments only, and often for a rather narrow class of labor such as "non-supervisory manufacturing workers."

Some economists believe, when measured correctly over the long run, the growth rate of a broad measure of worker compensation (including all workers engaged in the business sector) and the growth of worker productivity shows these to be effectively equal, as predicted by neoclassical theory. Specifically, between 1950 and 1995, real hourly output of American workers rose 144.7 percent while real hourly compensation increased 144.2 percent.

BIBLIOGRAPHY. Ronald G. Ehrenberg and Robert S. Smith, *Modern Labor Economics* (Addison Wesley, 2003); Bruce E. Kaufman and Julie L. Hotchkiss, *The Economics of Labor Markets* (South-Western, 2003); Campbell R. McConnell, Stanley L. Brue and David A. Macpherson, *Contemporary Labor Economics* (McGraw-Hill, 2003; Herbert Stein, "A Primer on Pay and Productivity," *The Wall Street Journal* (August 23, 1995).

THOMAS S. NESSLEIN
UNIVERSITY OF WISCONSIN, GREEN BAY

employment theory

SINCE THE MID-19TH CENTURY, the capitalist market economies have experienced significant economic growth. That is, over time production and income per person or household have risen. For example, from 1870 to the present, the UNITED STATES has experienced an average increase in per capita income of 1.8 percent per year.

Consequently, the bundle of goods and services that the average worker or family can buy today is more than 10 times higher than in 1870. The long-run rise in the standard of living, however, has not occurred without major fluctuations in production, incomes, and employment. Indeed, since 1870 the United States has experienced 10 significant decreases in the level of national production or GROSS DOMESTIC PRODUCT (GDP).

Severe downturns occurred in the early 1890s, in 1907, at the end of WORLD WAR I, and in the mid-1970s as a result of the world ENERGY crisis. Of course, the most severe downturn was the world-wide Great DEPRESSION of the 1930s. The United States entered the Great Depression in the fall of 1929 and by 1933, the level of U.S. national production had fallen by one-third and unemployment had risen up to 19 percent. The U.S. economy did not fully recover from the Great Depression until after WORLD WAR II. Clearly, the Great Depression was a horrendous waste of economic resources. Production, not undertaken because of idle factories and unemployed workers, is lost forever. Moreover, the Great Depression visited great personal costs on individual workers and their families because of increased poverty, ill health, alcoholism, marital strife, and divorce. Clearly, a precise understanding of the causes of economic downturns under capitalism is of great importance.

Causes of economic fluctuations. The causes of economic fluctuations in capitalist market economies and what potential government policies, if any, are capable of lessening their severity has long been one of the most controversial subjects in economic theory. Historically, economists, and others, have advanced many alternative theories to explain fluctuations in national production and employment. Some economists have argued that a capitalist economy has strong tendencies toward full employment unless struck by shocks such as wars and political instability. Others have argued that RECESSIONS (mild economic downturns) or depressions (severe economic downturns) are largely a monetary phenomenon created by an insufficient supply of money to support a full-employment level of national production. Economic historians have often focused on the impact of product innovations as a source of booms and busts in market economies. Included here are major technological innovations such as the steam engine, the RAILROAD, the harnessing of electricity as a power source, the AUTOMOBILE, and most recently, the telecommunications and COMPUTER revolutions.

Moreover, one prominent neoclassical economist, William Stanley JEVONS, suggested that economic fluctuations were largely related to the 11-year cycle of sunspots. The connection here is that sunspots, actually solar magnetic storms, were argued to have a major adverse effect on the earth's climate. In turn, the subsequent disruption of agricultural production was then argued to spread to the economy in general. Finally, many contemporary economists have stressed that recessions and depressions are largely linked to decreases in total spending in the economy (aggregate demand), especially from sharp declines in business investment spending (i.e., spending on production plants, machinery, and equipment) and/or spending on a country's exports.

Let us then turn to a concise description and evaluation of key theories of fluctuations in national production and employment. The historical evolution of employment theory is stressed here. In this regard, Stanley L. Brue and Jacob Oser note: "New scholarship in economics normally is connected to a previous body of thought, and while it may alter or transform the older tradition, it rarely replaces it."

Employment theory: the classical school. The father of the modern discipline of economics, Adam SMITH, was the leader of what has come to be called the classical school. Other prominent members of this 18th- and 19th-century school of thought include David RICARDO, Thomas MALTHUS, and John Stuart MILL. A fundamental belief of most classical economists was that a capitalist market economy would lead to a steady economic development and a rising level of national production and employment. In their view, a market economy has a strong tendency to fully employ all workers. In short, no tendency exists for involuntary unemployment.

The fundamental basis for this belief was known as SAY'S LAW of Markets. In essence, Say's Law asserts that "supply creates its own demand." In other words, every dollar of production generates a dollar of income to someone in the economy. Thus, there is always sufficient income created to buy whatever output is produced in a market economy. This is essentially true. But even some classical economists, for example, Malthus, were skeptical that Say's Law always ensured full employment. Does a dollar of income generated in some time period always result in a dollar of spending in that time period? Do not households and firms save a part of their income? Will not the leakage of saving out of the economy's income-expenditure stream imply that a dollar of production and income need not generate a dollar of effective demand, that is, spending in the marketplace? And if so, excess production and unemployment would result, certainly in the short run.

The classical school had two basic answers to the questions noted above. First, classical economists argued that both saving and business investment are largely determined by the INTEREST RATE and that changes in the interest rate will prevent any major deficiency in total spending (aggregate demand) in the economy. For example, assume that in a given year households begin to save more of their income. The increased supply of saving was asserted to cause the interest rate to fall. In turn, this would induce business firms to borrow these savings and increase their spending on plants and machinery. Consequently, it was believed that, via interest-rate adjustments, every dollar of saving would be injected back into the economy's income-expenditure stream in the form of business-investment spending.

Classical economists bolstered their arguments concerning full employment by asserting that if unemployment did emerge, such unemployment would be very brief. In their view, any surplus of labor (unemployment) would quickly cause wages to fall, thus inducing firms to hire all workers willing to work at the prevailing market wage.

Although the classical theory of employment was strongly challenged by many critics of capitalism during the 19th and early 20th centuries, it effectively remained the dominant view until undermined by the world-wide Great Depression and the elegant and rigorous presentation of a dramatically different theory of employment by British economist John Maynard KEYNES.

Employment theory: the Keynesian view. In his book *The General Theory of Employment, Interest, and Money* (1936), Keynes successfully challenged the classical orthodoxy and revolutionized thinking about the workings of the national (macro) economy. Keynes rejected Say's Law and the existence of the alleged automatic adjustment mechanisms.

First, he strongly challenged the view that saving and investment flows would be kept in balance by interest-rate adjustments. In essence, Keynes rejected the classical assumption that the interest rate was the primary determinant of both saving and business investment. Rather, he argued, the amount of household saving in a given year primarily depends on the household's current-year income.

On the other hand, the amount of business-investment spending in a given year depends largely on the many factors that influence the expected future profitability of new plants and machinery. Consequently, from this perspective there is no reason to believe that every dollar leaking out of the income-expenditure stream in the form of saving will be quickly returned in the form of business-investment spending. Moreover, Keynes argued that wage-cuts throughout the economy would fail to return the economy to full employment. Keynes argued here that classical theory was guilty of a basic logical error, namely, what is valid with respect to one firm in isolation may not be valid when applied to all firms across the economy. That is, if one firm faces falling wages, while prices and wages are stable across the economy, then the particular firm has a clear incentive to hire more workers. But if all firms experience falling wages, then firms in general will experience falling demand and prices for their products, and will have little or no incentive to hire additional workers.

Consequently, Keynes believed the classical theory to be fundamentally wrong. In essence, Keynes stood classical theory on its head. Instead of beginning with the idea that "supply creates its own demand," Keynes argued that the fundamental perspective should be that total spending in the economy (aggregate demand) determines supply, that is, the level of national production and employment in a given time period. Concomitantly, Keynes recognized that a fundamental assumption underpinning classical theory was the assumption of perfect wage-price flexibility in the economy. In the long run, this may be a good assumption. In the short run, however, and given the institutional and structural features of capitalist economies of the 1930s, Keynes argued that one should see wages and prices as more or less fixed. As a consequence, Keynes recognized that without price adjustments possible in the short run,

changes in aggregate demand would lead to quantity adjustments in terms of production and employment.

Moreover, assuming a world of fixed prices, even small changes in aggregate demand would become magnified over time via what has become known as the Keynesian multiplier process. In brief, the logic of the Keynesian multiplier is as follows. An increase, say, in business investment of $10 billion will generate over time more than a $10 billion in increase in aggregate demand and national production. Why? $10 billion more business-investment spending will increase aggregate demand and national production by $10 billion. This is the initial and direct result. But in an economy with unemployed resources and fixed prices and wages, the increase in national production is not limited to the $10 billion initial increase in business-investment spending. The increase of $10 billion in national production generates $10 billion more in income to resource suppliers throughout the economy. They, in turn, spend a fraction of the increase in income and save the remainder. The increase in consumer spending, however, again raises aggregate demand and national production, but by some fraction of the initial increase. And again, the increase in national production generates additional income and the process continues on. Of course, with the leakage of saving out of the income-expenditure stream at each round of the multiplier process, the process does not continue forever. However, Keynesian economists tend to believe that for every dollar increase in, say, business investment or government spending, aggregate demand and national production will be multiplied several times.

Likewise, a large multiplier effect suggests to them that a market economy will be extremely susceptible to downturns in aggregate demand, as even small decreases in business investment, consumer spending, and/or export spending will drive down national production substantially, leading to high unemployment. Since Keynesian economists believe there are no automatic adjustment mechanisms that will return the economy to full employment, it follows that the insufficiency of aggregate demand can and should be remedied by expansionary stabilization policies. The two basic stabilization policies are FISCAL POLICY (changes in government spending and taxes) and MONETARY POLICY (changes in the money supply). Keynesian economists have tended to strongly favor expansionary fiscal policy, in particular, increases in government expenditures.

Employment theory: monetarism and the new classical economics. Without a doubt, Keynesian economic theory has made a lasting contribution to understanding the causes of fluctuations in national production and employment. Nevertheless, changes in the structure and institutions of modern market economies as well as advances in economic research have led to significant modification of Keynesian theory.

Beginning in the early 1950s, a key competitor to Keynesian orthodoxy emerged.

Led by Professor Milton FRIEDMAN of the University of Chicago, this challenge to Keynesian economics came to be labeled MONETARISM. In 1976, Friedman was awarded the Nobel Prize in Economics, largely for his work in developing the modern quantity theory of money. In distinct contrast to Keynesian theory that tends to downplay the influence of changes in the money supply on aggregate demand, output, and prices, the modern quantity theory asserts a strong and direct link. Monetarists thus place much greater emphasis on monetary relative to fiscal policy as a stabilization policy instrument.

In addition, monetarists believe that Keynesian theory tends to greatly exaggerate the multiplier effect induced by expansionary fiscal policy via deficit financing. Monetarists maintain that there is a strong crowding-out effect that greatly reduces the size of the Keynesian multiplier. For example, assume that Congress increases government spending on public infrastructure and must finance this increased spending by borrowing. In turn, the increased borrowing by the government is asserted to raise the interest rate, thus depressing or crowding-out interest-sensitive business spending, as well as spending on houses and big-ticket consumer durables (e.g., cars). In theory, the presence of a crowding-out effect implies that the expansionary impact of, say, an increase in government spending is offset in whole or part.

Another line of monetarist attack is to argue that a market economy is much more stable than that predicted by Keynesian theory. Again, a key reason that Keynesian theory predicts a large multiplier effect is the assumption that households will spend a high proportion (i.e., 90 percent or more) of any change in their current-year income. Friedman and other economists (including Albert Ando and Franco MODIGLIANI) developed theories where consumer or household spending is related largely to a long-run measure of income labeled permanent or lifetime income. If, in fact, consumer expenditures are tied more to lifetime income, as opposed to current-year income, then changes in current-year income have greatly reduced impact on current-year consumer spending. In short, in such a world the strength of the multiplier process would be substantially reduced and fluctuations in business investment, export spending, and so on, would not result in major fluctuations in national production and employment.

Finally, since the mid-1970s a major new school of thought has asserted itself. This school is often labeled the new classical economics. Most new classical economists hold two fundamental views of the modern market economy. First, they assert that modern market economies such as the United States exhibit strong competition in most markets and that prices and wages are highly flexible, even over a very few years. Second, they tend to believe that economic agents—consumers, workers, managers, etc.—are rational and make their decisions about future values of economic variables by incorporating all available current and past information.

That is, economic agents are assumed to be much more forward-looking than assumed by previous theory that was grounded, often implicitly, on the idea that people formed their predictions of future economic variables by looking only at the past, what is called "adaptive expectations." The new theory, rational expectations theory, was developed by Nobel laureate Robert LUCAS of the University of Chicago. A key implication of new classical assumptions of highly flexible prices and rational expectations held by economic decision-makers is that the modern market economy adjusts much more rapidly to various kinds of shocks, economic or political. Consequently, the ability of public policies to improve the short-run performance of a market economy via active stabilization is viewed by new classical economists as greatly circumscribed.

Finally, in addition to the above theoretical considerations, most economists of whatever school recognize that major structural and institutional changes have occurred in market economies since the Great Depression. Many of the changes work to reduce the instability of a market economy. One major institutional change has been the growth of the modern welfare state. The modern welfare state has several features that, to a degree at least, automatically regulate aggregate demand, and in the process, tend to stabilize the economy. For example, assume that the economy begins to slide into a recession. As production and incomes fall, tax revenues from income, payroll, and sales taxes fall, thus supporting after-tax incomes. At the same time, rising unemployment results in a rise in unemployment insurance payments, food stamps, welfare assistance, and so on. Clearly, these so-called automatic stabilizers have greatly helped to lessen fluctuations in national production and employment.

BIBLIOGRAPHY. Jacob Oser and Stanley L. Brue, *The Evolution of Economic Thought* (South-Western, 1988); N. Gregory Mankiw, *Principles of Macroeconomics* (Worth Publishing, 2003); Campbell R. McConnell and Stanley L. Brue, *Macroeconomics* (McGraw-Hill, 1996); William J. Baumol and Alan S. Blinder, *Economics: Principles and Policies* (South-Western, 1998); Todd G. Buchholz, *New Ideas from Dead Economists* (Penguin, 1990); James Tobin, "Price Flexibility and Output Stability: an Old Keynesian View," *Journal of Economic Perspectives* (v.7, 1993); David Laidler, "Monetarism: an Interpretation and an Assessment," *Economic Journal* (v.91, 1981); Milton Friedman, "The Quantity Theory of Money—A Restatement," *Studies in the Quantity Theory of Money* (University of Chicago Press, 1956); Milton Friedman, *A Theory of the Consumption Function* (Princeton University Press, 1957); Albert Ando and Franco Modigliani, "The Life Cycle Hypothesis of Saving: Aggregate Implications and Tests," *American Economic Review* (v.53, March, 1963); David Laidler, "The New-Classical Contribution to Macroeconomics," *Banca Nazionale Del Lavaro Quarterly Review* (March, 1986); Rodney Maddock and Michael Carter, "A Child's Guide to Rational Expectations," *Journal of Economic Literature* (1982); N. Gregory Mankiw, "The Reincarnation of Keynesian Economics," *European Economic Review* (v.36, 1992).

THOMAS S. NESSLEIN
UNIVERSITY OF WISCONSIN, GREEN BAY

energy

FOSSIL FUELS—COAL, OIL, and natural gas—supply about 85 percent of primary energy consumption in the UNITED STATES. Coal provides approximately 54 percent of the U.S. electricity supply. Oil is used primarily for transportation fuels, but also for power production, for heat and as a feedstock for chemicals. The United States imports over half of the oil it uses. Natural gas (NG) is a relatively clean-burning fossil fuel, used mostly for space- and water-heating in buildings and running industrial processes. The new trend in small-scale, gas-turbine power plants has increased the demand for NG.

In the production of electricity, no new nuclear fission power plants have been built in the United States since the 1970s. Some plants were abandoned before startup, and others were taken out of production.

Renewable (naturally replenished) energy offers alternatives to both traditional fossil fuels and nuclear

The rise of capitalism echoes the exponential rise in energy consumption, especially of electricity, in the United States.

power. Biomass, solar, wind turbine, geothermal, hydroelectric, and hydrogen energy sources are among the many considered.

The development of capitalism echoes the rise of energy business: The five largest oil companies operating today in the United States control roughly 61 percent of the domestic retail gasoline market, 47 percent of the domestic oil refinery market, and 41 percent of domestic oil exploration and production. The five corporations are: EXXON-MOBIL, BP Amoco-Arco, Chevron-Texaco, Phillips-Tosco, and Marathon. These five corporations control 15 percent of the world's oil production.

The structure of the petroleum industry, internal to the United States, has also been changing. Smaller companies have gained a larger role in the development of U.S. oil and gas resources. The share of production from non-majors (independent oil and gas producers, pipeline companies, foreign-based companies, and a variety of other companies) has been generally increasing since 1986. These smaller companies tend to drill smaller fields and have faster depletion rates than the majors. However, with access to advanced technologies, the smaller companies have been able to reduce their finding costs to levels comparable to those of the majors.

The U.S. NG pipeline network has grown extensively over the past decade to meet the increasing demand for NG as a fuel and for transportation of the commodity. In addition to physically expanding the network, the companies engaged in NG pipeline transportation have also transformed the ways in which they transact business, while being consolidated into a smaller number of corporate entities through mergers and acquisitions. While the U.S. NG pipeline industry has undergone a major restructuring during the past decade, it has not been fully deregulated. Although NG pipelines can no longer buy and sell gas, many aspects of their operations and business practices are still subject to regulatory oversight. For instance, the Federal Energy Regulatory Commission (FERC) still determines a company's rate-setting methods, sets rules on business practices, and has approval authority on the building of new pipelines and the expansion of existing ones. Pipelines that are not governed by the FERC are regulated by state authorities.

The upward growth trend in coal production began in 1961. The growth during the 1990s included a strike-related downturn in production in 1993, and regional contrasts in production patterns. From 1986 to 1997, coal production increased by 22 percent, while the number of operating coal mines in the country declined by 59 percent, from 4,424 in 1986 to 1,828 in 1997. Coal prices decreased by 45 percent in real dollar terms. Significant adaptations supporting these inter-related trends include: increased average mine size; shutting down less competitive properties; concentration of productive capacity among fewer, large companies; significant gains in coal industry productivity; and fiscal discipline imposed by vigorous competition.

The U.S. electric power industry is changing to be more competitive. In some states, retail electricity customers can now choose their electricity-generation (power production itself, not transmission and distribution) company. New computerized wholesale electricity-trading markets are now operating in many regions of the country. The number of independent power producers and power marketers competing in these new retail and wholesale power markets has increased substantially over the past few years. However, a power crisis in California in 2001 showed that there are some definite kinks in the operation of this new de-regulated industry.

The major energy-using economic sectors are industry, transportation, residential/commercial, and agriculture. Agriculture is generally small, 2 to 5 percent of total energy use. In industrialized countries, the "Big 3 Sectors" are about even. In developing countries, industry uses most of the energy. Worldwide, the distribution is approximately: industry 40 percent; transportation 20 percent; and residential/commercial 40 percent.

Energy production is not environmentally friendly. When fossil fuels and biomass energy sources are combusted, or oxidized, among the probable by-products are carbon dioxide, sulfur dioxide, and small particles. The first has been scientifically linked with global warming, and the second and third with respiratory ailments. Nuclear power plants, barring accidents, give off relatively little radioactivity. Spent nuclear fuel storage is a problem due to the high radioactivity and long half-lives of the elements. Large hydroelectric dams disrupt natural habitats downstream, and displace people in areas flooded to create huge artificial lakes. Geothermal steam may include contaminants. It is difficult to find noxious by-products of wind and solar energy.

Scientists are mostly in agreement that energy use is a contributor to the Greenhouse Effect, a term that refers to the rising temperature of the Earth's atmosphere. Due to greenhouse gases, the atmosphere absorbs more infrared energy than it re-radiates to space, resulting in a net increase in surface temperature. A small rise in temperature can induce many other changes, for example, in sea level, cloud cover and wind patterns.

Energy policy is often directed at: exploration for, and development of, energy resources; research on, and development of, technologies that produce or use energy products; economic incentives for adjusting energy-related behavior according to social priorities; and legal restrictions on the supply of, and/or demand for, energy.

In 2001, U.S. national energy policy contained the following actions: direct federal agencies to conserve energy use at their facilities, especially during periods of peak demand; increase funding for renewable energy and energy-efficiency research and development programs

Nuclear power plants producing electricity remain a controversial energy source in most Western countries.

that are performance-based and cost-shared; create an income tax credit for the purchase of hybrid and fuel-cell vehicles; extend the Department of Energy's "Energy Star" efficiency program to include schools, retail buildings, health-care facilities, and homes; fund the federal government's Intelligent Transportation Systems Program—the fuel cell-powered transit bus program, and the clean buses program; and provide a tax incentive and streamline regulations to accelerate the development of clean combined-heat-and-power technology.

The debate goes on as to whether energy is a "special" commodity, and as such, needs government intervention to have smoothly functioning markets. On the one hand, there are a federal Department of Energy and numerous regulatory agencies. On the other hand, many of the traditionally regulated markets are being opened up to competition. The best compromise will inevitably contain elements of both.

BIBLIOGRAPHY. Richard Bonskowski, "The U.S. Coal Industry in the 1990's: Low Prices and Record Production," at www.eia.doe.gov; Hong Kong Observatory, "Greenhouse Effect," www.hko.gov.hk; William Liggett, "The Changing Structure of the Electric Power Industry 2000: An Update," www.eia.doe.gov; Jack J. Kraushaar and Robert A Ristinen, *Energy and Problems of a Technical Society* (John Wiley and Sons, 1993); G. Tyler Miller, *Living in the Environment* (Wadsworth/Thompson, 2003); *National Energy Policy Development Group*, www.whitehouse.gov; James Tobin, "Natural Gas Transportation: Infrastructure Issues and Operational Trends," www.eia.doe.gov; Union of Concerned Scientists, www.ucsusa.org; U.S. Dept. of Energy, www.energy.gov; U.S. Environmental Protection Agency, www.epa.gov.

JOHN SORRENTINO, PH.D.
MAHBUB RABBANI, M.A,
TEMPLE UNIVERSITY

Engel, Ernst (1821–96)

BORN IN DRESDEN, GERMANY, Ernst Engel received early training at a mining academy in Germany and, in 1847 went to study at the École des Mînes in Paris, FRANCE, where he came under the influence of Frédéric Le Play, one of the founding fathers of quantitative socioeconomic research. During a subsequent stay in BELGIUM, he became acquainted with Adolphe Quételet and was strongly impressed by his faith in the possibility of discovering quantitative social laws based on statistical regularities.

Upon his return to Germany, Engel took up statistics as a profession. He became director of the statistical bureaus of the Kingdom of Saxony (1850–58) and Prussia (from 1861 until his retirement in 1882) and taught statistics at the University of Berlin. He was also a co-founder of the Verein für Sozialpolitik, a research association set up in 1872 by a group of reform-minded social scientists, journalists, and public officials to promote empirical investigations of economic and social conditions. This institution has remained the leading association of economists in Germany until the present day.

Engel made a number of significant contributions to social science. He conducted the first empirical study of a demand curve. He pioneered the method of household expenditure diaries, evaluating the spending records of German housewives. In his little book of 1883, *The Economic Value of Man*, Engel defined what is now known as an equivalent measurement scale, to give appropriate weights to persons of different ages and sexes. In order to compare families of different sizes, he took the average consumption of an infant as unity and added a tenth for each year of growth until 20 years for females and 25 years for males. This unit of consumption was called a "quet" in honor of Quételet. Engel's methodology and substantive findings have influenced socioeconomic researchers from Lujo Brentano and Ferdinand Tönnies in Germany to Maurice Halbwachs in France and Carroll D. Wright in the United States.

Engel is best known for his studies of changes in expenditure patterns of households as incomes change. What is now called Engel's Law, first formulated in 1857, states that, with given tastes or preferences, the proportion of income spent on food diminishes as incomes increase. Based on a budget study of 153 Belgian families, Engel derived the following generalizations:

1. the percentage spent on food decreases as income rises

2. the percentage spent on housing stays about the same

3. the percentage spent on clothing stays the same (or increases)

4. the percentage spent on luxury items increases.

Income-expenditure curves of this sort are now called Engel Curves. From such curves it is possible to obtain income elasticities, showing the ratio of percentage change in expenditure on a consumption item to a percentage change in income.

Income-expenditure elasticities according to Engel's Law would be expected to be something like this: food – inelastic ($e < 1$); housing – unitary elastic ($e = 1$); clothing – unitary elastic ($e = 1$) or elastic ($e > 1$); and luxuries – elastic ($e > 1$).

If the quantity demanded increases proportionally with income (and the Engel Curve is upward-sloping), the good is a normal good. If demand rises proportionally more than income, the good is a luxury good. Otherwise (if the Engel Curve is downward-sloping), the good is an inferior (or necessary) good.

The economist Henrik Houthakker stated that, "Of all the empirical regularities observed in economic data, Engel's Law is probably the best established." In fact, numerous empirical studies carried out in many countries have found the percentage of expenditure for basic necessities of life decreasing, and that for all other consumption goods increasing, as income levels increase. The Law has attained importance in development economics. Poor countries spend much more of their GROSS DOMESTIC PRODUCT (GDP) on food than rich ones. While the proportion is around 10 percent in the United States, it can be over 50 percent in least-developed countries.

BIBLIOGRAPHY. J.M. Collette, "Empirical Enquiries and the Assessment of Social Progress in Western Europe: A Historical Perspective" *Social Policy and Development Programme Paper* (United Nations Research Institute for Social Development, 2000); A. Desrosières, *The Politics of Large Numbers: A History of Statistical Reasoning* (Harvard University Press, 1998); H.S. Houthakker, "An International Comparison of Households Expenditure Patterns Commemorating the Centenary of Engel's Law," *Econometrica* (v.25, 1957); S. Prais, S. and H.S. Houthakker, *The Analysis of Family Budgets.* (Cambridge University Press, 1971); G.J. Stigler, "The Early History of Empirical Studies of Consumer Behavior," *Journal of Political Economy* (v.62, 1954).

WOLFGANG GRASSL, PH.D.
HILLSDALE COLLEGE

Engels, Friedrich (1820–95)

A PHILOSOPHER AND SOCIOLOGIST, most well known as Karl MARX's faithful lifetime friend and ally, Friedrich Engels was born in Barmen as the eldest son of a successful German industrialist.

Engels' father was a well-to-do manufacturer and also a staunch Protestant. He tried to raise his son in the same creed, but young Engels showed his resilience very early. In his early 20s, he became a follower of the left wing of the Hegelian philosophy. His philosophical and political pamphlets were applauded in radical circles. He also wrote *Condition of the Working Classes in England* (1844), a credible piece of factual research nourished by direct observation and highly praised by Marx.

Engels met Marx in Paris, and the two men became close friends. Engels shared Marx's views on capitalism and after their first meeting he wrote that there was virtually "complete agreement in all theoretical fields." In 1846, socialists in England held a conference in London where they formed the Communist League. Engels attended as a delegate and took part in developing a strategy of action. In 1848, he and Marx wrote a pamphlet for the organization, the famous *Communist Manifesto*. In this brochure, Marx and Engels present their vision of history and social progress as driven by the "development of productive forces." At each stage of this development there are two main classes, defined by their relationship to the ownership of the means of production, whose struggle for economic and political power shapes social institutions and other non-economic parts of human life. The *Communist Manifesto* gives an account of the achievements of capitalism that is nothing short of glowing ("the bourgeoisie, during its rule of scarce one hundred years, has created more massive and more colossal productive forces than have all preceding generations together").

Marx and Engels go on to assert, however, that the very progress capitalism had achieved in freeing the development of productive forces from the fetters of the past, would lead to an increasing conflict between the bourgeoisie and proletariat. The proletariat, which in the dialectic vision of the class struggle is the progressive class under capitalism, the *Communist Manifesto* predicted, would win in this struggle and establish a new classless society with unlimited potential for economic development. Paradoxically, according to some experts, the prediction itself largely turned out to be true for advanced industrialized nations, although it happened without the proletarian revolution and in a way that was generally incompatible with the logic of class struggle envisioned by Marx and Engels.

After being expelled from several European countries for his involvement in the revolutionary movement, Marx finally settled in London in 1849 and had no source of income; Engels went back to work for his father in Germany in order to support Marx and his family. Engels continued his fairly successful business career together with revolutionary activities until 1869,

when he retired from business to solely serve the cause of Marxist socialism for the rest of his life. His most significant work during these years until his death in 1895 was to edit and publish the two last volumes of *Capital* that Marx left unfinished. In particular, Engels was left to struggle with the so-called transformation problem between the first and the third volumes of *Capital*.

According to Marx's theory of surplus value, the basis for capitalist profits should be proportional to the amount of living labor employed. But in reality, more mechanized processes that employ more capital goods and less labor tend to earn the same rate of profit on total capital invested as do the less mechanized processes. This implies that surplus value is not a function of labor employed alone.

The solution, apparently outlined by Marx himself and refined and published by Engels, basically amounts to changing the logic of analysis in the first volume in favor of a different logic of analysis in the third volume. Engels' preoccupation with this problem might have been in part responsible for his not noticing new trends of thought in economics that had emerged by that time (in particular, he "did not notice" Alfred MARSHALL's *Principles of Economics* published in 1890). All this contributed to the increased isolation of Marxism and especially of its communist wing from subsequent progress in mainstream economics and social thought.

After the death of Marx in 1883, Engels, in his own words, had to play the first fiddle for the first time. He did it through his writings that suggested the "orthodox" ways of interpreting Marx and through advising numerous newly emerging Marxist groups in various countries. Sometimes Engels tried to serve as a moderating influence, raising his voice against extreme emphasis on revolutionary violence. He could not, however, prevent the message of Marx ending up as the basis for the Leninist-Stalinist orthodoxy, shaping some of the most oppressive totalitarian regimes of the 20th century. Engels died in 1895 long before it all happened, but his name, just as the name of Marx, cannot be disassociated from that tragic history.

BIBLIOGRAPHY. Joseph A. Schumpeter, *Capitalism, Socialism, and Democracy* (Harper, 1950); Karl Marx and Friedrich Engels, *Manifesto of the Communist Party* (International Publishers, 1948); David Riazanov (Goldendach) *Karl Marx and Friedrich Engels* (International Publishers, 1927); Paul A. Samuelson, "Understanding the Marxian Notion of Exploitation: A Summary of the So-Called Transformation Problem Between Marxian Values and Competitive Prices," *The Journal of Economic Literature* (v.9/2, 1971).

SERGUEY BRAGUINSKY
STATE UNIVERSITY OF NEW YORK, BUFFALO

English Civil War

PART OF A LARGER STRUGGLE over the constitution of England's government, the English Civil War lasted from 1642 to 1649. The war was set against the background of the reigns of two Stuart kings, James I (1603–25) and Charles I (1625–49), who sought to expand the power of the English monarchy at the expense of the Parliament.

Charles I wanted Parliament to approve the levying of taxes to pay for the increased costs of government and the King's foreign policy endeavors, that included a costly war with Spain. Parliament refused to agree to the increased taxes. In fact, in 1628 its lower body, the House of Commons, passed the Petition of Right, which made it illegal to enact taxes without the consent of Parliament.

Charles had no intention of granting so much power to Parliament, for he sought to govern according to the divine right of kings, whereby he viewed himself as responsible only to God for his actions. From 1629 to 1640, he refused to call another Parliament and set out to rule on his own, raising taxes on his own authority. The most noteworthy fiscal act was his extension of the collection of Ship Money, a form of revenue designed to pay for the country's navy and defense. Traditionally, this tax had been imposed on coastal ports involved in shipping. Charles began to collect Ship Money from across England, including towns and counties in the interior. His actions sparked opposition not only because of their economic impact, but also because they infringed on traditional local rights.

Charles' religious policies also alienated important segments of the population and eventually brought a further clash involving the issue of taxation. In the mid-1500s the Protestant Reformation began to challenge the Anglican Church, the national church of England, that no longer accepted the authority of the Pope of Rome but still maintained many traditional Roman Catholic rites and doctrines, including the authority of bishops.

These challenges came primarily from the Calvinist forms of the Protestant belief. Scotland adhered to a Calvinist reform called Presbyterianism (from the word *presbyter*, in this sense meaning minister or elder). Presbyterians generally sought to eliminate the role and power of bishops in the church. They also advocated a simpler ritual. In these ways any return to the Catholic or Anglican traditions—that maintained a strong role for bishops and more elaborate ritual—was a threat to the Calvinist reforms. England's Puritans shared such Calvinist beliefs with the Scottish Presbyterians; it is no accident that North America was colonized by many of these religious reformers in the 1600s as they sought liberty in the New World to build their lives according to their beliefs, free from the volatile mix of politics, religion, and war in 17th-century England and Scotland.

Charles' religious policies alienated the Presbyterians in Scotland as well as the Puritans in England, many of whom were gentry and members of Parliament. Although the Stuarts were a Scottish line of royalty, it must be remembered that the monarchs of Europe were intermarried and brought with them the influences not necessarily of the lands they ruled, but of the environment and family in which they were raised. Charles' grandmother, Mary Queen of Scots, had important family ties to French royalty and Catholicism. When Charles became king, his actions confirmed the fears of reformers that he wanted to suppress the influence of Puritans and Presbyterians.

Charles married Henrietta Maria, a Catholic and sister of King Louis XIII of FRANCE. Also, under Charles the leading bishop in England, the Archbishop of Canterbury, sought to introduce more ritual into church life. When Charles tried to impose the Anglican *Book of Common Prayer* on the Scottish Presbyterians, the Scots rebelled.

Charles needed more revenue in order to suppress this uprising; to do this he was compelled to convene another Parliament in 1640. This assembly, known as the "Long" Parliament because it lasted, in various forms, until 1660, did not support the king. In fact, it severely restricted his power and brought to a head the dispute over royal authority. The Long Parliament not only prohibited taxes that were imposed without its consent, but also abolished those taxes, such as Ship Money, that had been levied by the king alone. It also eliminated the Star Chamber (named because it convened in a room decorated with stars), which was a council set up by King Henry VII a century earlier, because it adjudicated without a jury and represented royal authority. The Parliament also passed the Triennial Act, which called for parliaments to meet at least once every three years with or without royal consent. The Long Parliament, however, became divided over religious policy when its more radical Puritan members sought to eliminate bishops from the church and to establish a Presbyterian order. When Charles tried to arrest the radicals, England found itself in civil war.

The Royalists (also called Cavaliers), supporters of the king, were opposed by the Parliamentarians (whom the Royalists derisively called Roundheads because of the short hair that they wore). The Parliamentarians were victorious in the first phase of the war, which lasted from 1642 to 1646. They were aided by Scotland, which supported the Calvinist cause. Moreover, in 1645 the Parliamentarians created what is known as the New Model Army, which fought with a religious zeal driven by the radical Puritans. King Charles surrendered to the

Parliamentarians in 1646, but a new phase of the war began in 1648 when Charles escaped.

That same year Charles was captured again. The Parliamentarians' leader Oliver Cromwell (1599–1658), dismissed all but 53 members of the House of Commons (it had begun in 1640 with about 500), leaving what is known as the Rump Parliament. Cromwell, a Puritan and a member of the Long Parliament, was the head of a mounted regiment that he had formed (called the Ironsides) and a leader of the New Model Army. The dismissal purged Parliament of the more conservative Presbyterians, who wanted to establish a state church, in favor of the more radical Independents, who helped institute a policy of religious toleration for all—except for Unitarians, atheists, Roman Catholics, and staunch Anglicans.

The Rump Parliament tried and convicted the king of treason, beheading him on January 30, 1649. Even by 17th-century standards of violence and punishment, this was a shocking step to many people in Europe, for the members of the Rump Parliament had become regicides. The original dispute over royal power reached a conclusion that suppressed the power of kings completely: in 1649, Cromwell proclaimed the creation of an English republic, or Commonwealth, with himself as Lord Protector. The Commonwealth ruled on the basis of the Instrument of Government, the only time that England has had a written constitution. Cromwell found it difficult to rule, and the one-time defender of the rights of Parliament dispersed the remaining Rump Parliament in 1653. Thereafter, he ruled not through cooperation with the gentry, but as a dictator by military force.

The policies of religious toleration and the unprecedented involvement of common people in English political life aided the emergence of a variety of groups, many of which Cromwell suppressed. The most well-known groups were the Diggers (who repudiated private ownership of property and occupied common lands), the Levellers (who advocated a democratic republic, a written constitution, and a natural right to suffrage), the Fifth Monarchy Men (an extremist millenarian sect), and the Quakers. Cromwell died in 1658, naming his son as his successor. But England wearied of the arbitrariness of rule under the Commonwealth, and restored the monarchy in 1660 when Charles' son, Charles II, took the throne after an 11-year exile.

BIBLIOGRAPHY. C. Hibbert, *Cavaliers and Roundheads: The English Civil War, 1642–1649* (Macmillan, 1993); L.J. Reeve, *Charles I and the Road to Personal Rule* (Cambridge University Press, 1989); Anthony Fletcher, *The Outbreak of the English Civil War* (New York University Press, 1981); A. Fraser, *Cromwell, The Lord Protector* (Knopf, 1973); I. Gentles, *The New Model Army in England, Ireland, and Scotland,* *1645–1653* (Blackwell, 1992); Ronald Hutton, *The British Republic, 1649–1660* (St. Martin's Press, 2000); Christopher Hill, *Intellectual Origins of the English Revolution* (Clarendon Press, 1997).

GEORGE KOSAR
BRANDEIS UNIVERSITY

ENI

THE ENTE NAZIONALE IDROCARBURI (National Hydrocarbon Board) was established in 1953 to promote and develop ITALY's energy sector at a time when the country was completely unable to satisfy the increasing demand. Under the direction of Enrico Mattei (1906–62), ENI created new forms of contracts designed to improve the relationships between Italy and countries producing oil. These innovative contracts allowed local governments to participate more significantly in the management of oil concessions, leading to the producers' complete control of their resources.

Because of his views on the producers' role, Mattei often clashed with big corporations such as Esso (now ExxonMobil) and Shell and his death remains one of many Italian business mysteries. In addition to this foreign action, Mattei successfully persuaded Italy's industry to convert to natural gas since this was the country's main source of energy. ENI's PRIVATIZATION began in 1995, and approximately 70 percent of the company's activities now comprise international markets. In 2002, ENI ranked as the 71st largest company in the world with more than $44 billion in revenue.

BIBLIOGRAPHY. Nico Perrone, *Mattei il nemico italiano: politica e morte del presidente dell'ENI attraverso i documenti segreti, 1945-1962* (Leonardo, 1989); F. Venanzi and M. Faggiani, *ENI: Un'autobiografia* (Sperling & Kupfer, 1994); "Global 500: World's Largest Companies," *Fortune* (July 2002).

LUCA PRONO, PH.D.
UNIVERSITY OF NOTTINGHAM, ENGLAND

Enron

FORMED IN 1985, ENRON WAS the result of the merging of Houston Natural Gas and InterNorth. At the time of merger, the primary business of the newly formed company was the distribution of natural gas through interstate pipelines. The company experienced a phenomenal growth as a result of its expansion into electricity production and distribution, and trading commodities globally. In December 2001, the company filed for bankruptcy under Chapter 11 (reorganization) so that it could be protected from creditors' claims.

In just 15 years, Enron grew from nowhere to be America's seventh largest company, employing 21,000 people in more than 40 countries. At its peak, Enron's worth was estimated at about $70 billion and its shares traded at $90 per share. Enron's bankruptcy has been described as the second largest bankruptcy in the world history (after WorldCom). The rise and fall of Enron attracted widespread attention from academics, news media, stock exchanges, and regulatory agencies including the SECURITIES AND EXCHANGE COMMISSION (SEC), lawmakers, and also from the general public. What went wrong? What lessons can be learned and what are its implications on securities laws, accounting practices, campaign contributions reforms, and lobbying practices? Enron's story is now included as a topic of discussion in the auditing classes required for undergraduate and graduate level accounting students at many business schools throughout the country.

After its formation in 1985, Enron continued to build power plants and operate gas lines, but it became better known for its unique and creative trading businesses. After energy deregulation, the profit margin for Enron decreased suddenly and it started looking for other businesses. First it started buying and selling gas and electricity futures. It then introduced a new concept in commodities trading business. It created new markets for such "new commodities" as broadcast time for advertisers, weather futures, and internet bandwidth.

In order to finance its expansion, the company needed money from stockholders as well as from creditors. Enron created other companies and then established over 12 partnerships with the newly created corporations. Using and manipulating the complicated accounting rules to its advantage, it was successful in hiding loans that were primarily meant for Enron but concealed through these partnerships. Using this "off balance sheets financing," Enron was successful in concealing these loans and related interest charges. Expenses were understated by not reporting them properly while revenues were overstated by including sales to companies related to Enron. Top management was paid excessive salaries, bonuses, and other benefits. The problems resulting from its aggressive accounting practices eventually started to surface.

In October 2001, Enron reported its first quarterly loss in four years. In November 2001, it admitted to have overstated its earnings back to 1997 by about $600 million. Shares prices plunged to $4 per share, and its bonds that were issued to creditors officially became junk. On December 2, 2001, Enron applied for bankruptcy protection.

In the middle of all this, its auditors, Arthur Anderson, came under tremendous criticism from shareholders and employees of the company as well as from media, governmental, and regulatory agencies. They all wondered why the auditors did not catch this wrongdoing? The U.S. Justice Department charged Anderson for not following the Generally Accepted Auditing Standards and obstructing justice. The obstruction of justice charge mainly resulted from shredding the important audit-related documents after a court subpoenaed them.

The thousands of shareholders who saw their investment value drain down to zero are the primary people affected by Enron's collapse. Then, there are the thousands of employees who not only lost their jobs, but also saw the value of their pension funds plunge, as most of them had a significant portion of their retirement funds invested in Enron's stock. Other victims of Enron include financial institutions that lent money to the company; bondholders who loaned money to the company hoping to receive a decent return on their loans; the accounting profession, whose public credibility was damaged; and the stock market in general, because public trust in financial reporting was jeopardized.

As a result of the Enron situation, as well as other companies in similar straits, many accounting reforms were instituted both by the accounting profession as well as by lawmakers. In January 2002, the Sarbanes-Oxley Act, designed to raise standards of corporate accountability and prevent wrongdoing, was passed by the U.S. Congress.

The Act restricts consulting work that auditors perform for their publicly traded audit clients. It enforces new quality standards for the auditing firms and addresses such issues as the independence of the auditor, conflict of interest, and reinforces a public company's audit committees.

The 2002 law also requires a public company to assume more responsibility for the numbers in financial reports. It requires the CHIEF EXECUTIVE OFFICER (CEO) and the CHIEF FINANCIAL OFFICER (CFO) of these companies to attach a statement with the financial statements certifying the appropriateness of the financial statements and disclosures contained in the financial and reports submitted by them. It also embodies such issues as personal loans to officers, insider trading, etc.

Finally, the Sarbanes-Oxley Act imposes severe penalties in the case of misrepresentations and material inaccuracies included in financial and other reports.

The American Institute of Certified Public Accountants has issued exposure drafts of seven new auditing standards and invited discussion on them. Furthermore, on January 22, 2003, the SEC approved rules to implement the independence of auditors and other provisions of Sarbanes-Oxley Act.

Enron's financial calamity has had longer-term effects as well: Investors, in general, are expected to be more cautious and diligent about investing in any company, and to do the necessary analysis, research, and other homework before making their investment decisions.

BIBLIOGRAPHY. *Journal of Accountancy* (2001, 2002); Financial Accounting Standards Board, www.fasb.org; American Institute of Certified Public Accountants, www.aicpa.org; Enron, www.enron.com; Canadian Broadcasting Company, www.cbc.ca; BBC News, www.news.bbc.co.uk; National Public Radio, www.npr.org/news; Arthur Anderson, www.anderson.com.

SYED MOIZ, PH.D.
MARIAN COLLEGE

enterprise

PERHAPS DESCRIBED AS entrepreneurial projects that redirect human activity, enterprises take place within markets and organizations. ENTREPRENEURs undertake enterprises to replace existing states of affairs that they perceive with preferred alternatives that they imagine. Planning an enterprise means deciding between different means to achieve preferred ends. Such PLANNING takes place among many people, each with their own plans, and within existing institutions. The undertaking of an enterprise, in turn, alters the environment that it enters.

There are two main types of economic enterprises. Free market, or private enterprise aims toward profit through voluntary trade. Political enterprises make use of governmental agencies to affect wealth transfers. These two different types of enterprise yield distinct results, for those who implement and react to entrepreneurial action.

The planning of an enterprise takes place in four steps. Entrepreneurs gather data, perform calculations of value, execute their plans, and monitor results to detect and correct errors. The simultaneous coordination of many different plans requires that each incorporate into their plans all relevant data from other plans. Entrepreneurs acquire data for their enterprises through COMPETITION, and while competition informs and leads to coordination, its self-serving nature leads some to doubt its desirability.

Though entrepreneurs conduct private enterprise to earn profit, they benefit consumers in the process. This notion might seem odd, but since entrepreneurs must attract consumers to gain market share, they will serve consumer interests as an unintended consequence of pursuing their own selfish ambitions. As Adam SMITH put it, "It is not from the benevolence of the butcher, the brewer, or the baker, that we expect our dinner, but from their regard to their own interest. We address ourselves, not to their humanity but to their advantages."

The price system. The free enterprise system enables many businesses to coordinate their activities among each other. The price system, under free enterprise, works as a communications network and to inform sellers what buyers want most and least. They also inform buyers which products draw upon scarce resources the most, and therefore require the greatest conservation. Excessively high prices leave businesses with too many products and too few customers. This puts pressure on businesses to cut prices.

Conversely, excessively low prices leave markets with too many buyers for too few products. This prompts entrepreneurs to increase prices. In competitive markets, price adjustments lead to the greatest number of feasible trades and improve the allocation of resources.

The free enterprise system enables the decentralized planning of production. Prices inform and coordinate the activities of many independent individuals. Through competition, the plans of many adjust into a coherent set of plans for production based on specialization and division of labor. Price and quantity adjustments in markets reflect the reactions of consumers and entrepreneurs to each other's actions. Self-serving behavior in competitive markets leads to the unintended consequence of cooperation in planning production. The obvious lure of profits and subtle workings of the competitive free enterprise system create a cooperative order throughout society.

Entrepreneurs improve economic efficiency by being alert to profit opportunities. They notice a lower-cost means of satisfying consumer demand can earn higher profits, at least temporarily. Absent barriers to implementing more efficient means, others will emulate these methods. This emulation increases competition, reduces prices, and drives profitability down to competitive levels. By noticing better ways of serving customers, alert entrepreneurs improve economic efficiency while earning profit.

Free enterprise is an adaptive and innovative system. Organizational, legal, product, and technological innovations alter the outcomes of production and commerce. By adopting more productive or lower-cost methods businesses increase their odds of surviving competition. Free enterprise works as a natural selection process to weed out inferior products, technologies, strategies, and institutions.

Evolution of enterprise. This selection process applies to the evolution of business organization. Organizational innovations work to reduce costs and increase productivity. Business organizations exist because the costs in using markets sometimes exceed administrative costs in business. Entrepreneurs can hire consultants and independent contractors out of markets, or can organize firms with regular employees. By hiring consultants and independent contractors, entrepreneurs save on the cost of monitoring regular employees. On the other hand, contracting for temporary specialists entails its own costs. As market conditions change, entrepreneurs continually adapt the organization of their businesses.

Much of the pressure for reforming businesses comes from financial markets. The corporate form of ownership enables owners to delegate responsibility to managers. This also poses an informational problem. Corporate officers can abuse their authority at the expense of shareholders. As CHIEF EXECUTIVE OFFICER of RJR Nabisco, Ross Johnson spent corporate money lavishly on himself and others in this company. His management resulted in a low stock price, and an opportunity to change the management. Johnson attempted a leveraged buyout, but failed. Had Johnson succeeded, he would have been saddled with a large debt load that would have restricted him from wasting company funds. The new owners did assume a massive debt load. The result of this buy-out was that ownership became more concentrated, and the financing of this ownership shifted to debt.

Private institutions evolve and adapt to minimize many kinds of problems. The financial structure and internal organization of business, integration of industry, and terms of legal contracts all change as market conditions change. If businesses have trouble contracting with each other across stages of production, they can integrate vertically or laterally. In addition to organizational innovations, private enterprise often generates technological and product innovation.

Innovative enterprises. Combinations of different types of innovations sometimes produce unusual enterprises that produce surprising results. Tom Bourland launched one example of an unusual enterprise as a wildlife manager for 1.2 million acres of land for International Paper (IP). Bourland founded the company's Wildlife and Recreation program and began charging fees to hunters and campers. Once IP began earning profit from this new source, it changed its methods for harvesting trees in ways that increased the animal population and better preserved forests. By noticing a profit opportunity, Bourland changed IP's business practices in a way that simultaneously increased profits and addressed the concerns of conservationalists.

Hugh Macrae established a private network of hiking trails on Grandfather Mountain in North Carolina. This enterprise began in 1885, and has continued for more than a century. Over time, some changes have come: Macrae's descendents widened a horse trail to permit access by cars. Some of the scenic and environmental properties of this area came under threat by a federal highway project promoted by Franklin Delano ROOSEVELT. The owners managed to alter these plans, to preserve the scenic and ecological properties of the land. Some people are quick to criticize entrepreneurial capitalism for promoting environmental degradation. It is important to note that business enterprise aims toward what people value. Since many do value natural scenes and ecology, enterprises can earn profits in preserving nature.

John David ROCKEFELLER revolutionized the energy industry with a series of technological and organizational innovations. During the 19th century, many people used whale-oil lamps for light. Rockefeller set up kerosene refineries that provided a cheaper source of light for consumers, and also averted the imminent extinction of whales.

Rockefeller competed aggressively for market share and entered the kerosene market faced with a selling price of over $1 per gallon. Through vigorous competition, he pushed this price down by 90 percent, and earned a fortune for himself in the process. He was able to reduce his prices because innovations reduced his average costs from 3 cents to 0.29 cents per gallon. Rockefeller reduced his costs in many ways; one was to produce products he needed within his own organization whenever outsiders charged too much. Rockefeller built his own barrels, self-insured his business, and installed plumbing using people inside his own organization. Rockefeller also negotiated low rail rates for shipping his oil and bought out competitors. By buying out competitors, he ended inefficient procedures in these companies, and integrated their more cost-effective practices into his own.

Political enterprises. Political enterprises also aim toward profit and alter the economic environment. Political entrepreneurs lobby the government for income transfers, and there are many ways of affecting such transfers.

So long as new sellers can enter a market, incumbent sellers will lose market share if they raise prices above competitive levels. Legal entry barriers to a market are necessary for a single incumbent seller to sell as a monopolist, or several sellers to organize as and sell as a CARTEL. Legal entry barriers to markets enable entrepreneurs to raise prices and increase profits.

In a competitive political environment, entrepreneurs will bid away the expected gains from monopoly privilege. Such political enterprises not only reduce total market sales, they expend resources on a wasteful competition for special privileges.

The explicit purpose of antitrust laws is to reign in the excesses of private enterprise. Available data on industries initially accused of monopolistic pricing show that they increased output and reduced prices faster than in the rest of the economy. These companies acquired higher market share through superior efficiency and price-cutting, not through market power.

Antitrust laws have been used against companies that win market share through superior efficiency. ALCOA gained a high percentage of the primary market for aluminum. The judge in this case criticized ALCOA for doubling and redoubling its' capacity. The price of aluminum was $5 per pound in 1887, but fell to 50 cents in 1899, 38 cents in 1910, 22 cents in 1937, and 15 cents in 1941. Since output rose and prices fell in this market, it seems clear that ALCOA won market share through improved efficiency.

Entrepreneurs who fail in economic enterprises sometimes turn to seeking profit through political enterprise. Since political enterprises often restrict competition, raise prices, and lower output, it is often at odds with economic enterprises.

Other methods of transferring include lobbying for subsidies or regulations and initiating lawsuits. There may be circumstances that warrant transfers, but it is important to note that enterprises that transfer existing wealth do not create new wealth. Since all enterprises expend resources, purely redistributive enterprises reduce total wealth.

Enterprise can be either productive or wasteful. Within the context of secure property rights and voluntary trade, private enterprise is a competitive and creative process that drives the evolution of organizations, products, and technology. In contrast, political enterprise is a process by which a privileged few benefit from restricted trade and forced transfers.

BIBLIOGRAPHY. Armen Alchian, "Uncertainty and Evolution, and Economic Theory," *The Journal of Political Economy* (v.58/3, 1950); Terry Anderson, *Enviro-Capitalists* (Rowman and Littlefield, 1997); Dominick Armentano, *Antitrust and Monopoly* (John Wiley & Sons, 1981); Bryan Burrough and John Helyar, *Barbarians at the Gate: The Fall of RJR Nabisco* (HarperCollins, 1993); R.H. Coase, "The Nature of the Firm," *Economica* (v.4/16, 1937); F.A. Hayek, "The Use of Knowledge in Society," *The American Economic Review* (v.35/4, 1945); Michael C. Jensen, "Takeovers: Their Causes and Consequences," *The Journal of Economic Perspectives* (v.2/1, 1988).

D.W. MacKenzie
George Mason University

entrepreneur

ALTHOUGH THE LATE 1990s cult of the business executive faded within a few years, the activities of entre-

preneurs and their firms continue to represent a significant salient feature of modern capitalism in the eyes of even the casual observer of contemporary economic matters. Accordingly, it is somewhat puzzling for the beginning student of economics to find hardly any reference to entrepreneurship in an introductory textbook. This absence is due to the fact that the traditional analysis of markets emphasizes how firms choose their optimal course of action in response to a set of given and understood data. As William Baumol remarked more than three decades ago, the model describes the domain of business decision-making by reference to a class of well-defined problems "which need no entrepreneur for their solution."

The lack of emphasis on the role of entrepreneurship stems also from the practice of approaching the study of markets by focusing on the concept of perfect COMPETITION. While this is an important intellectual exercise, the realities of modern capitalist economies cannot be assimilated to the perfectly competitive economy of the textbook variety. Accounts of the defining institutional features of capitalist market economies and of the latter's long-term economic performance have to be sought elsewhere. Any historical or institutional account of the successes of capitalistic economies will pay only scant attention to the efficiency of perfectly competitive markets, and place entrepreneurs at or near center stage, delving into the transformations wrought on production and business activities by innovative firms over the last two centuries or so.

It will focus on factors like the dramatic changes in the market for automobiles that resulted from the strategy pursued by Henry FORD, or the concert of industrial and financial tactics adopted by the robber barons who dominated American capitalism at the end of the 19th century. Rather than illustrating the good deeds of Adam SMITH's invisible hand guiding the market economy, these accounts will detail the good and bad deeds of many visible hands, pursuing their own interests, propelling industries forward, and resisting adverse changes. These visible hands capture the role of entrepreneurship under capitalism.

Entrepreneurs and capitalism. The concept of entrepreneurship is central to accounts of capitalist development that emphasize its revolutionary nature and the pervasive impact of change on economic decisions. In this connection, entrepreneurship ought to be distinguished on a conceptual level from management or administration. The distinctive feature of entrepreneurial activity is that it focuses on carrying out something new and untried, on being first to exploit a possibly fleeting opportunity for personal gain. On the contrary, administration is concerned with the management of known and predictable processes, whose ends and means are well understood. Furthermore, it would be a mistake to identify the entrepreneur with the owner of the resources that are mobilized in order to carry out the entrepreneurial activity.

The requirement that entrepreneurial acts be distinguished by an element of novelty carries the implication that their outcome cannot be predicted reliably. Accordingly, it is common to characterize the entrepreneur as an individual bearing a risk of a rather special quality of his or her own volition, a conduct that is motivated by the expectation of personal gain. Within the context of business activities, entrepreneurship manifests itself in a variety of guises, including but not limited to the introduction of new products or new organizational practices.

Inasmuch as the lure of personal profit is the relevant inducement, it follows clearly that although customarily associated with the conduct of business, entrepreneurship can be exercised in any domain of human activity where novel opportunities for profit can be identified and pursued. Instances of these opportunities are the potential profits from arbitrage created by changes in prices for goods at different locations. Accordingly, an entrepreneur could benefit from his or her knowledge of such opportunities by buying goods at the low-price location and selling goods at the high-price location (note that these actions will reduce future arbitrage profits by reducing the price differential).

The role of the entrepreneur. The early analysis of capitalist market economies by the likes of Smith and other 19th-century economists clearly accounted for the profit motive of business, but their concept of entrepreneur or undertaker was typically defined as the individual responsible for organizing production. While useful for distinguishing it from the owner of capital, this definition of entrepreneurship blurs into that of management, and unlike the modern usage of the term, it does not emphasize the innovative nature of entrepreneurial activities, or its risk. The role of the entrepreneur as innovator receives a more emphatic discussion in Karl MARX's analysis of capitalist development. Marx describes the capitalist's pursuit of increased surplus value as occurring through the introduction of improved methods of production. Successful innovation of this sort rewards the capitalist entrepreneur with an increase in profits, at least until the new method of production becomes commonplace among other capitalists in the trade.

The role of entrepreneurial activity in sustaining the change of capitalist production methods, receives a more thorough analysis in the work of Joseph A. SCHUMPETER, an Austrian economist whose admiration for the achievements of capitalism was overwhelmingly based on its ability to sustain economic change. He argued:

Capitalism, then, is by nature a form or method of economic change and not only never is but never can be stationary. And this evolutionary character of the capitalist process is not merely due to the fact that economic life goes on in a social and natural environment which changes and by its change alters the data of economic action; this fact is important and these changes (wars, revolutions, and so on) often condition industrial change, but they are not its prime movers. The fundamental impulse that sets and keeps the capitalist engine in motion comes from the new consumers' goods, the new methods of production or transportation, the new markets, the new forms of industrial organization that capitalist enterprise creates.

Entrepreneurs are identified by their function, described as "to reform or revolutionize the pattern of production by exploiting an invention or, more generally, an untried technological possibility for producing a new commodity or producing an old one in a new way." Schumpeter clearly distinguishes the act of invention from that of innovation, the latter only being the province of the entrepreneur. While inventions could create unexploited opportunities for profiting from innovation, the inventor need not be either aware of them or capable of pursuing them effectively. On the other hand, the specialized focus of entrepreneurial activity is to scan the business environment for profit opportunities and to undertake the actions necessary to realize them. Accordingly, the successful entrepreneur primarily relies on his or her skills at acquiring and interpreting information and formulating conjectures about technological and market conditions. Further, a successful entrepreneur has to get things done and therefore needs personal qualities of leadership and self-confidence in order to overcome hurdles of different kinds.

An important element of Schumpeter's ideas is the belief that entrepreneurs carry out the important social function of promoting economic development even while pursuing innovative success for their own personal profit. Though the latter is largely the result of the monopolistic conditions created by innovation, Schumpeter understood these conditions to be temporary, and in any event a more desirable state of affairs from the viewpoint of social welfare than a world of perfect competition without innovation. The activities of imitators would progressively reduce the profits accruing to any innovator through the competitive mechanism, while subsequent innovations could recreate monopoly conditions, altering the structure of industries and forcing competitors to fight for their survival. The continuing efforts of entrepreneurs are therefore crucial for fueling the process of creative destruction that in Schumpeter's mind keeps the capitalist engine running.

In practice, Schumpeter observed a considerable change in the identity of the real-world actors who succeeded in carrying out the entrepreneurial function. While his early views on the matter underscore the individualistic nature of entrepreneurial activity, later in his life, Schumpeter witnessed the widespread rise to industrial dominance of large corporations whose innovative successes were increasingly based on continuing investment in research and development activities.

This development was part of broader organizational transformations in the nature of the business enterprises of modern capitalist systems. Small owner-managed firms had increasingly given way in industry after industry to firms whose activity was coordinated by hierarchies of professional managers, a transition that has been argued by Alfred Chandler to demarcate the end of the era of personal capitalism and the dawn of managerial capitalism. Differences among economists in the interpretation of these transformations focus on the social function of entrepreneurs and their future prospects.

Schumpeter interpreted the professionalization of business management as indicative that planning routines were beginning to encroach upon the domain of entrepreneurial activity and rapidly eroding its social value:

> For, on the one hand, it is much easier now than it has been in the past to do things that lie outside familiar routine—innovation itself is being reduced to routine. Technological progress is increasingly becoming the business of teams of trained specialists who turn out what is required and make it work in predictable ways. The romance of earlier commercial adventure is rapidly wearing away, because so many more things can be strictly calculated that had of old to be visualized in a flash of genius.

Schumpeter predicted, then, that entrepreneurs would soon cease to be necessary to keep the capitalist engine running. Furthermore, he associated the declining importance of entrepreneurial activity with the demise of capitalism itself as a form of economic change. Although coming to this conclusion from a rather different angle than Marx, Schumpeter predicted that capitalism would be supplanted by a socialist order dominated by large bureaucratic enterprises routinely pursuing innovation, whose management would become a matter of current administration. In spite of Schumpeter's erroneous predictions, attention should be called to the fact that he considered entrepreneurs to be an essential aspect of capitalist economies. Their pursuit of profit opportunities through innovation was the most important trait of competitive process in markets, a process that he considered to be a long distance from the textbook model of perfect competition.

Social value. Unlike Schumpeter, Thorstein VEBLEN reflected upon the transformation of industrial enterprise as sanctioning the subordination of the industrial activity (the machine process), whose commitment to the production of goods contributed to the social product, to the principles of business enterprise. The latter he considered to be directed to the accumulation of wealth as a result of arbitrage between purchase and sale prices. The subordination of industrial firms to the principles of business realized by the large corporations propelled the businessman or entrepreneur to a position of greater control over the economic welfare of the community. Contrary to Schumpeter's belief in the social value of the entrepreneurial function, Veblen characterizes the relationship between the interests of the entrepreneur and that of the community's welfare as antagonistic:

> The economic welfare of the community at large is best served by a facile and uninterrupted interplay of the various processes which make up the industrial system at large; but the pecuniary interests of the businessmen in whose hands lies the discretion in the matter are not necessarily best served by an unbroken maintenance of the industrial balance. Especially is this true as regards those greater businessmen whose interests are very extensive.

Furthermore, contrary to Schumpeter, who regarded the changes in industrial activity wrought by innovative entrepreneurs to actuate a socially beneficial process of creative destruction, Veblen considered the changes incidental to the businessman's pursuit of his own pecuniary gain to be on the whole hostile to the interests of the community:

> To the businessman who aims at a differential gain arising out of interstitial adjustments or disturbances of the industrial system, it is not a material question whether his operations have an immediate furthering or hindering effect upon the system at large. The end is pecuniary gain, the means is disturbance of the industrial system. . . . His gains (or losses) are related to the magnitude of the disturbances that take place, rather than to their bearing upon the welfare of the community.

The outcome of this management of industrial affairs through pecuniary transactions, therefore, has been to dissociate the interests of those men who exercise the discretion from the interests of the community.

Neither the growing size of the corporate enterprise of the early 20th century, nor its progressive bureaucratization led American economist Frank KNIGHT to believe that the scope for entrepreneurial activity, and its economic and social value, were waning. Knight considered entrepreneurship to be primarily concerned with decision-making under conditions of uncertainty that make the task of predicting the consequences of business actions especially difficult. The transformation of business firms could be interpreted accordingly as the evolution of social arrangements for dealing with the presence of business risk, a risk associated with "the exercise of judgment in the making of decisions by the business man," that is, to entrepreneurial activity.

Whereas insurance firms can achieve predictability of outcomes by pooling independent risks, business risks weighing on the prospects of an enterprise cannot be so reduced according to Knight because of the MORAL HAZARD involved in insuring an entrepreneur against the consequences of the exercise of his own judgment.

Knight perceives the entrepreneur himself to be the party who can best undertake the pooling of business risks associated with his own judgment by expanding his control over an increasing range of decisions. Thus, instead of reducing the scope for entrepreneurial decision-making, the large enterprise provides the institutional vehicle for increasing the scope of operations and the range of decisions placed under the control of a single entrepreneur.

In Knight's view, the emergence of corporations controlled by entrepreneurial managers represents an effective institutional response to the presence of uncertainty in economic affairs. Drawing an important distinction between quantifiable risk and uncertainty, he argues that uncertainty thus exerts a fourfold tendency to select men and specialize functions:

1. an adaptation of men to occupations on the basis of kind of knowledge and judgment

2. a similar selection on the basis of degree of foresight, for some lines of activity call for this endowment in a very different degree from others

3. a specialization within productive groups, the individuals with superior managerial ability (foresight and capacity of ruling others) being placed in control of the group and the others working under their direction

4. those with confidence in their judgment and disposition to "back it up" in action specialize in risk taking.

These selection forces and the specialization of productive roles manifest themselves in the emergence of managerial entrepreneurs who specialize in the exercise of judgment and the taking of the attendant business risks. The difference between Schumpeter's and Knight's positions on the future of entrepreneurship hinged on the question of whether or not innovation would become routinized as a result of the growth of large industrial enterprises. The subsequent history of capitalist economies has sided with Knight on this matter. Entrepreneurship continues to play an important role in fostering innovation and there is hardly any evidence to support the notion that innovation has been routinized.

The fallacy of the Schumpeterian prophecy is likely due to his unnecessarily belittling view of planning activities and his underlying assumption that the growing sophistication of scientific and technological knowledge would have eliminated uncertainty from the business decisions that are the realm of entrepreneurial activity. Schumpeter conjures up a historical path of development along which the uncertainty surrounding economic decisions, which promotes and rewards entrepreneurial activity in the capitalist stage, will slowly vanish. As human knowledge, particularly scientific and technological, accumulates and reduces the impact of uncertainty on economic organization, business decisions become increasingly of the planning variety, heralding the beginning of a socialist stage of economic development.

In contrast to the Schumpeterian view, the Austrian economist Friedrich von HAYEK regarded planning as an activity requiring continuous adaptations to unpredictable changes in economic conditions. How effectively these adaptations will be made is at once an important determinant of social welfare and an important outcome of the economic organization of society, a central concern for Hayek and for the AUSTRIAN SCHOOL economists, more generally. From this vantage point, Hayek judged the decentralized decision-making typical of a market economy to be an effective organizational principle because each individual is motivated by the incentive of personal gain to behave in ways that foster efficient adaptations of society's economic plan to changes in economic conditions.

The gist of this invisible-hand-like argument is that changes in economic conditions have two kinds of consequences. First, they require that the economy-wide allocation of resources be adapted. Second, they create profit opportunities for those individuals who learn about the changes in economic conditions before the relevant adaptations have occurred. Since knowledge about changes is fragmented among many individuals and across different locations, decentralized decision-making induces the better-informed individuals to act in entrepreneurial fashion upon the emerging opportunities for profits. By doing so, they foster the efficient adaptations in the allocation of resources. Therefore, a fundamental aspect of entrepreneurship is the identification and exploitation of profit opportunities on the basis of superior knowledge.

Decision-making. If economic change and the fragmentation of knowledge about it are the basis for entrepreneurial decision-making, there is no reason to confine the latter's domain to technological or organizational innovation, or even just to business activity. Borrowing Geoffrey Hodgson's words (*Economics and Evolution*, 1994), Hayek's "molecular view of the modern economy in terms of entrepreneurial individuals" who exercise their judgment for the pursuit of personal gain, suggests that the institutional structure of the economy plays a critical role in determining the domain of entrepreneurship in different societies or at different times in history.

By recognizing the variety of purposes to which entrepreneurial judgment can be directed, these views are remarkably sophisticated and of phenomenal interest for anyone interested in interpreting and understanding the role of entrepreneurship in the contemporary organization of industry.

Entrepreneurs are "persons who are ingenious and creative in finding ways that add to their own wealth, power, and prestige," whose activities cannot be automatically considered as performing a valuable social function. Although the Schumpeterian view emphasizes the productive value of entrepreneurial activities aimed at the introduction of new technologies or new organizational practices, or the opening up of new markets, and so on, entrepreneurial judgment and efforts can be directed to individually profitable activities that are unproductive or even destructive of social value, as Veblen noticed at the dawn of the 20th century. The potential for conflict between the motives of individual entrepreneurs and broader social economic goals affects different societies in varying degrees and with different outcomes, as social, political, and economic institutions determine whether and how that potential is transformed into actual conflict. Thus, while in some countries the problem of unproductive and destructive entrepreneurship resurfaces only from time to time, and with relatively modest effects on social well being, in others it is endemic and plays an important role in explaining their difficulties in experiencing sustained economic development.

BIBLIOGRAPHY. Joseph A. Schumpeter, *Theory of Economic Development* (Transaction Publishers, 1934); Joseph A. Schumpeter, *Capitalism, Socialism, and Democracy* (HarperCollins, 1947); Thorstein B. Veblen, *The Theory of Business Enterprise* (Penguin, 1904); Frank Knight, *Risk, Uncertainty and Profit* (Beard Group, 1921); Friedrich von Hayek, "The Use of Knowledge in Society," *American Economic Review* (1945); William J. Baumol, *Entrepreneurship, Management, and the Structure of Payoffs* (MIT Press, 1993); Alfred Chandler Jr., *The Visible Hand* (Harvard University Press, 1977).

ROBERTO MAZZOLENI, PH.D.
HOFSTRA UNIVERSITY

equilibrium, partial/general

EQUILIBRIUM, ACCORDING TO Webster's *New Twentieth Century Dictionary*, is defined as "an even balance." In economics, this refers to a balancing between the desire of consumers to pay lower prices and producers to receive higher prices for various quantities of goods and services.

In a single market, say the unleaded 87-octane gasoline market, the quantity level at which consumers are willing to pay what producers will accept is an equilibrium quantity level. The price at which this happens is an equilibrium price. The equilibrium is called a partial equilibrium because the influences of the variables in all other markets are neutralized.

When equilibrium happens in all markets for goods and services simultaneously, it is called a general equilibrium. The variables in each market affect the activity in all markets. Economists have labored long and hard to show the existence and stability of both partial and general equilibrium under various simplifying assumptions. General equilibrium is the truer picture, but it is more difficult to specify and numerically compute. While this is true at a single point in time, the difficulty increases further when equilibrium systems are tracked over time.

General equilibrium. General equilibrium (hereafter, GE) analysis tries to give an understanding of the economy as a whole using a microeconomic or bottom-up approach. It starts with individual buyers and sellers in each particular market. GE models typically represent a collection of different goods and services markets, each good and service defined by a fixed level of quality. In a free-market economy, the prices and quantities of all goods and services are related to each other, albeit by decentralized decisions. Determining the equilibrium price-quantity pair of any one good or service would require information on the prices and quantities of all of the thousands of different goods and services that are available. A daunting task, to put it mildly.

Adam SMITH (1723–1790), a Scottish philosopher and the "father" of modern economics, portrayed an implicit GE framework in *The Wealth of Nations*: individuals, in pursuing their own self-interests, will generate the maximum general welfare of society as if guided by an invisible hand.

Leon WALRAS (1834–1910), a French engineer-economist, is widely regarded as the "father" of formal GE theory. He showed that under certain restrictive assumptions, the equilibrium prices and quantities for all goods and services in an economy could conceptually be determined as the solution to a series of simultaneous equations. Walras set forth the (then) new marginalist or neoclassical theory in a formal GE setting. The innovation of the approach to GE theory of the Belgium-born, Italian engineer-economist-sociologist, Vilfredo Pareto (1848–1923), was its focus on individual optimizing behavior in a price-taking, multi-market framework. He also discussed the social efficiency that results from independent decentralized decision making. Pareto justified the price-taking aspect of the theory on the basis of the impossibility of market manipulation by any individual, in a sufficiently complex economy. Mathematically, however, Pareto assumed that the functions involved were differentiable. Differentiability means that the analyst is able to compute the first (slope) and second (slope of the slope) derivatives of these functions. The Paretian model differs from the Walrasian model in that the "tastes-and-obstacles" structure of the former replaces the "demand-and-supply" functions of the latter.

Economics in the post-WORLD WAR II period retained the tastes-and-obstacles optimization structure of the Paretian system, but it essentially avoided its differentiability assumptions and effectively reproduced the same results without it. Seminal works of this period were those of Nobel Prize winners, Kenneth ARROW and Gerard DEBREU, in the 1950s. The question of whether their reliance on convexity (the property of a set of points that a line drawn between any two points on its boundary lies entirely in the set) is more "general" is a thorny issue.

Some economists and many non-economists criticize the intense mathematics that has been used to refine GE models in the decades following the early Arrow-Debreu formulations as being mere mental gymnastics with no hope of application. Mathematical economists argue that basic research on models such as these puts specific applications into broader perspective, and therefore, is important. The debate continues.

Modern GE models are typically complex, require strong assumptions, and are fed into computers to achieve numerical solutions. Wassily LEONTIEF created a particular type of quasi-GE model, input-output analysis. I-O analysis was partly inspired by the Walrasian analysis of GE via inter-industry flows. Each output is a linear "recipe" of all other outputs in the economy. The output of each industry in the solution of these simultaneous linear equations must cover all other industry demands and the demand of final users. I-O analysis has been a mainstay of economic policy and planning throughout the world for the past half-century. Computable GE models of economic systems need to make restrictions often similar to I-O analysis on the underlying mathematical functions. Herbert Scarf is generally thought to be the first pioneer in the use of these models in the 1960s.

Partial equilibrium. Alfred MARSHALL (1842–1924) used the partial equilibrium (PE) approach to analyze a single generic market. He devised the most famous model used in economics, the demand and supply ("scissors") model. Marshall postulated that when the expenditure on the good or service under study is a small portion of a consumer's total expenditure, only a small fraction of any additional dollar of wealth will be spent on this good or service.

Also, with similarly small substitution effects, or the changes in quantity that result from changes in the price of one good or service relative to others, the small size of the market under study leads the prices of other goods to be approximately unaffected by changes in this market. The advent of the PE approach brought with it the use of the Latin phrase, *ceteris paribus,* interpreted as "other things remaining equal."

In PE analysis, the determination of the equilibrium price-quantity pair for a good or service is simplified by just looking at the price of one good, and assuming that prices and quantities of all other goods and services remain constant. Partial equilibrium analysis is usually considered adequate when the item to be analyzed is fairly insignificant when compared to the economy as a whole.

However, with appropriate assumptions, economists can apply PE analysis to any market. PE models of markets, or of systems of related markets, determine prices, outputs, profits and other variables of interest adhering to the assumption that there are no feedback effects from these endogenous magnitudes to the underlying demand or cost curves that are specified in advance. An individual's wealth (the value of the assets that he or she owns) is often treated as exogenous (outside of the model) in partial equilibrium theory.

Market failure. Though GE is almost always a more theoretically correct approach than PE, the GE model that is based on the assumption of perfect COMPETITION theoretically breaks down in some cases. In other cases, this assumption precludes its applicability to various real-world situations.

Certain phenomena that occur in the real world cause theoretical trouble for the elegant GE models. They are known as sources of market failure. The market failure due to incomplete information is discussed below under Disequilibrium Economics. Externalities are costs or benefits arising from production or consumption that directly affect third parties. They are not recognized by markets. The presence of externalities often precludes the theoretical solution to GE models by making the equations interdependent. A monopoly is a firm that solely produces a particular good or service and has leverage over the price or quantity of that good or service. There is no supply curve in a monopoly market, and the marginal cost pricing of perfect competition is violated. GE models often are not applicable in the presence of a monopoly.

In the case of a (pure) public good, if one person or organization provides a good or service, then everyone else in a relevant group can use that good or service without paying for it (non-excludability), and that use will not diminish the use of anyone else (non-rivalry). The presence of public goods links the functions of the individuals, and demand is often under-revealed due to the free-rider problem. These phenomena cause trouble for the strict GE models. The theory of the second best deals with how an economy can reach its best allocation of resources in the presence of these sources of market failure. While a theoretical representation is sometimes possible, the computational difficulties are often insurmountable.

Disequilibrium economics. Carl MENGER (1840–1921), "father" of the AUSTRIAN SCHOOL of economics, is thought to have lead the discussion on the difference between equilibrium theory and what goes on in the real world. Among the component assumptions of perfect competition underlying GE and PE theory are perfect information and perfect mobility of economic agents.

There has been a growing trend in the economics literature to look at markets as dynamic processes instead of static objects. In the absence of perfect information, economic players may undertake search behavior to find an optimal price, or a certain quantity or quality of a good or service, in a geographical region. Less than perfect mobility may occur when a lucrative job opens up in another city for one spouse, while the other just found a lucrative job in the present city. The first spouse may not make the move, and the job may go unfilled. Equilibrium theory allows for no such complications.

BIBLIOGRAPHY. Alfred Marshall, *Principles of Economics* (Macmillan, 1890); Vilfredo Pareto, *Manual of Political Economy* (1906); James Quirk and Rubin Saposnik, *Introduction to General Equilibrium Theory and Welfare Economics* (McGraw-Hill); H.E. Scarf, "On the Computation of Equilibrium Prices," *Ten Economic Studies in the Tradition of Irving Fisher* (John Wiley, 1967); Leon Walras, *Elements of Pure Economics*, William Jaffé, trans. (Irwin, 1965); "General Equilibrium," www.wikipedia.org.

JOHN SORRENTINO, PH.D.
MAHBUB RABBANI, M.A.
TEMPLE UNIVERSITY

equity

IN ITS ONE-DIMENSIONAL accounting definition, equity equals assets minus liabilities, in which case shareholders' equity, net worth, and book value are all synonymous. Is that all there is to equity?

No, equity is, in fact, the backbone of a company's balance sheet as well as the designation for an individual's net worth. In the corporate classification, equity is detailed on a business enterprise's balance sheet and is part of the "right side of the balance sheet." It is what remains after assets and liabilities are netted. Therefore, equity is what the shareholders own, as opposed to what is owed. It is applied in the same sense as household equity, where a homeowner's equity is the difference between what a property is worth and what the owner owes on that property.

When we speak of equity most people think of homes. Without a doubt, many who own a home may have a good percentage of their total net worth in that property. The equity in the home is the difference between the fair market value of the property and the amount owed on the mortgage (the liability). The equity is built up not only by payments to principal of the mortgage, but by appreciation as well; how much the price or worth of a home increases over the years

The concept of corporate equity is quite similar, though it has scores of more complicated components. First, there is ownership interest in a corporation, which is in the form of capital stock—both common and preferred. Shareholders holding common stock receive voting rights and dividends in the case of payouts, but end up at the bottom of the hierarchy for the receipt of corporate assets in the case of liquidation. The other type of capital stock is preferred stock, and preferred stockholders are exactly that: they may receive identifiable dividends before any common shareholders receive them, and in the event of liquidation, preferred shareholders take precedence over common stockholders. There can be numerous categories of preferred stock, but further categorization has no bearing on the overall integrity of equity.

Another component of equity is retained earnings, the earnings that are retained by the corporation. Earnings may be retained to pay dividends to shareholders or to pay off debt, or the money may be earmarked for specific purpose such as in the case of restricted retained earnings. Additionally, since both common and preferred stock are carried at par value on a corporation's balance sheet, additional paid-in capital represents amounts received in excess of the par or stated value of the shares sold. Sometimes, simplified financial statements will not separate the stock value from the excess amounts paid in, but instead will lump together all amounts that stockholders have paid into the company in exchange for stock under paid-in capital.

So then, does equity just sit out there as the lingering end to an equation, or does it have a more significant representation overall?

Shareholder equity is representative of a measured amount of funds and it is never a residual amount. The true measurement of equity (outside of the balance sheet accounting equation) is not as simple as assets minus liabilities. Thus, equity is more accurately measured as the sum of paid-in capital (stock at par value, and any excess over that value) and earnings retained by the corporation.

One mistake that is often made is thinking that all equity represents a claim. Although preferred stock may represent a claim above that of the common shareholder, the equity of a common shareholder is not a claim against any assets of the corporation. That is because, as a rule, a company's balance sheet reflects its book value as opposed to its fair-market value. The left side of the balance sheet is represented by assets, which are at cost and not fair value, except for certain kinds of marketable securities. Consequently, since the right side of the balance sheet—with liabilities and equity—balances to the left side, there is no monetary amount embodied by the shareholders' claim. In any case, if a business is liquidated, the sale price rarely will equal its book value.

The conventional balance sheet measurement of equity does not tell us all we need to know about it, for there are many measurements of performance that the professional analyst or investor uses in order to determine whether or not a corporation has a good grasp on the maintenance of equity. For example, equity turnover is calculated by dividing a company's annual sales by the average stockholders' equity. This essentially calculates the return on equity and thus quantifies how well a company is using its equity to generate revenue. The analyst also looks at the equity multiplier, wherein assets are divided by the total common stockholders' equity as a way to measure leverage, or how much a company is relying on debt to finance its asset base.

So indeed, equity is at the nucleus of a corporation's (or an individual's) financial strength. Bear in mind that a profitable enterprise operates over the long run to earn a satisfactory return on its investment, and the higher the income, the more positive the flow into the company's equity accounts. And the bottom line is that a corporation has to maintain its equity, otherwise it goes bankrupt.

BIBLIOGRAPHY. Robert N. Anthony, *Tell It Like It Was: A Conceptual Framework for Financial Accounting* (Irwin, 1983); Jan R. Williams, Keith G. Stanga, and William W. Holder, *Intermediate Accounting* (Dryden, 1995); W.T. Baxter and Sidney Davidson, *Studies in Accounting Theory* (John Wiley and Sons, 1962).

KAREN DE COSTER
WALSH COLLEGE

Estonia

THE REPUBLIC OF ESTONIA is bordered by RUSSIA, LATVIA, the Gulf of Finland, and the Baltic Sea. With a population of 1.41 million (2002), Estonia gained its independence in 1918 after being ruled by a series of governments dominated by DENMARK, SWEDEN, GERMANY, and Russia. In 1940, the country was subjugated by the UNION OF SOVIET SOCIALIST REPUBLICS and forced into its ranks. Estonia regained its independence when the Soviet Union broke apart in 1991, and since 1994 Estonia has been developing a capitalist economy and nurturing political associations with the rest of the world.

Estonia is a parliamentary republic divided into 15 counties with a GROSS NATIONAL PRODUCT (GNP) in 2001 of approximately $14.3 billion. As a member of the WORLD TRADE ORGANIZATION (WTO), the country was expected to formally join the EUROPEAN UNION in 2004. Estonia's primary industries are engineering, electronics, wood and wood products, and textiles. Its major commodity is focused in the labor and services categories of the economy, with 69 percent of the labor force composed of service-oriented positions. It is no surprise then that some of its most dominant industries are transit, information technology, and telecommunications.

By joining the North Atlantic Treaty Organization (NATO) in March, 2004, Estonia established the political and military stability it needs to foster economic growth. As with its Baltic neighbors, Latvia and LITHUANIA, Estonia looks to its NATO, EU, and WTO memberships as catalysts for capitalistic success.

BIBLIOGRAPHY. *CIA Work Factbook* (2003); Estonian Ministry of Foreign Affairs, www.vm.ee.

ARTHUR HOLST, PH.D.
WIDENER UNIVERSITY

ethics

CAPITALISM IS INVOLVED with ethics in three major ways:

1. certain moral behaviors make capitalism possible

2. the values conducive to capitalism may come into conflict with other moral values

3. questions about how the world works can become conflated with moral issues leading to acrimonious debates and bad policy.

Moral behaviors make capitalism possible. Max Weber advanced the proposition that moral values shape economic life in *The Protestant Ethic and the Spirit of Capitalism.* More recently, in *The Fatal Conceit,* Friedrich von HAYEK argued that civilization depends on moral values; morals are not the product of reason; and living in civilization produces conflicts for people.

Hayek's notion of civilization is the "extended order." This is in contrast with the tribal order that he considers to be "natural," that is, the way people ended up as a result of biological evolution. The extended order depends on markets for its organization. Exchange permits specialization, which allows great productivity in the use of resources. This allows population growth, which has resulted in the predominance of the extended order over tribal organization.

Exchange depends on private property rights. Exchange outside of the natural tribe depends on the cessation of hostility to outsiders. This requires a suppression of the natural tribal instincts of people. In the tribe, property is communal. Tribes have solidarity within, but view foreigners as enemies.

In Hayek's analysis morals are neither the product of instinct nor reason. This goes against much of traditional moral philosophy, as well as against sociobiology. Sociobiologists have attempted to show that altruistic behaviors, such as childcare, can be explained as a product of natural selection. Hayek does not reject this explanation for some of the behaviors we call moral; however, wolves also behave altruistically toward fellow pack members. Hayek does not want to use the term "moral" for instinctive impulses. He reserves it for rules such as respecting property, being civil to non-tribe members, and various sexual restrictions. These are not instinctive. They must be taught. They are taught by rote during childhood so that they become virtually indistinguishable from instincts.

While one may come to see reasons for morals later in life, they are not passed on by an appeal to the intellect. This illuminates the role of institutions such as families, churches, and schools as bearers of civilization. If most citizens do not abide by these rules, police and courts cannot regulate people's behavior sufficiently to defend civilization.

The behavioral restraints that make civilization possible feel oppressive to individual citizens. Being naturally tribal, many people feel unsatisfied by "mass culture." The yearning for tribal solidarity leads them to seek identity in traditional cultures and in invented tribes oriented around specialized interests and activities. It also leads to political calls for collectivism, which almost always implies weakening private property rights.

Rather than being progressive, Hayek sees this as an atavistic animal impulse, as quaint as a war dance. At worst, requiring decisions about resource use to be communally approved could destroy the intricate market web that permits us to enjoy the benefits of specialized knowledge without personally having to possess that knowledge. If this were to happen, it is doubtful that present levels of population could be sustained.

Capitalism and conflicting values. In *Systems of Survival*, Jane Jacobs, like Hayek, views morals as products of evolution, but she differentiates between two major systems, which she calls "syndromes." These are the evolutionary result of two ways of making a living: taking and trading. The guardian syndrome developed from the activities of seizing, defending, and administering territory. It is the traditional moral system of the aristocracy. Among the 15 values that Jacobs associates with the guardians are: disdain for commerce, obedience and discipline, adherence to tradition, ostentatious display of status, and dispensing largesse.

The commercial syndrome is associated with trade. It is the middle-class value system. Within it, it is morally desirable to: get things through trading rather than force, respect contracts rather than hierarchies, be inventive and open to new ideas, and to be thrifty. There may be a third syndrome. The largesse of the aristocrats toward peasants creates expectations. Demands that corporations "give back to the community" or that elected officials must "take care of the working man" suggest a "peasant syndrome" that is the symbiotic counterpart of the guardian syndrome.

Jacobs argues that both moral systems are necessary for civilization. The existence of commerce depends on the guardians establishing and defending property rights. The guardians need the innovativeness and productivity of commerce for plentiful food and advanced weapons and equipment. Problems arise two ways. First, when the two systems mix they can produce "monstrous hybrids," such as police or judges selling their services or employees of a firm who, out of loyalty, turn a blind eye to fraud or theft. Second, a good deal of apparently irresolvable controversy results from clashes of values from the two systems.

Alasdair MacIntyre argues that many modern ethical disputes are irresolvable, because the values and principles that we have inherited are disconnected fragments of ethical systems that were originally embedded in now defunct cultures. It is as though we were trying to do science after a Dark Age with nothing to instruct us but single, half-charred pages and torn sections of books. This is one reason why the values that engender capitalism come into conflict with other values.

Among the legal, technical, and cultural changes that allowed capitalism to develop were the secularization of European society and the emergence of the middle class as a political and economic power. Modern cosmopolitan citizens have been influenced by a wide array of cultural, class, and religious backgrounds. While they may agree broadly about which moral values are desirable, there are great differences about what precisely are the meaning and significance of those values, and about their relative priority when they come into conflict with other things that are important. What follows is a brief discussion of some of the values that figure most prominently in connection to capitalism: prosperity, liberty, equality, and democracy.

Most things that people want to do require material means. Prosperity is simply having the means to accomplish one's goals. Aristotle cautioned that one should not confuse the means to a good life with a good life itself. This presumably is the underlying basis for much of the scorn directed at "materialism." Are very many people materialistic in this sense? Are "materialists" mindlessly trying to acquire things, or are they attempting to achieve goals, such as power, status, high self-esteem, security, or being loved? The critic may disapprove of these goals, or may think it fruitless to try to reach them by these means. The disapproval would be more accurately aimed at the goals or at the faulty reasoning than at a mythical quest for material things.

For Adam SMITH material prosperity had moral significance. Smith thought that poverty was a major cause of evil. In his *Theory of Moral Sentiments*, Smith explained the capacity for moral judgment as residing in an impartial spectator within us who judged our actions according to whether others would be sympathetic to them or not. This, Smith thought, was universal. The particular content of the spectator's judgment, however, was culturally determined. Cultures with a history of extreme poverty developed an indifference to suffering, their own and that of others, long after their material circumstances changed and this trait ceased to have survival value.

Smith's *The Wealth of Nations* is an important contribution to the literature of classical liberalism, not to be confused with the late 20th-century American variety. Classical liberalism is a political philosophy that places emphasis on individual liberty. To the classical liberals, "liberty" meant negative liberty. Rights are closely associated with liberty, in that they articulate what one is actually free to do. Freedom of speech in the negative sense means that others are obligated not to punish you for voicing unpopular opinions. The negativity is the nature of the obligation implied by such a right. Other people must not do something. If, on the other hand, freedom of speech were construed to mean that one is entitled to time on television, or that people had to listen, this would be a positive liberty. If one asserts that people have rights to adequate food, housing, or medical care, these are positive rights.

Historically, one of the most important rights asserted by classical liberals such as John LOCKE, was private property. Having property rights over something means not only that one can possess something, but also that one can determine the use of it, and transfer these rights to others. Private property rights are a foundation of a market system. Knowing that such rights are secure, stable, and well defined allows people to exert productive efforts on the things they own with the expectation that they will reap the rewards. Why make long-lasting improvements to the soil, for example, if your land is subject to capricious confiscation by the authorities? Positive rights typically conflict with the right to private property. A right to adequate nutrition implies that someone else has an obligation to provide food.

Locke thought that unequal distribution of wealth was an inevitable consequence of private property and the use of money. Differing talents, degrees of ambition, and luck would cause differing success in accumulation. Locke thought this was justified since by agreeing to the use of money, people had agreed to the results.

Robert Nozick argues that inequality results from liberty. Even if everyone were given equal shares of the national income, people's individual preferences would cause them to spend this in different ways, for example, paying to see talented basketball players, that would cause the distribution of wealth to end up unequal.

The UNITED STATES *Declaration of Independence* proclaims that all men are created equal as a self-evident truth. Since people are obviously unequal in many ways, in what way was this meant? In the historical context in which it was written, the assertion of equality was in opposition to a European background of institutionalized privilege. It meant that people were equal in some moral or religious sense.

In attempting to implement this as a feature of political and civil life, one thing equality might mean is equal opportunity. People should be allowed to advance according to their performance, regardless of various accidents of birth. Lack of belief that opportunities really can be equal has led to some demands for equal results. The questions do not end here, however, because one must specify what exactly is supposed to be equal. Should it be money incomes, or physical quantities of things, or should it be happiness?

Democracy literally means "government by the people." What this definition practically implies is less than clear. Does it mean that decisions require unanimity, majority, or plurality? What, if any, are the limits of democratic power? Who are the people? Must they be males, adults, Caucasians, property owners, literate, and citizens? Since the collapse of eastern European communism in 1989, various forms of liberal democratic capitalism have become the predominant mode of economic and political organization. This is often referred to as "democracy." Since liberalism restrains the power of governments to interfere with individual liberties, and capitalism requires stable, secure property rights, this usage suggests that when people say "democracy," they are thinking of a form that is restricted by a constitution.

While liberalism in the classical sense is historically closely connected to capitalism, the compatibility of capitalism and democracy has been more tenuous. Lord J.E.E.D. Acton points out that the great gift of the ancient Greeks was not democracy, but the lesson that democracy needs to be restrained. Aristotle said that democracies are usually unable to resist the temptation to use the power of government to redistribute the wealth from the few to the many. In response, the rich organize to protect themselves leading perhaps to tyranny. This seems consistent with a pattern that occurred many times in the 20th century in Latin America. Capitalism depends on private property rights. People with little or no property may not view the defense of property as the most essential function of government.

Joseph SCHUMPETER saw a different way that democracy would threaten capitalism. He thought that the entrepreneurs, whose innovative spirit was vital to capitalism, came from the aristocracy. Administering a business after it matures is different from sensing an opportunity and creating a business to profit from it. As capitalism matured, Schumpeter thought that it would come to be dominated by mature businesses run by conservative bureaucrats. In a democratic system these corporate types would prevail. They would see no reason why an economy cannot be administered by a bureaucracy just like a large corporation. Thus, the success of capitalism would lead to SOCIALISM.

One way that capitalism is democratic is that resources are directed according to how consumers vote with their dollars. Sellers supply what people are willing to pay for. This is sometimes a source of tension. While the market system is responsible for average people enjoying unparalleled material wealth, it is in the form of cheeseburgers, mindless television shows, and sport utility vehicles rather than healthful vegetarian cuisine, Shakespeare, and emission-free electric cars.

Liberty, in the negative sense, is compatible, probably necessary for prosperity. Attempts to enforce material equality conflict with the right to private property, and therefore threaten prosperity. Democracy can be hostile to capitalism. Which of these is more important? If MacIntyre is correct, it may be impossible to settle such questions through reasoned argument. Isaiah Berlin sees danger in the belief that all good things must be capable of being brought into a "single harmony of truths." Following close behind is the belief that those who are privy to this truth should command those who are not. This was a driving force in the "isms" that were responsible for the convulsions of the 20th century. Tolerant societies based on the understanding that people have different goals in life and different moral priorities may be truer to the actual condition of the modern cosmopolitan world. Such pluralistic societies allow individuals the freedom to work out their own solutions, which may be the best we can hope for.

Moral issues conflated with questions about how the world works. Public debates over economic issues, especially concerning government policy, often find arguments over ethical values entangled with questions about how the world works. This can make such debates bitter when they come to be perceived as matters of good versus evil. It can also result in bad public policy if moral indignation overwhelms economic understanding.

A key point made by Smith, one that remains central to economists' understanding of the world, is that individual pursuit of self-interest can produce a desirable social outcome. According to Smith the self-interested individual is:

> . . . led by an invisible hand to promote an end which was no part of his intention. Nor is it always the worse for society that it was no part of it. By pursuing his own interest he frequently promotes that of society more effectually than when he really intends to promote it. I have never known much good done by those who affected to trade for the public good.

One frequently hears references, in public debates over contentious policy issues, to the motives of the actors: "Greedy multinational corporations move production overseas to cut labor costs." "Drug companies are making obscene profits from peoples' illness." If results matter, and if a market system really works like an "invisible hand," then people's motives might be irrelevant.

Economists often distinguish between positive and normative statements. A positive statement is an assertion of the truthfulness or falseness of an economic theory or fact. "Demand curves have negative slope" or "U.S. GDP rose 3 percent last year" are examples of positive economic statements. A normative statement is one that contains an assertion of ethical desirability, for example: "Everyone should earn enough to enjoy a decent standard of living." Differences over positive questions can, in principle if not always in practice, be settled by logic or observation. It is not entirely clear whether disputes over fundamental ethical values can be resolved by reason or evidence, without a crucial element of religious faith or something serving that function.

Milton FRIEDMAN once claimed that disagreements about public policy issues stem mainly from differing predicted effects of policies, not from "fundamental differences in basic values." Consider an issue such as the use of child labor in Third World factories to make athletic clothing for the rich world. Discussions about matters like this are often acrimonious because of a perceived unethical element. Children belong in school. Greedy corporations are exploiting them. Following closely behind is often a demand for action, perhaps a boycott or a law. The unintended results of these well-intended actions may be to harm the people they are designed to help. Boycotting clothing made by child labor might cause these children to lose their relatively desirable jobs working for multinational corporations. The alternative may be scavenging or prostitution. People opposing boycotts, or legal trade restrictions on clothing made using child labor, are not necessarily motivated by profits or indifferent to harsh conditions. They may think such measures will do more harm than good.

This is not to say that well-intended actions always produce bad results. But it does argue that policies and actions based only on moral indignation, in the absence of factual and contextual knowledge, can backfire. Economic analysis can help to clarify the actual choices and their costs and benefits.

BIBLIOGRAPHY. J.E.E.D. Acton, "The History of Freedom in Antiquity" in *Selected Writings of Lord Acton, Volume 1*(Liberty Fund,1998); Aristotle, *Politics, Book I,* translated by Benjamin Jowett, in *Aristotle's Politics and Poetics* (Viking, 1957); Isaiah Berlin, *Four Essays on Liberty* (Oxford University Press, 1969); Milton Friedman, "The Methodology of Positive Economics" in *Essays in Positive Economics* (University of Chicago Press, 1953); Friedrich von Hayek, *The Fatal Conceit* (University of Chicago Press, 1988); Jane Jacobs, *Systems of Survival* (Vintage Books, 1994); John Locke, *Of Civil Government, Second Essay* (Regnery, 1948); Alasdair MacIntyre, *After Virtue, Second Edition* (University of Notre Dame Press, 1984); Robert Nozick, *Anarchy, State and Utopia* (Basic Books, 1974); Joseph Schumpeter, *Capitalism, Socialism, and Democracy, Third Edition* (Harper Torchbooks, 1950); Adam Smith, *An Inquiry into the Nature and Causes of the Wealth of Nations* (Modern Library Edition, 1937); Max Weber, *The Protestant Ethic and the Spirit of Capitalism* (Scribner, 1930).

SAMUEL WESTON, PH.D.
UNIVERSITY OF DALLAS

Ethiopia

LOCATED IN THE HORN of Africa, Ethiopia is not only one of the oldest independent countries in Africa, it is also one of the oldest countries in the world. According to legend, the Queen of Sheba and the son of King Solomon founded the Ethiopian Empire. Ethiopia originally was a Christian country but Islam was introduced in the 7th century and grew rapidly. As a result, the country was cut off from European Christendom. The Portuguese attempted to re-convert Ethiopians to Christianity, leading to conflict and contributed to Ethiopia's isolationism until the mid-19th century. During the late 1930s and into WORLD WAR II, Ethiopia was invaded by the Italian Fascists. Ethiopia's emperor, Haile Selassie was forced into exile in England and did not return until

1941. In 1974, after a period of civil unrest, Selassie was deposed and a socialist government was installed. Pursuing communist policies, Ethiopia became a close allay of the SOVIET UNION and enjoyed economic support from the superpower.

But by the late 1970s and into the 1980s, a succession of droughts, famine, and insurrections led to the collapse of the government. A constitution was adopted in 1994 and in 1995 a federal republican government was elected. A long and bloody war (more than 80,000 dead) with Eritrea did not end until 2000. This conflict destroyed Ethiopia's mainly agricultural economy, and it remains one of the least developed countries in the world. Relying on massive food imports, Ethiopia had a GROSS DOMESTIC PRODUCT (GDP) of $46 billion with a population of 67.6 million in 2002.

BIBLIOGRAPHY. "The Department of State Background Note," www.state.gov; *CIA World Factbook* (2002); "Ethiopia, A Country Study," The Library of Congress, lcweb2.loc.gov.

LINDA L. PETROU, PH.D.
HIGH POINT UNIVERSITY

euro

SINCE JANUARY 1, 1999, the world has witnessed one of the most profound and far-reaching economic events of modern history. The EUROPEAN UNION (EU) launched the final stage of Economic and Monetary Union (EMU), thereby creating a new trans-European currency: the euro, adopted by 11 Member States on that day.

The 11 Member States were BELGIUM, GERMANY, SPAIN, FRANCE, IRELAND, ITALY, LUXEMBOURG, the NETHERLANDS, AUSTRIA, PORTUGAL, and Finland. GREECE became the 12th Member State to adopt the euro when the new euro banknotes and coins were introduced, and the euro became a physical reality across Europe, on January 1, 2002. Among the remaining Member States, Great Britain and Denmark chose not to participate. SWEDEN was not eligible because it had not been part of the European Monetary System.

The name, euro, was chosen by the European heads of state or government at the European Council meeting in Madrid in December 1995. The official abbreviation for the euro is EUR, and the sign or symbol for the new single currency is €. It looks like an E with two clearly marked, horizontal parallel lines across it, and was inspired by the Greek letter *epsilon*, in reference to the cradle of European civilization and to the first letter of the word Europe. The parallel lines represent the stability of the euro.

Why did the European Union create the euro? EMU is best understood as one component of the broader process of European political integration that began in the early 1950s. To this day, the legacy of armed conflict in Europe plays a crucial role in the process of European integration.

The greatest misconception about the euro is that it is fundamentally an economic project. In fact, the euro is an intensely political initiative that has been deeply entangled in European history for many years. Put simply, the euro has evolved as an essential step toward the ultimate goal of ever-closer political integration first outlined in the 1958 Treaty of Rome. The language of subsequent treaties makes it clear that the euro's introduction is based on far more than calculations of economic pros and cons.

Although the euro is the "child" of a wide range of political agenda, ambitious economic goals have played an important, if secondary, role since the very beginning. Clearly, political solidarity in Europe would hardly be furthered if the euro's creators believed that the new currency rested on a feeble economic footing. In fact, in the midst of political diversity, high-minded economic objectives have emerged as the most common answers to the "Why did they do this?" question. According to the Werner Report in 1970, in which EMU was first formally proposed: "Monetary union will make it possible to ensure growth and stability within the Community and reinforce the contribution it can make to economic and monetary equilibrium in the world and make it a pillar of stability." The 1992 Treaty on European Union itself cited: "the raising of the standard of living and the quality of life, and economic and social cohesion and solidarity among Member States" as its central goal.

Benefit of the euro. The euro's core economic benefits are direct, and include: the elimination of the need to exchange currencies of EMU members (this has been estimated to save as much as $30 billion per year); the elimination of excessive volatility among EMU currencies (fluctuations will only occur between the euro and the DOLLAR, the YEN, and the currencies of non-EMU nations); more rapid economic and financial integration among EMU members; a EUROPEAN CENTRAL BANK (ECB) that may conduct a more expansionary monetary policy than the generally restrictive one practically imposed in the past by the Bundesbank on the other EMU members; and greater economic discipline for countries, such as Italy and Greece, that seemed unwilling or unable to put their economic house in order without externally imposed conditions.

Other benefits of the euro for the EMU members are: moving away from the use of the dollar as an international currency (which currently confers about $8-10 billion in benefits to the United States, and the expectation is that the euro could provide similar benefits to the euro area); the reduced cost of borrowing in international financial markets (it has been estimated that the U.S. cost of borrowing on international financial markets is about 25-50 basis points lower than it would have been if the dollar were not used as an international currency, for a total saving of about $10 billion, and the expectation is that the euro area could gain as much); and last but not least, the increased economic and political importance that the EU will acquire in international affairs.

Problem with the euro. The most serious unresolved problem that the establishment of an ECB and the euro may create is how EMU Member States will respond to asymmetric economic shocks. It is almost inevitable that a large and diverse single currency-area face periodic asymmetric shocks that will affect various member nations differently and drive their economies out of alignment. In such a case, there is practically nothing that a nation so adversely affected can do. The nation cannot use its own monetary policy to overcome its particular problem, and EMU fiscal discipline would prevent it in the first place.

A single currency works well in the United States because if a region suffers an asymmetric shock, workers move quickly and in great numbers toward areas of

The symbol for the euro was inspired by the Greek letter epsilon; *the parallel lines represent stability.*

the nation with greater employment opportunities. This escape hatch is not generally available in Europe to the same extent as in the United States. In fact, the Organization for Economic Cooperation and Development (1986) and the European Commission (1990) found that labor mobility among EMU members is from two to three times lower than among U.S. regions because of language barriers, inflexible housing markets, and labor markets that remain regulated.

In addition to much greater regional and occupational labor mobility in the United States there is a great deal of federal fiscal redistribution in favor of the adversely affected region. In the euro area, on the other hand, fiscal redistribution cannot be of much help because the EMU budget is only about 1 percent of the EMU's GDP, and more than half of it is devoted to its Common Agricultural Policy. Furthermore, real wages are also somewhat more flexible downward in the United States than in the euro area. None of these escape valves are available to an EMU member adversely affected by a negative asymmetric shock. In fact, the difference in unemployment rates among EMU member nations is much higher than among U.S. regions.

There is also the question of the effectiveness of a euro-wide monetary policy on the various EMU members, although most economists believe that greater economic and financial integration enhances the effectiveness of the common monetary policy in member nations.

The impact of euro on business environments worldwide. Euro exchange rates set the tone for trade relations with euro areas, and businesses and investors worldwide are anxious to know whether the euro will be stronger or weaker than the national currencies that preceded it. When the euro is weak (meaning it trades at low levels against foreign currencies like the U.S. dollar), consumers pay lower prices for products imported from the euro zone. Non-European products can even be paid out of their own markets amid a deluge of cheap euro-area imports. When the euro is too weak, it sparks inflation and makes foreign borrowing by European firms and governments extremely expensive, thus destabilizing business environments. Alternatively, if the euro is strong, the export industries so crucial to European economic growth suffer, because non-euro area countries have to pay more to buy euro-denominated products. Simultaneously, euro-zone imports increase, galvanizing production in the region's main trading partners. The euro's stability, therefore, is at least as important as its strength, because a chronically unstable currency is the scourge of economic growth and investment. Unstable currencies rattle trade-dependent economies, destroy investments, and fracture business environments.

The strength of the euro is determined by a variety of factors. These include: the general level of economic and political stability; fiscal stability; the current account balance; INFLATION and INTEREST RATES; and the euro's use as an international reserve currency. As the euro transforms the area from 12 small, open nations, into one large, closed economy, the ECB might be likely to adopt a policy of benign neglect toward other currencies like the U.S. dollar. This may ultimately result in volatility similar to that seen in U.S. dollar markets.

The euro has become an important international reserve currency, not least by virtue of the fact that all previous euro-zone currencies, regardless of where they were held, converted into euros. It is highly unlikely, however, that the euro will pose a serious worldwide challenge to the U.S. dollar in the near future.

BIBLIOGRAPHY. Dominick Salvatore, "The European Monetary System: Crisis and Future" *Open Economies Review* (1996); International Monetary Fund, "The Real Effects of Monetary Policy in the European Union," *Working Paper no. 160* (1998); Christian N. Chabot, *Understanding the Euro: The Clear and Concise Guide to the New Trans-European Economy* (McGraw-Hill, 1999); European Commission, *Is the Commitment to Sound Public Finances Robust Enough in Europe?* (2001); Philip Arestis, Kevin McCauley, and Malcolm Sawyer, "The Future of the Euro: Is There an Alternative to the Stability and Growth Pact?" *Levy Institute Public Brief* (2001); Dominick Salvatore, *Eastern Economic Journal* (2002).

JIANG FUMING, PH.D.
CHARLES STUART UNIVERSITY, AUSTRALIA

European Central Bank

AN INDEPENDENT, SUPRANATIONAL central bank established in 1998, the European Central Bank (ECB) replaced the European Monetary Institute (EMI). Its headquarters are in Frankfurt, GERMANY. It implements MONETARY POLICY in the EURO area as recommended by the European System of Central Banks (ESCB). The ESCB is made of the ECB and the national central banks (NCB) of all EUROPEAN UNION (EU) member states and its primary objective is to maintain price stability. For all practical purposes, the ECB is the core of the ESCB (with the right to issue euros), and it implements the ESCB policies either itself or through the NCBs.

The ESCB, and hence the ECB, are charged to support the recommended economic policies in the European Union and to ensure the uninterrupted operation of the free and open market system. Additional tasks cover a wide range, from conducting foreign-exchange operations and managing foreign reserves of the EU member states, to promoting measures that guarantee smooth operation of the payments system. According to the Maastricht Treaty, which established the EU, the NCBs have been mandated to contribute foreign exchange reserves proportionate to their shares in the subscribed capital of the ECB. Eighty-five percent of the contributions were made in U.S. dollars and Japanese YEN, and the rest in gold. In return each contributing country was credited with a claim in euro equivalent. These reserves, amounting to €50 billion by January 4, 1999, provided the ECB its initial foreign exchange reserves to manage the euro.

The decision-making bodies of the ECB, which govern the ESCB, are the Governing Council and the Executive Board. The Governing Council is composed of the members of the Executive Board and the governors of the NCBs in the Euro area, each member with one vote. The Executive Board is composed of the President, the Vice-President, and four additional members. The Executive Board members are appointed for a non-renewable eight-year term, in order to free it from political pressure and to ensure independence and autonomy. The members are required to be of high professional status in international finance and banking, and are expected to be in common accord with the member state governments.

A third transitory decision-making body is the General Council. Its existence is the result of the fact that there are European Union countries that are not members of the euro area, and there are tasks previously performed by the EMI that need to be performed by the ECB. Thus the president and the vice-president of the ECB and the governors of all the central banks in the European Union constitute the General Council. The council's primary responsibility is to advise the process of fixing the exchange rates of the currencies of non-euro members.

The main responsibilities of the Governing Council are to formulate the monetary policy of the euro area by making decisions regarding monetary targets, major interest rates, and the supply of foreign exchange reserves in the ESCB. The Governing Council authorizes the issue of banknotes and coins within the euro area by the ECB and the NCBs. The Executive Board of the ECB is responsible for carrying out the policies decided by the Governing Council. The NCBs are an integral part of the ESCB and hence are expected to comply with the instructions of the ECB.

In addition to the supervision of the financial system in the euro area, the ECB implements the recommended monetary policies. The two major monetary-policy tools available to the ECB (and to the NCBs) are open market and credit operations and minimum reserves. The open market and credit operations refer to the purchase and/or sales, in the spot and forward markets, of financial claims and instruments. The purchase of financial claims and instruments indicates an increase in the money supply (expansionary monetary policy).

The sales of the financial claims and instruments, on the other hand, indicate a decrease in the money supply (contractionary monetary policy). The ECB can also implement monetary policy by changing the reserves, which the credit institutions are required to hold with the ECB and the NCBs. A decrease in the required reserves would mean the credit institutions would give more credits and the money supply would increase; an increase in the required reserve ratio would lower the money supply. Empowering the ECB with the right to levy financial sanctions in the case of non-compliance ensures compliance with its monetary policy.

Furthermore, the ECB (and the NCBs) can buy and sell foreign exchange, as well as foreign exchange denominated assets, in order to assure the smooth operation of the international payments system inside and outside the Euro area.

The ECB's firm commitment to price stability, and hence its emphasis on controlling monetary growth, have been the focus of a wide range of criticisms. A major argument has been that zealous dedication to keep inflation low leads to high unemployment and eventually to the erosion of labor's economic and social rights in Europe. A tight monetary policy, it is argued, would raise unemployment significantly, forcing the labor market to agree to lower wages and lower economic and social status.

BIBLIOGRAPHY. European Central Bank, www.ecb.int; European Central Bank: A Case Study, www.trema.com/case_studies; European Central Bank, *Protocol on the Statue of the European System of Central Banks and of the European Central Bank*, www.ecb.int (2002); Martin Feldtein, "The European Central Bank and the Euro: The First Year," *NBER Working Paper 7517* (National Bureau of Economic Research, 2000); O. Issing, V. Gaspar and I. Angelon, *Monetary Policy in the Euro Area* (Cambridge University Press, 2001).

M. ODEKON
SKIDMORE COLLEGE

European Union

A GROUP OF EUROPEAN countries that have integrated many of their economic activities and policy decisions, the European Union (EU) is the most comprehensive initiative of economic regional integration to date. As of January, 2003, the EU economy had almost the size of the UNITED STATES economy, and was already the world's major trading power.

The members of the EU have shared, since its inception, free internal trade and common customs duties and procedures. The free internal trade, as predicted, has induced significant trade growth among EU members. Until recently, these were probably the most prominent characteristics of the arrangement. Now, of a similar magnitude, the members also share a common currency: the EURO, used since 1999 for financial transactions and in circulation since January, 2002. Three EU members (DENMARK, SWEDEN, and the UNITED KINGDOM) have not yet adopted the euro as of early 2003, however.

The euro represented the consolidation of an evolving process of monetary and exchange rates coordination that began in 1979 with the European Monetary System (EMS). The EMS arose as a response to the economic instability that followed the breakdown of the BRETTON WOODS system in the early 1970s. Although the EMS worked similarly to Bretton Woods, inasmuch as the main goal in both cases was to limit exchange rates fluctuations, EMS was more flexible and was, naturally, restricted to the European countries.

The EMS worked well for more than 10 years, but in the early 1990s the increased financial volatility in world markets almost broke it down. By then, it became clear that the system would remain sustainable only if it were deepened. The choices were two: to eliminate monetary coordination altogether or to implement it fully. The second option was chosen and the EU members created the EUROPEAN CENTRAL BANK, with the goal of unifying monetary policy and creating a common currency. The choice was manifested in the Treaty of Maastricht (1992), establishing the timetable toward a single currency, and determining targets to be achieved by each EU member in terms of price and exchange rate stability, interest rates volatility, and budget deficits and public debt levels.

The deepening of integration that occurred with the introduction of the euro is expected to further increase trade and growth in Europe. As suggested in a study by Frankel and Rose (2002), belonging to a currency union tends to triple a country's trade with the other currency union members. Moreover, they find that each 3 percent increase in a country's overall trade induces a 1 percent increase in its per capita income. According to their estimates, the EU has therefore much to gain with the euro.

The EU has not always been as large and as integrated as it is now, however. It began as a much more modest initiative in the late 1940s aimed at integrating the coal and steel markets of its initial members: FRANCE, ITALY, (West) GERMANY, BELGIUM, LUXEMBOURG, and the NETHERLANDS. The initiative evolved to become a full customs union with the signature of the Treaty of Rome in 1957, which established the European Economic Community (EEC), the EU predecessor, in the following year. The initial goal was to create a common market, as well as to integrate the members' agricultural, transport

and commercial policies. Some observers argue, however, that the EEC's primary motivation was not really economic, but political, aimed at reducing the threat of future military conflicts in Europe.

From 1957 to today's currency union, the European integration process intensified gradually. Perhaps the clearest signal of the continuity of the process has been the membership evolution. The first expansion took place in 1973, with Denmark, IRELAND, and the United Kingdom joining. This first enlargement was accompanied by a deepening of integration, with some social and environmental regulations being added to the responsibility of the Community.

During the 1980s, three southern European countries were incorporated: GREECE in 1981, plus PORTUGAL and SPAIN in 1986. Finally, in 1995, three other nations obtained membership: AUSTRIA, FINLAND and SWEDEN. Just before this last expansion, the European single market came into effect in January, 1993, allowing goods and services, and also people and capital to move freely across the member countries.

It is noteworthy that six of the current members—Austria, Denmark, Finland, Portugal, Sweden and the United Kingdom—were previous participants of another, shallower, European integration initiative, the European Free Trade Association (EFTA), created in 1960. Progressively, however, the more deeply integrated arrangement in the European continent attracted most of the EFTA members.

In addition to the 15 full members (2003), the EU also has numerous free trade agreements with third countries. These include bilateral agreements with all EFTA members and with most central and eastern European, northern African, Middle Eastern, and Mediterranean countries. There are other agreements under negotiation as well, for instance with SOUTH AFRICA and with Mercosur, the southern Latin America regional bloc.

Perhaps even more significant are the EU projects of enlargement. In early 2003, negotiations for membership were under way with 13 central and eastern European countries, likely to be fully incorporated into the union in 2004. TURKEY, a candidate in 2003, will be the first Middle Eastern/Muslim/Asian country in the union if admitted. This new accession wave is likely to transform the EU into the largest economy in the world and one of its most populous, aggregating over half a billion consumers.

BIBLIOGRAPHY. The European Union, www.europa.eu.int; Jeffrey Frankel and Andrew Rose, "An Estimate of the Effect of Common Currencies on Trade and Income," *The Quarterly Journal of Economics* (v.117/2, 2002); Pavlos Karadeloglou, ed., *Enlarging the EU* (Palgrave Macmillan, 2002); John McCormick, *Understanding the European Union: A Concise In-*

troduction (Palgrave Macmillan, 1999); John Pinder, *The European Union: A Very Short Introduction* (Oxford University Press, 2001).

EMANUEL ORNELAS, PH.D.
UNIVERSITY OF GEORGIA

exchange rates

THE GLOBALIZATION OF the economic world forces us to recognize that few companies operate without dealing in other currencies. They may owe suppliers, sell products, or get or pay dividends or interest to owners or lenders in other countries. This exposure to foreign currencies introduces a special problem when making a financial FORECAST: exchange rates.

An exchange rate is simply a price. In other words, prices as we normally understand the term are themselves exchange rates: the price of a book, for example in the UNITED STATES, is the exchange rate between a particular good (the book) and DOLLARs. Suppose that it is quoted as $50, which means a book sells for $50, or can be bought at that price. It changes hands at an exchange rate of 1 book equals $50.

As far as the bookseller is concerned, that means "money can be bought" at the rate of $50 per book. From the bookseller's point of view, the price of $1 is 1/50th of a copy of this book. If its price were $55, the shop would only need to supply 1/55th of a copy in order to earn a dollar. Therefore, a rise in the price of the book, from $50 to $55, is the same as a fall in the price of money, from 1/50th to 1/55th of a book.

In the same way, an exchange rate of US$1.00= A$1.79 means that the price of an Australian dollar in U.S. currency is US$(1/1.79)=US$0.56. To an Australian, a U.S. dollar costs A$1.79. In general, the exchange rate of currency A in terms of currency B is the number of units of B needed to buy a unit of A. Therefore, an exchange rate can be defined as the price paid in domestic money to acquire one unit of a foreign money; the rate at which the money of one nation is exchanged for the money of another nation.

But money has not always been the currency of choice in history. For example, in Newfoundland's history, actual cash was scarce. The only medium of exchange for the great majority of Newfoundlanders for food, clothing, and other necessities was dried cod fish, which has often been referred to as "Newfoundland currency." The merchants carried out their business on what was known as the credit or truck system. They outfitted the fishermen in the spring, for which the fishermen paid with dried fish in the fall.

In the late 1700s, with the increase in population, coin became more common. It consisted mainly of British currency, but coins of other countries were also in circulation. As well, notes valued from five pounds to five shillings were available. Large transactions between firms were usually covered by Bills of Exchange, transferred from one firm to another in much the same way as banknotes are exchanged today.

Determinants of exchange rates. There are two different theories about what governs exchange rates: one theory proposes that it is relative purchasing power; the other that it is INTEREST RATES. The purchasing power theory suggests that exchange rates make the cost of goods the same in both countries in a free-trade world. If difference in the price of the same good offered in the two countries exists, someone will see the potential to profit and take that opportunity: they will buy the good at the lower price and offer it to buyers in the country where the good is commanding the higher price. This process is called arbitrage, and those acting on price differences are called arbitrageurs. Theoretically, exchange rates change only when there is a change in the rates of inflation in the two countries.

The purchasing power theory makes sense, but it does not take into account differences in actual costs of buying, moving the product, and reselling it, or any barriers to arbitrage created by the two countries. Because the purchasing power theory does not explain what actually occurs in the world very well, another theory was then developed.

This theory, called interest-rate parity, suggests that differences in interest rates, and changes in these differences, are at the heart of exchange rates. Theoretically, exchange rates make the real returns in the two countries the same: If real rates, the rates after subtracting the rate of inflation in each country from the nominal interest rate, are not the same, the potential exists to make a profit, and an arbitrageur will move in, take the profit, and make the expected real return the same. The mechanism to make the rates the same is the exchange rate between the two countries. Arbitrageurs move out of the currency of the country with the lower real rate of return, and thus create a demand for that currency. An increased demand for a currency puts pressure on the exchange rate, and it changes.

In fact, exchange rates are determined by a combination of such things as the differences in real interest rates, relative inflation, growth rates in available income, and perceptions about political and economic risk in the two countries.

Exchange rate systems. The post-WORLD WAR II history of the evolutionary development of currency systems has experienced two major phases, the first being the fixed-rate era known as BRETTON WOODS regime, that broke down in 1971, and the floating-rate period since then.

The world of international economic policy making at the end of World War II was dominated by two pre-occupations: first, to facilitate the reconstruction of European economies, and second, if possible, to prevent a return to the competitive devaluations and protectionism that had characterized the 1930s. To that end, the British and American governments established the INTERNATIONAL MONETARY FUND (IMF), which was intended to police a system of fixed-exchange rates known universally as the Bretton Woods system, after the small New Hampshire ski resort where the agreement was signed in 1944. Under the Bretton Woods system, countries undertook two major commitments: first to maintain convertibility and second, to preserve a fixed exchange rate until unambiguous evidence of "fundamental disequilibrium" appeared, at which point they were expected to devalue or revalue, as the case may be, in other words, announce a new (fixed) parity.

Convertibility turned out to be more a pious intention than a realistic objective; it was always more honored in the breach than the observance, with only the United States among the major economic powers ever permitting full freedom of capital movements.

The use of the U.S. dollar as a key currency in the Bretton Woods system created a dilemma. Chronic deficits in the U.S. balance of payments raised doubts about the continued convertibility of the dollar into gold and, therefore, the status of the dollar as a key currency was also doubted, but such deficits were required to increase international reserves. Sharp increases in the U.S. deficit in 1971 forced the abandonment of dollar convertibility into gold, shattering the Bretton Woods system.

Thus, a floating exchange rate was allowed, where the rates at which national currencies exchange for one another are determined by demand and supply of national currencies in foreign-exchange markets. One currency can depreciate or appreciate relative to another country's currency. When the dollar price of pounds increases, for example, from US$2 for £1 to US$3 for £1, we say that the value of the dollar has depreciated relative to the pound.

More generally, exchange-rate depreciation means that it takes more units of a country's currency (in this case U.S. dollars) to buy a single unit of some foreign currency (in this case British pounds sterling). Conversely, exchange-rate appreciation means that it takes fewer units of a country's currency to buy a single unit of some foreign currency. Some exchange rates are fixed: that is, the rate of exchange is set relative to some other currency, often the U.S. dollar. Fixed currency relationships can be changed by a country's governing body, usually its central bank.

For reasons that are not yet very clear, floating rates have proved extremely volatile, with violent short-term fluctuations and longer-run swings to apparent over- and under-valuation characterizing all the major currencies, including the U.S. dollar. Among the features of the international financial scene in recent years have been: the U.S. "twin deficit" problem, two OPEC (ORGANIZATION OF PETROLEUM EXPORTING COUNTRIES) oil shocks in the 1970s and a steeply falling oil price in the 1980s, a gathering crisis in international and U.S .domestic debt, the rapidly increasing importance of Japan and concomitant decline in the relative weight of the United States in world markets—all accompanied by an unprecedented degree of volatility and rapid innovation, both in the technology of executing transactions and in the range of financial instruments actually traded.

BIBLIOGRAPHY. C.F. Rowe, *The Book of Newfoundland* (1967); Diana R. Harrington, *Corporate Financial Analysis: Decisions in a Global Environment* (South-Western, 1993); John Jackson, Ron McIver, Campbell McConnell, *Economics* (1994); Laurence S. Copeland, *Exchange Rates and International Finance* (Longman, 1994); Jacques J. Polak, "Fifty Years of Exchange Rate Research and Policy at the International Monetary Fund," *IMF Staff Papers*, (v.42, 1995); David K. Eiteman, Arthur I. Stonehill, Michael H. Moffett, *Multinational Business Finance* (Addison Wesley, 2000).

JIANG FUMING, PH.D.
CHARLES STURT UNIVERSITY, AUSTRALIA

export and import

EXPORT IS A TERM USED for GOODS and services that are produced domestically but sold to another country or countries, while import is a term that denotes goods and services purchased from other country. Thus, export and import represent the exchange of goods and services between one country and another. This exchange, also known as international trade, occurs due to the non-availability of goods and services in a country and differences in cost production between countries.

Import and export are integral components of trade balance and, consequently, balance of payments. Trade surplus occurs when export proceeds are greater than import expenditures, while trade deficit emerges when domestic spending on foreign goods exceeds foreign purchases of domestically produced goods. However, regardless of whether countries run short-run trade deficits or surpluses, economists generally agree that international trade increases the economic welfare of trading countries as well as the world economy by broadening the range of goods and services available for consumption.

Specialized exports and imports. The differences in cost of production originate in the unequal endowment in resources required for the production in goods and services. The availability of certain types and quantities of raw materials, skill and size of labor force, the stock of capital and institutions differ among countries and play a pivotal role in determining the cost of production. Adam SMITH advanced the concept of absolute advantage by which countries should engage in trade of goods and services if foreign goods could be obtained with less resources than it would take to produce the respective goods and services domestically.

This would lead to the specialization in production of goods and services in which the country would have an absolute cost advantage. David RICARDO showed that countries would benefit from trade even if one country produced all of goods and services more expensively than the other country. According to his theory of comparative advantage, the gains from trade would materialize if relative costs of production of the different commodities were favorable, i.e. only comparative advantage would be required. Every nation must have a relative edge in efficiency in certain activities. Consequently, specialization would channel resources into the activities which countries have the most advantages or the least disadvantages for them, thus fostering international exchange of goods and services.

Modern economists further refined Ricardo's argument. The Hecksher-Ohlin-Samuelson theorem claims that countries will tend to export commodities that require more resources of which country is relatively well endowed. The theorem states that the main source of comparative advantage arises from the different relative factor endowments of the countries trading. This inevitably leads to the further specialization, increase of production and the enlargement of the markets, and some say, in turn, calls for arguments for removing all trade restrictions, or obstacles to FREE TRADE.

The debate between proponents of free trade and government control over foreign trade is as old as classical economics. The first proponents of free trade condemned the mercantilist point of view that trade deficits should be avoided. While mercantilists believed that the wealth of a nation was measured by the amount of gold that it amassed, and that the principal source of gold is export of commodities, Smith emphasized that what matters is not a stock of gold, but productivity—the ability to continuously lower the cost of production of goods and services. However, free trade advocates suffered a major setback in the Great DEPRESSION in the 1930s when economic protectionism became a dominant trend in the international trade.

Protectionism. The main feature of protectionism was the introduction of trade barriers such as TARIFFS and

Container shipping has become a predominant cargo transfer process for international export and import.

QUOTAS. A tariff is a tax levied on imported goods and services. Tariffs may take the form of a certain percentage of value, so-called *ad valorem* tariffs; an amount per unit, also known as a specific tariff; or a compound tariff, which represents a combination of *ad valorem* and specific tariffs.

The main rationale for introducing tariffs may span from simply raising the government revenue to conducting a particular economic policy. For a long time, the "infant industry" argument was a main vehicle behind introduction of tariffs. According to this argument, the introduction of tariffs was justified on the grounds that a new industry may be unable to withstand foreign competition during its infancy. Tariffs are intended to shelter an industry below optimum size and protection should be in place until the potential comparative advantage of the industry is realized.

The other rationales for introducing tariffs as an instrument of economic policy include: a) protection of strategically important industries; b) reduction of overall import level by making them more expensive relative to domestic production; c) prevention of dumping practices by raising the import prices of the dumped commodity to its economic level; d) reciprocity, that is retaliation against restrictive measures imposed by other countries.

Quotas are imposed limits on the quantity of goods produced or purchased. Import quotas are used to curtail or restrict the purchase of foreign commodities, while export quotas have been used to maximize the export revenue stream to countries producing primary products by restricting supply. The major disadvantage of quotas relative to tariffs is that quotas do not produce tariff revenue.

There are other sorts of non-tariff barriers besides quotas. The most popular among those is the voluntary export restraint, a mechanism by which an exporter voluntarily limits its quantity of exports, often under threat of tougher protective measures. Another popular form of non-tariff trade barriers is the legal requirements that artificially favor domestic operations.

Following the surge of protectionism in the 1930s the popularity of free trade argument was revived after World War II. The GENERAL AGREEMENT ON TRADE AND TARIFFS (GATT) was signed in 1947 and entered into effect on January 1, 1948. GATT was a multilateral trade agreement that set out the rules for international trade. The agreement called for the expansion of multilateral trade with gradual elimination of tariffs and other barriers to trade. Following the initial meeting in Geneva there were eight rounds of negotiations, including Kennedy round (1964–67), the Tokyo round (1973–79), ending with the Uruguay round (1986–93).

The Uruguay round reaffirmed the free-trade principles and focused on non-tariff trade barriers such as agricultural export subsidies, restriction on trade in banking, insurance, transport, and restrictions on foreign direct investment. The conclusion of the Uruguay round led to the establishment of the WORLD TRADE ORGANIZATION (WTO) in 1995. The WTO replaced GATT and provided the resources and the legal status for the resolution of trade disputes. It effectively introduced the monitoring and policing of multilateral trading system by imposing trade sanctions against a member country which refused to accept the WTO ruling over a trade dispute. In 2003, there were more than 130 countries who were members of the WTO.

There is also an increase in number of custom unions and free trade areas. A custom union represents a union of two or more countries within which trade restrictions are abolished but a common external tariff is established and applied against non-members. The EUROPEAN UNION, Mercosur, Caribbean Community and Common Market (CARICOM) are custom unions. A free trade area is a loose association of countries within which tariffs and other trade restrictions are removed. However, unlike a custom union in which member countries have a concerted commercial policy, each member country in free trade area retains its independent international trade policy with regard to countries outside the association. North American Free Trade Agreement (NAFTA), Latin American Integration Association (LAIA), and Association of South East Asian Nations are free trade areas.

Economic development. International trade, that is export and import, can also be analyzed within the framework of economic development. The expansion of an economy is often constrained by the country's balance of payments. In order to obtain sufficient foreign exchange, a country either can boost its exports, a principal foreign currency generator, or it needs to limit its imports, which are a major source of foreign expenditure. When the boost of exports becomes a principal strategy, economists characterize this path of development as an export-led growth or export-promotion. In the 1950s and early 1960s, ITALY and West GERMANY pursued export-led growth through the devaluation of the national currencies, which made their exports more competitive due to the lower prices. JAPAN and FRANCE, on the other hand, had chosen completely different growth strategies. Both countries protected domestic markets and used the expansion within the home markets as catalyst for the capture of foreign markets. Following the path of French and Japanese experience, Latin American economies became a cornerstone of import substitution strategy.

The import-substitution strategy in Latin America, however, was not successful. The initial growth in domestic production of consumer goods was followed by the rapid increase of imports of machinery and investment goods. Protected domestic industry was relatively inefficient and unable to compete on international markets. The particular problems arose when import substitution was relied on for a protracted period of time and extended to capital-extensive industries. The inefficiency of capital-intensive sectors spilled over to export sectors and severely limited economic growth and the development potential of several Latin American economies. The success of Japan and France and the problems encountered in Latin America led to the conclusion that import-substitution strategy can be pursued for a limited period of time in carefully chosen sectors. The protection, limited in time, can be provided only in those sectors in which firms could become competitive in the world markets.

The limits of import-substitution strategy prompted several developing countries to pursue an alternative development path. HONG KONG, South KOREA, SINGAPORE, and TAIWAN were among the first developing countries that followed the path of export-promotion, that is, the development of industries whose main markets are overseas. The success of export-promotion strategy rests upon relying on the most abundant production factors and diversification and expansion of non-traditional exports. The successful export-promotion strategy requires a number of supportive government policies such as competitive exchange-rate policy, deregulation of private industries, maintenance of infrastructure and transportation facilities, and reduction of overall rate of protection.

The role of export and import in the development of the world economy has steadily increased. Over the past 50 years, international trade has grown at annual rate of 6 percent, about 50 percent more than world output.

BIBLIOGRAPHY. Michael J. Trebilcock and Robert Howse, *Regulation of International Trade* (Routledge, 1998); U.S.

Customs Service, *Basic Guide to Importing* (NTC Publishing Group, 1995); Ken Albert Jones, *Export Restraint and the New Protectionism* (University of Michigan Press, 1994); Michael R. Czinkota (Editor), George Tesar, eds., *Export Policy: A Global Assessment* (Greenwood, 1982).

ZELJAN SCHUSTER, PH.D.
UNIVERSITY OF NEW HAVEN

externalities

AN EXTERNALITY EXISTS WHEN the actions of one agent (an individual or firm) affect the welfare of another agent. The term "externality" is derived from the fact that costs imposed on others are external to the decision-maker.

Externalities may be pecuniary or non-pecuniary. A pecuniary externality occurs when the actions of an agent affect the welfare of another through prices; for example, if a large number of immigrants join the labor force of a small town, the outward shift in labor supply will lower the market wage. Incumbent workers are worse off because of this wage reduction, but no inefficiency has resulted.

Non-pecuniary externalities, which do not operate through prices, do cause inefficiency; the remainder of this article refers exclusively to non-pecuniary externalities. An example of a non-pecuniary externality is the burning of coal by electricity-generation plants that results in the emission of sulfur dioxide, which causes acid rain, which damages property, the environment, and individuals' health. When deciding how much electricity to produce, the plant does not take into account the costs it imposes on others through acid rain; as a result, too much electricity is produced from a societal perspective.

Externalities may be either positive or negative, and result from either production or consumption. The previous example of a coal-fired power plant causing costly acid rain illustrates a negative externality in production. The presence of a negative externality in production implies that social costs exceed the private costs of production, with the result that a free market will produce a greater quantity than is socially optimal. A dual positive externality in production is generated when a farmer and beekeeper are located on adjacent properties; the farmer benefits from the beekeeper's production because the bees fertilize the farmer's crops and the beekeeper benefits from the farmer's production because the bees harvest pollen from the farmer's crops to make honey. A positive externality in production implies that social costs are less than the private costs of production, and as a result free markets will produce a smaller quantity than

is optimal. Smoking cigarettes generates a negative externality in consumption; second-hand smoke worsens the health of those nearby; in such a case, social benefits are less than the private benefits of consumption, so private markets will result in a higher quantity consumed than is socially optimal. Using breath mints generates a positive externality in consumption for the opposite reason: those nearby are made better off. In this case, social benefits exceed the private benefits of consumption, so private markets will result in a smaller quantity consumed than is socially optimal.

Social welfare is maximized by a free market when the private costs and private benefits of agents (individuals and firms) are equal to social costs and social benefits. The theorem of the invisible hand states that under perfect competition, utility-maximizing behavior on the part of individuals combined with profit-maximizing behavior on the part of firms leads to an outcome in which no one can be made better off without making someone else worse off (PARETO OPTIMALITY). However, the presence of externalities invalidates this theorem because private costs do not equal social costs, and/or private benefits do not equal social benefits. In order to bring about the socially optimal levels of production and consumption, policymakers seek to "internalize" externalities; in other words, to force private decision-makers to take into account the costs or benefits they impose on others or in other words to set private costs and benefits equal to the social costs and benefits. There are several strategies available to policymakers for internalizing externalities.

A.C. Pigou suggested that externalities could be internalized through taxes (for negative externalities) or subsidies (for positive externalities), the exact amount of which would be set equal to the value of the externality. Examples of such taxes are effluent fees on pollution, designed to force polluters to take into account the costs their pollution imposes on others.

Policymakers can also use quantity regulation to force markets to exchange the socially optimal quantity, or pollution regulation to cap external costs at their socially optimal level. For example, the U.S. government has outlawed smoking in public places, and sets emissions standards that limit the amount of sulfur dioxide and nitrous oxide that firms may emit. A variation of this approach is for the government to allocate to firms permits to release a specific amount of pollutant, and allow a free trade in the permits; this results in the pollution level being reduced in the most efficient way, as firms that can reduce cheaply will do so and sell their pollution permits to other firms that could only reduce their pollution at great cost.

A limitation of each of these solutions is that policymakers must have detailed information on the extent of external costs and benefits, or the socially optimal quantity. In many cases policymakers lack this detailed information, making it difficult for them to maximize social welfare in markets with externalities.

Ronald COASE proposed an ingenious solution to the problem of externalities that does not require the government to have any information about the value of external costs or benefits or about the optimal quantity. In a seminal 1960 article entitled "The Problem of Social Cost," Coase showed that the problem of externalities stems from unassigned property rights. For example, no one possesses property rights to the air; if citizens had property rights to the air, they could deny firms the right to pollute the air, or they could allow firms to pollute in exchange for payments that at least covered the external costs of pollution.

On the other hand, if firms had the property rights to the air, they could demand payments from citizens in exchange for not exercising the right to pollute. Coase noted that the solution to the problem of externalities was to assign the previously unassigned property rights, and allow the relevant parties to negotiate over the transfer of the rights. Coase noted that as long as negotiations were costless, the efficient outcome would result. For example, assume that polluting the air is worth $100 million to a firm, but that the pollution causes $1 billion in damage. If the property right to the air is assigned to the firm, a mutually beneficial transaction is for citizens to pay the firm some sum over $100 million in exchange for the firm not polluting. On the other hand, if property rights to the air are assigned to citizens, the citizens can refuse to allow the firm to pollute; the firm is willing to offer up to $100 million for the right to pollute, but that is not enough to compensate citizens for the $1 billion in damages they would suffer.

The key insight of what is known as the Coase Theorem is that no matter who is assigned the property rights initially, through negotiation the efficient outcome will result because the property rights will end up owned by the party that values them most. An important caveat is that while efficiency is not affected by the initial allocation of property rights, equity is an issue; the property right is valuable and both parties would like to be awarded it. The Coase Theorem revolutionized legal thinking and is one of the foundations of the field of law and economics.

BIBLIOGRAPHY. Ronald H. Coase, "The Problem of Social Cost," *Journal of Law and Economics* (1960); A.C. Pigou, *The Economics of Welfare* (Transaction Publishing, 1920).

JOHN CAWLEY, PH.D.
CORNELL UNIVERSITY

ExxonMobil

SINCE THE LATE 19TH CENTURY, petroleum has gained popularity as an energy source: world crude oil production grew from 20 million tons a year in 1900 to 3 billion tons by 1980. The modern petroleum industry is characterized by a vertical value chain involving crude oil exploration and transportation (pipelines, tankers), and refining and marketing.

In the United States, the early petroleum industry was dominated by the Standard Oil company. From its beginnings in Ohio in 1865, John D. ROCKEFELLER's petroleum interests came to control approximately 90 percent of total U.S. refining capacity by the 1880s. After an ANTITRUST investigation in 1911, Standard Oil was split into 34 separate firms to encourage competition in refining and marketing.

Following WORLD WAR II, both Exxon (formerly Standard Oil of New Jersey) and Mobil (formerly Standard Oil of New York) were part of the so-called "Seven Sisters," which initially controlled the huge Middle Eastern reserves, until the rise of the ORGANIZATION OF PETROLEUM EXPORTING COUNTRIES (OPEC) in the 1960s. Since then, changes in global crude oil supply conditions and in U.S. policy toward the petroleum industry have led to significant industry restructuring.

In 2001, ExxonMobil, formed by a $81 billion merger in 1998, was the world's largest private oil company by revenues), and ranked as the world's second largest company according to *Fortune* magazine. ExxonMobil is vertically integrated, as are the majority of its global competitors, operating in both "upstream" oil exploration and production and "downstream" refining and marketing. ExxonMobil has proven reserves of approximately 21.6 billion oil-equivalent barrels, and its refineries can handle more than 6 million barrels per day,

A gas station in New York is one of the 40,000 Exxon-Mobil outlets in 118 countries.

supplying refined products to more than 40,000 service stations in 118 countries.

ExxonMobil remains in a very good position for exploration and production in the Gulf of Mexico, West Africa, the Caspian Sea, and the Middle East. Downstream, ExxonMobil Chemical is also one of the largest global petrochemical companies, manufacturing a wide range of petrochemical products, with a leading position in paraxylene and polyolefins.

In 2001, total revenue amounted to $213.5 billion, with net income of $15.3 billion (7.2 percent). Of total revenue, petroleum and natural gas accounted for $192.7 billion (90 percent), and chemicals for the remaining 10 percent. ExxonMobil executives propose that their superior resource base, their investment in new technologies, their operational efficiency and their degree of vertical integration will allow them to continue to remain the world's pre-eminent energy company through the 21st century.

BIBLIOGRAPHY. F. Scherer, *Industry Structure, Strategy and Public Policy,*" F. Scherer (HarperCollins, 1996); J. Podolny and J. Roberts, *The Global Oil Industry* (Stanford University Press, 1998). www.exxonmobil.com; "Global 500: World's Largest Companies," *Fortune* (July, 2002).

CATHERINE MATRAVES
ALBION COLLEGE

Faneuil, Peter (1700–43)

ONE OF AMERICA'S first capitalists, little is known about Peter Faneuil's formative years, but it is believed he was born in Germany, the son of French Huguenot parents. The family's crest, which appeared on its coat of arms, was a grasshopper—probably a symbol of a family of farmers. This same family, generations later, migrated to London, England, where a Faneuil descendant held a seat on the London Exchange. Purportedly, his residence sported a grasshopper weathervane.

The Faneuils, who moved to America in the late 1600s, also claimed a similar weathervane over their home in New Rochelle, in the then-British-owned colony of New York. When Faneuil relocated to Boston, Massachusetts, is unknown, but by his early adulthood he had become one of the more affluent shippers and traders in town. His major trade was most likely codfish, a prevalent export of the area, which merchants traded for molasses and rum from the West Indies.

Faneuil saw the need for a central marketplace to benefit the local farmers who sold their livestock to buyers. Having the finances to build it, he chose architect John Smibert and declared the building would be his gift to the city he loved. He chose as the ideal site the commercially busy Dock Square. However, citizens rejected his idea because, according to historians, "it would bring all merchants and townsmen together in one spot with horses, carts, livestock, and produce (to cause) downtown Boston congestion." But, after he announced that he would add a meeting room over the market—to keep the convergence of traders off the sidewalks—the city seemed greatly appeased.

When erected, Faneuil Hall bore a copper grasshopper weathervane. Under its roof, commerce thrived. That might be the end of the story, had it not been for

the significant historical role the building was destined to play. By the 1760s, it quickly became the rendezvous place for the restless colonists opposing British King George's ever-expanding tax laws—such as the Sugar Tax of 1764 and the Stamp Act of 1765—unpopular decrees that eventually led to the AMERICAN REVOLUTIONARY WAR and independence. The meeting hall, on the second floor of the structure, was where John and Samuel ADAMS, Dr. Joseph Warren, and others planned

Quincy Market and Faneuil Hall now mark the Boston area where Peter Faneuil first had his central market.

their insurgence against England, including the revolt that became known as the Boston Tea Party, a few blocks from Faneuil Hall. Because of what took place under that grasshopper, Faneuil Hall is known today as the American "Cradle of Liberty."

After the Revolution, Faneuil Hall was expanded to better meet the commercial needs of the city. Architect Charles Bullfinch oversaw its refurbishment, a beautiful design maintained today and visible to thousands of sightseers annually.

BIBLIOGRAPHY. "Fanueil Hall," *Columbia Encyclopedia* (2003); Boston National Historical Park, www.nps.gov; Faneuil Hall, www.faneuilhallmarketplace.com.

JOSEPH GERINGER
SYED B. HUSSAIN, PH.D.
UNIVERSITY OF WISCONSIN, OSHKOSH

Fannie Mae

CREATED BY THE U.S. Congress in 1938, Fannie Mae (the Federal National Mortgage Association) is a corporation designed to promote home-ownership in the UNITED STATES. Fannie Mae does this by making funds available to institutions, such as banks, savings and loans, and mortgage companies, that then provide mortgages (promises that the homeowner will pay the holder of the mortgage a certain amount of money) to the general public. This steady source of funds from Fannie Mae to the lending institutions helps to keep mortgages more affordable and more widely available.

Originally establishing Fannie Mae as a federal agency, the federal government changed Fannie Mae's charter in 1968 to transform it into a stockholder-owned private corporation. In 1970, the federal government chartered Freddie Mac (the Federal Home Loan Mortgage Corporation), which is a very similar institution to Fannie Mae, thus creating competition in this particular market (the secondary market for mortgages). While essentially private corporations, both Fannie Mae and Freddie Mac have five members of their boards of directors appointed by the president of the United States.

Fannie Mae does not lend money directly to homebuyers. It is such institutions as mortgage companies, savings and loans, and commercial banks that lend money directly to individuals and families so that they can purchase a home. Once these institutions have created a mortgage they have two choices as to what to do with it. One, they can hold it in their portfolio, making money by collecting interest on it for the life of the mortgage. Or two, they can sell it and directly get cash or some other asset for the mortgage, rather than waiting for the interest to come in.

If they decide to sell their mortgages, they enter into what is called the secondary market. It is here that Fannie Mae (and other financial institutions) buys mortgages from the direct lenders. Fannie Mae either pays cash for the mortgages, which makes money immediately available to banks so that they can make more mortgages, or it issues mortgage-backed securities in exchange for pools (groups) of mortgages. These mortgage-backed securities are very liquid investments (almost like cash) for the banks and can be traded on Wall Street just like other securities. Either way, the direct lenders to the public acquire more funds to make more mortgages. It is in this way that Fannie Mae, through the secondary market, makes housing more affordable for the American public.

Fannie Mae is restricted by federal charter to buying residential mortgages within certain guidelines and limits. For example, the maximum limit for a one-family conventional loan that Fannie Mae was allowed to buy was, in 2003, $322,700. The loan limits are adjusted annually to reflect current market conditions. It is also directed by Congress to increase the availability and affordability of homeownership for low- to middle-income families.

In the multi-trillion dollar (of outstanding mortgage debt) HOUSING industry, Fannie Mae plays a large role, owning, or holding in trust, approximately 20 percent of all mortgages. In 2002 alone, it purchased (or guaranteed) $849 billion of mortgages, at a rate of over $2 billion every day of the year. Along with Freddie Mac, it has significant influence on homeownership in the United States.

The U.S. government decided long ago that it was desirable for Americans to live in homes that they owned themselves. So Fannie Mae, and later Freddie Mac, were established to help families pursue this particular facet of the "American Dream." Fannie Mae has been successful in this, and over the years it has helped finance purchases of homes for millions of families in the United States.

BIBLIOGRAPHY. Peter J. Wallison and Bert Ely, *Nationalizing Mortgage Risk: The Growth of Fannie Mae and Freddie Mac* (AEI Press, 2000); Fannie Mae, www.fanniemae.com; Freddie Mac, www.freddiemac.com.

PAUL A. SWANSON
WILLIAM PATERSON UNIVERSITY

fascism

SHORTLY AFTER WORLD WAR I, a new Italian political movement emerged under the former head of the

Italian Socialist Party, Benito Mussolini. It was known as Fascism, and won national attention by responding in kind to the violent tactics of Italy's revolutionary socialists and labor unions. Building on this success, Mussolini pressured King Victor Emmanuel to appoint him prime minister in 1922; he then moved toward dictatorship, banning all non-Fascist political parties by the late 1920s. The Fascists soon had many imitators around the world, most notably the National Socialist German Workers' Party under Adolf Hitler, prompting political analysts to transform the proper noun of "Fascism" into the generic concept of "fascism."

The extremism model versus the totalitarian model.
The most popular interpretation of fascism is that it is "right-wing extremism," standing in diametric opposition to the "left-wing extremism" of communism. This is not only the leading theory among political moderates: It was also the official position of the Communist International, which in 1935 defined fascism as the "overt, terrorist dictatorship of the most reactionary, chauvinist and imperialist elements of finance capital." The problem with the extremism model is that fascism and communism are similar in some ways. Most tellingly, both advocated and imposed a significantly larger role for government in the economy, almost always seen as a "left-wing" position. This is frankly admitted by socialists like Carl Landauer:

> In a history of socialism, fascism deserves a place not only as the opponent which, for a time, threatened to obliterate the socialist movement. Fascism is connected with socialism by many crosscurrents, and the two movements have some roots in common, especially the dissatisfaction with the capitalist economy of the pre-1918 type. . . . Fascism was ready to use forms of economic organization first suggested by socialists—and very likely that use of socialistic forms would have increased if fascism had not all but destroyed itself in causing the Second World War.

An alternative account is that both fascism and communism are forms of totalitarianism. The greater the power of the state, the more totalitarian it is. Historian Richard Pipes provides the canonical inventory: "an official, all-embracing ideology; a single party of the elect headed by a 'leader' and dominating the state; police terror; the ruling party's command of the means of communication and the armed forces; central command of the economy." The Soviet Union under Josef Stalin approximates the totalitarian pole, a pole that Hitler's Germany neared by the end of the war. The LAISSEZ-FAIRE minimal state stands at the opposite end of the spectrum.

Fascism as national socialism.
The most substantive objection to the totalitarian model is that fascists and communists have usually been violent enemies. How can they be ideological neighbors? What this question forgets is the old saying that "the heretic is worse than the infidel." Mussolini, Hitler, and other fascist leaders broadly accepted the economic outlook of their socialist rivals. But they split on the question of nationalism. Orthodox Marxism insisted that the fate of the nation was not of paramount interest to workers. Socialists were therefore obliged to oppose their own country's war efforts, and scorn the false god of patriotism.

The fascists took the opposite view. Only a deluded zealot could deny that the fate of Italy mattered for Italian workers. Just as members of the same economic class have interests in common, so do inhabitants of the same country. More importantly, ordinary people are highly susceptible to patriotic exhortations. Any political movement that hopes to succeed needs to integrate such feelings into its programs, not belittle them. Fascists accordingly replaced veneration of "the workers" with a fanatical devotion to "the nation," and concluded that Marxists were traitors.

Mussolini's transition from orthodox Marxism to fascism is a matter of public record. He rose to the highest level of the Italian Socialist Party, becoming the editor of its newspaper in 1912. By April 1914 he was, "in the judgment of sympathizers and opponents alike, the dictator of the Socialist Party," according to historian James A. Gregor. Vladimir Lenin himself publicly praised his radicalism. Yet Mussolini chaffed under his colleagues' internationalist scruples. He broke party discipline by advocating war against the Central Powers, and was expelled from the Socialist Party. Mussolini then opened a new newspaper, the *People of Italy*, to promote a synthesis of nationalism and socialism. Gregor explains:

> Mussolini insisted that the only socialism that would be viable in the twentieth century would be a socialism prepared to identify itself with the nation. . . . The commitment to national tasks involved fundamental common interests uniting all the special economic and parochial interests of the nation. . . . Mussolini's argument effectively identified traditional socialism as both antinational and antisocialist.

Hitler, in contrast, was never a Marxist; their "unpatriotic outlook" repelled him from the start. Yet he eagerly accepted the socialist label, even though it raised suspicions that "we were nothing but a species of Marxism. . . . For to this very day these scatterbrains have not understood the difference between socialism and Marxism," Hitler wrote. That difference is nationalism. Hitler hated the Marxists not for their economics, but because they "stabbed Germany in the back" during World War I with their revolutionary activities.

Indeed, he repeatedly claims that Marxism is pro-capitalist; it seeks "only to break the people's national and patriotic backbone and make them ripe for the slave's yoke of international capital and its masters, the Jews." For Hitler, preserving "the economic independence of the nation" from "the international stock exchange" is of paramount importance.

Fascist economic policies involved extensive government regulation, expansive public works, and generous social programs. Such policies had clear precedents in socialist legislation, but the fascists gave them a nationalist rationale: to heal internal class divisions, move towards economic autarchy, and prepare for war. As Hitler explained:

> The task of the state toward capital was comparatively simple and clear: it only had to make certain that capital remain the handmaiden of the state and not fancy itself the mistress of the nation. This point of view could then be defined between two restrictive limits: preservation of a solvent, national, and independent economy on the one hand, assurance of the social rights of workers on the other.

Fascists avoided the radical socialist policies of economy-wide nationalization of industry and collectivization of agriculture. But this deviation from orthodox Marxism was hardly unique to fascism: given these policies' devastating effect in the Soviet Union, most socialists wanted to avoid them. Historian Hermann Rauschning explains:

> Hitler had no intention, like Russia, of "liquidating" the possessing class. On the contrary, he would compel it to contribute by its abilities towards the building up of the new order. He could not afford to allow Germany to vegetate for years, as Russia had done, in famine and misery. Besides, the present owners of property would be grateful that their lives had been spared. They would be dependent and in a condition of permanent fear of worse things to come.

Economic policy under Italian fascism. Fascism reigned in Italy for over two decades. During the early years, the influence of national socialist doctrine on actual economic policy was relatively mild. Government's share of gross domestic product declined from 1922–26, as Italian industry recovered from post-World War I turmoil, though the depression restored it to earlier levels. Italian policy came into closer accord with national socialist ideology in the mid-1930s. Public works, state-enforced cartels, and welfare spending expanded significantly. The state bought assets of failing banks and corporations, eventually owning most of the banking sector and "a greater portion of the national economy than in any

other nation-state west of the Soviet Union," Stanley Payne explains in his *History of Fascism, 1914–1945.*

The 1935 conquest of Ethiopia pushed ITALY farther down the fascist road. Government spending rose to fund the war, then went even higher to pay for public works in the new colony. International sanctions to protest the war lasted only three months, but Mussolini used them to permanently reduce Italian dependence on foreign markets. The nationalization bent of fascist economic policy peaked in the last three years of World War II, when Mussolini became the semi-puppet ruler of German-occupied Italy. Mussolini then sought "revenge against the bourgeoisie and the rightist elite whom he believed had thwarted Fascism," Payne says, by subjecting industry to heavy government and worker control.

Economic policy under German National Socialism. The Nazis were far quicker to expand the role of government and cut ties with the world economy. In the first four years of their rule, the annual increase in real private consumption was 2.4 percent, versus an astronomical 19.7 percent for public consumption. Rearmament had priority, but real non-military government spending grew at an annual rate of 5.3 percent, according to economist Avraham Barkai. In spite of the rapid economic recovery, Nazi trade policy pushed imports below their depression levels, particularly in agriculture. Regulation expanded throughout the economy. Author David Schoenbaum provides a good summary:

> Wages, prices, working conditions, allocation of materials: none of these was left to managerial decision, let alone to the market. . . . Investment was controlled, occupational freedom was dead, prices were fixed. . . . Business, particularly big business, declined or flourished in direct proportion to its willingness to collaborate.

Unemployment rapidly fell during Hitler's early years, and his military buildup enjoyed most of the credit. But Nazi labor policy suggests a different mechanism: Wage ceilings and prohibition of militant union activity led to a significant reduction in workers' share of national income, making businesses much more eager to employ them.

WORLD WAR II brought more radical economic changes. The Nazis instituted state slavery, forcing millions of foreigners into involuntary, and often deadly, servitude. As the war progressed, Germany moved close to full fascism, ultimately conscripting women, the elderly, and even children for economic or military service.

Fascisms: divergence and convergence. In spite of the parallels, almost all observers acknowledge major differences between Italian Fascism and German National Socialism. Italian Fascism was far less murderous and militarily aggressive, and moderately less collectivist and internally repressive. Though Mussolini openly described his regime as "totalitarian" by 1925, his practice fell short of his rhetoric.

Furthermore, while Hitler borrowed many ideas from Mussolini, the fateful obsession with *Lebensraum*, or "living space," was unique to Nazism. Hitler was convinced that Germany was doomed to Malthusian starvation unless it could acquire more land: "The National Socialist movement must strive to eliminate the disproportion between our population and our area—viewing this latter as a source of food as well as a basis for power politics," Hitler wrote.

In spite of its superficial appeal, Hitler maintained that peaceful international commerce was shortsighted. He also rejected overseas colonization, arguing that other imperial powers had already occupied the areas "suited for settlement by Europeans." Therefore the only remaining option was "acquisition of new land in Europe itself," particularly in Russia. Hitler provides few specifics about the fate of the current occupants of his prospective conquests, but his subtext is genocidal. However paranoid Hitler's land fetish seems, his foolhardy sneak attack on the USSR suggests that he was sincere.

Conclusion. Since the end of World War II, "fascism" has been a term of abuse, automatically equated with whatever politics one happens to oppose. To understand fascism, we must study its theory and practice during the inter-war period, when millions openly accepted the label. Fascism was a Marxist heresy, a synthesis of socialism and nationalism. It made socialist ideas palatable to a broader audience by abandoning divisive class struggle in favor of unifying national struggle. Unlike modern democratic socialists, the fascists favored a large government role in alliance with corporate capital in the economy, but pragmatically distanced themselves from frightening Leninist measures like out-right expropriation.

BIBLIOGRAPHY. Avraham Barkai, *Nazi Economics: Ideology, Theory, and Policy* (Yale University Press, 1990); James A. Gregor, *The Faces of Janus: Marxism and Fascism in the Twentieth Century* (Yale University Press, 2000); Adolf Hitler, *Mein Kampf* (Houghton-Mifflin, 1971); Carl Landauer, *European Socialism: A History of Ideas and Movements* (University of California Press, 1995); Stanley Payne, *A History of Fascism, 1914–1945* (University of Wisconsin Press, 1995); Richard Pipes, *Russia Under the Bolshevik Regime* (Vintage Books, 1994); Hermann Rauschning, *The Voice of Destruction* (G.P. Putnam's Sons, 1940); David Schoenbaum, *Hitler's Social Revolution: Class and Status in Nazi Germany 1933–1939.* (W.W. Norton, 1980); R. Palmer Dutt, *Fascism and the Social Revolution* (International Publishers, 1935).

BRYAN CAPLAN, PH.D.
GEORGE MASON UNIVERSITY

Federal Reserve

THE FEDERAL RESERVE is the central bank of the United States. It was established through the Federal Reserve Act of 1913, in which the U.S. Congress attempted to create a safe, flexible, and stable monetary system. This Act was in response to the Panic of 1907 when many banks failed. Claiming that he knew nothing about economics, President Theodore ROOSEVELT left it to Congress to develop the new monetary institution. A *New York Times* poll of 90 members of Congress found that some wanted individual banks to issue notes, others favored a central bank, and still others supported issuing emergency currency in limited amounts. No one was definite on how to achieve any of these goals. By 1913, Congress agreed on the new Federal Reserve Act and left it to President Woodrow WILSON to implement its provisions. The Federal Reserve began operation on November 16, 1914.

Twelve Federal Reserve Districts were established, located in New York, Chicago, San Francisco, Philadelphia, Boston, Cleveland, St. Louis, Kansas City, Atlanta, Richmond, Dallas, and Minneapolis. The districts were chosen to best represent the population base at the beginning of the 20th century. Each of the 12 district banks is responsible for oversight of member banks within its district, and each member bank has its own Board of Directors that serves local business and economic interests. Paper money is issued under the authority of the Federal Reserve and is "legal tender for all debts, public and private."

The Federal Reserve Act of 1913 also extended the provision of the Aldrich-Vreeland Act of 1908, which permitted national currency associations to issue emergency currency, until June 30, 1915. This action provided the government with the power to handle the monetary crisis that resulted when WORLD WAR I broke out in Europe in 1914. By August, $208,810,790 of emergency notes had been issued, and World War I changed the entire future of the Federal Reserve system.

As the Federal Reserve system, popularly known as "the Fed," developed, its major duty evolved into overseeing the monetary policies of the United States by controlling the nation's supply of reserve money and overseeing the central supply of money and credit. The Fed can "tighten" the flow of money and credit when the economy is good or expand it when the economy is in crisis. One way that it exercises this power is through the 12-member Federal Open Market Committee, which buys and sells government securities and which can change the discount rate paid to the Federal Reserve by member banks who borrow money.

When these banks borrow from the Federal Reserve, it increases the amount of money paid to the United States government because the Federal Reserve is self-supporting, and all profits over a basic amount are paid into the U.S. Treasury. For example, in 2001, the Federal Reserve paid $27.14 billion to the government. Additional revenue is received from member banks through interest on government securities and service fees charged by the Federal Reserve. Critics of the Federal Reserve system claim that its policies are often short-sighted, and some go so far as to blame the Fed for the Great DEPRESSION. Supporters claim that the Federal Reserve has helped the United States to become a major economic power.

The Federal Reserve also supervises and regulates the banking industry, protects the credit rights of consumers, and provides support to government, the public, and American and foreign financial institutions. While the president of the United States has appointment power over major Federal Reserve officials and Congress has oversight powers, the Federal Reserve is an independent governmental body. The governing body of the entire Federal Reserve System is the Board of Governors. Seven governors are appointed by the president and confirmed by the Senate for 14-year staggered terms that may not be repeated. This means that every two years new appointments are made to the Board. Since the remaining members stay on the Board, Federal Reserve policy tends to remain stable when an election changes the party of the president.

The Chair and the Vice Chair of the Board of Governors are appointed by the president from among board members and confirmed by the Senate, but they serve four-year unlimited terms. In its early days, the Federal Reserve was often pressured by the president to further his own economic goals, but after 1951 the relationship developed into voluntary cooperation. The Chair of the Federal Reserve may remain in office even when an election changes the political party of the president, as was the case with Alan GREENSPAN, who remained Chair between the administrations of Bill CLINTON and George H. BUSH.

BIBLIOGRAPHY. "Board of Governors of the Federal Reserve System," www.federalreserve.gov; Elgin Grose Close, *Fifty Years of Managed Money: The Story of The Federal Reserve* (Spartan, 1966); Morris A. Copeland, *Our Free Enterprise Economy* (Macmillan, 1965); Paul A. Samuelson, *Economics* (McGraw-Hill, 1973); "Why A Federal Reserve System?" www.stls.frb.org.

ELIZABETH PURDY, PH.D.
INDEPENDENT SCHOLAR

Federal Trade Commission

AN INDEPENDENT AGENCY of the UNITED STATES, the Federal Trade Commission (FTC) was created in 1914. It consists of five commissioners appointed by the U.S. president with the advice and consent of the U.S. Senate. The commissioners serve staggered seven-year terms. No more than three commissioners can be from the same political party. The FTC has both rule-making authority as well as enforcement authority. When the FTC promulgates a rule pursuant to its statutory mandate, the rule has the force and effect of law.

The major grant of power to the FTC is contained in Section 5 of the Federal Trade Commission Act of 1914. This section prohibits "unfair methods of competition" as well as "unfair or deceptive acts or practices." The FTC has both consumer protection obligations and ANTITRUST enforcement powers. It also enforces a number of other consumer protection statutes either by itself or in conjunction with other federal agencies.

The broad legislative mandate of the FTC is in large part due to the history of government regulation of business in the late 19th and early 20th centuries. Congress enacted the Sherman Antitrust Act in 1890 in an attempt to eliminate monopolization and restraints of trade. The Sherman Act was a product of an era in which so-called robber barons and various big business trusts dominated American business. Subsequent interpretations of the Sherman Act by the U.S. Supreme Court severely restricted the reach of the Act. At the same time, large businesses were being created by way of mergers and stock acquisitions. These mergers were not subject to Sherman Act jurisdiction in most cases.

Congress viewed competition as the best means to advance consumer welfare and the economy. Monopolies and other accompanying restrictive business practices were viewed as antithetical to individual initiative, independence, and responsibility. Meanwhile, at the beginning of the 20th century, a consumer protection movement began to take hold in the United States. Certain business practices were viewed as unfair, including fraudulent, misleading and deceptive representations in advertising and marketing.

Structure of the FTC. In addition to the commission, the FTC consists of three bureaus and various regional offices. The Bureau of Competition is the antitrust arm of the FTC. Its purpose is to prevent business practices that restrain competition, such as monopolization and anticompetitive mergers. This bureau conducts investigations of individual companies, litigates cases before administrative law judges and federal courts, and engages in business and consumer education.

The Bureau of Consumer Protection is designed to protect consumers from unfair, deceptive, and fraudulent practices. The bureau enforces a number of specific consumer protection laws enacted by Congress, trade regulation rules promulgated by the FTC, and the general provisions of the FTC Act as they relate to consumer protection. The bureau conducts investigations of individual companies, engages in various law enforcement sweeps in cooperation with other federal agencies, litigates cases before administrative law judges and federal courts, and engages in business and consumer education. This bureau also conducts studies to evaluate the impact of proposed actions on consumer and consumer protection.

The Bureau of Economics provides economic analysis and support to both antitrust and consumer protection casework and rule making. It analyzes the impact of government regulations on competition and consumers, and provides various federal agencies and departments with economic studies of various markets and industries.

The FTC is geographically divided into seven regions with offices in major cities. These offices conduct investigations and litigation under the supervision of the Bureaus of Competition and Consumer Protection. They also provide advice to state and local officials on the implications of various proposed actions, provide outreach services to consumers and businesses, coordinate activities with state and local officials, and sponsor seminars for consumers, small businesses, and local authorities.

The FTC also maintains mission support offices, which include Administrative Law Judges, an Executive Director, a General Counsel, an Inspector General, a Secretary, and Legislative and Public Affairs offices.

Statutes enforced by the FTC. The FTC is responsible for enforcing a number of federal statutes in addition to the FTC Act itself. The FTC has specific authority regarding credit and credit practices under the Truth in Lending Act, the Fair Credit Billing Act, the Fair Credit Reporting Act, the Equal Credit Opportunity Act, the Consumer Leasing Act, and the Fair Debt Collection Practices Act. It regulates false advertising of food, drugs, and cosmetics under the Wheeler-Lea Act of 1938. It has regulatory, investigatory and reporting authority under the Public Health Cigarette Smoking Act of 1969 and the Comprehensive Smokeless Tobacco Health Education Act of 1986. Various fair packaging and labeling acts give the FTC broad authority to avoid misrepresentation in the sale of consumer goods.

Privacy and consumer information concerns led Congress to give the FTC expanded authority to protect consumers and their information. Included are the Telemarketing and Consumer Fraud and Abuse Prevention Act of 1994, the Children's Online Privacy Protection Act of 1998, the Identity Theft Assumption and Deterrence Act of 1998, and the Gramm-Leach-Bliley Act of 1999 regarding personal financial information.

Consumer protection under Section 5 of the FTC Act. The FTC Act prohibits unfair or deceptive acts or practices, and has established different standards for unfair

and for deceptive practices: A representation, omission, or practice is deceptive if it is likely to mislead consumers acting reasonably under the circumstances of a particular case; and it is material in the sense that it is likely to affect consumers' conduct or decisions with respect to the product or service in issue. The FTC has issued its own Federal Trade Commission Policy Statement on Deception to clarify its standards on this issue.

Unfairness was defined by Congress in a 1994 amendment to Section 5 of the FTC Act. An act or practice is unfair if the injury it causes or is likely to cause to consumers is substantial; not outweighed by countervailing benefits to consumers or to competition; and not reasonably avoidable by consumers themselves.

The FTC has issued policy statements and guides for specific areas. These include advertising, substantiation in advertising, bait advertising, deceptive pricing, use of the word "free," endorsements and testimonials, dietary supplements, eye-care surgery, food advertising, jewelry, furniture, and vocational and distance-education schools. These are in addition to the more general policy statements on deception and unfairness. The FTC also issues informational publications for both consumers and businesses with a view to educating people on their rights and obligations under the FTC Act.

Consumers and competitors do not have standing to sue under the FTC Act. Only the FTC can bring an action to enforce the statute. Because it has limited resources, the FTC normally investigates only matters of national concern and matters involving health and safety, as opposed to local matters or issues having only minor economic impacts. After conducting an investigation, the FTC staff makes a recommendation to the Commission to either close a case, settle a case, or proceed with a formal complaint. If a formal complaint is issued, the case is heard in a trial before an administrative law judge. The decision of the administrative law judge can be reviewed by the full Commission or it can be allowed to become a final decision. Appeals from a final decision are to the U.S. Circuit Court of Appeals and then to the U.S. Supreme Court.

The FTC can impose a range of civil penalties. A cease-and-desist order will require a business to stop a practice, provide substantiation for a claim, report periodically to the FTC about substantiation or other matters, and pay a fine up to $11,000 per day under the current version of the statute. The FTC can order corrective advertising as well as imposing other civil penalties in the form of consumer redress to people who purchased a product. This can result in the expenditure of millions of dollars.

The FTC enforcement of antitrust laws. The FTC has indirect authority to enforce the Sherman Act since, as the courts have held, any act or practice which violates the Sherman Act is also an unfair method of competition violating Section 5 of the FTC Act. The FTC has direct enforcement powers under the Clayton Antitrust Act to prohibit acquisitions, which may substantially lessen competition or tend to create a monopoly, as well as Clayton Act prohibitions on tying and exclusive dealing arrangements. Companies are required to file pre-merger notifications with the FTC and the Justice Department for transactions that satisfy certain thresholds under the Hart-Scott-Rodino Act amendments to the Clayton Act. The FTC also enforces the Robinson Patman Act, which prohibits certain forms of price discrimination that may lessen competition. Most of the FTC authority in this area is shared with the Antitrust Division of the Department of Justice.

The FTC administers only civil penalties for antitrust law violations. Included in these penalties are cease-and-desist orders, injunctions prohibiting mergers and acquisitions, and monetary penalties. In some cases the monetary penalties can be substantial. Criminal violations of the antitrust laws must be prosecuted by the Department of Justice.

BIBLIOGRAPHY. Federal Trade Commission, *Strategic Plan: Fiscal Years 2000–2005* (FTC, 2000); Robert V. Labaree, *The Federal Trade Commission: A Guide to Sources* (Garland Publishing, 2000); Patrick Murphy and William Wilkie, *Marketing and Advertising Regulation: The Federal Trade Commission in the 1990s* (University of Notre Dame Press, 1990); Lynda J. Oswald, *The Law of Marketing* (West Legal Studies in Business, 2002); Richard A. Posner, *Economic Analysis of Law* (Aspen Publishers, 2002); *U.S. Federal Trade Commission Handbook* (International Business Publications, 2000).

DAVID PAAS, J.D., PH.D.
HILLSDALE COLLEGE

federalism

FISCAL FEDERALISM is a decentralized system of government with taxation and fiscal responsibilities vested in both central and lower levels of government. The UNITED STATES has a federal system of government. In this system, there are many civil units with power to raise revenues and provide local services. Three levels of government consist of the federal, state, and local jurisdictions, which include counties, cities and towns, and smaller civil divisions such as villages and special districts with less than 1,000 residents.

The three basic functions of these governments are: the establishment of property right and regulation of private actions; determination of provisions of goods and services including national defense, homeland security, ed-

ucation, roads and health; and redistribution of income. State and local governments determine the provision of local services and their revenue needs.

These activities influence the economic decisions of the individuals and businesses and the course of the economy. Government employs about one fifth of the work force and constitutes nearly 25 percent of the GROSS DOMESTIC PRODUCT (GDP). In recent years, the share of the state and local governments has risen steadily. State governments spent $1.1 trillion in fiscal year 2000, exceeding the $1 trillion mark for the first time in U.S. history. Their revenues exceeded $1.3 trillion in the same year. Intergovernmental revenues totaled $274 billion or 22 percent, most of which came from the federal government. State and local governments employed more than 15 million full-time equivalent workers in 2000.

The decentralized system of government raises some important and interesting questions regarding relegation of responsibilities among these levels of government. In general, in a decentralized system citizens can influence the outcome of the political process according to their preferences for the level of government services and ways for raising revenues to pay for them. A major implication and consequence of this multilevel fiscal system is that when benefits are spatially separated, services are provided by separate units. Consequently, these units differ in size and fiscal capacity. Allowing for differences in taste and capacity to pay, people with similar incomes and tastes tend to live in the same jurisdictions. However, higher-income people have a tendency to move away from lower-income communities and the lower-income people to follow them.

Economic theory provides some insight into the consequences of alternative means of providing government services. Usually, public services are provided and financed in line with their relevant benefit regions. For that reason, the federal government provides services that are collectively consumed at the national level such as national defense and homeland security. It is clear that all citizens benefit from these services. On the other hand, state and local governments provide services such as education, police and fire protection, streetlights, and refuse removal. These services are spatially limited to the local residents.

The means of financing government services vary with local desires. Communities with strong preferences for certain programs can differ substantially in their menu of services and respective taxes. However, these decisions are not totally independent from those in other communities. Individuals search for the communities that best match their preferred level of services and corresponding tax liabilities. In the other words, they "vote with their feet." Thus, if a community decides to tax the rich more heavily than the poor and the middle-income, it most likely will erode its tax base as the rich leave and the poor and the middle-class move in.

Allowing diversity and differences in taste assures more flexibility and more choice and improved efficiency in allocation of resources according to citizens' tastes. However, it raises important concerns regarding inequities arising from differing fiscal capacities.

Variation in fiscal capacity among state and local governments requires special fiscal arrangements for coordination of services and expenditures among communities for various reasons. The higher level of governments may need to correct spillover of benefits, may want to advance an activity with social merit by providing a subsidy, and to some extent equalize the fiscal position of the lower-income jurisdictions, among other goals. The federal government provides grants to states for various purposes.

In 2001, per capita federal aid to state and local governments ranged from a maximum of more than $3,800 (for Alaska) to a minimum of $700 (for Nevada).

States also make grants to their own local subdivisions. Most of state grants are provided to reduce the effect of differences in sizes of the jurisdictions. States subsidize localities for education, public welfare and highway spending.

The globalization of the world economy has already altered the federal systems and has set the stage for new international institutions. For example, "Europe 1992" eliminated trade barriers among the European Community member states and established a central government authority. Originally, Alexis de Tocqueville, the French philosopher incorporated the U.S. federal experience into European thought particularly in Germany and France. He regarded the American decentralized form of government essential for a liberal and democratic society while he raised concern about its future.

The need to link separate communities in order to achieve common objectives is an old concept. Alliances of Greek city-states or mediaeval Italian towns were short-term alliance of this type. However, more permanent unions were less common and generally had weak central authorities. In the United States, the states originally formed a loose relationship with the Confederation—a weak central government. In 1789, that system was replaced by a new constitution, creating the modern United States and its current system of federalism. Alexander HAMILTON, John Jay, and James MADISON argued in favor of ratifying the federal constitution in the Federalist Papers.

As de Tocqueville expected, the future of American federalism remains uncertain. A ranking and comparison of key U.S. intergovernmental events, 1960–80 and 1980–95 has found that the role of the federal government in intergovernmental affairs has diminished. These trends will remain influential in forming the future of the decentralized system in the United States and in the emerging global economy.

BIBLIOGRAPHY. Michael Greve, "How to Promote Federalism and How Not to, Thoughts on Federalism," www.federalismproject.org; David H. Hyman, *Public Finance: A Contemporary Application of Theory to Policy* (Dryden Press HBJ, 2002); John Kincaid, "Federal Democracy and Liberty," (Symposium: Tocqueville and Democracy in America), *Political Science and Politics* (June 1999); Richard A. Musgrave and Peggy B. Musgrave, *Public Finance in Theory and Practice* (McGraw-Hill, 1976); Stephen Woodard, *The Simple Guide to the Federal Idea, from Ventotene, Federalism and Politics* (The Ventotene Papers of the Altiero Spinelli Institute for Federalist Studies, Ventotene, 1995).

SIMIN MOZAYENI, PH.D.
STATE UNIVERSITY OF NEW YORK, NEW PALTZ

feudalism

MOST SPECIFICALLY, feudalism is a term designating the predominant system of political organization of the European Middle Ages, arising in the wake of the disintegration of the Roman Empire after the 5th century. A vassal or political subordinate pledged fealty and military support to a political superior, his liege lord, in a ceremony that involved swearing fidelity and the performance of homage; in turn, the lord granted the vassal a "fief" or "feudum" (sometimes called a "benefice" in early sources), a coercive monopoly on the piece of territory he governed.

The parties to this arrangement are called "feudatories." The vassal could, in turn, subdivide his own fief. Thus, one individual could be a vassal to several lords. Feudalism should be seen as a complex, interlocking series of local arrangements. The vassal's obligations might include military service, garrison or court duty, relief (a tax on the hereditary status of the fief), aid (a system of extraordinary levies for particular circumstances), and hospitality. The liege pledged protection and justice for the vassal. This system, as a functioning means of government, peaked in the 12th and 13th centuries and was in decay by the late 15th century, giving rise especially in England to a decadent form called "bastard feudalism" in which the private armies of feudal peers vied for power. The period at the end of the 15th century saw the turn from feudal to absolutist monarchies, but important aspects of feudalism as a political arrangement persisted widely in continental Europe until the FRENCH REVOLUTION (1789), and its ceremonial vestiges are still apparent in those nations that retain a monarch, most notably in England. Originally, the term "feudal" described only the relationship between the noble and knightly or "armigerous" castes (those with a claim on a coat of arms). Feudal monarchies are characterized by the fragmentation of power and strong nobility (as opposed to absolutist monarchies, which seek centralized power and a weak nobility).

Feudal economics. The historian Georges Duby convincingly distinguished between feudalism as an economic system and as a political arrangement. In contemporary parlance, however, feudalism is frequently conflated with or understood to mean the manorial or seigniorial system, a system of land tenure that was the fundamental economic arrangement of medieval society after the early Middle Ages. It persisted formally and informally in parts of western Europe through 1789 and in Europe east of the Elbe River until 1848 or beyond.

In the manorial system, that had its roots in the large landed estates of the later Roman Empire, a local lord, typically a minor knight, but sometimes an abbot, managed the labor of local inhabitants, who would have been slaves in the Roman Empire, but whose status had been converted to that of a quasi-emancipation known as serfdom. They could no longer be purchased, but were still bound to remain on the land and obey the commands of the lord. The lord extracted rent from the tenants for land they tended, usually in the form of labor services. These inhabitants, frequently serfs, also cultivated the lord's land (the "demesne") and allowed his animals to graze on the common land. Peasants also paid taxes in kind for consumption of local resources (firewood or game) or use of common machinery (a portion of the flour from wheat ground in the manorial mill). Two primary organizational forms of seigneurialism were found in Europe: "Gutsherrschaft" east of the Elbe, in which the demesne comprised the largest portion of cultivated land, and "Grundherrschaft" in the west, where most land was cultivated by individual tenants. After the 12th century, most western European serfs could convert their labor obligations to fixed money rents and become free "villeins"; this system of emancipation was not possible in eastern Europe, where there were few individual tenants, and here, serfdom persisted much longer. The so-called disintegration of the manor in western Europe was typically favored by both peasants and lords. Peasants achieved greater freedom, particularly from hated labor obligations, and lords were rewarded with a cash payment and freed from paternalistic obligation to their tenants.

Although the terminology for describing the manorial system was derived from the European context and historians became increasingly ambivalent about its usefulness by the 1960s, Marc Bloch's use of the word "feudal" to describe a particular type of society has been expanded to explain arrangements in other parts of the world in other chronological phases (especially Japan, China, India, Latin America and Africa) despite the opposition of specialists to the designation in these contexts.

The arguments of Karl MARX regarding the historical stages of economic development made such usages common. For Marx, feudalism was an intermediate pre-requisite stage on the way to capitalism, in that the landlord did not completely control the means of production (as the capitalist later would), but could still appropriate the product. In this view, feudalism was challenged by the growth of trade and resulting markets for manufactured goods, which the feudal economy could not satisfy, both because seigneurs were primarily focused on political aims and not on standard-of-living issues, and because guild structure limited production to keep prices high. Because of these initial changes, capitalist production grew up around the feudal system, eventually causing landlords to orient themselves toward profit. Ultimately, then, they seek to enclose the common land of the manor in order to pursue profits, driving peasants off the land and into cities and providing the basis of the urban proletariat that will staff emergent capitalist factories.

Feudalism today. In most common usage today, feudal relations are found to occur whenever tenants pay rents to a monopolistic landlord class (the "seigneurie") that retains the non-economic coercive powers necessary to continue the subordination of the tenants, most typical as the economic mode of agrarian societies. The status of the peasants as serfs may be formally or informally codified. Arguably, this use of the term is most convincing to Marxist historians who understand the rise of free-wage labor from the decay of the manorial system, along with changes in the dominant mode of production, as the fundamental process that permitted capitalism to triumph. Similar assumptions, albeit from a different political perspective, underlay most of modernization theory as it developed after the 1950s.

A number of responses to such thinking emerged in the 1970s and 1980s. One of the most popular, DEPENDENCY THEORY, questioned the assumption that modern, industrialized capitalism was the most desirable end of economic development, and envisioned an alternative view of history in which Latin American arrangements were not viewed as anachronistic. These arguments have been confused by the multi-layered nature of much Third World economic activity; in Latin America, for instance, "feudal" features, such as the hierarchical organization of agrarian production in mines, workshops, plantations and haciendas, have co-existed from the beginning with capitalist commerce, wage labor and capital investment. In the wake of modernization theory, a number of creative attempts have been made to try to explain the persistence of feudal features in emergent or full-blown capitalist economies.

The most well known of these is the world-systems theory of Immanuel Wallerstein. According to this view, history should not be written from the perspective of the nation or region, but from a viewpoint that embraces different world areas organized economically: the most influential area is termed the "core," and areas with less political, economic, and social power are termed the "periphery." In this view, in the transition to the modern world, the core nations were those that most effectively navigated the transition from feudalism to capitalism, not only by giving rise to systems of wage-labor that replaced feudal arrangements, but also by developing effective mechanisms of labor control and strong coercive state apparatuses that defended and regulated these elements. Peripheral areas of the world that persisted in earlier means of production (either forced labor, as in the case of much of Latin America, or sharecropping, serfdom, or slavery) were forced into this position by the core powers so that the flow of resources and capital to the core powers could continue uninterruptedly. Critics of this system have argued that viewing the world economy as a system arranged by the core powers for their own benefit does not account for the constraints placed by indigenous history and circumstance.

"Feudal" continues to be a pejorative description from the modern perspective, and the debates of how allegedly feudal economies transformed themselves to capitalist production continue to be important as many seek the solutions to the economic problems of the Third World.

BIBLIOGRAPHY. Marc Bloch, *Feudal Society* (University of Chicago Press, 1961); Elizabeth A. R. Brown, "The Tyranny of a Construct: Feudalism and Historians of Medieval Europe," *American Historical Review* (1974); Jack Goody, "Economy and Feudalism in Africa," *Economic History Review* (v.22, 1969); John Whitney Hall, "Japanese Feudalism: A Reassessment," *Comparative Studies in Society and History* (v.5, 1962); Tulio Halperín-Donghi, "Dependency Theory and Latin American Historiography," *Latin American Research Review* (v.17, 1982); Barbara H. Rosenwein, *Negotiating Space: Power, Restraint and Privileges of Immunity in Early Medieval Europe* (Cornell University Press, 1999); Steve J. Stern, "Feudalism, Capitalism, and the World-System in the Perspective of Latin America and the Caribbean," *American Historical Review* (v.93, 1988); Immanuel Wallerstein, *The Modern World-System* (Academic Press, 1974–89).

SUSAN R. BOETTCHER, PH.D.
UNIVERSITY OF TEXAS, AUSTIN

Fiat

EVER SINCE JULY 11, 1899, when the *Società Anonima Fabbrica Italiana di Automobili-Torino* was formed, Fiat and the family that manages it, the Agnellis, have played a crucial part both in the development of Italian capitalism, and on the stage of Italian politics. Italian governments have always been more than willing to help out the Turin car industry both financially and politically.

The first car to be produced was a 4-horsepower engine capable of about 23 miles per hour, built by 150 workers. Other models soon followed and Fiat began to mass-produce cars and to expand to European and American markets. During the company's first 10 years, Fiat also diversified into the production of trucks, buses, trams, and marine and aero engines, and became involved in racing. With the rise to power of FASCISM in the late 1920s, Fiat had to stop its international expansion and focus on the domestic market. The most famous models of these years were the 508 Balilla (whose name paid homage to Benito Mussolini's dictatorship, meaning young fascist), first produced in 1932, and the 500 Topolino (1936), the smallest mass-produced car in the world at the time. In 1937, the famous Mirafiori plant started production, employing 22,000 workers.

The history of Fiat, after WORLD WAR II, is marked in equal measure by economic successes and severe financial crises. In the immediate postwar years, Fiat benefited from the financial aid of the MARSHALL PLAN and, under the leadership of Vittorio Valletta, was able to reconstruct its plants and launch new models such as the popular Fiat 500 and Fiat 600. In the late 1950s and in the 1960s, the Turin car industry exploited the years of Italian economic growth and expanded its domestic and international markets. The 1970s, on the contrary, were marked by social unrest and Fiat was shaken by workers' demonstrations supported by the major opposition party, the Italian Communist Party. This decade of turmoil and demands for fairer treatment of workers ended in 1980 with the March of the 40,000, a demonstration of white-collar professionals demanding an end to the workers' protests.

At the beginning of the new millennium, with the death of its charismatic president (and senator of the Italian Republic), Gianni Agnelli, Fiat faced new challenges. Despite the wealth of new models put on the market in the 1990s, the sales of the Turin-based group have diminished considerably and the partnership established with America's GENERAL MOTORS has only partially recovered financial losses. The group has also been at the center of several legal investigations for political corruption in Operation "Clean Hands" (*Mani Pulite*), a reform movement that swept away many of Italy's ruling politicians. Still, in 2002, Fiat ranked as the 49th largest company in the world with revenues of nearly $52 billion.

BIBLIOGRAPHY. Alan Friedman, *Agnelli: Fiat and the Network of Italian Power* (Penguin Books, 1989); Angiolo Silvio Ori, *Storia di una dinastia: gli Agnelli e la Fiat: cronache non autorizzate dei cento anni della più grande industria italiana* (Editori Riuniti, 1996); "Global 500: World's Largest Companies," *Fortune* (July 2002).

LUCA PRONO, PH.D.
UNIVERSITY OF NOTTINGHAM, ENGLAND

Fillmore, Millard (1800–74)

THE 13TH PRESIDENT of the UNITED STATES, Millard Fillmore was born in Cayuga County, New York. He had no formal education, but was tutored by a young teacher, Abigail Powers, whom he later married. As a young adult Fillmore moved to Buffalo where he was admitted to the Bar in 1823. He began his political career helping to organize the Antimasonic Party and served in the state legislature (1829–31), where he worked for the abolition of imprisonment for debt. In 1832, he was elected to the U.S. Congress, but as the Antimasonic Party fell apart, Fillmore did not seek re-election in 1834. Two years later he successfully ran as a Whig candidate for Congress and was subsequently re-elected three more times.

In Congress, Fillmore supported strong protectionist legislation, including the Whig Tariff of 1842. He also supported the anti-slavery faction of the Whig Party but tended to take moderate positions, believing that while slavery was evil, its existence in the American South was guaranteed by the U.S. Constitution.

In 1848, Fillmore received the party's nomination for vice president, balancing the Whig Party ticket of presidential nominee, Southern slave-owner Zachary TAYLOR.

When Taylor died suddenly in 1850, Fillmore became president and acted to resolve the growing crisis over the expansion of slavery by supporting the Compromise of 1850. Part of the Compromise was the infamous Fugitive Slave Act, which required Northern states to assist in the recapture of escaped slaves and their return to the South.

Although a supporter of high tariffs, Fillmore also supported foreign trade. He sent Commodore Perry to open trade relations with JAPAN and signed commercial treaties with many other countries. Moreover, he supported a failed effort to build a canal connecting the Atlantic and Pacific oceans through Nicaragua.

Fillmore was in favor of improvements to the nation's transportation infrastructure, such as canals and RAILROADS. Reduced transportation costs allowed him to sign into law a significant reduction in postal rates.

During his three years in office, the federal budget remained under $50 million, with budget surpluses of about $4 million each year.

Fillmore's support for the Compromise of 1850 so outraged abolitionists that the party's anti-slavery faction withheld its support at the 1852 convention, costing him the nomination. Four years later Fillmore accepted the presidential nomination of the American Party (the "Know-Nothings"), a strong anti-Catholic, anti-foreigner party. Fillmore, however, focused on the need for national unity. He lost overwhelmingly.

During the AMERICAN CIVIL WAR, Fillmore remained loyal to the Union, but strongly opposed many of President Abraham LINCOLN's wartime policies, including emancipation of the slaves. After the war, Fillmore supported President Andrew JOHNSON's conciliatory approach to Reconstruction and tended to support Democratic Party policies.

BIBLIOGRAPHY. Robert G. Ferris, *The Presidents* (Interpretive Publications, 1977); Robert J. Raybach, *Millard Fillmore* (American Political Biography Press, 1992); Robert J. Scarry, *Millard Fillmore* (McFarland, 2001).

MICHAEL J. TROY, J.D.
THOMAS D. JEITSCHKO, PH.D.
MICHIGAN STATE UNIVERSITY

film and film industry

AS FYODOR DOSTOYEVSKY and Emile Zola wrote masterpiece novels about wealth and poverty in the 19th century, filmmakers throughout the world in the 20th century have created movies about work, money, financial empires, class conflicts, and other facets of capitalism. Feature films do not pretend to depict reality exactly as it is; these works are points of view, visions, social constructions, subjective representations of a specific context, as seen by artists, recreated by directors, scriptwriters, and actors. But many people use selected elements they see in movies as references about the way they behave, talk, see others, and represent other nations and foreign cultures. Therefore, films shouldn't be separated from their social, cultural, historical, and economic contexts.

For example, at any point, Soviet films produced under Josef Stalin were quite different from Hollywood movies, even during the same period. But oddly, it was easier to see a Hollywood film in the Soviet Union than to watch a Soviet movie in the UNITED STATES, anytime in 20th century. This raises the question of film distribution (discussed in the second part of this article). This entry will present a few examples of films using elements about capitalism, plus an overview of the film industry seen as a capitalist, sometimes monopolistic system.

Films about labor and capital. Even in the age of silent movies, class conflicts were represented in a masterly fashion in some feature films. The most perfect and unequalled example is probably Fritz Lang's *Metropolis* (1927). In a gigantic city of the future (inspired by Lang's first vision of New York City from 1924), a powerful man (Fredersen, the living symbol of the capitalist) rules masses of workers that are submitted as slaves to the machine's infernal cycles and cadences.

A young pacifist, Maria, tries to hold back rebellion among exhausted workers, but the insensitive master learns of her actions and sends a replicate robot to secretly replace the pacifist. The human-like robot raises a revolt that destroys the workers' city, but those lives are saved by the real Maria. This metaphoric story shows the conflicts between workers and leaders, but also contemporary themes such as the fear of machines, robots that can take humans' places, union assemblies, and in a way, aspects of industrial relations. This German film became popular again in 1984 when it was colorized, reedited and distributed from the United States with its new rock soundtrack. The original silent (and longer) version remains more difficult to find in video stores, mainly for distribution reasons.

Many other film classics could be mentioned. In the Soviet Union, director Serguey Eisenstein created his first film, *Strike* (1924), which showed a rebellion among workers who were manipulated and punished during a strike. After the silent era, French film *A nous la liberté* (1931), directed by René Clair, presents a hobo who becomes the owner of a big firm. When he retires, he gives his enterprise to its employees. Clearly influenced by Clair's previous film, Charles Chaplin's *Modern Times* (1936) is perhaps the most famous, although not the first film about capitalism, with assembly lines, machines, bosses, economic crisis, workers' demonstrations, and strikes.

Another French film, *Le roman d'un tricheur* (Sacha Guitry, 1936), shows the story of an elegant man who became rich in casinos by cheating. His life was centered on his fascination with gambling.

Orson Welles's *Citizen Kane* (1941) is a sly presentation of the life of millionaire William Randolph Hearst and his affair with actress Marion Davies. We see the rise and fall of a narcissus businessman, who successfully buys newspapers, builds an empire, and therefore tries to control people's opinions.

A rather melodramatic masterpiece is *Bicycle Thief* (1948), the great Italian film directed by Vittorio De Sica that won many awards. After WORLD WAR II, a poor unemployed man needs a bicycle in order to get his first job in two years. After many sacrifices, he buys a bicycle but it soon gets stolen. The police can't help him so he tries to save his job by looking for the thief. As a last resource, he steals a bicycle and is arrested. Hollywood proposed Cary Grant for the leading role, but De Sica preferred to choose an unknown worker to obtain more realism.

Perhaps the most eloquent film about capitalism was praised in the 1960 Moscow Film Festival; it is a Japanese drama without dialogue, titled *The Island* (1960), directed by Kaneto Shindo. It is the strongest example of the criticisms of capitalism: a couple of poor laborers, with their two sons, live and work endlessly on a farm they don't own on a dry island. One day, when they capture a big fish, they sell it alive to a restaurant in the city, instead of cooking it. They buy clothes for the children with the money they earned. The scene when they respectfully offer all their harvest to their landlord is eloquent.

During the 1970s, many films dealt with union issues, such as an Italian drama, *The Working Class Goes to Heaven* (1971), written and directed by Elio Petri, and the American film *Norma Rae* (1979), directed by Martin Ritt, with Sally Field. Another American movie titled *Wall Street* (by Oliver Stone, 1987) was adapted from Kenneth Lipper's book. It showed a case of insider trading (an intentional tort) with a corrupted broker. On a more sarcastic note, *Roger and Me* (1990), directed by Michael Moore, is an unusual documentary about a man (the filmmaker) who tries to meet General Motors' chairman of the board to discuss why 35,000 workers in Flint, Michigan, were fired. The powerful boss remains unreachable, almost an abstraction.

As for comedies, the film *Tommy Boy* (P. Segal, 1995) shows how complicated it is for a son to succeed his father at the head of a big enterprise. Woody Allen's *Small Time Crooks* (2000) depicts a funny case of an unwanted success-story. Three criminals prepare a strategy to attack a bank; they slyly hide their plans by opening a little bakery commerce as a facade. But their honest business becomes a huge success while their crime strategy fails.

The film industry. The film industry, especially in the United States, is an aggressive universe. As Douglas Gomery explains, movies can sometimes be lucrative but they are always expensive to produce. Half of their budget usually goes to advertising and promotion. The American film industry has globalized since the 1920s, forming a group usually known as the majors, a group in competition with virtually all other film producers in the world. These seven major producers and distributors of motion picture and television programs are: Metro-Goldwyn-Mayer; Paramount Pictures Corporation; Walt Disney Company; Twentieth Century Fox Film Corp.; Universal Studios; Sony Pictures Entertainment; and Warner Bros., now part of AOL-Time Warner. These companies are represented by the Motion Picture Association of America (MPAA), one of the most powerful private organizations in the world.

The dominant American film industry has been criticized over the years. As opposed to most democratic countries, the U.S. film market (in theaters as well as on television) seems to be, in the main, closed to foreign productions; it has been described by American scholar Janet Wasko as "a more or less closed market through a form of de facto protectionism."

Capitalist extremes and excesses seem to characterize much of the motion pictures industry. In the American domestic market (that includes CANADA as well as the United States), the majors consider any other producer or distributor as a competitor. Producers share agreement exclusivities with specific distributors and exhibitors. This explains why foreign films are rarely offered on the big screens in movie theaters. According to American scholar Thomas Guback, "Market concentration and anti-competitive behavior are not unique to the motion picture business, although its history demonstrates how those conditions have characterized the industry." Guback adds: "In reality, the choice reduces itself, not to MONOPOLY or COMPETITION, but to monopoly, shared monopoly, or OLIGOPOLY. When that happens, rationalizations and legitimizations appear that either excuse monopoly or invent competition where it does not exist."

This dominant situation also repeats itself in many foreign countries. An illegal practice in the United States, block-booking, is often imposed on foreign exhibitors; this means they have to rent and schedule unwanted movies in order to obtain the few they really want. As scholar Ian Jarvie has explained, countries that would want to object to the American film presence have been threatened with a boycott menace; such was the case for a few months in England in 1948. It stopped when the UK film industry began to flourish again, during that U.S. boycott. In another article, Guback concludes about the Hollywood's world reputation: "American films and American companies are dominant, not because of the natural operation of marketplace forces, but because the marketplace has been made to operate in their favor."

People unaware of these sociological factors and economic structures often believe that American films are more visible or more popular because they are better, or because audiences would prefer them. This impression appears to be wrong. In fact, film domination can be explained in economic terms. Since this dominant position of the U. S. film industry has taken place for many generations, most American audiences wouldn't rapidly have the openness and curiosity to watch many foreign films. "Public taste in films has been formed and cultivated for decades by vertically integrated industry in which majors showed their films in their own theaters, and these acquired patterns of preference persist."

With a few exceptions, American audiences (of both movies and general television) are not exposed to foreign cultural products. They only see foreign universes through the lenses of American filmmakers. "Audiences can only be formed for films that are effectively available to them. The free-choice argument is no more than the myth of the consumer sovereignty which masks the demand created by film-distributing companies through massive advertising and promotion," explains author Pendakur Manjunath. The impact of this situation, which is perpetuated in many countries, is a feeble cultural diversity and a lack of dynamism in many cinematic arts.

BIBLIOGRAPHY. Douglas Gomery, "The Hollywood Film Industry: Theatrical Exhibition, Pay TV, and Home Video," *Who Owns the Media: Competition and Concentration in the Mass Media Industry* (Lawrence Erlbaum Associates, 2000); Thomas Guback, *The International Film Industry: Western Europe and America Since 1945* (Indiana University Press, 1969); Thomas Guback, "Theatrical Film," *Who Owns the Media: Competition and Concentration in the Mass Media Industry* (Knowledge Industry, 1982); Thomas Guback, "Non-Market Factors in the International Distribution of American Films," *Current Research in Film: Audiences, Economics, and Law* (Ablex Publications, 1985); Ian Jarvie, *Hollywood Overseas Campaign: The North Atlantic Movie Trade, 1920–1950* (Cambridge University Press, 1992); Toby Miller, ed., *Global Hollywood* (BFI Publishing, 2001); Pendakur, Manjunath, *Canadian Dreams, American Control: The Political Economy of the Canadian Film Industry* (Wayne State University Press, 1991); John Trumpbour, *Selling Hollywood to the World: U. S. and European Struggles for Mastery of the Global Film Industry, 1920–1950* (Cambridge University Press, 2002).

YVES LABERGE, PH.D.
INSTITUT QUÉBÉCOIS DES
HAUTES ÉTUDES INTERNATIONALES

finance

FINANCE IS A SUB-FIELD of economics that studies financial markets, financial instruments, and financial institutions. The basic function of the financial system is to intermediate financial funds between the net lenders and net borrowers. Net lenders lack sufficiently productive investment opportunities themselves, possess financial wealth, and thus are net savers. Net borrowers lack sufficient funds to undertake their productive investment opportunities, and thus are net spenders. Savers, spenders, and financial intermediaries are the main participants in financial markets. The financial intermediaries sit in between the savers and end-users of these financial funds, and facilitate exchange.

Financial markets include STOCK EXCHANGES, BOND markets, money markets, and foreign-exchange markets.

Financial intermediaries include deposit-taking banking institutions, investment banks, and venture capital firms. If funds directly flow from savers to end-users through financial markets, this is referred to as direct finance, and if they flow from savers to end-users through financial intermediaries, this is referred to as indirect finance. For instance, buying shares in a publicly traded company through a stockbroker is a form of direct finance, and buying shares in a mutual fund, which may in turn buy shares in a publicly traded company, is a form of indirect finance. Financial markets and intermediaries play several very important roles in capitalist economies. First, they help allocate resources towards their most efficient uses. Firms with the most productive investment opportunities do not necessarily possess undistributed profits that are sufficient to pay for the project. Financial markets help identify such projects, assess their relative profitability, and ultimately fund them. Second, financial markets help allocate resources over time. In the absence of direct or indirect finance, firms, households, and governments would have been required to spend out of their current incomes only. Financial markets allow households to borrow against their future income (in credit markets), firms to raise capital against their future profits (in equity markets), and governments to issue bills and bonds against their future revenues (in debt markets).

Third, financial markets enable participants to exchange risks, and therefore help share risks more efficiently.

Indicators of economic development. All of these basic functions of financial markets and intermediaries have long been recognized as important indicators of economic development. At least since Joseph SCHUMPETER (1951), many economists have argued that a well-functioning, mature financial system is an important determinant of economic growth. Many development economists have, for example, observed that restrictive regulations (financial repression) on financial markets can hinder economic growth by discouraging savings and allocating resources toward unproductive uses. These restrictions have included foreign-exchange controls, and interest-rate ceilings on demand deposits paid by banking institutions. Binding interest-rate ceilings either reduce the incentives to save, and thus curtail the amount of funds available for end-users, or encourage different (and less productive) forms of saving, such as in the form of precious metals.

Since the early 1990s, there has been a worldwide tendency toward liberalizing financial markets in an attempt to put finance at the service of economic growth and development. While the economic consequences of financial repression for economic development appear to be rather uncontroversial, there has been some disagreement over the desirable speed and form of financial liberalization and de-regulation in both developed and developing countries. For example, countries that have liberalized their financial markets seem to become vulnerable to currency and banking crises. At least for the banking sector, one of the determinants of crisis subsequent to liberalization is whether there exists effective banking regulation and supervision. When financial liberalization takes place within a "weak" institutional environment, it tends to result in costly bank failures, financial turmoil, and economic recessions. As well, a gradual approach to liberalization tends to reduce the likelihood of crisis.

Why does financial liberalization lead to costly outcomes? The reason is that inappropriate institutional arrangements exacerbate some of the basic problems that are inherent in finance and financial markets. The identification, analysis, and assessment of such basic problems, which essentially give rise to the discipline of finance and financial economics, extend beyond the narrower analysis of banking and financial crises. The two most basic issues underlying finance are asymmetric information and pricing of risk. The first issue is very relevant for the study of financial institutions, and the second is crucial for the study of financial instruments.

Theory of finance. One of the premises of the theory of finance is that informational problems give rise to financial institutions that attempt to mitigate these problems. The problems originate from the prevalence of asymmetric information, whereby one of the parties to a financial contract commands more or better information about the possible outcomes of the contract. Consider, for example, a bank loan. Deposit-taking banks intermediate between depositors (net savers) and firms (net spenders), and this intermediation typically takes the form of a loan contract. The contract stipulates the amount of the loan (principal), the maturity date, and the interest payment dates and amounts. The difference between the interest received from the loan and the interest paid to the depositors is the net revenue of the bank. The bank faces a default risk. Part of this default risk is related to asymmetric information because the borrowers typically have superior information regarding their project and their own abilities than the bank. In the presence of asymmetric information the bank will only have imperfect ways of distinguishing between the "good" and the "bad" projects (borrowers).

Asymmetric information leads to two separate problems, adverse selection and MORAL HAZARD. Adverse selection, in the case of a loan contract, suggests that a higher interest rate would only attract riskier investment projects (with possibly higher expected returns). This increases the bank's loan portfolio because as the interest rate rises, low risk-low return borrowers will be discouraged, potentially leaving those borrowers with no intentions to pay their loans back. Thus, adverse selection refers to the situation in which a bank's own actions increase the default risk it faces before the transaction occurs.

Moral hazard, in the context of a bank loan, corresponds to riskier behavior by the borrower after the bank extends a loan. Banks typically have imperfect ability to monitor and control the actions of the borrowers. Further, once the loan is disbursed the borrower may have incentives to shirk, or undertake riskier and undesirable activities. Thus, the actions of the borrower increase the default risk that the bank faces after the transaction occurs.

Moral hazard and adverse selection, within the broader theme of asymmetric information, have proven to be very useful concepts in analyzing and understanding the functioning of financial markets, financial instruments, and institutions. For example, asymmetric information helps us understand why debt or equity financing may be more attractive for certain firms. Small firms tend to use debt financing, such as bank loans, more heavily than equity financing, which gives shareholders claims over the firm's profits and net assets. The reason is that small firms are relatively less well known, and savers may have more difficulty assessing the viability of the firm's business, but may be in a better position to value its fixed assets and collateral. Given such informational problems, and given that shareholders are residual claimants, net savers may prefer debt financing over equity financing. Thus, informational issues determine the method of financing.

Such informational issues also have implications for the theory of corporate finance, which otherwise views the choice between debt and equity financing as irrelevant for the value of the firm. This is the celebrated irrelevance result of Franco MODIGLIANI and Merton C. MILLER (1958), and has since then been revisited by applying the tools of asymmetric information.

Asymmetric information. Similar problems related to asymmetric information help in understanding why certain financial intermediaries, and banks, in particular, do exist at all. Reliable and useful information is crucial for savers who would like to minimize their losses for a given level of risk. To this end, they search for, and evaluate different investment projects that are potentially profitable. And, if a project is promising, they have to write a contract with the borrower. Once the contract is written, they have to monitor the actions of the borrower to ensure that the loan is used for the appropriate project. However, information gathering and processing, writing contracts, and auditing are all costly, especially for small lenders. Banks can reduce these costs if they:

1. Gather and process information, and avoid duplication by otherwise unrelated depositors

2. Build expertise in writing contracts and reduce transactions costs

3. Act as a delegated monitor on behalf of the depositors.

However, large savers may themselves fulfill these functions at low costs, and may prefer direct finance. As well, even small savers may have less difficulty in obtaining and processing reliable information about big firms. Consequently, bank financing may be more suitable for small firms with limited credit history. Overall, issues related to information help explain why direct and indirect finance can coexist, despite the fact that ultimately they both serve the same function.

Indeed, although their basic function is the same, and they try to solve identical problems, financial intermediation and institutions have evolved very differently in different countries. For instance, as of 1995, in the United States, bank loans accounted for only 17 percent of the total credit market debt by companies, whereas in GERMANY it was 66 percent, and in JAPAN 60 percent. Clearly, in the United States, banks play a much smaller role in intermediation. Also, although banks are practically prohibited from holding equity shares in non-bank firms, German and Japanese banks hold (as of 1995) about 10–15 percent of the outstanding corporate equity. Further, American companies rely much more on direct finance to raise capital compared to their counterparts in Germany and Japan. In the United States, 54 percent of total credit market debt was intermediated in 1995, and in contrast it was 74 percent in Germany and 77 percent in Japan.

Why do such differences arise? Legal environments within which financial institutions operate differ across countries, and these differences are partly responsible for these outcomes. However, some of these legal institutions are themselves products of the past, and have themselves been influenced by financial and banking sector developments. For example, despite their similarities in their economic structures and legal environments, CANADA had only one bank failure throughout the 20th century, while the United States experienced numerous banking crises (especially during the early 1930s). These events have, in turn, shaped the financial legislation and current financial institutions in the two countries in different ways. With the internationalization of finance, cross-country differences in financial institutions and their roles in the economy may disappear over time, but it is worth noting that both legal and financial institutions tend to evolve with tremendous inertia.

Regardless of contemporary cross-country differences in the relative significance of direct versus indirect finance, well-developed financial markets in individual countries tend to offer very similar products or instruments to net savers, spenders, and intermediaries. These instruments range from rather mundane debt contracts such as loans from financial intermediaries, short-term bills and long-term bonds to more complex and exotic DERIVATIVE securities such as options, futures, and swaps. Some of these products fulfill the traditional function of financial markets, and transfer funds from net savers to net spenders.

Risk traders. Recently, however, most of the growth in volume of trade and advances in financial innovations have taken place in markets, which exchange contracts that help insure against certain risks. In fact, the spectrum of products available appears to be limited only by the imagination of the market participants and their willingness to write contracts that trade these risks. Sometimes alternative instruments are available to insure against a given risk, which are traded in different markets. For instance, wheat farmers, who wish to reduce the price risk they face, can sell their crop in the futures market before the harvest, and secure themselves a price. Commodity exchanges specialize in public trading of such (standardized) instruments (e.g., futures). Many more such products are also traded in the "over-the-counter" markets where financial institutions offer custom-tailored products (e.g., forwards). There are also dealer markets in which only members (such as large banks) trade large volumes of financial assets (foreign exchange) and instruments (swaps).

As in the case of financial intermediaries which attempt to address asymmetric information problems, financial markets in general tackle one fundamental problem: How to price risk? All financial instruments that are traded in financial markets carry risks. These risks range from the traditional default risk to price risk associated with individual commodities or assets. In all cases, the risks arise because there is fundamental uncertainty about the underlying commodity or asset's future value. The wheat farmer, for example, by selling his crop in the futures market, downloads the price risk to the other party. Hence the farmer should be willing to pay a price for selling the risk. Similarly, share prices should reflect the buyers' willingness to pay today for the present value of future dividends and capital gains. Asset-pricing studies how these shares are priced and future earnings are discounted. These pricing issues are studied in financial economics.

In the last 30 years, perhaps no sub-field of economics other than finance has experienced such an explosion of theoretical and applied research. This is partly because modern finance, with its emphasis on information economics and uncertainty, is a relatively young field. Partly, however, this growth reflects the symbiosis between the academic research and practical applications that is unparalleled in other fields.

The impact of academic research on certain financial markets has been phenomenal. For instance, the Black-Scholes-Merton formula (1973) for pricing an option has arguably been the single most important factor for the rapid increase in trading and much wider use of options contracts. The discovery of this formula allowed risks associated with options contracts to be priced very accurately and by using information that is available at low cost. It also led to the introduction of a range of products that have considerably expanded the eventualities that can be insured against. Although the support for research in financial economics is sometimes at the whims of the markets, and likewise the interest in research in finance appears to be cyclical, it promises to be an exciting field to study in the years to come.

BIBLIOGRAPHY. John H. Cochrane, *Asset Pricing* (Princeton University Press, 2001); Alsi Demirgüç-Kunt and Enrica Detragiache, "The Determinants of Banking Crises in Developing and Developed Countries," *IMF Staff Papers* (v.45, 1998); Carlos F. Díaz-Alejandro, "Good-bye Financial Repression, Hello Financial Crash," *Journal of Development Economics* (v.19, 1985); John C. Hull, *Introduction to Futures and Options Markets* (Prentice Hall, 1995); Graciela L. Kaminsky and Carmen M. Reinhart, "The Twin Crises: The Causes of Banking and Balance-of-payments Problems," *American Economic Review* (v.89, 1999); Ross Levine, "Financial Development and Growth: Views and Agenda," *Journal of Economic Literature* (v.35, 1997); Ronald McKinnon, *Money and Capital in Economic Development* (Brookings Institution, 1973); Frederic S. Mishkin, *The Economics of Money, Banking, and Financial Markets* (HarperCollins, 1995); Franco Modigliani and Merton H. Miller, "The Cost of Capital, Corporation Finance, and the Theory of Investment," *American Economic Review* (v.48, 1958); Stephen Ross, "Finance," *The New Palgrave: A Dictionary of Economics* (Macmillan Press, 1987); Joseph A. Schumpeter, *The Theory of Economic Development: An Inquiry into Profits, Capital, Credit, Interest, and the Business Cycle* (Harvard University Press, 1951); Edward S. Shaw, *Financial Deepening in Economic Development* (Oxford University Press, 1973).

TALAN IŞCAN
DALHOUSIE UNIVERSITY

financial institutions

FINANCIAL INSTITUTIONS, or financial intermediaries, are major participants in organized financial markets. They provide indirect finance through the services of an institutional "middle-man" that channels funds from savers to those who ultimately make capital investment. The principal reason for the existence of financial institutions is the fact that financial markets are imperfect; that is, securities buyers and sellers do not have full access to information.

The main problems arising from asymmetric information are adverse selection and MORAL HAZARD. Adverse selection refers to the potential for the least creditworthy borrowers to be the most likely to seek to issue financial instruments, while moral hazard pertains to the possibility that an initially creditworthy borrower may undertake actions that reduce his creditworthiness after receiving funds from a lender. Financial institutions are needed to resolve the problems caused by market imperfections.

Another reason for the existence of financial intermediaries is the existence of economies of scale, or reduction in average operating costs that can be achieved by pooling savings together and spreading management costs across many people. Financial institutions seek customers, both lenders and borrowers, by differentiating and advertising financial products. These products can be differentiated, either by PRICE (i.e., INTEREST RATE) or by variations in maturities fees, and auxiliary services. The non-price differentiation is especially important when interest rates are regulated and/or fixed by tacit or explicit collusion.

Balancing funds and credit. Financial intermediaries balance the demand for CREDIT with their available funds by adjusting interest rates and terms of loans. Borrowers are often classified in terms of risk and charged rates according to their classification. Financial firms produce financial services and include depository and non-depository institutions. Depository institutions consist of commercial banks, savings institutions, and credit unions. The non-depository institutions include finance companies, mutual funds, securities firms, insurance companies, and pension funds.

The depositary institution accepts deposits from surplus units and provides credit to deficit units through loans and purchases of securities. Depositary institutions are a major and the most popular type of financial intermediary. Commercial banks are the most dominant depositary institution.

Banks originated in the earliest civilizations as depositors for gold and silver. These institutions evolved into merchant banking firms and ultimately to modern banks. Commercial banks issue checking deposits and specialize in making loans, and they collect information about creditworthiness of individuals and businesses that desire loans. The principal assets of commercial banks are various loans, i.e., commercial loans, consumer loans, interbank loans, investment in securities, eurodollar loans, repurchase agreements, real estate loans, and fixed assets. The main liabilities of commercial banks include various deposits, such as transaction deposits, saving deposits, time deposits and money market deposits, borrowing from other banks, including borrowing from the Federal Reserve banks, eurodollar borrowings, and repurchase agreements.

The major sources of revenue for banks are interest revenues on loans and securities. They incur costs in the form of deposit interest expense, real resource costs incurred in providing deposit-related services, and real resources costs incurred in extending and monitoring loans.

Commercial banks serve both the private and public sectors since households, businesses, and government agencies utilize their services. There are currently more than 8,000 commercial banks in the United States. Banks are regulated to enhance safety and soundness of the financial system without hampering efficiency. Regulation focuses on six criteria: capital, asset quality, management, earnings, liquidity, and sensitivity to financial market conditions.

Saving institutions also known as thrift institutions include saving and loan associations (S&Ls), which are the dominant type, and savings banks. Some thrift operations are independent financial institutions, while others are subsidiaries of financial conglomerates. Saving institutions can be either stock-owned or owned by depositors (mutual). While most of the savings institutions are mutual, many of them shift their ownership structure from depositors to shareholders, which allow them to obtain additional capital by issuing stock. In addition, stock-owned institutions provide their owners greater potential to benefit from their performance. This, however, makes stock-owned institutions more susceptible to takeovers, while it is virtually impossible to take a control of a mutual institution.

The main sources of funds for savings institutions are deposits, borrowed funds, and CAPITAL. Unlike the commercial banks, which concentrate on commercial loans, savings and loan associations traditionally have specialized in extending mortgage loans to individuals who wish to purchase homes. The vast majority of the mortgages originated are for homes with only 10 percent being designated for commercial properties. Savings banks are similar to savings and loans although they have more diversified uses of funds.

A credit union is a depository institution that accepts deposits and makes loans to only a closed group of individuals. These institutions are nonprofit and they restrict their business to the credit-union members. Credit unions specialize in making consumer loans and use most of their funds to provide loans to their members.

Federal regulation. The federal regulation of depositary institution in the United States started with the Banking Act of 1933 and the formation of the Federal Deposit Insurance Corporation, which supervised the nation's taxpayer-guaranteed deposit insurance system for commercial banks and saving institutions. In 1999, Congress passed the Financial Service Modernization Act of 1999, which allowed for direct competition between depositary and non-depositary financial institutions. Traditional rationales for government regulation of depositary financial institutions include a) maintaining depositary institution liquidity, b) assuring bank solvency by limiting failures, c) promoting an efficient financial system, and d) protecting customers.

Non-depositary institutions generate funds from sources other than deposits. Finance companies specialize in making loans to relatively high-risk individuals and businesses. While the functions of finance companies overlap with the functions of depository institutions, the finance companies concentrate on a different segment of financial market. Consumer finance companies concentrate on providing direct loans to consumers, while sales finance companies concentrate on purchasing credit contracts from retailers and dealers. The major sources of funds for finance companies are loans from banks, commercial papers, deposits, bonds, and capital. Finance companies use funds for consumer loans, business loans and leasing as well as real estate loans. They compete with savings institutions in providing consumer loans, and succeed in increasing their market share when savings institutions experience financial problems.

Insurance companies specialize in trying to limit the adverse-selection and moral-hazard problems. There are two basic kinds of insurance companies. Life insurance companies charge premiums for policies that insure people against the financial consequences associated with death. They offer special financial instruments known as annuities. These instruments guarantee the holder fixed or variable payments at some future date. Property and casualty insurers insure risk relating to property damage and liabilities originating from by injuries or deaths by accidents or adverse natural events. Insurance companies invest the proceeds received from selling insurance in stocks and bonds, and their overall performance is linked to the performance of the stocks and bonds in which they invest.

Pension funds are institutions that specialize in managing funds that individuals save for retirement. The pension funds create financial instruments known as pension annuities, which are similar to the annuities offered by life insurance companies. However, unlike the life insurance annuities, the pension annuities apply only to the future event of retirement. The principal reasons for people using pension funds instead of saving on their own is asymmetric information; that is, the fact that those who operate pension funds may be better informed about financial markets than individual savers. In addition, many people would find monitoring their financial instruments very costly on a day-by-day basis and they would rather entrust the management of the respective instruments to pension funds.

Mutual funds are the dominant non-depositary financial institution. They sell shares to surplus units and use the funds received to purchase a portfolio of securities. Investment companies operate mutual funds. Mutual funds concentrate their investment either in capital market securities, such as stock and bonds, or money market securities. The latter are known as money market mutual funds. Mutual funds became very popular during the 1970s and 1980s when the assets held in these funds grew over 60 times initial levels. In 2003, more than 7,000 mutual funds were in operation.

Securities firms primarily provide brokerage and investment banking services. In addition, these firms often act as dealers and as advisors on mergers and other forms of corporate restructuring. Their principal sources of funds are insurance premiums and earnings from investments, while the main uses of funds are purchases of long-term government and corporate securities.

The regulation of financial institutions has been reduced and managers have been granted more flexibility to offer services that could increase cash flow and value. Deregulation allowed financial institutions more opportunities to capitalize on economies of scale. The consolidation of commercial banks resulted in the higher volume of services produced and lowered the average cost of providing the respective service. The reduction of regulation has prompted mergers of commercial banks and savings institutions, securities firms, finance companies, mutual funds, and insurance companies. These financial conglomerates enable customers to obtain all of their financial services from a single financial institution.

The global expansion of financial institutions is another dominant trend. Commercial banks and insurance companies have expanded globally through international mergers. An international merger between financial institutions enables the merged company to offer the services of both entities to all customers. The rationales for international financial intermediation are the same as the justification for domestic intermediation.

BIBLIOGRAPHY. Graham Bannock, et al., *The Penguin Dictionary of Economics* (Penguin Books, 1998); John Eatwell, Murray Milgate, Peter Newman, eds., *The New Palgrave A Dictionary of Economics* (The Stockton Press, 1991); Charles Geist, *Wall Street—A History* (Oxford University Press, 1997); Jeff Madura, *Financial Markets and Institutions* (South-Western, 2003); Roger Miller and David VanHoose, *Money, Banking, and Financial Markets* (South-Western, 2004); David William Pearce, *The MIT Dictionary of Modern Economics* (MIT Press, 1992); Marcia Stigum, *The Money Market* (Dow-Jones-Irwin, 1990).

ZELJAN SCHUSTER, PH.D.
UNIVERSITY OF NEW HAVEN

financial statement

A FINANCIAL STATEMENT is a report that summarizes the financial condition of an entity. The entity may be an individual, partnership, or business organization. There are actually a number of different types of financial statements including, but not limited to, the balance sheet, the income statement, and the statement of cash flows.

The balance sheet is a snapshot that basically summarizes asset, liabilities and net worth at some point in time. A company's total assets is the value of all it owns including cash, inventories, land, plant, and equipment. Total liabilities is the total amount the company owes others, that is, owes to creditors, including the pensions owed to retired employees. The balance sheet should give a good financial picture indicating assets owned and liabilities owed.

An accounting identity implies that assets must equal liabilities plus net worth. Thus, net worth provides information as to what the firm is currently worth. It also provides information as to the size of the company. Note that items are generally reported on the balance sheet at historical cost. A balance sheet is also referred to as a statement of financial position. A consolidated balance sheet includes figures for all subsidiaries.

The income statement summarizes income and expenses and may also summarize retained earnings in the case of a corporation and capital accounts in the case of a partnership. This profit and loss statement provides details as to a firm's or organization's financial operations over a specific period of time, for example, a year. The statement will include a reporting of net profit or loss for the particular period. It will include an accounting of revenues, costs, and expenses for this period of time. Note that items on the income statement are usually reported on an accrual basis, meaning that they are recorded when expenses are accrued or revenue is earned and not when they are paid or received.

The income statement is sometimes referred to as a statement of operation or profit and loss statement. In a company's annual report, the income statement gives the cumulative earnings and profitability resulting from the previous year's operations. It is in this statement that the company reports total income as well as the cost of sales. Thus, it is the income statement that provides information as to whether the firm was profitable or not.

The statement of cash flows records the comings and goings of cash at the firm. Simply defined, CASH FLOW is net income less noncash revenues plus depreciation and any other items charged to reserves that were not actually paid out in dollars. Thus, the statement of cash flows differs from the income statement and the balance sheet in that the latter two statements record items on an accrual basis. There are several sections of the statement of cash flows.

One section reports the activities of the firm that are related to the generation of income and include income, expenses, and changes in working capital items. This section is aptly called cash flows from operating activities. Another section reports cash flows that arise from the purchase or sale of physical assets or long-term financial assets. Note that long-term financial assets are generally not as liquid as cash and are therefore not cash equivalent. An asset that is cash equivalent is generally considered to be as safe and as liquid as cash itself. Loosely speaking, these are assets with a maturity of three months or less such as Treasury bills, short-term certificates of deposit, and money-market funds. The cash flow that is related to the raising of funds from investors and the returns to investors is summarized in the section referred to as cash flows from financing activities.

Typically, a balance sheet, an income statement, and a statement of cash flows comprise important financial statements for a firm and are used to evaluate the condition and performance of the firm. These statements are typically included in a company's annual report as well. The financial statement may thus be used to evaluate the historical or past performance of the firm and enables an assessment of the firm's strong points as well as weak points. In fact, other common financial statements include a statement of stockholder's equity and a statement of changes in financial positions. The former may provide information about the firm's debt and whether it is retaining profits. The latter statement gives information on whether working capital is increasing or decreasing. Thus, financial statements provide a basis for analyzing a company and providing tools for proper planning.

BIBLIOGRAPHY. P.A. Argenti, *The Fast Forward MBA Pocket Reference* (John Wiley & Sons, 1997); D.J. Leahigh, *A Pocket Guide to Finance* (The Dryden Press, 1996). G. Warfield, *How to Read and Understand the Financial News* (Harper Perennial, 1994).

BRADLEY T. EWING, PH.D.
TEXAS TECH UNIVERSITY

Finland

AT ONE TIME an exclusively agricultural country known for its crops, forests, and fishing, Finland has become industrialized. In reviewing the decades following WORLD WAR II, a war that put Finland face to face with a near state of ruin, the nation has steadily progressed toward joining a more global economic environment.

Finland's strategy has been to address concerns over a lack of balanced trade and the worries of high inflation and unemployment. By the mid-1960s, 20 years after the war ended, the majority of Finns worked in one of many major industries. And the shift continues today, away from farming and agriculture. Manufacturing, trade, and transportation now dominate the country's economy.

Finland's economy is based on free market principles, its capital output relatively parallel with its European neighbors, FRANCE, GERMANY, and the UNITED KINGDOM. Its main sector, manufacturing, involves the production of steel and iron, metal products, petroleum, ships, machinery, chemicals, clothing, and electronics. Of this latter industry, manufacturing cellular phones is a booming industry in Finland, and has high growth projections into the 21st century.

A member of the EUROPEAN UNION (EU) since 1995, and one of the first to adopt the EURO currency, Finland's principal trade partners include Germany, Great Britain, JAPAN, RUSSIA, SWEDEN, and the UNITED STATES. Transportation equipment, ships, clothing, and food are Finland's chief exports.

Agriculture, though no longer the mainstay, maintains a prestige of its own in the form of livestock (poultry, hogs, sheep, cattle, and reindeer) and hay, barley, wheat, and potatoes. Its timber industry, which has always been one of Europe's largest, has not given up that honor. Daily, shippers send Finnish wood and paper products throughout the world.

Despite a jump in unemployment, late 2002 statistics indicate a stable economic future. With a GROSS DOMESTIC PRODUCT (GDP) of $133.5 billion, and a population of just over 5.1 million, Finland has matched per capita income with its Western European counterparts.

BIBLIOGRAPHY. *Guide to Scandinavia and Finland* (Michelin Publications, 1996); Finland Statistics, www.finland.stat.fi; *CIA World Factbook* (2003).

JOSEPH GERINGER
SYED B. HUSSAIN, PH.D.
UNIVERSITY OF WISCONSIN, OSHKOSH

fiscal policy

FISCAL POLICY IS concerned with government purchases, TAXES, and transfer payments. Economists generally agree that fiscal policy has important effects on the economy. Fiscal policy can change the course of the economy through changes in spending and taxes. Policymakers may help restore the economy to its full potential when output falls below the full-employment level. An increase in government expenditures affects the aggregate spending and brings it to a new level. A tax cut increases consumers' disposable income, leading to more aggregate spending. Both changes stimulate the economy and move it closer to a full-employment level of output.

The difference between taxes and spending fiscal policies lies in their relative effect on the economy. A $100 increase in government purchases is a direct addition to spending. Whereas, the same amount of tax cut to individuals can induce additional consumption expenditures. Through these channels, governments can counteract any spending shocks. In reality, these processes are often slow and difficult to synchronize with what the economy needs at the time.

Fiscal-policy instruments can be slow for several reasons. Usually, implementation of a fiscal change may take several months. The legislative process alone could take many months or even longer to adopt a policy. In the United States, a tax bill originates in the House of Representatives and then goes to the Senate.

Usually, this political process is complex. Taxes usually change distribution of income and therefore the cost of a tax cut and its benefits affects different groups of individuals differently. Each party tries to please its constituency. Legislators could drag on arguments for changes in the tax bill. After the House resolves the representatives' differences the bill goes to the Senate. The Senate usually modifies the bill and sends it to the conference committee to resolve the differences. Then the bill goes to the president who would either sign it into a law or veto it. Even if the president approves the bill, the implementation phase of the law and the time necessary for its effect on the deriving sectors of the economy delay the effect on the aggregate economy. And if the president vetoes the bill, the process can add many additional months to this delay. Depending on the extent of the downturn, the policy may by then have unintended adverse effects on the course of the economy.

Any change in government spending or transfers could be as lengthy as a tax change. Consequently, a fiscal stimulus could take effect long after the economy has recovered. In that case, the policy would destabilize the economy and move it in the wrong direction.

Furthermore, effective fiscal-policy instruments should be countercyclical and thus temporary. Yet, the reality is different. Reversing taxes and government expenditures or transfer payments are politically very difficult. In the past, many temporary tax changes have become permanent. The public is never happy to lose a tax cut. And the government is usually reluctant to reverse a tax increase that provides revenues for a program.

Similarly, new government expenditures are likely to become permanent because the public is never happy to lose its benefits.

Another important consideration is the interaction of fiscal policy and monetary policy. Some economists believe that even if the government tried to stabilize the economy with fiscal-policy instruments, the FEDERAL RESERVE could counteract it through the monetary channels. The Federal Reserve affects the course of the economy through the monetary policy instruments to keep the economy as close as possible to its potential level. They could perceive a fiscal policy change as another shock and try to counteract it. For example, if the government cuts taxes to expand the output, the Fed could counteract it by a contractionary move to reduce output.

Furthermore, a restrictive monetary policy could more than offset the expansionary effects of fiscal policy, or vise versa, and pull the economy in the opposite direction. Yet, the two policies could work in the same direction. For example, a tax cut accompanied with lower short-term interest rates will stimulate the economy through fiscal and monetary channels to boost spending, which in turn boosts output. Monetary and fiscal polices are both instruments for promoting economic growth.

In recent years, the federal budget deficit has been the subject of a lively debate in the political arena and in academe. Government may be forced to incur debt to stabilize the economy and promote growth. Borrowing is an alternative to current taxation as a mean of financing government expenditures. A budget deficit is the excess of government outlays compared to its receipts from tax revenues, fees, and charges. Since 1970, federal government outlays have exceeded receipts for most years. And they have increased as a percentage of GROSS NATIONAL PRODUCT (GDP). As a result, interest payments on these loans have constituted an increasing share of the federal expenditures. In 1985, Congress adopted the Gramm-Rudman-Hollings Act to establish a plan for reducing the federal budget deficit. The Budget Enforcement Act of 1990 was passed to enforce the Gramm-Rudman-Hollings Act. Its enactment set new rules and put a cap on defense and international and domestic spending and required a new budget process: "pay-as-you-go" system for new programs and tax cuts. This act aimed to reduce the budget deficit significantly.

The budget imbalances reflect the level of economic activity as well as the structural imbalances between revenues and expenditures. Thus, the federal budget deficit can be divided into a cyclical component and a structural component. The fluctuations in economic activity associated with BUSINESS CYCLES affect the size of the federal budget deficit substantially. The Office of Management and Budget estimated in 1989 that each one percentage point decrease in the growth rates of real GROSS NATIONAL PRODUCT (GNP) and a one percentage point of unemployment would increase the federal budget deficit by $7.7 billions in that year. The high-employment budget deficit has on average been less than two percent of GNP in most years.

It is clear that fiscal policy can be used to fight recession and inflation. However, some changes in government receipts and expenditures reflect discretionary changes in the laws that govern fiscal policy. Changes in the levels of these items can also result automatically from changes in economic conditions—real output, unemployment, and the price level. In general, when the economic activity rises, government receipts rise and expenditures fall.

In recent years, attention has also turned to the long-term effects of taxes on economic growth. While the current reform agenda revolves around the tax base, the rates, and tax deductions and exemptions, a great deal of debate looms around the effect of taxation on savings, investment, and international market conditions and their impacts on domestic economic goals and objectives for growth

Slogans such as "No New Taxes" or "Balance the Budget" are to get the attention of voters. These are simple messages that ignore the seriousness of economic policy. If we decide to devote more resources to improving public health and social security, national defense, and homeland security, and to protect our environment, or to other problems markets cannot solve, we need to accept their opportunity cost. Some economists believe that "fiscal policy echoes the thunder of world history."

The government today has the responsibility to control financial panics and prevent depressions. The government has also the ability to minimize the ups and downs of the business cycles to prevent high levels of unemployment and to promote long-term economic growth. Taxes and expenditures are extremely powerful instruments for social changes.

BIBLIOGRAPHY. Henry J. Arron and William G. Gale, eds., *Economic Effects of Fundamental Tax Reform* (Brookings Institute, 1996); David N. Hyman, *Public Finance, A Contemporary Application of Theory to Policy* (Dryden HBJ Press, 2000); Marc Liberman and Robert Hall, *Introduction to Economics* (South-Western, 1999); Paul A. Samuelson and William D. Nordhaus, *Economics* (McGraw-Hill, 2000); Joseph Stiglitz, *Principles of Macroeconomics* (W.W. Norton, 1996).

SIMIN MOZAYENI, PH.D.
STATE UNIVERSITY OF NEW YORK, NEW PALTZ

Fisher, Irving (1867–1947)

"THE GREATEST OF America's scientific economists up to our own day" (according to Joseph SCHUMPETER in 1948) is probably best known for being wrong.

In the summer of 1929 Fisher stated, in his nationally syndicated weekly newspaper column, that he believed the economy had hit a new plateau, and that increases in productivity would ensure a bright macroeconomic future. In October of that same year, the Great DEPRESSION wiped out his own fortune (his inventions had made him a millionaire) and the fortunes of his countrymen. Fisher's attempt to "talk up" the market would stalk him to his end. It is an unfortunate way for this great economist to be remembered, since he made important contributions to nearly every discipline of economic theory.

His dissertation on mathematical economics, *Mathematical Investigations in the Theory of Value and Prices* (1892), was hailed by Paul SAMUELSON as "the greatest doctoral dissertation in economics ever written." He was an important early advocate of the marginalist position in MICROECONOMICS, and of an extremely sophisticated version of the Quantity Theory of Money in MACROECONOMICS.

His disquisitions upon the *Theory of Interest* (1930) and *The Purchasing Power of Money* (1911) underlie modern theories of intertemporal choice and the making of index numbers. Economists still refer to the "Fisher Equation" wherein the real interest rate equals the nominal rate minus the inflation rate (approximately). His econometric investigations (he was a founder and the first president of the Econometric Society) and data collection, that he personally financed, helped every economist to understand macroeconomic fluctuations. As a public intellectual, Fisher crusaded for a consumption tax, advances in public health (including universal health insurance), Prohibition, eugenics ("race hygiene"), and world peace.

BIBLIOGRAPHY. William J. Barber, ed., *The Works of Irving Fisher* (Pickering and Chatto, 1997); Hans Edi-Loef, ed., *Economics of Irving Fisher* (Edward Elgar, 1999).

KEVIN R FOSTER, PH.D.
CITY COLLEGE OF NEW YORK

Fisk, James Jr. (1835–72)

AN AMERICAN RAILROAD magnate notorious for his corrupt business practices, Jim Fisk was born in Pownal, Vermont and died in New York City. Fisk joined the Jordan Marsh Company in 1860 as a wholesale salesman, where he secured large government textile orders by distributing cash to legislators, and acquired scarce cotton for the company by smuggling it out of the Confederacy during the AMERICAN CIVIL WAR. Bought out in 1864, Fisk next made a fortune by selling Confederate bonds short in England before news of the South's

defeat spread widely. By 1867, he was a millionaire living in New York City. Rotund, bejeweled, and with a scandalous personal life, Fisk cut a colorful figure.

Joining with Daniel Drew and Jay GOULD to oppose Cornelius VANDERBILT for control of the Erie Railroad, Fisk became managing director of the line in 1868. When Vanderbilt began buying Erie stock, the trio issued new stock. Vanderbilt replied with a contempt of court order that forced the group to flee to New Jersey to avoid arrest. To get back into New York, they bribed the New York state legislature to pass legislation legalizing their stock over-issue. Although a popular and profitable RAILROAD, the Erie never paid a dividend because Fisk kept it in debt to finance his lavish lifestyle and manipulations. Besides engaging in insider trading, he bribed legislators and judges to gain competitive advantages. Fisk died at the hands of a rival for his mistress's affections.

BIBLIOGRAPHY. W.A. Swanberg, *Jim Fisk: The Career of an Improbabe Rascal* (Scribner, 1959); Marshall P. Stafford, *The Life of James Fisk, Jr.: A Full and Accurate Narrative of All the Enterprises in Which He Was Engaged* (Ayer, 1981).

CARYN E. NEUMANN, PH.D.
OHIO STATE UNIVERSITY

Fogel, Robert (1926–)

WINNER OF 1993 Nobel Prize in Economics (jointly with Douglass NORTH), Robert Fogel was cited by the Nobel Committee for "renewed" research in economic history by rigorously "applying economic theory and quantitative methods in order to explain economic and institutional change." The prize endorsed the "cliometric" revolution that transformed the practice of economic history beginning in the late 1950s. "Cliometrics" takes its name by adding the suffix "metrics" (to measure) to "Clio" (the Greek Muse of history). The essence of cliometrics is to unite economic theory with measurement to explain history. Fogel did more to advance the cliometric approach than anyone else.

Fogel attended Cornell University, where he majored in history with an economics minor and became president of the campus branch of American Youth for Democracy, a communist organization. After graduating in 1948, he became a professional organizer for the Communist Party.

But, in 1956, Fogel enrolled in Columbia University's graduate economics program and gave up his radicalism. At this time, economic historians were beginning to take an increasingly quantitative approach that made use of explicit mathematical economic models. Fogel was a pioneer, using these methods in his master's thesis, which studied the land grants given to the Union Pacific Railroad. After teaching at the University of Rochester, Fogel accepted an appointment at the University of Chicago, where he spent the bulk of his career, aside from a six-year move to Harvard from 1975–81.

Fogel's first major book, *Railroads and American Economic Growth* (1964), tested economic historian W.W. Rostow's thesis that RAILROADS had propelled the entire American economy to "take-off" into sustained economic growth. His "counterfactual" argument shocked traditional historians, because the model involved rewriting history to create a larger canal network that would have been built in the absence of railroads. Despite considerable initial skepticism and numerous attempts at refutation, Fogel successfully convinced the vast majority of historians that railroads were *not* indispensable to 19th-century American economic growth.

Fogel's best-known and most controversial book (written with Stanley Engerman), *Time on the Cross: The Economics of American Negro Slavery*, won the 1975 Bancroft Prize and was widely discussed in the press and on television. After demonstrating that slavery was profitable and prospering on the eve of the Civil War, it boldly argued that the material standards of living of American slaves were higher than many had thought, and that slave plantations were considerably more efficient than Northern farms and free Southern farms at turning the inputs of LAND, LABOR, and CAPITAL into output and revenue.

Many critics questioned these statistical findings, and many objected that the book viewed SLAVERY from the slaveowners' perspective—without condemning the institution's immorality. Fogel took these comments to heart and his sequel, *Without Consent or Contract* (1989), included lengthy treatments of abolitionism and the political realignment of the 1850s, which led to the downfall of American slavery. Most economic historians now accept the conclusion that slave agriculture was more efficient, but opinions are divided on the material conditions of slaves.

Fogel's most recent path-breaking research project examines historical links among the economy, nutrition, health, and mortality.

BIBLIOGRAPHY. Barry Eichengreen, "The Contributions of Robert W. Fogel to Economics and Economic History," *Scandinavian Journal of Economics* (1994); Robert Fogel, *A Life of Learning*, American Council of Learned Societies (1996); Claudia Goldin, "Cliometrics and the Nobel," *Journal of Economic Perspectives* (1995).

ROBERT WHAPLES
WAKE FOREST UNIVERSITY

Ford Motor Company

CELEBRATING ITS 100th anniversary on June 16, 2003, Ford Motor Company was founded by Henry FORD along with 11 investors. In 1919, the original investors and other stockholders were bought out, making the Ford family the sole owners of the company, and opening the door to expansion without resistance. Today, Ford employs 350,000 people around the world.

In 1956, Ford had its Initial Public Offering, selling 10.2 million shares—the largest IPO in United States history at the time, and leaving family ownership at 22 percent. Diversification followed the IPO, including creating Ford Credit, its leasing arm, in 1959. Ford further diversified in 1987, buying the Hertz Corporation and moving into the rental car market. The company addressed its need for quality parts and distribution by acquiring Electric Autolite Company in 1961, which evolved into Ford's Motorcraft brand of manufacturing and distribution in 1972. Further, beginning in 1991, Ford offered automotive service to its Ford, Lincoln, and Mercury brands through its Quality Care service at its dealerships.

Ford's history of development and diversification clearly paid off in the early 1990s. In 1993, five of the top eight selling vehicles in the United States were Ford products.

To ensure its continued success in the future, Ford merged its North American and European operations and moved to a global management team in 1995.

Product innovations, acquisitions and mergers also comprise Ford's history, particularly since the late 1970s. An early merger occurred in the mid-1940s, when Ford merged its Mercury and Lincoln brands for a 10-year period. Today, the brands are independent within the Ford family of products. Beginning with its 25 percent equity interest of Mazda in 1979, less than 10 years later, Ford became the majority owner of Aston Martin Lagonda, Ltd., in 1987 and bought all outstanding stock in 1994. In between its initial acquisition and full ownership of Aston Martin, Ford acquired Jaguar in 1990. Keeping strides at the same time with innovation, in 1992, the Ford F-Series trucks held the top spot in U.S. vehicle sales for the 10th year in a row.

Ford targeted the mid-size family car as a strategic cornerstone of worldwide development in 1988, introducing the same vehicle with different names domestically and abroad, known in the United States as the Ford Contour and Mercury Mistique and as the Mondeo in Taiwan, Europe, and the Middle East. The addition of Volvo to the Ford family came in 1999, at an acquisition price of $6.45 billion. Land Rover is the latest addition to the Ford portfolio of vehicles.

Ford posted revenues of $162.4 billion in 2001, with Ford Financial Services (Ford Credit and the Hertz

Corporation) accounting for $30.9 billion of the revenue stream. Ford sold 6,991,000 vehicles in 2001, a 5.8 percent decrease from 2000, posted its first quarterly loss in 10 years, and consequently reduced its annual common and Class B stock dividends from 60 to 40 cents in 2002. On the positive side, Ford boosted research investment in 2001 to $7.4 billion and ranked second worldwide in Group Market Share, trailing General Motors by 2.2 percent.

Ford is engaged in RESEARCH AND DEVELOPMENT (R&D) projects that are examining the use of hydrogen fuels. One project aims to put experimental fuel-cell powered vehicles on the road (in California) while another project is aimed at exploring alternatives to imported oil as a long-run strategy.

As Henry Ford's great grandson, Bill Ford Jr., leads the company into the future, he hopes to turn the company back toward the greatness and profitability it once enjoyed. In 2002, Ford has managed to cut costs and post a small profit. But, it's no easy time in the automobile industry. Competitiveness is at an all time high, both from domestic and foreign competitors. Price wars are stiff, with manufacturers competing on rebate and free financing offers. While the future of Ford is unclear, its current CEO is dedicated to upholding the family name.

BIBLIOGRAPHY. www.ford.com; Betsy Morris, "Can Ford Save Ford?" *Fortune* (2002); *Connecting with Society: Our Learning Journey: 2001 Corporate Citizenship Report*, Ford Motor Company (2002).

AUDREY D. KLINE, PH.D.
UNIVERSITY OF LOUISVILLE

Ford, Gerald R. (1913–)

BORN IN OMAHA, Nebraska, and christened Leslie King, Jr., Gerald R. Ford became the 38th president of the UNITED STATES. His parents were divorced when he was two and his mother remarried. He took the name of his stepfather, Gerald R. Ford, and grew up in Grand Rapids, Michigan.

Ford attended the University of Michigan where he studied economics and political science and played center on two national-championship football teams. Graduating from Yale University in 1941 with a law degree, Ford was subsequently admitted to the Michigan Bar.

During WORLD WAR II, Ford served four years in the U.S. Navy. After practicing law for several years, he ran for U.S. Congress in 1948. In 1963, while still a Republican congressman he was named by President Lyndon JOHNSON to the Warren Commission investigating the assassination of President John F. KENNEDY.

Ford described himself as "a moderate on domestic issues, a conservative in fiscal affairs, and a dyed-in-the-wool internationalist." He supported U.S. actions in the VIETNAM WAR and kept a low profile on civil rights issues. Elected by his colleagues in 1965 as House of Representatives minority leader, Ford served 25 years in the House before he was nominated by President Richard NIXON in 1973 to the office of vice president under the provision of the 25th Amendment upon the resignation of Spiro T. Agnew.

When Nixon resigned on August 9, 1974, Ford was sworn in as president saying that "our long national nightmare is over." President Ford was the first nonelected vice-president and president in U.S. history. During his time in office he tried to restore public confidence in the national leadership and in the institutions of government. Ford's "honeymoon" with Congress and the pubic ended on September 8, 1974, when he pardoned Nixon. Ford always felt that the nation was still consumed by Nixon and the Watergate scandal, and that without a presidential pardon, the nation would never heal.

Ford's first year in office was dominated by severe economic problems, including both inflation and recession. Unemployment was over 9 percent, new housing starts were at their lowest in years, new-car sales were down sharply, and inflation was at 12 percent. In foreign policy, American prestige was at an all-time low: the Vietnam War ended in 1975 with the collapse of South Vietnam and the evacuation of American citizens. When Ford ran for election to the presidency, he first had to campaign against Ronald Reagan for the Republican nomination. Ford won the nomination and selected Senator Robert Dole of Kansas as his running mate. Still dealing with the fallout of his Nixon pardon, a slow economic recovery, and an upstart Democratic candidate named Jimmy CARTER, Ford lost the presidential election of 1976.

Most historians credit Ford as a decent and honest man who entered into the office of president under unusual and difficult circumstances, a president whose integrity went far toward healing the wounds of Watergate. In economic terms, he inherited a crippled economy but was unable to reverse the ravages of inflation and unemployment. Tip O'Neill, the Democratic Speaker of the House of Representatives, in his memoirs said about Ford: "God has been good to America, especially during difficult times. . . . he gave us Gerald Ford—the right man at the right time who was able to put our nation back together again. Nothing like Watergate had ever happened before in our history, but we came out of it strong and free, and the transition from Nixon's administration to Ford's was a thing of awe and dignity."

BIBLIOGRAPHY. "Gerald Rudolph Ford," www.infoplease.com; Bob Woodward, *Shadow: Five Presidents and the*

Legacy of Watergate (Simon & Schuster, 1999); David Gergen, *Eyewitness to Power* (Simon & Schuster, 2000); Tip O'Neill with William Novak, *Man of the House: The Life and Political Memoirs of Speaker Tip O'Neill* (Random House, 1987).

LINDA L. PETROU, PH.D.
HIGH POINT UNIVERSITY

Ford, Henry (1863–1947)

AN AMERICAN INNOVATOR in the automobile industry, Henry Ford's production techniques became standardized throughout the manufacturing world in the early 20th century. The FORD MOTOR COMPANY, which he founded in 1903, was the largest automobile manufacturer in the world in the 1910s and 1920s with over 15 million Model T Fords sold between 1908 and 1927. With the announcement of a "Five Dollar Day" in 1914, Ford also popularized the idea of mass-production workers as consumers. The company was eclipsed by General Motors after 1930, but the Ford Motor Company remained the second-largest auto maker at the time of Ford's death in 1947.

Ford was the oldest surviving son of William Ford, who emigrated from Ireland in the 1840s, and Mary (Litigot) Ford. The Fords settled in the farming community of Dearborn, just west of Detroit, Michigan, and Henry Ford was born there on July 30, 1863. Before establishing his own farm holdings in Dearborn, William Ford worked as a railroad carpenter. His son inherited his mechanical aptitude and as a child earned money by repairing neighbors' watches.

Inspired by the sight of a steam-driven engine that could be used for threshing or sawing, Ford moved to Detroit when he was 16 years old to work in the Flower and Brothers Machine Shop. He remained in Detroit until 1882, working for three years at the Detroit Dry Dock Company's engine works. Ford then returned to Dearborn and worked for the Westinghouse Company as a repairman of their steam engines in southern Michigan for the next decade. After Ford married Clara Bryant on April 11, 1888, the couple settled on an 8-acre farm in Dearborn. By the time their only child, Edsel, was born in 1893, the Fords had moved back to Detroit, where Henry became the chief engineer of the Detroit Illuminating Company.

Always fascinated by engine design and application, Ford experimented with gasoline-powered internal combustion engines throughout the 1890s. On June 4, 1896, Ford and a group of friends tested their first automobile, comprised of two bicycles harnessed together and powered by a gas engine. After testing a number of prototypes over the next three years, Ford and a group of

investors established the Detroit Automobile Company in August 1899. The company lasted just over a year before closing, the fate of most of the thousands of automobile ventures that were started during the era. Ford attracted new investors in the Henry Ford Motor Company after winning an auto race in Grosse Pointe, Michigan, in October 1901. Ford left the company within a year after a series of arguments with its principal investors; under a new name, the Cadillac Corporation, the company eventually became the luxury division of Ford's chief rival, General Motors.

On June 16, 1903, Ford incorporated the Ford Motor Company with its principal assembly plant on Mack Avenue in Detroit. The Ford Model A—a moderately priced automobile featuring an innovative, vertically operating engine with cylinders that gave more power with less friction—was an instant success with 658 cars sold in its first season. In 1907, countering conventional wisdom in the industry, Ford decided to concentrate on lower-priced automobiles with the Model N, starting at $700. The decision led Ford to a million-dollar profit that year, with 8,243 Model N automobiles sold for gross revenues of over $4.7 million. Sales of the Model N increased to 10,000 in 1908. Despite refinements in his Mack Avenue assembly lines, Ford could not keep up with demand.

Ford's new factory in Highland Park, Michigan, opened in December 1909, as a state-of-the-art manufacturing facility. Each step in the production process was routinized through the intensive use of machinery that deskilled the labor process. The mechanization of production, standardization of the components, and constant planning and refining of the manufacturing process came to be known as "Fordism." Yet Fordism went far beyond the factory-shop floor. In order to combat the high absenteeism and turnover that Highland Park's never-ending assembly lines produced—in 1913, the annual turnover rate of the plant's labor force was 380 percent, with 10 percent of workers being absent on any given day—Ford announced an incentive pay plan in January, 1914, heralded as a "Five-Dollar Day." In actuality, the plan retained the basic daily wage rate of $2.34 for an eight-hour day, with profit-sharing incentives making up the difference. As an essential part of Fordism, the higher-wage rates recognized that mass-production workers were to be transformed into consumers of mass-production items, including automobiles.

The Ford Motor Company was the pre-eminent automobile manufacturer in the world during the first quarter of the 20th century: between 1908 and 1927, the Ford Motor Company sold over 15 million Model T automobiles. By 1930, however, General Motors had surpassed Ford by offering annual style updates and credit-purchasing options on its cars, two actions that

Henry Ford resisted. Ford's outside interests, including the sponsorship of a "Peace Ship" to negotiate an end to World War I and his ownership of an openly anti-Semitic newspaper, the *Dearborn Independent,* added to the company's loss of dominance in its market.

Ford was also plunged into controversy over the use of brutal and illegal tactics to keep labor unions out of his factories in the 1930s, including the infamous Battle of the Overpass outside of the company's River Rouge plant on May 26, 1937. Several union organizers were beaten and the event tarnished Ford's reputation as a down-to-earth man of integrity. Ford finally signed a collective bargaining agreement with the United Automobiles Workers union in June, 1941, after all of the other major automobile manufacturers had done so.

Ford had ceded some managerial control of the Ford Motor Corporation to his son, Edsel, in the 1930s, although he continually frustrated his son's attempts to modernize the company's administrative and marketing procedures. Tensions between father and son led to Edsel Ford's premature death in 1943, which forced his father to resume leadership of the company even though he had not fully recovered from a stroke suffered five years earlier. In 1945, Ford's grandson, Henry Ford II, assumed the presidency of the company. On April 7, 1947, Henry Ford died in Dearborn at his Fair Lane estate, a site adjacent to the Greenfield Village historical site and museum that he had established in 1928.

Although the Ford Motor Company had declined somewhat since its heydays in the 1910s and 1920s, it remained the second-largest automobile maker in the world at the time of its founder's death. The production techniques and higher wages that Ford pioneered had also become standardized throughout the automotive sector and in many other mass-production industries as well.

BIBLIOGRAPHY. Neil Baldwin, *Henry Ford and the Jews: The Mass Production of Hate* (Public Affairs, 2001); Ray Batchelor, *Henry Ford, Mass Production, Modernism, and Design* (University of Manchester Press, 1995); Michel Beaud, *A History of Capitalism, 1500–2000* (Monthly Review Press, 2001); David Brody, *Workers in Industrial America: Essays on the Twentieth Century Struggle* (Oxford University Press, 1993); Henry Ford, *My Life and Work* (Garden City Publishing Company, 1922); Stephen H. Norwood, *Strikebreaking and Intimidation: Mercenaries and Masculinity in Twentieth-Century America* (University of North Carolina Press, 2002); Allan Nevins and Frank Ernest Hill, *Ford: The Times, the Man, and the Company* (Charles Scribner's Sons, 1954).

TIMOTHY G. BORDEN, PH.D.
INDEPENDENT SCHOLAR

forecast

A FORECAST IS AN educated guess about the future, usually made in order to guide decisions in a variety of fields including business, economics, finance, marketing, and government. They are made by and used by both the private and public sectors.

Typically, there is a forecast object—what is going to be forecast. It may be sales, prices, GROSS DOMESTIC PRODUCT (GDP), growth rates, etc. Once chosen, modern forecasting usually involves the statistical analysis of data and a projection, perhaps into the future, of what is a likely outcome. A good forecasting model produces forecasts that are statistically close to the actual outcome.

To the extent that the forecast of some object differs from the actual outcome, there is a forecast error. For example, consider a simple forecasting model that predicts tomorrow's numerical value of the DOW JONES Industrial Average, a common stock price index, will be equal to today's value. If today the Dow Jones Industrial Average were at 9,000 points then this simple forecast model indicates that tomorrow it will also be at 9,000. That is, the expected value of the Dow Jones index is 9,000. Of course, anyone who follows the financial news will know that the stock market may go up or down from one day to the next.

Thus, the forecast is likely to have an error associated with it. If the value tomorrow actually turns out to 9,500, then the forecast error is simply the difference between the actual value (9,500) and the forecast (9,000) or 500 points. One may be able to improve the performance of the forecasting model, in the sense of reducing the size of the forecast error, by including other information into the model. The essence of forecasting is to construct the best-fitting, best-performing models at lowest cost. There are a variety of measures of model performance, however, and the size of the forecast error is just one of them.

In general, though, a good forecast will perform well by some standard and will utilize relevant and available information. The form of the forecasting model may become quite complex and may involve the use of sophisticated statistical techniques. However, all forecasts typically attempt to predict the value of something (i.e., the object) given limited information and rely on data and observations to do so. A forecast may even be augmented with subjective information as well.

In any case, models that use only one variable as a predictor are said to be univariate in nature while models that incorporate more than one variable are multivariate. Generally speaking, a forecast is a predicted value of some object and is made knowing that there is an error associated with it. Thus, a forecast is not written in stone, but instead should be used as one tool for making better decisions.

BIBLIOGRAPHY. Francis X. Diebold, *Elements of Forecasting*, (South-Western, 2001); T.C. Mills, *The Econometric Modelling of Financial Time Series*, (Cambridge University Press, 1999); H.H. Stokes and H.M. Neuburger, *New Methods in Financial Modeling: Explorations and Applications* (Quorum Books, 1998).

BRADLEY T. EWING, PH.D.
TEXAS TECH UNIVERSITY

Fortis

WITH MAIN OFFICES located in Brussels, BELGIUM, Fortis is an international financial services provider active in the fields of insurance, banking, and investments. The company ranks among the top 20 of Europe's most influential financial investors.

Known as the "Muscles from Brussels" for its aggressive role in the insurance and banking sectors, Fortis sells life and non-life insurance, such as health, auto, and fire, through independent agents and brokers, financial planners, and through the company's Fortis Bank branches.

Fortis Bank offers consumer and commercial banking services, asset management, private banking, investment banking, access to financial markets, and other financial services.

Within its home market of the Benelux countries—Belgium, the NETHERLANDS, and LUXEMBOURG—Fortis enjoys a vanguard position, serving corporate and public clients. Outside its geographic home market, Fortis focuses on selected banking and insurance segments most in demand.

Fortis' commercial growth has been a barometer to watch as it consistently ranks in the top 100 of *Fortune* magazine's lists of largest companies in the world, coming in at number 85 in 2002 with just over $40 billion in revenue. Financial targets for the company include growth of net operating profit per share of at least 12 percent, and return on equity of at least 15 percent.

BIBLIOGRAPHY. *Plunkett's Financial Services Industry Almanac 2002–2003* (Plunkett Research, Ltd., 2002); "Global 500: The World's Largest Companies," *Fortune* (July, 2002); Fortis, www.fortis.com.

JOSEPH GERINGER
SYED B. HUSSAIN, PH.D.
UNIVERSITY OF WISCONSIN, OSHKOSH

France Telecom

WITH A WORKFORCE of more than 200,000, a client base of 92 million, France Telecom is definitely one of the world's telecommunications industry giants. France Telecom and its subsidiaries provide a range of services to residential, professional, and large-business customers, primarily in FRANCE.

To call France Telecom a "telephone company" would be to underestimate its magnitude—as well as its strategic plans. In a market under full development and often chaotic, the group has set its sights on becoming a principal European player. With 56 million direct subscribers in more than 75 countries, and 206,000 service customers, France Telecom has also expanded with a wider range of products and services to fit a larger customer base. These include local telephone service, long distance, data transmission, mobile phone service, multimedia products, cable television, internet services, and audiovisual diffusion.

The mobile phones division serves 17.8 million clients in its native France and 12.5 million throughout the UNITED KINGDOM. This division manages the company's entire mobile telephone business—from conception of services and installation to network maintenance and commercialization.

The internet division manages public internet access—including network, cable, and satellite—in France, SPAIN, BELGIUM, the NETHERLANDS, and MOROCCO (through access provider Wanadoo).

A division called Fixed-Line Services and Distribution France monitors product and service marketing for telephone service and supplies. It also governs France Telecom's 700 "boutiques," where, across Europe, the company's phone-associated products are sold over the counter.

Corporate Solutions helps medium-sized and multinational clients in 220 countries manage their telecommunications needs. Handling the majority of consulting is subsidiary Equant, which promotes applicable sales solutions. The central function of the RESEARCH AND DEVELOPMENT (R&D) and Information Technology (IT) branches—which are interrelated—is to maintain and keep current the company's information systems technology. Supervising national and international networks for the entire product line is the Networks and Operators division. Comprising this branch are French Long Distance and Telecom Marine (dedicated to underwater networks).

The origins of France Telecom date back to the WORLD WAR II years, when the government foresaw the need of advanced telephone communications. The National Center for Telecommunication Research, created in 1944, monitored the upgrading of the phone system over the next 26 years until a department, entitled Head of Telecommunications, took over the reins of the industry. Renamed France Telecom in 1988, it became the country's autonomous provider of service.

France Telecom enjoyed a prosperous 2002 with consolidated revenues of 46.6 billion EUROS (up almost nine percent from the previous year) and an operating income of 6.8 billion euros (up 31 percent).

BIBLIOGRAPHY. France Telecom, "Investor Relations," www.francetelecom.com/en; "Global 500: World's Largest Companies," *Fortune* (July, 2002); "France Telecom," Hoover's, www.hoovers.com.

JOSEPH GERINGER
SYED B. HUSSAIN, PH.D.
UNIVERSITY OF WISCONSIN, OSHKOSH

France

IN EXAMINING THE history of capitalism in France, it is worth looking at the subject chronologically, while addressing certain common themes that are pertinent to the French case across time. Such themes, which relate more broadly to debates on capitalism, include the role of the state in capitalist development, the social costs and gains of capitalism, the role of empires in the development of European capitalism, and the connection between the capitalist economy and the modern nation state.

Before the Revolution. In etymological terms, France was the origin of capitalism, even if its economy was rather less developed in a modern, capitalist sense than that of England and Holland in the 18th century, when the term *capitaliste* begins to be applied by French writers to that class of the rising bourgeoisie who preferred to invest spare capital in risk-based trading and industrial ventures, rather than in the traditional solidity of land that was preferred by the French aristocracy. The term originally had negative connotations, in that it was used by "old money" as means of expressing distaste for the recklessness and lack of class of bourgeois *arrivistes* whose attitudes toward wealth and the ideal society posed something of a threat to the entrenched power of the French aristocracy.

Those aristocrats, and the French monarchy at its apex, presided over a stagnant economy with low rates of growth, little innovation in either agricultural or industrial spheres, weak trading links, and a poorly developed banking sector. The emphasis upon continuity and tradition in the French system contrasted markedly with that of rival European powers such as the UNITED KINGDOM and the NETHERLANDS that were building national wealth and empires upon dynamic, post-feudal, increasingly urban, economies driven by powerful middle classes. Yet even while France, the pre-eminent political power in 18th-century Europe, seemed to lose that status through its relative economic under-performance,

some structural and economic changes were taking place on a localized level across the country.

As Roger Price notes, the period 1730–50 saw a growth in France's population, in prices, and in internal trade, and at this time it is arguable that a process of proto-industrialization (akin to that which preceded the English INDUSTRIAL REVOLUTION) was taking place with piecework being farmed out to cheap, rural labor, rising commercial profits, the development of better transport networks, and increasing mechanization. Such change was not immediately obvious, because it was piecemeal and slow, but that seemed to be the French way in such matters. Even today, France's modern economic history is not at all spectacular, yet its economy has always been among the six largest in the world.

The fact that France has always managed to slowly reposition its economy so that it maintained its relative strength has generated a considerable literature on the French Paradox, for in many ways it does seem strange that a country with a very weak economic base before the 1840s, a large peasantry until the 20th century, and a lack of economic dynamism among politicians or entrepreneurs, should perform so well in the long term. It has been suggested that it was precisely the persistent comparison between industrializing England and stagnant France in the later 18th century that forms the basis of the assumption that France suffered from a structurally weak economy.

France 1789–1848. There seems little doubt that the French Revolutions of 1789 and 1793 altered the structures of French politics and society in a way that served as a necessary precondition for 19th-century economic growth. Even if the "Bourgeois Revolution" did not finally end monarchic rule in France, or introduce much democracy, it brought to an end the absolute monarchy of the *Ancien Régime* and the anachronistic notions of national economic development that had prevailed under that system. Napoleon Bonaparte was able to institutionalize some of the principles of the Revolution, while pursuing his own militaristic aims, through a reorganization of government, the civil service, and the legal system. Crucially, these reforms increased the role of the bourgeoisie in public life. That rise was clear in the Revolution of 1830 when Charles X, the quasi-absolute monarch of the Restoration, was forced to cede power to the rival royal house of Orléans, which was more willing to accommodate the voice of the Parisian bourgeoisie in political decision-making.

The year 1830 also saw the French conquest of Algeria, which marked the beginning of France's acquisition of its modern empire. That empire was to play a major role in the development of French capitalism, for like other European powers, the French were to rely on their colonies as sources of cheap labor and raw materi-

Paris, the French capital, is the seat of an economy that consistently ranks as the sixth-largest in the world.

als, and as protected markets for exports from France. That economic historians now doubt the efficiency of such trading systems when applying cost-benefit analyses to modern imperialism is immaterial, for the key point is that French capitalism was based on an imperial system that was itself an outgrowth of the French Revolutionary notion of national superiority, and of the moral value of the export of French ideas and rule.

While the period 1830–48 did not see the most dynamic phase of French industrial growth, it was the moment when key industries such as the railways came into being, and with them came a particular cultural aspect of French capitalism which was the technocratic compromise between the state and private interests. When railways were invented and first developed in England, a vigorous debate began in France on how a national rail network should be developed. On one side of the debate was an unusual alliance of right-wing nationalists and the political left, who argued that the state had to take responsibility for the development of railways in France (either for reasons of national security, or because state control of economic development was a fundamentally good thing), while on the other were the bourgeois free-marketeers who advocated the private development of rail in France, and liberals who claimed that state subsidies for rail would act as a form of double taxation on the poorer social classes.

The state's compromise solution, in this case, was for it to develop the railway network, and to lease out the right to run rail services to private concessions (and to allow them to develop secondary rail routes). This effectively created a state-sanctioned OLIGOPOLY in the market, and it is perhaps not surprising that

there was considerable interpenetration of business and political spheres at this time, with similar oligopolies being created in other sectors such as banking and department stores. This cartelization reflected a more general French belief in the importance of protection within the national market, at the expense of free-market competition.

Although such policies are clearly inefficient in terms of orthodox economics, and certainly in terms of modern neo-liberalism, they have achieved convincing results in France. They also played their part in the development of a society in which power is concentrated in the hands of a politico-economic elite, and where the development of a culture of rights was notoriously slower to come into being than in comparable European states.

France 1848–1914. The period between the revolutions of 1848 and the WORLD WAR I was crucial in terms of the development of the modern French state and its capitalist economy. Many of the structural features of the French economy emerged in the period 1848–70, and the grounds of modern French Republican politics were formed in the nascent Third Republic. This was a period in which Karl MARX was greatly interested in France, and with good reason, for an archetypal capitalist state was coming into being, though it is interesting to note that Marx felt that the Commune of 1871—the last major, radical challenge to that state—was inadvisable given France's developmental level. Later writers have identified the Commune as the last moment of resistance to both the state-private economic compromise of burgeoning French capitalism, and to the Third Republic's political compromise between the forces of tradition and the moderate heirs to the Revolution of 1789.

The great changes of the period, and their human consequences, are catalogued by cultural producers such as Emile Zola, whose *Rougon-Macquart* cycle charted, among other things, the development of the French railway network; the modernization of French agriculture; emigration to the cities; the development of trade unions; the growth of the Paris BOURSE and of popular share-ownership and speculation; the development of the north as a heavy-industrial heartland; the increasing and novel stress on investment and risk in the French economy; and the great growth of the French banking sector at this time.

Texts such as Zola's show us the changing moral world of French society as it rapidly became capitalist, and the speed and universality of change as all were exposed to the new forces changing French society. It is, as French historians have noted, no coincidence, that as a single national market emerged in France a new kind of government came after 1870 that stressed nationality above all else; a government that instituted a series of administrative reforms (especially in the spheres of education and language) and stressed the creation of a single, unified, manageable state. It should also not seem coincidental that this period of confident national growth marked the most rapid expansion of the French Empire. Structural weaknesses, however, remained in the French economy, as evinced by the less convincing performance of the French economy after 1870, but the contours of capitalist France had now been drawn.

France 1914–45. World War I, which of course took place primarily on French and Belgian soil, left France in an economically and demographically precarious position in the interwar years. France, like other major powers, suffered from the instability of the world economy with, in particular, periods of high inflation, a weakening currency, budget deficits, and, Poincaré aside, a political class that had little skill in economic affairs or inclination to reflate the economy. German reparations could not fully cover the cost of rebuilding France's industrial capacity, and when the DEPRESSION hit France, its effects were felt rather later and for rather longer than in other states. This difference, and the relatively low levels of unemployment in France in the 1930s, has traditionally been explained by the fact that France still had a much larger agricultural sector than comparable economies. The rural economy was able to take on many of the urban workers who had lost industrial jobs, or at the very least families were able to rely on networks of kin for food, but this undynamic agricultural sector was obviously not the route out of the Depression. France's eventual economic recovery came under the vigorously interventionist Popular Front government of 1936–38, though this experiment in popular socialism was ended by France's rapid defeat by the Germans in 1940.

France's wartime collaborationist government under Maréchal Pétain had a rather incoherent belief in both tradition and technocracy, claiming its National Revolution would return France to its best (rightist, rural) traditions, while revolutionizing French industry. Neither of these policy directions were realized, primarily because the French economy was subservient to the German war machine. Price notes that "By 1943, 15 percent of the agricultural and 40 percent of industrial output was exported to Germany, and paid for largely by the French themselves in the form of occupation costs." In addition, the French sent more than 680,000 workers to German factories.

France after 1945. In the aftermath of WORLD WAR II, along with France's crushing defeat in 1940 and the failure of collaboration, it was clear that new economic and political priorities would be set in 1945. In the economic sphere, Charles DE GAULLE's natural distaste for capital-

ism was shown in the NATIONALIZATION of key industries such as coal, banking, and leading manufacturers such as Renault cars, and a new mood emerged in which, as Price notes, "It had become necessary for the state to assume control of the 'levers of command' and direct investment not simply into reconstruction, but additionally into a program of social and economic modernization impelled by a now widely shared perception of France as a backward, archaic society."

The Fourth Republic inaugurated a period of great economic growth, with the period 1945–75 known as the *trente glorieuses*, in which technocratic state planning, backed initially by the MARSHALL PLAN, redeveloped the French economy, placing a great emphasis on new technologies and on the production of consumer goods for an increasingly affluent society.

French prosperity became increasingly linked to that of its neighbors through the European Economic Community, and as France decolonized, much greater emphasis was placed on trade with immediate European neighbors than had been the case earlier in the century. While French growth outpaced most of its European rivals, it was also clear that the new technocratic model, which was little more than the old state-private compromise of the railways in a new guise, did not address some of the principal structural weaknesses in the French economy.

In particular, unemployment has been stubbornly high in France since the 1980s and the French economic system remains one in which the benefits of growth are concentrated in particular areas, while other regions (such as the north) are in long-term decline. A progressive system of taxation removes some inequities, but there is a sense that the postwar French state and economy have nevertheless concentrated benefits and growth on the middle and upper classes. Periodic expressions of public anger (such as in the riots of 1968) are a reminder of this. As France has become more integrated into a European and global economy it has also become clear that French governments have much less latitude in imposing their own, particularly French, solutions to economic problems. This became abundantly clear in the early 1980s when President François Mitterrand was forced by global markets to first abandon his program of nationalization and state intervention; and to later actively reverse his strategy, thus becoming the socialist president who introduced privatization to France.

BIBLIOGRAPHY. Roger Price, *A Concise History of France* (Cambridge University Press, 1993); John Ardagh, *France in a New Century* (Penguin, 1999); Martin S. Alexander, ed., *French History Since Napoleon* (Edward Arnold, 1999); Roger Magraw, *France 1800–1914: A Social History* (Longman, 2002); Emile Zola, *Les Rougon-Macquart* (Librairie J.

Corti, 1960–67); M.M. Postan and H.J. Habakkuk, eds., *The Cambridge Economic History of Europe* (Cambridge University Press, 1966); Carlo M. Cipolla, ed., *The Fontana Economic History of Europe* (Barnes & Noble, 1977).

WILLIAM GALLOIS, PH.D.
AMERICAN UNIVERSITY OF SHARJAH

franchising

IN THE *Webster's New World Dictionary of Media and Communications*, Richard Weiner defines a franchise as "a contractual agreement between a manufacturer, service organization, or other franchisers and independent businesspersons (franchisees) who purchase the right to own and operate a retail unit and/or to sell the franchised products or services."

Franchising depends upon a legal agreement, that can be seen symbolically as a sharing of reputations: the franchisee accepts to bring a high level of quality to his customers and promises to conform to the corporation's standard norms, and by doing so, benefits from a label's name, exclusive products, well-known logos, and large-scale advertising. In return, the franchisee hosts satisfied customers from previous experiences in other franchises; he helps the other members of the franchise by responding to the customers' needs and expectations. By doing so, he contributes to improve the corporation's reputation.

There are many kinds of franchising organizations. For instance, Yum! Brands Inc. operates 32,000 restaurants; their chains include Kentucky Fried Chicken, Pizza Hut, and Taco Bell; those three were spun off from Pepsi Cola Enterprises in the late 1990s. Also in the fast-food business, Wendy's International Inc. controls a system of fast-casual restaurants, with some 6000 Wendy's restaurants in operation in the United States and in 20 other countries; from that number, almost 5,000 Wendy's restaurants are franchisees while 1,300 others are operated by the company itself. In the hotel business, the Holiday Inn hotels and motels are mostly franchises.

In Canada, the hardware stores that are part of the chain Canadian Tire are also operated by franchisees. However, depending on circumstances, a store may decide at some point to disconnect itself from the group and to become independent, or even to join another group of franchisees; he has to abandon all the previous logos and promotional elements that used to identify his outlet as a member of the chain. As a notable exception in the food business, Darden Restaurants controls the Red Lobster Restaurants as well as the Olive Garden Restaurants, but none of their U.S. restaurants are franchises; more than 1,000 restaurants are therefore company-owned and the corporation is also partly controlled by General Mills.

Licensees are not franchisees but independent third parties, that operate under the terms of license agreements, known as a legal or official permission granted by a licensor to a licensee. Under negotiated and limited terms, a name, product, program, or other item may be licensed or sold for a specific period or under specific conditions.

Imagine that you're opening your own McDonald's. To do this, you have to buy a McDonald's franchise. In order to qualify for a conventional franchise, you have to have $175,000 (not borrowed). Your total costs to open the restaurant, however, will be anywhere from $430,000 to $750,000, which goes to paying for the building, equipment, etc. Forty percent of this cost has to be from your own (non-borrowed) funds.

You'll pay an initial franchise fee of $45,000 directly to McDonald's. The other costs go to suppliers, so this is the only upfront fee you pay to McDonald's. Then, you'll go through a rigorous nine-month training period where you'll learn about the McDonald's way of doing things—things like their standards for quality, service, value, formulas and specifications for menu items, their method of operation, and inventory control techniques. You'll have to agree to operate the restaurant from a single location, usually for 20 years, following their guidelines for decor, signage, layout and everything else that makes McDonald's McDonald's.

Once you've completed training and are ready to go, McDonald's will offer you a location they've already developed. The exterior of the building will be complete, but you will have to take care of interior additions such as kitchen equipment, seating, and landscaping. You'll get constant support from a McDonald's Field Consultant, who can advise you on details and will visit regularly. You'll pay McDonald's a monthly fee of 4 percent of your sales, and either a flat base rent or a percentage rent of at least 8.5 percent of your sales.

McDonald's, the epitome of capitalism. McDonald's *Summary Annual Report 2002* states that the whole network serves 46 million customers every day. With 30,000 quick-service restaurants in more than 100 countries, McDonald's has achieved more than a franchise system: it is as well a global concept of marketing, a kind of management school and an unquestionable symbol of capitalism. Apart from that huge network of franchisees, McDonald's also controls some 9,000 company-operated restaurants and some 4,000 affiliated restaurants, including U.S.-based partner brands such as Boston Market, Donatos Pizzeria, and Chipotle Mexican Grill.

In the United States, there are about 13,000 McDonald's restaurants. Although McDonald's is a publicly owned company whose 1.2 billion shares are negotiated on the NEW YORK STOCK EXCHANGE and can be bought by anyone, the corporation is often seen as one of the best-known symbols of the United States, along with other mega-corporations such as Coca-Cola, Ford, or Microsoft. Most McDonald's customers choose famous names and labels in order to get familiar formulas, guaranteed reliability, standard menus, predictable tastes, and also clean rest rooms, even in foreign countries. Sociologist Douglas Kellner explains that while in a McDonald's restaurant in downtown Taichung, Taiwan, he was amazed to see how Taiwanese youth had adopted McDonald's restaurants in an unusual way: "In search of a men's room, I noticed that the place was packed with students studying, young people talking, and couples coupling. My host said that in a crowded city, McDonald's was a good site for studying and socializing and obviously the locals were taking advantage of this. Obviously, the social purposes and functions were quite different there than in the U.S. McDonald's."

The much-publicized opening of the first McDonald's in Moscow, Russia, on January 31, 1990, was a cultural shock for Soviet consumers and a source of wry analysis for some Western commentators. The U.S. fast-food premiere near the Kremlin, once the bastion of communism, was a standard McDonald's restaurant like any other (managed by a Canadian entrepreneur), with the same standard menu. Soviet customers were surprised by McDonald's proven efficiency, the employees' smiles, and also were shocked by the high prices for meals.

Often criticized for its standardization processes, McDonald's has, however, inspired some sociologists who theorized about the globalizing consumer society in terms of the "McDonald-ization of society." Although American sociologist and author George Ritzer criticizes McDonald's food, that he perceives as saturated with salt, sugar, and fat, he nonetheless considers this ubiquitous concept as a modern example of Max Weber's rationalization theory. In fact, McDonald-ization is more than a social phenomena about labor, high scale production, and consumption in global capitalism. Douglas Kellner resumes Ritzer's McDonald-ization theory "as a set of processes geared at increasing efficiency, calculability, predictability, and control."

There are countless fast-food restaurant chains in the United States, but none is perhaps praised and criticized as much as McDonald's; this is sometimes the price to pay for fame. As a symbol of U.S. prosperity and a cultural icon, McDonald's has been the target of numerous anti-American demonstrations abroad, from people opposing the American, invasive cultural presence in certain foreign countries or protesting against allegations of hidden GMF (Genetically Modified Food) in corn and soy products.

The corporation has always responded to critics with an omnipresent advertising strategy and a strong social commitment in order to create a positive image of good corporate citizenship, and also by giving to countless charities and foundations. On the other side, McDonald's corporation has sometimes been the solvent victim of what could be seen as excessive exploitation from some unsatisfied customers, who, in some cases, picked up any excuse to ask for damages and financial compensation for incidents occurring outside McDonald's restaurants, such as coffee-burning, car-key losses, and even more surprising claims. What was called the Stella Liebeck Case in the 1990s ranks among the most famous ones: after being burned by McDonald's hot coffee while in a car, an elderly woman went to court against McDonald's; after a long mediated trial, she was awarded $160,000 in compensatory damages, and $480,000 in punitive damages.

Another much-publicized lawsuit was the "McDonald's fries" case when vegetarians' organizations were granted court approval and compensatory damages because the restaurant chain didn't specify that their french fries were sometimes made with beef fat and beef flavoring. Hindu groups also said they were offended, because of their religious diet, to eat beef without knowing it when ordering french fries, and asked for compensatory damages. According to CNN Money News, "McDonald's Corp. said it would pay $10 million to Hindu, vegetarian and other groups more than a year after a Seattle lawyer sued the fast-food chain, alleging it failed to disclose the use of beef flavoring in its french fries." Such lawsuits had moved on in the early 2000s to include claims that McDonald's was responsible for the growing epidemic of obesity in America's children. Clearly, success in the franchise business carries its own risks: As a franchisee, one carries all the positive and negative aspects of the parent corporation.

BIBLIOGRAPHY. Peter M. Birkeland, *Franchising Dreams: The Lure of Entrepreneurship in America* (University of Chicago Press, 2002); Douglas Kellner, Douglas, *McDonaldization Revisited, Critical Essays on Consumer Culture* (Praeger Press, 1998); McDonald's Corporation, *McDonald's Summary Annual Report 2002* (2003); Marion Nestle, *Food Politics: How the Food Industry Influences Nutrition and Health* (University of California Press, 2002); Thomas J. Peters and Robert H. Waterman, Jr., *In search of excellence: Lessons from America's Best-Run Companies* (Warner Books Inc., 1984); George Ritzer, *The McDonaldization of Society* (Pine Forge, 1996); Michael Schudson, "Delectable Materialism: Second Thoughts on Consumer Culture," *Consumer Society in American History: A Reader* (Cornell University Press, 1999); Richard Weiner. *Webster's New World Dictionary of Media and Communications* (Macmillan, 1996).

YVES LABERGE, PH.D.
INSTITUT QUÉBÉCOIS DES
HAUTES ÉTUDES INTERNATIONALES

Franklin, Benjamin (1706–90)

ONE OF THE MOST influential figures of American society in the 18th century, Benjamin Franklin helped shape the American way of life through his model of personal success and achievement, popularized in his famous *Autobiography*, written between 1771 and 1790. Published posthumously, the book has enjoyed a vast readership and, after no less than 400 editions over the last three centuries, it is still in print and tells the story of Franklin, the self-made man who emerged from obscurity to eminence. Franklin's rise to fame exemplified the American dream of individual success and social mobility. The 20th-century social theorist Max Weber has gone so far as to identify Franklin with the spirit of capitalism itself.

Franklin was born into a large family of 17 children. His parents considered sending him to the ministry but they could not afford to give him more than two years of elementary school. The young Franklin was apprenticed to his older brother James, a printer, as he was incredibly fond of reading. Yet, already at the age of 17, Franklin showed that individualist spirit for which he became famous. He left his brother and ran away to Philadelphia, the city where the secular and egalitarian values of the Enlightenment were beginning to flourish. There he helped to revitalize the *Pennsylvania Gazette* and, after marrying Deborah Read in 1729, he launched his famous publication *Poor Richard's Almanac* in 1732. The publication was a manual on how to get ahead in the world ("time is money" was one of its mottos) and, in two decades of publication, sales reached 10,000 copies every year, making it a phenomenal bestseller in the small literate population of the American colonies.

By 1757, Franklin had made a small fortune and, in addition to his economic successes, he had become widely known in American and European scientific circles for his reports of electrical experiments and theories. As a result, he was elected Fellow of the Royal Society of London in 1756 and important universities such as Harvard, Yale, William and Mary, St. Andrews, and Oxford awarded him honorary degrees. The latter part of Franklin's life saw him start a long career as a politician. He would be chief spokesman for the British colonies in debates with the British king's ministers about self-government, and would have a hand in the writing of the *Declaration of Independence*. Franklin also played a crucial and historical role in securing financial and military aid from FRANCE during the AMERICAN REVOLUTION. At the age of 81, Franklin was the oldest delegate at the Constitutional Convention in 1787, and presented an important motion concerning the election of representatives in proportion to the population and the election of two senators by each state. Just five months before his death, Franklin signed a public note as president of the Pennsylvania Society for Promoting the Abolition of Slavery, containing a national policy of emancipation.

Franklin is a transitional figure between Puritanism and the American Enlightenment and his journey from Puritan Boston to Philadelphia is symbolic of this transition. Franklin gave material grounding to the rhetoric of Puritanism, sharing its emphasis on regeneration but adopting a crucially different perspective. According to the Puritans, only God's grace could purge the self from evil, while Franklin believed that man was perfectly able to make himself good. His *Autobiography* is the applied illustration of the "bold and arduous project of arriving at moral perfection," documented by the famous charts of weeks and days. Franklin starts and ends each day with a self-questioning and an introspection typical of Puritans: "What good shall I do this day?" and "What good have I done today?" According to Franklin, doing good meant to become a useful citizen. As Kenneth Silverman points out, in Franklin's project "the fervent Puritan hope for self-transformation has become the American passion for self-improvement."

Franklin's *Autobiography* and his proverbs in *Poor Richard's Almanac* celebrate the strength of the American middle-class, its quest for progress and scientific knowledge and its unashamed search for personal wealth. Franklin's own story and maxims honor economic individualism and upward mobility. His autobiography traces Franklin's progress from his low beginnings and his obscure family to his international reputation through his strict work ethic: "I was seen at no places of idle diversion. I never went out a-fishing or shooting; a book, indeed, sometimes debauched me from my work; but that was seldom, snug and gave no scandal." In this characterization of Franklin's persona, there are nuances of the Puritan doctrine of the Calling, yet, as Silverman points out, the text "reverses the Puritan ethos. It praises not copying one's family, but surpassing it, not deferring to one's elders but outfoxing them, trusting and assigning authority not to others and to God but to oneself. . . . It remains the classic statement of the American dream of material success."

Franklin's detractors have focused precisely on his gospel of social mobility and have identified him with the greedy American capitalist spirit. These critiques have been as international as Franklin's career. William Carlos Williams' *In the American Grain* (1925) exposed Franklin's impact on the aggressively acquisitive mood in American society and D.H. Lawrence described him as "the first dummy American." Weber has taken Franklin's writings as documents of the capitalist spirit, which they contain "in almost classical purity." Weber quotes Franklin's proverbs according to which "time is money" and that "money is of the prolific, generating nature" and concludes that Franklin's philosophy is one of avarice. Its peculiar ethic, Weber argues, "appears to be the ideal of the honest man of recognized credit, and above all the idea of a duty of the individual toward the increase of his capital, which is assumed as an end in itself."

It is this attitude of "worldly asceticism," this accumulation of wealth "combined with the strict avoidance of all spontaneous enjoyment of life," which, to Weber, is responsible for the establishment of the "iron cage" where we are all confined. Franklin embodies the capitalist ethos which makes the accumulation of wealth an end in itself thus conferring to "material goods . . . an increasing and finally an inexorable power over the lives of men as at no previous period in history."

BIBLIOGRAPHY. Nian-Sheng Huang, *Benjamin Franklin in American Thought and Culture, 1790–1990* (American Philosophical Society, 1994); Kenneth Silverman, "From Cotton Mather to Benjamin Franklin," *Columbia Literary History of the United States* (Columbia University Press, 1988); Max Weber, *The Protestant Ethic and the Spirit of Capitalism* (Routledge, 2001).

LUCA PRONO, PH.D.
UNIVERSITY OF NOTTINGHAM, ENGLAND

free trade

ECONOMIST ADAM SMITH (1723–90) first championed free trade as a systematic economic theory in his book *Wealth of Nations* (1776). Smith's ideas ran counter to the prevailing economic theories of his day, particularly MERCANTILISM, or the governmental regulation of the economy. As a concept, free trade has been controversial ever since. Today, most professional economists support the notion, despite the frequent criticism it receives from political groups across the ideological spectrum.

Free trade does not have a single, unified definition, but generally refers to trade between nations without any artificial barriers put in place by the government. When each side is engaged in free trade, they face prices determined by the global marketplace. In practice, free trade allows nations to trade with one another without restrictions, giving every nation the right to EXPORT AND IMPORT goods priced at the discretion of the market. In contrast, governments opting to limit free trade place restrictive policies (such as TARIFFS) against imported goods to artificially favor products produced within the nation, therefore protecting its own producers and manufacturers from foreign competition.

Free trade may seem like a relatively straightforward idea, but it is a hot topic in today's global economy. Free trade is used to defend or punish a nation's trade policy and is also utilized as a diplomatic tool in determining relations between countries or blocks of countries. In these instances, free trade becomes a plank in the ideological battle between nations, and a fierce issue among a variety of activists within and outside a given country. At the heart of free trade is the notion that the open exchange of goods between nations is a favorable development and benefits the global economy.

Smith's framework. Smith outlined his thoughts about free trade in lectures at Glasgow University in the 1760s, building on the work of earlier economic thinkers. By the time *Wealth of Nations* was published, Smith developed the theory into a coherent framework. He felt Great Britain should be a free port with all duties and customs eradicated.

Smith described the objective of mercantilist policy to diminish as much as possible the importation of foreign commodities and to increase the exportation of domestically produced products and merchandise. He examined the "economy-wide" impact of tariffs on imports and concluded that such policies led to higher prices, monopolistic practices in the home market, laziness, and poor management.

The foundation of Smith's thoughts on free trade centered on each individual's natural right to participate in the economy. Citizens sought to improve their own station by providing goods and services to others. In turn, their efforts enhanced the national economy through an efficient allocation of resources. In this system, COMPETITION defined the economic marketplace, not the government.

In Smith's view, however, the government did have a place in the economy, primarily allowing the "invisible hand" of the market to run more efficiently. And, in some cases, tariffs were necessary, such as in supporting an industry essential for national defense.

Smith's call for free trade was not a ploy to win favor among England's merchants. He believed in free trade because he believed it would benefit common people the most. Dedicated to the market economy, Smith concluded that even the poor and politically inept could prosper in an open financial system. In contrast, Smith thought that a state-controlled economy only enabled those close to the leadership to thrive and become rich.

Smith criticized merchants who lobbied for trade restrictions and disparaged governments that gave in to such pressure. In his view, tariffs harmed consumers because domestic merchants raised prices without the competition from foreign manufacturers. He also blasted governments that enacted retaliatory tariffs, because justifying them was difficult and more a political ploy than sound economic theory.

Free trade post-Smith. Smith's *Wealth of Nations* had some immediate impact on economic thought, but it took about 25 years for it to be considered a landmark work. The classical economists of the 19th century favored free trade and advocated its adoption despite the political chaos across Europe. Following the Napoleonic War, Britain adopted free trade policies that stimulated tremendous growth in world trade through the early 20th century.

After America won independence from England, the new nation embraced Smith and free trade as a counter to the mother country's harsh mercantilist trade restrictions. The idea of free trade became part of the revolutionary cause in the new nation. While the newly formed United States enacted some tariffs to protect burgeoning industries from foreign competition, free trade reigned.

In 1817, British politician and economist David RICARDO (1772–1823) published *The Principles of Political Economy and Taxation*, which outlined the Law of Comparative Advantage. Ricardo used the law to demonstrate that global trade is mutually beneficial, even when one nation is more productive than another. Comparative advantage assumes that even the poorest nation will have an advantage in some area. When the two nations trade, it becomes a win-win situation because trading is economically efficient.

For example, if an American buys a British good with dollars, the British merchant is likely to buy an item with dollars, or trade those dollars for pounds. Both nations become wealthier because nations become wealthy by producing and consuming goods and services. The total output rises, which is good for both economies. Tariffs, however, constrict growth and are debilitating to the nation erecting them, since its citizens will not have access to cheaper goods, thus forcing them to buy artificially higher-priced merchandise from domestic manufacturers.

The Law of Comparative Advantage is more problematic in modern times, but it still has many followers. Critics say that one of the basic assumptions of the theory is that capital (money) is immobile, which is simply no longer true. GOODS, CAPITAL, and LABOR all freely move across international boundaries with little more than a touch of a keystroke or simple computer transactions.

Early 20th century. Free trade suffered a severe blow in the 1920s when John Maynard KEYNES—considered one of the most influential economists of all time—suggested that it was wise to use tariffs in some instances to increase output and employment. Although Keynes actually advocated a pragmatic free-trade philosophy, his retreat from the idea weakened its place among economists.

In the UNITED STATES, powerful business and labor groups lobbied Congress for highly protective tariffs, which they believed would protect the domestic economy from foreign competition, thus preserving American jobs and wages. Congress passed two harsh tariffs, the Fordney-McCumber (1922) and the Smoot-Hawley (1930) tariffs. Rather than strengthen the U.S. economy, these measures disrupted global trade and caused credit imbalances that contributed to the Great DEPRESSION. Other nations acted similarly and put up their own tariffs in the face of economic collapse, thus exacerbating the effects of the Depression.

The overwhelming destruction caused by two world wars, however, gave new momentum to the idea of free trade. Economic and political thinkers viewed global free trade as a means to restoring quality of life, particularly in areas suffering the most from the ravages of war. In certain nations across Europe, Japan, and parts of the Far East, people were starving. Given its economic strength, the United States was called upon to open its markets to the world. At the end of WORLD WAR II, the United States clearly dominated the world economy, owning half the supply of monetary gold and producing half the world's GROSS NATIONAL PRODUCT (GNP).

As a result, the United States and Great Britain led a delegation of 45 nations in an economic planning session at BRETTON WOODS (New Hampshire) in 1944 to set up the WORLD BANK, which would regulate the reconstruction of devastated nations and prod their economies back to life. In addition, they also established the INTERNATIONAL MONETARY FUND (IMF) to stabilize exchange rates and balance of payments. These organizations solidified the postwar economy, while also clearly confirming the supremacy of the United States and Western Europe in economic affairs. The next step was to formalize an agreement on free trade.

President Franklin D. ROOSEVELT and his successor, Harry TRUMAN, both supported the expansion of international trade. The breakdown of free trade in the early decades of the 20th century, they believed, led to the prolonged Depression and the rise of totalitarian dictatorships, resulting in debilitating warfare. The Bretton Woods conference solidified the idea that global economics would adhere to a capitalistic system of free trade of goods and money. Despite the support for an organization to regulate free trade at the executive level, early efforts to form an international trade organization (ITO) failed to be ratified in the United States. Government officials continued to push for trade agreements.

Late 20th century. In 1948, Truman forced the nation to adhere to the GENERAL AGREEMENT ON TARIFFS AND TRADE (GATT) through executive agreement, which set up reciprocal trade between nations and had 23 initial participants. Immediately successful, the first round of GATT negotiations led to 45,000 tariff concessions. Later GATT talks further reduced trade barriers, eliminated discriminatory practices, and led to dispute resolution through mediation. From the birth of GATT to 1957, world trade jumped 77 percent, enabling western Europe and Japan to rebuild.

The recovery of GERMANY and JAPAN after the devastation of World War II (dubbed an "economic miracle" in the press) was directly attributed to the increased trade promoted by GATT. By the early 1950s, Japan and the European Common Market used U.S. economic assistance and the reduced tariffs negotiated in GATT talks to achieve economic growth rates that doubled increases in the United States. In 1964–67, the Kennedy Round, named in honor of the late president, achieved tariff cuts worth $40 billion.

The most ambitious free-trade talks took place during the Uruguay Round (1986–94). Both agriculture and service industries were discussed for the first time during the Uruguay Round. More importantly, the idea for the WORLD TRADE ORGANIZATION (WTO) took shape there. The first international trade organization to be ratified by the U.S. Congress (1996), the WTO subsumed GATT and became the primary authority governing free trade worldwide. The WTO has legal authority to settle disputes between nations. At the turn of the 21st century, 124 nations belonged to the WTO.

The WTO continued to evolve to include technologies that had a profound influence on the global economy. In 1997, 69 governments agreed to a policy regarding telecommunications services. The same year, 40 governments agreed to eliminate tariffs on information technology products, while 70 members set policies covering trade related to banking, insurance, securities, and financial information.

Large corporations have been the most ardent supporters of free trade in modern times. Corporate leaders argue that free trade increases wages and gives people access to more goods as markets expand. Critics, however, see free trade as a means of exporting manufacturing and production to areas where labor is least expensive and usurping the power of labor unions.

The North American Free Trade Agreement (NAFTA), a trilateral trade agreement between the United States, CANADA, and MEXICO is an example of the arguments for and against free trade. NAFTA talks began under President George H.W. BUSH, who later signed the treaty in late 1992. President Bill CLINTON then aggressively supported the agreement, later ratified in 1994. NAFTA gradually eliminated tariffs for the three, reduced barriers to trade and investment, and exempted corporations from many state, local, and national regulations. A panel of trade officials and lawyers from each country handles disputes in secret negotiations.

Large corporations in the three nations lobbied hard for NAFTA, arguing that it would spread prosperity. Opponents, however, questioned what the agreement would mean for workers, small businesses, and the environment. They viewed NAFTA as a way for corporations to outsource production to nations without strict labor laws or environmental protection.

The fierce debates over the ratification of NAFTA, however, pale in comparison with the storms of protest waged against the WTO. In 1999, when the organization attempted to launch a round of talks in Seattle, Washington, waves of protestors took to the streets calling for fair free trade between rich and poor nations. Critics of the WTO considered the organization a tool of wealthy Western nations to keep Third World nations dependent upon their goods. Suddenly, the WTO became the focal point for many activist groups, from labor unions to militant environmental groups. WTO negotiations in Doha, Qatar, two years later were more successful, but the gap between the rich and poor members still perplexes the organization.

Supporters of the WTO, in contrast, point to the substantial increases in world trade since the various organizations have been in place to regulate it. In the span between 1950 and 2000, total trade jumped 22 times it's previous level.

The present and future of free trade. President George W. BUSH unveiled an ambitious trade agenda early in his administration, including agreements with CHILE and SINGAPORE, the 35 democracies in the Western Hemisphere, and a global free-trade accord with the 144 nations of the WTO. Bush set off a wave of protest, however, when he pushed for unilateral authority to negotiate trade agreements without amendments (known as "fast track").

Nations will continue to argue for and against free trade and protectionist policies. Since World War II, the global economy has become increasingly important for nations of all sizes. Powerful countries, like the United States, have taken steps to formalize global trade, but these issues are burdened with controversy.

For example, China entered the WTO in December 2001, after 15 years of negotiations, despite the country's poor human rights record. The desire to gain access to the world's largest emerging economy by corporate and government officials offset the issues that confounded environmental and human-rights activists.

Historically, the idea of free trade in the United States has been used to justify many of the nation's political and diplomatic moves, such as the Open Door policy in China and the paternal control the nation has exerted over Central and South America for more than a century. In this light, free trade has been overlooked as an idea central to the American vision of supremacy in world affairs. In the United States and other democratic/capitalistic nations, free trade is no longer just an economic theory. Free trade is equated with freedom.

Thus, a country that does not permit or promote free trade is charged with denying its citizens with a basic human right.

Today, free trade is so closely linked to capitalism that its legitimacy can no longer be questioned, because casting doubt on free trade is akin to criticizing capitalism. The protestors who marched against the WTO in Seattle, for example, were roundly criticized in the media and denounced as anarchists and hooligans.

Free markets, competition, and private OWNERSHIP are ideas firmly rooted in the American psyche and have been spread worldwide. To "do business" with the United States, nations are encouraged to adopt the same beliefs in capitalism and its tenets.

BIBLIOGRAPHY. Todd G. Buchholz, *New Ideas from Dead Economists: An Introduction to Modern Economic Thought* (New American Library, 1989); Alfred E. Eckes, Jr., *Opening America's Market: U.S. Foreign Trade Policy Since 1776* (University of North Carolina Press, 1995); H. Peter Gray, *Free Trade or Protection? A Pragmatic Analysis* (Macmillan, 1985); Douglas A. Irwin, *Against the Tide: An Intellectual History of Free Trade* (Princeton University Press, 1996); Diane B. Kunz, *Butter and Guns: America's Cold War Economic Diplomacy* (Free Press, 1997); John R. MacArthur, *The Selling of "Free Trade:" NAFTA, Washington, and the Subversion of American Democracy* (University of California Press, 2001); Henri Miller, ed., *Free Trade Versus Protectionism* (H.W. Wilson, 1996); Harry Shutt, *The Myth of Free Trade: Patterns of Protectionism Since 1945* (Blackwell, 1985).

BOB BATCHELOR
INDEPENDENT SCHOLAR

French Revolution

A SUCCESSION OF EVENTS (1789–99) known as the French Revolution temporarily replaced absolutist monarchy with a republic; hastened the dissolution of serfdom; gave birth to the modern concept of human rights; introduced LIBERALISM and nationalism; and, bequeathed a model of popular insurrection that inspired generations to come.

By the second half of the 18th century a series of costly wars had drained the treasury of the French monarchy that was detached from reality and largely inept to govern. Almost 50 percent of the tax revenue was earmarked for debt payments while 25 percent went to maintain the military, not leaving enough resources to run the country. The intervention in the AMERICAN REVOLUTION produced no material advantages that could have compensated for the military expenses.

The first two estates (or classes), the clergy and nobility, were tax-exempt despite being the largest landowners. The third estate (over 90 percent of the population), a diverse social group ranging from upwardly mobile bourgeoisie to unskilled day laborers and peasants, united only by legal status, and having no political voice, carried the tax burden. The rigid Old Regime, founded on the feudal orders from the Middle Ages, had become outdated and it ceased to correspond with social reality.

In 1877, Louis XVI called an Assembly of Notables to gain support for the introduction of general tax on all landed property. The disenchanted nobility, whose economic base was in a relative decline, refused to give up their privileges. Hoping for broad political reforms, the nobility forced Louis XVI to convene the Estates-General, the representative body of all three estates that had not met since 1614. The King acquiesced anticipating the radical but diverse third estate would make the clergy and nobility more tractable. Yet, the third estate, dominated by lawyers and parish priests, proved to be more homogenous than the first two internally divided estates.

The meeting of the Estates-General in May 1789 became deadlocked over the voting protocol because the third estate demanded representation equal to that of the clergy and nobility. Contemporary intellectuals supported the demands for change by arguing the third estate constituted the true strength of the French nation. The third estate seceded on June 17, 1789, called itself the National Assembly, and swore the Tennis Court Oath pledging not to disband until they had written a new constitution. Louis XVI reluctantly capitulated and allowed all three estates to meet to draft a new constitution.

The events took a violent turn on July 14, 1789, when a Parisian mob, angered by high bread prices and fearing Louis XVI would use force to disband the National Assembly, stormed the Bastille (the royal prison) in search for weapons and food. A great fear swept rural France as peasants burned chateaux and expelled the landowners. After abolishing feudalism, on August 26, 1789, the National Assembly enacted the Declaration of the Rights of Man and the Citizens.

The Constitution of 1791 established a moderate constitutional monarchy and enacted constructive reforms. Civil rights were granted to all citizens and the nobility was eliminated as a legally defined class. The patchwork of provinces was replaced with 83 departments, and a unified system of weights and measures was introduced. However, the action against the Catholic Church, the confiscation of property and giving the state control over the clergy, was denounced by the Papacy and even the peasantry considered it to be too radical.

Attempted foreign invasions, domestic insurrection, and the deteriorating economic situation split the revolutionary coalition between the radical Jacobins and the more moderate Girondins. Both factions wanted to defend the Revolution but disagreed on the means. The Jacobins' radicalism prevailed and they established a revolutionary Commune in Paris. A new National Convention, that vested executive power in the Committee of Public Safety composed of 12 men led by Maximilian Robespierre, was elected on a franchise of universal male suffrage to draft a new republican constitution and to abolish the monarchy. Louis XVI, who had tried to flee the country, was beheaded in January 1793, and France was proclaimed a republic.

Robespierre and the Committee of Public Safety established the Reign of Terror in 1793. This was an attempt to save the Revolution by introducing a planned economy, mass executions, and French nationalism. The Jacobins instituted the wildly unpopular military draft by arguing the French soldiers were fighting for the French nation not the monarchy. The Jacobins centralized the administration, and established revolutionary tribunals throughout the nation that guillotined the real and suspected enemies of the Revolution. The regime also mandated a new egalitarian dress code, created a new calendar, and established a new religion, the Cult of the Supreme Being.

The Thermidorean Reaction of July 1794, ended the Reign of Terror, which had its merits because it brought the inflation under control, generated a sense of national unity, and succeeded in holding revolutionary France together. Robespierre was executed, the Commune was disbanded, and the Committee of Public Safety was stripped of its powers and replaced by the Directory.

The period of the Directory marked a return of moderate constitutionalism of the early revolutionary period. Deputies were elected on the basis of wealth or service in the Republican army. Legislative authority was vested in two legislative bodies, the Council of Ancients and the Council of Five Hundred. Executive power was in the hands of a five-man Directory elected by the Council of Ancients from a list of candidates presented by the Council of Five Hundred. The Directory was never popular because it was autocratic.

Napoleon Bonaparte, a young successful general and a national hero, overthrew the Directory in 1799, established himself as a military dictator, and soon became as powerful as any absolute monarch France had ever seen.

BIBLIOGRAPHY. Bronislaw Baczko, *Ending the Terror: The French Revolution After Robespierre* (Cambridge University Press, 1994); J. F. Bosher, *The French Revolution* (W.W. Norton, 1989); William Doyle, *The Oxford History of the French Revolution* (Cambridge University Press, 1989); Ferenc Feher, ed., *The French Revolution and the Birth of Modernity* (University of California Press, 1990); Lynn Hunt, ed., *The French Revolution and Human Rights: A Brief Documentary History* (Palgrave Macmillan, 1996); Georges Lefebvre, *Coming of the French Revolution, 1789* (Princeton University Press, 1989); Simon Schama, *Citizens: A Chronicle of the French Revolution* (Knopf, 1990).

JOSIP MOCNIK
BOWLING GREEN STATE UNIVERSITY

Frick, Henry Clay (1849–1919)

GROWING UP IN Westmoreland County, Pennsylvania, with limited formal education, Henry Clay Frick rose to become the largest producer of coke from coal, forming Frick & Company in 1871.

He began by buying out competitors during the Panic of 1873, and by age 30, he was a millionaire. Andrew CARNEGIE, a champion of the Bessemer process of steel making, which depended on coke, soon brought Frick into Carnegie Brothers Inc. to supply coke to his mills. Frick was given large holdings in Carnegie's company, and made chairman in 1889. He reorganized Carnegie into the world's largest coke and steel company by buying out competitors, acquiring railroad securities and, in the Lake Superior region, iron ore lands.

In keeping with Frick's strident vertical integration tactics, during the 1892 labor strike at the Homestead Works of Carnegie Steel Company, Frick took actions to eliminate the unions at the mills. Carnegie, who had given Frick orders to break the union, however, was in Europe when Frick reduced workers' wages, laid them off, hired strikebreakers, and used the Pinkerton detective agency to protect replacement workers. The violence and deaths that followed led to a major setback for the labor movement, and an assassination attempt on Frick from anarchist Alexander Berkmann.

Carnegie attempted to distance himself from Frick and the violence, and eventually Frick resigned from the company. Frick's entrepreneurial ventures continued in 1900 when he formed St. Clair Steel Company, with the largest coke works in the world. He directed the newly created United States Steel Corporation, and later invested in real estate in Pennsylvania and New York. In downtown Pittsburgh, Frick purchased the Frick building, William Penn Hotel, Union Arcade and Frick Annex and, to house his art collection a mansion in New York City. The mansion and art collection, a reflection of his appreciation for aesthetic values and the affection he held for his family, was willed to the public and opened as a museum in 1935.

BIBLIOGRAPHY. George Harvey, *Henry Clay Frick, the Man* (Scribner's, 1928); Martha Sanger, *Henry Clay Frick: An Intimate Portrait* (Abbeville Press, 1998); Howard Zinn, *A People's History of the United States* (Harper Perennial, 1990).

CRISTINA ZACCARINI
ADELPHI UNIVERSITY

Friedman, Milton (1912–)

IN 1976, THE NOBEL PRIZE in Economics went to Milton Friedman, a well-known and well-respected economist, advocate and champion of individual freedom and LAISSEZ-FAIRE policies. For his award, the Nobel committee honored his "achievements in the fields of consumption analysis and monetary history and theory, and his demonstration of the complexity of the stabilization policy."

Regarded as the leader of the CHICAGO SCHOOL of monetary economics, or MONETARISM, Friedman has for many years stressed the importance of quantity of money as an instrument of government policy and as a determinant of BUSINESS CYCLES and INFLATION.

Milton Friedman, a proponent of monetarism, also stressed individual freedom and laissez-faire economics.

Mixing economics with his social views, he has long supported public policy that favors individual rights. Alongside his scientific work, he found time to write and co-author several books on this subject, produce an ongoing column for *Newsweek* magazine for 18 consecutive years, and host a television show, *Free To Choose*, for the Public Broadcasting System.

Friedman was the fourth and last son of poor immigrant parents living in Brooklyn, New York. Jeno Friedman and his wife Sarah (Landau), eked out a living for their family, eventually moving to Rahway, New Jersey, seeking better opportunity. While Sarah ran a tiny dry goods store, Jeno ventured through a number of menial jobs, but always managing to feed and clothe his family. The warm Friedman family atmosphere, despite tough times, never waned, Friedman remembered.

An excellent student throughout his years at Rahway Elementary School, Friedman desired a college degree. His mother agreed that he should better himself and, despite the fact that her husband Jeno had died and that it wouldn't be easy financially, she saw to it that her boy realized his dream. She, and her two daughters remaining at home, pitched in. Friedman entered Rutgers University in 1928, greatly assisted by a competitive scholarship. Before, during and after each semester, he waited tables, clerked, and picked up whatever job he could find to supplement tuition funds.

A mathematics major, he soon changed his objective when confronted by two particular professors who inadvertently changed his direction. Arthur F. Burns shaped his understanding of economic research and Homer Jones introduced him to rigorous economic theory, leaving their pupil captivated. It was on the latter's recommendation that, when Friedman graduated from Rutgers in 1932, the University of Chicago offered the eager young man a tuition scholarship to complete his postgraduate degree.

Friedman was off to Chicago. In his autobiography for the Nobel Committee, Friedman recalled that experience. "My first year in Chicago was, financially, my most difficult year; intellectually, it opened new worlds." There, he came in contact with a brilliant roster of economists and mathematicians, among them professors Jacob Viner and Lloyd Mints, who introduced him to a vibrant educational atmosphere from which, he added, "I never recovered."

During that period, 1932–34, Friedman happened to form another kind of relationship from which would be formed a lifelong partnership, with his future wife, Rose. "In the words of the fairy tale, we lived happily ever after," Friedman attests. "(Rose) has been an active partner in all my professional work ever since."

Fulfilling a yearlong fellowship at New York City's Columbia University—where he steeped himself in the complexities of mathematical economics—Friedman returned to Chicago in 1935 as research assistant to Professor Henry Schultz, recent author of the insightful *Theory and Measurement of Demand.* Invited to design a large consumer budget study sponsored by the National Resources Committee, Friedman headed to Washington, D.C. The assignment proved to be a fortuitous experience as it provided him with the fundamental component that later led to his *Theory of the Consumption Function*—and, thus, his Noble Prize three decades later.

Friedman's evolving work in consumption and its relation to income analysis continued to drive him through the following couple of years. He tossed concepts back and forth with his wife, as well as with two personal friends, Dorothy Brady and Margaret Reid, who at the time were involved in consumption studies of their own. He also put his knowledge to practical use, co-writing *Incomes from Independent Professional Practice* with Columbia University's Simon KUZNETS. The book, published in 1937, focuses on the results of their research on professional income.

The 1940s and 1950s kept Friedman progressive. During World War II, he worked on wartime tax policy for the U.S. Treasury and as a mathematical statistician for Columbia University. After the war, he rejoined the University of Chicago to teach economic theory. One highlight from the 1950s was his tenure as a Fulbright Visiting Professor at Cambridge University, where he interestingly found his views balanced between the conservative and liberal economists.

Throughout the 1960s, Friedman became increasingly prominent in the public arena, serving in 1964 as economic adviser to Barry Goldwater, then for Richard NIXON's presidential campaign. In the meantime, he continued to teach at the University of Chicago until his retirement in 1977. Still, he never retreated from the front lines. He vocally supported the development of international currency markets; he incited a campaign to enact constitutional restrictions on government spending and taxes; and he opposed President Bill CLINTON's strategy to nationalize health care.

President George W. BUSH recently presented Friedman with a Lifetime Achievement Award. In doing so, the president cited, "[He] has never claimed that free markets are perfect. Yet, he has demonstrated that even an imperfect market produces better results than arrogant experts and grasping bureaucrats."

BIBLIOGRAPHY. Milton and Rose Friedman, *Capitalism and Freedom* (University of Chicago Press, 2002); Milton Friedman, *Essays in Positive Economics* (University of Chicago Press, 1966); www.laissezfairebooks.com; "Milton Friedman Autobiography," www.nobel.se; "Nobel Prize Internet Archive," www.almaz.com.

JOSEPH GERINGER
SYED B. HUSSAIN, PH.D.
UNIVERSITY OF WISCONSIN, OSHKOSH

Frisch, Ragnar (1895–1973)

IN 1969, the Nobel Prize Committee presented its first-ever award for achievements in Economic Sciences. Sharing the honors were Ragnar Anton Kittil Frisch from Oslo, Norway, and Netherlands-born economist Jan TINBERGEN. Both men's accomplishments were impressive, for both had separately and individually developed and applied their own dynamic models for the analysis of economic processes. But, what makes Frisch especially noteworthy is that, while Tinbergen created an original macroeconomic model, it was Frisch who had developed the thought process of, and coined the phrase for, both MACROECONOMICS and MICROECONOMICS. The former refers to the study of aggregate economies, the latter to single firms and industries.

To Frisch, economics was an exact science, as firm and undeniable as the logic found under a microscope. Throughout his career, he insisted that what he called ECONOMETRICS be regarded as having "a relevance to concrete realities."

Born in Oslo, his father had predetermined that he would carry on the long lineage of the Frisch family gold and silverworks, an occupation that had maintained the Frisch ancestors since the days of Norwegian King Christian IV in the 1600s. To please the elder Frisch, the son began an apprenticeship in the traditional business, earning the title of goldsmith. But, Frisch's mother saw to it that he be given an opportunity to attend Oslo University to experience a broader lifestyle and, perhaps, find his personal calling.

"We perused the (college) catalogue and found that economics was the shortest and easiest study," Frisch later recollected. "That is the way it happened."

Evidently it was a perfect match. He obtained his degree in 1919 and traveled abroad to study economics and mathematics throughout Europe and the United States. Returning to Oslo, he earned a Ph.D. in mathematical statistics and won a teaching position with the university in 1925. Within six years he was appointed director of research at the university's newly completed Economic Research Institute. Today, that same center is renamed in Frisch's memory.

He remained with the university throughout his career, a popular lecturer and writer. His work on econometrics proved to be a fundamental contribution to the field of economics.

BIBLIOGRAPHY. K.N. Edvardsen, *Ragnar Frisch, An Annotated Biography* (University of Oslo Press, 1998); "Ragnar Frisch Autobiography," www.nobel.se; *The Concise Encyclopedia of Economics* (Liberty Fund, Inc., 2002).

JOSEPH GERINGER
SYED B. HUSSAIN, PH.D.
UNIVERSITY OF WISCONSIN, OSHKOSH

Fujitsu Limited

THOUGH BASED in Tokyo, JAPAN, Fujitsu has operations worldwide and sells products ranging from air conditioners to telephone systems. Founded in 1935, Fujitsu has grown to become a global provider of customer-focused information technology and communications solutions. The corporation has claimed a commitment to step-ahead technology and hour-by-hour quality. Fujitsu's ingredients of success consist of "pace-setting technologies, high reliability/performance computing, and telecommunications platforms (supported by) a worldwide corps of systems and service experts."

Among its computer products are PCs, servers, peripherals, and software. The company's other lines include telecommunications network equipment, consumer electronics (especially televisions and car audio components), semiconductors, and information technology services (consulting, systems integration, and support). Fujitsu also owns Japan's top internet services provider, "Nifty."

Fujitsu's devotion to value-difference policies have generated what has become known as its "Lifecycle Solutions," a one-stop-shopping, customized, formatted continuum of strategic pursuits aimed at minimizing costs of their customers' operations. The package, flexible customer to customer, includes: complete hardware, software and infrastructure services; holistic solutions; integrated solutions; comprehensive solutions to increase productivity; and solutions concentrating on ensuring a competitive edge.

One of Fujitsu's most recent offerings is a business collaboration platform called "Interstage." It presents customers with the means to direct new business ventures by using Fujitsu's provision World Wide Web services that fuse with broadband internet technology. Recording $40 billion in revenue in 2002, Fujitsu ranked 88th on *Fortune* magazine's list of the largest companies in the world.

BIBLIOGRAPHY. *Plunkett's E-Commerce & Internet Business Almanac 2001–2002* (Plunkett Research, Ltd., 2001); *Plunkett's InfoTech Industry Almanac 2001–2002* (Plunkett Research, Ltd., 2001); "Global 500: The World's Largest Companies," *Fortune* (July 2002); Fujitsu, www.fujitsu.com; Fujitsu "Product Page," www.fcpa.com.

JOSEPH GERINGER
SYED B. HUSSAIN, PH.D.
UNIVERSITY OF WISCONSIN, OSHKOSH

functions of money

PRINCIPAL CAPABILITIES common to all generally accepted forms of MONEY that include medium of exchange, store of wealth, unit of account, and means of deferred payment are described as the functions of money. Some form of money has characterized nearly every civilization throughout history and continues to be a significant part of almost every culture in the world today. While the type of money may vary considerably throughout history and across the world, common features can be found.

Prior to money systems, societies relied primarily on BARTER to exchange with one another. The ability to barter was extremely important due to the fact that it made specialization and the division of labor possible. Without barter, individuals and societies would have had to remain self-sufficient making specialization, along with all of its benefits, impossible. As a method of exchange, however, barter exhibited several significant shortcomings. For one, barter required the double coincidence of wants, a condition relatively easy to achieve in a simple society but quite difficult in a rapidly developing economy. A large number of potential exchange rates along with issues of portability, divisibility, durability, measuring value and assessing quality were all problems that plagued barter systems and, in some cases, caused individuals to exchange far less than they would have had barter not been so cumbersome.

Over time, societies recognizing the benefits of exchange and the problems of barter began to adopt certain commodities to circulate as mediums of exchange. Cattle, skins, wheat, wampum, tobacco, and a variety of other items served as such media of exchange in colonial America. For example, rather than trading his shoes directly for cheese, a colonial shoemaker would sell his shoes for tobacco and then use the tobacco to buy cheese from the dairy farmer. This situation was far superior to that of direct barter for several reasons. First, by offering the dairy farmer tobacco rather than shoes, the shoemaker was able to overcome the potential problem of the double coincidence of wants. While the dairy farmer might already have a closet full of shoes and hence would be completely disinterested in obtaining any more, the dairy farmer would definitely be interested in acquiring tobacco, if for no other reason than because he could turn around easily and sell the tobacco to the bartender in exchange for a pint of whiskey

Without some generally accepted medium of exchange, in this case tobacco, the shoe salesman would have been unable to eat his cheese until he found a dairy farmer in need of shoes. Likewise, the dairy farmer would have had to do without his whiskey unless he could find a bartender in need of cheese. Because the dairy farmer and bartender knew they could exchange the tobacco for whatever products they desired, each was willing to accept the tobacco, not for immediate consumption, but as money—something that could be used to purchase goods and services. Having a generally accepted medium of exchange led to a tremendous increase in economic activity as it became much easier and much less costly to exchange.

Virtually everything could be, and in fact many things have been, used as money throughout history. Certain items, however, ultimately prevailed as common types of money, namely precious metals, coins, and eventually paper currency. Even so, one can still find examples of individuals using commodities as money (e.g., cigarettes in prisons and POW camps). Whether or not a commodity evolves into a generally accepted form of money depends on its ability to perform at least one of four functions: serve as an effective medium of exchange, store of wealth, unit of account, or means of deferred payment. To serve as a medium of exchange money must be widely accepted as payment for goods and services. Sellers must be willing to accept money in lieu of items as well as repayment of debt. One of the most significant benefits of having a universally recognized medium of exchange is that it reduces the problem of the double coincidence of wants.

This means more exchange, greater specialization, more economic activity and economic growth. Gresham's Law, while it does not disappear completely, becomes much less of an issue with a generally accepted medium of exchange particularly with coins and paper currency. Gresham's Law refers to the fact that, whenever possible, low rather than high quality commodities typically will be offered as payment for goods and services.

Having a relatively uniform medium of exchange reduces the probability of this occurring and increases the likelihood that individuals will exchange with one another.

Because most individuals do not spend all of their income at once, the ability to save or accumulate wealth is extremely important. Individuals throughout the years and across cultures can and have stored their wealth in a variety of different assets. Wealth in many ancient civilizations was measured by the number of cattle that an individual owned. Under MERCANTILISM, a nation's wealth was measured in terms of its accumulation of gold. Today real estate, rare artwork, and corporate jets are indications of wealth. When seeking a store of wealth, items with relatively stable values will be preferred to those whose future value is very uncertain. Common stores of wealth in the United States today include savings accounts, certificates of deposit (CDs), and money-market mutual funds, all of whose future values are known with relative certainty. There is little doubt that a $5,000 savings account, for example, will be worth $5,000 plus interest one, two, or ten years in the future. This, of course, ignores the effects of inflation as

well as the possibility that this individual might not be able to retrieve the cash in her savings account should her bank become insolvent. The existence of the Federal Deposit Insurance Corporation (FDIC) makes the latter highly improbable.

Having money function as a store of wealth rather than individuals relying on tomatoes or sheep to accumulate wealth is essential in a capitalist economy because it makes possible and fosters saving. The ability to save is extremely important because it allows people to time their purchases better, thereby getting more satisfaction from their budgets, and it makes capital accumulation possible for those who want to spend more than their current incomes.

Closely related, the last two functions of money are intricately tied to money's ability to facilitate exchange. As a unit of account, money is used to assign values (i.e., PRICES) to goods and services. In the absence of a generally accepted form of money, as in a barter system, numerous exchange rates would exist as a cow, for example, might be worth 20,000 tomatoes, 500 chickens, 200 sweaters, or 50 cords of firewood. By adopting an official unit of account (e.g., the dollar in the United States), just one exchange rate would exist in the market, and that would be the dollar value of the cow. Transactions costs would be significantly reduced by use of a standard unit of account, and consequently individuals would be more likely to exchange with one another. By acting as a standard unit of account as well as a relatively stable store of wealth, money also typically operates as a means of deferred payment by which individuals can safely make arrangements to carry out transactions at a later date.

The ability of an item to perform at least one of these four functions contributes to its adoption as money. The official definitions of the money supply in the United States (M1, M2, and M3) include only those things that are commonly used as either a medium of exchange, store of wealth, unit of account, or means of deferred payment.

BIBLIOGRAPHY. Glyn Davies, *A History of Money from Ancient Times to the Present Day* (University of Wales Press, 1996); R. Glenn Hubbard, *Money and the Financial System and the Economy* (Addison-Wesley, 2002); Frederic S. Mishkin, *The Economics of Money, Banking, and Financial Markets* (Addison-Wesley, 2002); Gary M. Walton and Hugh Rockoff, *History of the American Economy* (South-Western, 2001); Jack and J. McIver Weatherford, *The History of Money: From Sandstone to Cyberspace* (Three Rivers Press, 1998).

KRISTIN KUCSMA, PH.D.
SETON HALL UNIVERSITY

G

G8 Summit

THE ANNUAL MEETINGS of the heads of state of the major industrial countries are referred to as the G8 Summits (well known as the G7 before RUSSIA counted as the eighth country). These forums provide leaders an opportunity to discuss domestic and/or international financial, economic, political issues of mutual interest, and corresponding policies.

In 1975, the heads of six industrial countries, namely the UNITED KINGDOM, FRANCE, GERMANY, ITALY, JAPAN, and the UNITED STATES met in Rambouillet, France, to discuss the effectiveness of their economic and financial policies and institutions in dealing with the economic conditions of the time.

The following year, CANADA joined the group at their meeting in Puerto Rico, and the so-called Group of Seven (G7) was formed. In 1977, the European Community (now the EUROPEAN UNION) became an observer at these meetings, and was allowed to participate in discussions. Russia was invited to join in political discussions in 1994, and was accepted as a full member of the forum in 1998. Thus the Group of Eight (G8) came into existence. Annual meetings of the G8 take place in the home country of its chair, which rotates among the heads of the state. Since 1998, the G8 summits have been preceded by meetings among foreign and finance ministers. The so-called "sherpas," trusted aides to the heads of states, prepare the agendas for the summits based on the discussions at these preliminary meetings. (The word sherpa originates with the mountain-dwelling people of Nepal and Sikkim who have an excellent reputation for trekking and leading.)

The major goals of the annual summits are to promote growth in the world economy and to maintain stability in the international financial markets. Over the years, however, the agendas of these meetings have expanded to include non-economic issues. The early 1970s were marked by an oil crisis resulting from an unprecedented increase in oil prices, the collapse of the BRETTON WOODS pegged exchange-rate system, and the simultaneous rise of INFLATION and UNEMPLOYMENT in major industrial countries. A second oil crisis in the late 1970s exacerbated these economic ills. It is therefore not surprising that the G7 annual meetings between 1976 and 1981 focused on economic issues such as growth, unemployment, oil prices, inflation, and exchange-rate stability.

The second cycle of the group's annual gatherings, between 1982–88, focused similarly on economic issues, but more on those with an international flavor as a result of the advent of GLOBALIZATION. Globalization, defined as internationalization of economic activity, has rendered economies more interdependent than ever before. The increased interdependence has also raised the potential that disturbances, especially financial disturbances, will spread rapidly among countries. Hence, the goal of summits shifted toward increasing cooperation among industrial countries to guarantee that the domestic and external markets would continue to function efficiently. Other issues that gained prominence throughout the second cycle included the Uruguay Round of trade negotiations, exchange-rate stability, agricultural policies, and debt relief after the world debt crisis of 1983.

At the same time, the summits incorporated discussions among leaders on contemporary non-economic issues, for example the Iran-Iraq war and the Chernobyl nuclear disaster. Political issues began to play an even more important role in the third cycle of meetings. During this time, the G7/G8 discussed the implications of the Tiananmen Square massacre in CHINA, the political transformation of Eastern Europe, war in Bosnia, genocide in Rwanda, political reforms in Russia, and human rights. They also discussed related economic issues such as debt-relief to developing countries, the formation of the WORLD TRADE ORGANIZATION (WTO), and the stability in the global economy.

The fourth, most recent, cycle (1996–2003) coincides with Russia's full membership to the summit. This fourth cycle is also marked by an increased interest from G8 leaders in international political and social issues. In addition to the usual concern with economic and financial stability in the rapidly globalizing environment, recent topics have included transnational organized crime, corruption, illicit drugs, terrorism, infectious diseases, arms control, democracy and human rights, global warming, landmines, food safety, biotechnology, the mapping of the human genome, the political situation in the Middle East, and social and economic challenges posed by the aging populations.

An area that has increasingly attracted the group's attention in this cycle is Africa. In 1996 in Lyon, France, the group formed the New Global Partnership for Development (NEPAD), recognizing that while development is ultimately the developing country's responsibility, industrial countries also should support their efforts and facilitate their transition and adjustment to the global market economy. Concern with Africa culminated at the 2002 Kananaskis, Canada, summit with the formation of the G8 Africa Action Plan to support the NEPAD. This plan commits the G8 members to increase aid especially to those African countries that have taken measures to reform their economic and political structures in line with the recommendations of NEPAD, and have taken the necessary initial steps to implement free market- and democracy-oriented policy measures.

The two other general areas that have gained prominence in the fourth cycle are debt relief and the environment. In Cologne, Germany, in 1999, the G8 launched the Cologne Debt Initiative to relieve the Heavily Indebted Poor Countries (HIPC) from their unsustainable heavy debt by increasing the official development assistance (ODA), on one hand, and by supporting efforts for economic and political democratization, on the other. These efforts to reduce poverty are also supplemented by the recommendation that developing countries liberalize their external sector, promote private investment, and increase overall investment outlays in health, education, and social programs to fight poverty.

While discussions concerning the environment have routinely been part of the G7/G8 summits, they have become significantly more detailed and substantive in the fourth cycle. With the Denver, Colorado summit in 1997, the group shifted its focus to sustainable development and protection of the environment. Specific topics included global warming, deforestation, safe water, sustainable use of oceans and seas, and desertification. A wide spectrum of policy recommendations was examined, ranging from cooperation between industrial and developing countries concerning green technology transfer, to the use of private sector based free-market reforms in solving environmental problems.

The diverse array of issues discussed at G7/G8 Summits demonstrates the flexibility of these meetings in incorporating pressing contemporary topics and problems into their agendas. On the other hand, the summits could be criticized for being too unfocused to succeed in implementing their policy recommendations. The exception to this criticism is the clear modern focus on globalization and its sustainability. In all the recent G7/G8 Summits, implicitly or explicitly, the leaders have promoted economic and financial stability and discussed coordinated measures to strengthen globalization. Trade and financial market liberalization, coupled with the emphasis on free markets and private investment, have been policy recommendations regarding almost every global economic issue.

The ANTI-GLOBALIZATION movement, including environmental non-governmental organizations (NGOs), church and labor groups, leftist political organizations, civil rights groups, students, and also anarchists, not only questions the legitimacy of G7/G8 Summits on the basis of their non-democratic composition, but also argues that free-market oriented globalization has left many economically disadvantaged groups outside of the process. Those left out are deprived of the benefits of globalization, reinforcing poverty and increasing economic inequality. Many within the anti-globalization movement regard the G7/G8 summits as forums where transnational corporations strengthen their global economic power by promoting neo-liberal policies via international financial institutions, the INTERNATIONAL MONETARY FUND (IMF), WORLD BANK, and the WTO.

Anti-globalization advocates ask for a limit to corporate power and thus a limit on the exploitation of labor, the economically disadvantaged, and the environment. Anti-globalization groups have actively demonstrated against the G8 Summits in recent years, in some cases more peacefully than in others. At the Genoa, Italy, summit in 2001, the police killed one demonstrator during protest violence.

In spite of these criticisms and its limited success, the G8 Summit continues; at the very least, it serves a purpose in bringing the major world leaders together and engaging them in a dialog about current economic, political, and social issues.

BIBLIOGRAPHY. T. Barry, "G8: Failing Model of Global Governance," *Foreign Policy in Focus,* VII (2002); Nicholas Bayne, *Hanging in There: The G7 and G8 Summit in Maturity and Renewal (*Ashgate, 2000); P. Hajnal and J. Kirton, "The

Evolving Role and Agenda of the G7/G8: A North American Perspective," *NIRA Review* (v.5/10, 2000); P. Hajnal, *The G7/G8 System: Evolution, Role and Documentation* (Ashgate, 1999); S. Ostry, "Globalization and the G8: Could Kananaskis Set a New Direction?" (O.D. Skelton Memorial Lecture, Queens University, March, 2002); University of Toronto G8 Information Center, www.g7.utoronto.ca.

M. ODEKON
SKIDMORE COLLEGE

Galbraith, John Kenneth (1908–)

PERHAPS THE MOST illuminating fact about John Kenneth Galbraith is that he started to write his classic book, *The Affluent Society* (1958), as a treatise on poverty. As he did more research, it dawned on him that the idea of affluence was more important for understanding post-WORLD WAR II American capitalism. He scrapped the original book, and, in the process created a revolution in economic thought about capitalism. Political economists before him, Thomas MALTHUS, David RICARDO, Karl MARX, believed in SCARCITY and an iron law of wages that doomed workers to starvation and misery. As Galbraith saw it, this presumption had to be thrown out if post-war capitalism were to be understood.

Before writing *The Affluent Society*, Galbraith had already been an active observer of, and participant in, modern capitalism. During the war, he worked for the Office of Price Administration (OPA), but was pushed out for his views on regulation. His first major work, *American Capitalism* (1952), published when he had become an economics professor at Harvard University. In the book, he explained that smaller firms were disappearing, being gobbled up by a "small number of corporations." Previous political economists such as Adam SMITH believed market competition ensured that no business would grow too strong. Thus, Galbraith's conclusions would seem to be gloomy, as he saw power concentrating in a smaller number of hands. But he assured his readers that countervailing power—the regulatory activities of government, the growth of labor unions, the rise of consumer groups, and even the mundane activities of chain stores and retail buyers—could check the growing power of corporations.

Galbraith did see an amassing of power in the hands of the American corporation, and he was one of the first economists to seriously study advertising and the rise of the CONSUMER culture. Delineating a "Dependence Effect," Galbraith argued that corporations created "needs" in order to nurture consumption for an abundant amount of goods. "If production is to increase," Galbraith explained, "the wants must be effec-

tively contrived." Clearly, Galbraith did not care for the adverse impacts of the postwar economy. For example, he complained about the ugliness of billboards and the unnecessary waste of consumer culture. He consistently bemoaned the selfishness inherent in consumerism, as seen in his more recent work such as *The Culture of Contentment* (1992). But Galbraith's most important concern centered on how "private opulence," that is abundant consumer goods, existed alongside "public squalor."

Galbraith argued that as American corporations pumped out goods for private consumption, public goods such as schools fell into disrepair. He described how Americans bought efficient, comfortable cars but traveled on ugly highways into desiccated cities and polluted parks. In noting this contradiction, Galbraith made clear that he was a "liberal," someone who believed that public spending should make up for the shortcomings of capitalist markets. He called on governments to address the poverty that affluence failed to alleviate—especially that which resided in "rural and urban slums." Not surprisingly, Galbraith advised Adlai Stevenson, the Democratic Party contender for president during the 1950s, and then worked for John F. KENNEDY and Lyndon B. JOHNSON.

While he worried about the shortcomings of consumer capitalism, Galbraith continued to believe in self-correcting forces (countervailing power) and grew increasingly optimistic during the 1960s. In *The New Industrial State* (1967), he extended some earlier arguments he had made about a "new class" of employees in American corporations. Here Galbraith picked up on a long line of social thought, one that extended from the iconoclastic economic thinker Thorstein VEBLEN. Veblen recognized that as businesses grew in size, more managerial power was ceded to engineers and other professionals. Galbraith recognized that the number of white-collar employees had continued to grow since after World War II, further displacing the power of corporate chiefs and those who owned capital. For him, an "educational and scientific elite" played an increasing role in managing corporations. Being educated and critical-minded, this new class looked upon advertising with "disdain," as too manipulative for their ideals. Galbraith called this a paradox. He explained, "The economy for its success requires organized bamboozlement [through advertising]. At the same time it nurtures a growing class which feels itself superior to such bamboozlement and deplores it as intellectually corrupt." Thus, the possibilities for change—for emphasizing values other than consumption and private profit—resided within corporations.

Another source of optimism for Galbraith was the "technostructure," marking corporate life. He recognized that as corporations centralized their power and encouraged steady consumption on the part of increasing numbers of Americans (supported via advertising), they developed a massive bureaucratic infrastructure to manage these challenges. The modern corporation, for Galbraith, was "no longer subordinate to the market" celebrated by classical liberals like Smith. If anything, the corporation planned economic activities by projecting costs and manipulating needs to sustain itself. It became more reliant upon the federal government in the process, not only for such things as highways but for direct subsidies, as in the case of defense contracts. Though there was a pernicious side to all this, Galbraith believed it pointed to a more planned economy that might actually benefit Americans. The new class and its technostructure showed that corporate production was no longer haphazard but increasingly attuned to planning.

Of course, this optimism balanced itself against worries, not just about consumer culture but more mundane things like inflation. Galbraith believed inflation was a new type of problem endemic to postwar economic prosperity. As wages went up within an "affluent society," corporations raised prices. This "wage-price spiral" was especially evident in the highly unionized sector of the American economy (e.g., steel). Though trained as a Keynesian economist, Galbraith broke with certain Keynesian tenets. He argued, "The preoccupation of Keynesian economics with depression has meant that inflation control has been handled by improvisation."

Indeed, Galbraith rejected a tendency among some Keynesians to shy away from direct regulation of the economy (settling instead for occasional fiscal stimuli). Instead, Galbraith drew upon his own career at the OPA, arguing that a return to price control would probably be necessary to head off inflation. He illustrated that when government stopped using price control mechanisms in the wake of World War II, inflation shot up. Against more conservative critics, Galbraith asserted that price control could be used much more flexibly than it was during the war. Most importantly, he urged liberals to remain more open toward direct interventions in the economy to address inflation as well as other problems.

This is what made Galbraith a quintessential liberal in relation to modern capitalism. He believed in the regulatory power of government and wanted a much more vibrant public sector that could address issues of education, health, and income redistribution. Galbraith was politically active in the Democratic Party, but he became increasingly alienated due to the VIETNAM WAR. After 1968, he invested less and less time in politics. In 2003, he continued to write, in very accessible ways about difficult economic problems, but none of his more recent books reached the stature of *The Affluent Society*.

BIBLIOGRAPHY. John Kenneth Galbraith, *The Affluent Society* (Houghton Mifflin, 1976); *American Capitalism* (Houghton Mifflin, 1962); "Are Living Costs Out of Control?" *The Atlantic Monthly* (1957); *A Life in Our Times* (Houghton Mifflin, 1981); Loren Okroi, *Galbraith, Harrington, Heilbroner: Economics and Dissent in an Age of Optimism* (Princeton University Press, 1988); Ron Stanfield, *John Kenneth Galbraith* (St. Martin's Press, 1996).

KEVIN MATTSON, PH.D.
UNIVERSITY OF OHIO

gambling and lotteries

GAMBLING IS A HUGE business in the UNITED STATES and the rest of the world. While the dollar value of total gambling is difficult to measure because a significant portion of wagering, particularly sports betting, occurs illegally, the gross gambling revenue in the United States in 2000 was from various sources: card rooms, $884.6 million; casinos, $27.2 billion; charitable games and bingo, $2.4 billion; Native American reservations $12.2 billion; legal bookmaking (primarily sports betting), $125.9 million; lotteries, $17.6 billion; and pari-mutuel (including horse and dog racing), $3.8 billion; for a grand total of $63.3 billion.

As the term "gross gambling revenue" refers to total wagers less winnings, it substantially understates total funds wagered. For example, wagering in legal bookmaking totaled $2.3 billion in 2000 compared to gross gambling revenue of only 5 percent of this amount which represents the casinos' take. Similarly, a gambler may play dozens of hands of blackjack while ending up just breaking even. While hundreds of dollars of individual bets have been made, the gross gambling revenue from this gambler is zero.

Total wagering is, of course, much harder to measure, but is roughly twice the gross gambling revenue for lotteries, ten times gross gambling revenue for pari-mutuel betting, and roughly fifteen times gross gambling for casino and Indian gaming.

Commonly played games of chance come in many forms. Casino gambling includes table games such as roulette and craps, card games such as blackjack, the most popular casino card game in the United States, and baccarat, a popular French casino card game, and coin-operated slot machines and video slots. The payoffs from table games average about 98 percent of money wagered and slot machines vary between 90 percent and 98 percent. In the United States, as of 2001, 11 states had commercial gambling and another 23 had casinos operated by Native American tribes on reservations.

Another 40 states had state-run lotteries. These agencies typically offer a mix of instant-win scratch-off cards and online drawing games offering large prizes at large odds. Typical payoffs for state lotteries are among the lowest in the gambling industry, with returns averaging between 40 percent and 60 percent. Pari-mutuel gambling is offered at horse and dog racetracks in 41 states. Pari-mutuel betting, which averages a 90 percent return, is unique in that the amount of the prize won depends on the number of other bettors and winners. The house makes its profit by taking a portion of all bets placed known as the vigorish.

Sports betting in the United States is legal only in the state of Nevada, although it is estimated that illegal sports betting exceeds legal betting by a factor of 100. Sports bookies work to adjust the odds and payoffs so that an even amount of play enters in on each side of a bet, and then make their profit just as in pari-mutuel betting. Card rooms are offered by casinos to allow gamblers to play directly against other bettors. Again, the house simply retains a portion of all money wagered.

Lotteries and gambling have existed in many forms throughout history. Lotteries are mentioned in the Bible, the ancient Greeks, Romans, and Egyptians were known to have played dice, and the Hun Dynasty in CHINA created Keno in 100 B.C.E. to pay for defense. Privately run gambling houses have often been discouraged by governments that did not wish to allow competition with official sources of gambling that contributed to government revenue. The first legally recognized public gaming houses came about in the 17th century in ITALY, and the modern term, casino, derives from these "small houses" or *casini*. Lotteries were common in post-Renaissance Europe and spread to the New World with the European colonists. Lotteries were sponsored by such notable early Americans as Benjamin FRANKLIN, George WASHINGTON, and John HANCOCK to finance public expenditures, such as equipment for the Continental Army and Faneuil Hall in Boston. Harvard, Yale, Columbia, and Princeton, as well as other numerous churches and colleges all sponsored lotteries to raise funds for early construction.

Beginning in the 1820s, corruption in lotteries became widespread and, lacking effective means to regulate the industry, state governments began to ban lotteries. By 1878, all states except for Louisiana had banned the sale of lottery tickets. Casino gambling and card-playing remained popular through the western United States, but gradually states outlawed public gaming as well. In 1909, Nevada became the last state to outlaw casino gambling, and coupled with court decisions in 1905 that effectively ended the Louisiana Lottery, the United States entered a 20-year period of prohibition on all types of gambling.

Nevada re-legalized casinos in 1931, but its action was not followed by another state until New Jersey rati-

Gambling and lotteries are a $63 billion (or more) business— the size of a small nation's gross domestic product.

fied gambling in Atlantic City in 1978. Racetracks, however, were re-established in 21 states during the 1930s, and many other states took small steps toward a general legalization of gambling by allowing small-stakes charitable gambling and bingo throughout the 1940s and 1950s. For example, nearly every state allowed the sale of raffle tickets to aid civic organizations. In 1964, New Hampshire introduced the first state-run lottery in 60 years and was slowly followed by other states, with a large number of states offering lotteries for the first time in the late 1980s. CANADA offered the first provincial lottery in Manitoba and Québec in 1970. In 1988, federal laws allowed increased cooperation among state lottery associations and the first large multi-state lottery, Powerball, was formed.

The gambling industry underwent a significant legal change in 1987 when the U.S. Supreme Court affirmed the right of Native American tribes to offer high-stakes gaming. This decision ushered in a wave of new casinos located on reservation lands. In response, many states legalized non-tribal casinos, although casino operation in these states was generally restricted to designated areas. For example, gambling in Illinois and Iowa was restricted to large riverboats, and gambling in Colorado, South Dakota, and Kansas was limited to historical areas such as Deadwood, Dodge City, and Cripple Creek. The historical capital of gambling, Las Vegas, responded to the increased competition for gambling dollars by building more and more lavish and extravagant casinos, and changing the image of the city from a gambler's paradise to a more family-oriented vacation destination. The latest innovation in the gaming trade has been the advent of a rapidly growing internet gambling industry.

Many groups look upon the gambling industry with disfavor for several reasons. First, many object to gambling on religious grounds. Both Islam and conservative Christianity place prohibitions on games of chance. Next, many argue that gambling preys upon the poor who may see a big payoff in the lottery or casino as their only ticket out of poverty. Gambling, as a large cash business, is also looked upon as a haven for money laundering. Until recently, Las Vegas was considered to have strong ties to organized-crime figures. Finally, many worry about the destructive effects of gambling on those with addiction problems.

BIBLIOGRAPHY. Charles Clotfelter and Philip Cook, *Selling Hope* (Harvard University Press, 1989); National Association of State and Provincial Lotteries, www.naspl.org; American Gaming Association, www.americangaming.org; William Eadington, "The Economics of Casino Gambling," *Journal of Economic Perspectives* (1999).

VICTOR MATHESON, PH.D.
WILLIAMS COLLEGE

game theory

IT IS A RARE PERSON who has not had the experience of playing a game. However, most people do not analyze the structure of the game in terms of its basic elements: players, rules, strategies, timing, outcomes, and payoffs.

Game theory is a branch of mathematics with applications in computer science, economics, engineering, and other disciplines. Players can be nature itself, individuals, spouses, computers, sports clubs, regions, nations, and groups of nations. Rules may include a marriage contract, the three-second lane violation in basketball, and the Geneva Convention on armed forces engaged in warfare. Strategies can range from "increasing charitable donations for tax reduction purposes" to "using Agent Orange to defoliate Vietnamese jungles." Timing may involve who shoots first between two gunslingers, or waiting to ask Dad or Mom for the car keys until after they have eaten. Outcomes and payoffs can be different, but they both result from choosing strategies. Student X may have

chosen the strategy of "studying instead of enjoying leisure" to obtain an SAT score of 1500 (outcome). The payoff is getting into a top-tier college. What is extremely attractive about game theory is its ability to be as general or specific as one needs it to be.

Modern game theory became a prominent branch of mathematics after the 1944 publication of *The Theory of Games and Economic Behavior* by John von Neumann and Oskar Morgenstern. This work contained the method for finding optimal solutions for two-person, zero-sum games.

A 2001 motion picture, *A Beautiful Mind*, popularized the life of John NASH. Around 1950, Nash developed a definition of an optimum outcome for multi-player games now known as the Nash Equilibrium. The concept was further refined by Reinhart SELTEN. These men were awarded the Nobel Prize in Economics in 1994 for their work on game theory, along with John HARSANYI. The latter had developed the analysis of games with incomplete information. The literature on game theory has blossomed in the past several decades, as have its applications to real-world problems.

Anatomy of a game. There are two distinct but related ways of describing a game mathematically. The extensive form is the most detailed way. It describes play by means of a game tree that explicitly indicates when players move, which moves are available, and what they know about the moves of other players and the "state of nature" when they move. Most importantly, it specifies the payoffs that players receive at the end of the game. Equilibria in such games are often attained by examining the payoffs at the right of the tree, and working one's way left to the choices that would have been made by each player to get there.

A "pure" strategy is a set of instructions. Generally, strategies are contingent responses. An alternative to the extensive form is the normal or strategic form. This is less detailed than the extensive form, specifying the list of strategies available to each player and the payoffs that accrue to each when the strategies meet. A game in normal form is specified by:

1. A set, I_n, of n players

2. Strategy sets, $S_1, S_2, ..., S_n$ for each player

3. Real-valued payoff functions, $M_i(s_1, s_2, ... s_n)$ for each player i, and strategies, $s_i \, 0S_i$, chosen by each.

A zero-sum game is one in which the total payoff to all players in the game adds to zero. In other words, each player benefits only at the expense of others. Chess and Poker are zero-sum games, because one wins exactly the amount one's opponents lose. Business, politics, and the Prisoners' Dilemma (next section), for example, are non-zero-sum games because some outcomes are good for all players or bad for all players.

It is easier, however, to analyze a zero-sum game, and it turns out to be possible to transform any game into a zero-sum game by adding an additional dummy player often called "the board," whose losses compensate for the players' winnings. A constant-sum game is a game in which for every combination of strategies the sum of the players' payoffs is the same. In the game of squash, the constant is 100.

A cooperative game is one in which the players may freely communicate among themselves before making game decisions and may make bargains to influence those decisions. Parker Brothers' Monopoly is a cooperative game, while the Prisoners' Dilemma is not. A complete-information game is a game in which each player has the same game-relevant information as every other player. Chess and the Prisoners' Dilemma are complete information games, while poker is not.

The Prisoners' Dilemma game. The normal form of a game is often given in matrix form. The table below is the normal form matrix for former Princeton Professor Albert Tucker's Prisoners' Dilemma game. In this game, the two players were partners in a crime and have been captured by the police. The police can prove that the two committed a minor crime, but cannot prove that they also committed a major crime. They need at least one confession for that. The payoffs in Table 1 are negative because they represent years in jail. If both prisoners choose "not confess," they both get one year in jail for the minor crime. If one confesses and the other doesn't, the confessor goes home and the non-confessor gets 8 years. If they both confess, they each get 5 years. Each suspect is placed in a separate room, and offered the opportunity to confess to the crime. The rows of the matrix correspond to the strategies of player 1. The columns are headed by the strategies for player 2. Each cell in the table gives the payoff to player 1 on the left and player 2 on the right. The total payoff to both players is "highest" if neither confesses and each receives only 1 year.

However, each player reasons as follows: if the other player does not confess, it is best for me to confess (0 instead of -1). If the other player does confess, it is also best for me to confess (-5 instead of -8). So no matter what either thinks the other player will do, it is best to confess. This is called a dominant strategy for each player. The theory predicts, therefore, that each player following her own self-interest will result in confessions by both players.

Each player choosing her dominant pure strategy will result in a Nash Equilibrium in this game. In a Nash Equilibrium, no player would want to change strategies from what she has already chosen. This result casts doubt on Adam SMITH's notion that the individual pursuit of self-interest will lead to the best outcome for the group.

Table 1: *Prisoners' Dilemma*

Player 1	Player 2		
		not confess	confess
	not confess	-1, -1	-8, 0
	confess	0, -8	-5, -5

Some games do not have an equilibrium set of pure strategies, but may have an equilibrium in mixed strategies. A mixed strategy is a strategy that assigns a probability less than one to each of the pure strategies available to the player, with all probabilities adding to one. Of course, each pure strategy can be written as a mixed strategy with its own probability equal to one, and all other probabilities equal to zero. If $(s_1, s_2, ..., s_m)$ are m pure strategies a player can choose, and $(p_1, p_2, ..., p_m)$ are the probabilities assigned by the player to these strategies, then $(p_1*s_1, p_2*s_2, ⌋, p_m*s_m)$ is a mixed strategy. This complicates the payoffs that result from the use of strategies by each player and expected payoffs (payoffs weighted by probabilities) become relevant.

Even though it has an equilibrium in pure strategies, the Prisoners' Dilemma game, as shown in the table, can be used to illustrate the concepts of mixed strategy and expected payoff. If player 1 assigns a probability of .5 (the expected value of heads in, say, a fair coin toss) to each of "not confess" and "confess," then she creates a mixed strategy. If player 2 assigns .25 and .75 (by, say, spinning a needle over a 4-quadrant circle with 3 marked "confess") to "not confess" and "confess," then player 2 can expect a payoff of .25*[.5*(-1) + .5*(-8)] = .25*[-4.5] = -1.125 for choosing "not confess" and .75*[.5*(0) + .5*(-5)] = .75*[-2.5] = 1.875 for choosing "confess." The same process can be done for player 1.

Each player can have infinitely many mixed strategies, even when there is a finite number of pure strategies. Under certain mathematical conditions, it can be shown that a Nash Equilibrium in mixed strategies exists for games with a finite number of pure strategies. Equilibria in mixed strategies have come under attack as mixed strategies are thought not to be commonly used, and the assumption that each player guesses the other's probabilities is thought to be fairly far-fetched.

Games with coalition formation. Suppose that there are more than two players in a game. A coalition is a group of players that band together to obtain the benefits of coordinating strategies. There is the possibility that any two players may form a coalition against the third. As the number of players grows, the number of possible coalitions grows, but the costs of getting groups to coalesce may also increase. A game in characteristic function form involves a real-valued function defined over sets of players. It is called a "characteristic function" (hereafter, c.f.), and it assigns values in the game to various coalitions. A c.f., v, for a non-zero sum game with v as the "empty" coalition, and R, S as two arbitrary non-overlapping coalitions, must satisfy:

4. $v(v) = 0$
5. $v(R\chi S) \ni v(R) + v(S)$.

Inequality 5) is known as the property of superadditivity, which means that the bigger coalition can get a payoff at least as big as the sum of the payoffs to the separate coalitions. An example of the superadditivity of payoffs to coalitions is labor unions in general. In most cases, the total wages paid to labor after negotiating as a coalition with management is greater than what each worker might have negotiated separately. The United Auto Workers and the Major League Baseball Players' Association are live examples of this.

The discussion of equilibria for games in characteristic function form quickly gets mathematically technical. Therefore, the interested reader is directed to the sources listed in the Bibliography at the end of this article.

The bargaining problem. Besides proposing an equilibrium for non-cooperative games, Nash addressed the same issue for cooperative games. Suppose that two players are at a status quo level of "well-offness" and can negotiate so that each would become better off. If u_i is the utility or well-offness level of player i, and d_i is the value of that well-offness in the status quo, then Nash proposed finding the best solution for both players simultaneously by maximizing the following function for players 1 and 2 over the set of possible outcomes:

6. $U = (u_1 - d_1) * (u_2 - d_2)$.

Subtracting off the d-levels essentially eliminates any status quo bias in favor of one or the other, to assess what is the maximum improvement that can happen. The multiplicative nature of the function ties the well-offness of each to that of the other. For games with n>2 players, the function in 6) becomes the product of $(u_i - d_i)$ for all i.

Economics and the theory of games. As noted at the very outset, the real birth of the theory of games occurred in a book by a mathematician and an economist. The notions of self-interest, utility, and optimization created early links between game theory and economics. The key link is rationality, the attribute of people that guides them to do things in their own self-interest only if the perceived benefits exceed the perceived costs. Economics, especially in its neoclassical form, is based on the assumption that human beings, and the institutions they create, are absolutely rational in their economic choices. Specifically, the assumption is that each person or institution maximizes her or its

rewards (e.g., profits, incomes, or subjective benefits) in the circumstances that she faces. The game theory framework is ideal for this. Perhaps the three most famous of the economics applications of game theory are the game formulation of equilibrium in a duopoly (two-firm) market devised by Augustin Cournot (1801–77), the game view of member producers deciding to cheat or not in a cartel (group of producers agreeing to coordinate economic decisions; e.g., OPEC), and a game formulation of an economy in which the core (a set allocations of resources that dominate all allocations in terms of the utility of each individual) is achievable through the coordination of competitive market prices. In some of these models, the strategies are not disjoint entities, but choices among infinitely many points on continuous functions.

Market failures such as the overexploitation of fisheries, global warming, and inadequate resources committed to research are additional examples of games. In this realm, the individual pursuing self-interest is pitted against the broader goals of society. Modern game theory texts are filled with examples like these, and game theory itself is also permeating texts in many other disciplines. Over time, the payoffs to this phenomenon will be revealed.

BIBLIOGRAPHY. H. Scott Bierman and Luis Fernandez, *Game Theory with Economic Applications* (Addison-Wesley, 1993); Avinash Dixit and Susan Skeath, *Games of Strategy* (W.W. Norton, 1999); Duncan R. Luce and Howard Raiffa, *Games and Decisions* (John Wiley & Sons, 1967); Alvin Roth, "Al Roth's game theory page," www.economics.harvard.edu; Thomas C. Schelling *The Strategy of Conflict* (Oxford University Press,1963); John Von Neumann and Oskar Morgenstern, *The Theory of Games and Economic Behavior* (Princeton University Press, 1944); J.D. Williams, *The Compleat Strategist* (Dover, 1954).

JOHN SORRENTINO, PH.D.
MAHBUB RABBANI, M.A.
TEMPLE UNIVERSITY

gangsters

PERHAPS AN EXTREME example of criminal capitalism in modern times, gangsters have been present throughout human history. The best-known gangsters are the Mafia, whose groups date back to feudal times in Sicily, ITALY. Gangs of men were used to protect the estates of absentee landlords. As time progressed, the gangs evolved into criminal bands, and by the 19th century the mafia consisted of a criminal network that dominated Sicily. Toward the end of the 19th century, some members of the Mafia immigrated to the UNITED STATES and soon many were involved in American organized crime.

The term gangster can apply to any member of a criminal gang, yet it is most often used in connection with notorious leaders of organized crime. Some infamous criminals that come to mind are Al Capone and "Bugsy" Siegel. These high-profile men were part of the gangster's heyday in the United States during the 1920s.

In many ways, gangsters and the economic system of capitalism are intertwined. Gangsters have been portrayed as ruthless businessmen or cunning entrepreneurs. With the influx of new people to America during the late 19th and early 20th centuries, immigrants had to compete to survive. There was an unwritten message to new Americans that opportunities must be seized.

In the case of gangsters, these opportunities were seized using illegal means. Paying no heed to laws making their activities illegal, the gangsters of the day provided services for which customers were willing to pay. These "services" included gambling, prostitution, liquor, racketeering, and drugs.

Just one example of the quintessential gangster-capitalist is Al Capone. Born January 17, 1899, Alphonse Capone was the son of Italian immigrants who had come to America five years earlier to build new lives. Capone grew up in the streets of Brooklyn, New York, where he met his criminal mentor, Johnny Torrio. Torrio was a pioneer in the development of modern criminal enterprise: With his administrative and organizational talents he was able to transform crude racketeering into a form of corporate structure. As Torrio's business expanded and opportunities emerged, he took young Capone under his wing and guided him into a life of crime.

By 1921, Capone had advanced from Torrio's employee to his partner. He helped to manage, maintain, and control operations in illegal bootlegging, gambling, and prostitution. Capone and other gangsters were aided in their crimes by corrupt politicians. By buying off the politicians and law enforcement officers, gangsters were able to operate rather freely without concern of punishment.

By 1927, Capone was an extremely wealthy and powerful man. At the end of 1925, Torrio had retired leaving Capone his legacy of nightclubs, whorehouses, gambling joints, breweries, and speakeasies. With his power, Capone came to view himself as a hero to Italian immigrants. Indeed, his bootlegging operations alone employed thousands of people, many of whom were poor Italian natives desperate for work in America.

As Capone's wealth and power grew, so did the animosity of competing gangsters. One such rival was Bugs Moran. Capone decided to eliminate Moran as a threat and this decision led to the infamous Saint Valentine's Day Massacre. On February 14, 1929, Capone and his allies arranged the assassination of six of Moran's men using a cunning plan of trickery. Though the plan failed to kill Moran, it brought Capone to the nation's attention.

Soon enough Capone was cited as the public's number-one enemy by President Herbert HOOVER. Though government prosecutors had trouble finding evidence to support charges against Capone dealing with criminal activities, they did have another tactic with which to pursue him. In 1927, the U.S. Supreme Court ruled that bootleggers must report and pay income tax on their illegal bootlegging businesses. This ruling stated that even though reporting and paying tax on illegally gained revenues was self-incrimination, it was not unconstitutional. Thus, prosecutors could arrest and try Capone for tax evasion. On October 17, 1931, Capone was found guilty of some of the tax charges against him and he was sentenced to 11 years in a federal penitentiary.

The story of Al Capone is a tale that reflects the high point of the gangsters' glory days in America. When Prohibition was repealed in America in 1933 much of the capital and revenue of the gangsters was removed. Organized crime still exists in America but not in the spotlight as it did in the Prohibition era.

Since the dissolution of the SOVIET UNION, and the subsequent embrace of capitalism in the former communist republics, RUSSIA has become a prime location for organized crime. As Russia undergoes the transformation from a socialist economy to a capitalist economy, there are many overlapping and conflicting laws regarding the economy. There is confusion over which laws are valid when presidential decrees and parliamentary legislation conflict. Another factor is the overlapping jurisdictions of administrative offices. With all of this confusion, it is easy to see how organized crime can flourish. The public is willing to pay gangsters to ensure that their businesses can survive. It is hoped that as the Russian economy settles, and becomes more organized, the power of these modern gangsters will diminish.

Still, it seems that gangsters are an inevitable part of the growing pains as capitalist economies develop.

BIBLIOGRAPHY. Laurence Bergreen, *Capone: The Man and the Era* (Touchstone, 1996); John Kobler, *Capone: The Life and World of Al Capone* (DaCapo, 1992); Robert A. Rockaway, *But He Was Good to His Mother: The Lives and Crimes of Jewish Gangsters* (Geffen, 2000); Vadim Volkov, *Violent Entrepreneurs: The Use of Force in the Making of Russian Capitalism* (Cornell University Press, 2002).

CHRIS HOWELL
RED ROCKS COLLEGE

Garfield, James (1831–81)

THE 20TH PRESIDENT of the UNITED STATES, James Abrams Garfield was born in Cuyahoga County, Ohio.

His father died when he was two, leaving his mother to raise five children with little money. At 16, Garfield began working on a canal barge, but after becoming sick, he decided to pursue an education. After graduating from Williams College in 1856, he became a college president, professor, and part-time preacher. He later studied law and joined the bar.

In 1858, Garfield was elected to the Ohio State Senate where he was a strong anti-slavery advocate and a vocal opponent of secession. He campaigned vigorously for Abraham LINCOLN in 1860. When the AMERICAN CIVIL WAR broke out, he helped recruit the 42nd Ohio Infantry and received a commission as a lieutenant colonel. A combination of his abilities, bravery, and good political connections allowed him to rise to major general. While serving in the field, his friends nominated him for Congress. He was elected to a seat in the U.S. House of Representatives in 1862. Despite his election, he remained in the field until Congress reconvened in late 1863.

Representative Garfield was a radical Republican. He supported strong protections for the freedmen and tough military measures to suppress the former rebels. He was one of the House leaders who successfully impeached President Andrew JOHNSON in 1868.

After the war, Garfield strongly supported moving the currency back to the specie standard. This meant that money would be backed by gold or silver, preventing currency inflation. This position was especially controversial in the west, where farmers hoped to escape their debts through high inflation. Garfield, however, viewed it as a moral issue, arguing that inflation was a form of legalized theft. He was also considered a moderate supporter of tariffs and civil service reform.

In 1872, Garfield was one of many Congressmen embarrassed by involvement in the Credit Mobilier scandal. Congressmen received stock and generous dividends from a railroad company that had been given lucrative government contracts. Although the scandal ended many political careers, Garfield's involvement was relatively minor and left him unscathed. He had also received other payments from government contractors while serving in the House, which, although legal at that time, seemed ethically questionable to many reformers.

Garfield sat on the election commission in 1876 that controversially awarded the presidency to Republican Rutherford B. HAYES.

In a special election in January, 1880, Garfield was elected to the U.S. Senate. But before he could take his seat, he went to the Republican Convention in support of John Sherman for president. The convention became deadlocked. In order to block an attempt by supporters of former President Ulysses GRANT to take the nomination, the other major candidates compromised by nominating a surprised Garfield on the 36th ballot.

After the election, there was an unusually large flurry of demands for patronage government jobs. Garfield had long been in favor of civil service reform, though he was not considered a particularly strong advocate. He spent much of his first months dealing with job controversies. In July 1881, a disgruntled (and probably insane) office seeker, named Charles Guiteau, shot the president in the back. Garfield lingered for months before dying in September. Outrage over the assassination resulted in the passage of the Pendleton Act in 1883, one of the first major legislative acts aimed at civil service reform.

BIBLIOGRAPHY. Harry James Brown and Frederick D. Williams, eds., *The Diary of James A. Garfield* (Michigan State University Press, 1967-1982); Allan Peskin, *James A. Garfield: A Biography* (Kent State University Press, 1978); Charles E. Rosenberg, *The Trial of the Assassin Guiteau* (University of Chicago Press, 1968).

MICHAEL J. TROY, J.D.
THOMAS D. JEITSCHKO, PH.D.
MICHIGAN STATE UNIVERSITY

Gates, William Henry III (1955–)

BILL GATES IS THE CO-FOUNDER, chief software architect, chairman, and former CHIEF EXECUTIVE OFFICER of the MICROSOFT Corporation. Gates is reported to be the richest American in history, the richest person in the world, and has been called the most successful entrepreneur in history.

Born in Seattle, Washington, his parents sent young Gates, a precocious child and ravenous reader, to an intense college preparatory school that rented mainframe-computer time from Computer Center Corporation for its students. Gates became addicted to the machine, as was his new friend Paul Allen (with whom Gates would eventually form Microsoft). Gates, Allen, and some other friends formed a computer club that volunteered to fix programming bugs for the Computer Center Corporation in exchange for computer time, and later wrote a payroll program for another local company.

Gates was admitted to Harvard University in 1973 but spent more time playing with the university's computers than concentrating on his studies. When Allen (who followed Gates out to Massachusetts) found an advertisement for the Altair 8080, an assembly-required microcomputer, Gates and Allen wrote a BASIC (a programming language) program for the Altair and sold it to the company. Within a year, Gates had dropped out of Harvard and formed with Allen the Microsoft Corporation that, by 1978, had sales exceeding $1 million.

After a brief stay in Albuquerque, New Mexico, Microsoft moved to the outskirts of Seattle in 1979, partly because Gates wanted to be closer to his family. After Allen was diagnosed with Hodgkin's disease in 1982 and left the company, Gates took over sole control of Microsoft. The company's continuing success made Gates a billionaire by 1986; at only 31 years old, he was the youngest billionaire in history.

At Microsoft, Gates is notorious for his focus, his total awareness of his products, and his confrontational management style. Gates insists workers argue with each other to fully examine ideas, and he has been known to verbally attack employees if he feels they are not properly prepared. In the early days of Microsoft, when it was still a reasonably small company, Gates insisted all decisions come through him; he preferred an open management style to bureaucracy (which became unavoidable in light of the company's enormous growth rate). Even today, Gates prefers informal management and tries to keep the atmosphere at company headquarters informal.

When dealing with competing companies, however, Gates is often notoriously ruthless. When Microsoft contemplated entering the internet service market by buying America Online, Gates told AOL chairman Steve Case, "I can buy 20 percent of you or I can buy all of you, or I can go into this business myself and bury you." Gates has also been accused of obsessing over his competition (in particular the Apple Macintosh system).

In 1998, Gates relinquished the titles of president and chief executive officer at Microsoft to Steve Ballmer, a friend of Gates from Harvard hired for his management (rather than technical) prowess. By adopting the title of chief software architect, Gates announced, allowed him to focus on Microsoft's products and less on business operations. Industry critics speculated the move less reflected Gates's desire to concentrate on technology than on his unsuitability for corporate management.

Gates has long been driven by a vision of computers entering all aspects of people's lives. In the early days of Microsoft, the Gates-penned company motto was "A computer on every desktop and in every home." Since then, this vision has expanded to include software spreading beyond computers, into every aspect of a person's life. Gates engineered the development of WebTV in an attempt to bring the internet to people without computers, and is a fervent supporter of developing software to integrate home appliances and computers. Gates' Lake Washington estate embodies this omnipresence of technology approach, as it is used as a testing grounds for many Microsoft-constructed home automation products. Gates spelled out his visions of technology in two best-selling books: 1995's *The Road Ahead* and 1999's *Business @ the Speed of Thought*.

Gates has also been an active philanthropist from the early days of Microsoft. In 1984, Gates and Allen donated $2.2 million to their old prep school for a science and math center. Gates also donated the profits from both his books to charities supporting technology education. Gates has also supported computer-in-library programs and global health organizations with billions of dollars in donations. Gates is particularly interested in lowering the price and raising the availability of prescription drugs and vaccines, one of the key goals of his charity foundation.

BIBLIOGRAPHY. Janet Lowe, *Bill Gates Speaks: Insight from the World's Greatest Entrepreneur* (John Wiley & Sons, 1998); David Bank, *Breaking Windows: How Bill Gates Fumbled the Future of Microsoft* (The Free Press, 2001); *Inside Out: Microsoft: In Our Own Words* (Warner Books, 2000); Jeanne M. Lesinski, *Bill Gates* (Lerner Publications, 2000).

MIKE S. DUBOSE
BOWLING GREEN STATE UNIVERSITY

General Agreement on Tariffs and Trade (GATT)

GATT CAME INTO EXISTENCE on January 1, 1948, with 23 original members, in the aftermath of WORLD WAR II as part of an attempt by the victorious allies to structure an economic world order that would better suit the realities of post-world-war life. It was ended at the conclusion of the Uruguay Round of talks in 1994 to be replaced by the WORLD TRADE ORGANIZATION (WTO), by which time it had grown to over 125 members, regulated some 90 percent of international trade, and had succeeded in reducing average international trade tariffs from 40 percent to about 4 percent.

The period prior to WORLD WAR I had seen increasing GLOBALIZATION and liberalization of international trade in a world system featuring strong nation-state alliances buttressed by the colonization of much of the third world. However, the war itself and the settlement that followed it did much to destroy that system and the institutional replacement for international alliances—the League of Nations—was not strong enough to prevent nations relapsing increasingly into a series of protectionist measures that further diminished confidence, and then contributed to reduced economic growth.

The UNITED STATES, in particular, with a large domestic market and few overseas connections compared with European powers, favored an isolationist stance with a strong protectionist element that contributed significantly to the stock market crash of 1929 and the subsequent Great DEPRESSION. World War II provided a stimulus to the American economy such that at the conclusion of the fighting, the United States was recognized as the emergent world economic leader.

Postwar discussions of the shape and nature of an international economic order that would help prevent the same economic problems (stimulated by the work of John Maynard KEYNES), as well as contributing to maintaining international peace in the face of the Cold War, centered on the creation of three institutions—the WORLD BANK, the INTERNATIONAL MONETARY FUND (IMF), and the International Trade Organization (ITO). ITO was intended to be the body which would regulate international trade and ensure fair play. However, America was mindful of its economic strength, which it wished to deploy in bilateral rather than multilateral forums, and its strong balance of payments surplus, and Congress refused to approve the Treaty of Havana that would have confirmed membership in the ITO. As a result, the ITO plan was abandoned, since it would have been impossible to operate without the support of the United States. In its place, the GATT was born, as an interim institution that was never, in fact, succeeded by the UN-sponsored successor to ITO that had been expected.

The main purpose of the GATT was to hold a series of negotiations at which tariff rates could be agreed upon. The principles by which the GATT was to operate included non-discrimination, most favored nation (MFN) status, and reciprocity. The principle of non-discrimination means that goods, once they have passed beyond a country's borders, must be treated as if they were domestic goods and be free from any discrimination or bias. MFN status means that all parties bind themselves to the idea that treatment extended to one party must be extended to all other members of the agreement. Reciprocity means that a privilege such as reducing a tariff—which is not enforceable in a commercial treaty such as provided by the GATT—should also be granted by the receiving nation and, indeed, all other nations that are signatory to the agreement.

Since GATT had little in the way of full-time staff or resources to support its workings, negotiations were frequently lengthy and inconclusive. Although some headline agreements were reached, this was often largely because strong nations were able to exclude issues that appeared to be troublesome, and deal with weaker nations on a bilateral basis so that they could enforce terms that would have been recognized as unfair by the international community at large. Hence, agriculture, heavily subsidized in Europe and even more so in the United States, has been excluded from GATT discussions. Similarly, textiles and garment manufacturers, in which the developing world has long had a competitive advantage due to lower LABOR costs, was dealt with by the Multifiber Agreement. This arose as a result of multilateral discussions in the GATT, contrary to the principles of the institution which enabled devel-

oped countries to enter into bilateral arrangements with lesser-developed countries (initially those such as JAPAN and HONG KONG) about how much in the way of imports of particular textiles they would accept. Formal acceptance of this arrangement by the GATT has subsequently cost the developing world many billions of dollars in lost sales as they have been unable to penetrate the markets of developed countries, markets in which they have definite advantages to the extent that GATT seemed to promise.

In recent years, other issues and forms of trade have increased significantly in importance in the world of international trade. In particular, trade in service and intellectual property have become of considerable importance as, in the face of increased competitiveness from low-labor-cost countries such as CHINA and VIETNAM not previously part of the capitalist system, profitability has come increasingly to depend on possession of knowledge, brand, and other value-added and capital-intensive assets.

The developed nations called for these areas to be included in GATT; agriculture and similar industries have been resolutely placed out of bounds. The Uruguay Round concluded with the expansion of GATT's efforts into the World Trade Organization (WTO) to include many of those issues requested by the developed nations.

Eight rounds of talks were held by the GATT before its abolition and, perhaps inevitably, given the nature of a weakly enforceable agreement structure with complex issues, many participants and a dynamic environment, success varied among the different rounds. Those of particular significance included the Kennedy Round of 1964–67, the Tokyo Round of 1973–79, and the Uruguay Round of 1986–94, all of which were in fact held in Geneva, Switzerland. This period witnessed numerous important changes in international arrangements that had an impact upon GATT negotiations.

For example, the rise of the "East Asian Tigers" (SOUTH KOREA, TAIWAN, HONG KONG and SINGAPORE) demonstrated in different ways that free trade was not always necessary for rapid economic growth by some lesser-developed nations. Similarly the spread of multinational enterprise units and their importance to the world economy, and the increasing pace of globalization, have considerably lessened the importance of many nation-states as actors in international trade.

However, it is slightly unfair to criticize the GATT for failing to deal with issues that were unanticipated at its formation, and that it did not have the resources with which to adapt itself. For example, environmental degradation and the need for SUSTAINABLE DEVELOPMENT were not recognized as important issues in the middle, and indeed the later part of the 20th century, when it was believed that exploitation of natural resources and overall economic growth could continue indefinitely.

At the same time, relative success in removing or reducing tariff barriers in a number of important industries led to attention being switched to non-tariff barriers (i.e., those designed, at least in part, with a view to maintaining labor protection or environmental standards). This led to increasing friction with trade unions, non-governmental organizations, and social activists whose role has been to protect those standards.

BIBLIOGRAPHY. Kyle Bagwell and Robert W. Staiger, "Economic Theory and the Interpretation of GATT/WTO," *American Economist* (v.46/2, 2002); Edward M. Graham, "Should There Be Multinational Rules on Foreign Direct Investment?" *Governments, Globalization and International Business* (Oxford University Press, 1997); Robert A. Isaak, *International Political Economy: Managing World Economic Change* (Prentice Hall, 1991); Richard Pomfret, *International Trade: An Introduction to Theory and Policy* (Blackwell, 1991).

JOHN WALSH, PH.D.
SHINAWATRA UNIVERSITY, THAILAND

General Electric

A DIVERSE SERVICE AND technology company, General Electric (GE) owes its beginnings to the famous inventor and innovator, Thomas EDISON. GE is the only company listed on the Dow Jones Industrial Index of 1896 that is still listed today. The company's success and longevity have involved power generation, financial services, aircraft, plastics, television, and other products, and it employs over 300,000 people in 100 different company divisions today.

GE traces its origins to the 1878 Edison Electric Light Company. An 1892 merger between the Edison General Electric Company and the Thomson-Houston Electric Company created the General Electric Company. The company had 2001 net earnings of over $14 billion on international revenues of $50 billion. Its market capitalization is estimated at an astounding $263 billion. Recent GE corporate leaders, such as Jack Welch, have been lauded as the new form of CHIEF EXECUTIVE OFFICER who can transform traditional industry companies to take advantage of emerging markets.

Along the way, GE has been involved in a large number of innovations with over 67,000 patents and two Nobel Prizes in about a century of operation. GE has been responsible for making available a vast array of products, processes, and services. Some of these are the tungsten filaments for lighting that helped bring artificial light to the world as a tool. The man-made diamond, the first television broadcast, the magnetron,

the microwave, improved Magnetic Resonance Imaging (MRI) and CT scanners, digital x-ray imaging, new plastics, applications in the communication industries, and much more have been spawned in the labs inspired by Edison so many years ago at his Menlo Park laboratory.

Some of the most important developments and products include inexpensive light bulbs in 1879; x-ray machines in 1896; the first radio broadcast in 1906; the first electric-generator-propelled ship in 1912; the electric system for the Panama Canal in 1914; and in 1918, the development of the magnetron vacuum tube for control of microwaves, and the first trans-Atlantic radio power generator.

During the 1920s, GE scientists designed the sources of power behind record-setting airplanes and racecars, and the first television broadcasts. In the 1930s, GE helped spread electric technology to the home by building power generation systems and home appliances that became standard after the 1940s. Between the 1930s and 1950s, the GE Credit Company allowed many consumers to acquire the tools of tomorrow on payment plans. During WORLD WAR II, GE pioneered the television station, the first American jet engine, and jumpstarted the field of atmospheric science with forays into rainmaking, or cloud seeding.

In the 1950s, GE popularized its innovations in plastics and home appliances. In the 1960s, GE played an integral role, from products to service, in placing the first human on the moon. During the 1970s, GE power sources became a norm for most commercial aircraft. In the 1980s, GE developed fiber optics and began to expand operations into new markets such as the launch of CNBC, a cable news network.

GE continues to diversify today with offerings in insurance, finance, and entertainment to supplement its traditional business of power generation and electrical and plastics products. The General Electric tradition of scientific advancement, beyond market profit, also continues with experiments in the world of the very small and very extreme using super magnets, space-age materials, and GE power sources for the experiments, often carried out with GE scientific involvement.

BIBLIOGRAPHY. C. Bramsen, *Wilhelm Meyer and the Establishment of General Electric in China* (Curson Press, 2000); T. Sekiguchi, *Welfare Capitalism and the Workers in GE's Schenectady Works*, The Institute of Business Research (Chuo University, 1995); R. Schatz, *A History of Labor at General Electric and Westinghouse, 1923-1960* (University of Illinois Press, 1983); R. Slater, *Jack Welch and the GE Way* (McGraw-Hill, 1999).

CHRIS HOWELL
RED ROCKS COLLEGE

General Motors

COMMONLY CITED FOR decades as the largest corporation in the world, General Motors (GM) traces its history to the Olds Motor Vehicle Company, organized by Ransom E. Olds, in 1897. The next century would see incredible development and expansion in the automotive industry, with GM a leader worldwide.

In 1899, a merger between Olds Motor Vehicle and Olds Gasoline Engine Works formed Olds Motor Works, leading to the first automobile manufacturing factory in the United States. In short order, Cadillac came into existence, organized by Henry M. Leland in 1902, followed by the incorporation of Buick Motor Company a year later. Billy Durant took control of Buick in 1904 and subsequently organized General Motors Company on September 16, 1908.

GM purchased Oldsmobile in November of the same year and purchased a 50 percent interest in Oakland Motor Car Company (later to become Pontiac) the following year. Later in 1909, GM expanded once more, adding Cadillac to its fleet with a purchase price of $5.5 million. Expansion continued throughout 1909, with AC Spark Plug (known as Champion Ignition Company) joining GM, followed by the acquisition of Rapid Motor Vehicle Company, the forerunner of GMC Truck, and Reliance Motor Truck Company. In an effort to grow even more, Durant attempted to buy Ford Motor Company the same year but was denied a loan request of $9.5 million.

By 1910, however, GM finances were precarious. Facing financial collapse, loans were secured to keep GM afloat and Durant was removed from his leadership role. In 1911, GM President James J. Storrow created the Engineering Department, which would become the GM Research Department in November 1911. Continuing with its expansion, General Motors Truck Company (today known as GMC) was organized in July 1911, followed by the incorporation of Chevrolet Motor Company in November 1911. Simultaneously, GM Export Company was put into place to handle sales of GM products abroad.

Expansion continued throughout the 1920s, with GM's first European assembly plant established in 1923 under the leadership of Chairman Alfred P. Sloan. Sloan's focus in the 1924 annual report was to declare GM's strategy of "A car for every purse and purpose." This strategy certainly fit well, given the pace of acquisitions, development, and expansion of GM products in its first 30 years of business. Expansion continued, with GM establishing its presence in England, Brazil, Argentina, Spain, Paris, Berlin, South Africa, Australia, New Zealand, Japan, Egypt, Uruguay, India, Germany, and China by 1930.

GM's impressive growth was marked by the production of its 25-millionth car on January 11, 1940. With the onset of World War II, GM lost control of Adam Opel AG to the NAZI government, shut down operations in Japan, and devoted all of its production to the beginning war effort.

1953 brought about the introduction of one of Chevrolet's most famous products, the Corvette. The late 1960s saw more expansion in GM's product lines with the introduction of the Chevrolet Camaro in 1967 and the Pontiac Firebird the following year (but listing a 1967 production year). Much to the chagrin of muscle-car enthusiasts, both vehicles were discontinued in 2002. In other arenas, GM produced the navigation system for the Apollo 11, guiding the first landing on the moon.

GM continued its acquisitions in early 1971, acquiring a 34.2 percent interest in Isuzu Motors Ltd. It entered into a joint venture in IRAN in 1972 but pulled out in December 1978 (at the time of the Islamic Revolution). At the same time as it launched its venture in Iran, GM entered into a joint venture with Shinjin Motor Co. of Seoul, South Korea. This would become Daewoo Motor Company in 1982. GM held a 50 percent interest in the company until 1992.

With the oil embargo of 1974, GM moved forward with a strategy of downsizing its products. The Chevrolet Chevette was introduced in 1975, with smaller models of Chevrolet, Pontiac, Oldsmobile, Buick, and Cadillac being introduced in 1976.

The 1980s saw the introduction of GM's Saturn Corporation, with production beginning in 1990. GM further diversified by acquiring Electronic Data Systems Corporation (EDS), a data processing and telecommunications company. The late 1980s featured the redesign of GM's fleet of mid-sized cars and the introduction of SmartLease, a GM consumer-leasing program. It also formed a joint venture with Volvo for its heavy truck business and introduced its Geo line of vehicles. By the close of the decade, GM had purchased a 50 percent interest in Saab Automobile AB of Sweden.

The early 1990s saw another management change, with John F. Smith, Jr. being named chief executive officer of GM. A reorganization effort ensued, establishing two primary operations for GM, its North American Operations and General Motors International Operations. Further, GM released the 5 percent rebate GM Mastercard. In the mid-1990s, GM's sales outside North America exceeded 3 million vehicles for the first time.

In 2000, GM increased its equity in Saab to 100 percent. It also entered into e-business partnerships with Sony, NetXero, and AmericaOnline, created a strategic alliance with Fiat, broke ground for a new $1 billion manufacturing complex in Michigan, increased its equity share of Suzuki to 20 percent, and announced the planned discontinuation of the Oldsmobile brand.

In 2003, GM revolved around six fundamental values for its business, including continuous improvement, customer enthusiasm, innovation, integrity, teamwork, and individual respect and responsibility. GM posted a net profit margin of only 0.3 percent in 2001. However, in the third quarter of 2002, GM posted a 30 percent improvement in earnings compared with the same period in 2001. The improvements are attributed to strong market performance and cost-cutting measures. Earnings were reported at $696 million, compared with $527 million in the third quarter of 2001.

BIBLIOGRAPHY. *General Motors Corporation Annual Reports*, www.gm.com (2002 and 2001); Alfred P. Sloan, *My Years with General Motors* (Doubleday, 1996).

AUDREY D. KLINE, PH.D.
UNIVERSITY OF LOUISVILLE

Generally Accepted Accounting Principles (GAAP)

THE ACRONYM FOR Generally Accepted Accounting Principles, GAAP provides the standards, rules, and conventions that accountants follow in recording financial transactions and preparing financial statements. Following GAAP essentially means the "accepted way" of doing accounting.

GAAP was largely developed and saw most of its growth throughout the 1930s. This was spurred by several earlier factors, including the establishment of the corporate form of business which saw the separation of management and ownership; the introduction of the income tax in 1913; the stock market crash and the ensuing DEPRESSION; and the regulatory period of 1933–34, which saw the establishment of the SECURITIES AND EXCHANGE COMMISSION (SEC), the regulation of securities trading, and full disclosure to investors.

In 1934, the SEC was given statutory authority to develop accounting standards, but instead, it left the private sector standard-setting bodies, such as the American Institute for Certified Public Accountants (AICPA), to do the bulk of the governing work.

The question becomes, then, what exactly is GAAP, and who presides over it?

First, the accounting industry is governed by various authoritative bodies, and their respective influence on accounting standards is given on the basis of the authoritative rank of each group's literature. This is arranged into what is known as the GAAP hierarchy. The GAAP hierarchy is established by the Financial Accounting Standards Board (FASB). FASB is the designated organization within the accounting industry that establishes

GAAP. Though the SEC has statutory authority to establish standards for publicly held companies, it has long relied on the private sector to do this. Consequently, the SEC does indeed recognize GAAP standards as authoritative.

At the top of the five-category hierarchy, there is the FASB Statements and Interpretations. Also on par with the FASB Statements is the Accounting Principles Board (APB) Opinions and Accounting Research Bulletins.

The next category establishes the significance of FASB Technical Bulletins, AICPA Industry Audit and Accounting Guides, and AICPA Statements of Position. The third category is consensus positions of the FASB Emerging Issues Task Force (EITF) and AICPA Practice Bulletins. The fourth category includes AICPA Accounting Interpretations, FASB Questions and Answers, and prevalent industry practices. Finally, the last and least authoritative level in the GAAP hierarchy is composed of FASB Concept Statements, AICPA Issues Papers, and accounting textbooks and journal articles.

However, GAAP is not a fixed set of rules. Since there is no official, published list of principles, accountants must be familiar with this hierarchy, and the available sources within each category, in order to make proper judgments in a hazy and sometimes ambiguous environment.

The ambiguity contention then brings us to GAAP and its fundamental objectives. It was originally intended to be a set of principles, which are fundamental concepts and not specific rules to guide conduct. Though the rules, practices, conventions, and procedures used by accountants are subject to change, the purpose of the implementation of GAAP was to give the accounting industry a guiding set of principles to prevail throughout changes in the business environment and actual accounting practices.

GAAP principles, however, are mostly derived from tradition or specific practice over time. This is what has caused GAAP to be critically referred to, by its critics, as mere "working rules of practice" as opposed to an actual model set of principles.

However, the major components of GAAP are principle-based, while the various conventions and practices for the various components are generally driven by accepted norms, rules, and conventions within the industry. And the GAAP hierarchy lays out which authoritative sources shall guide the recording of transactions.

Indeed, principles and rules of conduct are very distinct. For example, assorted accounting measurements may have several accepted procedures or rules for financial statement representation; however, GAAP requires that these procedures follow the consistency principle, meaning that measurements are not subject to the whims of deliberate misrepresentation from one accounting period to the next. In other words, a company adopting a certain accounting principle to disclose specified information must use that principle in the same manner from one period to the next, and if that principle changes, that fact must be disclosed along with the effects of the change.

Another broad GAAP principle is the asset/liability measurement principle, that measures assets and liabilities by different attributes that depend on the nature of the asset/liability, and the relevance and reliability of the attribute measured. GAAP also has broad principles dealing with disclosure, the matching of revenues and expenses, revenue recognition, and the monetary unit assumption.

GAAP principles, overall, are those that have substantial authoritative support, and they are principles that are evaluated on the basis of how much they contribute to the objectives of the financial-reporting process. On the whole, the basic emphasis is to have a pervasive impact on the form and content of financial statements so that they are understandable to external users.

In any case, if GAAP is, by some appearances, just a "suggested" list of principles, why do accountants need to follow them? Accountants need to follow GAAP because even though they are referred to as principles, they are similar to laws within our legal system. For example, certified public accountants routinely AUDIT companies to determine if their financial statements are prepared according to GAAP. These audit findings will be published along with the company's financial statements. Keep in mind there is an immense amount of legitimacy placed on the external auditor's report, a report that essentially states whether or not GAAP was followed in a consistent manner. Most outside users of financial statements, except perhaps those dealing with smaller businesses, require externally audited financial statements that concur with GAAP. This compliance helps maintain creditability with creditors and stockholders because it reassures outsiders that a company's financial reports accurately portray its financial position.

GAAP, however, has had some setbacks in the era of corporate collapse during the early 2000s. The accounting scandals surrounding ENRON, WORLDCOM, Xerox, and other corporate giants play a large role in the revamping of principles-based accounting, the industry's ability to continue self-regulating, and the authoritative hierarchy within the industry.

Enron was the first spectacle to bring critical attention to GAAP and its ability to be effective. By late 2001, all major media markets were focused on Enron and its financial woes as it was revealed that Enron's off-balance-sheet accounting had not disclosed losses from a number of complex partnerships. Before that, Enron had been bumping up its revenues via a loophole in accounting rules because the FASB just could not make up its mind about how energy contracts should be accounted for and, at some point or other, decided that each company had a free hand to do what it wanted.

What followed was a media barrage on the entire accounting industry, as one scandal after another was revealed: Enron, WorldCom, Xerox, Global Crossing, Tyco, Halliburton, Qwest Communications, K-Mart, and so on. Financial statements from years back were restated, losses were revealed, stock prices dove, and 2002 saw the world's largest bankruptcies. Previously, the media couldn't have cared about accounting, but now, not only were accountants the new objects of ridicule, but GAAP, formerly an industry-only utterance, became a household word.

Though GAAP clearly had solid principles to determine revenue recognition rules, the allowable degree for deviation was so great that it was exploited by Enron in an attempt to prop up the appearance of booming profits. The fallout for GAAP was that it was said to be, essentially, not tough enough with its principles, and therefore, allowed for deceptive accounting practices far too easily. So again, where GAAP encounters problems is when companies are left free to pursue aggressive accounting tactics, though they are not necessarily illegal.

This wave of corporate accounting scandals ushered in a new era of regulation to the accounting industry. Perhaps the new regulatory oversight, as government adopts a new get-tough policy on deceptive corporate accounting, will prove to be more cumbersome than advantageous. Alas, the increased involvement from the public sector may prove to be detrimental in terms of competition, because the costs of wide-ranging oversight, political lobbying, and compliance to the various new rules will likely prohibit those on the margin from competing in businesses under less vigorous oversight conditions.

Change is inevitable, however, in terms of ultimate accounting principles, practices, and oversight. As the various governing and advisory bodies within the accounting industry adapt to ever-changing economic phenomena, up-and-down markets, and more burdensome regulatory oversight, opinions about the perceived benefits or harm to third-party financial statement users will be the driving influence in the way that GAAP is further developed, defined, and administered.

In conclusion, the implication sometimes is that GAAP is not as soundly principle-based as it could or should be, and that it is perhaps using misleading terminology to reflect that it is. However, the greatest challenge to the accounting profession is not to nitpick at the difference between terminologies, but rather to fully develop underlying postulates and concepts so that a principle-based system such as GAAP can keep pace with the needs of a rapidly changing business system.

BIBLIOGRAPHY. Morton Backer, *Modern Accounting Theory* (Thomson, 1966); Joel G. Siegel and Jae K. Shim, *Barrons Business Guide: Dictionary of Accounting Terms* (Barrons, 2000); Robert N. Anthony, *Tell It Like It Was: A Conceptual Framework for Financial Accounting* (Irwin, 1983); Jan R. Williams, Keith G. Stanga, and William W. Holder, *Intermediate Accounting* (Dryden Press, 1995); Maurice Moonitz and A.C. Littleton, *Significant Accounting Essays* (Garland, 1965); W.T. Baxter and Sidney Davidson, *Studies in Accounting Theory* (John Wiley & Sons, 1962).

KAREN DE COSTER
WALSH COLLEGE

Georgia

LOCATED IN THE Caucasus Mountains, along the eastern coast of the Black Sea, Georgia's history dates back 2,500 years. It has retained its distinctive culture (and its own language, Georgian) over this long period in spite of sieges and occupations by Persians, Arabs, Turks, Mongols, and Russians. Its dominant religious faith has been Orthodox Christianity since its conversion in the 4th century A.D.

In 1801, RUSSIA incorporated Georgia into its empire. The Russian Empire collapsed in the February 1917, Revolution, after which the first Republic of Georgia was proclaimed, on May 26, 1918. In March 1921, Georgia was incorporated into the SOVIET UNION. The most well-known Georgian in the Soviet leadership was Joseph Stalin, whose surname by birth was Dzhugashvili.

Georgia proclaimed its independence from the Soviet Union on April 9, 1991, but has continually been beset with its own national separatist movements. Its government was somewhat stabilized by presidential elections in 1995 (which twice have chosen Edouard Shevardnadze, Soviet foreign minister under Mikhail GORBACHEV). Nevertheless, corruption and violence are widespread in Georgian political and economic life. The provinces of Abkhazia and South Ossetia and other areas that are not Georgian have produced refugee problems and threaten the stability of the region. Georgia hopes that its strategic location between the oil-rich Caspian Sea and the Black Sea will boost its economy through the construction across its territory of the Baku-Tbilisi-Ceyhan oil pipeline.

Georgia, with a population of five million people, had a GROSS DOMESTIC PRODUCT (GDP) of $15.5 billion in 2001; the majority of production coming from agriculture, mining, machinery, and chemicals.

BIBLIOGRAPHY. Ronald Grigor Suny, *The Making of the Georgian Nation* (Indiana University Press, 1994); Jonathan Aves, *Georgia, From Chaos to Stability?* (Royal Institute of International Affairs, 1996); David M. Lang, *A Modern History of Soviet Georgia* (Grove Press, 1962); CIA World Factbook (2002).

GEORGE KOSAR
BRANDEIS UNIVERSITY

Germany

THE ECONOMIC FATE of Germany is closely tied to the effort to unite Europe economically as the EUROPEAN UNION (EU). The success of this new form of capitalism beyond the nation-state, with free-market economies, and outside of national planned economies, will largely depend on the economic fortune and future of countries such as Germany and FRANCE in the EU.

Moderate summers and rainy winters characterize the German climate and make for well-watered, high-yield soils. The Alps form the southern border with AUSTRIA and SWITZERLAND, and mountain ranges also define the southeast border with the CZECH REPUBLIC. The eastern border with POLAND has the Oder and Neisse Rivers. The north consists of the European plain and the Baltic Sea. To the west is the Rhine River drainage and BELGIUM, LUXEMBOURG, and France. The Danube River starts in the Black Forest and becomes a major waterway for Europe. Many of the European rivers are linked by canal systems through Germany.

Historically, Germany was a group of small states that shared common cultural, but not political borders, before unification under Otto von BISMARCK in the 1870s. However, the capitalist tradition was strong in German states going back to the time of the Hausa Baltic seafaring states and continuing through German gun-making communities associated with early gunpowder weapons in Europe.

During the rise of the Prussian State in 1815 and after, the small German state economies became linked with military production and a significant civilian sector was always present as evidenced by the Weimar Republic period. The military-economic linkage increased with WORLD WAR I in the beginning of the 20th century. After the war, the German state collapsed and the economy became part of the global DEPRESSION of the 1930s, only to be renewed with a re-emerging military-based economy under Adolf Hitler.

After WORLD WAR II, the German state was divided between the SOVIET UNION (East Germany) and the western allies (West Germany). The Soviet economy, based in Russia as a socialist, state-run economy controlled East Germany until the economic and political reunification in late 1980s and early 1990s. West Germany followed the path of capitalism and is currently trying to re-integrate its East German territories back into a capitalist economy, albeit with great deal of trouble.

In early 2003, the Bundesrepublik Deutschland (The Federal Republic of Germany) had a coalition government headed by Chancellor Gerhard Schröder since 1998. Its two main economic goals are internal and external in nature. Internally, Germany needs to rebuild the civilization of infrastructure of the former socialist East German territory. After a generation of socialist economic activity, even the East German citizens are unfamiliar with what this will mean exactly, and re-education is a big part of the effort. Historians suggest it will likely take one or two generations of East Germans absorbed into West German capitalism before full reunification becomes a reality.

Externally, Germany hopes to lead the way to European economic unity with the EU. This is no easy task either, as the different European communities are united mainly by sharing the same subcontinent and general history. The multitude of languages, cultures, and monetary systems, however is offset by reasonably similar transportation and civilization infrastructures, at least in the European states outside of the eastern block dominated by Soviet rule for the last half century.

Essentially, Germany faces the same internal economic difficulties as the EU faces externally. There is the question of how to integrate former socialist economies and civilization infrastructures of the last half-century with the traditional capitalist economies of Western Europe. Additionally, there are the dynamics of democratic social states in the west such as the Scandinavian states or the NETHERLANDS, and small states such as Luxembourg integrated with large states such as France or Germany.

A key component to the EU is the monetary system and Germany has led the way as the banking and finance center of Europe, and in adopting the EURO currency. Germany has 82 million people. Most are German-speakers and are united by a sense of German culture. The capital has been moved back to Berlin in an effort to aid the economy of East Germany. The GROSS DOMESTIC PRODUCT (GPD) per capita was $25,000 (2000), the GDP real growth 3 percent (2000). The labor force of about 41 million has a 9 to 10 percent unemployment rate. This is due to 17-percent unemployment rates in the former socialist East German territory, and to an influx of refugees and job seekers from less economically robust areas of the globe. Inflation is low at 2 to 3 percent per year and foreign debt is $2 billion.

Chancellor Schröder has enacted tax reforms, the shutdown of nuclear plants, and the importation of 20,000 computer specialists to help boost the economy since 2000. In dealing with cross-European issues, moves toward organic animal husbandry and away

from industrial production have stemmed mad-cow and hoof-and-mouth disease impacts.

The launch of the EURO in 1999 by the EUROPEAN CENTRAL BANK (ECB) is centered in the German finance and banking centers. So far, the euro's volatile performance versus the U.S. dollar is of concern. The ECB raised interest rates five times in 2000 alone to combat this instability but such moves are dangerous for the already high unemployment rate in Europe.

Tax rates have been modified to move away from a more socialist past and toward a market-oriented future. Corporate top tax rates will drop from 52 to 39 percent by 2005. The lack of trained computer professionals (employment experts cite the need for 450,000) has only been partially addressed by importing foreign professionals. Retraining of East German citizens is a likely move in the future to lower unemployment and boost the economy.

Germany is the world's second-largest exporter, averaging over $400 billion annually but its trade deficit grew to $23.5 billion by 2001. Transnational companies based in Germany such as Dresdner Bank, DAIMLER-CHRYSLER, T-Mobile, and re-insurers in the insurance industry are concerned. Drops in the German stock market reflect this, and the German government has responded by retooling the education system to move Germany into competitiveness in the technology sector. However, the experience of recent U.S. economic slowdowns in this sector may call such a strategy into question.

The German economy is often described as a social-market economy based on industry and the service sector. Free enterprise is sometimes subordinate to political goals and exports are key for the long-term. The emerging East German market has increased imports and may help to increase domestic consumption as its citizens transition to capitalism. Basically a new generation and economy will have to grow out of the two, older economies of the pre-unification era. With such internal division, economists see two ways to look at Germany's entry into and leadership of the EU.

One view suggests that the time is right for the EU and Germany. Germany is transitioning internally anyway with reunification and might as well transition externally too. This combination of internal and external economic change could just propel the German economy into a position of global pre-eminence. Another view is not so positive. Germany's internal troubles should first be resolved or it should first become entrenched in the EU economy, but should not do both at the same time. The stress on the economy could be too much and an economic collapse may be likely.

The current economy of Germany is providing data on both of these views but the results are hard to interpret for the long-term. More and more Germans speak

English and French as well as German. In the 1980s, privately owned companies were allowed into the public broadcasting fields of radio and television. Most of the 600 daily newspapers are now dominated by private enterprises. Advertising now plays a key role in much of media. Germany's entry into the EU meant further markets for its export products, beyond its main North American markets for automobiles and other high-end products. The low performance of the euro gave North American U.S. dollar-holders good incentive to trade with countries using the euro. Now over half of German export trade is with EU countries.

But problems abound. Indications are, that despite high-quality export products in aircraft, motor vehicles, heavy machinery, precision instruments, office equipment, and electrical engineering products, success in foreign markets for German products is tied more to trade liberalization, reduced tariffs, and collapsing competitor statist economies like JAPAN, than to Germany's excellent quality and service reputation. So even if East Germany is brought up to West German standards of capitalism, the EU members will have to do the same for benefits to be realized in Germany.

The agriculture sector accounts for only 1 percent of the GDP and employs 4 percent of the workforce. Yet one-fifth of all imports are foodstuffs. Recently, West German farmers have migrated to the east to start new farms or become advisors for the old East German cooperative farms. EU policy now links German farms, many below fifty hectares. The EU sets farm prices, marketing quotas, and exchange rates. This makes it difficult for Germany to become self-sufficient and create internal food production-consumption cycles that would benefit farmers and the economy. To combat this, the German Ministry of Food, Agriculture, and Forestry has enacted national policy within the EU framework to preserve efficient farmsteads with tax incentives, grants, and subsidies as well as a social security system.

The farming dilemma is a vital problem throughout the EU and Germany. Europe, known for its small farms and high quality, fresh produce and meats, is unlike the North American, mass-production approach to food production and consumption. Much of the local economy in rural areas is based on this organic, daily version of farm-to-market economics. Farmer protests from France to Ireland, to Eastern Europe indicate the importance of balancing local, state, and EU economic needs.

In 2000, German products were exported to France (11 percent), United States (10 percent), United Kingdom (8 percent), Italy (7 percent), the Netherlands (6 percent), Belgium/Luxembourg (5 percent), Austria (5 percent), Spain (5 percent), Switzerland (4 percent), and Poland (3 percent). Imports for the same year were France (10 percent), the Netherlands (9 percent), United States (8 percent), United Kingdom (7 percent), Italy (7

percent), Belgium/Luxembourg (5 percent), Japan (5 percent), Austria (4 percent), Switzerland (4 percent), and China (3 percent).

Such numbers indicate intricate linkages between the German economy and import/export. Membership in the EU and the incorporation and subsidization of East Germany into the German economy are potential threats to the delicate balances in the German trade-driven economy.

The industrial sector accounted for 36 percent of the GDP in 1999 and employed 36 percent of the workforce. Traditional industries like steel and shipbuilding have contracted or even changed their focus to survive. For instance, the traditional heavy industry conglomerate Preussag is changing operations toward tourism as of 1999. Elsewhere, even the vaunted German automobile industry has moved toward transnational corporate status to remain competitive with global and EU market changes. The combination of the American car company Chrysler and the German company Daimler-Benz is a prime example. West German industry is modernizing with electronics while East German industry has lagged far behind with high wages and worker productivity sometimes 70 percent below that of West Germany.

Tourism accounts for 16 percent of the GDP and 16 percent of the workforce employed. Most visitors are from the Netherlands, the United States, the United Kingdom, Italy, and Switzerland. Increasing private sector operations in tourism are helping to lead the way in economic growth for German service industries.

In the energy sector, mining accounts for 1 percent of the GDP and 1 percent of the workforce. Other than large supplies of brown and black coal, and huge potential deposits of lignite in East Germany, most German energy resources are imported. High cost of extraction in East Germany and EU resistance to pollution from brown coal has affected internal energy production. Brown coal, in particular, has caused air and water pollution from the Black Forest to the Netherlands, but the alternative has been a 40-percent production of German electricity from nuclear power. The German Green Party, part of the coalition government of Schröder, has been actively pressing for the curtailing of nuclear activity in Germany. This has further exacerbated German energy import dilemmas. Germany now imports 40 percent of its energy consumption as oil. Natural gas imports account for 20 percent, and nuclear energy for most of the rest.

Germany has eight major stock exchanges located in Frankfurt, Munich, Berlin, Dusseldorf, Hamburg, Stuttgart, Hanover, and Bremen. The Frankfurt exchange still handles over half of all the volume as of 2002, despite the move of the capital to Berlin. Together the eight exchanges are second only to the London Stock Exchange (LSE) in Europe. However, the eight exchanges are still separate and indicate the regional nature of much of the German economy. A bold move to combine the Frankfurt Stock Exchange with the London Stock Exchange in 2000 could have helped integrate the hesitant United Kingdom into the EU. Instead, the move was derailed by the LSE, partly on concerns of lack of German stock-exchange unity according to some analysts.

A sophisticated system of banking forms the financial structure behind German economic might. The central bank of Deutsche Bundesbank operates on behalf of the European Central Bank. Many banks have shareholdings in industry companies and bank members are also board members for such companies. This relationship is dangerous as the German industry sector contracts to a lesser position within the German economy. Potential contraction of German industry would seriously impact the German banks, and thus the Deutsche Bundesbank, and likely the ECB as well.

Some positive signs for German capitalism are evident as well. The deregulation of public phone companies led the DEUTSCHE TELECOM company to gain control of 99 percent of local telephone connections. Costs for customers were dramatically reduced by up to 85 percent for domestic long-distance calls. Deutsche Telecom, or T-Online and T-Mobile, as they are known in the internet and cell phone markets, also controls the internet access market in Germany and cell phone operations are spreading into North America and beyond.

Additionally, national transportation and communication infrastructures are some of the best in the world. Government ministries are excellent harbingers of economic policy and are generally proactive rather than reactive when problem-solving. So, usually, Germany gets results when addressing economic issues, such as mad-cow disease, and is considered a leader in economic problem solving and PLANNING.

The economic future of German capitalism is clearly one of increasing privatization, pro-growth policies by the German government, and further integration within the EU. Germany should be a leader within banking and finance in the EU. German reliance on external energy will likely shrink its industrial sector but the potential for consumption and production in eastern Germany is intriguing.

BIBLIOGRAPHY. R. Deeg, *Finance Capitalism Unveiled: Banks and the German Political Economy* (University of Michigan Press, 1999); P. Dininio, *The Political Economy of East German Privatization* (Praeger, 1999); Federal Statistics Office of Germany, www.statistik-bund.de; R. Harding and W. Paterson, *The Future of the German Economy: An End to the Miracle* (Manchester University Press, 2003); B. Heitger and L. Waverman, eds., *German Unification and the International Economy* (Routledge, 1993); G. Herrigel, *Industrial Constructions: The Sources of German Industrial Power* (Cambridge University Press, 1996); T. Lange and J.R. Shackleton, eds., *The Political Economy of German Unification* (Berhhahn Books, 1998); P. Koslowsk, ed., *Theory of Capitalism in the German Economic Tradition* (Springer Verlag, 2000); K. Yamamura and W. Streeck, eds., *The End of Diversity: Prospects for German and Japanese Capitalism* (Cornell University Press, 2003).

CHRIS HOWELL
RED ROCKS COLLEGE

globalization

AS THE SPREAD OF WORLDWIDE, interconnected business, globalization provides an archetype of perceived class conflict; what one sees depends upon one's angle of vision.

From the commanding heights of the owners and managers of the media, industrial, commercial, and international financial institutions looking down, 21st-century globalization is greater, wider, and thicker global interdependence than that which has been growing for centuries in the form of expanded trade, environmental interdependence, and cultural exchange.

However, from the grassroots perspective of the poor and dispossessed, unemployed and underemployed, downsized, restructured, and dislocated workers and migrant populations, the officially encouraged higher mobility of capital in contemporary globalization is an ongoing disaster, which began with the movement toward deregulation in the UNITED STATES in the late 1970s. To the immediate victims of Joseph SCHUMPETER's "creative destruction," and from the perspectives of overworked environmental, human rights, peasant, and labor organizers who care, globalization is disastrous.

From the heights, globalization is the freeing up of international capital through corporate structures, the result of the neo-liberal convergence, where mobile capital in the form of transnational corporations, enabled by free trade and deregulation from national political barriers, will increase the living standards of all countries.

Or, looking from below, it is a race to the bottom, where stateless corporations play nations, communities, ecosystems, and workers against one another by demanding concessions of wages, taxes, environmental standards, and quality of life, while seeking to maximize profits. They feel the advocates of free trade show little serious regard to democratic processes, environmental degradation, or labor standards, that are tacked on as if after-thoughts to international trade agreements.

Without meaning to minimize the very many diverse forms of globalization, we will focus largely on the economic conditions surrounding globalization.

Early globalization. Here are a few examples of early or thin globalization: the spread of Christianity and Islam, the plagues that swept Europe, and the Silk Road that connected medieval Europe and Asia. Luxury goods and spices traveled over the Silk Road to elite customers among the European populations, all classes of whom suffered from the viruses that accompanied the traders. The invention of Chinese fireworks designed for entertainment value, quickly provided increased coercive capacity of European explorers and conquerors with new weapons, as they began their domination of indigenous peoples in the 16th century.

Later, at the beginning of the INDUSTRIAL REVOLUTION, a passage from Karl MARX's and Friedrich ENGEL's *Communist Manifesto* captures the ambiguity of the spread of global capital: "All old established national industries have been destroyed or are being destroyed . . . in place of the old local and national seclusion and self-sufficiency, we have intercourse in every direction, universal interdependence of nations."

Around the turn of the 19th century, many theorists of international politics including Princeton University's Woodrow WILSON began to think about what came to be known as liberal internationalism; the development of international law and institutions and free trade as democratic, stabilizing, and peaceful substitutions for secret alliances and wars conducted by aristocratic European elites to correct imbalances of power. This globalization had its idealist spokespersons, as well as its policy planners of brutal and forced colonization, interventions, and gunboats. In many cases it was hard to distinguish between the idealists and colonizers.

WORLD WAR I interrupted the progress of "free" trade. International organizations surrounding the League of Nations proved as ineffectual in dealing with threats to national security as with economic integration and stabilization issues. As the world DEPRESSION spread globally in 1929, "beggar thy neighbor" protectionist policies typified national economies in the 1930s. WORLD WAR II brought a completely globalized military world, eventually leading to two alliance systems and the ability of United States forces to project its power anywhere on the globe, rationalized by containment of the communist "threat." The close of the war brought a new paradigm for globalization and international organizations. Recognizing a need for national autonomy, as well as a need to protect national economies and populations, the UNITED NATIONS (UN), designed by the victorious powers, built a regulated international monetary system along with ten-year plans to end tariff barriers to trade, and increase international economic integration.

The postwar period turned out to be a time of very rapid growth for the United States and Western industrial nations, and of prolific plan-making, but little economic growth for the poor nations or the second-world socialist/communist nations. These countries largely fought amongst themselves and were uncoordinated and ineffectual in their efforts to provide an economic model to challenge free-enterprise international capitalism.

The development of the European economic common market, and the slow evolution of genuine mobility of labor and capital, supported by regional institutions and motivated by the apparent desire to prevent downward harmonization and improved social development throughout the European community, contrasted with the developments across the ocean. The outstanding economic success of the United States, its use of covert or overt means, including preventing international loans to achieve regime change of unfriendly nationalist leaders, some of whom valued care and concern for their own citizens above the right of free international investment, the international popularity of Hollywood portrayals of the world, the growth of multinational corporations (the majority headquartered in the United States), some with more resources than medium-sized nations, and the growing tendency to conduct business in American English using American legal, accounting, technical practices, probably inclined many observers and leaders of the world to equate late 20th-century globalization with Americanization.

Modern globalization. The fall of the Berlin Wall and disintegration of the Soviet empire seemed to accelerate the processes and deepen the consequences of America-centric international integration and globalization. The evolution of an unchallenged hyper-superpower, the apparent success and dominance of deregulation and privatization in the publicized economic policies of the successful candidates of both U.S. political parties, seemed very important in terms of establishing another new paradigm of globalization.

Deregulated and privatized globalization, dating from the late 1970s, has characterized the integrated practices of those institutions in the UN dealing with the international monetary regime—the WORLD BANK, the INTERNATIONAL MONETARY FUND (IMF), and the successor to the GENERAL AGREEMENT ON TARIFFS AND TRADE (GATT), the WORLD TRADE ORGANIZATION (WTO). The United States supplies the multilateral lending institutions with the most funds of all UN members, and has taken a pre-eminent position with near-veto power in developing lending policies and economic development models in the tool kits of UN financial lenders and managers.

This model of economic development for the poor and transitional countries of the world, is now identified as "the Washington Consensus" and is articulated by neo-liberal economists, whose views of mixed capitalist economics seem to neglect or forget that the regulation and tariff protection of infant industries was very important in allowing the United States and other great economic powers to successfully build their own economies.

For most developing countries, except those with oil to export, virtually the only way to engage in economic development is to secure international financing for projects beyond the capacities of their weak economies and revenue structures. To qualify for international loans from most major banks, the IMF or World Bank must certify the borrower's willingness to service the debt. IMF counselors have established a standard, which requires the loan recipient to agree to structural adjustment plans. These often include: trade liberalization to encourage international investors; reducing and ending tariffs that may have protected infant industry; privatization of public sector enterprises and rationalizing public sector work by downsizing and reducing the number of public employees; ending subsidies for food products and services; devaluation of local currency; and expanding export production.

From the perspective of the bankers, investors, and multinational corporations these structural adjustments provide a stable environment in which to invest, they hasten movement from barter to monetized economies, remove inefficiencies of publicly owned enterprises and surplus labor, and assure that at least the interest, if not the principal, on previous loans will be repaid.

From the perspective of the workers, farmers, and the poor, the effects of these policies have been to increase the cost of food and services, to increase the unemployment rate, often to discourage enforcement of labor law, thereby reducing union membership and power, lowering the number of school attendees and the availability of medical care, and driving many economic refugees behind the fences of international sweatshop and *maquiladora* or "offshore" production facilities. The Washington Consensus, in its structural adjustment plans, does not value well-paid labor as imports are to be discouraged and the increased money from exports should be used to service the debt. Companies threaten to move and thus further erode the bargaining power of workers, in both industrial and poor countries. Some are willing to abandon their disposable fixed capital, even after bargaining to gain concessions, in large part because of the incentives provided by the new host nation in the form of rapid depreciation, lower taxes, low or no environmental regulation, and wages a fraction of the rates at home, in pursuit of much higher profits and lower costs in even lower-wage countries.

A truly globalized world, international relations expert Joseph Nye points out, "would mean free flows of goods, people, and capital, and similar interest rates." But in modern globalization, close to 70 percent of the GOODS, which are exchanged, are transferred between branches of multinational corporations. Capital flows have increased in speed, frequency and volume ($150 billion per day in 1973; $1.5 trillion per day in 1995), and massive transfers happen instantaneously, sometimes with disastrous results, as with the 1997 ASIAN FINANCIAL CRISIS that affected the whole international community. Borders are still relatively impervious for people, who have little legal opportunity to move to high-wage nations, but who often feel blessed with good fortune of having any job and receiving a few dollars a day working in sweatshop conditions in what used to be called "duty free" or "off shore" zones.

Globalization certainly has not meant the creation of a universal community. In social and political terms, some citizens of the third world view the United States as "the great Satan." The major targets of the September 11, 2001 terrorists were economic and military symbols of America-centric globalization, the World Trade Center and the Pentagon, and perhaps the White House. The United States votes against the majority of the world in the UN General Assembly about 88 percent of the time. There are other aspects of globalization, for instance: U.S. fast-food culture is everywhere, even if it includes local recipes and specials on the menu, and has prompted an international "slow food" movement. Many U.S. standards are pervasive, including English spoken by all air-traffic controllers around the world, international internet protocols, securities laws and practices, and drug regulation, and most nations scorn the United States' refusal or inability to move to the metric system. It also appears many world leaders are repulsed by American capital punishment and the prevalence and hallowedness of gun ownership.

Interdependence and technology have clearly increased the speed and pervasiveness of both real and virtual viruses. Historians point out that it took 3,000 years for smallpox to reach every continent on the globe, while AIDS has only taken three decades. Various strains of the flu from across the oceans inspire the necessary flu shots every fall. Virus protection is also part of the clear growth industry of computer software, largely because it only took three days for the "Filipino Love Bug" to affect major computer systems all over the world. The speed, complexity, short reaction time, participation of hackers and networking interdependence of corporations and increased uncertainty, will very likely create greater instability and a number of panics in the future.

Differential consequences. Most of the indices of globalization reflect the great benefits that have accrued to the Western industrial nations and the financial elites in the third world. Until the recession beginning in 2000, per capita income in the United States, Europe, JAPAN, AUSTRALIA, and New Zealand had shown substantial increases. Although the disproportionate growth was in the top 10 percent of each population, many economists point out that the bottom 70 percent have had stagnant or declining incomes in the last three decades. For neo-liberal economists, the free market unfettered by government regulation has allowed tremendous increases in entrepreneurial creativity and economic growth. As Milton FRIEDMAN noted, advocates of freedom do not count the heads of those who succeed. What is important is the opportunity, even if it results in the richest three individuals in the world owning more wealth than the bottom 40 percent of the world's population. Aside from a few countries in east Asia, that had substantial economic growth until the late 1990s, the Latin American economy has stagnated for two decades, and economic growth of African nations has declined. About a 100th of the population of Africa has access to the internet.

Besides increased world per-capita income and growing inequality, there are some interesting economic effects. Critics of globalization point to a general belt-tightening over hungry stomachs, increasing joblessness, internal migration and suffering, structural adjustment plans that have predictable, and perhaps intended but unspoken results. Since there are few finished products that can compete with those from developed industrial producers, most of the legal exports to earn foreign exchange to service growing debt are primary commodities, such as ore, bananas, and coffee.

Other indebted states in the same climatic and geographic regions have to play by the same rules, thus increasing the supply of similar primary products. The market works well for these commodities, thus prices fall. As export prices decline by a third, the primary exporting country must produce 50 percent more to raise the same earnings. As each producer nation scrambles to increase production, prices fall further. Profits for the foreign and indigenous transporters, merchandisers, and owners increase and widen the gap between the rich and the poor. The benefits accrue to the importing nations with stable tax bases and high employment, as well as to fat bank accounts and investors seeking more profitable opportunities. This asymmetrically beneficial exchange usually flows to the same states that have adamantly refused to establish much sought-after commodity price agreements hoped for by the primary product exporters. The cumulative effect of worsening terms of trade, and less return for more work, increases the perception of illegitimate rules and practices controlled by the rich and successful states and their local allies.

Critics of globalization also point to another perverse consequence, clearly intended, and which benefits important political constituencies in the rich nations. As tariff barriers are removed, "inefficient" producers of commodities, such as food grains in poor countries can no longer compete with the often highly subsidized and high-technology industrial agribusinesses, which now have new markets for their corn, rice, and wheat. For example, price caps and subsidies for tortillas in MEXICO must be removed as part of the conditionality of the structural adjustment plans required of a debtor country, as well as, requirements of membership in the WTO and the North American Free Trade Agreement (NAFTA), but agricultural subsidies continue for the agribusiness exporters, in large part because of the power of important constituencies in industrial nations. Thus, subsistence farmers who used to be able to sell their small surplus are now required to participate in a monetized economy and to pay for "cheap" imported grain from the industrial societies in order to eat.

The falling prices of exports, and the non-competitiveness of indigenous grain producers facing agribusiness imports, has driven and will continue to drive many small producers into illegal crops, such as coca, heroin poppies, and marijuana. This will provide some cash to participate in the monetized economy, but not substantially increase the quality of caloric intake. It also provides a rationale for the industrial countries to continue their global war on drugs, and for enriching shady elites in both rich and poor nations who are not caught.

Economic downturns in developed countries increase the rigidity of debt servicing, thus there is more austerity for the indebted, less forgiveness of the poorest indebted countries, and growing transfer of wealth from the poor to the rich.

Reactions to the consequences of globalization. The articulated and rational critique of the consequences of the international political economy dominated by rules favorable to mobile capital and free enterprise (or no rules), have been around since the first radical challengers to capitalism in the 19th century. But the late 20th-century developments, perhaps fueled by the absence of working alternatives to democratic capitalism, have turned sporadic and unconnected protests into worldwide protests. Demonstrators shadow the industrial giants, the G-8, at international finance meetings regarding the WTO, the Multilateral Agreement on Investment, NAFTA, and the Free Trade Act of the Americas often in proximity to the IMF and World Bank institutions, organized by new and grassroots-accessible communication tools such as the internet. The effective organization of worldwide critics of the multilateral agreement on investment by Australian and Canadian net workers, brought a premature end to an agreement which would have benefited international investors protected by secret processes that seemed to give more rights to corporations than to citizens.

The growing perception that the rules and institutions of the global economy have lost their legitimacy, has led to a number of trends as we move into the 21st century. The U.S. drive for greater economic growth and more flexible sovereign autonomy may have motivated the superpower's unilateral withdrawal from a number of international treaties such as the Kyoto Protocol on global warming, the International Criminal Court, and anti-ballistic missile treaties. There are plausible claims that the United States may have, as its primary motivation in attacking the regime of Saddam Hussein, the desire to control directly the 13 percent of the world oil reserves underneath Iraqi territory.

In the early 2000s, the regular criticism of U.S. policies by most members of the United Nations seems to heighten the American willingness to go it alone and give up on multilateral institutions. Major critics of the current neo-liberal international monetary regime have won recent elections in Latin America. Participants of the World Social Forum, established in Porto Alegre, Brazil, in 1999 and founded as a counterpoint to the world economic forum held annually by the G8 SUMMIT in Davos, Switzerland, feel that it is possible to change the rules set by the current international monetary elite, particularly those dealing with a deregulated, pro-corporate model for the economy.

The current challengers will have to figure out how to convince electorates and the media about the need for greater autonomy for nations in how they participate in the world economy, for example, by regulating foreign investment to suit domestic needs. A specific idea has been floated: There could be a small fractional tax on global currency and financial transactions to deter some speculative capital flows and at the same time generate funds for development and debt-servicing by poor nations. Other items on the challengers' agenda include establishing more regulations at the international level to provide protections and standards for workers, the environment, and the poor that most industrial nations enacted to try to tame the extremes of capitalism, as noted by Charles Dickens and Karl Marx at the end of the 19th century and early years of the 20th century.

Absent a powerful government at the international level willing to enact regulations such as Franklin D. ROOSEVELT's NEW DEAL in the United States, this will be very difficult. Without the development of much more critical thinking in the United States about globalization and its relatively few beneficiaries, success of proposed reforms to globalizations seem doubtful.

BIBLIOGRAPHY. Daniel Drezner, "Bottom Feeders," *Foreign Policy* (November, 2000); Jeff Faux, "The Global Alternative," *The American Prospect* (July 2001); Thomas Friedman, *The Lexus and the Olive Tree* (Anchor Books, 2000); William Greider, *One World, Ready or Not: The Manic Logic of Global Capitalism* (Touchstone, 1998); Joseph Nye, *The Para-*dox of American Power* (Oxford University Press, 2002); Joseph Stiglitz, *Globalization and its Discontents* (W.W Norton, 2002).

CHARLES WEED, PH.D.
KEENE STATE COLLEGE

gold standard

EXPRESSING THE VALUE of a country's currency in the form of gold was first established by England in the 18th century, and the gold standard existed in some form throughout the 19th century. However, the use of gold as a medium of payment has been in existence for centuries: It was perhaps the only universal form of currency. The introduction of paper money and coinage was made for convenience and safety; carrying gold was not a very safe activity, thus paper currency and coinage became a medium of exchange.

In the UNITED STATES, there existed a bimetal standard, using both gold and silver. However, by the middle of the 19th century, the United States converted to a full gold standard and fixed the price of gold in 1834, at $20.67 per ounce. This price did not change until the initial demise of the gold standard during WORLD WAR I.

The idea behind the gold standard was for every participating country to fix the price of gold according to their currency, then the exchange rate between currencies could be easily calculated. Since the price of gold was fixed in various countries, the prices of commodities were also fixed and over time these prices had a tendency of moving together. This was a de facto, fixed-exchange-rate system that was adopted by the member countries.

The gold standard required that the member countries follow certain rules. First, the price of gold had to be fixed in terms of the local currency. Second, member nations had to allow for free import and export of gold. Third, the country had to allow for free conversion of the domestic currency in lieu of gold and vice versa. Fourth, the country could not impose any restriction on the coinage of gold, and gold had to be considered legal tender within the country.

Once all this was achieved, the country saw an automatic adjustment of its balance of payments, due to the existence of the gold standard system. This system was also referred to as the Classical Gold Standard system. The outcomes of the gold standard system followed the classical principles of equilibrium, and the idea that very little government intervention was required.

The benefit of the gold standard was that the U.S. domestic economy saw very little inflation. From 1870–1914 the inflation rate in the United States averaged about 0.1 percent. A similar comparison from 1946–90 saw U.S. inflation at an average of 4.2 percent. The price stability is achieved by adhering to the rules mentioned earlier. As the domestic economy demands more foreign commodities, it results in an outflow of gold. This causes a decline in the money supply that will result in a reduction in the price level. In the foreign country, the inflow of gold in lieu of the commodities sold will increase the money supply and thus cause an increase in the price level. The pattern of trade will reverse and now the foreign country starts importing more commodities. Trade balance will thus be achieved in both countries.

Any discovery of gold will lead to temporary changes in the price level, but the long-run effect is negligible. The discovery of gold in California is one such example of instability in the United States. With the California Gold Rush of 1848, the money supply in the United States increased, which, in turn, increased nominal income and thus lead to an increase in imports. With the resultant increase in the gold outflow from the United States, this caused a trade deficit in the United States and a trade surplus in the exporting nations. Although initially the discovery of gold led to an increase in the amount of output produced, it eventually led to only an increase in the price level.

The gold standard allowed for stable prices in the member countries, however, it did not allow for any possibility of using macroeconomic policies to address any problems in the economy. Thus, while price fluctuations were held under check, the output fluctuated significantly.

As Europe and North America plunged into World War I, member nations started overlooking the rules of the gold standard and thus the entire system was abolished. Between World War I and II, a makeshift arrangement was created that aimed to bring some stability into the system. The Great DEPRESSION, it is argued by some, was precipitated by the inaction of the U.S. government that was required by the gold standard system to not act in response to the economic alarms of 1929–30.

After WORLD WAR II, in a meeting at BRETTON WOODS, New Hampshire, world leaders and economists devised an alternative plan to address the issue of price stability and removing the uncertainty over trading with each other. The plan called for the U.S. DOLLAR to be the primary currency. The value of gold was fixed at $35 per ounce and the value of the other currencies was fixed against the U.S. dollar. The countries were encouraged to hold dollar-denominated assets, as they were assured that the United States would exchange the dollar bills for gold at the fixed exchange rate.

This system performed well in the 1950s and 1960s, when the U.S. currency was considered to be the most valuable asset in the world. In the late 1960s, the United States started experiencing a trade deficit and a loss of competitiveness. This coupled with a declining value of the dollar, forced many nations to relinquish the dollar and ask for gold in exchange for it. President Richard NIXON signed an order in 1971 that eliminated the gold standard system. Currencies thus did not have any backing, other than the government's seal.

There is still some support in academia and the business community to revert back to the gold standard system. The attraction primarily stems from the price stability that is possible. Another benefit, as viewed by these individuals, is the lack of control exhibited by policy makers. The assumption here is that human intervention is based on personal agenda and not sound economic principles, thus it is liable to do more harm than good. Also, the gold standard system was a fixed-exchange rate system. With all the fluctuations in the exchange rates in the world today it seems preferable to revert to a fixed-exchange rate system.

The gold standard system was a very useful tool for a specific time in human history. Under current circumstances, when the focus is on targeting both inflation and unemployment, using Keynesian type policies, it is not possible to see how the gold standard could be revived. Present-day economies are unwilling to forgo control over economic policies and rely on a system of gold inflow and outflow to bring domestic equilibrium. Nonetheless, the gold standard system allows world economies and academics to critically evaluate present economic policies based on the outcomes achieved under the gold standard system.

BIBLIOGRAPHY. Michael Bordo, "Gold Standard," www.econlib.org/library; Brad DeLong, "Why Not the Gold Standard? Talking Points on the Likely Consequences of Re-Establishment of a Gold Standard," www.j-bradford-delong.net; Dominick Salvatore, *International Economics* (Prentice Hall, 2002); Robert Carbaugh, *International Economics* (Southwestern, 2001); Campbell McConnell and Stanley Brue, *Economics: Principles, Problems and Policies* (McGraw-Hill, 2002).

JAISHANKAR RAMAN, PH.D.
VALPARAISO UNIVERSITY

goods

THINGS THAT SATISFY human needs and desires, goods are often physical objects, such as cars and loaves of bread, but they can also be intangible, such as software and technological methods. Goods can satisfy human needs either directly, like a loaf of bread, or indirectly, like the oven and ingredients used to make the bread.

As central as goods are to any economic system—and indeed, to human survival itself—modern economists spend very little time thinking about what they are. Many undergraduate economics textbooks contain no definition of the term, though they discuss various types of goods at great length. Even some dictionaries of economics fail to define the term "good."

The reason for this apparent lack of interest is that by the end of the 20th century, economists had settled most of the fundamental questions about goods. A few disputes still remained, such as whether the value of goods could be quantified, or whether a consumer truly could be indifferent between two goods. But on the big issues of what goods are and why they are valuable, economists—though probably not people in general—are in almost unanimous agreement.

Goods satisfy human needs and desires, but not all goods are studied by economics. In order to be an economic good, a good must be scarce—that is, there must be less of the good than would satisfy all human desires for it. If a good is not scarce, it is a "free good" and is not studied by economics. Breathable air, for example, is a good, but is not now an economic good because it is not scarce compared to human needs for it. Drinkable water, on the other hand, has become sufficiently scarce that bottled water sales are booming in many areas.

The economic value of goods is determined by three main factors:

1. the intensity of human need and/or desire

2. scarcity

3. the availability of substitutes.

Thus, the value of goods combines both subjective (human need or desire) and objective (scarcity, availability of substitutes) elements.

In economics, these factors are often expressed in terms of SUPPLY and DEMAND curves that show how the quantities supplied and demanded of a good change based on changes in the price. For normal goods, consumers tend to buy more at lower prices and less at higher prices. Conversely, suppliers tend to produce less at lower prices and more at higher prices. A demand curve shows the different quantities of a good that consumers will want to buy at different prices. A supply curve shows the different quantities of a good that producers will want to make and sell at different prices.

The price at which consumers want to buy the same quantity that suppliers want to sell is called the market-clearing price and is the economic value of the good. This value can easily change, such as when consumer tastes shift or a new substitute comes onto the market.

Historically, the value of goods was thought to be derived from the labor required to make them. The two most famous advocates of this view were Adam SMITH, best known as a free-market supporter and founder of modern economics; and Karl MARX, best known as a social-control supporter and a founder of communism.

Smith's version of the labor theory of value was more sophisticated than Marx's, mainly because Smith was inconsistent about applying the theory and Marx wasn't. Smith wrote that: "Labor alone, therefore, never varying in its own value, is alone the ultimate and real standard by which the value of all commodities can at all times and places be estimated and compared. It is their real price: money is their nominal price only."

However, only 26 pages later in his *Wealth of Nations*, Smith modifies his theory and observes that supply and demand are key determinants of the economic value of goods: "The market price of every particular commodity is regulated by the proportion between the quantity which is actually brought to market, and the demand of those who are willing to pay the natural price of the commodity." In his personal life, Smith was notoriously absent-minded, and that trait occasionally seemed to serve him well in economics when he forgot the flawed labor theory of value and relied on his observation of markets.

Marx dealt with the same problem by distinguishing between the use value and the exchange value of commodities (goods). Marx argued that although exchange value was affected by other factors, the use value of a good was determined solely by the amount of labor required to produce it: "A use-value, or useful article, has value only because human labor in the abstract has been embodied or materialized in it. How, then, is the magnitude of this value to be measured? Plainly, by the quantity of the value-creating substance, the labor, contained in the article."

A modern variant of the labor theory of value is the cost-of-production theory: that the fair price of a good is the cost of making it, plus a small amount of profit. This is the common-sense view of many people. However, goods' cost of production does not reflect their actual economic value, and economics has nothing to say about what prices are "fair."

There are two main types of goods. Consumer goods are those that directly satisfy human needs and desires. Examples of consumer goods are bread, automobiles, comic books, shoes, and music compact discs. Capital goods are those used to create consumer goods. That is, capital goods are those that indirectly satisfy human needs and desires by helping produce goods that satisfy them directly. Examples of capital goods are flour (to make bread), steel, glass, and rubber (to make automobiles), paper and ink (to print comic books), leather (to make shoes) and petroleum by-products (to make compact discs).

Whether a good is a consumer good or a capital good depends on its use. The same good can be a consumer good in one use and a capital good in another use. For example, if a computer is used for playing games, it is a consumer good. If the same computer is used a few hours later for writing a business report, it is a capital good.

Substitutes are goods that, as their name implies, can substitute for each other. A jacket and a sweater are substitutes; taking the bus or riding a bicycle is a substitute for driving a car. The availability of attractive substitutes tends to reduce the economic value of goods. Conversely, the absence of substitutes tends to increase the economic value of goods. If two goods are substitutes for each other, an increase in the price of one tends to increase the demand for the other because the substitute has become less attractive.

Complementary goods are those that go together and are less attractive alone. Gasoline and automobiles are an example of complementary goods. The availability of complementary goods tends to increase the economic value of goods for which they are complementary. Conversely, the absence of complementary goods tends to decrease the economic value of their complements. If two goods are complementary, an increase in the price of one tends to decrease the demand of the other because the two goods are normally used together.

Giffen goods are an unusual class of consumer goods in that people buy more of them at higher prices. This is an unusual but not unheard-of phenomenon. The appeal of higher-priced Giffen goods is due mainly to:

1. consumers' perception that a higher price means higher quality

2. consumers' sense of social status attached to paying a higher price for certain goods.

Thus, consumers might prefer an expensive compact disc player because they assume it is of higher quality than a cheaper model, even if they can't hear any difference. Likewise, they might prefer an expensive pair of sneakers because of the social status attached to the brand-name logo they bear, even though the sneakers are no better in manufacturing quality than much cheaper brands.

Public goods are those that are scarce and valuable but considered difficult to sell as commercial products. A public good is "an economic good which, by its nature, cannot be provided separately to each individual, but must be provided, or not provided, to all the members of a pre-existing group," explains economist David Friedman. The problem in providing public goods in a commercial market is that, because such goods must be provided to all people in the market, then if they are provided at all, they cease to be scarce and producers find it difficult to charge for them. If some consumers decide not to pay for the public good, they still receive it: they are "free riders" on the producers and on those who pay for the good. For those reasons, public goods are usually provided by governments and supported by taxes. However, some economists contend that there are no public goods; other economists argue that most goods claimed as public goods could be provided as commercial products.

BIBLIOGRAPHY. Ludwig von Mises, *Human Action* (Mises Institute, 1998); Adam Smith, *The Wealth of Nations* (University of Chicago Press, 1976): Karl Marx, *Capital*, (Modern Library, 1960): David Friedman, *The Machinery of Freedom* (Arlington House Publishers, 1978); Murray N. Rothbard, *Power and Market* (Institute for Humane Studies, 1970).

SCOTT PALMER, PH.D.
RGMS ECONOMICS

Gorbachev, Mikhail (1931–)

LEADER OF THE SOVIET UNION from 1985 to 1991, Mikhail Gorbachev was born in the village of Privolnoye and raised in Stavropol, an agricultural region of southern Russia. He grew up on a collective farm and was influenced by both of his grandfathers. One of them, a *kulak* (relatively prosperous peasant) taught him a work ethic; the other, a committed communist, helped form Gorbachev's political outlook. Gorbachev distinguished himself early in life. While in high school he won the Hero of Socialist Labor award for his work as a tractor driver.

This earned him a scholarship to the prestigious Moscow State University. Instead of studying engineering or some technical trade, a path to professional success that was quite popular at the time, Gorbachev studied law, receiving a degree in 1955. While in Moscow he married Raisa Maksimova Titorenko, a woman who would attract much attention in both the Soviet Union and abroad in the 1980s with her glamorous and sophisticated demeanor, a role quite unlike the usual wives of Soviet leaders, who kept low profiles in public life. He joined the Communist Party in 1952, a move necessary for further professional advancement in a socialist country where the government owned and operated all institutions, and where Party officials ran the government.

Gorbachev returned to Stavropol, where he served as first secretary in organizations of increasing importance: from 1958 to 1962 he served in the Stavropol Territory Komsomol (Young Communist League), the leading Party-run youth organization; in 1966 he was on the Stavropol City Communist Party Committee;

from 1970 to 1978 he led the Stavropol Territory Communist Party Committee. In 1967, he earned a graduate degree in agronomy. In 1971, he became a member of the Central Committee of the Communist Party of the Soviet Union. The Central Committee was important because its members, several hundred in number, were all leading Party officials who elected the Politburo, a committee of 10-15 men who ran the country.

Gorbachev did more than just obtain leadership positions. Through his diligence, engaging manner, and public speaking ability, he gained the attention of Soviet leaders. It didn't hurt that Stavropol was a vacation spot for the Communist elite. In the early 1970s, he was in charge of improving agriculture and undertook various reforms to increase production. His experimentation focused on trying to reduce bureaucracy and give incentives for extra work. He broke up large collective farms and promoted the use of small work teams that could work on their own. In the 1970s, few Soviet leaders undertook initiatives with their own ideas. Gorbachev's telegenic presence became an even greater asset at a time when more and more Soviet citizens were purchasing televisions.

Yuri Andropov, head of the KGB (state security service) recognized Gorbachev's dynamism and effectiveness as a leader and brought him to Moscow as a lower member of the Politburo, the top committee that governed the country. Gorbachev was put in charge of agricultural affairs in 1978. Andropov promoted Gorbachev as someone capable of leading the nation through its serious systemic problems.

Andropov was more aware than most officials of the moribund nature of the Soviet economy and bureaucracy. After the older generation of communist leaders died (Leonid Brezhnev in 1982, Yuri Andropov in 1984, and Konstantin Chernenko in 1985), Gorbachev was chosen as the new Soviet leader at the age of 54, the youngest man to hold the position since Josef Stalin in the 1920s. This meant that he held the top Party post, general secretary of the Communist Party.

Within his first two years Gorbachev worked to bring in a new generation of leaders, decentralized power to local officials, and in 1989 organized the first free, competitive elections in Russia since 1917. He carried two broad programs: *glasnost* or openness, which allowed freedom of speech; and *perestroika* or economic restructuring, which sought to break down the old centralized administrative command structure of the Soviet economy. Gorbachev also signed an Intermediate Nuclear Forces (INF) arms-limitation treaty with the UNITED STATES in 1987, and encouraged the Soviets' Eastern European "satellite" countries to liberalize economically and politically. In 1989, he ended the Soviet occupation of Afghanistan, 10 years after the Soviet invasion that had brought an end to the period of *détente* (when East and West had sought a relaxation of Cold War tensions). Gorbachev also released political prisoners and permitted greater numbers of Soviet citizens to emigrate, a move that began the largest wave of immigration to Israel since the creation of that state in 1948.

The new political liberties contributed to Gorbachev's fall from power and the dissolution of the Soviet Union. Long-suppressed national tensions in the Baltics, other Slavic republics such as Belarus and Ukraine, as well as Soviet republics in the Caucasus and Central Asia, sought autonomy or outright independence. In August 1991, while Gorbachev was vacationing on the Black Sea, Soviet hardliners attempted a coup d'etat against Gorbachev and the government in an effort to halt the breakdown of the Union, which was made up of 15 constituent socialist republics and hundreds of nationalities. Although the coup failed, afterward Gorbachev found himself powerless over the new authority of Boris Yeltsin, who had been elected president of the Russian Republic of the Soviet Union. On December 8, 1991, Russia, Belarus, and Ukraine agreed to form the Commonwealth of Independent States, a loose confederation of almost all of the Soviet republics. The CIS made the Soviet Union obsolete, and on December 25, 1991, Gorbachev resigned his position and dissolved the Union of Soviet Socialist Republics.

Although Gorbachev unsuccessfully ran for president of Russia in 1996, he has been active in various endeavors. He won the Nobel Peace Prize in 1990. In 1993, he became president of the Green Cross International, an environmental organization that he founded. He also heads the Gorbachev Foundation, established in December 1991, a self-described international nongovernmental foundation for socio-economic and political studies.

BIBLIOGRAPHY. A. Brown, *The Gorbachev Factor* (Oxford University Press, 1996); Richard Sakwa, *Gorbachev and His Reforms, 1985-1990* (Prentice Hall, 1991). Mikhail Gorbachev, *Perestroika: A New Thinking for Our Country and the World* (Collins, 1987); Stephen White, *Gorbachev in Power* (Cambridge University Press, 1990); Anders Aslund, *Gorbachev's Struggle for Economic Reform* (Cornell University Press, 1991).

GEORGE KOSAR, PH.D.
BRANDEIS UNIVERSITY

Gordon, Robert J. (1940–)

ONE OF THE MOST PROLIFIC contemporary economists, Robert J. Gordon has fundamentally advanced our knowledge of MACROECONOMICS processes, economic growth and economic policy, by addressing economic theory, empirical testing of theory, and detailed methodology of measuring relevant variables.

Gordon attended Harvard and Oxford universities before earning his Ph.D. at the Massachusetts Institute of Technology in 1967. Most recently the Stanley Harris Professor of the Social Sciences at Northwestern University, Gordon was appointed professor of economics at Northwestern University in 1973. Previously, he taught at Harvard University and the University of Chicago. He has spent more than 25 years as a research associate at the National Bureau of Economic Research. In addition, Gordon has served as a research Fellow at the Centre for Economic Policy Research in London, a senior advisor to the Brookings Panel of Economic Activity, and on the Economic Advisory Panel of the Congressional Budget Office and the Economic Advisory Panel of the Bureau of Economic Analysis.

Gordon has examined the causes and consequences of inflation and unemployment, theoretically and empirically. He has modeled and estimated PHILLIP'S CURVE relationships between inflation and unemployment, along with a host of related dynamics of wage growth, output growth, and productivity growth. His work has helped explain the inflation of the 1970s, and the productivity slowdown of the 1970s and 1980s. This work has enhanced our understanding of key macroeconomic dynamics such as BUSINESS CYCLES and changes in the rate of UNEMPLOYMENT consistent with constant INFLATION.

Gordon's related work on precise measurement of prices, output, and productivity, at both industry and aggregate levels, has broached many of the subtleties of accounting for quality change in specific rapidly evolving industries, such as computers or banking. Gordon's work has influenced revisions of the Consumer Price Index and estimates of trends in productivity growth.

His analysis of macroeconomic variables and business cycles extends to international and historical dimensions. He has compared U.S., European, and Japanese performance with respect to productivity, wages, and unemployment. Gordon has also examined long-term productivity growth in the United States, price movements and U.S. policy between 1890 and 1980, and compared current and late 19th-century technical change.

Recently, Gordon has emerged as a leading skeptic of "new economy" arguments, that he claims overestimate the significance of information-based technical change in the 1990s. Gordon was one of the first to argue that the productivity boom of the 1990s was fragile because it partially reflected the upward swing of a strong business cycle as well as a temporary surge in computer investment.

Overall, Gordon's work has contributed to the development of capitalism by offering substantial theoret-ical, empirical and measurement tools relevant to business cycles, economic growth, inflation, unemployment and related policies.

BIBLIOGRAPHY. Robert J. Gordon and W. Franz, "German and American Wage and Price Dynamics: Differences and Common Trends," *European Economic Review* (v.37/2, 1993); Robert J. Gordon, "The Productivity Slowdown, Measurement Issues, and the Explosion of Computer Power," *Brookings Papers on Economic Activity* (v.19/2, 1988); Robert J. Gordon, "Does the New Economy Measure Up to the Great Inventions of the Past?" *Journal of Economic Perspectives* (v.14/4, 2000).

WILLIAM D. FERGUSON
GRINNELL COLLEGE

Gould, Jay (1836–92)

BORN IN NEW YORK as Jason, Jay Gould has come to be known as one of the most ruthless financiers in American capitalist history. He rose to control over half the railroad mileage in the southwest, New York City's elevated railroads, and the Western Union Telegraph Company.

Beginning at age 21 with $5,000, Gould speculated in the securities of small railroads. He became director of the Erie Railroad by joining with James FISK and Daniel Drew to defeat Cornelius VANDERBILT for control of the railroad, often using unscrupulous tactics such as issuing false stock and bribing regulators to legalize fraud.

In 1869, along with Fisk, Gould manipulated and cornered the gold market, resulting in the "Black Friday" panic that ruined many investors. Due to public protest, Gould and his group were forced out of the Erie Railroad.

Subsequently, Gould bought into the Union Pacific Railroad and other western lines, eventually gaining control of four major railroads. His intent was not to build and grow these rail lines but to manipulate their stock for his personal profit.

Leaving $77 million upon his death, Gould is best known in the annals of 19th-century capitalism as one of the "robber barons."

BIBLIOGRAPHY. "The Robber Barons," www.pbs.org; Maury Klein, "Overrated and Underrated Robber Baron," www.americanheritage.com; "Jay Gould" *Encyclopaedia Britannica* (2000).

LINDA L. PETROU, PH.D.
HIGH POINT UNIVERSITY

Grant, Ulysses S. (1822–85)

THE 18TH PRESIDENT of the UNITED STATES, Hiram Ulysses Grant was born in rural Ohio. His father arranged for Grant's appointment to West Point military academy without his knowledge. Upon arrival, Grant found that he had been mistakenly listed as Ulysses Simpson Grant—the name he went by from then on. After graduation, Grant served with distinction in the MEXICAN-AMERICAN WAR. Peacetime, however, proved frustrating. Underpaid, forced to leave his family behind, and dealing with a difficult commanding officer, Grant resigned from the army in 1854. He tried a series of civilian jobs but was unsuccessful. Then, the AMERICAN CIVIL WAR began.

Grant commanded the 21st Illinois Regiment before being appointed general. A string of advances in Tennessee brought him to national prominence, and after his capture of Vicksburg, in 1863, and other successes, President Abraham LINCOLN put him in command of all U.S. forces.

Grant proposed an ambitions plan to make simultaneous movements on all fronts. The South had great generals, but was not well enough equipped to compete with the North on all fronts at the same time. Despite suffering bloody losses, Grant continued to advance. Within a year, the South was decimated and Confederate commander General Robert E. Lee surrendered.

Grant remained commander of the army after the war. President Andrew JOHNSON appointed him acting secretary of war, but when the removal of Grant's predecessor resulted in Johnson's impeachment, Grant decided to resign the Cabinet position.

Grant was the overwhelming choice for president in 1868. He entered office with no clear agenda and let Congress set policy. The main issue of the day was Reconstruction, rebuilding the South after the war. Grant supported efforts to protect the rights of the freedmen against a hostile white majority, but the efforts proved half-hearted, as Southern whites were able to retake control.

During the Civil War, the federal government had issued paper money without any backing by specie (gold or silver). Grant agreed to redeem the greenbacks for specie. This prevented runaway inflation, but upset westerners who hoped that inflation would reduce their debts.

Grant's two presidential terms are mainly remembered for their scandals. One was an attempt by two speculators to corner the gold market in 1869. Their attempt counted on the government not to release gold reserves as the price increased. Grant's brother-in-law and senior officials were in on the deal. However, when the attempt resulted in financial panic and caught Grant's attention, he fired those responsible and released government gold into the market.

The Credit Mobilier scandal involved stock sales to key government officials, including Vice President Schuyler Colfax, at reduced prices. Congress then gave the company lucrative government contracts and stockholders garnered hefty dividends. Congress considered impeaching Colfax. Though not pursued, he did not run again in 1872.

Grant was never implicated personally in any of the scandals. However, he was criticized for standing by his aides even after their guilt was well known and for failing to set stronger ethical standards.

Many Republican leaders encouraged Grant to run for a third term, but the Party decided against it due to the precedent of a two-term limit. His name was proposed again at the 1880 convention, but he was not nominated. Grant left office destitute, and proceeded to engage in business ventures that failed. To support himself, he began writing his memoirs, which were published posthumously.

BIBLIOGRAPHY. Ulysses S. Grant, *Personal Memoirs* (1886, William Konecky, 1999); Brooks Simpson, *The Reconstruction Presidents* (University Press of Kansas, 1998); Jean Edward Smith, *Grant* (Simon & Schuster, 2001).

MICHAEL J. TROY, J.D.
THOMAS D. JEITSCHKO, PH.D.
MICHIGAN STATE UNIVERSITY

Greece

THE COUNTRY OF GREECE, located in southeast Europe in the Balkan region, has a Mediterranean climate, a mountainous landscape and over 2,000 islands with vast access to the Mediterranean Sea.

The country has a population of more than 10 million people with 60 percent living in cities such as the ancient capital of Athens. The major ethnicity and language is Greek, the official religion is Greek Orthodoxy, and the currency is the euro. Currently, Greece is a multiparty republic with a developing private enterprise economy based on agriculture, manufacturing, and tourism.

Beginning with the Minoan civilization on Crete, the Greek peninsula has been a major influence on the development of Western civilization, including some components of capitalism. For instance, classical Greece had an economy based on markets but lacked full private ownership of surplus production. Interestingly, the role of seafaring for movement of goods and development of communication and exchange standards was a key to both ancient and modern Greek economic systems, capitalist and otherwise.

After the conquest of Greece by the Macedonians and Alexander the Great in the 4th century B.C.E., Greek culture was spread throughout the Macedonian Empire including the Hellenistic forms of the Greek economic systems. These systems would later influence Roman economic systems including old-world land and sea trade, much like modern global capitalism.

During the medieval period, Greece became a colony of various empires including the Eastern Orthodox Byzantine Empire, the Muslim Ottoman Turkish Empire, and at times, the Roman Catholic Austrian Habsburg Empire. Often utilized as a mercantile colony, Greece was unable to develop any permanent economic system of its own. Only in 1832 would it emerge independent from the Ottoman colonial and economic system. Even then, the Greek economy was often controlled by financial linkages with the great powers of Europe, including RUSSIA, England, and FRANCE. Permanent Greek independence did not manifest itself until after WORLD WAR I, when the turbulent Balkan region calmed. However, 20th-century capitalism failed to establish a lasting presence in Greece because of the WORLD WAR II Nazi occupation.

After the war, Greece fell into civil war with communist and capitalist forces vying for control. The strife lasted until 1949 when communist forces were defeated. However, the civil war left Greece with a mixed legacy concerning beliefs on communist and capitalist economic systems.

The ancient Greek tradition of seafaring helped capitalism gain a permanent foothold in Greece during the 20th century. It was a complex and fascinating set of events that led to the emergence of capitalism with Greek shipping empires. Rather than capitalism emerging from within Greece, it came from outside.

Greece, after centuries of external control, had little to offer in terms of surplus internal resources for a capitalist market. Instead, enterprising capitalists such as Aristotle Onassis turned to external resources in other capitalist markets before importing those resources back into Greece. For instance, Onassis borrowed funds and bought Canadian ships anchored in Rotterdam, the Netherlands, with Panamanian flags to establish his early shipping fleet. Greek shipping magnates became middlemen for moving World War II and Cold War resources around the globe. This planted the seeds of capitalism within Greece despite an uncooperative government and socialist-oriented economy. In particular, the role of oil in and after the Cold War provided opportunity for Greek capitalists to move foreign resources with foreign-built ships. This created links between Greece and a capitalist, Western economic system, culminating with Greece joining the North Atlantic Treaty Organization in 1952 and the EUROPEAN UNION in 1981.

The economy of modern Greece is still weak, but is expanding with the aid of outside sources. In 2000, the GROSS DOMESTIC PRODUCT (GDP) of Greece was estimated to be $181.9 billion. Greece's GDP breaks down into three categories. Services account for 62 percent, industry accounts for 23 percent, and agriculture accounts for 15 percent.

Tourism is Greece's largest industry and it is also the nation's only source of foreign-exchange earnings. Much of Greece's capitalist economy depends on the roles of importing and exporting. In 2000, Greece's imports were valued at $33.9 billion with its exports totaling only $15.8 billion. In recent years, Greece has worked to strengthen its economy by becoming a part of international economic systems. The country's economic expansion has resulted greatly from government programs, economic aid from the UNITED STATES, trade with the Middle East, and trade with other members of the EUROPEAN UNION.

BIBLIOGRAPHY. *Mark Kishlansky,* "Civilization in the West," (Encyclopedia Ameriana 2002); Andrew A. Freris, *The Greek Economy in the Twentieth Century* (Palgrave Macmillan, 1986); Jon V. Kofas, *Financial Relations of Greece and the Great Powers, 1832–1862* (Columbia University Press, 1981).

CHRIS HOWELL
RED ROCKS COLLEGE

The quaint villages of ancient Greece are one reason tourism is the nation's largest industry in the 2000s.

Greenspan, Alan (1926–)

A ONE-TIME ADVOCATE of the GOLD STANDARD who became chairman of the U.S. FEDERAL RESERVE system, Alan Greenspan presided over both the economic boom of the mid-1990s and the first deep recession of the 21st century.

Born on March 6, 1926 in New York City, Greenspan studied economics at New York University, where he earned his B.S. in 1948 and his M.A. in 1950. He began an economics Ph.D. program at Columbia University in 1950, but had to drop out for lack of money and take a job as an economist. NYU finally awarded Greenspan his economics Ph.D. in 1977 after he had already served (1974–77) as chairman of the COUNCIL OF ECONOMIC ADVISORS for President Gerald Ford. He also received honorary degrees from Harvard, Yale, and Notre Dame universities.

Though best known as a banker and economist, Greenspan started out as a student at New York's famous Julliard School of Music and found his first job in the late 1940s as a saxophone player in a swing band.

After leaving Columbia in 1954, Greenspan co-founded the economic consulting firm of Townsend-Greenspan & Co. and served as its chairman from 1954–74 and 1977–87. His career as a private-sector economic consultant was punctuated by frequent involvements in government, the first of which was as a policy advisor to the presidential campaign of Richard M. NIXON (1967–68). He was recruited for the post by his former bandmate Leonard Garment, who had become a lawyer and one of Nixon's campaign managers. After serving on Gerald Ford's economic team, President Ronald REAGAN appointed Greenspan chairman of the National Commission on Social Security Reform (1981–83), and then chairman of the U.S. Federal Reserve (the Fed), where he filled an unexpired term from 1987–91 and was reappointed by President William J. Clinton in 1992 to a 14-year term as chairman.

In 2000, Greenspan was awarded the Légion d'Honneur, the French government's highest honor. In 2002, he was made an honorary Knight Commander of the British Empire by the government of the United Kingdom.

During his tenure as Fed chairman, Greenspan's reputation at any given moment closely tracked the performance of the U.S. economy and stock market. In the last months of the 1990s economic boom, Senator Phil Gramm (himself a former economics professor) hailed Greenspan as "the greatest central banker in the history of the world." Two laudatory books told his story. However, after the recession of 2001 began and the stock market began to slide, Greenspan was criticized for his apparent failure to recognize and stop the economic "bubble" that had artificially inflated the late-1990s U.S. economy to unsustainable levels.

Indeed, Greenspan had in 1996 warned against the "irrational exuberance" of the U.S. stock market, but he had taken no action for fear of causing the recession, which by then was inevitable. Five years later, the recession began—worse than it might have been if the Federal Reserve had acted in 1996.

Greenspan's public statements as Fed chairman tended to be vague but reassuring, as befitted a man from whom a careless remark could send stock prices plummeting. Earlier in his career, however, he did not shy away from controversy. As a friend and confidant of novelist Ayn RAND from the 1950s on, Greenspan wrote in favor of the gold standard and for the repeal of ANTITRUST laws.

In 1962, Greenspan wrote of "the destructiveness of compromise, of mixed premises and mixed purposes." Given the pragmatism with which he guided the Federal Reserve through good economic times and bad—compromising when necessary, improvising when helpful—the mature Greenspan seemed to have reconsidered those youthful sentiments.

BIBLIOGRAPHY. R.W. Bradford, "Alan Greenspan—Cultist?" *The American Enterprise* (September 9, 1997); "Almighty Alan Greenspan," *The Economist* (January 6, 2000); Bob Woodward, *Maestro: Greenspan's Fed and the American Boom* (Simon & Schuster, 2000); Justin Martin, *Greenspan: The Man Behind Money* (Perseus Publishing, 2000); Alan Greenspan, "Gold and Economic Freedom" and "Antitrust," *Capitalism: The Unknown Ideal* (New American Library, 1967); Alan Greenspan, "The Crisis Over Berlin," *The Objectivist Newsletter* (v.1/1, 1962).

SCOTT PALMER, PH.D.
RGMS ECONOMICS

gross domestic product (GDP)

GDP IS THE BROADEST measure of an economy's output and can be defined as the market value of all final goods and services produced within a country during a given period of time. To understand this definition it is best to consider each phrase separately.

The market value: GDP adds together the market values of the many different types of goods and services produced in a modern economy to give a single measure of economic activity.

Of all: GDP is a comprehensive measure and includes all goods and services bought and sold legally in markets. However, goods and services produced and consumed in the home and those traded in black markets are excluded.

Final goods and services: To prevent double counting of transactions GDP includes only the value of the final goods and services, which are the end products of the production process. Intermediate goods and services such as the steel used in the production of a car are excluded.

Produced: GDP measures current production. Goods and services sold in second-hand markets are excluded since these were counted when they were originally purchased.

Within a country: GDP includes all goods and services produced with the geographical boundaries of a country, regardless of the nationality of the producer. It excludes all production by domestic producers within the geographical boundaries of a foreign country.

During a given period of time: GDP is a flow variable measured over a period of time, usually quarterly or yearly. Quarterly data is seasonally adjusted by government statisticians to remove the effects of the regular seasonal changes in an economy's production of goods and services for example, the effect of increased production during the Christmas period.

GDP can be measured by one of three methods. The output method sums the value added by all firms in the economy, at each stage of the production process. Value added is the market value of a good or service, minus the cost of inputs purchased from other firms. For example, assume GENERAL MOTORS produces a car using $8,000 of steel bought from U.S. STEEL, and sells the final product for $20,000. The value added by U.S. Steel is $8,000 and the value added by General Motors is $12,000. Summed, the value added by each firm equals the market value of the car.

The expenditure method measures GDP as the sum of expenditure on all final goods and services in four broad expenditure categories; personal household consumption expenditure (C), private investment expenditure (I), government purchases of goods and services (G), and net export expenditure (NX)—domestic goods and services sold abroad (exports) minus foreign goods and services purchased by domestic households (imports). Imports are subtracted because C, I, and G include domestic expenditure on foreign goods and services. The relationship between GDP and total expenditure on domestically produced goods and services can be expressed by the national income identity:

$$GDP = C + I + G + NX$$

The income method measures GDP as the total income generated by production. When a good or service is sold the total revenue from sales is distributed to workers and to the owners of the capital. Therefore, GDP = labor income + capital income. Labor income accounts for approximately 75 percent of GDP and includes income from employment and income from self-employment. Capital income accounts for the remaining 25 percent of

GDP and includes payments to the owners of physical capital and the total profits of businesses of all types. Thus, GDP can be measured in three ways; as the total production of goods and services in an economy, as total expenditure on the economy's goods and services, or as total income in an economy.

So far we have discussed nominal GDP, which measures the value of final goods and services produced using current prices. However, comparing nominal GDP from one year to the next does not permit us to compare the quantities of goods and services produced in those two years. Changes in nominal GDP between two time periods may reflect only changes in prices, not changes in production. Real GDP measures the value of goods and services produced using the prices prevailing in a base year. For example, if the base year is 2000 then real GDP in 2003 is calculated using the 2003 quantities valued at 2000 prices. Real GDP is therefore unaffected by changes in prices and provides an accurate measure of changes in the quantity of goods and services produced. Several years can be compared using the base-year prices and the resultant figures will be an accurate reflection of production increase, or in some cases, decrease over time. Comparing real GDP from one year to another enables us to say whether the economy has produced more or fewer goods.

It was not until WORLD WAR II that the need to accurately measure a nation's output of goods and services became paramount in government planning. During this period, economic measurement was developed principally by two economists working separately, but following parallel ideas, Simon KUZNETS in America, and Richard STONE in the UNITED KINGDOM. Their Nobel Prize-winning work became the internationally accepted basis for measuring national output. During World War II, the calculation of GDP, gross national product as it was then known, was used to monitor and adjust industrial war effort. Today, measures of change in real GDP are used to determine whether an economy is doing well or poorly in terms of economic growth. In addition, measures of real GDP are often considered to be an indicator of the economic well-being or standard of living of the population within a country.

Certainly countries with higher per-capita levels of real GDP enjoy a greater abundance of consumer goods, greater life expectancy, lower infant and child mortality rates, better medical facilities, more doctors, and greater access to education. However, it has been argued that because GDP measures only the value of market-based activities, it can, at best, be only an imperfect measure of economic well-being.

For example, because GDP measures only the production of goods and services it ignores totally how those goods and services are produced. The current debate reflects the fact that measures of GDP do not take into account the effects of environmental degradation, the rate of resource depletion, or indeed the pollution caused by industry. It could be argued that a measure of the value of these negative consequences of economic growth should be used to offset measures of increases in GDP. Such environmental effects are subjective and it is therefore almost impossible to obtain a unified widely accepted measure. It follows then that achieving a consensus as to the value of such negative consequences is difficult. Because of the effects on resources and environment and because such negative costs are not reflected in GDP, critics charge that government policies which are based on GDP statistics are fundamentally flawed.

In addition, GDP cannot measure the distribution of goods and services within society. By using it as a standard measure of society's well-being, the overlying assumption is that all members of that society enjoy life to the same standards—we know that is not the case.

GDP ignores the added value placed on goods by ensuring they are produced in a humane, democratic working environment that provides an acceptable standard of living for the workforce. Measuring only the quantity of output GDP ignores the added value of well-being. However, as with environmental impacts, achieving useable figures to measure these concepts is a difficult and time-consuming process.

Using a single index value compiled from separate indicators, such as unemployment rates, infant mortality rates, homeless rates, health care coverage and income levels, may overcome some of these problems. Although common indicators such as these are readily available, the problem is in deciding which indicators should be included with the possibility that including the wrong indicators may compound the nature of the problem.

There are other common factors that have an adverse effect on the accuracy of GDP. The UNDERGROUND ECONOMY is supported by those who work or conduct their daily business on a cash basis and avoid paying any contributions to the Internal Revenue Service. There is no way to accurately measure the amounts involved but no one doubts that it has a negative effect on GDP. Some goods and services are excluded from GDP because they are not sold on the open market. The husband who cuts the lawn on the weekend, the grandparent who babysits—social tasks such as these, that clearly have an economic value, are not included when calculating GDP.

GDP should be used cautiously when employed to make comparisons over time or across countries. When the value of the negative consequences of economic growth are taken into account, a high GDP might not always be an indication that a country's economy is making true economic growth.

BIBLIOGRAPHY. N. Gregory Mankiw, *Principles of Economics* (Harcourt, 2001); Robert H. Frank and Ben S. Bernanke, *Principles of Economics* (McGraw-Hill, 2001); Richard G. Lipsey, *An Introduction to Positive Economics* (Weidenfeld and Nicolson, 1987); United Nations, *Human Development Report* (UN, 1999); Michael Parkin and David King, *Economics* (Addison-Wesley, 1995).

DEREK RUTHERFORD YOUNG, PH.D.
UNIVERSITY OF DUNDEE, SCOTLAND

gross national product

SINCE VALORIZATION (to maintain and enhance value) is the main driving force of material productions under capitalism, it is necessary to have a quantitative measure of all value-producing activities and the resultant commodities. Gross national product (GNP) is one such yardstick. GNP measures the money value of all final commodities produced by the residents of a country no matter where, within or without the national boundaries, the production was carried out within a given period of time, generally a year, and calculated at current market prices. Because it is impractical to catalog and track long and numerous lists of quantities, kinds and types of commodities, it is customary to reduce them to their common-value denominator of MONEY to arrive at an aggregate measure of all production. The term "final product" implies that no intermediate products will be counted. An illustration might be to count the value of bread but not that of flour used as raw material for bread making. This obviates double counting since the value of flour is included in that of the bread.

The gross in GNP refers to the fact that the depreciation of capital has not been taken into account yet. When that is done, GNP is transformed into net national product. The total output is measured as a sum of all commodities multiplied by their corresponding market prices, (e.g., 5 loaves of bread at $3.00 each contributes $15 worth of GNP), and is classified as nominal GNP. Clearly, if only prices increase and the actual output remains the same, the GNP (nominal) would increase. To assess the changes in economic production, therefore, one can measure output at constant prices, i.e., to adjust for inflation and arrive at real GNP. The changes in real GNP reflect the changing level of actual production. Real GNP per capita, then, can gauge the average potential standard of living for a country.

GNP data over time indicate how the economy is progressing—too slow, fast, or just right—to make intertemporal comparisons. The size and the rate of growth of GNP are obviously a major determinant in the standard of living. One can thus use GNP figures for different countries to make comparisons of relative prosperity between different communities. These are essentially measures of economic well-being comparing different countries or tracking a specific country over time—a valuable piece of sociological knowledge by itself. After all, the value of production forms the basis of provisioning our income required to carry on the daily life and its transactions. This, however, does not place these data collection efforts at the center of economic decision-making.

With the advent of Keynesian formulation (circa 1930s) of the dynamics of a market economy, the emphasis of information procurement has shifted from welfare comparisons to policy-making instruments. Keynesian analysis suggested that the level of production, employment and income is directly related to the expenditures on goods and services (i.e., the level of "effective aggregate demand"). The role of expenditures in the performance of the economy, therefore, takes center stage.

The type of expenditure and its decision mechanism takes on an added significance. The expenditures, therefore, are divided into sectors of domestic consumers, investors, governments, and foreign buyers, because each one is typically regulated by different forces, which in turn can be affected by appropriate and commensurate policy measures. While Keynesian theory established the determinants of national production and income, Keynesian policy proscribed the need for collective action. The governments are to adopt economic policies to promote large enough expenditures for socially desirable levels of employment and income distribution. To carry out this responsibility, the governments need reliable and accurate estimates of national income, expenditure, the size and direction of change in response to specific policy steps and the sites and modalities of the system to induce and initiate fruitful changes. It is the acceptance of this challenge and its consequent contingencies that necessitates most governments to collect, classify, and disseminate national accounts of income and expenditure—the GNP being the foremost category.

The modern-day battery of fiscal and monetary policy measures are based on the direction and rate of change of GNP data. In a Keynesian world, if the unemployment level is higher than socially desirable, the government is to increase expenditures or reduce taxes to increase aggregate demand to promote higher production which, in turn, would lead to higher employment—this is FISCAL POLICY. Or the FEDERAL RESERVE bank can increase money supply, reduce INTEREST RATES thus fueling expenditures to the same effect—the expression of MONETARY POLICY. In the event of an inflationary period—when prices are increasing at a fast enough clip to be detrimental to social well-being—these fiscal and monetary policies could be applied in reverse to achieve a social optimum. Needless to say that the complexities of economic policy diagnostics and practical implementation are much more vexing than this abstract presentation. The point, however, is to highlight the centrality and importance that an accurate assessment of GNP has acquired.

Given that GNP as a category is so crucial to welfare comparisons and policy prescriptions, it is advisable to examine the robustness of this yardstick. To the extent that GNP records only market transactions, its frequent invocation in comparisons to less economically developed countries can be very misleading. To wonder how an average Indian citizen, for example, can live for a year with less than $500 worth of income is to ignore that a self-sufficient, rural-based peasantry has limited interaction with the market. Hence, even its meager income in GNP terms is grossly under-estimated. Likewise, for BARTER transactions in the advanced countries when, for instance, a plumber fixes the leaky faucet of an auto mechanic in exchange for a tune-up. Trade in illegal commodities—as in alcohol during the Prohibition era—is not counted for moral and practical reasons. Even though rental value of owner-occupied residences is estimated and included in GNP, the value of household production—cooking, cleaning, babysitting, etc., which could likewise be estimated, is excluded to prompt some to indicate gender bias.

Environmental degradation is not deducted but any restorative activity is taken as a positive entry, thereby puffing up GNP figures. Government transactions are assessed at cost rather than market price, which can introduce distortions. No allowance is made for labor depreciation (as opposed to capital depreciation which is allowed) and no account taken of leisure—the ultimate utility good the desire for which balances the income-generating incentive of work. With all these and other theoretical pitfalls, in addition to the herculean task of tracking down different bits of relevant data, GNP is still the most widely used indicator of economic activity, and no other measure of comparable acceptability has been devised despite numerous theoretical albeit debatable innovations.

As of 1991, the United States has adopted a slightly modified but essentially similar measure of output called GROSS DOMESTIC PRODUCT (GDP). GDP measures all production within the national boundaries regardless of the ownership of the means of production—meaning that whatever production is carried out by residents as well as foreigners but within the national territory is counted as part of U.S. GDP. This leads to GNP being equal to GDP plus the income earned by U.S. residents from factors of production outside the country minus the value of income earned by foreigners from factors of production in the country. Even though this transformation has been occasioned in response to international income accounting practices, the two measures generate similar figures for the economic output of the United States.

BIBLIOGRAPHY. R.I. Downing, *National Income and Social Accounts* (Melbourne University Press, 1969); R.H. Parker and G.C. Harcourt, *Readings in the Concept and Measurement of Income* (Cambridge University Press, 1969); A.W. Smith, *Demystifying Economics* (Ironwood Publications, 2000).

SYED B. HUSSAIN, PH.D.
UNIVERSITY OF WISCONSIN, OSHKOSH

growth

ECONOMIC GROWTH REFERS to a continual increase in a country's ability to produce goods and services. The amount of goods and services produced by an economy at a given period of time, usually a year, is called the GROSS DOMESTIC PRODUCT (GDP). When GDP is adjusted for the general increase in prices (i.e., inflation), it is termed "real GDP." Economic growth can thus be defined as a sustained increase in real GDP.

Economist Adam SMITH put together the first theory of economic growth in 1776. Defining labor's productivity as the output per person employed in the work force, Smith's theory can be summarized as follows: An increase in the division of labor increases labor's productivity. The increase in productivity, in turn, raises output, income, and the demand for goods and services; this creates larger markets that further increase the division of labor.

Hence, there is a virtuous circle linking the division of labor and the size of the market. For Smith, this virtuous circle could, however, be broken in the absence of "good" governments. A good government enforces property rights and maintains order. If, for instance, a government were to implement monopolies or take measures that limit the expansion of international trade, this would break the virtuous circle. Since monopolies restrict output and charge higher prices, the increase in productivity would not lead to increased output, and the circle would be broken.

In 1798, the Reverend Thomas MALTHUS put forward a theory of economic growth casting doubts on Smith's virtuous circle. Malthus believed that population expanded at a geometric rate, doubling every 30 years or so, while land grew very slowly. This divergence in the growth rate of the two factors of production (resources) would lead to a fall of a worker's marginal contribution to food production. Combined with a growing population, per capita food production (i.e., the amount of food produced divided by the number of people) would fall gradually and this would lead to a decline of standards of living toward subsistence levels. Malthus believed that if people could limit their progeny, a constant state of subsistence level could be avoided; otherwise rising death and famines would result. Malthus thus offers a very negative and pessimistic view of the theory of economic development and growth.

In the 1940s, economists Roy HARROD and Evsey Domar developed independently a model to help explain the role of CAPITAL ACCUMULATION (i.e., investment) in the growth process, known as the Harrod-Domar model. It suggests that saving provides the funds that are borrowed for investment purposes. More physical capital is needed to stimulate economic growth. With increased economic growth comes higher income and therefore higher levels of saving. Saving, in turn, leads to higher investment.

We thus have a virtuous circle between capital accumulation, income, savings, and investment. An implication of the model is that economic growth requires policies that encourage higher saving. Unfortunately, the virtuous circle of the Harrod-Domar model leads to the fact that if an economy strays from its optimal growth path it either explodes or implodes. This unrealistic characteristic lead to the search for alternative models, the most famous being the neoclassical growth model, usually associated with Robert SOLOW.

Nobel Prize-winning economist Solow expanded the Harrod-Domar model by introducing labor and technology into the growth equation. By doing so, economic growth could only result either from increases in the quantity and quality of labor (i.e., population growth and education), or increases in the capital stock (i.e., factories, equipment, buildings) through saving and investment, or technological progress.

Another finding of the neoclassical growth theory is that an economy always converges towards a steady-state rate of growth. More precisely, closed economies (those with no international trade with the rest of the world) with lower saving rates will tend to grow more slowly than those with higher saving rates, and will converge to lower per capital levels of income in the short-run. In contrast, open economies will converge at higher levels of income in the short-run. Technical progress played a key role in the Solow model. In the long run, technical progress becomes the main determinant of economic growth. The problem, though, was that technology was assumed to be exogenously determined (that is, determined independently of all other factors). So, what makes people better off in the long run in per-capita terms? The neoclassical response will be: technology. But if one were to ask about the determinants of technology, the neoclassical economists could provide no explanation.

In the 1990s, a new growth theory, known as endogenous growth theory, came into existence due to the growing dissatisfaction with the idea of exogenous technical progress and per capita income convergence arising out of the neoclassical theory. Pioneers of this new view include economists Robert LUCAS and Paul Romer. In an endogenous growth framework, the rate of growth of output depends on aggregate stock of capital (both physical and human) and on the level of research and development in an economy. Endogenous growth theories also explain the persistent differences in growth rates between countries and the importance of research and human capital development in permanently increasing the growth rate of an economy. A consequence of that view, for instance, is that a recession in a country, whether temporary or prolonged, could lead to a permanent increase in the output gap between itself and the rest of the world.

Sources of economic growth include increases in factors of production (LABOR, CAPITAL, LAND) and technology. Indeed, a country can increase production (grow) if it increases the amount of resources used or makes better use of existing factors of production. Resources (factors of productions) and technical progress (innovation) are all important determinants of the growth rate of an economy. Various policies can be used to improve the economic growth rate (mostly through their impacts on resources and technology); they include investing in human capital, creating policies to stimulate savings, encouraging international trade, and subsidizing research and development.

Barriers to economic growth are somewhat related to the sources of growth and include the lack of technical knowledge or a slowdown in technical progress; the lack of capital and skilled labor needed to manufacture goods and services; a rapid population growth; and a large foreign debt. Current research in economics shows that the quality of institutions is also an important determinant of economic growth/slowdown. Countries with poor institutions (i.e., high corruption, weak judicial systems) tend to grow slower than countries with strong institutions. The recent economic crises in Southeast Asia and Russia are examples of the importance of institutions and the role of the state in economic growth and development. Another example comes from African countries that are well endowed with natural resources but are still lagging behind the rest of the world; their low growth rates seem to be due mostly to the high levels of grand corruption of their top government officials who frequently engage in "white elephant" projects.

BIBLIOGRAPHY. Adam Smith, *An Inquiry into the Nature and Causes of the Wealth of Nations* (Renascence Editions); Thomas Malthus, *Essay on the Principle of Population* (Great Mind Series); Roy Harrod, "An Essay in Dynamic Theory," *Economic Journal* (Blackwell Publishing, 1939); Evsey Domar, "Expansion and Employment," *American Economic Review* (American Economic Association 1947); Robert Solow, "A Contribution to the Theory of Economic Growth," *Quarterly Journal of Economics* (MIT Press, 1956); Howard Pack, "Endogenous Growth Theory: Intellectual Appeal and Empirical Shortcomings," *Journal of Economic Perspectives* (AEA, 1994).

ARSÈNE A. AKA, PH.D.
CATHOLIC UNIVERSITY OF AMERICA